"E. J. W. GIBB MEMORIAL"
NEW SERIES XIX

AVERROES'
TAHAFUT AL-TAHAFUT

(*The Incoherence of the Incoherence*)

TRANSLATED FROM THE ARABIC
WITH INTRODUCTION AND NOTES
BY
SIMON VAN DEN BERGH

VOLUMES I AND II

PUBLISHED BY
THE TRUSTEES OF THE
"E. J. W. GIBB MEMORIAL"
AND DISTRIBUTED BY
LUZAC AND COMPANY LIMITED
P.O. BOX 157, 46 GREAT RUSSELL STREET,
LONDON WC1B 3PE

All rights reserved. No part of this book
may be reproduced in any form, by mimeograph
or any other means without permission in
writing from the publishers.

© EJW Gibb Memorial Trust 1954
Reprinted 1969
Reprinted as one volume 1978

ISBN 0 906094 04 6

Produced in association with
Book Production Consultants, Cambridge, England

Reprinted at the University Press, Cambridge

THIS VOLUME
IS ONE OF A SERIES
PUBLISHED BY THE TRUSTEES OF
THE "E. J. W. GIBB MEMORIAL"

The funds of this Memorial are derived from the Interest accruing from a Sum of money given by the late MRS GIBB *of Glasgow, to perpetuate the Memory of her beloved Son*

ELIAS JOHN WILKINSON GIBB

and to promote those researches into the History, Literature, Philosophy and Religion of the Turks, Persians and Arabs, to which, from his Youth upwards, until his premature and deeply lamented Death in his forty-fifth year, on December 5, 1901, his life was devoted.

تِلْكَ آثَارُنَا تَدُلُّ عَلَيْنَا * فَانْظُرُوا بَعْدَنَا إِلَى ٱلْآثَارِ

"*These are our works, these works our souls display;
Behold our works when we have passed away.*"

CLERK OF THE TRUST
P. R. Bligh, F.C.A.
c/o Spicer and Pegler
Leda House, Station Road
Cambridge, England

VOLUME I

PREFACE

I wish to express my warmest thanks to the Trustees of the Gibb Memorial Fund for making the publication of this work possible, and especially to Professor Sir Hamilton Gibb, who asked me to undertake the work and who has not only read the proofs but has continually given me his interest and encouragement. I am also deeply indebted to Dr. R. Walzer, who has read the proofs, carefully checked the references in my notes, and composed the indexes and the Greek–Arabic and Arabic–Greek vocabularies. I have also to thank Dr. S. M. Stern for his help in completing the subject-index. Finally, I wish to pay a tribute to one who is no longer amongst us, Father Maurice Bouyges, without whose admirable text the work could never have been undertaken.

> The marginal numbers in Vol. I refer to the text of Father Bouyges's edition of the *Tahafut al Tahafut* in his *Bibliotheca Arabica Scholasticorum*, vol. iii, Beyrouth, 1930.

> The asterisks indicate different readings from those to be found in Bouyges's text: cf. the Appendix, Vol. I, pp. 364 ff.

CONTENTS
(VOLUME I)

INTRODUCTION *Page* ix

TRANSLATION

THE FIRST DISCUSSION 1
Concerning the Eternity of the World
- THE FIRST PROOF — 1
- THE SECOND PROOF — 37
- THE THIRD PROOF — 57
- THE FOURTH PROOF — 58

THE SECOND DISCUSSION 69
The Refutation of their Theory of the Incorruptibility of the World and of Time and Motion

THE THIRD DISCUSSION 87
The demonstration of their confusion in saying that God is the agent and the maker of the world and that the world in His product and act, and the demonstration that these expressions are in their system only metaphors without any real sense

THE FOURTH DISCUSSION 156
Showing that they are unable to prove the existence of a creator of the world

THE FIFTH DISCUSSION 170
To show their incapacity to prove God's unity and the impossibility of two necessary existents both without a cause

THE SIXTH DISCUSSION 186
To refute their denial of attributes

THE SEVENTH DISCUSSION 221
To refute their claim that nothing can share with the First its genus, and be differentiated from it through a specific difference, and that with respect to its intellect the division into genus and specific difference cannot be applied to it

THE EIGHTH DISCUSSION 235
To refute their theory that the existence of the First is simple, namely that it is pure existence and that its existence stands in relation to no quiddity and to no essence, but stands to necessary existence as do other beings to their quiddity

THE NINTH DISCUSSION 241
To refute their proof that the First is incorporeal

CONTENTS

THE TENTH DISCUSSION 250
To prove their incapacity to demonstrate that the world has a creator and a cause, and that in fact they are forced to admit atheism

THE ELEVENTH DISCUSSION 255
To show the incapacity of those philosophers who believe that the First knows other things besides its own self and that it knows the genera and the species in a universal way, to prove that this is so

THE TWELFTH DISCUSSION 269
About the impotence of the philosophers to prove that God knows Himself

THE THIRTEENTH DISCUSSION 275
To refute those who affirm that God is ignorant of the individual things which are divided in time into present, past, and future

THE FOURTEENTH DISCUSSION 285
To refute their proof that heaven is an animal moving in a circle in obedience to God

THE FIFTEENTH DISCUSSION 293
To refute the theory of the philosophers about the aim which moves heaven

THE SIXTEENTH DISCUSSION 300
To refute the philosophical theory that the souls of the heavens observe all the particular events of this world

ABOUT THE NATURAL SCIENCES 311

THE FIRST DISCUSSION 316
The denial of a logical necessity between cause and effect

THE SECOND DISCUSSION 333
The impotence of the philosophers to show by demonstrative proof that the soul is a spiritual substance

THE THIRD DISCUSSION 356
Refutation of the philosophers' proof for the immortality of the soul

THE FOURTH DISCUSSION 359
Concerning the philosophers' denial of bodily resurrection

APPENDIX: Changes proposed in the Arabic Text 365

INDEX of Proper Names 374

(VOLUME II)
NOTES 1
Index of Proper Names mentioned in the Introduction and in the Notes 207
Index of Subjects mentioned in the Notes 211
Some contradictions in Aristotle's System 215
Arabic–Greek Index to the Notes 216
Greek–Arabic Index to the Notes 218

INTRODUCTION

IF it may be said that Santa Maria sopra Minerva is a symbol of our European culture, it should not be forgotten that the mosque also was built on the Greek temple. But whereas in Christian Western theology there was a gradual and indirect infiltration of Greek, and especially Aristotelian ideas, so that it may be said that finally Thomas Aquinas baptized Aristotle, the impact on Islam was sudden, violent, and short. The great conquests by the Arabs took place in the seventh century when the Arabs first came into contact with the Hellenistic world. At that time Hellenistic culture was still alive; Alexandria in Egypt, certain towns in Syria—Edessa for instance—were centres of Hellenistic learning, and in the cloisters of Syria and Mesopotamia not only Theology was studied but Science and Philosophy also were cultivated. In Philosophy Aristotle was still 'the master of those who know', and especially his logical works as interpreted by the Neoplatonic commentators were studied intensively. But also many Neoplatonic and Neopythagorean writings were still known, and also, very probably, some of the old Stoic concepts and problems were still alive and discussed.

The great period of translation of Greek into Arabic, mostly through the intermediary of Christian Syrians, was between the years 750 and 850, but already before that time there was an impact of Greek ideas on Muhammadan theology. The first speculative theologians in Islam are called Mu'tazilites (from about A.D. 723), an exact translation of the Greek word σχισματικοί (the general name for speculative theologians is Mutakallimun, διαλεκτικοί, dialecticians, a name often given in later Greek philosophy to the Stoics). Although they form rather a heterogeneous group of thinkers whose theories are syncretistic, that is taken from different Greek sources with a preponderance of Stoic ideas, they have certain points in common, principally their theory, taken from the Stoics, of the rationality of religion (which is for them identical with Islam), of a *lumen naturale* which burns in the heart of every man, and the optimistic view of a rational God who has created the best of all possible worlds for the greatest good of man who occupies the central place in the universe. They touch upon certain difficult problems that were perceived by the Greeks. The paradoxes of Zeno concerning movement and the infinite divisibility of space and time hold their attention, and the subtle problem of the status of the non-existent, a problem long neglected in modern philosophy, but revived by the school of Brentano, especially by Meinong, which caused an endless controversy amongst the Stoics, is also much debated by them.

A later generation of theologians, the Ash'arites, named after Al Ash'ari, born A.D. 873, are forced by the weight of evidence to admit a certain irrationality in theological concepts, and their philosophical speculations, largely based on Stoicism, are strongly mixed with Sceptical theories. They hold the middle way between the traditionalists who want to forbid all reasoning on religious matters and those who affirm that reason unaided by revelation is capable of attaining religious truths. Since Ghazali founds his attack against the philosophers on Ash'arite principles, we may consider for a moment some of their theories. The difference between the Ash'arite and Mu'tazilite conceptions of God cannot be better expressed than by the following passage which is found twice in Ghazali (in his *Golden Means of Dogmatics* and his *Vivification of Theology*) and to which by tradition is ascribed the breach between Al Ash'ari and the Mu'tazilites.

'Let us imagine a child and a grown-up in Heaven who both died in the True Faith, but the grown-up has a higher place than the child. And the child will ask God, "Why did you give that man a higher place?" And God will answer, "He has done many good works." Then the child will say, "Why did you let me die so soon so that I was prevented from doing good?" God will answer, "I knew that you would grow up a sinner, therefore it was better that you should die a child." Then a cry goes up from the damned in the depths of Hell, "Why, O Lord, did you not let us die before we became sinners?"'

Ghazali adds to this: 'the imponderable decisions of God cannot be weighed by the scales of reason and Mu'tazilism'.

According to the Ash'arites, therefore, right and wrong are human concepts and cannot be applied to God. 'Cui mali nihil est nec esse potest quid huic opus est dilectu bonorum et malorum?' is the argument of the Sceptic Carneades expressed by Cicero (*De natura deorum*, iii. 15. 38). It is a dangerous theory for the theologians, because it severs the moral relationship between God and man and therefore it cannot be and is not consistently applied by the Ash'arites and Ghazali.

The Ash'arites have taken over from the Stoics their epistemology, their sensationalism, their nominalism, their materialism. Some details of this epistemology are given by Ghazali in his autobiography: the clearness of representations is the criterion for their truth; the soul at birth is a blank on which the sensations are imprinted; at the seventh year of a man's life he acquires the rational knowledge of right and wrong. Stoic influence on Islamic theology is overwhelming. Of Stoic origin, for instance, are the division of the acts of man into five classes; the importance placed on the motive of an act when judging its moral character; the theory of the two categories of substance and accident (the two other categories, condition and relation, are not considered by the Muslim theologians to pertain to reality, since they are subjective); above all, the fatalism and determinism in Islam which is often regarded as a feature of the Oriental soul. In the Koran, however, there is no definite theory about free will. Muhammad was not a philosopher. The definition of will in man given by the Ash'arites, as the instrument of unalterable fate and the unalterable law of God, is Stoic both in idea and expression. (I have discussed several other theories in my notes.)

Sometimes, however, the theologians prefer to the Stoic view the view of their adversaries. For instance, concerning the discussion between Neoplatonism and Stoicism whether there is a moral obligation resting on God and man relative to animals, Islam answers with the Neoplatonists in the affirmative (Spinoza, that Stoic Cartesian, will give, in his *Ethica*, the negative Stoic answer).

The culmination of the philosophy of Islam was in the tenth and eleventh centuries. This was the age also of the great theologians. It was with Greek ideas, taken in part from Stoics and Sceptics, that the theologians tried to refute the ideas of the philosophers. The philosophers themselves were followers of Aristotle as seen through the eyes of his Neoplatonic commentators. This Neoplatonic interpretation of Aristotle, although it gives a mystical character to his philosophy which is alien to it, has a certain justification in the fact that there are in his philosophy many elements of the theory of his master Plato, which lend themselves to a Neoplatonic conception. Plotinus regarded himself as nothing but the commentator of Plato and Aristotle, and in his school the identity of view of these two great masters was affirmed. In the struggle in Islam between Philosophy and Theology, Philosophy was defeated, and the final blow to the philosophers was given in Ghazali's attack on Philosophy which in substance is incorporated in Averroës' book and which he tries to refute.

Ghazali, who was born in the middle of the eleventh century, is one of the most remarkable and at the same time most enigmatic figures in Islam. Like St. Augustine, with whom he is often compared, he has told us in his autobiography how he had to pass through a period of despair and scepticism until God, not through demonstration but by the light of His grace, had given him peace and certitude. This divine light, says Ghazali, is the basis of most of our knowledge and, he adds, profoundly, one cannot find proofs for the premisses of knowledge; the premisses are there and one looks for the reasons, but they cannot be found. Certitude is reached, he says, not through scholastic reasoning, not through philosophy, but through mystical illumination and the mystical way of life. Still Ghazali is not only a mystic, he is a great dogmatist and moralist. He is regarded as Islam's greatest theologian and, through some of his books, as a defender of Orthodoxy. It is generally believed that the *Tahafut*, the book in which he criticizes Philosophy, was written in the period of his doubts. The book, however, is a Defence of Faith, and though it is more negative than positive, for it aims to destroy and not to construct, it is based on the theories of his immediate predecessors, many of whose arguments he reproduces. Besides, he promises in this book to give in another book the correct dogmatic answers. The treatise to which he seems to refer does not contain anything but the old theological articles of faith and the Ash'arite arguments and solutions. But we should not look for consistency in Ghazali; necessarily his mysticism comes into conflict with his dogmatism and he himself has been strongly influenced by the philosophers, especially by Avicenna, and in many works he comes very near to the Neoplatonic theories which he criticizes. On the whole it would seem to me that Ghazali in his attack on the philosophers has taken from the vast arsenal of Ash'arite dialectical arguments those appropriate to the special point under discussion, regardless of whether they are destructive also of some of the views he holds.

Averroës was the last great philosopher in Islam in the twelfth century, and is the most scholarly and scrupulous commentator of Aristotle. He is far better known in Europe than in the Orient, where few of his works are still in existence and where he had no influence, he being the last great philosopher of his culture. Renan, who wrote a big book about him, *Averroès et l'Averroïsme*, had never seen a line of Arabic by him. Lately some of his works have been edited in Arabic, for instance his *Tahafut al Tahafut*, in a most exemplary manner. Averroës' influence on European thought during the Middle Ages and the Renaissance has been immense.

The name of Ghazali's book in which he attacks the philosophers is *Tahafut al Falasifa*, which has been translated by the medieval Latin translator as *Destructio Philosophorum*. The name of Averroës' book is *Tahafut al Tahafut*, which is rendered as *Destructio Destructionis* (or *destructionum*). This rendering is surely not exact. The word 'Tahafut' has been translated by modern scholars in different ways, and the title of Ghazali's book has been given as the breakdown, the disintegration, or the incoherence, of the philosophers. The exact title of Averroës' book would be *The Incoherence of the Incoherence*.

In the *Revue des Deux Mondes* there was an article published in 1895 by Ferdinand Brunetière, 'La Banqueroute de la Science', in which he tried to show that the solutions by science, and especially by biology, of fundamental problems, solutions which were in opposition to the dogmas taught by the Church, were primitive and unreasonable. Science had promised us to eliminate mystery, but, Brunetière said, not only had it not removed it but we saw clearly that it would never do so. Science had been able neither to solve, nor even to pose, the questions that mattered: those that touched the origin of man, the laws of his conduct, his future destiny. What Brunetière tried to do, to defend Faith by showing up the audacity of Science in its attempt to solve ultimate problems, is exactly the same as Ghazali tried to do in relation to the pretensions of the philosophers of his time who, having based themselves on reason alone, tried to solve all the problems concerning God and the world. Therefore a suitable title for his book might perhaps be 'The Bankruptcy of Philosophy'.

In the introduction to his book Ghazali says that a group of people hearing the famous names Socrates, Hippocrates, Plato, and Aristotle, and knowing what they had attained in such sciences as Geometry, Logic, and Physics, have left the religion of their fathers in which they were brought up to follow the philosophers. The theories of the philosophers are many, but Ghazali will attack only one, the greatest, Aristotle; Aristotle, of whom it is said that he refuted all his predecessors, even Plato, excusing himself by saying 'amicus Plato, amica veritas, sed magis amica veritas'. I may add that this well-known saying, which is a variant of a passage in Plato's *Phaedo* and in Aristotle's *Nicomachean Ethics*, is found in this form first in Arabic. One of the first European authors who has it in this form is Cervantes (*Don Quijote*, ii, c. 52). I quote this saying—Ghazali adds—to show that there is no surety and evidence in Philosophy. According to Ghazali, the philosophers claim for their metaphysical proofs the same evidence as is found in Mathematics and Logic. But all Philosophy is based on supposition and opinion. If Metaphysics had the same evidence as Mathematics all philosophers would agree just as well in Philosophy as in Mathematics. According to him the translators of Aristotle have often misunderstood or changed the meaning and the different texts have caused different controversies. Ghazali considers Farabi and Avicenna to be the best commentators on Aristotle in Islam, and it is their theories that he will attack.

Before entering into the heart of the matter I will say a few words about Ghazali's remark that Metaphysics, although it claims to follow the same method as Mathematics, does not attain the same degree of evidence. Neither Aristotle nor his commentators ever asked the question whether there is any difference between the methods of Mathematics and Metaphysics (it is a significant fact that most examples of proof in the *Posterior Analytics* are taken from Mathematics) and why the conclusions reached by Metaphysics seem so much less convincing than those reached by Mathematics. It would seem that Metaphysics, being the basis of all knowledge and having as its subject the ultimate principles of things, should possess, according to Aristotle, the highest evidence and that God, as being the highest principle, should stand at the beginning of the system, as in Spinoza. In fact, Aristotle could not have sought God if he had not found Him. For Aristotle all necessary reasoning is deductive and exclusively based on syllogism. Reasoning—he says—and I think this is a profound and true remark—cannot go on indefinitely. You cannot go on asking for reasons infinitely, nor can you reason about a subject which is not known to you. Reason must come to a stop. There must be first principles which are immediately evident. And indeed Aristotle acknowledges their existence. When we ask, however, what these first principles are, he does not give us any answer but only points out the Laws of Thought as such. But from the Laws of Thought nothing can be deduced, as Aristotle acknowledges himself. As a matter of fact Aristotle is quite unaware of the assumption on which his system is based. He is what philosophers are wont to call nowadays a naïve realist. He believes that the world which we perceive and think about with all it contains has a reality independent of our perceptions or our thoughts. But this view seems so natural to him that he is not aware that it could be doubted or that any reason might be asked for it. Now I, for my part, believe that the objectivity of a common world in which we all live and die is the necessary assumption of all reasoning and thought. I believe indeed, with Aristotle, that there are primary assumptions which cannot be deduced from other principles. All reasoning assumes the existence of an objective truth which is sought and therefore is assumed to have an independent reality of its own. Every thinking person is conscious of his own identity and the identity of his fellow beings from whom he accepts language and thoughts and to whom he can communicate his own ideas and emotions. Besides, all conceptual thought implies universality, i.e. belief in law and in objective necessity. I can only infer from Socrates being a man that he is mortal when I have assumed that the same thing (in this case man in so far as he is man) in the same conditions will always necessarily behave in the same way.

In his book Ghazali attacks the philosophers on twenty points. Except for the last two points which are only slightly touched by Averroës, Averroës follows point for point the arguments Ghazali uses and tries to refute them. Ghazali's book is badly constructed, it is unsystematic and repetitive. If Ghazali had proceeded systematically he would have attacked first the philosophical basis of the system of the philosophers—namely their proof for the existence of God, since from God, the Highest Principle, everything else is deduced. But the first problem Ghazali mentions is the philosphers' proof for the eternity of the world. This is the problem which Ghazali considers to be the most important and to which he allots the greatest space, almost a quarter of his book. He starts by saying rather arbitrarily that the philosophers have four arguments, but, in discussing them, he mixes them up and the whole discussion is complicated by the fact that he gives the philosophical arguments and theological counter-arguments in such an involved way that the trend is sometimes hard to follow. He says, for instance, page 3, that to the first arguments of the philosophers there are two objections. The first objection he gives on this page, but the second, after long controversy between the philosophers and theologians, on page 32. I will not follow here Ghazali and Averroës point for point in their discussions but will give rather the substance of their principal arguments (for a detailed discussion I refer to my notes).

The theory of the eternity of the world is an Aristotelian one.

Aristotle was, as he says himself, the first thinker who affirmed that the world in which we live, the universe as an orderly whole, a cosmos, is eternal. All the philosophers before him believed that the world had come into being either from some primitive matter or after a number of other worlds. At the same time Aristotle believes in the finitude of causes. For him it is impossible that movement should have started or can continue by itself. There must be a principle from which all movement derives. Movement, however, by itself is eternal. It seems to me that this whole conception is untenable. If the world is eternal there will be an infinite series of causes and an infinite series of movers; there will be an infinite series, for instance, of fathers and sons, of birds and eggs (the example of the bird and egg is first mentioned in Censorinus, *De die natali*, where he discusses the Peripatetic theory of the eternity of the world), and we will never reach a first mover or cause, a first father or a first bird. Aristotle, in fact, defends the two opposite theses of Kant's first antinomy. He holds at the same time that time and movement are infinite and that every causal series must be finite. The contradiction in Aristotle is still further accentuated in the Muhammadan philosophers by the fact that they see in God, not only as Aristotle did, the First Mover of the movement of the universe, but that they regard Him, under the influence of the Plotinian theory of emanation, as the Creator of the universe from whom the world emanates eternally. However, can the relation between two existing entities *qua* existents be regarded as a causal one? Can there be a causal relation between an eternally unchangeable God and an eternally revolving and changing world, and is it sense to speak of a creation of that which exists eternally? Besides, if the relation between the eternal God and the eternal movement of the world could be regarded as a causal relation, no prior movement could be considered the cause of a posterior movement, and sequences such as the eternal sequence of fathers and sons would not form a causal series. God would not be a first cause but the Only Cause of everything. It is the contradiction in the idea of an eternal creation which forms the chief argument of Ghazali in this book. In a later chapter, for instance, when he refutes Avicenna's proof for God based on the Aristotelian concepts 'necessary by itself', i.e. logical necessity, and 'necessary through another', i.e. ontological necessity, in which there is the usual Aristotelian confusion of the logical with the ontological, Ghazali's long argument can be reduced to the assertion that once the possibility of

INTRODUCTION xvii

an infinite series of causes is admitted, there is no sense in positing a first cause.

The first argument is as follows. If the world had been created, there must have been something determining its existence at the moment it was created, for otherwise it would have remained in the state of pure possibility it was in before. But if there was something determining its existence, this determinant must have been determined by another determinant and so on *ad infinitum*, or we must accept an eternal God in whom eternally new determinations may arise. But there cannot be any new determinations in an eternal God.

The argument in this form is found in Avicenna, but its elements are Aristotelian. In Cicero's *Academics* we have a fragment of one of Aristotle's earlier and more popular writings, the lost dialogue *De philosophia*, in which he says that it is impossible that the world could ever have been generated. For how could there have been a new decision, that is a new decision in the mind of God, for such a magnificent work? St. Augustine knows this argument from Cicero and he too denies that God could have a *novum consilium*. St. Augustine is well aware of the difficulty, and he says in his *De civitate dei* that God has always existed, that after a certain time, without having changed His will, He created man, whom He had not wanted to create before, this is indeed a fact too profound for us. It also belongs to Aristotle's philosophy that in all change there is a potentiality and all potentiality needs an actualizer which exists already. In the form this argument has in Avicenna it is, however, taken from a book by a late Greek Christian commentator of Aristotle, John Philoponus, *De aeternitate mundi*, which was directed against a book by the great Neoplatonist Proclus who had given eighteen arguments to prove the eternity of the world. Plato himself believed in the temporal creation of the world not by God Himself but by a demiurge. But later followers of Plato differed from him on this point. Amongst the post-Aristotelian schools only the Stoics assumed a periodical generation and destruction of the world. Theophrastus had already tried to refute some of the Stoic arguments for this view, and it may well be that John Philoponus made use of some Stoic sources for his defence of the temporality of the world.

The book by Proclus is lost, but John Philoponus, who as a Christian believes in the creation of the world, gives, before refuting them, the arguments given by Proclus. The book by Philoponus was translated into Arabic and many of its arguments are reproduced in the Muhammadan controversies about the problem (arguments for the temporal creation of the world were also given by Philoponus in a work against Aristotle's theory of the eternity of the world, arguments which are known to us through their quotation and refutation by Simplicius in his commentary on *Physics* viii; one of these arguments by Philoponus was well known to the Arabs and is also reproduced by Ghazali, see note 3. 3). The argument I have mentioned is the third as given by Proclus. Philoponus' book is extremely important for all medieval philosophy, but it has never been translated into a modern language and has never been properly studied. On the whole the importance of the commentators of Aristotle for Arabic and medieval philosophy in general has not yet been sufficiently acknowledged.

To this argument Ghazali gives the following answer, which has become the classic reply for this difficulty and which has been taken from Philoponus. One must distinguish, says Philoponus, between God's eternally willing something and the eternity of the object of His Will, or, as St. Thomas will say later, 'Deus voluit ab aeterno mundus esset sed non ut ab aeterno esset'. God willed, for instance, that Socrates should be born before Plato and He willed this from eternity, so that when it was time for Plato to be born it happened. It is not difficult for Averroës to refute this argument. In willing and doing something there is more than just the decision that you will do it. You can take the decision to get up tomorrow, but the actual willing to get up can be done only at the moment you do it, and there can be no delay between the cause and the effect. There must be added to the decision to get up the impulse of the will to get up. So in God there would have to be a new impulse, and it is just this newness that has to be denied. But, says Averroës, the whole basis of this argument is wrong for it assumes in God a will like a human will. Desire and will can be understood only in a being that has a need; for the Perfect Being there can be no need, there can be no choice, for when He acts He will necessarily do the best. Will in God must have another meaning than human will.

Averroës therefore does not explicitly deny that God has a will, but will should not be taken in its human sense. He has much the same conception as Plotinus, who denies that God has the power to do one of two contraries (for God will necessarily always choose the best, which implies that God necessarily will always do the best, but this in fact annuls the ideas of choice and will), and who regards the world as produced by natural necessity. Aristotle also held that for the

INTRODUCTION

Perfect Being no voluntary action is possible, and he regards God as in an eternal blissful state of self-contemplation. This would be a consequence of His Perfection which, for Averroës at least, involves His Omniscience. For the Perfect the drama of life is ended: nothing can be done any more, no decision can be taken any more, for decisions belong to the condition of man to whom both knowledge and ignorance are given and who can have an hypothetical knowledge of the future, knowing that on his decisions the future may depend and to whom a sure knowledge of the future is denied. But an Omniscient Being can neither act nor decide; for Him the future is irremediable like the past and cannot be changed any more by His decisions or actions. Paradoxically the Omnipotent is impotent. This notion of God as a Self-contemplating Being, however, constitutes one of the many profound contradictions in Aristotle's system. And this profound contradiction is also found in all the works of Aristotle's commentators. One of Aristotle's proofs for the existence of God—and according to a recent pronouncement of the Pope, the most stringent—is the one based on movement. There cannot be an infinite series of movers; there must be a Prime Agent, a Prime Mover, God, the originator of all change and action in the universe. According to the conception of God as a Self-Contemplating Being, however, the love for God is the motive for the circular motion of Heaven. God is not the ultimate Agent, God is the ultimate Aim of desire which inspires the Heavens to action. It is Heaven which moves itself and circles round out of love for God. And in this case it is God who is passive; the impelling force, the efficient cause, the spring of all action lies in the world, lies in the souls of the stars.

Let us now return to Ghazali. We have seen that his first argument is not very convincing, but he now gives us another argument which the Muhammadan theologians have taken from John Philoponus and which has more strength. It runs: if you assume the world to have no beginning in time, at any moment which we can imagine an infinite series must have been ended. To give an example, every one of us is the effect of an infinite series of causes; indeed, man is the finite junction of an infinite past and an infinite future, the effect of an infinite series of causes, the cause of an infinite series of effects. But an infinite series cannot be traversed. If you stand near the bed of a river waiting for the water to arrive from an infinitely distant source you will never see it arriving, for an infinite distance cannot be passed. This is the argument given by Kant in the thesis of his first antimony. The curious fact is that the wording in Kant is almost identical with that of John Philoponus.

The answers Averroës gives are certainly not convincing. He repeats the Aristotelian dictum that what has no beginning has no end and that therefore there is never an end of time, and one can never say that at any moment an infinite time is ended: an infinite time is never ended. But this is begging the question and is surely not true, for there are certainly finite times. He denies that an infinite time involves an infinite causal series and the negation of a First Cause. The series involved is but a temporal sequence, causal by accident, since it is God who is its essential cause. Averroës also bases his answer on the Aristotelian theory that in time there is only a succession. A simultaneous infinite whole is denied by Aristotle and therefore, according to Aristotle, the world must be limited in space; but in time, according to him, there is never a whole, since the past is no longer existent and the future not yet.

But the philosophers have a convincing argument for the eternity of the world. Suppose the world had a beginning, then before the world existed there was empty time; but in an empty time, in pure emptiness, there cannot be a motive for a beginning and there could be nothing that could decide God to start His creation. This is Kant's antithesis of his first antinomy. It is very old and is given by Aristotle, but it is already found in the pre-Socratic philosopher Parmenides. Ghazali's answer is that God's will is completely undetermined. His will does not depend on distinctions in outside things, but He creates the distinctions Himself. The idea of God's creative will is of Stoic origin. According to the Neoplatonic conception God's knowledge is creative. We know because things are; things are because God knows them. This idea of the creative knowledge of God has a very great diffusion in philosophy (just as our bodies live by the eternal spark of life transmitted to us by our ancestors, so we rekindle in our minds the thoughts of those who are no more); it is found, for instance, in St. Augustine, Thomas Aquinas, Spinoza, and Kant—who calls it *intellektuelle Anschauung*, intellectual intuition, and it is also used by the Muhammadan philosophers when it suits them. Against Ghazali's conception, however, Averroës has the following argument: If God creates the world arbitrarily, if His Will establishes the distinctions without being determined by any reason, neither wisdom nor goodness can be attributed to Him. We have here a difficulty the Greeks had seen already. Either God is beyond the laws of thought and of morals and then He is neither good nor wise, or He Himself stands under their dominion and then He is not omnipotent.

Another argument for the eternity of the world is based on the eternity of time: God cannot have a priority to time, as the theologians affirm, because priority implies time and time implies movement. For the philosophers God's priority to the world consists solely in His being its simultaneous cause. Both parties, however, seem to hold that God's existence does not imply time, since He exists in timeless eternity. But in this case, what neither of the parties has seen, no causal relation between God and the world can exist at all, since all causation implies a simultaneous time.

We come now to the most important argument which shows the basic difference between the philosophical and theological systems. For Aristotle the world cannot have come to be because there is no absolute becoming. Everything that becomes comes from something. And, as a matter of fact, we all believe this. We all believe more or less unconsciously (we are not fully aware of our basic principles: a basement is always obscure) in the dictum *rien ne se crée, rien ne se perd*. We believe that everything that comes to be is but a development, an evolution, without being too clear about the meaning of these words (evolution means literally 'unrolling', and Cicero says that the procession of events out of time is like the uncoiling of a rope—*quasi rudentis explicatio*), and we believe that the plant lies in the seed, the future in the present. For example: when a child is born we believe it to have certain dispositions; it may have a disposition to become a musician, and when all the conditions are favourable it will become a musician. Now, according to Aristotle, becoming is nothing but the actualization of a potentiality, that is the becoming actual of a disposition. However, there is a difficulty here. It belongs to one of the little ironies of the history of philosophy that Aristotle's philosophy is based on a concept, i.e. potentiality, that has been excluded by a law that he was the first to express consciously. For Aristotle is the first to have stated as the supreme law of thought (or is it a law of reality?) that there is no intermediary between being and non-being. But the potential, i.e. the objective possible, is such an intermediary; it is namely something which is, still is not yet. Already the Eleatics had declared that there is no becoming, either a thing is or it is not. If it is, it need not become. If it is not—out of nothing nothing becomes. Besides, there is another difficulty which the Megarians have shown.

You say that your child has a disposition to become a musician, that he can become a musician, but if he dies as a child, or when conditions are unfavourable, he cannot become a musician. He can only become one when all the conditions for his being a musician are fulfilled. But in that case it is not possibly that he will be a musician, necessarily he will be one. There is in fact no possibility of his being a musician before he actually is one. There is therefore no potentiality in nature and no becoming of things out of potencies. Things are or are not. This Megarian denial of potentiality has been taken over by the Ash'arites, and Ghazali in this book is on the whole, although not consistently, in agreement with them. I myself regard this problem as one of the cruces of philosophy. The Ash'arites and Ghazali believed, as the Megarians did, that things do not become and that the future does not lie in the present; every event that occurs is new and unconnected with its predecessor. The theologians believed that the world is not an independent universe, a self-subsistent system, that develops by itself, has its own laws, and can be understood by itself. They transferred the mystery of becoming to the mystery of God, who is the cause of all change in the world, and who at every moment creates the world anew. Things are or are not. God creates them and annihilates them, but they do not become out of each other, there is no passage between being and non-being. Nor is there movement, since a thing that moves is neither here nor there, since it moves—what we call movement is *being* at rest at different space-atoms at different time-atoms. It is the denial of potentiality, possibility *in rerum natura*, that Ghazali uses to refute the Aristotelian idea of an eternal matter in which the potentialities are found of everything that can or will happen. For, according to Aristotle, matter must be eternal and cannot have become, since it is, itself, the condition for all becoming.

It may be mentioned here that the modern static theory of movement is akin to the Megarian–Ash'arite doctrine of the denial of movement and becoming. Bertrand Russell, for instance, although he does not accept the Megarian atomic conception, but holds with Aristotle that movement and rest take place in time, not in the instant, defines movement as *being* at different places at different times. At the same time, although he rejects the Megarian conception of 'jumps', he affirms that the moving body always passes from one position to another by gradual transition. But 'passing' implies, just as much as 'jumping', something more than mere being, namely, the movement which both theories deny and the identity of the moving body.

On the idea of possibility another argument for the eternity of the world is based. It is affirmed that if the world had been created an infinite number of possibilities of its creation, that is, an eternal duration of its possibility, would have preceded it. But nothing possible can be eternal, since everything possible must be realized. The idea that everything possible has to be realized is found in Aristotle himself, who says that if there could be an eternal possible that were not realized, it would be impossible, not possible, since the impossible is that which will never be realized. Aristotle does not see that this definition is contrary to the basic idea of his own philosophy—the reality of a possibility which may or may not become real—and that by declaring that the possible will have to happen he reduces it to a necessity, and by admitting that everything that happens had to happen he denies that the possibility of its not happening could precede it, i.e. he accepts, in fact, the Megarian conception of possibility which he himself had tried to refute. Averroës, who agrees with his master on this point, is not aware either of the implication of the definition. On the other hand, the Ash'arites, notwithstanding their denial of potentiality, maintain that for God everything is possible, a theory which implies objective possibility (the same inconsistency was committed by the Stoics). Both philosophers and theologians, indeed, hold about this difficult problem contradictory theories, and it is therefore not astonishing that Ghazali's and Averroës' discussion about it is full of confusion (for the details I refer to my notes).

In the second chapter Ghazali treats the problem of the incorruptibility of the world. As Ghazali says himself, the problem of the incorruptibility of the world is essentially the same as that of its being uncreated and the same arguments can be brought forward. Still, there is less opposition amongst the theologians about its incorruptibility than about its being uncreated. Some of the Mu'tazilites argued, just as Thomas Aquinas was to do later, that we can only know through the Divine Law that this world of ours will end and there is no rational proof for its annihilation. Just as a series of numbers needs a first term but no final term, the beginning of the world does not imply its end. However, the orthodox view is that the annihilation of the world, including Heaven and Hell, is in God's power, although this will not happen. Still, in the corruptibility of the world there is a new difficulty for the theologians. If God destroys the world He causes 'nothingness', that is, His act is related to 'nothing'. But can an act be related to 'nothing'? The question as it is posed seems to rest on a confusion between action and effect, but its deeper sense would be to establish the nature of God's action and the process by which His creative and annihilating power exercises itself. As there cannot be any analogy with the physical process through which our human will performs its function, the mystery of His creative and annihilating action cannot be solved and the naïve answers the theologians give satisfy neither Averroës nor Ghazali himself. Averroës argues that there is no essential difference between production and destruction and, in agreement with Aristotle, he affirms that there are three principles for them: form, matter, and privation. When a thing becomes, its form arises and its privation disappears; when it is destroyed its privation arises and its form disappears, but the substratum of this process, matter, remains eternally. I have criticized this theory in my notes and will only mention here that for Aristotle and Averroës this process of production and destruction is eternal, circular, and reversible. Things, however, do not revolve in an eternal cycle, nor is there an eternal return as the Stoics and Nietzsche held. Inexorably the past is gone. Every 'now' is new. Every flower in the field has never been, the up-torn trees are not rooted again. 'Thou'll come no more, Never, never, never, never, never!' Besides, Averroës, holding as he does that the world is eternally produced out of nothing, is inconsistent in regarding with Aristotle production and destruction as correlatives.

In the third chapter Ghazali maintains that the terms acting and agent are falsely applied to God by the philosophers. Acting, according to him, can be said only of a person having will and choice. When you say that fire burns, there is here a causal relation, if you like, but this implies nothing but a sequence in time, just as Hume will affirm later. So when the philosophers say that God's acting is like the fire's burning or the sun's heating, since God acts by natural necessity, they deny, according to Ghazali, His action altogether. Real causation can only be affirmed of a willing conscious being. The interesting point in this discussion is that, according to the Ash'arites and Ghazali, there is no causation in this world at all, there is only one extra-mundane cause which is God. Even our acts which depend on our will and choice are not, according to the Ash'arites, truly performed by ourselves. We are only the instruments, and the real agent is God. But if this is true, how can we say that action and causation depend on will and choice? How can we come to the idea of any causal action in God depending on His Will if we deny generally that there is a causal relation between will and action? The same contradiction is found in modern philosophy in Mach. Mach holds that to speak of causation or action in material things—so to say that fire burns—is a kind of fetishism or animism, i.e. that we project our will and our actions into physical lifeless things. However, at the same time he, as a follower of Hume, says that causation, even in acts caused by will, is nothing but a temporal sequence of events. He denies causation even in voluntary actions. Therefore it would follow that the relation of willing and acting is not different from the relation of fire and burning and that there cannot be any question of fetishism or animism. According to such a theory there is no action at all in the universe but only a sequence of events.

Then, after a second argument by which Ghazali sets out to show that an eternal production and creation are contradictions in terms, since production and creation imply the generation of something after its non-existence, he directs a third argument against the Neoplatonic theory, held by the philosophers, of the emanation of the world from God's absolute Oneness.

Plotinus' conception of God is prompted by the problem of plurality and relation. All duality implies a relation, and every relation establishes a new unity which is not the simple addition of its terms (since every whole is more than its parts) and violates therefore the supreme law of thought that a thing is what it is and nothing else. Just as the line is more than its points, the stone more than its elements, the organism transcending its members, man, notwithstanding the plurality of his faculties, an identical personality, so the world is an organized well-ordered system surpassing the multitude of the unities it encloses. According to Plotinus the **Force** binding the plurality into unity and the plurality of unities into the **all**-containing unit of the Universe is the Archetype of unity, the ultimate, primordial Monad, God, unattainable in His supreme Simplicity even for thought. For all thought is relational, knitting together in the undefinable unity of a judgement a subject and a predicate. But in God's absolute and highest Unity there is no plurality that can be joined, since all joining needs a superior joining unit. Thus God must be the One and the Lone, having no attribute, no genus, no species, no universal that He can share with any creatures of the world. Even existence can be only referred to Him when it expresses not an attribute, but His very Essence. But then there is no bridge leading from the stable stillness of His Unity to the changing and varied multiplicity of the world; all relation between Him and the world is severed. If the One is the truly rational, God's rationality can be obtained only by regarding His relation to the world as irrational, and all statements about Him will be inconsistent with the initial thesis. And if God is unattainable for thought, the very affirmation of this will be self-contradictory.

Now, the philosophers in Islam hold with Plotinus that although absolutely positive statements are not admissible about God, the positive statements made by them can be all reduced to negative affirmations (with the sole exception, according to Averroës, of His possessing intellect) and to certain relative statements, for neither negations nor *external* relations add anything to His essence.

In this and several following chapters Ghazali attacks the philosophers from two sides: by showing up the inanity of the Plotinian conception of God as pure unity, and by exposing their inconsistency in attributing to Him definite qualities and regarding Him as the source of the world of variety and plurality.

The infinite variety and plurality of the world does not derive directly from God according to the philosophers in Islam, who combine Aristotle's astronomical view of animate planets circling round in their spheres with the Neoplatonic theory of emanation, and introduce into the Aristotelian framework Proclus' conception of a triadic process, but through a series of immaterial mediators. From God's single act—for they with Aristotle regard God as the First Agent—only a single effect follows, but this single effect, the supramundane Intellect, develops in itself a threefoldness through which it can exercise a threefold action. Ghazali objects in a long discussion that if God's eternal action is unique and constant, only one single effect in which no plurality can be admitted will follow (a similar objection can be directed against Aristotle, who cannot explain how the plurality and variety of transitory movements can follow from one single constant movement). The plurality of the world according to Ghazali cannot be explained through a series of mediators. Averroës, who sometimes does not seem very sure of the validity of mediate emanation, is rather evasive in his answer on this point.

In a series of rather intricate discussions which I have tried to elucidate in my notes, Ghazali endeavours to show that the proofs of the philosophers for God's uniqueness, for their denial of His attributes, for their claims that nothing can share with Him His genus and species, that He is pure existence which stands in no relation to an essence, and that He is incorporeal, are all vain. The leading idea of the philosophers that all plurality needs a prior joining principle, Ghazali rejects, while Averroës defends it. Why—so Ghazali asks, for instance—since the essence in temporal things is not the cause of their existence, should this not be the case in the Eternal? Or why should body, although it is composite according to the philosophers, not be the First Cause, especially as they assume an eternal body, since it is not impossible to suppose a compound without a composing principle? From the incorporeality of God, the First Principle, Avicenna had tried to infer, through the disjunction that everything is either matter or intellect, that He is intellect (since the philosophers in Islam hold with Aristotle and in opposition to Plotinus that God possesses self-consciousness). Ghazali does not admit this disjunction and, besides, argues with Plotinus that self-consciousness implies a subject and an object, and therefore would impede the philosophers' thesis of God's absolute unity.

The Muhammadan philosophers, following Aristotle's Neoplatonic commentators, affirm that God's self-knowledge implies His knowledge of all universals (a line of thought followed, for instance, by Thomas Aquinas and some moderns like Brentano). In man this knowledge forms a plurality, in God it is unified. Avicenna subscribes to the Koranic words that no particle in Heaven or Earth escapes God's knowledge, but he holds, as Porphyry had done before, that God can know the particular things only in a universal way, whatever this means. Ghazali takes it to mean that God, according to Avicenna, must be ignorant of individuals, a most heretical theory. For Averroës God's knowledge is neither universal nor particular, but transcending both, in a way unintelligible to the human mind.

One thing, however, God cannot know according to Avicenna (and he agrees here with Plato's *Parmenides*) and that is the passing of time, for in the Eternal no relation is possible to the fleeting 'now'. There are two aspects of time: the sequence of anteriority and posteriority which remains fixed for ever, and the eternal flow of the future through the present into the past. It will be eternally true that I was healthy before I sickened and God can know its eternal truth. But in God's timeless eternity there can be no 'now' simultaneous with the trembling present in which we humans live and change and die, there is no 'now' in God's eternity in which He can know that I am sickening now. In God's eternal stillness the fleeting facts and truths of human experience can find no rest. Ghazali objects, erroneously, I think, that a change in the object of thought need not imply a change in the subject of consciousness.

In another chapter Ghazali refutes the philosophers' proof that Heaven is animated. He does not deny its possibility, but declares that the arguments given are insufficient. He discusses also the view that the heavens move out of love for God and out of desire to assimilate themselves to Him, and he asks the pertinent question—already posed by Theophrastus in his *Metaphysics*, but which scandalizes Averroës by its prosaicness—why it is meritorious for them to circle round eternally and whether eternal rest would not be more appropriate for them in their desire to assimilate themselves to God's eternal stability.

In the last chapter of this part Ghazali examines the philosophers' symbolical interpretation of the Koranic entities 'The Pen' and 'The Tablet' and their theories about dreams and prophecy. It is interesting to note that, although he refutes them here, he largely adopts them in his own *Vivification of Theology*.

In the last part of his book Ghazali treats the natural sciences. He enumerates them and declares that there is no objection to them according to religion except on four points. The first is that there exists a logical nexus between cause and effect; the second, the self-subsistent spirituality of the soul; the third, the immortality of this subsistent soul; the fourth, the denial of bodily resurrection. The first, that there exists between cause and effect a logical necessity, has to be contested according to Ghazali, because by denying it the possibility of miracles can be maintained. The philosophers do not deny absolutely the possibility of miracles. Muhammad himself did not claim to perform any miracles and Hugo Grotius tried to prove the superiority of Christianity over Islam by saying 'Mahumetis se missum ait non cum miraculis sed cum armis'. In later times, however, Muhammad's followers ascribed to him the most fantastic miracles, for instance the cleavage of the moon and his ascension to Heaven. These extravagant miracles are not accepted by the philosophers. Their theory of the possibility of miracles is based on the Stoic–Neoplatonic theory of 'Sympathia', which is that all parts of the world are in intimate contact and related. In a little treatise of Plutarch it is shown how bodily phenomena are influenced by suggestion, by emotion and emotional states, and it is claimed by him, and later also by Plotinus, that the emotions one experiences cannot only influence one's own body but also other bodies, and that one's soul can exercise an influence on other bodies without the intermediary of any bodily action. The phenomena of telepathy, for instance the fascination which a snake has on other animals, they explained in this way. Amulets and talismans can receive through psychological influences certain powers which can be realized later. This explanation of occult phenomena, which is found in Avicenna's *Psychology*, a book translated in the Middle Ages, has been widely accepted (for instance, by Ghazali himself in his *Vivification of Theology*), and is found in Thomas Aquinas and most of the writers about the occult in the Renaissance, for instance Heinricus Cornelius Agrippa, Paracelsus, and Cardanus. It may be mentioned here that Avicenna gives as an example of the power of suggestion that a man will go calmly over a plank when it is on the ground, whereas he will hesitate if the plank be across an abyss. This famous example is found in Pascal's *Pensées*, and the well-known modern healer, Coué, takes it as his chief proof for the power of suggestion. Pascal has taken it from Montaigne, Montaigne has borrowed it from his contemporary the great doctor Pietro Bairo, who himself has a lengthy quotation from the *Psychology* of Avicenna. Robert Burton in his *Anatomy of Melancholy* also mentions it. In the Middle Ages this example is found in Thomas Aquinas. Now the philosophers limit the possibility of miracles only to those that can be explained by the power of the mind over physical objects; for instance, they would regard it as possible that a prophet might cause rain to fall or an earthquake to take place, but they refuse to accept the more extravagant miracles I have mentioned as authentic.

The theologians, however, base their theory of miracles on a denial of natural law. The Megarian–Ash'arite denial of potentiality already implies the denial of natural law. According to this conception there is neither necessity nor possibility *in rerum natura*, they are or they are not, there is no nexus between the phenomena. But the Greek Sceptics also deny the rational relation between cause and effect, and it is this Greek Sceptical theory which the Ash'arites have copied, as we can see by their examples. The theory that there is no necessary relation between cause and effect is found, for instance, in Galen. Fire burns but there is, according to the Greek Sceptics, no necessary relation between fire and burning. Through seeing this happen many times we assume that it will happen also in the future, but there is no necessity, no absolute certainty. This Sceptical theory is quasi-identical with the theory of Hume and is based on the same assumptions, that all knowledge is given through sense-impression; and since the idea of causation cannot be derived from sense experience it is denied altogether. According to the theory of the theologians, God who creates and re-creates the universe continually follows a certain habit in His creation. But He can do anything He desires, everything is possible for Him except the logically impossible; therefore all logically possible miracles are allowed. One might say that, for the theologians, all nature is miraculous and all miracles are natural. Averroës asks a good question: What is really meant by habit, is it a habit in man or in nature? I do not know how Hume would answer this question. For if causation is a habit in man, what makes it possible that such a habit can be formed? What is the objective counterpart of these habits? There is another question which has been asked by the Greek opponents of this theory, but which is not mentioned by Averroës: How many times must such a sequence be observed before such a habit can be formed? There is yet another question that might be asked: Since we cannot act before such a habit is formed—for action implies causation—what are we doing until then? What, even, is the meaning of 'I act' and 'I do'? If there is nothing in the world but a sequence of events, the very word 'activity' will have no sense, and it would seem that we would be doomed to an eternal passivity. Averroës' answer to this denial of natural law is that universals themselves imply already the idea of necessity and law. I think this answer is correct. When we speak, for instance, of wood or stone, we express by those words an hypothetical necessity, that is, we mean a certain object, which in such-and-such circumstances will necessarily behave in a certain way—that the behaviour of wood, for example, is based on its nature, that is, on the potentialities it has.

I may remark here that it seems to me probable that Nicholas of Autrecourt, 'the medieval Hume', was influenced by Ghazali's Ash'arite theories. He denies in the same way as Ghazali the logical connexion between cause and effect: 'ex eo quod aliqua res est cognita esse, non potest evidenter evidentia reducta in primum principium vel in certitudinem primi principii inferri, quod alia res sit' (cf. Lappe, 'Nicolaus von Autrecourt', *Beitr. z. Gesch. d. Phil. d. M.* B.vi, H.2, p. 11); he gives the same example of *ignis* and *stupa*, he seems to hold also the Ash'arite thesis of God as the sole cause of all action (cf. op. cit., p. 24), and he quotes in one place Ghazali's Metaphysics (cf. N. of Autrecourt, 'Exigit ordo executionis', in *Mediaeval Studies*, vol. i, ed. by J. Reginald O'Donnell, Toronto, 1931, p. 208). Now Nicholas's works were burnt during his lifetime in Paris in 1347, whereas the Latin translation of the *Tahafut al Tahafut* by Calo Calonymus was terminated in Arles in 1328.

The second point Ghazali wants to refute are the proofs for the substantiality and the spirituality of the soul as given by the philosophers. He himself does not affirm that the soul is material, and as a matter of fact he holds, in other books, the contrary opinion, but the Ash'arites largely adopted the Stoic materialism. The ten arguments of the philosophers for the spirituality of the soul derive all from arguments given by the Greeks. It would seem to me that Ghazali's arguments for the soul's materiality may be based on the Stoic answers (which have not come down to us) against the proofs of Aristotle and the later Platonists for the immateriality of the soul. There is in the whole discussion a certain confusion, partly based on the ambiguity of the word 'soul'. The term 'soul' both in Greek and Arabic can also mean 'life'. Plants and animals have a 'soul'. However, it is not affirmed by Aristotle that life in plants and animals is a spiritual principle. 'Soul' is also used for the rational part, the thinking part, of our consciousness. It is only this thinking part, according to Aristotle, that is not related to or bound up with matter; sensation and imagination are localized in the body, and it is only part of our thinking soul that seems to possess eternity or to be immortal. Now, most of the ten arguments derive from Aristotle and mean only to prove that the thinking part of our soul is incorporeal. Still the Muhammadan philosophers affirm with Plato and Plotinus that the whole soul is spiritual and incorruptible, and that the soul is a substance independent of the body, although at the same time they adopt Aristotle's physiological explanations of all the non-rational functions of the soul and accept Aristotle's definition of the 'soul' as the first entelechy of an organic body. On the other hand, the Muhammadan philosophers do not admit the Platonic theory of the pre-existence of the soul. Aristotle's conception of a material and transitory element in the soul and an immaterial and immortal element destroys all possibility of considering human personality as a unity. Although he reproaches Plato with regarding the human soul as a plurality, the same reproach can be applied to himself.

Neither the Greek nor the Muhammadan philosophers have ever been able to uphold a theory that does justice to the individuality of the human personality. That it is my undefinable ego that perceives, represents, wills, and thinks, the mysterious fact of the uniqueness of my personality, has never been apprehended by them. It is true that there is in Aristotle's psychology a faint conception of a functional theory of our conscious life, but he is unable to harmonize this with his psycho-physiological notions.

I have discussed in my notes the ten arguments and will mention here only two because of their importance. Ghazali gives one of these arguments in the following form: How can man's identity be attributed to body with all its accidents? For bodies are continually in dissolution and nutrition replaces what is dissolved, so that when we see a child, after separation from its mother's womb, fall ill a few times, become thin and then fat again, and grow up, we may safely say that after forty years no particle remains of what there was when its mother was delivered of it. Indeed, the child began its existence out of parts of the sperm alone, but nothing of the particles of the sperm remains in it; no, all this is dissolved and has changed into something else and then this body has become another. Still we say that the identical man remains and his notions remain with him from the beginning of his youth although all bodily parts have changed, and this shows that the soul has an existence outside the body and that the body is its organ. Now the first part of this argument, that all things are in a state of flux and that of the bodily life of man no part remains identical, is textually found in Montaigne's *Apology of Raymond de Sebond*. Montaigne has taken it from Plutarch, and the Arabic philosophers may have borrowed it from the same source from which Plutarch has taken it. The argument of the philosophers that matter is evanescent, but the soul a stable identity, which is also given by the Christian philosopher Nemesius in his *De natura hominis* (a book translated into Arabic), who ascribes it to Ammonius Saccas and Numenius, is basically Platonic and Neoplatonic, and strangely enough, although he refutes it here, it is adduced by Ghazali himself in his *Vivification of Theology*. Socrates says in the Platonic dialogue *Cratylus*: 'Can we truly say that there is knowledge, Cratylus, if all things are continually changing and nothing remains? For knowledge cannot continue unless it remains and keeps its identity. But if knowledge changes its very essence, it will lose at once its identity and there will be no knowledge.' Plotinus (*Enn.* iv. 7. 3) argues that matter, in its continual changing, cannot explain the identity of the soul. And he says in a beautiful passage (*Enn.* iv. 7. 10) the idea of which Avicenna has copied:

'One should contemplate the nature of everything in its purity, since what is added is ever an obstacle to its knowledge. Contemplate therefore the soul in its abstraction or rather let him who makes this abstraction contemplate himself in this state and he will know that he is immortal when he will see in himself the purity of the intellect, for he will see his intellect contemplate nothing sensible, nothing mortal, but apprehending the eternal through the eternal.'

This passage bears some relation to Descartes's dictum *cogito ergo sum*, but whereas Plotinus affirms the self-consciousness of a stable identity, Descartes states only that every thought has a subject, an ego. Neither the one, nor the other shows that this subject is my ego in the sense of my undefinable unique personality, my awareness who I am: that I am, for instance, John and not Peter, my consciousness of the continuity of my identity from birth to death, my knowledge that at the same time I am master and slave of an identical body, whatever the changes may be in that body, and that as long as I live I am a unique and an identical whole of body and soul. Plautus' Sosia, who was not a philosopher, expresses himself (*Amphitruo*, line 447) in almost the same way as Descartes—'sed quom cogito, equidem certo idem sum qui fui semper'—but the introduction of the words *semper* and *idem* renders the statement fallacious; from mere consciousness the lasting identity of my personality cannot be inferred.

Ghazali answers this point by saying that animals and plants also, notwithstanding that their matter is continually changing, preserve their identity, although nobody believes that this identity is based on a spiritual principle. Averroës regards this objection as justified.

The second argument is based on the theory of universals. Since thought apprehends universals which are not in a particular place and have no individuality, they cannot be material, since everything material is individual and is in space. Against this theory of universals Ghazali develops, under Stoic influence, his nominalistic theory which is probably the theory held by the Ash'arites in general. This theory is quasi-identical with Berkeley's nominalistic conception and springs from the same assumption that thinking is nothing but the having of images. By a strange coincidence both Ghazali and Berkeley give the example of a hand: when we have an idea of a hand as a universal, what really happens is that we have a representation of a particular hand, since there are no universals. But this particular hand is capable of representing for us any possible hand, just as much a big black hand as a small white one. The fallacy of the theory lies, of course, in the word 'representing', which as a matter of fact assumes what it tended to deny, namely, that we can think of a hand in general which has neither a particular shape, nor a particular colour, nor is localized in space.

The next point Ghazali tries to refute is the argument of the philosophers for the immortality of the soul. According to the philosophers, the fact that it is a substance independent of a body and is immaterial shows that a corruption of the body cannot affect it. This, as a matter of fact, is a truism, since the meaning of substantiality and immateriality for the philosophers implies already the idea of eternity. On the other hand, if the soul is the form of the body, as is also affirmed by them, it can only exist with its matter and the mortality of its body would imply its own mortality, as Ghazali rightly points out. The Arabic philosophers through their combination of Platonism and Aristotelianism hold, indeed, at the same time three theories inconsistent with each other, about the relation of body and soul: that the soul is the form of the body, that the soul is a substance, subsistent by itself and immortal, and that the soul after death takes a pneumatic body (a theory already found in Porphyry). Besides, their denial of the Platonic idea of pre-existence of the soul vitiates their statement that the soul is a substance, subsistent by itself, that is, eternal, ungenerated, and incorruptible. Although Averroës in his whole book tries to come as near to the Aristotelian conception of the soul as possible, in this chapter he seems to adopt the eschatology of the late Greek authors. He allows to the souls of the dead a pneumatic body and believes that they exist somewhere in the sphere of the moon. He also accepts the theory of the *Djinn*, the equivalent of the Greek *Daimones*. What he rejects, and what the philosophers generally reject, is the resurrection of the flesh.

In his last chapter Averroës summarizes his views about religion. There are three possible views. A Sceptical view that religion is opium for the people, held by certain Greek rationalists; the view that religion expresses Absolute Truth; and the intermediate view, held by Averroës, that the religious conceptions are the symbols of a higher philosophical truth, symbols which have to be taken for reality

INTRODUCTION

itself by the non-philosophers. For the unphilosophical, however, they are binding, since the sanctity of the State depends on them.

When we have read the long discussions between the philosophers and theologians we may come to the conclusion that it is sometimes more the formula than the essence of things which divides them. Both philosophers and theologians affirm that God creates or has created the world. For the philosophers, since the world is eternal, this creation is eternal. Is there, however, any sense in calling created what has been eternally? For the theologians God is the creator of everything including time, but does not the term 'creation' assume already the concept of time? Both the philosophers and theologians apply to God the theory that His will and knowledge differ from human will and knowledge in that they are creative principles and essentially beyond understanding; both admit that the Divine cannot be measured by the standards of man. But this, in fact, implies an avowal of our complete ignorance in face of the Mystery of God. Still, for both parties God is the supreme Artifex who in His wisdom has chosen the best of all possible worlds; for although the philosophers affirm also that God acts only by natural necessity, their system, like that of their predecessors, the Platonists, Peripatetics, and Stoics, is essentially teleological. As to the problem of possibility, both parties commit the same inconsistencies and hold sometimes that the world could, sometimes that it could not, have been different from what it is. Finally, both parties believe in God's ultimate Unity.

And if one studies the other works of Ghazali the resemblance between him and the philosophers becomes still greater. For instance, he too believes in the spirituality of the soul, notwithstanding the arguments he gives against it in this book; he too sometimes regards religious concepts as the symbols of a higher philosophical or mystical truth, although he admits here only a literal interpretation. He too sometimes teaches the fundamental theory of the philosophers which he tries to refute so insistently in our book, the theory that from the one supreme Agent as the ultimate source through intermediaries all things derive; and he himself expresses this idea (in his *Alchemy of Happiness* and slightly differently in his *Vivification of Theology*) by the charming simile of an ant which seeing black tracings on a sheet of paper thinks that their cause is the pen, while it is the hand that moves the pen by the power of the will which derives from the heart, itself inspired by the spiritual agent, the cause of causes. The resemblances between Ghazali and Averroës, men belonging to the same culture, indeed, the greatest men in this culture, seem sometimes greater than their differences.

Emotionally the difference goes deep. Averroës is a philosopher and a proud believer in the possibility of reason to achieve a knowledge of 'was das Innere der Welt zusammenhält'. He was not always too sure, he knew too much, and there is much wavering and hesitation in his ideas. Still, his faith in reason remains unshaken. Although he does not subscribe to the lofty words of his master that man because of the power of his intellect is a mortal God, he reproaches the theologians for having made God an immortal man. God, for him, is a dehumanized principle. But if God has to respond to the needs of man's heart, can He be exempt from humanity? Ghazali is a *mu'min*, that is a believer, he is a *muslim*, that is he accepts: his heart submits to a truth his reason cannot establish, for his heart has reasons his reason does not know. His theology is the philosophy of the heart in which there is expressed man's fear and loneliness and his feeling of dependence on an understanding and loving Being to whom he can cry out from the depths of his despair, and whose mercy is infinite. It is not so much after abstract truth that Ghazali strives; his search is for God, for the Pity behind the clouds.

IN THE NAME OF THE MERCIFUL AND COMPASSIONATE
GOD: AND AFTER PRAISE TO GOD AND BENEDICTION
UPON ALL HIS MESSENGERS AND PROPHETS:

THE aim of this book is to show the different degrees of assent[1] and conviction attained by the assertions in *The Incoherence of the Philosophers*, and to prove that the greater part has not reached the degree of evidence and of truth.

THE FIRST DISCUSSION
Concerning the Eternity of the World

Ghazali, speaking of the philosophers' proofs for the eternity of the world,[2] says:

Let us restrict ourselves in this chapter to those proofs that make an impression on the mind.

This chapter contains four* proofs.

THE FIRST PROOF

The philosophers say: It is impossible that the temporal should proceed from the absolutely Eternal. For it is clear—if we assume the Eternal existing without, for instance, the world proceeding from Him, then, at a certain moment, the world beginning to proceed from Him—that it did not proceed before, because there was no determining principle for its existence, but its existence was pure possibility*. When the world begins in time, a new determinant either does or does not arise. If it does not, the world will stay in the same state of pure possibility as before; if a new determinant does arise, the same question can be asked about this new determinant, why it determines now, and not before, and either we shall have an infinite regress or we shall arrive at a principle determining eternally.[3]

I say: This argument is in the highest degree dialectical and does not reach the pitch of demonstrative proof.[4] For its premisses are common notions, and common notions approach the equivocal, whereas demonstrative premisses are concerned with things proper to the same genus.[5]

For the term 'possible' is used in an equivocal way of the possible that happens more often than not, of the possible that happens less often than not, and of the possible with equal chances of happening, and these three types of the possible do not seem to have the same need for a new determining principle.[6] For the possible that happens more often than not is frequently believed to have its determining principle in itself, not outside, as is the case with the possible which has equal chances of happening and not happening.¹ Further, the possible resides sometimes in the agent, i.e. the possibility of acting, and sometimes in the patient, i.e. the possibility of receiving, and it does not seem that the necessity for a determining principle is the same in both cases. For it is well known that the possible in the patient needs a new determinant from the outside; this can be perceived by the senses in artificial things and in many natural things too, although in regard to natural things there is a doubt, for in most natural things the principle of their change forms part of them.² Therefore it is believed of many natural things that they move themselves, and it is by no means self-evident that everything that is moved has a mover and that there is nothing that moves itself.³ But all this needs to be examined, and the old philosophers have therefore done so. As concerns the possible in the agent, however, in many cases it is believed that it can be actualized without an external principle, for the transition in the agent from inactivity to activity is often regarded as not being a change which requires a principle; e.g. the transition in the geometer from non-geometrizing to geometrizing, or in the teacher from non-teaching to teaching.

Further, those changes which are regarded as needing a principle of change can sometimes be changes in substance, sometimes in quality, or in quantity, or in place.⁴

In addition, 'eternal' is predicated by many of the eternal-by-itself and the eternal-through-another.⁵ According to some, it is permissible to admit certain changes in the Eternal, for instance a new volition in the Eternal, according to the Karramites,⁶ and the possibility of generation and corruption which the ancients attribute to primary matter, although it is eternal.⁷ Equally, new concepts are admitted in the possible intellect although, according to most authors, it is eternal.⁸ But there are also changes which are inadmissible, especially according to certain ancients, though not according to others.

Then there is the agent who acts of his will and the agent which acts by nature, and the manner of actualization of the possible act is not the same for both agents, i.e. so far as the need for a new determinant is concerned.⁹ Further, is this division into two agents complete, or does demonstration lead to an agent which resembles neither the natural agent nor the voluntary agent of human experience?

All these are multifarious and difficult questions which need, each of them, a special examination, both in themselves and in regard to the opinions the ancients held about them. To treat what is in reality a plurality of questions as one problem is one of the well-known seven sophisms,[1] and a mistake in one of these principles becomes a great error by the end of the examination of reality.[2]

Ghazali says:

There are two objections to this. The first objection is to say: why* do you deny the theory of those who say that the world has been created by an eternal will which has decreed its existence in the time in which it exists; that its non-existence lasts until the moment it ceases and that its existence begins from the moment it begins; that its existence was not willed before and therefore did not happen, and that at the exact moment it began it was willed by an eternal will and therefore began?[3] What is the objection to this theory and what is absurd in it?

I say:

This argument is sophistical: although it is not allowable for him to admit the possibility of the actual effect being delayed after the actual cause, and in a voluntary agent, after the decision to act, he regards it as possible that the effect should be delayed after the will of the agent. It is possible that the effect should be delayed after the will of the agent, but its being delayed after the actual cause is impossible, and equally impossible is its being delayed after a voluntary agent's decision to act. The difficulty is thus unchanged, for he must of necessity draw one of these two conclusions: either that the act of the agent does not imply in him a change which itself would need an external principle of change, or that there are changes which arise by themselves, without the necessity of an agent in whom they occur and who causes them, and that therefore there are changes possible in the Eternal without an agent who causes them. And his adversaries insist on these two very points: (1) that the act of the agent necessarily implies a change[4] and that each change has a principle which causes it; (2) that the Eternal cannot change in any way. But all this is difficult to prove.[5]

The Ash'arites are forced to assume either a first agent or a first act of this agent, for they cannot admit that the disposition of the agent, relative to the effect, when he acts is the same as his disposition, when he does not act.[6] This implies therefore a new disposition or a new relation, and this necessarily either in the agent, or in the effect, or in both.[7] But in this case, if we posit as a principle that for each new disposition there is an agent, this new disposition in the first agent will either need another agent, and then this first agent was not the first and was not on his own account sufficient for the act but needed another, or the agent of the disposition which is the condition of the agent's act will be identical with the agent of the act. Then this act which we regarded as being the first act arising out of him will not be the first, but his act producing the disposition which is the condition of the effect will be anterior to the act producing the effect.[1] This, you see, is a necessary consequence, unless one allows that new dispositions may arise in the agents without a cause. But this is absurd, unless one believes that there are things which happen at haphazard and by themselves,[2] a theory of the old philosophers who denied the agent,[3] the falsehood of which is self-evident.

In Ghazali's objection there is a confusion. For our expressions 'eternal will' and 'temporal will' are equivocal, indeed contrary. For the empirical will is a faculty which possesses the possibility of doing equally one of two contraries and then of receiving equally one of the two contraries willed.[4] For the will is the desire of the agent towards action.[5] When the agent acts, the desire ceases and the thing willed happens, and this desire and this act are equally related to both the contraries. But when one says: 'There is a Willer who wills eternally one of two contraries in Himself', the definition of the will is abandoned, for we have transferred its nature from the possible to the necessary. If it is objected that in an eternal will the will does not cease through the presence of the object willed, for as an eternal will has no beginning there is no moment in it which is specially determined for the realization of the object willed, we answer: this is not obvious, unless we say that demonstrative proof leads to the existence of an agent endowed with a power which is neither voluntary nor natural, which, however, the Divine Law calls 'will', in the same way as demonstrative proof leads to middle terms between things which seemed at first sight to be contrary, without being really so, as when we speak of an existence which is neither inside nor outside the world.[6]

Ghazali answers, on behalf of the philosophers:

The philosophers say: This is clearly impossible, for everything that happens is necessitated and has its cause, and as it is impossible that there should be an effect without a necessitating principle and a cause, so it is impossible that there should exist a cause of which the effect is delayed, when all the conditions of its necessitating, its causes and elements are completely fulfilled. On the contrary, the existence of the effect, when the cause is realized with all its conditions, is necessary, and its delay is just as impossible as an effect without cause. Before the existence of the world there existed a Willer, a will, and its relation to the thing willed. No new willer arose, nor a new will, nor a new relation to the will—for all this is change; how then could a new object of will arise, and what prevented its arising before? The condition of the new production did not distinguish itself from the condition of the non-production in any way, in any mode, in any relation—on the contrary, everything remained as it was before. At one moment the object of will did not exist, everything remained as it was before, and then the object of will existed. Is not this a perfectly absurd theory?

I say:

This is perfectly clear, except for one who denies one of the premises we have laid down previously. But Ghazali passes from this proof to an example based upon convention,[1] and through this he confuses this defence of the philosophers.

Ghazali says:

This kind of impossibility is found not only in the necessary and essential cause and effect but also in the accidental* and conventional. If a man pronounces the formula of divorce against his wife without the divorce becoming irrevocable immediately, one does not imagine that it will become so later.[2] For he made the formula through convention and usage a cause of the judgement, and we do not believe that the effect can be delayed, except when the divorce depends on an ulterior event, e.g. on the arrival of tomorrow or on someone's entering the house, for then the divorce does not take place at once, but only when tomorrow arrives or someone enters the house; in this case the man made the formula a cause only in conjunction with an ulterior event. But as this event, the coming of tomorrow and someone's entering the house, is not yet actual, the effect is delayed until this future event is realized. The effect only takes place when a new event, i.e. entering the house or the arrival of tomorrow, has actually happened. Even if a man wanted to delay the effect after the formula, without making it dependent on an ulterior event, this would be regarded as impossible, although it is he himself who lays down the convention and fixes its modalities. If thus in conventional matters such a delay is incomprehensible and inadmissible, how can we admit it in essential, rational, and necessary causal relations? In respect of our conduct and our voluntary actions, there is a delay in actual volition only when there is some obstacle. When there is actual volition and actual power and the obstacles are eliminated, a delay in the object willed is inadmissible.[3] A delay in the object willed is imaginable only in decision, for decision is not sufficient for the existence of the act;[4] the decision to write does not produce the writing, if it is not, as a new fact, accompanied by an act of volition, i.e. an impulse in the man which presents itself at the moment of the act. If there is thus an analogy between the eternal Will and our will to act, a delay of the object willed is inadmissible, unless through an obstacle, and an antecedent existence of the volition is equally inadmissible, for I cannot will to get up tomorrow except by way of decision. If, however, the eternal Will is analogous to our decision, it does not suffice to produce the thing decided upon, but the act of creation must be accompanied by a new act of volition, and this brings us again to the idea of a change. But then we have the same difficulty all over again. Why does this impulse or volition or will or whatever you choose to call it happen just now and not before? There remain, then, only these alternatives: either something happening without a cause, or an infinite regress. This is the upshot of the discussion: There is a cause the conditions of which are all completely fulfilled, but notwithstanding this the effect is delayed and is not realized during a period to the beginning of which imagination cannot attain and for which thousands of years would mean no diminution; then suddenly, without the addition of any new fact, and without the realization of any new condition, this effect comes into existence and is produced. And this is absurd.

I say:

This example of divorce based on convention seems to strengthen the argument of the philosophers, but in reality it weakens it. For it enables the Ash'arites to say: In the same way as the actual divorce is delayed after the formula of divorce till the moment when the condition of someone's entering the house, or any other, is fulfilled, so the realization of the world can be delayed after God's act of creation until the condition is fulfilled on which this realization depends, i.e. the moment when God willed it. But conventional things do not behave like rational. The Literalists, comparing these conventional things to rational, say: This divorce is not binding and does not become effective through the realization of the condition which is posterior to the pronouncement of the divorce by the divorcer, since it would be a divorce which became effective without connexion with the act of the divorcer.[1] But in this matter there is no relation between the concept drawn from the nature of things and that which is artificial and conventional.

Then Ghazali says, on behalf of the Ash'arites:

The answer is: Do you recognize the impossibility of connecting the eternal Will with the temporal production of anything, through the necessity of intuitive thought or through a logical deduction, or—to use your own logical terminology—do you recognize the clash between these two concepts through a middle term or without a middle term?[2] If you claim a middle term—and this is the deductive method—you will have to produce it, and if you assert that you know this through the necessity of thought, why do your adversaries not share this intuition with you?[3] For

THE FIRST DISCUSSION

the party which believes in the creation of the world in time through an eternal Will includes so many persons that no country can contain them and no number enumerate them, and they certainly do not contradict the logically minded out of obstinacy, while knowing better in their hearts. A proof according to the rules of logic must be produced to show this impossibility, as in all your* arguments up till now there is only a presumption of impossibility and a comparison with our decision and our will; and this is false, for the eternal Will does not resemble temporal volitions, and a pure presumption of impossibility will not suffice without proof.

I say:

This argument is one of those which have only a very feeble persuasive power. It amounts to saying that one who claims the impossibility of delay in an effect, when its cause with all its conditions is realized, must assert that he knows this either by a syllogism or from first principles; if through a syllogism, he must produce it—but there is none; if from first principles, it must be known to all, adversaries and others alike. But this argument is mistaken, for it is not a condition of objective truth that it should be known to all. That anything should be held by all does not imply anything more than its being a common notion, just as the existence of a common notion does not imply objective truth.[1]

Ghazali answers on behalf of the Ash'arites:

If it is said, 'We know by the necessity of thought that, when all its conditions are fulfilled, a cause without effect is inadmissible and that to admit it is an affront to the necessity of thought,' we answer: what is the difference between you and your adversaries, when they say to you, 'We know by the necessity of thought the impossibility of a theory which affirms that one single being knows all the universals, without this knowledge forming a plurality in its essence or adding anything to it, and without this plurality of things known implying a plurality in the knowledge'?[2] For this is your theory of God, which according to us and our science is quite absurd. You, however, say there is no analogy between eternal and temporal knowledge. Some of you acknowledge the impossibility involved, and say that God knows only Himself and that He is the knower, the knowledge and the known, and that the three are one. One might object: The unity of the knowledge, the knower, and the known is clearly an impossibility, for to suppose the Creator of the world ignorant of His own work is necessarily absurd, and the Eternal—who is far too high to be reached by your* words and the words of any heretics—could, if He knows only Himself, never know His work.

I say:

This amounts to saying that the theologians do not gratuitously and without proof deny the admitted impossibility of a delay between the effect and its cause, but base themselves on an argument which leads them to believe in the temporal creation of the world, and that they therefore act in the same way as the philosophers, who only deny the well-known necessary plurality of knowledge and known, so far as it concerns their unity in God, because of a demonstration which, according to them, leads them to their theory about Him. And that this is still more true of those philosophers who deny it to be necessary that God should know His own work, affirming that He knows only Himself. This assertion belongs to the class of assertions whose contrary is equally false.[1] For there exists no proof which refutes anything that is evidently true, and universally acknowledged. Anything that can be refuted by a demonstrative proof is only supposed to be true, not really true.[2] Therefore, if it is absolutely and evidently true that knowledge and known form a plurality, both in the visible and in the invisible world, we can be sure that the philosophers cannot have a proof of this unity in God; but if the theory of the plurality of knowledge and known is only a supposition, then it is possible for the philosophers to have a proof. Equally, if it is absolutely true that the effect of a cause cannot be delayed after the causation and the Ash'arites claim that they can advance a proof to deny it, then we can be absolutely sure that they cannot have such a proof. If there is a controversy about questions like this, the final criterion rests with the sound understanding[3] which does not base itself on prejudice and passion, when it probes according to the signs and rules by which truth and mere opinion are logically distinguished. Likewise, if two people dispute about a sentence and one says that it is poetry, the other that it is prose, the final judgement rests with the 'sound understanding' which can distinguish poetry from prose, and with the science of prosody. And as, in the case of metre, the denial of him who denies it does not interfere with its perception by him who perceives it, so the denial of a truth by a contradictor does not trouble the conviction of the men to whom it is evident.

This whole argument is extremely inept and weak, and Ghazali ought not to have filled* his book with such talk if he intended to convince the learned.

And drawing consequences which are irrelevant and beside the point, Ghazali goes on to say:

But the consequences of this argument cannot be overcome. And we say to them: How will you refute your adversaries, when they say the eternity of the world is impossible, for it implies an infinite number and an infinity of unities for the spherical revolutions, although they can be divided by six, by four, and by two.[1] For the sphere of the sun revolves in one year, the sphere of Saturn in thirty years, and so Saturn's revolution is a thirtieth and Jupiter's revolution—for Jupiter revolves in twelve years—a twelfth of the sun's revolution. But the number of revolutions of Saturn has the same infinity as the revolutions of the sun, although they are in a proportion of one to thirty and even the infinity of the sphere of the fixed stars which turns round once in thirty-six thousand years is the same as the daily revolution which the sun performs in twenty-four hours. If now your adversary says that this is plainly impossible, in what does your argument differ from his? And suppose it is asked: Are the numbers of these revolutions even or uneven or both even and uneven or neither even nor uneven? If you answer, both even and uneven, or neither even nor uneven, you say what is evidently absurd. If, however, you say 'even' or 'uneven', even and uneven become uneven and even by the addition of one unit and how could infinity be one unit short? You must, therefore, draw the conclusion that they are neither even nor uneven.

I say:

This too is a sophistical argument. It amounts to saying: In the same way as *you* are unable to refute *our* argument for the creation of the world in time, that if it were eternal, its revolutions would be neither even nor uneven, so *we* cannot refute *your* theory that the effect of an agent whose conditions to act are always fulfilled cannot be delayed. This argument aims only at creating and establishing a doubt, which is one of the sophist's objectives.

But you, reader of this book, you have already heard the arguments of the philosophers to establish the eternity of the world and the refutation of the Ash'arites. Now hear the proofs of the Ash'arites for their refutation and hear the arguments of the philosophers to refute those proofs in the wording of Ghazali!†

I say:

This is in brief that, if you imagine two circular movements in one and the same finite time and imagine then a limited part of these movements in one and the same finite time, the proportion between the parts of these two circular movements and between their wholes will be the same. For instance, if the circular movement of Saturn in the period which we call a year is a thirtieth of the circular movement of the sun in this period, and you imagine the whole of the circular movements of the sun in proportion to the whole of the

† [Here, in the Arabic text, the last passage of Ghazali, which previously was given only in an abbreviated form, is repeated in full.]

circular movements of Saturn in one and the same period*, necessarily the proportion between their wholes* and between their parts will be the same.[1] If, however, there is no proportion between two movements in their totality, because they are both potential, i.e. they have neither beginning nor end but there exists a proportion between the parts, because they are both actual, then the proportion between the wholes is not necessarily the same as the proportion between the parts—although many think so, basing their proof on this prejudice —for there is no proportion between two magnitudes or quantities which are both taken to be infinite.[2] When, therefore, the ancients believed that, for instance, the totality of the movements of the sun and of Saturn had neither beginning nor end, there could be no proportion between them, for this would have implied the finitude of both these totalities, just as this is implied for the parts of both. This is self-evident. Our adversaries believe that, when a proportion of more and less exists between parts, this proportion holds good also for the totalities, but this is only binding when the totalities are finite.[3] For where there is no end there is neither 'more' nor 'less'. The admission in such a case of the proportion of more and less brings with it another absurd conscquence, namely that one infinite could be greater than another. This is only absurd when one supposes two things actually infinite, for then a proportion does exist between them.[4] When, however, one imagines things potentially infinite, there exists no proportion at all. This is the right answer to this question, not what Ghazali says in the name of the philosophers.

And through this are solved all the difficulties which beset our adversaries on this question, of which the greatest is that which they habitually formulate in this way: If the movements in the past are infinite, then no movement in the actual present can take place, unless an infinite number of preceding movements is terminated.[5] This is true, and acknowledged by the philosophers, once granted that the anterior movement is the condition for the posterior movement's taking place, i.e. once granted that the existence of one single movement implies an infinite number of causes. But no philosopher allows the existence of an infinite number of causes, as accepted by the materialists, for this would imply the existence of an effect without cause and a motion without mover.[6] But when the existence of an eternal prime mover had been proved, whose act cannot be posterior to his being, it followed that there could as little be a beginning for

THE FIRST DISCUSSION

his act as for his being; otherwise his act would be possible, not necessary, and he would not be a first principle.[1] The acts of an agent who has no beginning have a beginning as little as his existence, and therefore it follows necessarily that no preceding act of his is the condition for the existence of a later, for neither of them is an agent by itself and their sequence is accidental. An accidental infinite, not an essential infinite, is admitted by the philosophers; nay, this type of infinite is in fact a necessary consequence of the existence of an eternal first principle.[2] And this is not only true for successive or continuous movements and the like, but even where the earlier is regarded as the cause of the later, for instance the man who engenders a man like himself.[3] For it is necessary that the series of temporal productions of one individual man by another should lead upwards to an eternal agent, for whom there is no beginning either of his existence or of his production of man out of man. The production of one man by another *ad infinitum* is accidental, whereas the relation of before and after in it is essential. The agent who has no beginning either for his existence or for those acts of his which he performs without an instrument, has no first instrument* either to perform those acts of his without beginning which by their nature need an instrument.[4]

But since the theologians mistook the accidental for the essential, they denied this eternal agent; the solution of their problem was difficult and they believed this proof to be stringent. But this theory of the philosophers is clear, and their first master Aristotle has explained that, if motion were produced by motion, or element by element, motion and element could not exist.[5] For this type of infinite the philosophers admit neither a beginning nor an end, and therefore one can never say of anything in this series that it has ended or has begun, not even in the past, for everything that has an end must have begun and what does not begin does not end. This can also be understood from the fact that beginning and end are correlatives. Therefore one who affirms that there is no end of the celestial revolutions in the future cannot logically ascribe a beginning to them, for what has a beginning has an end and what has no end has no beginning, and the same relation exists between first and last; i.e. what has a first term has also a last term, and what has no first term has no last term, and there is in reality neither end nor beginning for any part of a series that has no last term, and what has no beginning for any of its parts has no end for any of them either. When, therefore, the theologians ask the philosophers if the movements which precede the present one are ended, their answer is negative, for their assumption that they have no beginning implies their endlessness. The opinion of the theologians that the philosophers admit their end is erroneous, for they do not admit an end for what has no beginning.[1] It will be clear to you that neither the arguments of the theologians for the temporal creation of the world of which Ghazali speaks, nor the arguments of the philosophers which he includes and describes in his book, suffice to reach absolute evidence or afford stringent proof*. And this is what we have tried to show in this book. The best answer one can give to him who asks where in the past is the starting-point of His acts, is: The starting-point of His acts is at the starting-point of His existence; for neither of them has a beginning.

And here is the passage of Ghazali in which he sets forth the defence of the philosophers against the argument built on the difference in speed of the celestial spheres, and his refutation of their argument.

Ghazali says:

If one says, 'The error in your argument consists in your considering those circular movements as an aggregate of units, but those movements have no real existence, for the past is no more and the future not yet; "aggregate" means units existing in the present, but in this case there is no existence.'

Then he says to refute this:

We answer: Number can be divided into even and uneven; there is no third possibility, whether for the numbered permanent reality, or for the numbered passing event. Therefore whatever number we imagine, we must believe it to be even or uneven, whether we regard it as existent or non-existent; and if the thing numbered vanishes from existence, our judgement of its being even or uneven does not vanish or change.[2]

I say:

This is the end of his argument. But this argument—that the numbered thing must be judged as even or uneven, whether it exists or not—is only valid so far as it concerns external things or things in the soul that have a beginning and an end. For of the number which exists only potentially, i.e. which has neither beginning nor end, it cannot truly be said that it is even or uneven, or that it begins or ends; it happens neither in the past nor in the future, for what exists potentially falls under the law of non-existence.[3] This is what the philosophers meant when they said that the circular movements of the past and the future are non-existent.[4] The upshot of this

THE FIRST DISCUSSION

question is: Everything that is called a limited aggregate with a beginning and an end is so called either because it has a beginning and end in the world exterior to the soul, or because it is inside, not outside, the soul. Every totality, actual and limited in the past, whether inside or outside the soul, is necessarily either even or uneven. But an unlimited aggregate existing outside the soul cannot be other than limited so far as it is represented in the soul, for the soul cannot represent unlimited existence. Therefore also this unlimited aggregate, as being limited in the soul, can be called even or uneven; in so far, however, as it exists outside the soul, it can be called neither even nor uneven. Equally, past aggregates which are considered to exist potentially outside the soul, i.e. which have no beginning, cannot be called even or uneven unless they are looked upon as actual, i.e. as having beginning and end. No motion possesses totality or forms an aggregate, i.e. is provided with a beginning or an end, except in so far as it is in the soul, as is the case with time.[1] And it follows from the nature of circular movement that it is neither even nor uneven except as represented in the soul. The cause of this mistake is that it was believed that, when something possesses a certain quality in the soul, it must possess this quality also outside the soul, and, since anything that has happened in the past can only be represented in the soul as finite, it was thought that everything that has happened in the past must also be finite outside the soul. And as the circular movements of the future are regarded by the imagination* as infinite, for it represents them as a sequence of part after part,[2] Plato[3] and the Ash'arites believed that they might be infinite, but this is simply a judgement based on imagination, not on proof. Therefore those* who believe—as many theologians have done—that, if the world is supposed to have begun, it must have an end, are truer to their principles[4] and show more consistency.

Ghazali says after this:

And we say moreover to the philosophers: According to your principles it is not absurd that there should be actual units, qualitatively differentiated, which are infinite in number; I am thinking of human souls, separated through death from their bodies. These are therefore realities that can neither be called even nor uneven. How will you refute the man who affirms that this is necessarily absurd in the same way as you claim the connexion between an eternal will and a temporal creation to be necessarily absurd? This theory about souls is that which Avicenna accepted, and it is perhaps Aristotle's.

I say:

This argument is extremely weak. It says, in brief, 'You philosophers need not refute our assertion that what is a logical necessity for you is not necessary, as you consider things possible which your adversaries consider impossible by the necessity of thought. That is to say, just as you consider things possible which your adversaries consider impossible, so you consider things necessary which your adversaries do not consider so. And you cannot bring a criterion for judging the two claims.' It has already been shown in the science of logic that this is a weak rhetorical or sophistical kind of argument.[1] The answer is that what *we** claim to be necessarily true is objectively true, whereas what *you* claim as necessarily absurd is not as you claim it to be. For this there is no other criterion than immediate intuitive apprehension,[2] just as, when one man claims that a line is rhythmical and another denies it, the criterion is the intuition of the sound understanding.

As for the thesis of a numerical plurality of immaterial souls, this is not a theory acknowledged by the philosophers,[3] for they regard matter as the cause of numerical plurality[4] and form as the cause of congruity in numerical plurality. And that there should be a numerical plurality without matter, having one unique form, is impossible. For in its description one individual can only be distinguished from another accidentally, as there is often another individual who participates in this description,[5] but only through their matter do individuals differ in reality. And also this: the impossibility of an actual infinite is an acknowledged axiom in philosophical theory, equally valid for material and immaterial things. We do not know of any one who makes a distinction here between the spatial and the non-spatial, with the single exception of Avicenna.[6] I do not know of any other philosopher who affirms this, it does not correspond with any of their principles and it makes no sense, for the philosophers deny the existence of an actual infinite equally for material and for immaterial things, as it would imply that one infinite could be greater than another. Perhaps Avicenna wanted only to satisfy the masses, telling them what they were accustomed to hear about the soul. But this theory is far from satisfactory. For if there were an actual infinite and it were divided in two, the part would equal the whole; e.g. if there were a line or a number actually infinite in both directions and it were divided in two, both the parts and the whole would be actually infinite; and this is absurd.[7] All this is simply the consequence of the admission of an actual and not potential infinite.

Ghazali says:

If it is said, 'The truth lies with Plato's theory of one eternal soul which is only divided in bodies and returns after its separation from them to its original unity',[1] we answer: This theory is still worse, more objectionable and more apt to be regarded as contrary to the necessity of thought. For we say that the soul of Zaid is either identical with the soul of Amr or different from it; but their identity would mean something absurd, for everyone is conscious of his own identity and knows that he is not another, and, were they identical, their knowledge, which is an essential quality of their souls and enters into all the relations into which their souls enter, would be identical too.[2] If you say their soul is unique and only divided through its association with bodies, we answer that the division of a unity which has no measurable volume* is absurd by the necessity of thought. And how could the one become two, and indeed a thousand, and then return to its unity? This can be understood of things which have volume and quantity, like the water of the sea which is distributed into brooks and rivers and flows then back again into the sea, but how can that which has no quantity be divided?[3] We seek to show by all this that the philosophers cannot shake the conviction of their adversaries that the eternal Will is connected with temporal creation, except by claiming its absurdity by the necessity of thought, and that therefore they are in no way different from the theologians who make the same claim against the philosophical doctrines opposed to theirs. And out of this there is no issue.

I say:

Zaid and Amr are numerically different, but identical in form. If, for example, the soul of Zaid were numerically different from the soul of Amr in the way Zaid is numerically different from Amr, the soul of Zaid and the soul of Amr would be numerically two, but one in their form, and the soul would possess another soul.[4] The necessary conclusion is therefore that the soul of Zaid and the soul of Amr are identical in their form. An identical form inheres in a numerical, i.e. a divisible, multiplicity, only through the multiplicity of matter. If then the soul does not die when the body dies, or if it possesses an immortal element, it must, when it has left the bodies, form a numerical unity.[5] But this is not the place to go deeper into this subject.

His argument against Plato is sophistical. It says in short that the soul of Zaid is either identical with the soul of Amr or different from it; but that the soul of Zaid is not identical with the soul of Amr and that therefore it is different from it. But 'different' is an equivocal term, and 'identity' too is predicated of a number of things which are also called 'different'.[6] The souls of Zaid and Amr are one in one sense and many in another; we might say, one in relation to their form, many in relation to their substratum. His remark that division can only be imagined of the quantitative is partially false; it is true of essential division, but not of accidental division, i.e. of those things which can be divided, because they exist in the essentially divisible.[1] The essentially divisible is, for example, body; accidental division is, for instance, the division of whiteness, when the bodies in which it is present are divided, and in this way the forms and the soul are accidentally divisible, i.e. through the division of the substrate. The soul is closely similar to light: light is divided by the division of illuminated bodies, and is unified when the bodies are annihilated, and this same relation holds between soul and bodies.[2] To advance such sophistical arguments is dishonest, for it may be supposed that he is not a man to have overlooked the points mentioned. What he said, he said only to flatter the masses of his times, but how far removed is such an attitude from the character of those who seek to set forth the truth![3] But perhaps the man may be forgiven on account of the time and place in which he lived; and indeed he only proceeded in his books in a tentative way.[4]

And as these arguments carry no evidence whatsoever, Ghazali says:

> We want to show by all this that the philosophers cannot shake the conviction of their adversaries that the eternal Will is connected with temporal creation, by claiming its absurdity by the necessity of thought, and that therefore they do not distinguish themselves from the theologians, who make the same claim against the philosophical doctrines opposed to theirs. And out of this there is no issue.

I say:

When someone denies a truth of which it is absolutely certain that it is such-and-such, there exists no argument by which we can come to an understanding with him; for every argument is based on known premisses about which both adversaries agree.[5] When each point advanced is denied by the adversary, discussion with him becomes impossible, but such people stand outside the pale of humanity and have to be educated. But for him who denies an evident truth, because of a difficulty which presents itself to him there is a remedy, i.e. the solution of this difficulty. He who does not understand evident truth, because he is lacking in intelligence, cannot be taught anything, nor can he be educated.[6] It is like trying to make the blind imagine colours or know their existence.

Ghazali says:

The philosophers may object: This argument (that the present has been preceded by an infinite past) can be turned against you, for God before the creation of the world was able to create it, say, one year or two years* before He did, and there is no limit to His power; but He seemed to have patience and did not create. Then He created. Now, the duration of His inactivity is either finite or infinite. If you say finite, the existence of the Creator becomes finite; if you say infinite, a duration in which there is an infinite number of possibilities receives its termination.[1] We answer: Duration and time are, according to us, created, but we shall explain the real answer to this question when we reply to the second proof of the philosophers.[2]

I say:

Most people who accept a temporal creation of the world believe time to have been created with it. Therefore his assertion that the duration of His inactivity was either limited or unlimited is untrue. For what has no beginning does not finish or end. And the opponent does not admit that the inactivity has any duration at all. What one has to ask them about the consequences of their theory is: Is it possible, when the creation of time is admitted, that the term of its beginning may lie beyond the real time in which we live?[3] If they answer that it is not possible, they posit a limited extension beyond which the Creator cannot pass, and this is, in their view, shocking and absurd. If, however, they concede that its possible beginning may lie beyond the moment of its created term, it may further be asked if there may not lie another term beyond this second. If they answer in the affirmative—and they cannot do otherwise—it will be said: Then we shall have here a possible creation of an infinite number of durations, and you will be forced to admit—according to your argument about the spherical revolutions—that their termination is a condition for the real age which exists since them. If you say what is infinite does not finish, the arguments you use about the spherical revolutions against your opponents your opponents will use against you* on the subject of the possibility of created durations. If it is objected that the difference between those two cases is that these infinite possibilities belong to extensions which do not become actual, whereas the spherical revolutions do become actual, the answer is that the possibilities of things belong to their necessary accidents and that it does not make any difference, according to the philosophers, if they precede these things or are simultaneous with them, for of necessity they are the dispositions* of things.[4] If, then, it is impossible that before the existence of the present spherical revolution there should have been infinite spherical revolutions, the existence of infinite possible revolutions is equally impossible. If one wants to avoid these consequences, one can say that the age of the world is a definite quantity and cannot be longer or shorter than it is, in conformity with the philosophical doctrine about the size of the world.[1] Therefore these arguments are not stringent, and the safest way for him who accepts the temporal creation of the world is to regard time as of a definite extension and not to admit a possibility which precedes the possible;[2] and to regard also the spatial extension of the world as finite. Only, spatial extension forms a simultaneous whole; not so time.

Ghazali expounds a certain kind of argument attributed to the philosophers on this subject against the theologians when they denied* that the impossibility of delay* in the Creator's act after His existence is known by primitive intuition:[3]

> How will you defend yourselves, theologians, against the philosophers, when they drop this argument, based on the necessity of thought, and prove the eternity of the world* in this way, saying that times are equivalent so far as the possibility that the Divine Will should attach itself to them is concerned, for what differentiates a given time from an earlier or a later time? And it is not absurd to believe that the earlier or the later might be chosen when on the contrary you theologians say about white, black, movement, and rest that the white is realized through the eternal Will although its substrate accepts equally black and white. Why, then, does the eternal Will attach itself to the white rather than to the black, and what differentiates one of the two possibles from the other for connexion with the eternal Will? But we philosophers know by the necessity of thought that one thing does not distinguish itself from a similar except by a differentiating principle, for if not, it would be possible that the world should come into existence, having the possibility both of existing and of not existing, and that the side of existence, although it has the same possibility as the side of non-existence, should be differentiated without a differentiating principle. If you answer that the Will of God is the differentiating principle, then one has to inquire what differentiates the Will, i.e. the reason why it has been differentiated in such or such way. And if you answer: One does not inquire after the motives of the Eternal,[4] well, let the world then be eternal, and let us not inquire after its Creator and its cause, since one does not inquire after the motives of the Eternal! If it is regarded as possible that the Eternal should differentiate one of the two possibles by chance, it will be an extreme absurdity to say that the world is differentiated in differentiated forms which might just as well be other-

wise, and one might then say that this has happened by chance in the same way as you say that the Divine Will has differentiated one time rather than another or one form rather than another by chance. If you say that such a question is irrelevant, because it refers to anything God can will or decide, we answer that this question is quite relevant, for it concerns any time and is pertinent for our opponents to any decision God takes.

We answer: The world exists, in the way it exists, in its time, with its qualities, and in its space, by the Divine Will and will is a quality which has the faculty of differentiating one thing from another,[1] and if it had not this faculty, power in itself would suffice.[2] But, since power is equally related to two contraries[3] and a differentiating principle is needed to differentiate one thing from a similar, it is said that the Eternal possesses besides His power a quality which can differentiate between two similars.[4] And to ask why will differentiates one of two similars is like asking why knowledge must comprehend the knowable, and the answer is that 'knowledge' is the term for a quality which has just this nature. And in the same way, 'will' is the term for a quality the nature or rather the essence of which is to differentiate one thing from another.

The philosophers may object: The assumption of a quality the nature of which is to differentiate one thing from a similar one is something incomprehensible, nay even contradictory, for 'similar' means not to be differentiated, and 'differentiated' means not similar. And it must not be believed that two blacks in two substrates are similar in every way, since the one is in one place and the other in another, and this causes a distinction; nor are two blacks at two times in one substrate absolutely similar, since they are separated in time, and how could they therefore be similar in every way? When we say of two blacks that they are similar, we mean that they are similar in blackness, in their special relation to it—not absolutely. Certainly, if the substrate and the time were one without any distinction, one could not speak any more of two blacks or of any duality at all. This proves that the term 'Divine Will' is derived from our will, and one does not imagine that through our will two similar things can be differentiated.[5] On the contrary, if someone who is thirsty has before him two cups of water, similar in everything in respect to his aim, it will not be possible for him to take either of them. No, he can only take the one he thinks more beautiful or lighter or nearer to his right hand, if he is right-handed, or act from some such reason, hidden or known. Without this the differentiation of the one from the other cannot be imagined.

I say:

The summary of what Ghazali relates in this section of the proofs of the philosophers for the impossibility of a temporal proceeding from an eternal agent is that in God there cannot be a will. The philosophers could only arrive at this argument after granting to their opponents that all opposites—opposites in time,[6] like anterior and posterior, as well as those in quality, like white and black—are equivalent in relation to the eternal Will. And also non-existence and existence are, according to the theologians, equivalent in relation to the Divine Will. And having granted their opponents this premiss, although they did not acknowledge its truth, they said to them: It is of the nature of will that it cannot give preponderance to one thing rather than to a similar one, except through a differentiating principle[1] and a cause which only exist in one of these two similar things; if not, one of the two would happen by chance—and the philosophers argued for the sake of discussion, as if they had conceded that, if the Eternal had a will, a temporal could proceed from an eternal. As the theologians were unable to give a satisfactory answer, they took refuge in the theory that the eternal Will is a quality the nature of which is to differentiate between two similar things, without there being for God a differentiating principle which inclines Him to one of two similar acts; that the eternal Will is thus a quality like warmth which gives heat or like knowledge which comprehends the knowable.[2] But their opponents, the philosophers, answered: It is impossible that this should happen, for two similar things are equivalent for the willer, and his action can only attach itself to the one rather than to the other through their being dissimilar, i.e. through one's having a quality the other has not. When, however, they are similar in every way and when for God there is no differentiating principle at all, His will will attach itself to both of them indifferently and, when this is the case—His will being the cause of His act—the act will not attach itself to the one rather than to the other, it will attach itself either to the two contrary actions simultaneously or to neither of them at all, and both cases are absurd. The philosophers, therefore, began their argument, as if they had it granted to them that all things were equivalent in relation to the First Agent, and they forced them to admit that there must be for God a differentiating principle which precedes Him, which is absurd. When the theologians answered that will is a quality the nature of which is to differentiate the similar from the similar, in so far as it is similar, the philosophers objected that this is not understood or meant by the idea of will. They therefore appear to reject the principle which they granted them in the beginning.[3] This is in short the content of this section. It waves the argument from the original question to the problem of the will; to shift one's ground,[4] however, is an act of sophistry.

Ghazali answers in defence of the theological doctrine of the Divine Will:

There are two objections: First, as to your affirmation that you cannot imagine this, do you know it by the necessity of thought or through deduction? You can claim neither the one nor the other. Your comparison with our will is a bad analogy, which resembles that employed on the question of God's knowledge. Now God's knowledge is different from ours in several ways which we acknowledge. Therefore it is not absurd to admit a difference in the will. Your affirmation is like saying that an essence existing neither outside nor inside the world, neither continuous with the world nor separated from it, cannot be understood, because we cannot understand this according to our human measure; the right answer is that it is the fault of your imagination, for rational proof has led the learned to accept its truth. How, then, will you refute those who say that rational proof has led to establishing in God a quality the nature of which is to differentiate between two similar things? And, if the word 'will' does not apply, call it by another name, for let us not quibble about words! We only use the term 'will' by permission of the Divine Law.[1] It may be objected that by its conventional meaning 'will' designates that which has desire, and God has no desire, but we are concerned here with a question not of words but of fact. Besides, we do not even with respect to our human will concede that this cannot be imagined. Suppose two similar dates in front of a man who has a strong desire* for them, but who is unable to take them both. Surely he will take one of them through a quality in him the nature of which is to differentiate between two similar things. All the distinguishing qualities you have mentioned, like beauty or nearness or facility in taking, we can assume to be absent, but still the possibility of the taking remains. You can choose between two answers: either you merely say that an equivalence in respect to his desire cannot be imagined—but this is a silly answer, for to assume it is indeed possible—or you say that if an equivalence is assumed, the man will remain for ever hungry and perplexed, looking at the dates without taking one of them, and without a power to choose or to will, distinct from his desire.[2] And this again is one of those absurdities which are recognized by the necessity of thought. Everyone, therefore, who studies, in the human and the divine, the real working of the act of choice, must necessarily admit a quality the nature of which is to differentiate between two similar things.

I say:

This objection can be summarized in two parts: In the first Ghazali concedes that the human will is such that it is unable to differentiate one thing from a similar one, in so far as it is similar, but that a rational proof forces us to accept the existence of such a quality in the First Agent. To believe that such a quality cannot exist would be like believing that there cannot exist a being who is neither inside nor outside the world. According to this reasoning, will, which is attributed to the First Agent and to man, is predicated in an equivocal way, like knowledge and other qualities which exist in the Eternal in a different way from that in which they exist in the temporal, and it is only through the prescription of the Divine Law that we speak of the Divine Will. It is clear that this objection cannot have anything more than a dialectical value. For a proof that could demonstrate the existence of such a quality, i.e. a principle determining the existence of one thing rather than that of a similar, would have to assume things willed that are similar; things willed are, however, not similar, but on the contrary opposite, for all opposites can be reduced to the opposition of being and not being, which is the extreme form of opposition; and opposition is the contrary of similarity.[1] The assumption of the theologians that the things to which the will attaches itself are similar is a false one, and we shall speak of it later. If they say: we affirm only that they are similar in relation to the First Willer, who in His holiness is too exalted to possess desires, and it is through desires that two similar things are actually differentiated,[2] we answer: as to the desires whose realization contributes to the perfection of the essence of the willer,[3] as happens with our desires, through which our will attaches itself to the things willed—those desires are impossible in God, for the will which acts in this way is a longing for perfection when there is an imperfection in the essence of the willer; but as to the desires which belong to the essence of the things willed,[4] nothing* new comes to the willer from their realization. It comes exclusively to the thing willed, for instance, when a thing passes into existence from non-existence, for it cannot be doubted that existence is better for it than non-existence. It is in this second way that the Primal Will is related to the existing things, for it chooses for them eternally the better of two opposites, and this essentially and primally. This is the first part of the objection contained in this argument.

In the second part he no longer concedes that this quality cannot exist in the human will, but tries to prove that there is also in us, in the face of similar things, a will which distinguishes one from the other; of this he gives examples. For instance, it is assumed that in front of a man there are two dates, similar in every way, and it is supposed that he cannot take them both at the same time. It is supposed that no special attraction need be imagined for him in either of them, and that nevertheless he will of necessity distinguish one of them by taking it. But this is an error. For, when one supposes such a thing, and a willer whom necessity prompts to eat or to take the date, then it is by no means a matter of distinguishing between two similar things when, in this condition, he takes one of the two dates. It is nothing but the admission of an equivalence of two similar things; for whichever of the two dates he may take, his aim will be attained and his desire satisfied. His will attaches itself therefore merely to the distinction between the fact of taking one of them and the fact of leaving them altogether; it attaches itself by no means to the act of taking one definite date and distinguishing this act from the act of leaving the other (that is to say, when it is assumed that the desires for the two are equal); he does not prefer the act of taking the one to the act of taking the other, but he prefers the act of taking one of the two, whichever it may be, and he gives a preference to the act of taking over the act of leaving.[1] This is self-evident. For distinguishing* one from the other means giving a preference* to the one over the other, and one cannot give a preponderance to one of two similar things in so far as it is similar to the other—although in their existence as individuals they are not similar since each of two individuals is different from the other by reason of a quality exclusive to it.[2] If, therefore, we assume that the will attaches itself to that special character of one of them, then it can be imagined that the will attaches to the one rather than the other because of the element of difference existing in both. But then the will does not attach itself to two similar objects, in so far as they are similar. This is, in short, the meaning of Ghazali's first objection. Then he gives his second objection against those who deny the existence of a quality, distinguishing two similar objects from one another.

Ghazali says:

The second objection is that we say: You in your system also are unable to do without a principle differentiating between two equals, for the world exists in virtue of a cause which has produced it in its peculiar shape out of a number of possible distinct shapes which are equivalent; why, then, has this cause differentiated some of them? If to distinguish two similar things is impossible, it is irrelevant whether this concerns the act of God, natural causality, or the logical necessity of ideas.[3] Perhaps you will say: the universal order of the world could not be different from what it is; if the world were smaller or bigger than it actually is, this order would not be perfect, and the same may be asserted of the number of spheres and of stars. And perhaps you will say: The big differs from the small and the many from the few, in so far as they are the object of the will, and therefore they are not similar but different; but human power is too feeble to perceive the modes of Divine Wisdom in its determination of the measures and qualities of things; only in some of them can His wisdom be perceived, as in the obliquity of the ecliptic in relation to the equator, and in the wise contrivance of the apogee and the eccentric sphere.[1] In most cases, however, the secret is not revealed, but the differences are known, and it is not impossible that a thing should be distinguished from another, because the order of the world depends on it; but certainly the times are absolutely indifferent in relation to the world's possibility and its order, and it cannot be claimed that, if the world were created one moment later or earlier, this order could not be imagined; and this indifference is known by the necessity of thought.—But then we answer: Although we can employ the same reasoning against your argument in the matter of different times, for it might be said that God created the world at the time most propitious for its creation, we shall not limit ourselves to this refutation, but shall assume, according to your own principle, a differentiation in two points about which there can be no disagreement: (1) the difference in the direction of spherical movement; (2) the definite place of the poles in relation to the ecliptic in spherical movement.[2] The proof of the statement relating to the poles is that heaven is a globe, moving on two poles, as on two immovable points, whereas the globe of heaven is homogeneous and simple, especially the highest sphere, the ninth,[3] which possesses no stars at all, and these two spheres[4] move on two poles, the north and the south. We now say: of all the opposite points, which are infinite, according to you philosophers, there is no pair one could not imagine as poles. Why then have the two points of the north and south pole been fixed upon as poles and as immovable; and why does the ecliptic not pass through these two poles, so that the poles would become the opposite points of the ecliptic?[5] And if wisdom is shown in the size and shape of heaven, what then distinguishes the place of the poles from others, so that they are fixed upon to serve as poles, to the exclusion of all the other parts and points? And yet all the points are similar, and all parts of the globe are equivalent. And to this there is no answer.

One might say: Perhaps the spot in which the point of the poles is, is distinguished from other points by a special quality, in relation to its being the place of the poles and to its being at rest, for it does not seem to change its place or space or position or whatever one wishes to call it; and all the other spots of the sphere by turning change their position in relation to the earth and the other spheres and only the poles are at rest; perhaps this spot was more apt to be at rest than the others. We answer: If you say so, you explain the fact through a natural differentiation of the parts of the first sphere; the sphere, then, ceases to be homogeneous, and this is in contradiction with your principle, for one of the proofs by which you prove the necessity of the globular shape of heaven, is that its nature is simple, homogeneous, and without differentiation, and the simplest shape is the globe; for the quadrangle and the hexagon and other figures demand a salience and a differentiation of the angles,[1] and this happens only when its simple nature is added to. But although this supposition of yours is in contradiction with your own theory, it does not break the strength of your opponents' argument; the question about this special quality still holds good, namely, can those other parts accept this quality or not? If the answer is in the affirmative, why then is this quality limited to a few only of those homogeneous parts? If the answer is negative, we reply: the other parts, in so far as they constitute bodies, receiving the form of bodies, are homogeneous of necessity, and there is no justification for attributing this special quality to this spot exclusively on account of its being a part of a body and a part of heaven, for the other parts of heaven participate in this qualification. Therefore its differentiation must rest on a decision by God, or on a quality whose nature consists in differentiating between two similars. Therefore, just as among philosophers the theory is upheld that all times are equivalent in regard to the creation of the world, their opponents are justified in claiming that the parts of heaven are equivalent for the reception of the quality through which stability in position becomes more appropriate than a change of position. And out of this there is no issue.

I say:

This means in brief that the philosophers must acknowledge that there is a quality in the Creator of the world which differentiates between two similars, for it seems that the world might have had another shape and another quantity than it actually has, for it might have been bigger or smaller. Those different possibilities are, therefore, equivalent in regard to the determination of the existence of the world. On the other hand, if the philosophers say that the world can have only one special shape, the special quantity of its bodies and the special number of them it actually has, and that this equivalence of possibilities can only be imagined in relation to the times of temporal creation—since for God no moment is more suitable than another for its creation—they may be told that it is possible to answer this by saying that the creation of the world happened at its most propitious moment. But we, the theologians say, want to show the philosophers two equivalent things of which they cannot affirm that there exists any difference between them; the first is the particular direction of the spherical movement and the second the particular position of the poles, relative to the spheres; for any pair whatever of opposite points, united by a line which passes through the centre of the sphere, might constitute the poles. But the differentiation of these two points, exclusive of all other points which might just as well be the poles of this identical sphere cannot happen except by a quality differentiating between two similar objects. If the philosophers assert that it is not true that any other place on the sphere might be the seat for these poles, they will be told: such an assertion implies that the parts of the spheres are not homogeneous and yet you have often said that the sphere is of a simple nature and therefore has a simple form, viz. the spherical. And again, if the philosophers affirm that there are spots on the sphere which are not homogeneous, it will be asked how these spots came to be of a heterogeneous nature; is it because they are a body or because they are a celestial body? But the absence of homogeneity cannot be explained in this way. Therefore—Ghazali says—just as among philosophers the theory is upheld that all times are equivalent in regard to the creation of the world, the theologians are justified in claiming that the parts of heaven are equivalent in regard to their serving as poles, and that the poles do not seem differentiated from the other points through a special position or through their being in an immovable place, exclusive of all other places.

This then in short is the objection; it is, however, a rhetorical one, for many things which by demonstration can be found to be necessary seem at first sight merely possible.[1] The philosophers' answer is that they assert that they have proved that the world is composed of five bodies: a body neither heavy nor light, i.e. the revolving spherical body of heaven[2] and four other bodies, two of which are earth, absolutely heavy, which is the centre of the revolving spherical body, and fire, absolutely light, which is seated in the extremity of the revolving sphere; nearest to earth is water, which is heavy relatively to air, light relatively to earth; next to water comes air, which is light relatively to water, heavy relatively to fire. The reason why earth is absolutely heavy is that it is farthest away from the circular movement, and therefore it is the fixed centre of the revolving body; the reason why fire is absolutely light is that it is nearest to the revolving sphere; the intermediate bodies are both heavy and light, because they are in the middle between the two extremes, i.e. the farthest point and the nearest.[3] If there were not a revolving body, surely there would be neither heavy nor light by nature, and neither high nor low by nature,[4] and this whether absolutely or relatively; and the bodies would not differ by nature in the way in which, for instance, earth moves by nature to its specific place and fire moves by nature to another place, and equally so the intermediary bodies. And the world is only finite, because of the spherical body, and this because of the essential and natural finiteness of the spherical body, as one single plane circumscribes it.[1] Rectilinear bodies are not essentially finite,[2] as they allow of an increase and decrease; they are only finite because they are in the middle of a body that admits neither increase nor decrease, and is therefore essentially finite. And, therefore, the body circumscribing the world cannot but be spherical, as otherwise the bodies would either have to end in other bodies, and we should have an infinite regress, or they would end in empty space, and the impossibility of both suppositions has been demonstrated.[3] He who understands this knows that every possible world imaginable can only consist of these bodies, and that bodies have to be either circular—and then they are neither heavy nor light—or rectilinear—and then they are either heavy or light, i.e. either fire or earth or the intermediate bodies; that these bodies have to be either revolving, or surrounded by a revolving periphery, for each body either moves from, towards, or round the centre; that by the movements of the heavenly bodies to the right and to the left[4] all bodies are constituted and all that is produced from opposites is generated; and that through these movements the individuals of these four bodies never cease being in a continual production and corruption.[5] Indeed, if a single one of these movements should cease, the order and proportion of this universe would disappear, for it is clear that this order must necessarily depend on the actual number of these movements—for if this were smaller or greater, either the order would be disturbed, or there would be another order—and that the number of these movements is as it is, either through its necessity for the existence of this sublunary world, or because it is the best.[6]

Do not ask here for a proof for all this, but if you are interested in science, look for its proof, where you can find it. Here, however, listen to theories which are more convincing than those of the theologians and which, even if they do not bring you complete proof, will give your mind an inclination to lead you to proof through scientific speculation. You should imagine that each heavenly sphere is a living being, in so far as it possesses a body of a definite measure and shape and moves itself in definite directions, not at random. Anything of this nature is necessarily a living being; i.e.

when we see a body of a definite quality and quantity move itself in space, in a definite direction, not at random, through its own power, not through an exterior cause, and move in opposite directions at the same time, we are absolutely sure that it is a living being, and we said only 'not through an exterior cause' because iron moves towards a magnet when the magnet is brought to it from the outside—and besides, iron moves to a magnet from any direction whatever.[1] The heavenly bodies, therefore, possess places which are poles by nature, and these bodies cannot have their poles in other places, just as earthly animals have particular organs in particular parts of their bodies for particular actions, and cannot have them in other places, e.g. the organs of locomotion, which are located in definite parts. The poles represent the organs of locomotion in animals of spherical form, and the only difference in this respect between spherical and non-spherical animals is that in the latter these organs differ in both shape and power, whereas in the former they only differ in power.[2] For this reason it has been thought on first sight that they do not differ at all, and that the poles could be in any two points on the sphere. And just as it would be ridiculous to say that a certain movement in a certain species of earthly animal could be in any part whatever of its body, or in that part where it is in another species, because this movement has been localized in each species in the place where it conforms most to its nature, or in the only place where this animal can perform the movement, so it stands with the differentiation in the heavenly bodies for the place of their poles. For the heavenly bodies are not one species and numerically many, but they form a plurality in species, like the plurality of different individuals of animals where there is only one individual in the species.[3]

Exactly the same answer can be given to the question why the heavens move in different directions: that, because they are animals, they must move in definite directions, like right and left, before and behind, which are directions determined by the movements of animals, and the only difference between the movements of earthly animals and those of heavenly bodies is that in the different animals these movements are different in shape and in power, whereas in the heavenly animals they only differ in power. And it is for this reason that Aristotle thinks that heaven possesses the directions of right and left, before and behind, high and low.[4] The diversity of the heavenly bodies in the direction of their movements rests on their diversity of species, and the fact that this difference in the directions of their movements forms the specific differentia of their species is something proper to them. Imagine the first heaven as one identical animal whose nature obliges it—either by necessity or because it is for the best—to move with all its parts in one movement from east to west. The other spheres are obliged by their nature to have the opposite movement. The direction which the body of the universe is compelled to follow through its nature is the best one, because its body is the best of bodies and the best among the moving bodies must also have the best direction. All this is explained here in this tentative way, but is proved apodictically in its proper place. This is also the manifest sense of the Divine Words, 'There is no changing the words of God',[1] and 'There is no altering the creation of God'.[2] If you want to be an educated man, proceeding by proof, you should look for the proof of this in its proper place.

Now if you have understood all this, it will not be difficult for you to see the faults in Ghazali's arguments here about the equivalence of the two opposite movements in relation to each heavenly body and to the sublunary world. On first thoughts it might be imagined that the movement from east to west might also belong to other spheres besides the first, and that the first sphere might equally well move from west to east. You might as well say* that the crab could be imagined as having the same direction of movement as man. But, as a matter of fact, such a thought will not occur to you about men and crabs, because of their difference in shape, whereas it might occur to you about the heavenly spheres, since they agree in shape.[3] He who contemplates a product of art does not perceive its wisdom if he does not perceive the wisdom of the intention embodied in it, and the effect intended.[4] And if he does not understand its wisdom, he may well imagine that this object might have any form, any quantity, any configuration of its parts, and any composition whatever. This is the case with the theologians in regard to the body of the heavens, but all such opinions are superficial. He who has such beliefs about products of art understands neither the work nor the artist, and this holds also in respect of the works of God's creation. Understand this principle, and do not judge the works of God's creation hastily and superficially—so that you may not become one of those about whom the Koran says: 'Say, shall we inform you of those who lose most by their works, those who erred in their endeavour after the life of this world and who think they are doing good deeds?'[5] May God make us perspicacious and lift from us the veils of ignorance; indeed He is the bounteous, the generous! To contemplate the various actions of the heavenly bodies is like contemplating the kingdom of heaven, which Abraham contemplated, according to the words of the Koran: 'Thus did we show Abraham the kingdom of heaven and of the earth, that he should be of those who are sure.'[1]

And let us now relate Ghazali's argument about the movements.

Ghazali says:

The second point in this argument concerns the special direction of the movement of the spheres which move partially from east to west, partially in the opposite direction, whereas the equivalence of the directions in relation to their cause is exactly the same as the equivalence of the times. If it is said: If the universe revolved in only one direction, there would never be a difference in the configuration of the stars, and such relations of the stars as their being in trine, in sextile, and in conjunction[2] would never arise, but the universe would remain in one unique position without any change; the difference of these relations, however, is the principle of all production in the world—we answer: Our argument does not concern the difference in direction of movement; no, we concede that the highest sphere moves from east to west and the spheres beneath it in the opposite direction, but everything that happens in this way would happen equally if the reverse took place, i.e. if the highest sphere moved from west to east and the lower spheres in the opposite direction. For all the same differences in configuration would arise just as well. Granted that these movements are circular and in opposite directions, both directions are equivalent; why then is the one distinguished from the other, which is similar to it?[3] If it is said: as the two directions are opposed and contrary, how can they be similar?—we answer: this is like saying 'since before and after are opposed in the existing world, how could it be claimed that they are equivalent?' Still, it is asserted by you philosophers that the equivalence of times, so far as the possibility of their realization and any purpose one might imagine in their realization is concerned, is an evident fact. Now, we regard it as equally evident that spaces, positions, situations, and directions are equivalent so far as concerns their receiving movement and any purpose that might be connected with it. If therefore the philosophers are allowed to claim that notwithstanding this equivalence they are different, their opponents are fully justified in claiming the same in regard to the times.*

I say:

From what I have said previously, the speciousness of this argument and the way in which it has to be answered will not be obscure to you. All this is the work of one who does not understand the exalted natures of the heavenly bodies and their acts of wisdom for the sake of which they have been created, and who compares God's knowledge with the knowledge of ignorant man.

THE FIRST DISCUSSION

Ghazali says:

If it is said: as the two directions are opposed and contrary, how can they be similar?—we answer: this is like saying 'since before and after in the existing world are opposed, how could it be claimed that they are equivalent?' Still, it is asserted by you philosophers that the equivalence of times so far as the possibility of their realization, and any purpose one might imagine in their realization is concerned, is an evident fact. Now, we regard it as equally evident that spaces, positions, situations, and directions are equivalent so far as concerns their receiving the movement and any purpose that might be connected with it.

I say:

The falsehood of this is self-evident. Even if one should admit that the possibilities of man's existence and non-existence are equivalent in the matter out of which he has been created, and that this is a proof for the existence of a determining principle which prefers his existence to his non-existence, still it cannot be imagined that the possibilities of seeing and not seeing are equivalent in the eye.[1] Thus no one can claim that the opposite directions are equivalent, although he may claim that the substratum for both is indifferent, and that therefore out of both directions similar actions result.[2] And the same holds good for before and after: they are not equivalent, in so far as this event is earlier and that event later; they can only be claimed to be equivalent so far as their possibility of existence is concerned.[3] But the whole assumption is wrong: for essential opposites also need essentially opposite substrata and a unique substratum giving rise to opposite acts at one and the same time is an impossibility.[4] The philosophers do not believe that the possibilities of a thing's existence and of its non-existence are equivalent at one and the same time; no, the time of the possibility of its existence is different from the time of the possibility of its non-existence,[5] time for them is the condition for the production of what is produced, and for the corruption of what perishes.[6] If the time for the possibility of the existence of a thing and the time for the possibility of its non-existence were the same, that is to say in its proximate matter, its existence would be vitiated, because of the possibility of its non-existence, and the possibility of its existence and of its non-existence would be dependent only on the agent, not on the substratum.[7]

Thus he who tries to prove the existence of an agent in this way gives only persuasive, dialectical arguments, not apodictic proof. It is believed that Farabi and Avicenna followed this line to establish that every act must have an agent, but it is not a proof of the ancient philosophers, and both of them merely took it over from the theologians of our religion.¹ In relation, however, to the temporal creation of the world—for him who believes in it—before and after cannot even be imagined,² for before and after in time can only be imagined in relation to the present moment,³ and as, according to the theologians, there was before the creation of the world no time, how could there be imagined something preceding the moment when the world was created? A definite moment cannot be assigned for the creation of the world, for either time did not exist before it, or there was an infinite time, and in neither case could a definite time be fixed to which the Divine could attach itself.⁴ Therefore it would be more suitable to call this book 'Incoherence' without qualification rather than 'The Incoherence of the Philosophers', for the only profit it gives the reader is to make him incoherent.

Ghazali says:

If, therefore, the philosophers are allowed to claim that, notwithstanding this equivalence, they are different, their opponents are fully justified in claiming the same in regard to times.

I say:

He wants to say: If the philosophers are justified in claiming a difference in the direction of movement, the theologians have the right to assert a difference in times, notwithstanding their belief in their equivalence. This is only a verbal argument, and does not refer to the facts themselves, even if one admits an analogy between the opposite directions and the different times,* but this is often objected to, because there is no analogy between this difference in times and directions.⁵ Our adversary, however, is forced to admit that there is an analogy between them, because they are both claimed to be different, and both to be equivalent! These, therefore, are one and all only dialectical arguments.

Ghazali says:

The second objection⁶ against the basis of their argument is that the philosophers are told: 'You regard the creation of a temporal being by an eternal as impossible, but you have to acknowledge it too, for there are new events happening in the world and they have causes. It is absurd to think that these events lead to other events *ad infinitum*, and no intelligent person can believe such a thing. If such a thing were possible, you need not acknowledge a creator and establish a necessary being on whom possible existences depend. If, however, there is a limit for those events in which their sequence ends, this limit will be the eternal and then

THE FIRST DISCUSSION

indubitably you too acknowledge the principle that a temporal can proceed from an eternal being.'[1]

I say:

If the philosophers had introduced the eternal being into reality from the side of the temporal by this kind of argument, i.e. if they had admitted that the temporal, in so far as temporal, proceeds from an eternal being, there would be no possibility of their avoiding the difficulty in this problem. But you must understand that the philosophers permit the existence of a temporal which comes out of a temporal being *ad infinitum* in an accidental way, when this is repeated in a limited and finite matter—when, for instance, the corruption of one* of two things becomes the necessary condition for the existence of the other. For instance, according to the philosophers it is necessary that man should be produced from man on condition that the anterior man perishes so as to become the matter for the production of a third.[2] For instance, we must imagine two men of whom the first produces the second from the matter of a man who perishes; when the second becomes a man himself, the first perishes, then the second man produces a third man out of the matter of the first, and then the second perishes and the third produces out of his matter a fourth, and so we can imagine in two matters an activity continuing *ad infinitum*, without any impossibility arising. And this happens as long as the agent lasts, for if this agent has neither beginning nor end for his existence, the activity has neither beginning nor end for its existence, as it has been explained before.[3] And in the same way you may imagine this happening in them in the past: When a man exists, there must before him have been a man who produced him and a man who perished, and before this second man a man who produced him and a man who perished, for everything that is produced in this way is, when it depends on an eternal agent, of a circular nature in which no actual totality can be reached.[4] If, on the other hand, a man were produced from another man out of infinite matters, or there were an infinite addition of them, there would be an impossibility, for then there could arise an infinite matter and there could be an infinite whole. For if a finite whole existed to which things were added *ad infinitum* without any corruption taking place in it, an infinite whole could come into existence, as Aristotle proved in his *Physics*.[5] For this reason the ancients introduce an eternal absolutely unchanging being, having in mind not temporal beings, proceeding from him in so far as they are temporal, but beings proceeding from him as being eternal generically,[1] and they hold that this infinite series is the necessary consequence of an eternal agent, for the temporal needs for its own existence only a temporal cause.[2] Now there are two reasons why the ancients introduce the existence of an eternal numerically unique being which does not suffer any change. The first is that they discovered that this revolving being is eternal, for they discovered that the present individual is produced through the corruption of its predecessor and that the corruption of this previous individual implies the production of the one that follows it, and that it is necessary that this everlasting change should proceed from an eternal mover and an eternal moved body, which does not change in its substance,[3] but which changes only in place so far as concerns its parts,[4] and approaches certain of the transitory things and recedes from certain of them, and this is the cause of the corruption of one half of them and the production of the other half.[5] And this heavenly body is the being that changes in place only, not in any of the other kinds of change,[6] and is through its temporal activities the cause of all things temporal; and because of the continuity of its activities which have neither beginning nor end, it proceeds from a cause which has neither beginning nor end. The second reason why they introduce an eternal being absolutely without body and matter is that they found that all the kinds of movement depend on spatial movement,[7] and that spatial movement depends on a being moved essentially by a prime mover, absolutely unmoved, both essentially and accidentally,[8] for otherwise there would exist at the same time an infinite number of moved movers, and this is impossible.[9] And it is necessary that this first mover should be eternal, or else it would not be the first. Every movement, therefore, depends on this mover and its setting in motion essentially, not accidentally. And this mover exists simultaneously with each thing moved, at the time of its motion, for a mover existing before the thing moved*—such as a man producing a man—sets only in motion accidentally, not essentially; but the mover who is the condition of man's existence from the beginning of his production till its end, or rather from the beginning of his existence till its end, is the prime mover. And likewise his existence is the condition for the existence of all beings and the preservation[10] of heaven and earth and all that is between them.[11] All this is not proved here apodictically, but only in the way we follow here and which is in any case more plausible for an impartial reader than the arguments of our opponents.

If this is clear to you, you certainly are in no need of the subterfuge by which Ghazali in his argument against the philosophers tries to conciliate them with their adversaries in this matter; indeed these artifices will not do, for if you have not understood how the philosophers introduce an eternal being into reality, you have not understood how they settle the difficulty of the rise of the temporal out of the eternal; they do that, as we said, either through the medium of a being eternal in its essence but generable and corruptible in its particular movements, not, however, in its universal circular movement,[1] or through the medium of what is generically eternal[2]—i.e. has neither beginning nor end—in its acts.

Ghazali answers in the name of the philosophers:

The philosophers may say, 'we do not consider it impossible that any temporal being, whatever it may be, should proceed from an eternal being, but we regard it as impossible that the first temporal should proceed from the eternal, as the mode of its procession does not differ from that which precedes it, either in a greater inclination* towards existence or through the presence of some particular time, or through an instrument, condition, nature, accident, or any cause whatever which might produce a new mode. If this therefore is not the first temporal, it will be possible that it should proceed from the eternal, when another thing proceeds from it, because of the disposition of the receiving substratum, or because the time was propitious or for any other reason.'[3]

Having given this reply on the part of the philosophers, Ghazali answers it:

This question about the actualization of the disposition, whether of the time and of any new condition which arises in it, still holds good, and we must either come to an infinite regress or arrive at an eternal being out of which a first temporal being proceeds.

I say:

This question is the same question all over again as he asked the philosophers first,[4] and this is the same kind of conclusion as he made them draw then, namely that a temporal proceeds from an eternal, and having given as their answer something which does not correspond with the question, i.e. that it is possible that a temporal being should proceed from the Eternal without there being a first temporal being, he turns the same question against them again. The correct answer to this question was given above: the temporal proceeds from the First Eternal, not in so far as it is temporal but in so far as it is eternal, i.e. through being eternal generically, though temporal in its parts. For according to the philosophers an eternal being out of which a temporal being proceeds essentially[1] is not the First Eternal, but its acts, according to them, depend on the First Eternal; i.e. the actualization of the condition for activity of the eternal, which is not the First Eternal, depends on the First Eternal in the same way as the temporal products depend on the First Eternal and this is a dependence based on the universal, not on individuals.[2]

After this Ghazali introduces an answer of the philosophers, in one of the forms in which this theory can be represented, which amounts to this: A temporal being proceeding from an eternal can only be represented by means of a circular movement which resembles the eternal by not having beginning or end and which resembles the temporal in so far as each part of it is transient, so that this movement through the generation of its parts is the principle of temporal things, and through the eternity of its totality the activity of the eternal.

Then Ghazali argues against this view, according to which in the opinion of the philosophers the temporal proceeds from the First Eternal, and says to them:

Is this circular movement temporal or eternal? If it is eternal, how does it become the principle for temporal things? And if it is temporal, it will need another temporal being and we shall have an infinite regress. And when you say that it partially resembles the eternal, partially the temporal, for it resembles the eternal in so far as it is permanent and the temporal in so far as it arises anew, we answer: Is it the principle of temporal things, because of its permanence, or because of its arising anew? In the former case, how can a temporal proceed from something because of its permanence? And in the latter case, what arises anew will need a cause for its arising anew, and we have an infinite regress.[3]

I say:

This argument is sophistical. The temporal does not proceed from it in so far as it is eternal, but in so far as it is temporal; it does not need, however, for its arising anew a cause arising anew, for its arising anew is not a new fact, but is an eternal act, i.e. an act without beginning or end. Therefore its agent must be an eternal agent, for an eternal act has an eternal agent, and a temporal act a temporal agent. Only through the eternal element in it can it be understood that movement has neither beginning nor end, and this is meant by its permanence, for movement itself is not permanent, but changing.

And since Ghazali knew this, he said:

In order to elude this consequence the philosophers have a kind of artifice which we will expose briefly.

Ghazali says:

THE SECOND PROOF OF THE PHILOSOPHERS CONCERNING THIS PROBLEM[1]

They assert that he who affirms that the world is posterior to God and God prior to the world cannot mean anything but that He is prior not temporally but essentially,[2] like the natural priority of one to two, although they can exist together in temporal existence, or like the priority of cause to effect, for instance the priority of the movement of a man to the movement of his shadow which follows him, or the movement of the hand to the movement of the ring, or the movement of the hand in the water to the movement of the water, for all these things are simultaneous, but the one is cause, the other effect, for it is said that the shadow moves through the movement of the man and the water through the hand in the water, and the reverse is not said although they are simultaneous.[3] If this is what you mean by saying that God is prior to the world, then it follows that they must both either be temporal or eternal, for it is absurd that the one should be temporal and the other eternal.[4] If it is meant that God is prior to the world and to time, not essentially, but temporally, then there was, before the existence of the world and of time, a time in which the world was non-existent, since non-existence preceded the world and God preceded it during a long duration which had a final term but no initial one, and then there was before time an infinite time, which is self-contradictory. Therefore the assertion that time had a beginning is absurd. And if time—which is the expression of the measure of movement—is eternal, movement must be eternal. And the necessity of the eternity of movement implies the necessity of the eternity of the thing in motion, through the duration of which time endures.

I say:

The mode of their reasoning which he reproduces does not constitute a proof. It amounts to saying that the Creator, if He is prior to the world, must either be prior not in time, but in causation, like the priority of a man to his shadow, or prior in time, like a builder to a wall.[5] If He is prior in the same way as the man is prior to his shadow, and if the Creator is eternal, then the world too is eternal. But if He is prior in time, then He must precede the world by a time which has no beginning, and time will be eternal, for if there is a time before the actual, its starting-point cannot be imagined. And if time is eternal, movement too is eternal, for time cannot be understood without motion. And if motion is eternal, the thing in motion will be eternal, and its mover will necessarily be eternal too. But this proof is unsound, for it is not of the nature of the Creator to be in time, whereas it belongs to the nature of the world to be so; and for this very reason it is not true that He is either simultaneous with it or prior to it in time or in causation.¹

Ghazali says:

The objection to this is: Time is generated and created, and before it there was no time at all. The meaning of our words that God is prior to the world and to time is: He existed without the world and without time, then He existed and with Him there was the world and there was time. And the meaning of our words that He existed without the world is: the existence of the essence of the Creator and the non-existence of the essence of the world, and nothing else. And the meaning of our words that He existed and with Him there was the world is: the existence of the two essences, and nothing else. And the meaning of priority: the uniqueness of His existence, and nothing else. And the world is like a singular person; if we should say, for instance: God existed without Jesus, then He existed with Jesus—these words contain nothing but, first, the existence of an essence and the non-existence of an essence, then, the existence of two essences, and there is no need to assume here a third essence, namely time, although imagination cannot desist from assuming it. But we should not heed the errors of the imagination.²

I say:

These words are erroneous and mistaken, for we have already proved that there are two kinds of existence: one in the nature of which* there is motion and which cannot be separated from time; the other in the nature of which there is no motion and which is eternal and cannot be described in terms of time. The first is known by the senses and by reason; the existence of the second—in the nature of which there is neither motion nor change—is known by proof to everyone who acknowledges that each motion needs a mover and each effect a cause, and that the causes which move each other do not regress infinitely, but end in a first cause which is absolutely unmoved. And it has also been established that the entity in the nature of which there is no movement is the cause of the entity in the nature of which there is movement. And it has been proved also that the entity in the nature of which there is motion cannot be separated from time, and that the entity in the nature of which there is no movement is entirely free from time. Therefore the priority of the one entity over the other is based neither on a priority in time, nor on the priority of that kind of cause and effect, which belongs to the nature of things in motion, like the priority of a man to his shadow. For this reason anyone who compares the priority of the unmoved being to the thing in motion to the priority existing between two things in motion is in error; since it is only true of each one in pairs of moving things that, when it is brought in relation to the other, it is either simultaneous with it or prior or posterior in time to it. It is the later philosophers of Islam who made this mistake, since they enjoyed but slight comprehension of the doctrine of the ancients. So the priority of this one being to the other is the priority of the unchanging timeless existence to the changing existence which is in time, and this is an altogether different type of priority. It is therefore not true of these existences that they are simultaneous, or that the one precedes the other, and Ghazali's observation that the priority of the Creator to the world is not a temporal priority is true. But the posteriority of the world to the Creator, since He does not precede the world in time, can only be understood as the posteriority of effect to cause,[1] for posteriority and priority are opposites which are necessarily in one genus, as has been shown in the sciences.[2] Since therefore this priority is not in time, the posteriority also cannot be in time, and we have the same difficulty all over again: how can the effect be delayed after the cause when the conditions of acting are fulfilled?[3] The philosophers, however, since they do not recognize a beginning in the totality of this existence in motion, are not touched by this difficulty, and it is possible for them to indicate in what way the temporal beings proceed from the eternal. One of their proofs* that existence in motion has no beginning, and that in its totality it does not start, is that, when it is assumed to start, it is assumed to exist before its existence, for to start is a movement, and movement is of necessity in the thing in motion,[4] equally whether the movement is regarded as taking place in time or at an instant.[5] Another proof is that everything that becomes has the potentiality of becoming before it actually becomes, although the theologians deny this (a discussion with them on this point will follow); now potentiality is a necessary attribute of being in motion, and it follows necessarily that, if it were assumed to become, it would exist before its existence.[6] What we have here are only dialectical arguments; they have, however, a much greater plausibility than what the theologians advance.

As for Ghazali's words:

If we should say, for instance, that God existed without Jesus, and then He existed with Jesus, these words contain nothing but, first, the existence of an essence and the non-existence of an essence, then, the existence of two essences, and there is no need to assume here a third essence, namely time.

I say:

This is true, provided that Jesus' posteriority is not regarded as an essential temporal posteriority, but, if there is a posteriority, it is an accidental posteriority, for time precedes this posterior entity*, i.e. it is a necessity of Jesus' existence that time should precede Him and that His existence should have begun, but the world is not subject to such a necessity, except in so far as it is a part of a moving existence beyond which time extends in two directions,[1] as happens to Jesus* and other transitory individuals.[2] Nothing of this is proved here; here it is simply explained that the objection is not valid. In addition, what he says afterwards of the proofs of the philosophers is untrue.

70 Answering in the name of the philosophers, Ghazali says:

One might say that our expression 'God existed without the world' means a third thing, besides the existence of one being and the non-existence of another, because, if we should suppose that in the future God should exist without the world, there would be in the future the existence of one being and the non-existence of another, still it would not be right to say 'God existed without the world', but we should say 'God will exist without the world', for only of the past do we say 'God existed without the world'; and between the words 'existed' and 'will exist' there is a difference, for they cannot replace each other. And if we try to find out where the difference between the two sentences lies, it certainly does not lie in the words 'existence of one being' and 'non-existence of another being', but in a third entity, for if we say of the non-existence of the world in the future 'God was without the world', it will be objected: this is wrong, for 'was' refers only to the past. This shows therefore that the word 'was' comprises a third entity, namely the past, and the past by itself is time, and through another existent it is movement, for movement passes only through the passing of time. And so it follows necessarily that, before the world, a time finished which terminated in the existence of the world.[3]

I say:

In this in brief he shows that when it is said 'such-and-such was without such-and-such' and then 'such-and-such was with such-and-such' a third entity is understood, namely time. The word 'was' shows this, because of the difference in the meaning of this concept in the past and in the future, for if we assume the existence of one thing with the non-existence of another in the past, we say 'such a thing existed without such a thing', but when we assume the non-existence of the one with the existence of the other in the future, we say 'such a thing will exist without such a thing', and the change in meaning implies that there is here a third entity. If in our expression 'such-and-such existed without such-and-such' the word 'existed' did not signify an entity, the word 'existed' would not differ from 'will exist'. All this is self-evident, but it is only unquestionable in relation to the priority and posteriority of things which are by nature in time. Concerning the timeless the word 'was' and the like indicate in such a proposition nothing but the copula between predicate and subject, when we say, for example, 'God was indulgent and compassionate';[1] and the same holds when either predicate or subject is timeless, e.g. when we say 'God was without the world, then God was with the world'. Therefore for such existents the time-relation to which he refers* does not hold. This relation is, however, unquestionably real when we compare the non-existence of the world with its existence, for if the world is in time, the non-existence of the world has to be in time too. And since the non-existence and the existence of the world cannot be in one and the same time, the non-existence must precede; the non-existence must be prior and the world posterior to it, for priority and posteriority in the moving can only be understood in this relation to time. The only flaw in this argument is to assume this relation between God and the world. Only in this point is the argument which Ghazali relates faulty and does it fail to constitute a proof.

Then Ghazali gives the theologians' objection to this argument of the philosophers:[2]

The primitive meaning of the two words is the existence of one thing and the non-existence of another. The third element which is the connexion* between the two words is a necessary relation to us. The proof is that, if we should suppose a destruction of the world in the future and afterwards a second existence for us, we should then say 'God was without the world', and this would be true, whether we meant its original non-existence or the second non-existence, its destruction after its existence. And a sign that this is a subjective relation is that the future can become past and can be indicated by the word 'past'.[3] All this[4] is the consequence of the inability of our imagination to imagine the beginning of a thing without something preceding it, and this 'before' of which the imagination cannot rid itself is regarded as a really existing thing, namely time. This resembles the inability of the imagination to admit a limited body, e.g. overhead, without anything beyond its surface, so that it is imagined that behind the world there is a space either occupied or empty; and when it is said there is above the surface of the world no beyond and no farther extension, this is beyond the grasp of the imagination. Likewise, when it is said that there is no real anterior to the existence of the world, the imagination refuses to believe it. But the imagination may be called false in allow-ing above the world an empty space which is an infinite extension by our saying to it: empty space cannot be understood by itself, for extension is the necessary attribute of a body whose sides comprise space;[1] a finite body implies the finiteness of extension, which is its attribute, and the limitation of occupied space; empty space is unintelligible, therefore there is neither empty nor occupied space behind the world, although the imagination cannot admit this. And in the same way as it is said that spatial extension is an attribute of body, temporal extension is an attribute of motion, for time is the extension of movement just as the space between the sides of a body is the extension of space. And just as the proof that the sides of a body are finite prevents the admission of a spatial extension behind the world, so the proof of the finite character of movement in both directions prevents the supposition of a temporal extension behind the world, although the imagination, subject to its illusion and supposition, admits it and does not hold back from it. There is no difference between temporal extension, which is apprehended as divided through the relation of before and after, and spatial extension, which is apprehended as divided through the relation of high and low.[2] If it is therefore permissible to admit a highest point above which there is nothing, it is equally permissible to admit a beginning, not preceded by anything real, except through an illusion similar to that which permits a beyond for the highest space. This is a legitimate consequence; notice it carefully, as the philosophers themselves agreed that behind the world there is neither empty nor occupied space.

I say:

There are two parts to this objection; the first is that, when we imagine the past and the future, i.e. the prior and the posterior, they are two things existing in relation to our imagination, because we can imagine a future event as becoming past and a past event as having been future. But if this is so, past and future are not real things in themselves and do not possess existence outside the soul; they are only constructs of the soul. And when movement is annihilated, the relation and measure of time will not have sense any more.

The answer is that the necessary connexion of movement and time is real and time is something the soul constructs in movement,[3] but neither movement nor time is annihilated: they are only abolished in those things which are not subject to motion, but in the existence of moving things or in their possible existence time inheres necessarily. For there are only two kinds of being, those that are subject to motion and those that are not, and the one kind cannot be converted into the other, for otherwise a conversion of the necessary into the possible would become possible.[4] For if movement were impossible and then afterwards occurred, the nature of things which are not subject to motion would have changed into the nature of things subject to motion, and this is impossible. This is a consequence of the fact that motion inheres necessarily in a substratum. If movement were possible before the existence of the world, the things which are subject to movement would be necessarily in time, for movement is only possible in what is subject to rest,[1] not in absolute non-existence, for in absolute non-existence there is no possibility whatever, or one would have to admit that absolute non-existence could be converted into existence.[2] Therefore, the non-existence or privation[3] which necessarily precedes the occurrence of a thing has to be connected with a substratum, and will be disconnected from it when the substratum actually receives this occurrence, as happens with all contraries. For instance, when a warm thing becomes cold, the essence of warmth does not change into coldness; it is only the receptacle and the substratum of warmth that exchange their warmth for coldness.

The second part of this objection—and it is the most important of these objections—is sophistical and malicious. It amounts to saying that to imagine something before the beginning of this first movement (which is not preceded by any moving body) is like the illusion that the end of the world, for example, its highest part, ends necessarily either in another body or in empty space, for extension is a necessary attribute of body, as time is a necessary attribute of movement. And if it is impossible that there should be an infinite body, it is impossible that there should be an infinite extension, and, if it is impossible that there should be infinite extension, it is impossible that every body should end in another body or in something which has the potentiality of extension, i.e. for instance, emptiness, and that this should continue without end.[4] And the same applies to movement which has time as a necessary attribute, for if it is impossible that there should be infinite past movements* and there exists therefore a first movement with a finite initial term, it is impossible that there should exist a 'before' before it, for, if so, there would be another movement before the first.

This objection is, as we said, malicious, and belongs to the class of sophistical substitutions—you will recognize what I mean if you have read the book *On sophistic refutations*.[5] In other words, Ghazali treats the quantity which has no position and does not form a totality, i.e. time and motion, as the quantity which possesses position and totality, i.e. body.[6] He makes the impossibility of endlessness in the latter a proof of its impossibility in the former, and he deals with the act of the soul when it imagines an increase in the one quantity which is assumed to be actual, i.e. body, as if it concerned both quantities. This is a manifest error. For to imagine an increase in actual spatial magnitude, so that it must end in another actual spatial magnitude, is to imagine something which does not exist in the essence and definition of spatial magnitude, but to imagine priority and posteriority in a movement that occurs is to imagine something that belongs to its essence. For a movement can only occur in time, i.e. time has to pass beyond its beginning. For this reason one cannot represent a time the initial term of which is not the final term of another time, for the definition of 'the instant' is that it is the end of the past and the beginning of the future,[1] for the instant is the present which necessarily is the middle between the past and the future, and to represent a present which is not preceded by a past is absurd.[2] This, however, does not apply to the point, for the point is the end of the line[3] and exists at the same time as the line, for the line is at rest. Therefore one can imagine a point which is the beginning of a line[4] without its being the end of another line, but the instant cannot exist without the past and the future, and exists necessarily after the past and before the future, and what cannot subsist in itself cannot exist before the existence of the future without being the end of the past. The cause of this error is the comparison of the instant with the point. The proof that each movement which occurs is preceded by time is this: everything must come to exist out of a privation, and nothing can become in the instant—of which it can be truly said that its becoming is a vanishing[5]—and so it must be true that its privation must be in another moment than that in which it itself exists, and there is time between each pair of instants, because instant is not continuous with instant, nor point continuous with point.[6] This has been proved in the sciences. Therefore before the instant in which the movement occurs there must necessarily be a time, because, when we represent two instants in reality, there must necessarily be time between them.

And what is said in this objection that 'higher' resembles 'before' is not true, nor does the instant resemble the point, nor the quantity which possesses position the quantity which does not possess position.[7] He who allows the existence of an instant which is not a present, or of a present which is not preceded by a past, denies time and the instant, for he assumes an instant as having the description which we have mentioned,[8] and then assumes a time which has no

THE FIRST DISCUSSION

beginning—which is a self-contradictory assumption. It is, therefore, wrong to ascribe to an act of imagination the fact that there is a prior event for every occurrence, for he who denies priority denies the event in time. The contrary is the case with the man who denies the real character of the high*, for he denies the absolutely high and, when he denies the absolutely high, he denies also the absolutely low,[1] and when these two are denied, also the heavy and the light are denied[2] and the act of the imagination that a body with straight dimensions must end in another body is not false; no, this is a necessary truth, for the body with straight dimensions has the possibility of increasing, and what has this possibility is not limited by nature.[3] Therefore the body with straight surfaces must end in the circumscribing circular body, since this is the perfect body which is liable neither to increase nor to decrease. Therefore when the mind seeks to imagine that the circular body must end in another body, it imagines the impossible. These are all matters of which the theologians and those who do not start their inquiry in the proper scientific order are unaware.

Further, the relation between time and motion is not the same as that between spatial limit and spatial magnitude, for the spatial limit is an attribute of spatial magnitude, in so far as it inheres in it, in the way that the accident inheres in its substratum and is individualized by the individuality of its substratum and is indicated by pointing at its substratum and by its being in the place in which its substratum is.[4] But this is not the case with the necessary relation between time and motion. For the dependence of time on motion is much like the dependence of number on the thing numbered:[5] just as number does not become individualized through the individuation of the thing numbered, nor pluralized through its plurality, so it stands with the relation between time and movement.[6] Time, therefore, is unique for all movement and for each thing moving, and exists everywhere, so that if we should suppose people confined from youth in a cave in the earth, still we should be sure that they would perceive time, even if they did not perceive any of the movements which are perceived in the world.[7] Aristotle therefore thought that the existence of movements in time is much like the existence of the things numbered in number,[8] for number is not pluralized through the plurality of the things numbered, nor is it localized through the individuation of the places numbered. He thought, therefore, that its specific quality was to mesaure the movements and to measure the existence of moving things, in so far as they are moving, as number counts the individual moving things, and therefore Aristotle says in his definition of time that it is the number of movement according to the relations of anterior and posterior.[1] Therefore, just as the supposition that a thing numbered occurs does not imply that number comes into existence, but it is a necessary condition for the occurrence of a thing numbered that number should exist before it, so the occurrence of movement implies that there was time before it. If time occurred with the occurrence of any individual movement whatever, time would only be perceived with that individual movement.[2] This will make you understand how different the nature of time is from the nature of spatial magnitude.

Ghazali answers on behalf of the philosophers:

It may be said: This comparison[3] is lame, for there is neither above nor below in the world; for the world is spherical, and in the sphere there is neither above nor below; if the one direction is called above, because it is overhead, and the other below, because it is under foot, this name is always determined[*] in relation to you, and the direction which is below in relation to you is above in relation to another, if you imagine him standing on the other side of the terrestrial globe with the sole of his foot opposite the sole of your foot. Yes, these parts of heaven which you reckon above during the day are identical with what is below during the night, and what is below the earth comes again above the earth through the daily revolution. But it cannot be imagined that the beginning of the world becomes its end. If we imagined a stick with one thick and one thin end and we agreed to call the part nearest the thin end 'above' and the other 'below', there would not arise from this an essential differentiation in the parts of the world; it would simply be that different names would have been applied to the shape of the stick, so that if we substituted the one name for the other, there would be an exchange of names, but the world itself would remain unchanged. So 'above' and 'below' are a mere relation to you without any differentiation in the parts and places of the world. The non-existence, however, preceding the world and the initial term of its existence are essential realities, a substitution or a change of which cannot be imagined. Nor can it be imagined that the non-existence which is supposed to occur at the disappearance of the world and which follows the world can become the non-existence preceding it. The initial and final terms of the world's existence are permanent essential terms, in which no change can be imagined through the change of the subjective relation to them, in contrast with 'above' and 'below'. Therefore we philosophers, indeed, are justified in saying that in the world there is neither 'above' nor 'below', but you theologians have not the right to assert that the existence of the world has neither a 'before' nor an 'after'.

And when the existence of 'before' and 'after' is proved, time cannot mean anything but what is apprehended through the anterior and the posterior.[1]

I say:

This answer given in the name of the philosophers is extremely unsound. It amounts to saying that 'above' and 'below' are relative to us and that therefore imagination can treat them as an infinite sequence, but that the sequence of 'before' and 'after' does not rest on imagination—for there is here no subjective relation—but is a purely rational concept. This means that the order of above and below in a thing may be reversed in imagination, but that the privation before an event and the privation after an event, its before and its after, are not interchangeable for imagination. But by giving this answer the problem is not solved,[2] for the philosophers think that there exists a natural above[3] to which light things move and a natural below to which heavy things move, or else the heavy and the light would be relative and exist by convention, and they hold* that in imagination the limit of a body, having by nature its place above, may end either in occupied or in empty space.[4] And this argument is invalid as a justification of the philosophers for two reasons. First, that the philosophers assume an absolute above and an absolute below, but no absolute beginning and no absolute end; secondly that their opponents may object that it is not the fact of their being relative that causes the imagination to regard the sequence of low and high as an infinite series, but that this happens to the imagination because it observes that every spatial magnitude is continuous with another spatial magnitude, just as any event is preceded by another event. Therefore Ghazali transfers the question from the words 'above' and 'below' to 'inside' and 'outside'[5] and he says in his answer to the philosophers:

There is no real difference in the words 'above' and 'below', and therefore there is no sense in defining them, but we will apply ourselves rather to the words 'inside' and 'outside'. We say: The world has an inside and an outside; and we ask: Is there outside the world an occupied or empty space? The philosophers will answer: There is outside the world neither occupied nor empty space, and if you mean by 'outside' its extreme surface, then there is an outside, but if you mean anything else, there is no outside.[6] Therefore if they ask us theologians if there is anything before the existence of the world, we say: If you mean by it the beginning, i.e. its initial term, then there is a before, just as there is an outside to the world according to your explanation that that is its ultimate limit and its final plane, but if you mean anything else, then there is not, in analogy with your answer.

If you say: A beginning of existence, without anything preceding it, cannot be understood, we say: A limit of a body existing without anything outside it cannot be understood.[1] If you say: Its exterior is its furthest plane and nothing else, we say: Its before is the beginning of its existence, nothing else. The conclusion is that we say: We affirm that God has an existence without the world's existing, and this assumption again does not force us to accept anything else. That to assume more rests on the act of imagination is proved by the fact that imagination acts in the same way in regard to time as in regard to place, for although our opponents believe in the eternity of the world, their imagination is willing to suppose it created; whereas we, who believe in its creation, are often allowed by our imagination to regard it as eternal. So much as far as body is concerned; but to revert to time, our opponents do not regard a time without a beginning as possible, and yet in opposition to this belief their imagination can represent it as a possible assumption, although time cannot be represented by the imagination in the way that body is represented, for neither the champion nor the opponent of the finitude of body can imagine a body not surrounded by empty or occupied space; the imagination simply refuses to accept it. Therefore one should say: a clear thinker pays no attention to the imagination when he cannot deny the finitude of body by proof, nor does he give attention to the imagination when he cannot deny the beginning of an existence without anything preceding it, which the imagination cannot grasp. For the imagination, as it is only accustomed to a body limited by another body or by air, represents emptiness in this way, although emptiness, being imperceptible,[2] cannot be occupied by anything. Likewise the imagination, being only accustomed to an event occurring after another event, fears to suppose an event not preceded by another event which is terminated. And this is the reason of the error.[3]

I say:

Through this transference, by his comparing the time-limit with the spatial limit in his argument against the philosophers, this argument becomes invalid and we have already shown the error through which it is specious and the sophistical character of the argument, and we need not repeat ourselves.

Ghazali says:

The philosophers have a second way of forcing their opponents to admit the eternity of time. They say: You do not doubt that God was able to create the world one year, a hundred years, a thousand years, and so *ad infinitum*, before He created it and that those possibilities are different in magnitude and number. Therefore it is necessary to admit before the existence of the world a measurable extension, one part of which can be longer than another part, and therefore it is necessary that something should have existed before the existence of the world. If you say the word 'years' cannot be applied before the creation and revolution of heaven, let us drop the word 'years' and let us give another turn to our argument and say: If we suppose that from the beginning of the world till now the sphere of the world has performed, for instance, a thousand revolutions, was God able to create a second world before it, which, for example, would have performed eleven hundred revolutions up to now? If you deny it, it would mean that the Eternal had passed from impotence to power or the world from impossibility to possibility, but if you accept it, and you cannot but accept it, it may be asked if God was able to create a third world which would have performed twelve hundred revolutions up to now and you will have to admit this. We philosophers say: Then, could the world which we called by the order of our supposition the third, although as a matter of fact it is the first, have been created at the same time as the world we called the second, so that the former would have performed twelve hundred revolutions and the latter eleven hundred revolutions, it being understood that both, in revolving, complete the same distance at the same speed? If you were to admit this, you would be admitting something absurd, for it would be absurd that in that case the number of the two revolutions, having the same speed and finishing at the same moment, should be different. But, if you answer that it is impossible that the third world which has up to now performed twelve hundred revolutions could have been created at the same time as the second world which has up to now performed eleven hundred revolutions, and that on the contrary it must have been created the same number of years earlier than the second, as the second has been created before the first—we call it first, as it comes first in order, when in imagination we proceed from our time to it—then there exists a quantity of possibility double that of another possibility, and there is doubtless another possibility which doubles the whole of the others. These measurable quantitative possibilities, of which some are longer than others by a definite measure, have no other reality than time, and those measurable quantities are not an attribute of the essence of God, who is too exalted to possess measure,[1] nor an attribute of the non-existence of the world, for non-existence is nothing and therefore cannot be measured with different measures. Still, quantity is an attribute which demands a substratum, and this is nothing other than movement, and quantity is nothing but the time which measures movement. Therefore also for you theologians there existed before the world a substratum of differentiated quantity, namely time, and according to you time existed before the world.[2]

I say:
The summary of this argument is that, when we imagine a movement, we find with it an extension which measures it, as if it were its measurement, while reciprocally the movement measures the extension,[3] and we find that we can assume in this measure and this

extension a movement longer than the first supposed movement, and we affirm through the corresponding and congruous units of this extension that the one movement is longer than the other.[1] If therefore for you theologians the world has a certain extension from its beginning till now—let us suppose, for instance, a thousand years—and since God according to you is able to create before this world another world, we may suppose that the extension He can give it will be longer than the extension of the first world by a certain definite quantity, and that He can likewise create a third world before this second and that the existence of each of them must be preceded by an extension through which its existence can be measured.[2] If this is true, and there is an infinite regress of this possibility of anterior worlds, there is an extension which precedes all these worlds. And this extension which measures all of them cannot be absolute non-existence, for non-existence cannot measure; it has, therefore, to be a quantity, for what measures a quantity has to be quantity itself, and the measuring quantity is that which we call time. And it is clear that this must precede in existence anything we imagine to occur, just as the measure must precede the measured in existence. If this extension which is time were to occur at the occurrence of the first movement, then it would have to be preceded by an extension which could measure it, in which it could occur, and which could be like its measurement. And in the same way any world which could be imagined would have to be preceded by an extension which measures it. Therefore this extension has no beginning, for if it had a beginning it would have to have an extension which measured it, for each event which begins has an extension which measures it and which we call time.

This is the most suitable exposition of this argument, and this is the method by which Avicenna proves infinite time,[3] but there is a difficulty in understanding it, because of the problem that each possible has one extension and each extension is connected with its own possible and this forms a point of discussion;[4] or one must concede that the possibilities prior to the world are of the same nature as the possible inside the world, i.e. as it is of the nature of this possible inside the world that time inheres in it, so also with the possible which is prior to the world. This is clear concerning the possible inside the world, and therefore the existence of time may be imagined from it.[5]

Ghazali says:

THE FIRST DISCUSSION

The objection is that all this is the work of imagination, and the most convenient way of refuting it is to compare time with place; therefore we say: Was it not in God's power to create the highest sphere in its heaven a cubit higher than He has created it? If the answer is negative, this is to deny God's power, and if the answer is affirmative, we ask: And by two cubits and by three cubits and so on *ad infinitum*? Now we affirm that this amounts to admitting behind the world a spatial extension which has measure and quantity, as a thing which is bigger by two or three cubits than another occupies a space bigger by two or three cubits, and by reason of this there is behind the world a quantity which demands a substratum and this is a body or empty space. Therefore, there is behind the world empty or occupied space. And how can you answer this? And likewise we may ask, whether God was not able to create the sphere of the world smaller than He has created it by a cubit or two cubits? And is there no difference between those two magnitudes in regard to the occupied space taken away from them and the space they still occupy, for the occupied space withdrawn is bigger when two cubits are taken away than when one cubit is taken away? And therefore empty space has measure. But emptiness is nothing; how can it have measure? And our answer is: 'It belongs to the illusion of imagination to suppose possibilities in time before the existence of the world', just as your answer is: 'It belongs to the illusion of imagination to suppose possibilities in space behind the existence of the world.' There is no difference between those two points of view.[1]

I say:
This consequence is true against the theory which regards an infinite increase in the size of the world as possible, for it follows from this theory that a finite thing proceeds from God which is preceded by infinite quantitative possibilities. And if this is allowed for possibility in space, it must also be allowed in regard to the possibility in time, and we should have a time limited in both directions*, although it would be preceded by infinite temporal possibilities. The answer is, however, that to imagine the world to be bigger or smaller does not conform to truth but is impossible. But the impossibility of this does not imply that to imagine the possibility of a world before this world is to imagine an impossibility, except in case the nature of the possible were already realized and there existed before the existence of the world only two natures, the nature of the necessary and the nature of the impossible.[2] But it is evident that the judgement of reason concerning the being of these three natures is eternal, like its judgement concerning the necessary and the impossible.

This objection, however, does not touch the philosophers, because they hold that the world could not be smaller or bigger than it is,

If it were possible that a spatial magnitude could infinitely increase, then the existence of a spatial magnitude without end would be possible and a spatial magnitude, actually infinite, would exist, and this is impossible and Aristotle has already shown the impossibility of this.[1] But against the man who believes in this possibility, because the contrary would imply a denial of God's power, this argument is valid, for this spatial possibility is just as much a purely rational concept[2] as the possibility of temporal anteriority according to the philosophers. Therefore, he who believes in the temporal creation of the world and affirms that all body is in space, is bound to admit that before the creation of the world there was space, either occupied by body, in which the production of the world could occur, or empty, for it is necessary that space should precede what is produced.[3] The man who denies empty space and affirms the finiteness of body—like* certain later Ash'arites who, however, separated themselves from the principles of the theologians; but I have not read it in their books and it was told to me by some who studied their doctrines[4]—cannot admit the temporal production of the world. If the fact of this extension which measures movement and which stands in relation to it as its measurement were indeed the work of an illusion—like the representation of a world bigger or smaller than it really is—time would not exist, for time is nothing but what the mind perceives of this extension which measures movement. And if it is self-evident that time exists, then the act of the mind must necessarily be a veracious one, embodying reason, not one embodying illusion.

Ghazali says:

It has been objected:[5] we declare that what is not possible is what cannot be done and increase or decrease in the size of the world is impossible, and therefore could not be brought about.[6]

I say:

This is the answer to the objection of the Ash'arites that to admit that God could not have made the world bigger or smaller is to charge Him with impotence, but they have thereby compromised themselves, for impotence is not inability to do the impossible, but inability to do what can be done.[7]

Ghazali, opposing this, says:

This excuse is invalid for three reasons: The first is that it is an affront to reason, for when reason regards it as possible that the world might be bigger or smaller than it is by a cubit, this is not the same as regarding it as possible to identify black with white and existence with non-existence;

impossibility lies in affirming the negative and the positive at the same time, and all impossibilities amount to this. This is indeed a silly and faulty assertion.¹

I say:

This statement is, as he says, an affront to reason, but only to the reason of him who judges superficially; it is not an affront to true reason, for a statement about its being possible or not² requires a proof. And therefore he is right when he declares that this is not impossible in the way in which the assumption that black might be white is impossible, for the impossibility of the latter is self-evident. The statement, however, that the world could not be smaller or larger than it is is not self-evident. And although all impossibilities can be reduced to self-evident impossibilities, this reduction can take place in two ways. The first is that the impossibility is self-evident; the second is that there follows sooner or later from its supposition an impossibility of the same character as that of self-evident impossibilities.³ For instance, if it is assumed that the world might be larger or smaller than it is, it follows that outside it there would be occupied or empty space. And from the supposition that there is outside it occupied or empty space, some of the greatest impossibilities follow: from empty space the existence of mere extension existing by itself; from occupied space a body moving either upward or downward or in a circle which therefore must be part of another world. Now it has been proved in the science of physics that the existence of another world at the same time as this is an impossibility⁴ and the most unlikely consequence would be that the world should have empty space: for any world must needs have four elements and a spherical body revolving round them. He who wants to ascertain this should look up the places where its exposition is demanded—this, of course, after having fulfilled the preliminary conditions necessary for the student to understand strict proof.⁵

Then Ghazali mentions the second reason:

If the world is in the state it is, without the possibility of being larger or smaller than it is, then its existence, as it is, is necessary, not possible. But the necessary needs no cause. So say, then, as the materialists do that you deny the creator and that you deny the cause of causes! But this is not your doctrine.⁶

I say:

To this the answer which Avicenna gives in accordance with his doctrine is quite appropriate.¹ According to him necessity of existence is of two kinds: the necessary, existent by itself, and the necessary, existent through another. But my answer on this question is still more to the point: things necessary in this sense need not have an agent or a maker; take, for example, a saw which is used to saw wood—it is a tool having a certain determined quantity, quality, and matter, that is, it is not possible for it to be of another material than iron and it could not have any other shape than that of a saw or any other measure than the measure of a saw. Still nobody would say that the saw has a necessity of being.² See, therefore, how crude this mistake is! If one were to take away the necessity from the quantities, qualities, and matters of things produced by art, in the way the Ash'arites imagine this to happen concerning the created in relation to the creator, the wisdom which lies in the creator and the created would have been withdrawn, any agent could be an artificer and any cause in existence a creator. But all this is a denial of reason and wisdom.³

Ghazali says:

The third reason is that this faulty argument authorizes its opponent⁴ to oppose it by a similar one, and we may say: The existence of the world was not possible before its existence, for indeed possibility—according to your theory—is coextensive with existence, neither more nor less.⁵ If you say: 'But then the eternal has passed from impotence to power', we answer: 'No, for the existence was not possible and therefore could not be brought about and the impossibility of a thing's happening that could not happen does not indicate impotence.' If you say: 'How can a thing which is impossible become possible?' We answer: 'But why should it be impossible that a thing should be impossible at one moment and possible at another?'⁶ If you say: 'The times are similar,' the answer is: 'But so are the measures, and why should one measure be possible and another, bigger or smaller by the width of a nail, impossible?'⁷ And if the latter assumption is not impossible, the former is not impossible either.' And this is the way to oppose them.

But the true answer is that their supposition of possibilities⁸ makes no sense whatever. We concede only that God is eternal and powerful, and that His action never fails, even if He should wish it. And there is nothing in this power that demands the assumption of a temporal extension, unless imagination, confusing God's power with other things*, connects it with time*.⁹

I say:

The summary of this is that the Ash'arites say to the philosophers: this question whether the world could be larger or smaller is impossible according to us; it has sense only for the man who believes in a priority of possibility in relation to the actualization of a thing, i.e. the realization of the possible. We, the Ash'arites, however, say: 'Possibility occurs together with the actuality as it is, without adding or subtracting anything.'

Now my answer is that he who denies the possibility of the possible before its existence denies the necessary, for the possible is the contrary of the impossible without there existing a middle term, and, if a thing is not possible before its existence, then it is necessarily impossible.[1] Now to posit the impossible as existing is an impossible falsehood, but to posit the possible as existing is a possible, not an impossible, falsehood.[2] Their assertion that possibility and actuality exist together is a falsehood, for possibility and actuality are contradictory, and do not exist together in one and the same moment. The necessary consequence for them is that possibility exists neither at the same time as the actuality nor before it.[3] The true consequence for the Ash'arites in this discussion is not that the eternal passes from impotence to power, for he who cannot do an impossible act is not called impotent, but that a thing can pass from the nature of the impossible to the nature of existence, and this is like the changing of the necessary into the possible. To posit a thing, however, as impossible at one time and possible at another does not cut it off from the nature of the possible, for this is the general character of the possible; the existence of anything possible, for instance, is impossible at the moment when its contrary exists in its substratum.[4] If the opponent concedes that a thing impossible at one time is possible at another, then he has conceded that this thing is of the nature of the absolutely possible[5] and that it has not the nature of the impossible. If it is assumed that the world was impossible for an infinite time before its production, the consequence is that, when it was produced, it changed over from impossibility to possibility.[6] This question is not the problem with which we are concerned here, but as we have said before, the transference from one problem to another is an act of sophistry.

And as to his words:

But the true answer is that their supposition of possibilities makes no sense whatever. We concede only that God is eternal and powerful and that His action never fails, even if He should wish it. And there is nothing in this power that demands the assumption of a temporal extension, unless imagination confusing God's power with other things* connects with it time*.

I say:

Even if there were nothing in this supposition—as he says—that implies the eternity of time, there is something in it that demands that the possibility of the occurrence of the world and equally of time should be eternal. And this is that God never ceases to have power for action, and that it is impossible that anything should prevent His act from being eternally connected with His existence; and perhaps the opposite of this statement indicates the impossibility better still, namely, that He should have no power at one time but power at another, and that He could be called powerful only at definite limited times, although He is an eternal and perpetual being. And then we have the old question again whether the world may be either eternal or temporal, or whether the world cannot be eternal, or whether the world cannot be temporal, or whether the world may be temporal but certainly cannot be eternal, and whether, if the world is temporal, it can be a first act or not. And if reason has no power to pronounce for one of these opposite propositions, let us go back to tradition, but do not then regard this question as a rational one! We say that the First Cause cannot omit the best act and perform an inferior, because this would be an imperfection; but can there be a greater imperfection than to assume the act of the Eternal as finite and limited, like the act of a temporal product, although a limited act can only be imagined of a limited agent, not of the eternal agent whose existence and action are unlimited? All this, as you see, cannot be unknown to the man who has even the slightest understanding of the rational. And how can it be thought that the present act proceeding from the Eternal cannot be preceded by another act, and again by another, and so in our thinking infinitely, like the infinite continuation of His existence? For it is a necessary consequence that the act of Him whose existence time cannot measure nor comprehend in either direction cannot be comprehended in time nor measured by a limited duration. For there is no being whose act is delayed after its existence, except when there is an impediment which prevents its existence from attaining its perfection,[1] or, in voluntary beings, when there is an obstruction in the execution of their choice. He, therefore, who assumes that from the Eternal there proceeds only a temporal act presumes that His act is constrained in a certain way and in this way therefore does not depend on His choice.

THE THIRD PROOF FOR THE ETERNITY
OF THE WORLD

Ghazali says:

They insist on saying: The existence of the world is possible before its existence, as it is absurd that it should be impossible and then become possible;[1] this possibility has no beginning, it is eternally unchangeable and the existence of the world remains eternally possible, for at no time whatever can the existence of the world be described as impossible; and if the possibility never ceases, the possible, in conformity with the possibility, never ceases either; and the meaning of the sentence, that the existence of the world is possible, is that the existence of the world is not impossible; and since its existence is eternally possible, it is never impossible, for if it were ever impossible, it would not be true that the existence of the world is eternally possible; and if it were not true that the existence of the world is eternally possible, it would not be true that its possibility never ceases; and if it were not true that its possibility never ceases, it would be true that its possibility had begun; and if it were true that its possibility had begun, its existence before this beginning would not be possible and that would lead to the assumption of a time when the world was not possible and God had no power over it.

I say:

He who concedes that the world before its existence was of a never-ceasing possibility must admit that the world is eternal, for the assumption that what is eternally possible[2] is eternally existent implies no absurdity.[3] What can possibly exist eternally must necessarily exist eternally, for what can receive eternity cannot become corruptible, except if it were possible that the corruptible could become eternal.[4] Therefore Aristotle has said that the possibility in the eternal beings is necessary.[5]

Ghazali says:

The objection is that it is said that the temporal becoming of the world never ceased to be possible, and certainly there is no time at which its becoming could not be imagined. But although it could be at any time, it did not become at any time whatever, for reality does not conform to possibility, but differs from it.[6] You yourself hold, for instance, in the matter of place, that the world could be bigger than it is, or that the creation of an infinite series of bodies above the world is possible, and that there is no limit to the possibilities of increase in the size of the world, but still the actual existence of absolutely infinite occupied space and of any infinite and limitless being is impossible. What is said to be possible is an actual body of a limited surface, but the exact size of this body, whether it is larger or smaller, is not specified. In the same way, what is possible is the coming into existence of the world in time, but the exact time of its coming into existence whether earlier or later, is not specified. The principle of its having come into being is specified and this is the possible, nothing else.[1]

I say:

The man who assumes that before the existence of the world there was one unique, never-ceasing possibility must concede that the world is eternal. The man who affirms, like Ghazali in his answer, that before the world there was an infinite number of possibilities of worlds, has certainly to admit that before this world there was another world and before this second world a third, and so on *ad infinitum*, as is the case with human beings, and especially when it is assumed that the perishing of the earlier is the necessary condition for the existence of the later.[2] For instance, if God had the power to create another world before this, and before this second world yet another, the series must continue infinitely, or else we should arrive at a world before which no other world could have been created (however, the theologians do not affirm this nor use it as a proof for the temporal production of the world).[3] Although the assumption that before this world there might be an infinite number of others does not seem an impossible one, it appears after closer examination to be absurd, for it would follow from it that the universe had the nature of an individual person in this transitory world, so that its procession from the First Principle would be like the procession of the individual person from Him—that is to say, through an eternal moving body and an eternal motion. But then this world would be part of another world, like the transient beings in this world, and then necessarily either we end finally in a world individually eternal or we have an infinite series. And if we have to bring this series to a standstill, it is more appropriate to arrest it at this world, by regarding it as eternally unique.

THE FOURTH PROOF

Ghazali says:

The fourth proof is that they say everything that becomes is preceded by the matter which is in it, for what becomes cannot be free from matter.[4] For this reason matter never becomes; what becomes is only the form, the accidents and the qualities which add themselves to matter.[5] The proof is that the existence of each thing that becomes must, before its becoming, either be possible, impossible, or necessary: it cannot be impossible, for the essentially impossible will never exist; it cannot be necessary, for the

THE FIRST DISCUSSION

essentially necessary will never be in a state of non-existence, and therefore it is the essentially possible.[1] Therefore, the thing which becomes has before its becoming the possibility of becoming, but the possibility of becoming is an attribute which needs a relation and has no subsistence in itself.[2] It needs, therefore, a substratum with which it can be connected, and there is no substratum except matter, and it becomes connected with it in the way in which we say this matter receives warmth and coldness, or black and white, or movement and rest, i.e. it is possible that these qualities and these changes occur in it and therefore possibility is an attribute of matter. Matter does not possess other matter,[3] and cannot become; for, if it did, the possibility of its existence would precede its existence, and possibility would subsist by itself without being related to anything else, whereas it is a relative attribute which cannot be understood as subsisting by itself. And it cannot be said that the meaning of possibility amounts to what can be done and what the Eternal had the power to do, because we know only that a thing can be done, because it is possible, and we say 'this can be done because it is possible and cannot be done because it is not possible';[4] and if 'this is possible' meant 'this can be done', to say 'this can be done because it is possible' would mean 'this is possible because it is possible', and this is a circular definition; and this shows that 'this is possible' is a first judgement in the mind, evident in itself, which makes the second judgement 'that it can be done' intelligible. It cannot be said, either, that to be possible refers to the knowledge of the Eternal, for knowledge depends on a thing known, whereas possibility is undoubtedly an object of knowledge, not knowledge;[5] further, it is a relative attribute, and needs something to which it can be related, and this can only be matter, and everything that becomes is preceded by matter.

I say:

The summary of this is that everything that becomes is possible before it becomes, and that possibility needs something for its subsistence, namely, the substratum which receives that which is possible. For it must not be believed that the possibility of the recipient is the same as the possibility of the agent. It is a different thing to say about Zaid, the agent, that he can do something and to say about the patient that it can have something done to it. Thus the possibility of the patient[6] is a necessary condition for the possibility of the agent, for the agent which cannot act is not possible but impossible. Since it is impossible that the possibility prior to the thing's becoming should be absolutely without* substratum, or that the agent should be its substratum or the thing possible—for the thing possible loses its possibility, when it becomes actual—there only remains as a vehicle for possibility the recipient of the possible, i.e. matter. Matter, in so far as it is matter, does not become; for if it did it would need other matter and we should have an infinite regress. Matter only becomes in so far as it is combined with form. Everything that comes into being comes into being from something else, and this must either give rise to an infinite regress and lead directly to infinite matter which is impossible, even if we assume an eternal mover, for there is no actual infinite; or the forms must be interchangeable in the ingenerable and incorruptible substratum, eternally and in rotation.[1] There must, therefore, be an eternal movement which produces this interchange in the eternally transitory things. And therefore it is clear that the generation of the one in each pair of generated beings is the corruption of the other; otherwise a thing could come into being from nothing, for the meaning of 'becoming' is the alteration of a thing and its change, from what it has potentially, into actuality. It is not possible that the privation itself should change into the existent, and it is not the privation of which it is said that it has become. There exists, therefore, a substratum for the contrary forms, and it is in this substratum that the forms interchange.

Ghazali says:

The objection is that the possibility of which they speak is a judgement of the intellect, and anything whose existence the intellect supposes, provided no obstacle presents itself to the supposition, we call possible and, if there is such an obstacle, we call it impossible and, if we suppose that it cannot be supposed not to be, we call it necessary.[2] These are rational judgements which need no real existent which they might qualify. There are three proofs of this. The first is: If possibility needed an existent to which it could be related, and of which it could be said that it is its possibility, impossibility also would need an existent of which it might be said that it is *its* impossibility; but impossibility has no real existence, and there is no matter in which it occurs and to which it could be related.

I say:

That possibility demands an existing matter is clear, for all true intellectual concepts need a thing outside the soul, for truth, as it has been defined, is the agreement of what is in the soul with what is outside the soul.[3] And when we say that something is possible, we cannot but understand that it needs something in which this possibility can be.[4] As regards his proof that the possible is not dependent on an existent, because the impossible is not dependent on an existent, this is sophistical. Indeed the impossible demands a substratum just as much as the possible does, and this is clear from the fact that the impossible is the opposite of the possible and opposite contraries undoubtedly require a substratum. For impossibility is the negation of possibility, and, if possibility needs a substratum, impossibility which is the negation of this possibility requires a substratum too, e.g. we say that the existence of empty space is impossible, because the existence of independent dimensions outside or inside natural bodies is impossible, or that the presence of opposites at the same time in the same substratum is impossible, or that the equivalence of one to two is impossible, i.e. in reality. All this is self-evident, and it is not necessary to consider the errors here committed.

Ghazali says:

The second proof is that the intellect decides that black and white are possible before they exist.[1] If this possibility were related to the body in which they inhere, so that it might be said that the meaning is that this body can be black and white, then white would not be possible by itself and possibility would be related only to the body. But we affirm, as concerns the judgement about black in itself, as to whether it is possible, necessary, or impossible, that we, without doubt, will say that it is possible. And this shows that the intellect in order to decide whether something is possible need not admit an existing thing to which the possibility can be related.

I say:

This is a sophism. For the possible is predicated of the recipient and of the inherent quality. In so far as it is predicated of the substratum, its opposite is the impossible, and in so far as it is predicated of the inherent, its opposite is the necessary.[2] Thus the possible which is described as being the opposite of the impossible is not that which abandons its possibility so far as it is actualized, when it becomes actual, because this latter loses its possibility in the actualizing process.[3] This latter possible is only described by possibility in so far as it is in potency, and the vehicle of this potency is the substratum which changes from existence in potency into existence in actuality.[4] This is evident from the definition of the possible that it is the non-existence which is in readiness to exist or not to exist.[5] This possible non-existent is possible neither in so far as it is non-existent nor in so far as it is actually existent.[6] It is only possible in so far as it is in potency, and for this reason the Muʿtazilites affirm that the non-existent is a kind of entity.[7] For non-existence is the opposite of existence, and each of the two is succeeded by the other, and when the non-existence of a thing disappears it is followed by its existence, and when its existence disappears it is succeeded by its non-existence. As non-existence by itself cannot change into existence, and existence by itself cannot change into non-existence, there must be a third entity which is the recipient for both of them, and that is what is described by 'possibility' and 'becoming' and 'change from the quality of non-existence to the quality of existence'. For non-existence itself is not described by 'becoming' or 'change'; nor is the thing that has become actual described in this way, for what becomes loses the quality of becoming, change, and possibility when it has become actual. Therefore there must necessarily be something that can be described by 'becoming' and 'change' and 'transition from non-existence to existence', as happens in the passage of opposites into opposites; that is to say, there must be a substratum for them in which they can interchange—with this one difference, however, that this substratum exists in the interchange of all the accidents in actuality, whereas in the substance it exists in potency.[1]

And we cannot think of regarding what is described by 'possibility' and 'change' as identical with the actual, i.e. which belongs to the becoming in so far as it is actual, for the former again vanishes and the latter must necessarily be a part of the product.[2] Therefore there must necessarily be a substratum which is the recipient for the possibility and which is the vehicle of the change and the becoming, and it is this of which it is said that it becomes, and alters, and changes from non-existence into existence. Nor can we think of making this substratum of the nature of the actualized, for if this were the case the existent would not become, for what becomes comes into being from the non-existent not from the existent.[3] Both philosophers and Mu'tazilites agree about the existence of this entity; only the philosophers are of the opinion that it cannot be exempt from a form actually existent, i.e. that it cannot be free from existence, like the transition, for example, from sperma to blood and the transition from blood to the members of the embryo.[4] The reason is that if it were exempt from existence it would have an existence of its own, and if it had an existence of its own, becoming could not come from it.[5] This entity is called by the philosophers '*hyle*', and it is the cause of generation and corruption. And according to the philosophers an existent which is free from *hyle* is neither generable nor corruptible.[6]

Ghazali says:

The third proof is that the souls of men, according to the philosophers, are substances which subsist by themselves[7] without being in a body or in matter or impressed on matter;[8] they had a beginning in time, according

THE FIRST DISCUSSION 63

to the theory of Avicenna and the acknowledged philosophers, they had possibility before their beginning, but they have neither essence nor matter[1] and their possibility is a relative attribute,[2] dependent neither on God's power nor on the Agent;[3] but on what then is it dependent? The difficulties are therefore turned against them themselves.

I say:

I do not know any philosopher who said that the soul has a beginning in the true sense of the word and is thereafter everlasting except —as Ghazali relates—Avicenna.[4] All other philosophers agree that in their temporal existence they are related to and connected with the bodily possibilities, which receive this connexion like the possibilities which subsist in mirrors for their connexion with the rays of the sun.[5] According to the philosophers this possibility is not of the nature of the generable and corruptible forms, but of a kind to which, according to them, demonstrative proof leads, and the vehicle of this possibility is of another nature than the nature of the *hyle*. He alone can grasp their theories in these matters who has read their books and fulfilled the conditions there laid down by them, and has besides a sound understanding and a learned master.[6] That Ghazali should touch on such questions in this way is not worthy of such a man, but there are only these alternatives: either he knew these matters in their true nature, and sets them out here wrongly, which is wicked; or he did not understand their real nature and touched on problems he had not grasped, which is the act of an ignoramus. However, he stands too high in our eyes for either of these qualifications. But even the best horse will stumble[7] and it was a stumble of Ghazali's that he brought out this book. But perhaps he was forced to do so by the conditions of his time and his situation.

Ghazali says, speaking on behalf of the philosophers:

It may be said: To reduce possibility to a judgement of the intellect is absurd, for the meaning of 'judgement of the intellect' is nothing but the knowledge of possibility, and possibility is an object of knowledge, not knowledge itself; knowledge, on the contrary, comprises possibility and follows it and depends on it as it is, and if knowledge vanished the object of knowledge would not, but the disappearance of the object of knowledge would imply the disappearance of knowledge. For knowledge and the object-known are two things, the former dependent on the latter, and if we supposed rational beings to turn away from possibility and neglect it, we should say: 'It is not possibility that is annulled, for the possibilities subsist by themselves, but it is simply that minds neglect them or that minds and rational beings have disappeared; but possibility remains,

109 without any doubt.[1] And the three proofs are not valid, for impossibility requires an existent to which it can be related, and impossibility means identifying two opposites, and if the substratum were white it could not become black as long as the white existed, and therefore we need a substratum, qualified by the quality during the inherence of which its opposite is spoken of as impossible in this substratum, and therefore impossibility is a relative attribute subsistent in a substratum and related to it. And where the necessary is concerned it is evident that it is related to necessary existence.

As concerns the second proof, that black is in itself possible, this is a mistake, for if it is taken, abstracted from the substratum in which it inheres, it is impossible, not possible; it only becomes possible when it can become a form in a body; the body is then in readiness for the interchange, and the interchange is possible for the body; but in itself black has no individuality, so as to be characterizable by possibility.

As concerns the third proof about the soul, it is eternal for one school of philosophers, and is only possible in the attaching of itself to bodies, and therefore against those philosophers the argument does not apply.[2] But for those who admit that the soul comes into existence—and one school of philosophers has believed that it is impressed on matter and follows its temperament, as is indicated by Galen in certain passages—it comes into existence in matter and its possibility is related to its matter.[3] And according to the theory of those who admit that it comes into existence, although it is not impressed on matter—which means that it is possible for the rational soul to direct matter—the possibility prior to the becoming is relative to matter,[4] and although the soul is not impressed on matter, it is attached to it, for it is its directing principle and uses it as an instrument, and in this way its possibility is relative to matter.[5]

I say:

What he says in this section is true, as will be clear to you from our explanation of the nature of the possible.

Then Ghazali, objecting to the philosophers, says:

And the answer is: To reduce possibility, necessity, and impossibility to rational concepts is correct, and as for the assertion that the concepts of reason form its knowledge, and knowledge implies a thing known, let them be answered: it cannot be said that receptivity of colour and ani-
110 mality and the other concepts, which are fixed in the mind according to the philosophers—and this is what constitutes the sciences—have no objects;[6] still these objects have no real existence in the external world, and the philosophers are certainly right in saying that universals exist only in the mind, not in the external world, and that in the external world there are only particular individuals, which are apprehended by the senses, not by reason; and yet these individuals are the reason why the mind abstracts from them a concept separated from its rational matter; therefore

receptivity of colour is a concept, separate in the mind from blackness and whiteness, although in reality a colour which is neither black nor white nor of another colour cannot be imagined,[1] and receptivity of colour is fixed in the mind without any specification—now, in the same way, it can be said that possibility is a form which exists in minds, not in the exterior world, and if this is not impossible for other concepts,[2] there is no impossibility in what we have said.[3]

I say:

This argument is sophistical because possibility is a universal which has individuals outside the mind like all the other universals, and knowledge is not knowledge of the universal concept, but it is a knowledge of individuals in a universal way which the mind attains in the case of the individuals, when it abstracts from them one common nature which is distributed among the different matters.[4] The nature, therefore, of the universal is not identical with the nature of the things of which it is a universal. Ghazali is here in error, for he assumes that the nature of possibility is the nature of the universal, without there being individuals on which this universal, i.e. the universal concept of possibility, depends. The universal, however, is not the object of knowledge; on the contrary through it the things become known, although it exists potentially in the nature of the things known;[5] otherwise its apprehension of the individuals, in so far as they are universals, would be false. This apprehension would indeed be false if the nature of the object known were essentially individual, not accidentally individual, whereas the opposite is the case: it is accidentally individual, essentially universal.[6] Therefore if the mind did not apprehend the individuals in so far as they are universal, it would be in error and make false judgements about them. But if it abstracts those natures which subsist in the individual things from their matter, and makes them universal, then it is possible that it judges them rightly; otherwise it would confuse those natures, of which the possible is one.

The theory of the philosophers that universals exist only in the mind, not in the external world, only means that the universals exist actually only in the mind, and not in the external world, not that they do not exist at all in the external world, for the meaning is that they exist potentially, not actually in the external world; indeed, if they did not exist at all in the outside world they would be false. Since universals exist outside the mind in potency and possibilities exist outside the soul in potency, the nature of universals in regard to this resembles that of possibilities. And for this reason Ghazali tried to deceive people by a sophism*, for he compared possibility to the universals because of their both being potentially in reality, and then he assumed that the philosophers assert that universals do not exist at all outside the soul; from which he deduced that possibility does not exist outside the soul. What an ugly and crude sophism!

112 Ghazali says:

As regards their assertion that, if it were assumed that rational beings had vanished or had neglected possibility, possibility itself would not have disappeared, we answer: 'If it were assumed that they had vanished, would not the universal concepts, i.e. the genera and species, have disappeared too?' and if they agree to this, this can only mean that universals are only concepts in the mind; but this is exactly what we say about possibility, and there is no difference between the two cases; if they, however, affirm that they are permanent in the knowledge of God,[1] the same may be said about possibility, and the argument is valid, and our aim of showing the contradiction in this theory has been attained.

I say:

This argument shows his foolishness and proneness to contradiction. The most plausible form in which it might be expressed would be to base it* on two premises: the first, that the evident proposition that possibility is partially individual, namely, outside the soul, partially universal, namely, the universal concept of the individual possibles, is not true; and the second, that it was said that the nature of the individual possibles outside the soul is identical with the nature of the universal of possibility in the mind; and in this case the possible would have neither a universal nor an individual nature, or else the nature of the individual would have to be identical with that of the universal. All this is presumptuous, and how should it be else, for in a way the universal has an existence outside the soul.

Ghazali says:

And as regards their subterfuge where the impossible is concerned, that it is related to the matter qualified by its opposite, as it cannot take the place of its opposite,[2] this cannot be the case with every impossible, for that God should have a rival is impossible, but there is no matter to which this impossibility could be related. If they say the impossibility of God's having a rival, means that the solitude of God in His essence and His uniqueness are necessary and that this solitude is proper to Him, we answer: This is not necessary, for the world exists with Him, and He is therefore not solitary. And if they say that His solitude so far as a rival is concerned is necessary, and that the opposite of the necessary is the impossible, and that the impossible is related to Him, we answer: In this case the solitude of God in regard to the world is different from His solitude in regard to His equal and in this case His solitude in regard to His rival is necessary, and in regard to the created world not necessary.[1]

I say:

All this is vain talk, for it cannot be doubted that the judgements of the mind have value only in regard to the nature of things outside the soul. If there were outside the soul nothing possible or impossible, the judgement of the mind that things are possible or impossible would be of as much value as no judgement at all, and there would be no difference between reason and illusion. And that there should be a rival to God is just as impossible in reality as God's existence is necessary in reality. But there is no sense in wasting more words on this question.

Ghazali says:

The subterfuge concerning the becoming of the souls is worthless too, for they have individual essences and a possibility prior to their becoming,[2] and at that time there is nothing with which they could be brought into relation.[3] Their argument contends that it is possible for matter that the souls direct it is a remote relation[4] and, if this satisfies you, you might as well say that the possibility of the souls' becoming* lies in the power of Him who can on His own authority produce them,[5] for the souls are then related to the Agent—although they are not impressed on Him—in the same way as to the body, on which they are not impressed either. And since the imprint is made neither on the one substrate nor on the other*, there is no difference between the relation to the agent and that to the patient.

I say:

He wants to force those who assume* the possibility of the soul's becoming without there being an imprint in matter to concede that the possibility in the recipient is like the possibility in the agent, because the act proceeds from the agent and therefore these two possibilities are similar. But this is a shocking supposition, for, according to it, the soul would come to the body as if it directed it from the outside, as the artisan directs his product, and the soul would not be a form in the body, just as the artisan is not a form in his product. The answer is that it is not impossible that there should be amongst the entelechies which conduct themselves like forms[6] something that is separate from its substratum as the steersman is from his ship[7] and the artisan from his tool, and if the body is like the instrument of the soul, the soul is a separate form, and then the possibility which is in the instrument is not like the possibility which is in the agent; no, the instrument is in both conditions, the possibility which is in the patient and the possibility which is in the agent, and therefore the instruments are the mover and the moved, and in so far as they are the mover, there is in them the possibility which is in the agent, and in so far as they are moved, the possibility which is in the recipient.[1]

But the supposition that the soul is a separate entity does not force them into the admission that the possibility which is in the recipient is identical[2] with the possibility which is in the agent. Besides, the possibility which according to the philosophers is in the agent is not only a rational judgement, but refers to something outside the soul.[3] Therefore his argument does not gain by assimilating one of these two possibilities to the other. And since Ghazali knew that all these arguments have no other effect than to bring doubts and perplexity to those who cannot solve them—which is an act of wicked sophists, he says:

And if it is said you have taken good care in all your objections to oppose the difficulties by other difficulties, but nothing of what you yourself have adduced is free from difficulty, we answer: the objections do show the falsity of an argument, no doubt, and certain aspects* of the problem are solved in stating the opposite view and its foundation.[4] We have not committed ourselves to anything more than to upsetting their theories, and to showing the faults in the consequence of their proofs so as to demonstrate their incoherence. We do not seek to attack from any definite point of view, and we shall not transgress the aim of this book, nor give full proofs for the temporal production of the world, for our intention is merely to refute their alleged knowledge of its eternity. But after finishing this book we shall, if it pleases God, devote a work to establishing the doctrine of truth, and we call it 'The Golden Mean in Dogmatic Beliefs'*,[5] in which we shall be engaged in building up, as in this book we have been in destroying.

I say:

To oppose difficulty with difficulty does not bring about destruction, but only perplexity and doubts in him who acts in this way, for why should he think one of the two conflicting theories reasonable and the opposite one vain? Most of the arguments with which this man Ghazali opposes the philosophers are doubts which arise when certain parts of the doctrine of the philosophers come into conflict with others, and when those differences are compared with each other; but this is an imperfect refutation. A perfect refutation would be one that succeeded in showing the futility of their system according to the facts themselves, not such a one as, for instance, his assumption that it is permissible for the opponents of the philosophers to claim that possibility is a mental concept in the same way as the philosophers claim this for the universal. For if the truth of this comparison between the two were conceded, it would not follow that it was untrue that possibility was a concept dependent on reality, but only either that the universal existed in the mind only was not true, or that possibility existed in the mind only was not true. Indeed, it would have been necessary for him to begin by establishing the truth, before starting to perplex and confuse his readers, for they might die before they could get hold of that book, or he might have died himself before writing it. But this book has not yet come into my hands[1] and perhaps he never composed it, and he only says that he does not base this present book on any doctrine, in order that it should not be thought that he based it on that of the Ash'arites. It appears from the books ascribed to him that in metaphysics he recurs to the philosophers. And of all his books this is most clearly shown and most truly proved in his book called *The Niche for Lights*.[2]

THE SECOND DISCUSSION

The Refutation of their Theory of the Incorruptibility of the World and of Time and Motion

Ghazali says:

Know that this is part of the first question, for according to the philosophers the existence of the world, having no beginning, does not end either; it is eternal, without a final term. Its disappearance and its corruption cannot be imagined; it never began to exist in the condition in which it exists[3] and it will never cease to exist in the condition in which it exists.

Their four arguments which we have mentioned in our discussion of its eternity in the past refer also to its eternity in the future, and the objection is the same without any difference. They say that the world is caused, and that its cause is without beginning or end, and that this applies both to the effect and to the cause, and that, if the cause does not change, the effect cannot change either; upon this they build their proof of the impossibility of its beginning, and the same applies to its ending. This is their first proof.

70   TAHAFUT AL TAHAFUT

The second proof is that an eventual annihilation of the world must occur *after* its existence, but 'after' implies an affirmation of time.

The third proof is that the possibility of its existence does not end, and that therefore its possible existence may conform to the possibility.[1] But this argument has no force, for we regard it as impossible that the world should not have begun, but we do not regard it as impossible that it should last eternally, if God should make it last eternally, for it is not necessary that what begins has also an end, although it is necessary for an act to have a beginning and an initial term. Only Abu Hudhail al-Allaf thought that the world must needs have an end, and he said that, as in the past infinite circular movements are impossible, so they are in the future;[2] but this is wrong, for the whole of the future never enters into existence either simultaneously or successively, whereas the whole of the past is there simultaneously but not successively.[3] And since it is clear that we do not regard the incorruptibility of the world as impossible from a rational point of view—we regard indeed its incorruptibility and corruptibility as equally possible—we know only through the Divine Law[4] which of the two possibilities will be realized. Therefore let us not try to solve this problem by mere reason!

I say:

His assertion that the argument of the philosophers for the eternity of the world in the past applies also to its eternity in the future is true, and equally the second argument applies to both cases. But his assertion that the third argument is not equally valid for the future and for the past, that indeed we regard the becoming of the world in the past as impossible, but that with the exception of Abu Hudhail al-Allaf, who thought that the eternity of the world was impossible in either direction, we do not regard its eternity in the future as absolutely impossible, is not true. For when it was conceded to the philosophers that the possibility of the world had no beginning and that with this possibility a condition of extension, which could measure this possibility, was connected in the same way as this condition of extension is connected with the possible existent, when it is actualized, and it was also evident that this extension had no initial term, the philosophers were convinced that time had no initial term, for this extension is nothing but time, and to call it timeless eternity[5] is senseless. And since time is connected with possibility and possibility with existence in motion, existence in motion has no first term either. And the assertion of the theologians that everything which existed in the past had a first term is futile, for the First exists in the past eternally, as it exists eternally in the future.[6] And their distinction here between the first term and its act[7] requires a proof,

THE SECOND DISCUSSION

for the existence of the temporal which occurs in the past is different from the existence of the eternal which occurs in the past. For the temporal which has occurred in the past is finite in both directions, i.e. it has a beginning and an end, but the eternal which has occurred in the past has neither beginning nor end.[1] And therefore, since the philosophers have not admitted that the circular movement has a beginning, they cannot be forced to admit that it has an end, for they do not regard its existence in the past as transitory, and, if some philosopher does regard it as such, he contradicts himself and therefore the statement is true that everything that has a beginning has an end.[2] That anything could have a beginning and no end is not true, unless the possible could be changed into the eternal, for everything that has a beginning is possible. And that anything could be liable to corruption and at the same time could be capable of eternity is something incomprehensible[3] and stands in need of examination. The ancient philosophers indeed examined this problem, and Abu Hudhail agrees with the philosophers in saying that whatever can be generated is corruptible, and he kept strictly to the consequence which follows from the acceptance of the principle of becoming. As to those who make a distinction between the past and the future, because what is in the past is there in its totality, whereas the future never enters into existence in its totality (for the future enters reality only successively), this is deceptive, for what is in reality past is that which has entered time and that which has entered time has time beyond it in both directions and possesses totality. But that which has never entered the past in the way the temporal enters the past can only be said in an equivocal way to be in the past; it is infinitely extended, with the past rather than in the past,[4] and possesses no totality in itself, although its parts are totalities. And this, if it has no initial term beginning in the past, is in fact time itself. For each temporal beginning is a present, and each present is preceded by a past, and both that which exists commensurable with time, and time commensurable with it, must necessarily be infinite. Only the parts of time which are limited by time in both directions can enter the past, in the same way as only the instant which is everchanging and only the instantaneous motion of a thing in movement in the spatial magnitude in which it moves can really enter the existence of the moved.[5] And just as we do not say that the past of what never ceased to exist in the past ever entered existence at an instant—for this would mean that its existence had a beginning and that time limited it in both directions—so it stands with that which is simultaneous with time, not in time. For of the circular movements only those that time limits enter into represented existence,[1] but those that are simultaneous with time do not afterwards enter past existence, just as the eternally existent does not enter past existence, since no time limits it. And when one imagines an eternal entity whose acts are not delayed after its existence—as indeed must be the case with any entity whose existence is perfect[2]—then, if it is eternal and does not enter past time, it follows necessarily that its acts also cannot enter past time, for if they did they would be finite and this eternal existent would be eternally inactive and what is eternally inactive is necessarily impossible. And it is most appropriate for an entity, whose existence does not enter time and which is not limited by time, that its acts should not enter existence either, because there is no difference between the entity and its acts. If the movements of the celestial bodies and what follows from them are acts of an eternal entity, the existence of which does not enter the past, then its acts do not enter past time either. For it is not permissible to say of anything that is eternal that it has entered past time, nor that it has ended, for that which has an end has a beginning. For indeed, our statement that it is eternal means the denial of its entering past time and of its having had a beginning. He who, assuming that it entered past time, assumes that it must have a beginning begs the question.[3] It is, therefore, untrue that what is coexistent with eternal existence, has entered existence, unless the eternal existence has entered existence by entering past time. Therefore our statement 'everything past must have entered existence' must be understood in two ways: first, that which has entered past existence must have entered existence, and this is a true statement; secondly, that which is past and is inseparably connected with eternal existence cannot be truly said to have entered existence, for our expression 'entered existence' is incompatible with our expression 'connected with eternal existence'. And there is here no difference between act and existence. For he who concedes the existence of an entity which has an eternal past must concede that there exist acts, too, which have no beginning in the past. And it by no means follows from the existence of His acts that they must have entered existence, just as it by no means follows from the past permanency of His essence that He has ever entered existence. And all this is perfectly clear, as you see.

Through this First Existent acts can exist which never began and will never cease, and if this were impossible for the act, it would be impossible, too, for existence, for every act is connected with its existent in existence. The theologians, however, regarded it as impossible that God's act should be eternal, although they regarded His existence as eternal, and that is the gravest error. To apply the expression 'production' for the world's creation as the Divine Law does is more appropriate than to use it of temporal production, as the Ash'arites did,[1] for the act, in so far as it is an act, is a product, and eternity is only represented in this act because this production and the act produced have neither beginning nor end. And I say that it was therefore difficult for Muslims to call God eternal and the world eternal, because they understood by 'eternal' that which has no cause.[2] Still I have seen some of the theologians tending rather to our opinion.[3]

Ghazali says:

Their fourth proof is similar to the third, for they say that if the world were annihilated the possibility of its existence would remain, as the possible cannot become impossible. This possibility is a relative attribute and according to them everything that becomes needs matter which precedes it and everything that vanishes needs matter from which it can vanish, but the matter and the elements do not vanish, only the forms and accidents vanish which were in them.

I say:

If it is assumed that the forms succeed each other in one substratum in a circular way and that the agent of this succession is an eternal one, nothing impossible follows from this assumption. But if this succession is assumed to take place in an infinite number of matters or through an infinite number of specifically different forms, it is impossible, and equally the assumption is impossible that such a succession could occur without an eternal agent or through a temporal agent. For if there were an infinite number of matters, an actual infinite would exist, and this is impossible. It is still more absurd to suppose that this succession could occur through temporal agents, and therefore from this point of view it is only true that a man must become from another man, on condition that the successive series happens in one and the same matter and the perishing of the earlier men can become the matter of the later. Besides, the existence of the earlier men is also in some respect the efficient cause and the instrument for the later—all this, however, in an accidental way, for those men are nothing but the instrument for the Agent, who does not cease to produce a man by means of a man and through the matter of a man. The student who does not distinguish all these points will not be able to free himself from insoluble doubts. Perhaps God will place you and us among those who have reached the utmost truth concerning what may and must be taught about God's infinite acts. What I have said about all these things is not proved here, but must be examined by the application of the conditions which the ancients have explained and the rules which they have established for scientific research. Besides, he who would like to be one of those who possess the truth should in any question he examines consult those who hold divergent opinions.[1]

Ghazali says:

The answer to all this has been given above. I only single out this question because they have two proofs for it.

The first proof is that given by Galen, who says: If the sun, for instance, were liable to annihilation, decay would appear in it over a long period. But observation for thousands of years shows no change in its size, and the fact that it has shown no loss of power through such a long time shows that it does not suffer corruption.[2] There are two objections to this: The first is that the mode of this proof—that if the sun suffers corruption, it must suffer loss of power, and as the consequence is impossible, the antecedent must be impossible too—is what the philosophers call a conjunctive hypothetical proposition,[3] and this inference is not conclusive, because its antecedent is not true, unless it is connected with another condition. In other words the falsehood of the consequence of the proposition 'if the sun suffers corruption, it must become weaker' does not imply the falsehood of the antecedent, unless either (1) the antecedent is bound up with the additional condition that, if it suffers corruption through decay, it must do so during a long period, or (2) it is seriously proved that there is no corruption except through decay. For only then does the falsehood of the consequence imply the falsehood of the antecedent. Now, we do not concede that a thing can only become corrupt through decay; decay is only one form of corruption, for it is not impossible that what is in a state of perfection should suddenly suffer corruption.

I say:

He says in his objection here to this argument that there is no necessary relation between antecedent and consequent, because that which suffers corruption need not become weaker, since it can suffer corruption before it has become weaker. The conclusion, however, is quite sound, when it is assumed that the corruption takes place in a natural way, not by violence, and it is assumed besides that the celestial body is an animal, for all animals suffer corruption only in a natural way—they necessarily decay before their corruption. However, our opponents do not accept these premises, so far as they concern heaven, without proof. And therefore Galen's statement is only of dialectical value. The safest way to use this argument is to say that, if heaven should suffer corruption, it would either disintegrate into the elements of which it is composed or, losing the form it possesses, receive another, as happens with the four elements when they change into one another. If, however, heaven passed away into the elements, those elements would have to be part of another world, for it could not have come into being from the elements contained in this world, since these elements are infinitely small, compared with its size, something like a point in relation to a circle.[1] Should heaven, however, lose its form and receive another there would exist a sixth element opposed to all the others, being neither heaven, nor earth, nor water, nor air, nor fire.[2] And all this is impossible. And his statement that heaven does not decay is only a common opinion, lacking the force of the immediately evident axioms; and it is explained in the *Posterior Analytics* of what kind these premises are.[3]

Ghazali says:

The second objection is that, if it were conceded to Galen that there is no corruption except through decay, how can it be known that decay does not affect the sun? His reliance on observation is impossible, for observations determine the size only by approximation, and if the sun, whose size is said to be approximately a hundred and seventy times that of the earth,[4] decreased, for instance, by the size of mountains the difference would not be perceptible to the senses. Indeed, it is perhaps already in decay, and has decreased up to the present by the size of mountains or more; but perception cannot ascertain this, for its knowledge in the science of optics works only by supposition and approximation. The same takes place with sapphire and gold, which, according to them, are composed out of elements and which are liable to corruption. Still, if you left a sapphire for a hundred years, its decrease would be imperceptible, and perhaps the decrease in the sun during the period in which it has been observed stands in proportion to its size as the decrease of the sapphire to its size in a hundred years. This is imperceptible, and this fact shows that his proof is utterly futile.

We have abstained from bringing many proofs of the same kind as the wise disdain. We have given only this one to serve as an example of what we have omitted, and we have restricted ourselves to the four proofs which demand that their solution should be attempted in the way indicated above.

I say:

If the sun had decayed and the parts of it which had disintegrated during the period of its observation were imperceptible because of the size of its body, still the effect of its decay on bodies in the sublunary world would be perceptible in a definite degree, for everything that decays does so only through the corruption and disintegration of its parts, and those parts which disconnect themselves from the decaying mass must necessarily remain in the world in their totality or change* into other parts, and in either case an appreciable change must occur in the world, either in the number or in the character of its parts. And if the size of the bodies could change, their actions and affections would change too, and if their actions and affections, and especially those of the heavenly bodies, could change, changes would arise in the sublunary world. To imagine, therefore, a dissipation of the heavenly bodies is to admit a disarrangement in the divine order which, according to the philosopher, prevails in this world. This proof is not absolutely strict.

Ghazali says:

The philosophers have a second proof of the impossibility of the annihilation of the world. They say: The substance of the world could not be annihilated, because no cause could be imagined for this and the passage from existence to non-existence cannot take place without a cause. This cause must be either the Will of the Eternal, and this is impossible, for if He willed the annihilation of the world after not having willed it, He would have changed; or it must be assumed that God and His Will are in all conditions absolutely the same, although the object of His Will changes from non-existence to existence and then again from existence to non-existence. And the impossibility of which we have spoken in the matter of a temporal existence through an eternal will, holds also for the problem of annihilation. But we shall add* here a still greater difficulty, namely, that the object willed is without doubt an act of the willer, for the act of him who acts after not having acted—even if he does not alter in his own nature—must necessarily exist after having not existed: if he remained absolutely in the state he was in before, his act would not be there. But when the world is annihilated, there is no object for God's act, and if He does not perform anything (for annihilation is nothing), how could there be an action? Suppose the annihilation of the world needed a new act in God which did not exist before, what could such an act be? Could it be the existence of the world? But this is impossible, since what happens is on the contrary the termination of its existence. Could this act then be the annihilation of the world? But annihilation is nothing at all, and it could therefore not be an act. For even in its slightest intensity an act

THE SECOND DISCUSSION

must be existent, but the annihilation of the world is nothing existent at all; how could it then be said that he who caused it was an agent, or he who effected it its cause?[1]

The philosophers say that to escape this difficulty the theologians are divided into four sects and that each sect falls into an absurdity.

I say:

He says here that the philosophers compel the theologians who admit the annihilation of the world to draw the consequence that from the Eternal, who produced the world, there proceeds a new act, i.e. the act of annihilation, just as they compelled them to draw this consequence in regard to His temporal production. About this problem everything has been said already in our discussion of temporal production, for the same difficulties as befall the problem of production apply to annihilation, and there is no sense in repeating ourselves. But the special difficulty he mentions here is that from the assumption of the world's temporal production it follows that the act of the agent attaches itself to non-existence,[2] so that in fact the agent performs a non-existing act and this seemed to all the parties too shocking to be accepted,[3] and therefore they took refuge in theories he mentions later. But this consequence follows necessarily from any theory which affirms that the act of the agent is connected with absolute creation—that is, the production of something that did not exist before in potency and was not a possibility which its agent converted from potency into actuality, a theory which affirms in fact that the agent created it out of nothing. But for the philosophers the act of the agent is nothing but the actualizing of what is in potency, and this act is, according to them, attached to an existent in two ways, either* in production, by converting the thing from its potential existence into actuality so that its non-existence is terminated, or* in destruction, by converting the thing from its actual existence into potential existence, so that it passes into a relative non-existence. But he who does not conceive the act of the agent in this way has to draw the consequence that the agent's act is attached to non-existence in both ways, in production as in destruction; only as this seems clearer in the case of destruction, the theologians could not defend themselves against their opponents. For it is clear that for the man who holds the theory of absolute annihilation the agent must perform something non-existent, for when the agent converts the thing from existence into absolute non-existence, he directs his first intention to something non-existent, by contrast with what happens when he converts it from actual existence into potential existence; for in this conversion the passage into non-existence is only a secondary fact. The same consequence applies to production, only here it is not so obvious, for the existence of the thing implies the annulment of its non-existence, and therefore production is nothing but the changing of the non-existence of a thing into its existence; but since this movement is directed towards production, the theologians could say that the act of the agent is attached solely to production. They could not, however, say this in regard to destruction, since this movement is directed towards non-existence. They have, therefore, no right to say that in production the act of the agent attaches itself only to production, and not to the annulment of non-existence, for in production the annulment of non-existence is necessary, and therefore the act of the agent must necessarily be attached to non-existence. For according to the doctrine of the theologians, the existent possesses only two conditions: a condition in which it is absolutely non-existent and a condition in which it is actually existent.[1] The act of the agent, therefore, attaches itself to it, neither when it is actually existent, nor when it is non-existent*. Thus only the following alternatives remain: either the act of the agent does not attach itself to it at all, or it attaches itself to non-existence,[2] and non-existence changes itself into existence. He who conceives the agent in this way must regard the change of non-existence itself into existence, and of existence itself into non-existence, as possible, and must hold that the act of the agent can attach itself to the conversion of either of these opposites into the other. This is absolutely impossible in respect to the other opposites, not to speak of non-existence and existence.[3]

The theologians perceived the agent in the way the weak-sighted perceive the shadow of a thing instead of the thing itself and then mistake the shadow for it.[4] But, as you see, all these difficulties arise for the man who has not understood that production is the conversion of a thing from potential into actual existence, and that destruction is the reverse, i.e. the change from the actual into the potential.[5] It appears from this that possibility and matter are necessarily connected with anything becoming, and that what is subsistent in itself can be neither destroyed nor produced.[6]

The theory of the Ash'arites mentioned here by Ghazali, which regards the production of a substance, subsistent in itself, as possible, but not so its destruction, is an extremely weak one, for the consequences which apply to destruction apply also to production, only, it was thought, because in the former case it is more obvious that there was here a real difference. He then mentions the answers of the different sects to the difficulty which faces them on the question of annihilation.[1]

Ghazali says:

The Mu'tazilites say: the act proceeding from Him is an existent, i.e. extinction, which He does not create in a substratum; at one and the same moment it annihilates* the whole world and disappears by itself, so that it does not stand in need of another extinction and thus of an infinite regress.[2]

And mentioning this answer to the difficulty, he says:

This is wrong for different reasons. First, extinction is not an intelligible existent, the creation of which can be supposed. Moreover, why, if it is supposed to exist, does it disappear by itself without a cause for its disappearance? Further, why does it annihilate the world? For its creation and inherence in the essence of the world are impossible, since the inherent meets its substratum and exists together with it if only in an instant; if the extinction and existence of the world could meet, extinction would not be in opposition to existence and would not annihilate it[3] and, if extinction is created neither in the world nor in a substratum, where could its existence be in order to be opposed to the existence of the world? Another shocking feature in this doctrine is that God cannot annihilate part of the world without annihilating the remainder; indeed He can only create an extinction which annihilates the world in its totality, for if extinction is not in a substratum, it stands in one and the same relation to the totality of the world.

I say:

The answer is too foolish to merit refutation. Extinction and annihilation are synonymous, and if God cannot create annihilation, He cannot create extinction either. And even if we suppose extinction to be an existent, it could at most be an accident, but an accident without a substratum is absurd. And how can one imagine that the non-existent causes non-existence? All this resembles the talk of the delirious.

Ghazali says:

The second sect, the Karramites, say that the act of God is annihilation, and annihilation signifies an existent which He produces in His essence and through which the world becomes non-existent.[4] In the same way, according to them, existence arises out of the act of creation which He produces in His essence and through which the world becomes existent. Once again, this theory is wrong as it makes the Eternal a substratum for temporal production*. Further it is incomprehensible, for creation and likewise annihilation cannot be understood except as an existence, related to will and power, and to establish another entity besides the will and the power and their object, the world, is inconceivable.

I say:

The Karramites believe that there are here three factors: the agent, the act—which they call creation—and an object, i.e. that to which the act attaches itself, and likewise they believe that in the process of annihilation there are three factors: the annihilator, the act—which they call annihilation—and a non-existent. They believe that the act inheres in the essence of the agent and according to them the rise of such a new condition[1] in the agent does not imply that the agent is determined by a temporal cause, for such a condition is of a relative and proportional type, and a new relation and proportion does not involve newness in the substratum; only those new events involve a change in the substratum which change the essence of the substratum, e.g. the changing of a thing from whiteness to blackness. Their statement, however, that the act inheres in the essence of the agent is a mistake; it is only a relation which exists between the agent and the object of the act which, when assigned to the agent, is called 'act' and when assigned to the object is called 'passivity'[2] Through this assumption the Karramites are not obliged to admit that, as the Ash'arites believed, the Eternal produces temporal reality[3] or that the Eternal is not eternal,[4] but the consequence which is forced upon them is that there must be a cause anterior to the Eternal, for, when an agent acts after not having acted, all the conditions for the existence of his object being fulfilled at the time he did not act, there must have arisen a new quality in the agent at the time when he acts, and each new event demands a new cause.[5] So there must be another cause before the first, and so on *ad infinitum*.

Ghazali says:

The third sect is that of the Ash'arites, who say that accidents pass away by themselves and cannot be imagined to persist, for if they persisted they could not, for this very reason, be imagined ever to pass away.[6] Substances do not persist by themselves either, but persist by a persistence added to their existence. And if God had not created persistence, substances would have become non-existent through the non-existence of persistence. This too is wrong, in so far as it denies the evidence of the senses by saying that black and white do not persist and that their existence is continually renewed; reason shrinks from this, as it does, too, from the statement that the body renews its existence at each moment, for reason judges that the hair which is on a man's head today is identical with, not similar to, the hair that was there yesterday, and judges the same about the black and the white.[1] There is yet another difficulty, namely, that when things persist through persistence, God's attributes must persist through persistence and this persistence persists through persistence and so on *ad infinitum*.[2]

I say:
This theory of the flux of all existing things is a useless one, although many ancients held it, and there is no end to the impossibilities it implies.[3] How could an existent come into existence, when it passes away by itself and existence passes away through its passing away? If it passed away by itself, it would have to come into existence by itself, and in this case that by which it becomes existent would be identical with that by which it passes away and this is impossible. For existence is the opposite of passing away, and it is not possible that two opposites should occur in the same thing in one and the same connexion. Therefore in a pure existent no passing away can be imagined, for if its existence determined its passing away, it would be non-existent and existent at one and the same moment, and this is impossible. Further, if the existents persist through the persistence of an attribute by itself, will this absence of change in them occur through their existence or through their non-existence? The latter is impossible, so it follows that they persist because of their existence. If, then, all existents must persist because they are existent, and non-existence is something that can supervene upon them, why in Heaven's name do we need this attribute of persistence to make them persist? All this resembles a case of mental disorder. But let us leave this sect, for the absurdity of their theory is too clear to need refutation.

Ghazali says:
The fourth sect are a group of Ash'arites who say that accidents pass away by themselves, but that substances pass away when God does not create motion or rest or aggregation and disintegration in them, for it is impossible that a body should persist which is neither in motion nor at rest, since in that case it becomes non-existent.[4] The two parties of the Ash'arites incline to the view that annihilation is not an act, but rather a refraining from acting, since they do not understand how non-existence can be an act. All these different theories being false—say the philosophers —it cannot any longer be asserted that the annihilation of the world is

possible, even if one were to admit that the world had been produced in time; for although the philosophers concede that the human soul has been produced, they claim the impossibility of its annihilation by means of arguments which are very close to those we have mentioned. For, according to the philosophers, nothing that is self-subsistent and does not inhere in a substratum[1] can be imagined as becoming non-existent after its existence, whether it is produced or eternal.[2] If one objects against them, that when water is boiled it disappears, they answer that it does not disappear, but is only changed into steam and the steam becomes water again, and its primary matter, i.e. its *hyle*, the matter in which the form of water inhered, persists when the water has become air, for the *hyle* only loses the form of water and takes up that of air; the air, having become cold again, condenses into water, but does not receive a new matter, for the matter is common to the elements and only the forms are changed in it.

I say:

He who affirms that accidents do not persist for two moments, and that their existence in substances is a condition of the persistence of those substances, does not know how he contradicts himself, for if the substances are a condition of the existence of the accidents—since the accidents cannot exist without the substances in which they inhere—and the accidents are assumed to be a condition for the existence of the substances, the substances must be necessarily a condition for their own existence; and it is absurd to say that something is a condition for its own existence. Further, how could the accidents be such a condition, since they themselves do not persist for two moments? For, as the instant is at the same time the end of their privation and the beginning of their period of existence, the substance must be destroyed in this instant, for in this instant there is neither anything of the privative period nor anything of the existent. If there were in the instant anything of the privative period or of the existent, it could not be the end of the former and the beginning of the latter.[3] And on the whole, that something which does not persist two moments should be made a condition for the persistence of something for two moments is absurd.[4] Indeed, a thing that persists for two moments is more capable of persisting than one which does not persist for two moments, for the existence of what does not persist for two moments is at an instant, which is in flux, but the existence of what persists for two moments is constant, and how can what is in flux be a condition for the existence of the constant, or how can what is only specifically persistent be a condition for the persistence of the

THE SECOND DISCUSSION

individually persistent? This is all senseless talk. One should know that he who does not admit a *hyle* for the corruptible* must regard the existent as simple and as not liable to corruption, for the simple does not alter and does not exchange its substance for another substance. Therefore Hippocrates says 'if man were made out of one thing alone, he could not suffer by himself'*,[1] i.e. he could not suffer corruption or change. And therefore he could not have become either, but would have to be an eternal existent. What he says here about Avicenna of the difference between the production and the destruction of the soul is without sense.[2]

Ghazali says, answering the philosophers:

The answer is: So far as concerns the different sects you have mentioned, although we could defend each of them and could show that your refutation on the basis of your principle is not valid, because your own principles are liable to the same kind of objection, we will not insist on this point, but we will restrict ourselves to one sect and ask: How will you refute the man who claims that creation and annihilation take place through the will of God: if God wills, He creates, and if He wills, He annihilates, and this is the meaning of His being absolutely powerful, and notwithstanding this He does not alter in Himself, but it is only His act that alters? And concerning your objection that, inasmuch as an act must proceed from the agent, it cannot be understood which act can proceed from Him, when He annihilates, we answer: What proceeds from Him is a new fact, and the new fact is non-existence, for there was no non-existence; then it happened as something new, and this is what proceeds from Him. And if you say: Non-existence is nothing, how could it then proceed from Him? we reply: If non-existence is nothing, how could it happen? Indeed, 'proceeding from Him' does not mean anything but that its happening is related to His power. If its happening has an intelligible meaning, why should its relation to His power not be reasonable?[3]

I say:

All this is sophistical and wrong. The philosophers do not deny that a thing becomes non-existent when a destroying agent destroys it; they only say that the destroying act does not attach itself to it, in so far as the thing becomes non-existent, but in so far as it changes from actual being to potential being, and non-existence results from this change, and it is in this way that non-existence is related to the agent. But it does not follow from the fact that its non-existence occurs after the act of the agent that the agent performs it primarily and essentially. For when it was conceded to Ghazali during the discussion of this problem that the non-existence of the corrupting thing will necessarily occur after the act of the corrupting agent, he drew the conclusion that its non-existence would follow essentially and primarily from the act, but this is impossible. For the agent's act does not attach itself to its non-existence in so far as it is non-existent, i.e. primarily and essentially. And therefore*, if the perceptible existences were simple, they could neither be generated nor destroyed except through the act of the agent being attached to their non-existence essentially and primarily. But the act of the agent is only attached to non-existence accidentally and secondarily through its changing the object from actual existence into another form of existence in an act followed by non-existence, as from the change of a fire into air there follows the non-existence of the fire. This is the philosophical theory of existence and non-existence.

Ghazali says:

And what is the difference between you and the man who denies absolutely that non-existence can occur to accidents and forms, and who says that non-existence is nothing at all and asks how then it could occur and be called an occurrence and a new event? But no doubt non-existence can be represented as occurring to the accidents, and to speak of it as occurring has a sense whether you call it something real or not. And the relation of this occurrence, which has a reasonable sense, to the power of the Omnipotent, also has an intelligible meaning.[1]

I say:

That non-existence of this kind occurs is true, and the philosophers admit it, because it proceeds from the agent according to a second intention and accidentally; but it does not follow from its proceeding or from its having a reasonable meaning that it happens essentially or primarily, and the difference between the philosophers and those who deny the occurrence of non-existence is that the philosophers do not absolutely deny the occurrence of non-existence, but only its occurring primarily and essentially through the agent. For the act of the agent does not attach itself necessarily, primarily, and essentially to non-existence, and according to the philosophers non-existence happens only subsequently to the agent's act in reality. The difficulties ensue only for those who affirm that the world can be annihilated in an absolute annihilation.

Ghazali says:

Perhaps the philosophers will answer: This difficulty is only acute for those who allow the non-existence of a thing after its existence, for those may be asked what the reality is that occurs. But according to us philosophers the existing thing does not become non-existent, for we understand by the fact that the accidents become non-existent the occurrence of their opposites, which are existing realities, and not the occurrence of mere non-existence which is nothing at all, and how could what is nothing at all be said to occur? For if hair becomes white, it is simply whiteness that occurs, for whiteness is something real; but one cannot say that what occurs is the privation of blackness.[1]

I say:

This answer on behalf of the philosophers is mistaken, for the philosophers do not deny that non-existence occurs and happens through the agent, not, however, according to a primary intention as would be the consequence for one who assumes that a thing can change into pure nothingness; no, non-existence, according to them, occurs when the form of the thing that becomes non-existent disappears, and the opposite form appears. Therefore the following objection which Ghazali makes is valid.

Ghazali says:

This is wrong for two reasons. The first is: Does the occurrence of whiteness imply the absence of blackness? If they deny it, this is an affront to reason, and if they admit it, it may be asked: Is what is implied identical with that which implies? To admit this is a contradiction, for a thing does not imply itself, and if they deny it, it may be asked: Has that which is implied an intelligible meaning? If they deny it, we ask, 'How do you know, then, that it is implied, for the judgement that it is implied presupposes that it has a sensible meaning?' If they admit this, we ask; 'Is this thing which is implied and has a sensible meaning, i.e. the absence of blackness, eternal or temporal?' The answer 'eternal' is impossible; if they answer 'temporal', how should what is described as occurring temporally not be clearly understood? And if they answer 'neither eternal nor temporal', this is absurd, for if it were said before the occurrence of whiteness that blackness was non-existent, it would be false, whereas afterwards it would be true.[2] It occurred, therefore, without any doubt, and this occurrence is perfectly intelligible and must be related to the Omnipotent.

I say:

This is an occurrence which is perfectly intelligible and must be related to the Omnipotent, but only accidentally and not essentially, for the act of the agent does not attach itself to absolute non-existence, nor to the non-existence of anything, for even the Omnipotent cannot bring it about that existence should become identical with non-existence.[3] The man who does not assume matter cannot be freed from this difficulty, and he will have to admit that the act of the agent is attached to non-existence primarily and essentially. All this is

145 clear, and there is no need to say more about it. The philosophers, therefore, say that the essential principles of transitory things are two: matter and form, and that there is a third accidental principle, privation, which is a condition of the occurrence of what becomes, namely as preceding it: if a thing becomes, its privation disappears, and if it suffers corruption, its privation arises.[1]

Ghazali says:

The second objection is that according to the philosophers there are accidents which can become non-existent otherwise than through their contrary, for instance, motion has no contrary, and the opposition between motion and rest is, according to the philosophers, only the opposition of possession and non-possession,[2] i.e. the opposition of being and not-being, not the opposition of one being to another being,[3] and the meaning of rest is the absence of motion, and, when motion ceases, rest does not supervene as its contrary, but is a pure non-existence.[4] The same is the case with those qualities which belong to the class of entelechies, like the impression of the sensible species on the vitreous humour of the eye[5] and still more the impression of the forms of the intelligibles on the soul; they become existent without the cessation of a contrary, and their non-existence only means the cessation of their existence without the subsequent occurrence of their opposites, and their disappearance is an example of pure non-existence which arises. The occurrence of such a non-existence is an understandable fact, and that which can be understood as occurring by itself, even if it is not a real entity, can be understood as being related to the power of the Omnipotent. Through this it is clear that, when one imagines an event as occuring through the eternal Will, it is unessential, whether the occurring event is a becoming or a vanishing.

I say:

On the contrary, when non-existence is assumed to proceed from the agent as existence proceeds from it, there is the greatest difference between the two. But when existence is assumed as a primary fact and non-existence as a secondary fact, i.e. when non-existence is assumed to take place through the agent by means of a kind of existence, i.e. when the agent transforms actual existence into poten-
146 tial existence by removing the actuality—which is a quality possessed by the substrate—then it is true. And from this point of view the philosophers do not regard it as impossible that the world should become non-existent in the sense of its changing into another form,[6] for non-existence is in this case only a subsequent occurrence and a secondary fact. But what they regard as impossible is that a thing should disappear into absolute nothingness, for then the act of the

agent would have attached itself to non-existence, primarily and essentially.

Throughout this discussion Ghazali has mistaken the accidental for the essential, and forced on the philosophers conclusions which they themselves regard as impossible. This is in general the character of the discussion in this book. A more suitable name, therefore, for this book would be 'The Book of Absolute Incoherence', or 'The Incoherence of Ghazali', not 'The Incoherence of the Philosophers', and the best name for my book 'The Distinction between Truth and Incoherent Arguments'.[1]

THE THIRD DISCUSSION

The demonstration of their confusion in saying that God is the agent and the maker of the world and that the world is His product and act, and the demonstration that these expressions are in their system only metaphors without any real sense

Ghazali says:

All philosophers, except the materialists, agree that the world has a maker, and that God is the maker and agent of the world and the world is His act and His work. And this is an imposture where their principle is concerned, nay it cannot be imagined that according to the trend of their principle the world is the work of God, and this for three reasons, from the point of view of the agent, from the point of view of the act, and from the point of view of the relation common to act and agent. As concerns the first point, the agent must be willing, choosing, and knowing what he wills to be the agent of what he wills, but according to them God does not will, He has no attribute whatever, and what proceeds from Him proceeds by the compulsion of necessity. The second point is that the world is eternal, but 'act' implies production. And the third point is that God is unique, according to their principles, from all points of view, and from one thing—according to their principles—there can only proceed one thing. The world, however, is constituted out of diverse components; how could it therefore proceed from Him?[2]

I say:

Ghazali's words 'The agent must be willing, choosing, and knowing what he wills to be the agent of what he wills' are by no means self-evident and cannot be accepted as a definition of the maker of the world without a proof, unless one is justified in inferring from the empirical to the divine. For we observe in the empirical world two kinds of agents, one which performs exclusively one thing and this essentially, for instance warmth which causes heat and coldness which causes cold; and this kind is called by the philosophers natural agents. The second kind of agents are those that perform a certain act at one time and its opposite at another; these, acting only out of knowledge and deliberation, are called by the philosophers voluntary and selective agents. But the First Agent cannot be described as having either of these two actions, in so far as these are ascribed to transitory things by the philosophers. For he who chooses and wills lacks the things which he wills, and God cannot lack anything He wills. And he who chooses makes a choice for himself of the better of two things, but God is in no need of a better condition. Further, when the willer has reached his object, his will ceases and, generally speaking, will is a passive quality and a change, but God is exempt from passivity and change.[1] God is still farther distant from natural action, for the act of the natural thing is a necessity in its substance, but is not a necessity in the substance of the willer, and belongs to its entelechy.[2] In addition, natural action does not proceed from knowledge: it has, however, been proved that God's act does proceed from knowledge. The way in which God becomes an agent and a willer has not become clear in this place, since there is no counterpart to His will in the empirical world. How is it therefore possible to assert that an agent can only be understood as acting through deliberation and choice? For then this definition is indifferently applied to the empirical and the divine, but the philosophers do not acknowledge this extension of the definition, so that from their refusal to acknowledge this definition as applying to the First Agent, it cannot be inferred that they deny that He acts at all.

This is, of course, self-evident and not the philosophers are impostors, but he who speaks in this way, for an impostor is one who seeks to perplex, and does not look for the truth. He, however, who errs while seeking the truth cannot be called an impostor, and the philosophers, as a matter of fact, are known to seek the truth, and therefore they are by no means impostors. There is no difference between one who says that God wills with a will which does not resemble the human will, and one who says that God knows through a knowledge which does not resemble human knowledge; in the same way as the quality of His knowledge cannot be conceived, so the quality of His will cannot be conceived.

THE THIRD DISCUSSION

Ghazali says:

We will now test each of these three reasons at the same time as the illusory arguments which the philosophers give in their defence.

The first reason. We say: 'Agent' means someone from whom there proceeds an act with the will to act according to choice and with the knowledge of the object willed. But according to the philosophers the world stands in relation to God as the effect to the cause, in a necessary connexion which God cannot be imagined to sever, and which is like the connexion between the shadow and the man, light and the sun, but this is not an act at all. On the contrary, he who says that the lamp makes the light and the man makes the shadow uses the term vaguely, giving it a sense much wider than its definition, and uses it metaphorically, relying on the fact that there is an analogy between the object originally meant by it and the object to which it is transferred, i.e. the agent is in a general sense a cause, the lamp is the cause of the light, and the sun is the cause of luminosity; but the agent is not called a creative agent from the sole fact that it is a cause, but by its being a cause in a special way, namely that it causes through will and through choice.[1] If, therefore, one said that neither a wall, nor a stone, nor anything inanimate is an agent,[2] and that only animals have actions, this could not be denied and his statement would not be called false. But according to the philosophers a stone has an action, namely falling and heaviness and a centripetal tendency, just as fire has an action, namely heating, and a wall has an action, namely a centripetal tendency and the throwing of a shadow, and, according to them each of these actions proceeds from it as its agent; which is absurd.[3]

I say:

There are in brief two points here, the first of which is that only those who act from deliberation and choice are regarded as acting causes, and the action of a natural agent producing something else is not counted among acting causes, while the second point is that the philosophers regard the procession of the world from God as the necessary connexion obtaining between shadow and the person, and luminosity and the sun, and the downward rolling in relation to the stone, but that this cannot be called an action because the action can be separated* from the agent.[4]

I say:

All this is false. For the philosophers believe that there are four causes: agent, matter, form, and end. The agent is what causes some other thing to pass from potency to actuality and from non-existence to existence; this actualization occurs sometimes from deliberation and choice, sometimes by nature, and the philosophers do not call a person who throws a shadow an agent, except metaphorically, because the shadow cannot be separated from the man, and by common consent the agent can be separated from its object, and the philosophers certainly believe that God is separated[1] from the world and according to them He is not to be classed with this kind of natural cause. Nor is He an agent in the sense in which any empirical agent, either voluntary or involuntary, is; He is rather the agent of these causes, drawing forth the Universe from non-existence to existence and conserving it,[2] and such an act is a more perfect and glorious one than any performed by the empirical agents. None of these objections therefore touch them, for they believe that God's act proceeds from Him through knowledge, not through any necessity which calls for it, either in His essence or outside His essence, but through His grace and His bounty.[3] He is necessarily endowed with will and choice in their highest form, since the insufficiency which is proper to the empirical willer does not pertain to Him. And these are the very words of Aristotle in one of his metaphysical treatises: We were asked how God could bring forth the world out of nothing, and convert it into something out of nothing, and our answer is this: the Agent must be such that His capacity must be proportionate to His power and His power proportionate to His will and His will proportionate to His wisdom, if not, His capacity would be weaker than His power, His power weaker than His will, and His will weaker than His wisdom. And if some of His powers were weaker than others, there would be no difference between His powers and ours, and imperfection would attach to Him as to us—a very blasphemous theory. But in the opposite case each of these powers is of the utmost perfection. When He wills He has the power, and when He has the power He has the capacity and all this with the greatest wisdom. And He exists, making what He wants out of nothing. And this is only astonishing through this imperfection which is in us.[4] And Aristotle said also: Everything that is in this world is only set together through the power which is in it from God; if this power did not exist in the things, they could not last the twinkling of an eye.[5]

I say:

Composite existence is of two classes; in the one class the composition is something additional to the existence of the composed, but in the other the composition is like the existence of matter and form and in these existents the existence cannot be regarded as anterior to the composition, but on the contrary the composition is the cause of their existence and anterior to it.[6] If God therefore is the cause of the composition of the parts of the world, the existence of which is in their composition, then He is the cause of their existence and necessarily he who is the cause of the existence of anything whatever is its agent. This is the way in which according to the philosophers this question must be understood, if their system is truly explained to the student.

Ghazali says, speaking on behalf of the philosophers:

The philosophers may say: we call an object anything that has no necessary existence by itself, but exists through another, and we call its cause the agent, and we do not mind whether the cause acts by nature or voluntarily, just as you do not mind whether it acts by means of an instrument or without an instrument, and just as 'act' is a genus subdivided into 'acts which occur by means of an instrument' and 'acts which occur without an instrument', so it is a genus subdivided into 'acts which occur by nature' and 'acts which occur voluntarily'. The proof is that, when we speak of an act which occurs by nature, our words 'by nature' are not contradictory to the term 'act'; the words 'by nature' are not used to exclude or contradict the idea of act, but are meant only to explain the specific character of the act, just as, when we speak of an act effected directly without an instrument, there is no contradiction, but only a specification and an explanation. And when we speak of a 'voluntary act', there is not a redundancy as in the expression a 'living being-man';[1] it is only an explanation of its specific character, like the expression, 'act performed by means of an instrument'. If, however, the word 'act' included the idea of will, and will were essential to act, in so far as it is an act, our expression 'natural act' would be a contradiction.

I say:

The answer, in short, has two parts. The first is that everything that is necessary through another thing is an object of what is necessary by itself,[2] but this can be opposed, since that through which the 'necessary through another' has its necessary existence need not be an agent, unless by 'through which it has its necessary existence' is meant that which is really an agent, i.e., that which brings potency into act.[3] The second part is that the term 'agent' seems like a genus for that which acts by choice and deliberation and for that which acts by nature; this is true, and is proved by our definition of the term 'agent'. Only this argument wrongly creates the impression that the philosophers do not regard the first agent as endowed with will. And this dichotomy that everything is either of necessary existence by itself or existent through another is not self-evident.

Ghazali, refuting the philosophers, says:

This designation is wrong, for we do not call any cause whatsoever an agent, nor any effect an object; for, if this were so, it would be not right to say that the inanimate has no act and that only the living exhibit acts—a statement generally admitted.

I say:

His assertion that not every cause is called an agent is true, but his argument that the inanimate is not called an agent is false, for the denial that the inanimate exhibits acts excludes only the rational and voluntary act, not act absolutely, for we find that certain inanimate things have powers to actualize things like themselves; e.g. fire, which changes anything warm* and dry into another fire like itself, through converting it from what it has in potency into actuality. Therefore fire cannot make a fire like itself in anything that has not the potency or that is not in readiness to receive the actuality of fire. The theologians, however, deny that fire is an agent, and the discussion of this problem will follow later. Further, nobody doubts that there are in the bodies of animals powers which make the food a part of the animal feeding itself and generally direct the body of the animal. If we suppose them withdrawn, the animal would die, as Galen says.[1] And through this direction we call it alive, whereas in the absence of these powers we call it dead.

Ghazali goes on:

If the inanimate is called an agent, it is by metaphor, in the same way as it is spoken of metaphorically as tending and willing, since it is said that the stone falls down, because it tends and has an inclination to the centre, but in reality tendency and will can only be imagined in connexion with knowledge and an object desired and these can only be imagined in animals.

I say:

If by 'agent' or 'tendency' or 'willing' is meant the performance of an act of a willer, it is a metaphor, but when by these expressions is meant that it actualizes another's potency, it is really an agent in the full meaning of the word.

Ghazali then says:

When the philosophers say that the term 'act' is a genus which is subdivided into 'natural act' and 'voluntary act', this cannot be conceded; it is as if one were to say that 'willing' is a genus which is subdivided into willing accompanied by knowledge of the object willed, and willing without knowledge of the object willed. This is wrong, because will necessarily implies knowledge, and likewise act necessarily implies will.

I say:

THE THIRD DISCUSSION

The assertion of the philosophers that 'agent' is subdivided into 'voluntary' and 'non-voluntary agent' is true, but the comparison with a division of will into rational and irrational is false, because in the definition of will knowledge is included, so that the division has no sense. But in the definition of 'act' knowledge is not included, because actualization of another thing is possible without knowing it. This is clear, and therefore the wise say that God's word: 'a wall which wanted to fall to pieces'[1] is a metaphor.

Ghazali proceeds:

When you affirm that your expression 'natural act' is not a contradiction in terms, you are wrong; there is as a matter of fact a contradiction when 'natural act' is taken in a real sense, only this contradiction is not at once evident to the understanding nor is the incompatibility of nature and act felt acutely, because this expression is employed metaphorically; for since nature is in a certain way a cause and the agent is also a cause, nature is called an agent metaphorically. The expression 'voluntary act' is as much redundant as the expression 'he wills and knows what he wills'.

I say:

This statement is undoubtedly wrong, for what actualizes another thing, i.e. acts on it, is not called agent simply by a metaphor, but in reality, for the definition of 'agent' is appropriate to it. The division of 'agent' into 'natural' and 'voluntary agent' is not the division of an equivocal term, but the division of a genus. Therefore the division of 'agent' into 'natural' and 'voluntary agent' is right, since that which actualizes another can also be divided into these two classes.

Ghazali says:

However, as it can happen that 'act' is used metaphorically and also in its real sense, people have no objection in saying 'someone acted voluntarily', meaning that he acted not in a metaphorical sense, but really, in the way in which it is said 'he spoke with his tongue', or 'he saw with his eye'. For, since one is permitted to use 'heart' metaphorically for 'sight', and motion of the head or hand for word—for one can say 'He nodded assent'—it is not wrong to say 'He spoke with his tongue and he saw with his eye', in order to exclude any idea of metaphor. This is a delicate point, but let us be careful to heed the place where those stupid people slipped.

I say:

Certainly it is a delicate point that a man with scientific pretensions should give such a bad example and such a false reason to explain the repugnance people seem to have in admitting the division of 'act' into 'natural' and 'voluntary act'. No one ever says 'He saw with his eye, and he saw without his eye' in the belief that this is a division of sight; we only say 'He saw with his eye' to emphasize the fact that real sight is meant, and to exclude the metaphorical sense of 'sight'. And the intelligent in fact think that for the man who understands immediately that the real meaning is intended, this connecting of sight with the eye is almost senseless. But when one speaks of 'natural' and 'voluntary act', no intelligent person disagrees that we have here a division of 'act'. If, however, the expression 'voluntary act' were similar to 'sight with the eye' the expression 'natural act' would be metaphorical. But as a matter of fact the natural agent has an act much more stable than the voluntary agent, for the natural agent's act is constant—which is not the case with the act of the voluntary agent.[1] And therefore the opponents of the theologians might reverse the argument against them and say that 'natural act' is like 'sight with the eye' and 'voluntary act' is a metaphor—especially according to the doctrine of the Ash'arites, who do not acknowledge a free will in man and a power to exercise an influence on reality. And if this is the case with the agent in the empirical world, how can we know that it is an accurate description of the real Agent in the divine world to say that He acts through knowledge and will?[2]

Ghazali says, speaking on behalf of the philosophers:

The philosophers may reply: The designation 'agent' is known only through language. However, it is clear to the mind that the cause of a thing can be divided into voluntary and non-voluntary cause, and it may be disputed whether or not in both cases the word 'act' is used in a proper sense, but it is not possible to deny this, since the Arabs say that fire burns, a sword cuts, that snow makes cold, that scammony purges, that bread stills hunger and water thirst, and our expression 'he beats' means he performs the act of beating, and 'it burns' it performs the act of burning, and 'he cuts' he performs the act of cutting; if you say, therefore, that its use is quite metaphorical, you are judging without any evidence.

I say:

This, in short, is a common-sense argument. The Arabs indeed call that which* exerts an influence on a thing, even if not voluntary, an agent, in a proper, not in a metaphorical, sense. This argument, however, is dialectical and of no importance.

Ghazali replies to this:

The answer is that all this is said in a metaphorical way and that only a voluntary act is a proper act. The proof is that, if we assume an event which is based on two facts, the one voluntary, the other involuntary, the mind relates the act to the voluntary fact. Language expresses itself in the same way, for if a man were to throw another into a fire and kill him, it is the man who would be called his killer, not the fire. If, however, the term were used in the same sense of the voluntary and the non-voluntary, and it were not that the one was a proper sense, the other a metaphorical, why should the killing be related to the voluntary, by language, usage, and reason, although the fire was the proximate cause of the killing and the man who threw the other into the fire did nothing but bring man and fire together? Since, however, the bringing together is a voluntary act and the influence of the fire non-voluntary, the man is called a killer and the fire only metaphorically so. This proves that the word 'agent' is used of one whose act proceeds from his will, and, behold, the philosophers do not regard God as endowed with will and choice.

I say:

This is an answer of the wicked who heap fallacy on fallacy. Ghazali is above this, but perhaps the people of his time obliged him to write this book to safeguard himself against the suspicion of sharing the philosophers' view. Certainly nobody attributes the act to its instrument, but only to its first mover.[1] He who killed a man by fire is in the proper sense the agent and the fire is the instrument of the killing, but when a man is burned by a fire, without this fact's depending on someone's choice, nobody would say that the fire burned him metaphorically. The fallacy he employs here is the well-known one *a dicto secundum quid ad dictum simpliciter*, e.g. to say of a negro, because his teeth are white, that he is white absolutely.[2] The philosophers do not deny absolutely that God wills, for He is an agent through knowledge and from knowledge, and He performs the better of two contrary acts, although both are possible; they only affirm that He does not will in the way that man wills.

Ghazali says, answering in defence of the philosophers:

If the philosophers say: We do not mean anything by God's being an agent but that He is the cause of every existent besides Himself and that the world has its subsistence through Him, and if the Creator did not exist, the existence of the world could not be imagined. And if the Creator should be supposed non-existent, the world would be non-existent too, just as the supposition that the sun was non-existent would imply the non-existence of light. This is what we mean by His being an agent. If our opponents refuse to give this meaning to the word 'act', well, we shall not quibble about words.

I say:

161 Such an answer would mean that the philosophers would concede to their opponents that God is not an agent, but one of those causes without which a thing cannot reach its perfection; and the answer is wrong, for against them it might be deduced from it that the First Cause is a principle, as if it were the form of the Universe, in the way the soul is a principle for the body; no philosopher, however, affirms this.

Then Ghazali says, answering the philosophers:

We say: Our aim is to show that such is not the meaning of 'act' and 'work'. These words can mean only that which really proceeds from the will. But you reject the real meaning of 'act', although you use this word, which is honoured amongst Muslims. But one's religion is not perfect when one uses words deprived of their sense. Declare therefore openly that God has no act, so that it becomes clear that your belief is in opposition to the religion of Islam, and do not deceive by saying that God is the maker of the world and that the world is His work, for you use the words, but reject their real sense!

I say:

This would indeed be a correct conclusion against the philosophers, if they should really say what Ghazali makes them say. For in this case they could indeed be forced to admit that the world has neither a natural nor a voluntary agent, nor that there is another type of agents besides these two. He does not unmask their imposture by his words, but he himself deceives by ascribing to them theories which they do not hold.

Ghazali says:

162 The second reason for denying that the world is according to the principle of the philosophers an act of God is based on the implication of the notion of an act. 'Act' applies to temporal production, but for them the world is eternal and is not produced in time. The meaning of 'act' is 'to convert from not-being into being by producing it' and this cannot be imagined in the eternal, as what exists already cannot be brought into existence. Therefore 'act' implies a temporal product, but according to them the world is eternal; how then could it be God's act?

I say:

If the world were by itself eternal and existent (not in so far as it is moved, for each movement is composed of parts which are produced), then, indeed, the world would not have an agent at all. But if the meaning of 'eternal' is that it is in everlasting production and that this production has neither beginning nor end, certainly the term 'production' is more truly applied to him who brings about an everlasting production than to him who procures a limited production. In this way the world is God's product and the name 'production' is even more suitable for it than the word 'eternity', and the philosophers only call the world eternal to safeguard themselves against the word 'product' in the sense of 'a thing produced after a state of non-existence, from something, and in time'.

Then Ghazali says, on behalf of the philosophers:

The philosophers may perhaps say: The meaning of 'product' is 'that which exists after its non-existence'. Let us therefore examine if what proceeds from the agent when He produces, and what is connected with Him, is either pure existence, or pure non-existence, or both together. Now, it is impossible to say that previous non-existence was connected with Him, since the agent cannot exert influence upon non-existence, and it is equally impossible to say 'both together', for it is clear that non-existence is in no way connected with the agent, for non-existence *qua* non-existence needs no agent at all. It follows therefore that what is connected with Him is connected with Him in so far as it is an existent, that what proceeds from Him is pure existence, and that there is no other relation to Him than that of existence. If existence is regarded as everlasting, then this relation is everlasting, and if this relation is everlasting, then the term to which this relation refers is the most illustrious and the most enduring in influence, because at no moment is non-existence connected with it. Temporal production implies therefore the contradictory statements that it must be connected with an agent, that it cannot be produced, if it is not preceded by non-existence, and that non-existence cannot be connected with the agent.

And if previous non-existence is made a condition of the existent, and it is said that what is connected with the agent is a special existence, not any existence, namely an existence preceded by non-existence, it may be answered that its being preceded by non-existence cannot be an act of an agent or a deed of a maker, for the procession of this existence from its agent cannot be imagined, unless preceded by non-existence; neither, therefore*, can the precedence of this non-existence be an act of the agent and connected with him, nor* the fact that this existence is preceded by non-existence. Therefore to make non-existence a condition for the act's becoming an act is to impose as a condition one whereby the agent cannot exert any influence under any condition.[1]

I say:

This is an argument put forward on this question by Avicenna from the philosophical side. It is sophistical, because Avicenna leaves out one of the factors which a complete division would have to state.[2]

For he says that the act of the agent must be connected either with an existence or with a non-existence, previous to it and in so far as it is non-existence, or with both together, and that it is impossible that it should be connected with non-existence, for the agent does not bring about non-existence and, therefore, neither can it effect both together. Therefore the agent can be only connected with existence, and production is nothing but the connexion of act with existence, i.e. the act of the agent is only bringing into existence,[1] and it is immaterial whether this existence be preceded by non-existence or not. But this argument is faulty, because the act of the agent is only connected with existence in a state of non-existence, i.e. existence in potentiality, and is not connected with actual existence, in so far as it is actual, nor with non-existence, in so far as it is non-existent. It is only connected with imperfect existence in which non-existence inheres. The act of the agent is not connected with non-existence, because non-existence is not actual; nor is it connected with existence which is not linked together with non-existence, for whatever has reached its extreme perfection of existence needs neither causation nor cause.[2] But existence which is linked up with non-existence only exists as long as the producer exists. The only way to escape this difficulty is to assume that the existence of the world has always been and will always be linked together with non-existence, as is the case with movement, which is always in need of a mover. And the acknowledged philosophers believe that such is the case with the celestial world in its relation to the Creator, and *a fortiori* with the sublunary world. Here lies the difference between the created and the artificial, for the artificial product, once produced, is not tied up with non-existence which would be in need of an agent for the continued sustenance of the product.[3]

Ghazali continues:

And your statement, theologians, that what exists cannot be made to exist, if you mean by it, that its existence does not begin after its non-existence, is true; but if you mean that it cannot become an effect[4] at the time when it exists, we have shown that it can only become an effect at the time when it exists, not at the time when it does not exist. For a thing only exists when its agent causes it to exist, and the agent only causes it to exist at the time when, proceeding from it, it exists, not when the thing does not exist; and the causation is joined with the existence of the agent and the object, for causation is the relation between cause and effect. Cause, effect, and causation are simultaneous with existence and there is no priority here, and therefore there is causation only for what exists, if

THE THIRD DISCUSSION

by 'causation' is meant the relation through which the agent and its object exist. The philosophers say: It is for this reason that we have come to the conclusion that the world, which is the work of God, is without beginning and everlasting, and that never at any moment was God not its agent, for existence is what is joined with the agent and as long as this union lasts existence lasts, and, if this union is ever discontinued, existence ceases. It is by no means what you theologians mean, that if the Creator were supposed to exist no longer, the world could still persist; you, indeed, believe that the same relation prevails as between the builder and the building, for the building persists when the builder has disappeared. But the persistence of the building does not depend on the builder, but on the strength of the structure in its coherence, for if it had not the power of coherence—if it were like water, for example—it would not be supposed to keep the shape which it received through the act of the agent.[1]

I say:

Possibly the world is in such a condition, but in general this argument is not sound. For it is only true that the causing agent is always connected with the effect*, in so far as the effect actually exists without this actuality's having any insufficiency and any potency, if one imagines that the essence of the effect* lies in its being an effect, for then the effect can only be an effect through the causation of the agent. But if its becoming an effect through a cause is only an addition to its essence, then it is not necessary that its existence should cease when the relation between the causing agent and the effect is interrupted. If, however, it is not an addition, but its essence consists in this relation of being an effect, then what Avicenna says is true. However, it is not true of the world, for the world does not exist on account of this relation, but it exists on account of its substance and the relation is only accidental to it.[2] Perhaps what Avicenna says is true concerning the forms of the celestial bodies, in so far as they perceive the separate immaterial forms; and the philosophers affirm this, because it is proved that there are immaterial forms whose existence consists in their thinking, whereas knowledge in this sublunary world only differs from its object because its object inheres in matter.[3]

Ghazali, answering the philosophers, says:

Our answer is that the act is connected with the agent only in so far as it comes into being, but not in so far as it is preceded by non-existence nor in so far as it is merely existent. According to us the act is not connected with the agent for a second moment after its coming to be, for then it exists; it is only connected with it at the time of its coming to be in so far

167 as it comes to be and changes from non-existence into existence. If it is denied the name of becoming, it cannot be thought to be an act nor to be connected with the agent. Your statement, philosophers, that a thing's coming to be means its being preceded by non-existence, and that its being preceded by non-existence does not belong to the act of the agent and the deed of the producer, is true; but this prior non-existence is a necessary condition for the existent's being an act of the agent. For existence not preceded by non-existence is everlasting, and cannot be truly said* to
5 be an act of the agent. Not all conditions necessary to make an act an act need proceed from the agent's act; the essence, power, will, and knowledge of the agent are a condition of his being an agent, but do not derive from him. An act can only be imagined as proceeding from an existent, and the existence, will, power, and knowledge of the agent are a condition of his being an agent, although they do not derive from him.[1]

I say:
All this is true. The act of the agent is only connected with the
10 effect, in so far as it is moved, and the movement from potential to actual being is what is called becoming. And, as Ghazali says, non-existence is one of the conditions for the existence of a movement through a mover. Avicenna's argument that when it is a condition for the act of the agent to be connected with the existence, the absence of this connexion implies that the agent is connected with its opposite, i.e. non-existence, is not true. But the philosophers affirm that there are existents whose essential specific differences consist in motion, e.g. the winds[2] and so on;[3] and the heavens and the sublunary bodies belong to the genus of existents whose existence lies in
168 their movement, and if this is true, they are eternally in a continual becoming. And therefore, just as the eternal existent is more truly existent than the temporal, similarly that which is eternally in becoming is more truly coming to be than that which comes to be only during a definite time.[4] And if the substance of the world were not in this condition of continual movement, the world would not, after
5 its existence, need the Creator, just as a house after being completed and finished does not need the builder's existence, unless that were true which Avicenna tried to prove in the preceding argument, that the existence of the world consists only in its relation to the agent; and we have already said that we agree with him so far as this concerns the forms of the heavenly bodies.

Therefore the world is during the time of its existence in need of the presence of its agent for both reasons together, namely, because
10 the substance of the world is continually in motion and because its

form, through which it has its subsistence and existence, is of the nature of a relation, not of the nature of a quality, i.e. the shapes and states which have been enumerated in the chapter on quality.[1] A form which belongs to the class of quality, and is included in it, is, when it exists and its existence is finished, in no need of an agent. All this will solve the problem for you, and will remove from you the perplexity which befalls man through these contradictory statements.[2]

Ghazali says, on behalf of the philosophers:

The philosophers might say: If you acknowledge that it is possible that the act should be simultaneous with the agent and not posterior to it, it follows that if the agent is temporal the act must be temporal, and if the agent is eternal the act must be eternal. But to impose as a condition that the act must be posterior in time to the agent is impossible, for when a man moves his finger in a bowl of water, the water moves at the same time as the finger, neither before nor after, for if the water moved later than the finger, finger and water would have to be in one and the same space before the water disconnected itself,[3] and if the water moved before the finger, the water would be separated from the finger and notwithstanding its anteriority* would be an effect* of the finger performed for its sake.[4] But if we suppose the finger eternally moving in the water, the movement of the water will be eternal too, and will be, notwithstanding its eternal character, an effect and an object, and the supposition of eternity does not make this impossible. And such is the relation between the world and God.

I say:

This is true in so far as it concerns the relation of movement and mover, but in regard to the stable existent or to that which exists without moving or resting by nature (if there exist such things*) and their relation to their cause, it is not true.[5] Let us therefore admit this relation between the agent and the world only in so far as the world is in motion. As for the fact that the act of every existent must be conjoined with its existence, this is true, unless something occurs to this existent which lies outside its nature, or one or another accident occurs to it,[6] and it is immaterial whether this act be natural or voluntary. See, therefore, what the Ash'arites did who assumed an eternal existent, but denied that He acted during His eternal existence, but then, however, allowed this agent to act eternally in the future, so that the eternal existence of the Eternal would become divided into two parts, an eternal past during which He does not act and an eternal future during which He acts! But for the philosophers all this is confusion and error.

Ghazali answers the philosophers on the question of priority:

We do not say that the simultaneity of agent and act is impossible, granted that the act is temporal, e.g. the motion of the water, for this happens after its non-being and therefore it can be an act, and it is immaterial whether this act be posterior to the agent or simultaneous with him. It is only an *eternal* act that we consider impossible, for to call an act that which does not come into being out of not-being is pure metaphor and does not conform to reality.[1] As to the simultaneity of cause and effect, cause and effect can be either both temporal or both eternal, in the way in which it may be said that the eternal knowledge is the cause of the fact that the Eternal is knowing; we are not discussing this, but only what is called an act.[2] For the effect of a cause is not called the act of a cause, except metaphorically.[3] It can only be called an act on condition that it comes into being out of non-being. And if a man thinks he may describe the everlasting Eternal metaphorically as acting on something, what he thinks possible is only the use of a metaphor.[4] And your argument, philosophers—that if we suppose the movement of the water to be eternal and everlasting with the movement of the finger, this does not prevent the movement of the water from being an act—rests on a confusion, for the finger has no act, the agent is simply the man to whom the finger belongs, that is the man who wills the movement; and, if we suppose him to be eternal, then the movement of the finger is his act, because every part of this movement comes out of not-being,[5] and in this sense it is an act. So far as the motion of the water is concerned, we do not say that it occurs through the act of this man—it is simply an act of God.[6] In any case, it is only an act in so far as it has come to be, and if its coming to be is everlasting, it is still an act, because it has come to be.

Then Ghazali gives the philosophers' answer:

The philosophers may say: 'If you acknowledge that the relation of the act to the agent, in so far as this act is an existent, is like the relation of effect and cause and you admit that the causal relation may be everlasting, we affirm that we do not understand anything else by the expression "that the world is an act" than that it is an effect having an everlasting relation to God. Speak of this as an "act" or not just as you please, for do not let us quibble about words when their sense has once been established.'

Ghazali says:

Our answer is that our aim in this question is to show that you philosophers use those venerable names without justification, and that God according to you is not a true agent, nor the world truly His act, and that you apply this word metaphorically—not in its real sense. This has now been shown.

I say:

In this argument he supposes that the philosophers concede to him that they only mean by God's agency that He is the cause of the world, and nothing else, and that cause and effect are simultaneous.[1] But this would mean that the philosophers had abandoned their original statement, for the effect follows only from its cause, in so far as it is a formal or final cause, but does not necessarily follow from its efficient cause, for the efficient cause frequently exists without the effect's existing.[2] Ghazali acts here like a guardian who tries to extract from his ward the confession* of having done things he did not allow him to do. The philosophers' theory, indeed, is that the world has an agent acting from eternity and everlasting, i.e. converting the world eternally from non-being into being. This question was formerly a point of discussion between Aristotelians and Platonists. Since Plato believed in a beginning of the world, there could not in his system be any hesitation in assuming a creative agent for the world. But since Aristotle supposed the world to be eternal, the Platonists raised difficulties against him, like the one which occupies us here, and they said that Aristotle did not seem to admit a creator of the world. If was therefore necessary for the Aristotelians to defend him with arguments which establish that Aristotle did indeed believe that the world has a creator and an agent.[3] This will be fully explained in its proper place.

The principal idea is that according to the Aristotelians the celestial bodies subsist through their movement, and that He who bestows this movement is in reality the agent of this movement and, since the existence of the celestial bodies only attains its perfection through their being in motion, the giver of this motion is in fact the agent of the celestial bodies. Further, they prove that God is the giver of the unity through which the world is united, and the giver of the unity which is the condition of the existence of the composite; that is to say, He provides the existence of the parts through which the composition occurs, because this action of combining is their cause (as is proved), and such is the relation of the First Principle to the whole world. And the statement that the act has come to be,[4] is true, for it is movement, and the expression 'eternity' applied to it means only that it has neither a first nor a last term. Thus the philosophers do not mean by the expression 'eternal' that the world is eternal through eternal constituents,[5] for the world consists of movement. And since the Ash'arites did not understand this, it was difficult for them to attribute eternity at the same time to God and to the world. Therefore the term ' eternal becoming' is more appropriate to the world than the term 'eternity'.

173 Ghazali says:

The third reason why it is impossible for the philosophers to admit according to their principle that the world is the act of God is because of a condition which is common to the agent and the act, namely, their assertion that out of the one only one can proceed.[1] Now the First Principle is one in every way, and the world is composed out of different constituents. Therefore according to their principle it cannot be imagined that the world is the act of God.

I say:

If one accepts this principle, and its consequences, then indeed the answer is difficult. But this principle has only been put forward by the later philosophers of Islam.[2]

Then Ghazali says, on behalf of the philosophers:

The philosophers may say perhaps: The world in its totality does not proceed from God without a mediator; what proceeds from Him is one single existent, and this is the first of the created principles, namely, abstract intellect, that is a substance subsisting by itself, not possessing any volume, knowing itself and knowing its principle, which in the language of the Divine Law is called 'angel'. From it there proceeds a third principle, and from the third a fourth, and through this mediation the existent beings come to be many. The differentiation and multiplicity of the act can proceed either from a differentiation in active powers, in the way that we act differently through the power of passion and through the power of anger; or through a differentiation of matters, as the sun whitens a garment which has been washed, blackens the face of man, melts certain substances and hardens others; or through a differentiation of instruments, as one and the same carpenter saws with a saw, cuts with an axe, bores with an awl;[3] or this multiplication of the act can proceed through mediation, so that the agent does one act, then this act performs another act, and in this way the act multiplies. All these divisions are impossible in the First Principle, because there is no differentiation nor duality, nor multiplicity in His essence, as will be proved in the proofs of His unity.

174 And there is here neither a differentiation of matters—and the very discussion refers to the first effect, which is, for example, primary matter, nor a differentiation of the instrument, for there is no existent on the same level as God—and the very discussion refers to the coming into existence of the first instrument. The only conclusion possible is that the multiplicity which is in the world proceeds from God through mediation, as has been stated previously.[4]

I say:

This amounts to saying that from the One, if He is simple, there can proceed only one. And the act of the agent can only be differentiated and multiplied either through matters (but there are no matters where He is concerned), or through an instrument (but there is no instrument with Him). The only conclusion therefore is that this happens through mediation, so that first the unit proceeds from Him, and from this unit another, and from this again another, and that it is in this way that plurality comes into existence.

Then Ghazali denies this, and says:

We answer: The consequence of this would be that there is nothing in the world composed of units, but that everything that exists is simple and one, and each unit is the effect of a superior unit and the cause of an inferior, till the series ends in an effect which has no further effect, just as the ascending series ends in a cause which has no other cause. But in reality it is not like this, for, according to the philosophers, body is composed of form and *hyle*, and through this conjunction there arises one single thing; and man is composed out of body and soul and body does not arise out of soul, nor soul out of body: they exist together through another cause. The sphere, too, is, according to them, like this, for it is a body possessing a soul and the soul does not come to be through the body, nor the body through the soul; no, both proceed from another cause. How do these compounds, then, come into existence? Through one single cause? But then their principle that out of the one only one arises is false. Or through a compound cause? But then the question can be repeated in the case of this cause, till one necessarily arrives at a point where the compound and the simple meet. For the First Principle is simple and the rest are compound, and this can only be imagined through their contact.[1] But wherever this contact takes place, this principle, that out of the one only one proceeds, is false.

I say:

This consequence, that everything which exists is simple, is a necessary consequence for the philosophers, if they assume that the First Agent is like a simple agent in the empirical world. But this consequence is binding only upon the man who applies this principle universally to everything that exists.[2] But the man who divides existents into abstract existents and material, sensible existents, makes the principles to which the sensible existent ascends different from the principles to which the intelligible existent ascends, for he regards as the principles of the sensible existents matter and form, and he makes some of these existents the agents of others, till the heavenly body is reached, and he makes the intelligible substances ascend to a first principle which is a principle to them, in one way analogous to a formal cause, in another analogous to a final cause, and in a third way analogous to an efficient cause. All this has been proved in the works of the philosophers, and we state* this proposition here only in a general way. Therefore these difficulties do not touch them. And this is the theory of Aristotle.[1]

About this statement—that out of the one only one proceeds—all ancient philosophers were agreed,[2] when they investigated the first principle of the world in a dialectical way (they mistook this investigation, however, for a real demonstration), and they all came to the conclusion that the first principle is one and the same for everything, and that from the one only one can proceed. Those two principles having been established, they started to examine where multiplicity comes from. For they had already come to the conclusion that the older theory was untenable. This theory held that the first principles are two, one for the good, one for the bad; for those older philosophers did not think that the principles of the opposites could be one and the same; they believed that the most general opposites which comprehend all opposites are the good and the bad, and held therefore that the first principles must be two.[3] When, however, after a close examination, it was discovered that all things tend to one end, and this end is the order which exists in the world, as it exists in an army through its leader, and as it exists in cities through their government,[4] they came to the conclusion that the world must have one highest principle; and this is the sense of the Holy Words 'If there were in heaven and earth gods beside God, both would surely have been corrupted'.[5] They believed therefore, because of the good which is present in everything, that evil occurs only in an accidental way,[6] like the punishments which good governors of cities ordain; for they are evils instituted for the sake of the good, not by primary intention.[7] For there exist amongst good things some that can only exist with an admixture of evil, for instance, in the being of man who is composed of a rational and an animal soul. Divine Wisdom has ordained, according to these philosophers, that a great quantity of the good should exist, although it had to be mixed with a small quantity of evil, for the existence of much good with a little evil is preferable to the non-existence of much good because of a little evil.[8]

Since therefore these later philosophers were convinced that the first principle must of necessity be one and unique, and this difficulty about the one occurred, they gave three answers to this question. Some, like Anaxagoras and his school, believe that plurality is only introduced through matter,[1] some believe that plurality is introduced through the instruments, and some believe that plurality comes only through the mediators; and the first who assumed this was Plato.[2] This is the most convincing answer, for in the case of both the other solutions one would have to ask again; from where does the plurality come in the matters and in the instruments? But this difficulty touches anyone* who acknowledges that from the one only one can proceed: he has to explain how plurality can derive from the one. Nowadays, however, the contrary of this theory, namely, that out of the one all things proceed by one first emanation, is generally accepted, and with our contemporaries we need discuss only this latter statement.[3]

The objection which Ghazali raises against the Peripatetics, that, if plurality were introduced through mediators, there could only arise a plurality of qualitatively undifferentiated agglomerates which could only form a quantitative plurality, does not touch them. For the Peripatetics hold that there exists a twofold plurality, the plurality of simple beings, those beings namely that do not exist in matter, and that some of these are the causes of others and that they all ascend to one unique cause which is of their own genus, and is the first being of their genus, and that the plurality of the heavenly bodies only arises from the plurality of these principles; and that the plurality of the sublunary world comes only from matter and form and the heavenly bodies.[4] So the Peripatetics are not touched by this difficulty. The heavenly bodies are moved primarily through their movers, which are absolutely immaterial, and the forms of these heavenly bodies are acquired from these movers and the forms in the sublunary world are acquired from the heavenly bodies and also from each other, indifferently, whether they are forms of the elements which are in imperishable prime matter[5] or forms of bodies composed out of the elements, and, indeed, the composition in this sublunary world arises out of the heavenly bodies.[6] This is their theory of the order which exists in the world. The reasons which led the philosophers to this theory cannot be explained here, since they built it on many principles and propositions, which are proved in many sciences and through many sciences in a systematic way. But when the philosophers of our religion, like Farabi and Avicenna, had once conceded to their opponents that the agent in the divine world is like the agent in the empirical, and that from the one agent there can arise but one object (and according to all the First was an absolutely simple unity), it became difficult for them to explain how plurality could arise from it. This difficulty compelled them finally to regard the First as different from the mover of the daily circular movement; they declared that from the First, who is a simple existent, the mover of the highest sphere proceeds, and from this mover, since he is of a composite nature, as he is both conscious of himself and conscious of the First, a duality, the highest sphere, and the mover of the second sphere, the sphere under the highest can arise. This, however, is a mistake,[1] according to philosophical teaching, for thinker and thought are one identical thing in human intellect and this is still more true in the case of the abstract intellects.[2] This does not affect Aristotle's theory, for the individual agent in the empirical world, from which there can only proceed one single act, can only in an equivocal way be compared to the first agent.[3] For the first agent in the divine world is an absolute agent, while the agent in the empirical world is a relative agent, and from the absolute agent only an absolute act which has no special individual object can proceed. And thereby Aristotle proves that the agent of the human intelligibles is an intellect free from matter, since this agent thinks all things,[4] and in the same way he proves that the passive intellect is ingenerable and incorruptible,[5] because this intellect also thinks all things.

According to the system of Aristotle the answer on this point is that everything whose existence is only effected through a conjunction of parts, like the conjunction of matter and form, or the conjunction of the elements of the world, receives its existence as a consequence of this conjunction. The bestower of this conjunction is, therefore, the bestower of existence. And since everything conjoined is only conjoined through a unity in it, and this unity through which it is conjoined must depend on a unity, subsistent by itself, and be related to it, there must exist a single unity, subsistent by itself, and this unity must of necessity provide unity through its own essence.[6] This unity is distributed in the different classes of existing things, according to their natures, and from this unity, allotted to the individual things, their existence arises; and all those unities lead upwards to the First Monad, as warmth which exists in all the individual warm things proceeds from primal warmth, which is fire, and leads upwards to it.[7] By means of this theory Aristotle connects sensible existence with intelligible, saying that the world is one and proceeds from one, and that this Monad is partly the cause of unity, partly the cause of plurality. And since Aristotle was the first to find this solution, and because of its difficulty, many of the later philosophers did not understand it, as we have shown. It is evident, therefore, that there is a unique entity from which a single power emanates through which all beings exist. And since they are many, it is necessarily from the Monad, in so far as it is one, that plurality arises or proceeds or whatever term is to be used.[1] This is the sense of Aristotle's theory, a sense very different from that in which those thinkers believe who affirm that from the one only one can proceed. See therefore how serious this error proved among the philosophers! You should, therefore, see for youself in the books of the ancients whether these philosophical theories are proved, not in the works of Avicenna and others who changed the philosophical doctrine in its treatment of metaphysics so much that it became mere guessing.

Ghazali says, on behalf of the philosophers:

It may be said: If the philosophical theory is properly understood, the difficulties disappear. Existents can be divided into what exists in a substratum, like accidents and forms, and what does not exist in a substratum. The latter can be divided again into what serves as a substratum for other things, e.g. bodies, and what does not exist in a substratum, e.g. substances which subsist by themselves. These latter again are divided into those which exert an influence on bodies and which we call souls, and those which exert an influence not on bodies but on souls, and which we call abstract intellects. Existents which inhere in a substratum, like accidents, are temporal and have temporal causes which terminate in a principle, in one way temporal, in another way everlasting, namely, circular movement. But we are not discussing this here. Here we are discussing only those principles which exist by themselves and do not inhere in a substratum, which are of three kinds: (1) bodies, which are the lowest type, (2) abstract intellects, which are not attached to bodies, either by way of action or by being impressed upon them, which are the highest type, and (3) souls, which are the intermediate agencies, attached to the bodies in a certain way, namely, through their influence and their action upon them, and which stand midway in dignity; they undergo an influence from the intellects and exert an influence upon the bodies.

Now the number of bodies is ten. There are nine heavens, and the tenth body is the matter which fills the concavity of the sphere of the moon.[2] The nine heavens are animated; they possess bodies and souls, and they have an order in existence which we shall mention here. From the existence of the First Principle there emanates the first intellect—an existent which subsists by itself, immaterial, not impressed on body, conscious of its principle and which we philosophers call First Intellect,[3] but which (for we do not quibble about words) may be called angel, or intellect, or what you will. From its existence there derive three things, an intellect, the soul, and the body of the farthest sphere, i.e. the ninth heaven.[4] Then from the second intellect there derive a third intellect and the soul and the body of the sphere of the fixed stars, then from the third intellect there derive a fourth intellect and the soul and the body of the sphere of Saturn, then from the fourth intellect there derive a fifth intellect and the soul and the body of the sphere of Jupiter, and so on till one arrives at the intellect from which there derive the intellect, the soul and the body of the sphere of the moon, and this last intellect is that which is called the active intellect. Then there follows that which fills the sphere of the moon, namely, the matter which receives generation and corruption from the active intellect and from the natures of the spheres. Then through the action of the movements of the spheres and the stars the matters are mixed in different mixtures from which the minerals, vegetables, and animals arise. It is not necessary that from each intellect another intellect should derive endlessly, for these intellects are of a different kind, and what is valid for the one is not valid for the other.[1] It follows from this that the intellects after the First Principle are ten in number and that there are nine spheres, and the sum of these noble principles after the First Principle is therefore nineteen; and that under each of the primary intellects there are three things, another intellect and a soul and body of a sphere. Therefore there must be in each intellect a triple character, and in the first effect a plurality can only be imagined in this way: (1) it is conscious of its principle, (2) it is conscious of itself, (3) it is in itself possible, since the necessity of its existence derives from another. These are three conditions, and the most noble of these three effects must be related to the most noble of these conditions.[2] Therefore the intellect proceeds from the first effect[3] in so far as the first effect is conscious of its principle; the soul of the sphere proceeds from the first effect, in so far as the first effect is conscious of itself; and the body of the sphere proceeds from the first effect, in so far as by itself the first effect belongs to possible existence. We must still explain why this triple character is found in the first effect, although its principle is only one. We say that from the First Principle only one thing proceeds, namely, the essence of this intellect through which it is conscious of itself. The effect, however, must by itself become conscious of its principle, and this kind of consciousness cannot derive from its cause. Also the effect by itself belongs to possible existence, and cannot receive this possibility from the First Principle, but possesses it in its own essence. We do indeed regard it as possible that one effect should proceed from the one, although this effect possesses by itself and not through its principle certain necessary qualities, either relative or non-relative.[4] In this way a plurality arises, and so it becomes the principle of the existence of plurality. Thus the composite can meet the simple, as their meeting must needs take place and cannot take place in any other manner, and this is the right and reasonable explanation, and it is in this way that this philosophical theory must be understood.[5]

THE THIRD DISCUSSION

I say:

All these are inventions fabricated against the philosophers by Avicenna, Farabi, and others. But the true theory of the ancient philosophers is that there are principles which are the celestial bodies, and that the principles of the celestial bodies, which are immaterial existents, are the movers of those celestial bodies, and that the celestial bodies move towards them in obedience to them and out of love for them, to comply with their order to move and to understand them, and that they are only created with a view to movement. For when it was found that the principles which move the celestial bodies are immaterial and incorporeal, there was no way left to them in which they might move the bodies other than by ordering them to move. And from this the philosophers concluded that the celestial bodies are rational animals, conscious of themselves and of their principles, which move them by command.[1] And since it was established—in the *De Anima*—that there is no difference between knowledge and the object of knowledge, except for the latter's being in matter,[2] of necessity the substance of immaterial beings—if there are such—had to be knowledge or intellect or whatever you wish to call it. And the philosophers knew that these principles must be immaterial, because they confer on the celestial bodies everlasting movement in which there is no fatigue or weariness,[3] and that anything which bestows such an everlasting movement must be immaterial, and cannot be a material power. And indeed the celestial body acquires its permanence only through these immaterial principles. And the philosophers understood that the existence of these immaterial principles must be connected with a first principle amongst them; if not, there could be no order in the world. You can find these theories in the books of the philosophers and, if you want to make sure of the truth in these matters, you will have to consult them. It also becomes clear from the fact that all the spheres have the daily circular movement, although besides this movement they have, as the philosophers had ascertained, their own special movements, that He who commands this movement must be the First Principle, i.e. God, and that He commands the other principles to order the other movements to the other spheres. Through this heaven and earth are ruled as a state is ruled by the commands of the supreme monarch, which, however, are transmitted to all classes of the population by the men he has appointed for this purpose in the different affairs of the state. As it says in the Koran: 'And He inspired every Heaven with its bidding.'[4]

This heavenly injunction and this obedience are the prototypes of the injunction and obedience imposed on man because he is a rational animal.[1] What Avicenna says of the derivation of these principles from each other is a theory not known amongst the ancients, who merely state that these principles hold certain positions[2] in relation to the First Principle, and that their existence is only made real through this relation to the First Principle. As is said in the Koran: 'There is none amongst us but has his appointed place.'[3] It is the connexion[4] which exists between them which brings it about that some are the effect of others and that they all depend on the First Principle. By 'agent' and 'object', 'creator' and 'creature', in so far as it concerns this existence nothing more can be understood than just this idea of connexion. But what we said of this connexion of every existent with the One is something different from what is meant by 'agent' and 'object', 'maker' and 'product' in this sublunary world. If you imagine a ruler who has many men under his command who again have others under their command, and if you imagine that those commanded receive their existence only through receiving this command and through their obedience to this command, and those who are under those commanded can only exist through those commanded, of necessity the first ruler will be the one who bestows on all existents the characteristic through which they become existent, and that which exists through its being commanded will only exist because of the first ruler. And the philosophers understood that this is what is meant by the divine laws when they speak of creation, of calling into existence out of nothing, and of command. This is the best way to teach people to understand the philosophical doctrine without the ignominy attaching to it, which seems to attach when you listen to the analysis Ghazali gives of it here. The philosophers assert that all this is proved in their books, and the man who, having fulfilled the conditions they impose,[5] is able to study their works will find the truth of what they say—or perhaps its opposite—and will not understand Aristotle's theory or Plato's in any other sense than that here indicated. And their philosophy is the highest point human intelligence can reach. It may be that, when a man discovers these explanations of philosophical theory, he will find that they happen not only to be true but to be generally acknowledged, and teachings which are generally acceptable are pleasing and delightful to all.[6]

One of the premises from which this explanation is deduced is that when one observes this sublunary world, one finds that what is called 'living' and 'knowing' moves on its own account in well-defined movements towards well-defined ends and well-defined acts from which new well-defined acts arise. For this reason the theologians say that any act can only proceed from a living, knowing being. When one has found this first premiss, that what moves in well-defined movements from which arise well-defined and ordered actions is living and knowing, and one joins to this a second premiss which can be verified by the senses, that the heavens move on their own account in well-defined movements from which there follow in the existents under them well-defined acts, order, and rank through which these existents under them receive their subsistence, one deduces from this, no doubt, a third principle, namely, that the heavenly bodies are living beings endowed with perception.[1] That from their movements there follow well-defined acts from which this sublunary world, its animals, vegetables, and minerals receive their subsistence and conservation,[2] is evident from observation, for, were it not that the sun in its ecliptic[3] approaches the sublunary world and recedes from it, there would not be the four seasons, and without the four seasons there would be no plants and no animals, and the orderly origination of elements out of each other necessary for the conservation of their existence would not take place. For instance, when the sun recedes towards the south the air in the north becomes cold and rains occur and the production of the watery element increases, whereas in the south the production of the airy element becomes greater; whereas in summer, when the sun approaches our zenith, the opposite takes place.[4] Those actions which the sun exercises everlastingly through its varying distance from the different existents which always occupy one and the same place are also found in the moon and all the stars which have oblique spheres, and they produce the four seasons through their circular movements, and the most important of all these movements, in its necessity for the existence and conservation of the creation, is the highest circular movement which produces day and night. The Venerable Book refers in several verses to the providential care for man which arises out of God's subjection of all the heavens to His bidding, as, for instance, in the Koranic verse 'And the sun and the moon and the stars are subjected to His bidding',[5] and when man observes these acts and this guidance which proceed necessarily and permanently from the movements of the stars, and sees how these stars move in fixed movements, and that they have well-defined shapes and move in well-defined directions towards well-defined actions in opposite motions, he understands that these well-defined acts can only arise from beings perceptive, living, capable of choice and of willing.

And he becomes still more convinced of this when he sees that many beings in this world which have small, despicable, miserable, and insignificant bodies are not wholly devoid of life, notwithstanding the smallness of their size, the feebleness of their powers, the shortness of their lives, the insignificance of their bodies; and that divine munificence has bestowed on them life and perception, through which they direct themselves and conserve their existence. And he knows with absolute certainty that the heavenly bodies are better fitted to possess life and perception than the bodies of this sublunary world, because of the size of their bodies, the magnificence of their existence, and the multitude of their lights,[1] as it says in the Divine Words: 'Surely the creation of the heavens and the earth is greater than the creation of man, but most men know it not.'[2] But especially when he notices how they direct the living beings of this sublunary world, does he understand with absolute certainty that they are alive, for the living can only be guided by a being leading a more perfect life.[3] And when man observes these noble, living, rational bodies, capable of choice, which surround us, and recognizes a third principle, namely, that they do not need for their own existence the providence with which they guide the sublunary world,[4] he becomes aware that they are commanded to perform these movements and to control the animals, vegetables, and minerals of this sublunary world, and that He who commands them is not one of them and that He is necessarily incorporeal (for, if not, He would be one of them) and that all these heavenly bodies control the existents which are under them, but serve Him, who for His existence is in no need of them. And were it not for this Commander, they would not give their care everlastingly and continuously to this sublunary world which they guide willingly, without any advantage to themselves, especially in this act. They move* thus by way of command and obligation the heavens which repair to them, only in order to conserve this sublunary world and to uphold its existence. And the Commander is God (glory be to Him), and all this is the meaning of the Divine Words 'We come willingly'.[5]

And another proof of all this is that, if a man sees a great many people, distinguished and meritorious, applying themselves to definite acts without a moment's interruption, although these acts are not necessary for their own existence and they do not need them, it is absolutely evident to him that these acts have been prescribed and ordered to them and that they have a leader who has obliged them in his everlasting service to act continually for the good of others.[1] This leader is the highest among them in power and rank and they are, as it were, his submissive slaves. And this is the meaning to which the Venerable Book refers in the words: 'Thus did we show Abraham the kingdom of heaven and the earth that he should be of those who are safe.'[2] And when man observes still another thing, namely, that all the seven planets in their own special movements are subservient to their universal daily motion and that their own bodies as parts of the whole are submissive to the universal body, as if they were all one in fulfilling this service, he knows again with absolute certainty that each planet has its own commanding principle, supervising it as a deputy of the first Commander. Just as, in the organization of armies, where each body of troops has one commander, called a centurion, each centurion is subordinate to the one Commander-in-chief of the army, so also in regard to the movements of the heavenly bodies which the ancients observed. They number somewhat more than forty, of which seven or eight[3]—for the ancients disagreed about this —dominate the others and themselves depend on the first Commander, praise be to Him! Man acquires this knowledge in this way, whether or not he knows how the principle of the creation of these heavenly bodies acts, or what the connexion is between the existence of these commanders and the first Commander. In any case he does not doubt that, if these heavenly bodies existed by themselves, that is, if they were eternal and had no cause, they might refuse to serve their own commanders or might not obey them, and the commanders might refuse to obey the first Commander. But, since it is not possible for them to behave in this way, the relation between them and the first Commander is determined by absolute obedience, and this means nothing more than that they possess this obedience in the essence of their being, not accidentally, as is the case in the relation between master and servant.[4] Servitude, therefore, is not something additional to their essence, but these essences subsist through servitude and this is the meaning of the Divine Words: 'There is none in the heavens or the earth but comes to the Merciful as a servant.'[5] And their possession is the kingdom of the heavens and the earth which God showed to Abraham, as it is expressed in the Devine Words: 'Thus did we show Abraham the kingdom of heaven and earth that he should be of those who are safe.'[1] Therefore you will understand that the creation of these bodies and the principle of their becoming cannot be like the coming to be of the bodies of this sublunary world, and that the human intellect is too weak to understand how this act works, although it knows that this act exists. He who tries to compare heavenly with earthly existence, and believes that the Agent of the divine world acts in the way in which an agent in this sublunary world works, is utterly thoughtless, profoundly mistaken, and in complete error.

This is the extreme limit we can reach in our understanding of the theories of the ancients about the heavenly bodies, of their proof for the existence of a Creator for these bodies who is immaterial, and of their statements concerning the immaterial existents under Him, one of which is the soul. But to believe in His existence as if He were the cause through which these bodies had been produced in time, in the way we see the production of the bodies of this sublunary world, as the theologians desired—this, indeed, is very difficult, and the premisses they use for its proof do not lead them where they desire. We shall show this later, when we discuss the different proofs for the existence of God.

And since this has been firmly established, we shall now go back to relate and refute in detail what Ghazali tells of the philosophers, and to show the degree of truth reached by his assertions, for this is the primary intention of this book.

Ghazali says, refuting the philosophers:

What you affirm are only suppositions and in fact you do nothing but add obscurities to obscurities. If a man were to say that he had seen such things in a dream, it would be a proof of his bad constitution, or if one should advance such arguments in juridical controversies, in which everything under discussion is conjectural, one would say these were stupidities which could not command any assent.

I say:

This is very much the way the ignorant treat the learned and the vulgar the eminent, and in this way, too, the common people behave towards the products of craftsmanship. For, when the artisans show the common people the products of their craftsmanship which possess many qualities from which they draw wonderful actions, the masses scoff* at them and regard them as insane, whereas in reality they themselves are insane and ignorant in comparison with the wise.[2] With such utterances as these the learned and the thoughtful need

THE THIRD DISCUSSION

not occupy themselves. What Ghazali ought to have done, since he relates these theories, is to show the motives which led to them, so that the reader might compare them with the arguments through which he wants to refute them.

Ghazali says:

The ways of refuting such theories are countless, but we shall bring here a certain number. The first is that we say: You claim that one of the meanings of plurality in the first effect is that it is possible in its existence, but we ask whether its being possible in its existence is identical with its being or something different? If you say 'identical', then no plurality proceeds from it, but if you say that it is different, why then do you not assert that there is a plurality in the First Principle, for it not only has existence, but is necessary in its existence, and existence and necessary existence are not identical. Therefore, because of this plurality in the First Principle, let us allow that different entities proceed from it. If it is said: 'Necessity of existence cannot mean anything but existence', we answer: 'Possibility of existence cannot mean anything but existence.' If, however, you say: 'Its existence can be known without its possibility being known, and therefore they are different,' we answer: 'In the same way the existence of the necessary existent can be known without its necessity being known, unless another proof is added,[1] let them therefore be different! Generally speaking, existence is a universal which can be divided into necessary and possible, and if the one specific difference is an addition to the universal, the other specific difference is also an addition, for both cases are the same.' If you say, 'It possesses the possibility of its existence through itself and its existence through another, how then can what it possesses through itself and what it possesses through another be identical?' we answer: 'How then can the necessity of its being be identical with its being, so that the necessity of its existence can be denied and its existence affirmed? And to God, the One, the Absolute Truth, negation and affirmation cannot be applied equivocally, for one cannot say of Him that He is and is not, or that His existence is at the same time necessary or not necessary; but it can be said of Him that He exists, but that His existence is not necessary, as it can be said of Him that He exists, but that His existence is not possible. And it is through this that His Unity can be recognized. But this unity in the First cannot be upheld*, if what you say is true, that possibility of existence is something different from the possible existent*.'[2]

I say:

Ghazali affirms that, when we say of a thing that it is possible in its existence, this must either mean that it is identical with its existence or different from it, i.e. something additional to its existence. If it is identical, there is no plurality, and the statement of the philosophers that there is a plurality in the possible existent has no sense. If, however, it is not identical, the philosophers will have to make the same admission about the necessary existent, i.e. that there is a plurality in it, but this is in contradiction to their own principle. This reasoning, however, is not valid, for Ghazali has overlooked a third case, namely, that necessity of being might be not something added to existence outside the soul but a condition[1] in the necessary existent which adds nothing to its essence; it might be said to refer to the denial of its being the effect of something else, a denial of that which is affirmed of all other entities,[2] just as, when we say of something that it is one, nothing additional to its essence existing outside the soul is meant—as is, on the contrary, the case when we speak of a white existent—but only a negative condition, namely, indivisibility.[3] In the same way, when we speak of the necessary existent, we mean by the necessity of His existence a negative condition which is the consequence of His existence, namely, that His existence is necessary through Himself, not through something else. And also when we speak of the existent which is possible through itself, it is not something additional to its essence outside the soul—as is the case with the real possible[4]—that should be understood, but merely that its essence determines that its existence can become necessary only through a cause; what is meant, therefore, is an essence which will not be by itself necessary in its existence when its cause is removed and therefore is not a necessary existent, i.e. it is denied the quality of necessary existence.[5] It is as if Ghazali said that the necessary existent is partially necessary through itself, partially through a cause, and that which is necessary through a cause is not necessary through itself.[6] Nobody doubts that these specific differences are neither substantial differences which divide the essence nor additions to the essence, but that they are only negative or relative relations, just as, when we say that a thing exists, the word 'exists' does not indicate an entity added to its essence outside the soul, which is the case when we say of a thing that it is white.[7] It is here that Avicenna erred, for he believed that unity is an addition to the essence and also that existence, when we say that a thing exists, is an addition to the thing.[8] This question will be treated later. And the first to develop this theory of the existent, possible by itself and necessary through another, was Avicenna;[9] for him possibility was a quality in a thing, different from the thing in which the possibility is, and from this it seems to follow that what is under the First is composed of two things,

THE THIRD DISCUSSION

one to which possibility is attributed, the other to which necessity is attributed; but this is a mistaken theory.[1] But he who has understood our explanation will not be concerned about the difficulty which Ghazali adduces against Avicenna. The only question he will have to ask, when he has understood the meaning of 'possibility of existence' for the first effect, is whether this possibility brings about a compound character in the first effect or not, for if the quality is relative, it does not bring about a compound character. For not all the different dispositions which can be imagined in a thing need determine additional qualities in its essence outside the soul; indeed, this is the case with the disposition of privations and relations, and for this reason certain philosophers do not count the category of relation among things which exist outside the soul, i.e. the ten categories.[2] Ghazali, however, implies in his argument that any additional meaning must apply to an additional entity actually outside the soul; but this is a mistake, and a sophistical argument.[3] This follows from his words:

Generally speaking, existence is a universal which can be divided into necessary and possible, and if the one specific difference is an addition to the universal, the other specific difference also is an addition, for both cases are the same.

But the division of existence into possible and necessary is not like the division of animal into rational and irrational, or into walking, swimming, and flying animals, for those things are additional to the genus and provide additional species—animality is their common concept and they are specific differences added to it. But the possible into which Avicenna divides existence is not an entity actually outside the soul, and his theory is wrong, as we said before. For the existence which for its existence is in need of a cause can, as an entity by itself, only be understood as non-existence—that is to say, anything that exists through another thing must be non-existent by itself, unless its nature is the nature of the true possible.[4] Therefore the division of existence into necessary and possible existence is not a valid one, if one does not mean by 'possible' the true possible; but we will treat of this later. The summary of what we said here is that the existent can be divided either into essential differences or into relative conditions or into accidents additional to its essence; out of the division into essential differences there must necessarily result a plurality of acts which arise out of the existent, but out of the division into relational and accidental dispositions no such plurality of different acts results. And if it should be claimed that out of relational qualities a plurality of acts results, well then, a plurality will proceed from the First Principle of necessity without need of the intervention of an effect as the principle of plurality; on the other hand, if it should be claimed that out of relational qualities no plurality of acts results, well then, out of the relational qualities of the first effect also there will result no plurality of acts, and this latter assumption is the better.[1]

Ghazali says:

How then can what it possesses through itself, and what it possesses through another, be identical?

But how can this same man who affirms that possibility exists only in the mind, say such a thing? Why then does he not apply this doctrine here, for it is not impossible for the one essence to be positive and negative in its relations without there resulting a plurality in this essence—which, however, Ghazali denies. But if you have understood this, you will be able to solve the problem Ghazali poses in this section.

If it is said: 'It follows from this that there is no composition, either in existence, necessary by itself, or in existence, necessary through another,' we answer: As to what is necessary through another, the mind perceives in it a composition through cause and effect; if it is a body*, there must be in it both a unity actually, and a plurality potentially;[2] if it is, however, incorporeal, the mind does not perceive a plurality either in act or in potency*.[3] For this reason the philosophers call this kind of existent simple, but they regard the cause as more simple than the effect and they hold that the First is the most simple[4] of them all, because it cannot be understood as having any cause or effect at all. But composition can be understood of the principles which come after the First; therefore, according to the philosophers, the second principle is more simple than the third, and it is in this way that their theory must be understood. The meaning of 'cause' and 'effect' in these existents is that a potential plurality (as it were) exists in them which shows itself in the effect, i.e. there proceeds out of it a plurality of effects which it never contains actually in any definite moment.[5] If the hearer has understood their theory in this way and accepted it, he will see that they are not affected by the objections of Ghazali. But one should not understand this theory in the way Ghazali does, namely, that out of the second principle, because it knows its own essence and knows its principle, and therefore possesses two forms or a dual existence, there proceed two different things, for this is a false theory. For this would mean that this second principle is composed of more than one form and that therefore this form[1] is one in its substratum, many by its definition, as is the case with the soul.[2] But the theologians keep tenaciously to this false explanation in their statements about the derivation of these principles from each other, as if they wanted to understand the divine through an analogy with perceptible acts; indeed, when metaphysics contains such theories, it becomes more conjectural than jurisprudence. You will have seen from this that the conclusion Ghazali wants the philosophers to draw concerning the plurality in the necessary existent, because of the plurality which he considers must exist in the possible existent, has no validity. For, if possibility were understood as real possibility, it would indeed imply here a plurality, but since this is impossible, according to what we have said and shall show later, nothing similar follows concerning the necessary existent. But if possibility is understood as being a concept of the mind, it follows that neither the necessary existent nor the possible existent must be regarded as composite for this reason; the only reason why composition must be admitted here is because of the relation of cause and effect.

Ghazali says:

The second objection is that we say: 'Is the knowledge the first effect has of its principle identical with its own existence and with the knowledge it has of itself?' If so, there is only a plurality in the expression used to describe the essence, not in the essence itself; if not, this plurality will exist also in the First, for He knows Himself and He knows others.

I say:

What is true is that the knowledge the first effect has of its principle is identical with its own essence and that the first effect belongs to the domain of relation and is therefore of a lesser rank than the First who belongs to the domain of what exists by itself. It is true, according to the philosophers, that the First thinks only His own essence—not something relative, namely, that He is a principle—but His essence, according to the philosophers, contains all intellects, nay, all existents, in a nobler and more perfect way than they all possess in reality, as we shall explain later.[3] Therefore this theory does not imply the abominable consequences he ascribes to it.[4]

Ghazali says:

It may be said by the philosophers that His knowing Himself is identical with His essence, and that he who does not know that he is a principle for others does not know his own essence, for knowledge conforms to the thing known and refers therefore to His essence.

I say:

This statement is wrong, for His being a principle is something relative and cannot be identical with His essence. If He could think that He is a principle, He would be conscious of the things the principle of which He is, in the way these things really exist, and in this case the higher would be perfected through the lower, for the thing known is the perfection of the knower according to the philosophers, as is set forth in the sciences about the human intellect.[1]

Ghazali says:

But we answer: In this case the knowledge the effect has of itself is identical with its essence, for it thinks with its substance and knows itself, and intellect and knower and thing known are all one. Therefore, if its knowing itself is identical with its essence, well then, let it think itself as the effect of a cause, for this it really is. But the intellect conforms to the thing known; therefore all this refers solely to its essence and so there is no plurality. If, indeed, there is a plurality, it must exist in the First. Therefore, let differentiation proceed from the First.

I say:

What he says here of the philosophers, about the exclusive existence of a plurality in the principles under the First Principle, is wrong and does not follow from their principles. There is, according to them, no plurality in these intellects, and they do not distinguish themselves by simplicity[2] and plurality, but only by being cause and effect. And the difference between the knowledge of the First Principle, as knowing itself, and the knowledge of the other principles, as knowing themselves, is that the First Principle thinks itself as existing by itself, not as being related to a cause, whereas the other intellects think themselves as related to their cause and in this way plurality is introduced into them. They need not all have the same degree of simplicity, since they are not of the same rank in relation to the First Principle and none of them is simple in the sense in which the First Principle is simple, because the First Principle is regarded as an existence by itself whereas they are in related existence.

And as to Ghazali's words:

Therefore, if its knowing itself is identical with its essence, well then, let it think itself as the effect of a cause, for this it really is. But the intellect conforms to the thing known, and therefore all this refers solely to its

THE THIRD DISCUSSION

essence and so there is no plurality. If, indeed, there is a plurality, it must exist in the First Principle.

I say:

It does not follow from the fact that intellect and the thing known are identical in the separate intellects that they are all similar in simplicity, for in this, according to the philosophers, some are superior to others in a greater or lesser degree; absolute simplicity is only found in the First Intellect, and the reason is that the essence of the First Intellect is subsistent by itself, and the other intellects, when they think themselves, are conscious that they subsist by it; if intellect and the intelligible were in each of them of the same degree of unity as in the First Principle, either the essence existing by reason of itself and the essence existing by reason of another would be congruous, or intellect would not conform to the nature of the intelligible thing;[1] which is impossible, according to the philosophers. All these arguments and their answers, as set forth by Ghazali, are dialectical and the only man who can—notwithstanding the deficiency of the human understanding concerning these questions—give a demonstrative argument about them is the man who knows (to begin with) what the intellect is, and the only man who knows what the intellect is is the man who knows what the soul is, and the only man who knows what the soul is is the man who knows what a living being is.[2] There is no sense in discussing these matters in a superficial way and according to the common notions, which do not contain specific knowledge and are not properly related to the problem. To discuss these questions, before knowing what the intellect is, is nothing more than babbling. The Ash'arites, therefore, when they relate the philosophical doctrines, make them extremely hateful and something very different from even the first speculation of man about what exists.

Ghazali says:

Let us therefore drop the claim of its absolute unity, if this unity is annulled through plurality of this kind.

I say:

Ghazali means that, when the philosophers assume that the First thinks its own essence and knows through this that it is the cause of others, they must conclude that it is not absolutely one. For it has not yet been proved that God must be absolutely one. This is the theory of some Peripatetics who interpreted it as the theory of Aristotle himself.[3]

Ghazali says:

If it is said that the First knows only its own essence, and the knowledge of its own essence is identical with its essence, for intelligence, thinker, and intelligible are all one and it does not know anything but itself—this can be refuted in two ways. First, because of its worthlessness this theory was abandoned by Avicenna and other philosophers of repute, who affirm that the First knows itself as the principle of what emanates from it and knows all other existents in their species by a universal thought, and not individually. For they repudiate the theory that there emanates out of the First Principle, which does not know what emanates from it, only one intellect; that its effect is an intellect from which there emanates an intellect and the soul and the body of a sphere, and that this intellect knows itself and its three effects, whereas its cause and principle knows only itself. For according to this theory the effect is superior to the cause, since from the cause only one thing emanates, whereas from the effect three things emanate; moreover, the First Principle knows only itself, but the effect knows its principle and effects besides itself. Who can be satisfied with the idea that such words can apply to the status of God, for indeed they make Him lower than any of His creatures, who know themselves and know Him, and he who knows Him and knows himself is of a nobler rank than He is, since He knows none but Himself. Their profound thoughts about God's glory end therefore in a denial of everything that is understood by His greatness, and assimilate the state of God to that of a dead body which has no notion of what happens in the world, with the sole exception that God possesses self-knowledge.[1] So does God deal with those who turn aside from His way and deviate from the path of His guidance, denying His words: 'I did not make them witnesses of the creation of the heavens and the earth nor of the creation of themselves,'[2] who think wicked thoughts about God,[3] who believe that the powers of man suffice to reach the essence of the divine, who, deceived in their minds, believe that the human understanding is competent to free itself from the authority of the prophets and from obedience to them. For no doubt they are now forced to acknowledge that the quintessence of their thought is reduced to absurdities which would make one wonder if they were told in a dream.

I say:

One who wants to enter deeply into these speculations must know that much of what is firmly established in the speculative sciences seems at first sight, and compared to the opinions the common man holds about them, like the visions of a dreamer, as Ghazali truly says; many of these truths are deduced from a different kind of premisses from that which satisfies the masses; indeed there is no other way for anyone to become convinced of their truth than that of comprehending them by logical proof and evidence. If, for example, the common man, and even he who has reached a somewhat higher degree of culture, is told that the sun, which appears to the eye as being the size of a foot, is about a hundred and seventy times bigger than the earth, he will say that it is absurd, and will regard him who believes it as a dreamer; and it is difficult for us to convince him through propositions which he can easily understand and acknowledge in a short time. The only way, indeed, to attain such knowledge is through deductive proof—that is, for the man who is amenable to proof. If it is the case even with geometrical questions and mathematical problems in general, that, when a solution is explained to the common man, it will appear to him fallacious and open to criticism at first sight and to have the character of a dream, how much more this will be the case in the metaphysical sciences, since for this kind of knowledge there are no plausible premises which satisfy the superficial understanding, by which I mean the understanding of the masses. One might say that the final knowledge the understanding can reach will seem to the common man at first sight something absurd. And this happens not only in the theoretical sciences but in the practical sciences as well. Therefore, the assumption that one of the sciences should vanish and then come into existence again, at first sight would seem to be impossible.[1] For this reason many have thought that those sciences are of supernatural origin and some attribute them to the Jinn, others to the prophets, so that Ibn Hazm goes so far as to affirm that the strongest proof of the existence of prophecy is the existence of these sciences.[2] Therefore, if a lover of truth finds a theory reprehensible and does not find plausible premises which remove its reprehensible character, he must not at once believe that the theory is false, but must inquire how he who puts it forward has arrived at it, must employ much time in learning this, and follow the systematic order corresponding to the nature of the topic. And if this is necessary in other sciences than metaphysics, how much more will this hold for metaphysics, since that science is so remote from the sciences built on common sense. Thus it should be learned that in metaphysics rhetorical reasoning cannot be applied, as it may be applied in other questions; for dialectics is useful and permissible in the other sciences but forbidden in this. For this reason most students of this science seek refuge in the theory that metaphysics is wholly concerned with the qualification of the substance[3] which the human mind cannot qualify, for if it could do so, the eternal and the transitory would be on the same level. If this is so, may God judge him who discusses these questions with common opinions and who argues about God without scientific knowledge. So it is often thought that the philosophers are extremely inefficient in this science, and for this reason Ghazali says that metaphysics is only conjectural.

But in any case* we shall try to show some plausible premises and true propositions—and we try this only because Ghazali gave such a false representation of this noble science and denied people the possibility of attaining happiness through excellent acts, and God is the inquirer and the reckoner[1]—in order to set out the motives which moved the philosophers to believe these theories about the First Principle and other existents, the limit which the human understanding can reach in this matter, and the doubts which beset these problems; and we shall show all this also in respect to the Muslim theologians and indicate how far their wisdom attained. We hope through this to help the lover of knowledge to find the truth, and to urge him to study the sciences of both parties, hoping also that God may assist him in all this!

We say:

The philosophers tried to acquire knowledge about reality through speculation alone, without relying on the words of anyone who should induce them to acquiesce in them without proof; on the contrary, sometimes through speculation they came into contradiction with the facts as shown by the senses.[2] They discovered that the sublunary world can be divided into two classes, the living and the inanimate, any instance of which only comes into being through something, called form, which is the entity by which it comes into being after having been non-existent; through something, called matter, out of which it comes into being; through something, called the agent, from which it comes into being; and through something, called the end, for the sake of which it comes into being; and so they established that there are four causes. And they found that the form by which a thing comes into being, i.e. the form of the thing generated, is identical with the proximate agent, from which it comes into being, either in species, like the generation of man out of man, or in genus, like the generation of the mule from a horse and a donkey.[3] And since, according to them, the causes do not form an infinite series, they introduced a primary, permanent efficient cause. Some of them believed that the heavenly bodies are this efficient cause,[4] some that it is an abstract principle, connected with the heavenly bodies, some that it is the First Principle, some again that it is a principle inferior to it,[1] and these philosophers thought it sufficient to regard the heavens and the principles of the heavenly bodies* as the cause for the coming into being of the elements,[2] since according to them they too need an efficient cause. As to the generation of living beings from each other in the sublunary world, the philosophers had, because of this faculty of life, to introduce another principle, which was the bestower of soul and of form, and of the wisdom which is manifested in this world. This is what Galen calls the formative faculty[3] and some regard it as an abstract principle,[4] some as an intellect, some as a soul,[5] some as the body of the heavens, and some as the First. Galen called this potency the demiurge[6] and was in doubt whether it is God or another principle. This faculty acts in the generative animals and in plants, and is needed still more in those plants and animals which have an equivocal generation.[7] This was the point they reached in the examination of the sublunary world.

When they had agreed that the heavens were the principles of the perceptible bodies, they investigated the heavens also and agreed that the heavenly bodies are the principles of the changeable perceptible bodies and of the species in the sublunary world, either by themselves or in combination with an abstract principle. And from their investigation of the heavenly bodies it appeared to them that these do not come into being in the way that the transitory things of the sublunary world come into being, for what comes into being, in so far as it comes into being, is seen to be a part of this perceptible world and its coming into being is only effected in so far as it is a part of it, for what has come into being has come into being out of something, through the act of something, by means of something, in time and in space. And they discovered that the celestial bodies are, as remote efficient causes, a condition for the coming into being of perceptible things. If, however, the celestial bodies themselves had come into being in this way, they would, as a condition of their becoming, have required prior to them other bodies which would have needed to be parts of another world, and there would be in this other world bodies like these, and if these bodies had also come into being, they would have required other celestial bodies before, and so *ad infinitum*.[8] And since this was established in this way and many others, they were convinced that the heavenly bodies neither come into being nor are destroyed in the way that sublunary things come into being and are destroyed, for 'coming into being' has no other definition or description[9] or explanation or meaning than that which we have laid down here. Then they found that the celestial bodies have also moving principles by means of which and by the agency of which they are moved. And when they investigated their principles, they found that the moving principles were neither bodies nor potencies in bodies. They are not bodies because they are the first principles of the bodies encircling the world; they are not potencies in bodies, i.e. their bodies are not a condition for their existence (as is the case in this sublunary world with the composite principles in animals), because any potency in a body is, according to the philosophers, finite, since it can be divided through the division of the body[1] and every body which can be divided is generable and corruptible, i.e. composed of matter and form, and the existence of its matter* is a condition for the existence of its form.[2] And again, if the principles of heavenly bodies were like the principles of earthly bodies, the former would be like the latter and would need other bodies prior to them.[3] Thus they were convinced of the existence of incorporeal principles which are not potencies in a body.

Moreover, they had already found, concerning the human intellect, that form has two modes of existence, a sensible existence in matter, as in the stone there is the form of the inorganic which exists in the matter outside the soul, and an intelligible existence, namely, perception and intellect, which is separate from matter and exists in the soul.[4] From this they concluded that these absolutely abstract existences are pure intellects, for if what* is separated from another is already intellect, how much better suited to be intellect will something be that is absolutely separate.[5] And so, of necessity, they deduced that the objects of thought of those intellects are the forms of the existents and of the order which exists in the world, as is the case with the human intellect, for the human intellect is nothing other than the perception of the forms of the existents, in so far as they are without matter. They concluded, therefore, that existents have two modes of existence, a sensible existence and an intelligible existence, and that the relation between sensible and intelligible existence is like the relation between the products of art and the arts of the craftsman,[6] and they believed therefore that the heavenly bodies are conscious of these principles and that they can only guide what exists in the sublunary world because they are animated. And when they compared the separate intellects with the human intellect, they found that these intellects are superior to the human intellect, although they have it in common with the human intellect that their intelligibles are the forms of existents, and that the form of each of these intellects is nothing but the forms and the order of the existents it perceives, in the way that the human intellect is nothing but the forms and the order of the existents it perceives. The difference between these two kinds of intellect is that the forms of the existents are a cause of the human intellect, since it receives its perfection through them, in the way that the existent is brought into being through its form, whereas the intelligibles of these intellects are the cause of the forms of the existents.[1] For the order and arrangement in the existents of this sublunary world are only a consequence and result of the order which exists in these separate intellects; and the order which exists in the intellect which is in us is only a consequence of the order and arrangement which it perceives in the existents, and therefore it is very imperfect, for most of this order and arrangement it does not perceive. If this is true, there are different degrees in the forms of the sensible existents; the lowest is their existence in matters, then their existence in the human intellect is superior to their existence in matters, and their existence in the separate intellects is still superior to their existence in the human intellect. Then again they have in the separate intellects different degrees of superiority of existence, according to the different degrees of superiority in these intellects in themselves.

And again when they investigated the body of the heavens they found that in reality it is one unique body similar to one single animal, and that it has one general movement—which is like the general movement of the animal which moves the whole body of the animal —namely, the daily movement, and they found that the other heavenly bodies and their individual movements were similar to the particular members of a single animal and its particular movements.[2] And they believed, because of this connexion between these bodies, their referring to one body and to one end, and their collaboration in one act—namely, the world in its totality—that they depended on one principle, as happens to different arts which aim at one product and which depend on one primary art. For this reason they believed that these abstract principles depend on a unique abstract principle which is the cause of all of them, that the forms and the order and arrangement in this principle are the noblest existence which the forms, the order, and the arrangement in all reality can possess, that this order and arrangement are the cause of all the orders and arrangements in this sublunary world, and that the intellects reach their different degrees of superiority in this, according to their lesser or greater distance from this principle. The First amongst all these principles thinks only its own essence and, by thinking its essence, thinks at the same time all existents in the noblest mode of existence and in the noblest order and arrangement. The substance of everything under the First Principle depends on the way in which it thinks the forms, order, and arrangement which exist in the First Intellect; and their greater or lesser superiority consists only in this. They conclude therefore that the inferior cannot think the superior in the way the superior thinks its own essence, nor does the superior think the inferior in the way the inferior thinks its own essence; this means that no one of any pair of existents can be of the same rank as its fellow, since if this were possible they would have become one and would not form a numerical plurality.[1] Because of this they say that the First thinks only its own essence, and that the next principle can think only the First, but cannot think what is under itself, because this is its effect and if it should think its effect, the effect would become a cause. The philosophers believe that the consciousness which the First has of its own essence is the cause of all existents, and that which each of the intellects inferior to it thinks is in part the cause of those existents the creation of which pertains especially to it, in part the cause of its own essence, i.e. the human intellect in its universality.[2]

It is in this way that the doctrine of the philosophers concerning these things and concerning the motives which lead them to these beliefs about the world must be understood. On examination they will not be less convincing than the motives of the theologians of our religion, first the Mu'tazilites and secondly the Ash'arites, which lead them to their view of the First Principle. They believed, namely, that there exists an essence—neither corporeal, nor in a body—which is living, knowing, willing, provided with power, speaking, hearing, and seeing,[3] while the Ash'arites, but not the Mu'tazilites, held besides that this essence is the agent of everything without intermediary[4] and knows them with an infinite knowledge, since the existents themselves are infinite.[5] The Ash'arites denied the existence of causes, and professed that this living, knowing, willing, hearing, seeing, powerful, speaking essence exists in continuous existence connected with everything and in everything. But this assumption may be thought to imply consequences open to criticism, for an essence with qualities as mentioned above must necessarily be of the genus of the soul, for the soul is an essence, incorporeal, living, knowing, provided with power, willing, hearing, seeing, speaking, and therefore these theologians assumed the principle of reality to be a universal soul, separated from matter in a way they did not understand.[1]

We shall now mention the difficulties which result from this assumption. The most obvious one concerning their theory of the qualities is that there must exist a composite, eternal essence and therefore an eternal compound, which contradicts the Ash'arite theory that every compound is temporal, because it is an accident and every accident is according to them a temporal product.[2] They assumed besides that all existents are possible acts, and they did not believe that there is in them an order, a proportion, and a wisdom which the nature of these existents requires;[3] no, they held that all things could be different from what they are and this applies necessarily also to the intellect;[4] still, they believed that in the products of art, to which they compared the products of nature, there exist order and proportion, and this was called wisdom, and they called the Creator wise.[5] The argument by which they tried to show that there is in the universe something like this principle was that they compared natural acts to acts of will and said that every act, in so far as it is an act, proceeds from an agent endowed with will, power, choice, life, and knowledge, and that the nature of an act, in so far as it is an act, demands this; and they tried to prove the truth of this by arguing that what is not living is inorganic and dead, and, since from the dead there cannot proceed any act, there does not proceed any act from what is not alive. Thus they denied the acts which proceed from natural things and moreover they refused to admit that the living beings which we see in the empirical world have acts; they said that these acts *seem* connected with the living in the empirical world, but their agent is only the living God in the divine world. But the logical conclusion for them would be that there is in the empirical world no life at all, for life is inferred from things in the empirical world, because of their acts;[6] and, further, it would be interesting to know how they arrived at this judgement about the divine world.[7]

The manner in which they established this creator was by assuming that every temporal product must have a cause, but that this cannot go on infinitely, and that therefore of necessity the series must end in an eternal cause; and this is true enough, only it does not follow from this that this eternal principle cannot be body. They need therefore the additional proposition that a body cannot be eternal, but this proposition causes them many difficulties. For it is not sufficient for them to prove that this world is produced, since it might still be argued that its cause is an eternal body which has none of the accidents, no circular movements, nor anything else, through which—although they themselves admitted an eternal composite being[1]—they proved that the heavens must be produced.[2] Now, having assumed that the heavenly body has been produced, they supposed that this production had taken place in quite a different way from what is understood by production in the empirical world.[3] In the empirical world, namely, things are produced from something, in time and space, and with a definite quality, not in their totality,[4] and in the empirical world there is no production of a body from that which is not a body. Nor did they suppose its agent to act like an agent in the empirical world, for the empirical agent changes one quality in the existent into another; it does not change absolute non-existence into existence—no, it brings the existent into a form and an intelligible quality through which this existent becomes another existent instead of this, different from it in substance, definition, name, and act, as it is expressed in the Divine Words: 'We have created man from [an extract of] clay, then we made him a clot in a sure depository, then we created the clot congealed blood, and we created the congealed blood a morsel, &c.'[5] It is for this reason that the ancient philosophers believed that the absolute existent neither comes into existence nor can be destroyed.

Now, if one concedes to the theologians that the heavens were created in time, they are unable to prove that they are the first of created things, as is the evident meaning of what is said in the Venerable Book in more than one verse, for instance, in the Divine Words, 'Do not those who misbelieve see that the heavens and the earth were both solid, &c.?'[6] and in the words, 'and His throne was upon the water',[7] and in the words, 'then He made for heaven and it was but smoke, &c.'[8] And as concerns this agent, according to the theologians, it creates the matter and the form of that which becomes, if they believe that it has a matter, or it creates the thing in its totality, if they believe it to be simple in the way they believe the atom to be simple;[9] and if this is so, this kind of agent changes either non-existence into existence, namely, when there is generation, that is when the atom, which according to them is the element of the bodies, comes into being; or existence into non-existence, namely, when there is destruction, that is, when the atom is destroyed. But it is clear that an opposite cannot be changed into its opposite, and that non-existence itself cannot become existence nor warmth itself cold. It is the privation which becomes existent, it is the warm thing which becomes cold and the cold thing which becomes warm, and for this reason the Mu'tazilites say that privation is an entity although they deprive this entity of the attribute of existence before the becoming of the world.[1] And their arguments by which they believe it can be proved that a thing does not come into being from another thing are incorrect. The most plausible of them is their affirmation that, if a thing came into being from another thing, this would imply an infinite regress. The answer is that this is only impossible for production in a straight line, which, indeed, needs an infinite existence in act; but, as to circular production, it is not impossible that, for instance, fire should come from air and air from fire *ad infinitum*, while the substratum is eternal. They support their theory of the temporal production of the universe by saying that that which cannot be devoid of things produced must itself be produced, and the universe, being the substratum of the things that are produced, must therefore be produced. The greatest mistake in this argument, when its premiss is conceded, is that it is a false generalization, for that which cannot be devoid of things produced in the empirical world is a thing produced out of something else, not out of nothing, whereas they assume that the universe is produced out of nothing. Further, this substratum which the philosophers call primary matter cannot be devoid of corporeality according to the philosophers, and, according to the philosophers, absolute corporeality is not produced.[2] Besides, the premiss which affirms that what cannot be devoid of things produced is produced, is only true when the things produced of which it cannot be devoid are individual things, but if the things produced are one generically, they have no initial term; and from whence then should it follow that their substratum must be produced?[3] And since among the theologians the Ash'arites understood this, they added to this proposition another, namely, that it is not possible that infinite generated things (i.e. without initial and final term) should exist, a proposition which the philosophers regard as necessary.[4] Such difficulties follow from the assumption of the theologians, and they are much more numerous than those which can be held against the philosophers.

And again their assumption that the identical agent which is the First Principle is an agent for everything in the world without an intermediary contradicts the evidence of the senses that things act upon other things. Their most convincing argument on this point is that, if the agent were an effect, this would lead to an infinite regress.[1] But this would only follow if the agent were agent only in so far as it is effect, and if what is moved were the mover, in so far as it is moved, but this is not the case; on the contrary the agent is only agent in so far as it is an actual existent, for the non-existent does not produce any effect.[2] What follows from this is not that there are no acting effects,[3] as the theologians thought, but that the acting effects end[4] in an agent which itself is not an effect at all. Further, the impossibility which is the consequence of their deduction is still greater than the impossibility which follows from the premises from which they draw this conclusion. For if the principle of the existents is an essence, endowed with life, knowledge, power, and will, and if these qualities are additional to its essence and this essence is incorporeal, then the only difference between the soul and this existent is that the soul is in a body and this existent is a soul which is not in a body. But that which has such a quality is necessarily composed of an essence and attributes, and each compound requires of necessity a cause for its being a compound, since a thing can neither be compounded by itself nor produced by itself, for producing, which is an act of the producer, is nothing but the putting together of the product. And, in general, just as for each effect there must be an agent, so for each compound there must be an agent which puts it together, for the putting together is a condition of the existence of the compound.[5] And nothing can be a cause of the condition of its own existence, because this would imply that a thing should be its own cause. Therefore the Mu'tazilites assumed that these attributes in the First Principle refer to its essence and are nothing additional to it, in the way in which this happens with many essential qualities in many existents, like a thing's being existent and one and eternal and so on.[6] This comes nearer to the truth than the theory of the Ash'arites,[7] and the philosophers' theory of the First Principle approaches that of the Mu'tazilites.

We have now mentioned the motives which led these two parties to their theories about the First Principle, and the conclusions which their adversaries can draw from them and hold against them. As concerns the objections against the philosophers, Ghazali has related them in full; we have answered some of them already, and we will answer some of them* later. The difficulties which beset the theologians we have shown in this discussion in detail.

THE THIRD DISCUSSION

We shall now return to distinguish the degree of conviction and plausibility reached by the different statements which Ghazali makes in this book, as we proposed to do, and we were only compelled to mention the plausible propositions which led the philosophers to their theories about the principles of the universe because they answer the objections which their adversaries, the theologians, adduce against them; on the other hand, we mentioned the difficulties which beset the theologians because it is only right that their arguments on this problem should be known and their views represented, since they are free to use them as they wish. It is right, as Aristotle says, that a man should adduce the arguments of his adversaries as he brings forward his own; that is, he should exert himself to find the arguments of his opponents in the same way as he exerts himself to find the arguments of his own school of thought, and he should accept the same kind of arguments from them as he accepts when he has found the arguments himself.[1]

We say: The objection that the First Principle, if it can think only its own essence, must be ignorant of everything it has created would be only a valid inference if the way it thinks its essence were to exclude all existents absolutely. But the philosophers mean only that the manner in which it thinks its own essence includes the existents in their noblest mode of existence, and that it is the intellect which is the cause of the existents; and that it is not an intellect because it thinks the existents, in so far as they are the cause of its thinking, as is the case with our intellect. The meaning of their words, that it does not think the existents which are under it, is that it does not think them in the way we think them, but that it thinks them in a way no other thinking existent can think them, for if another existent could think them in the way it thinks them, it would participate in the knowledge of God, and God is far too exalted for this.[2] This is a quality which is peculiar to God, and for this reason certain theologians concluded that God, besides the seven qualities which they attribute to Him, has yet another which is peculiar to Him.[3] Therefore His knowledge can be described neither as universal nor as individual, for both the universal and the individual are effects of existents, and the knowledge of both universal and individual is transitory.[4] We shall explain this still better when we discuss the question whether God knows individuals or does not know them, as the philosophers mostly assert when they pose this problem, and we shall explain that the whole problem is absurd in relation to God.[5] This problem as a whole is based on two necessary points. First, if God thought existents in such a way that they should be the cause of His knowledge, His intellect would necessarily be transitory and the superior would be brought into being through the inferior. Secondly, if His essence did not contain the intelligibles of all things and their order, there would exist a supreme intellect which would not perceive the forms of existents in their order and proportion.[1] And since these two cases are absurd,

228 it follows that when this principle thinks its own essence,* these existents exist in it in a nobler mode than that in which they exist by themselves. And that one and the same existent can have different degrees of existence can be shown from what occurs with colour*.[2] For we find that colour has different degrees of existence, some higher than others; the lowest degree is its existence in matter, a higher degree is its existence in sight, for it exists in such a way that the colour becomes conscious of itself,[3] whereas existence in matter is an inorganic existence without consciousness; further, it has been proved in the science of psychology that colour has also an existence in the imaginative faculty,[4] and this is a superior existence to its existence in the faculty of sight; it has equally been shown that it has an existence in the remembering faculty superior to that in the imaginative faculty,[5] and, finally, it has in the intellect an existence superior to all these existences. Now, in the same way, we are convinced that it has in the essence of the First Knowledge an existence superior to all its other existences, and that this is the highest degree of existence possible.

229 As for what Ghazali mentions concerning the philosophical theory of the order in the emanation of these separate principles and of the number of entities which emanate out of each of them, there is no proof that this really takes place and that this happens exactly in this way; and the form in which Ghazali relates it is therefore not to be found in the works of the ancient philosophers. But these philosophers all agree on the theory that the principles, both separate and non-separate, all emanate from the First Principle, and that through the emanation of this unique power the world in its totality becomes a unity, and that through this power all its parts are connected, so that the universe aims at one act, as happens with the one body of an animal; which, however, has different potencies, members, and acts; and indeed the world is according to the learned one and the same existent* only because of this one power which emanates from the First Principle.[6] And they agree about all this, because according to them

the heavens are like a single animal and the daily movement which
is common to all the heavens is like the animal's general movement in
space, and the particular movements which the different parts of
heaven have are like the particular movements of the members of the
animal. And the philosophers had already proved that there is one
power in the animal through which it becomes one and through
which all the potencies which it possesses tend towards one act, that
is, towards the preservation of the animal,[1] and all these potencies are
connected with the potency which emanates from the First Principle;
and if this were not the case, its parts would disconnect themselves
and it would not persist for the twinkling of an eye. If, however, it is
necessary that for a single animal there should be a single spiritual
potency,[2] permeating all its parts, through which the plurality of
potencies and bodies in it becomes unified, so that it can be said of its
bodies and potencies that they are one, and if, further, the relations of
individual beings to the universe in its totality are like the relation of
the parts of an animal to the animal itself,[3] it needs must be the case
that all the potencies in the particular parts of this unique animal and
in the psychological and intellectual motive powers of these parts
should be such that there is in them one single spiritual force which
connects all the spiritual and bodily potencies and which permeates
the universe in one and the same penetration.[4] If this were not the
case, no order and no proportion would exist. And in this way it is true
that God is the creator, supporter, and preserver of everything, and
to this the Divine Words apply: 'Verily, God supports the heavens and
the earth lest they should decline.'[5] And it in no way follows from
the fact that this one potency permeates many things that there
should be a plurality in it, as those thought who said that from the
First Principle there can in the first place emanate only one from
which plurality can then emanate; for this statement can only be
regarded as valid if the immaterial agent is compared to the material
agent. Therefore the term 'agent' can only be applied equivocally to
both the immaterial agent and the material. And this will explain to
you the possibility of the procession of plurality from the Monad.

Again, the existence of all other separate principles consists only
in the forms in which they conceive the First Principle, and it is
not impossible that this should be one identical thing, notwithstanding the difference of the forms in which they conceive it, in the same
way as it is not impossible that a plurality should be conceived
through one and the same form.[6] And we find, indeed, that all the

heavenly bodies in their daily movement, and the sphere of the fixed stars, conceive one identical form[1] and that they all, moving in this daily movement, are moved by one and the same mover, who is the mover of the sphere of the fixed stars; and we find, too, that they have also different particular movements. Therefore it needs must be that their movements proceed partly from different movers, partly—namely through the connexion of their movements with the first sphere—from one unique mover.[2] And just as the removal of an organ or a potency vital to the whole animal would invalidate all the organs and potencies of this animal, so the same applies to heaven with respect to its parts and its moving potencies, and in general with respect to the principles of the world and their parts in relation to the First Principle and in their mutual relations. According to the philosophers the world is closely similar to a single state: a state is upheld through one ruler and many deputies subordinate to him; all the deputies in the state are connected with the first ruler, because the authority of each of them is based on him alone, with respect to the ends and the order of the acts which lead to these ends for the sake of which these deputies exist; and so is the relation of the First Ruler in the world to His deputies. And it is evident to the philosophers that he who bestows on the immaterial existents their end is identical with him who bestows on them[3] their existence, for according to them form and end are identical in this kind of existent[4] and he who bestows on these existents both form and end is their agent. And therefore it is clear that the First Principle is the principle of all these principles, and that He is an agent, a form, and an end.[5] And as to His relation to the sensible existents, He is—since He bestows on them the unity which causes their plurality and the unification of their plurality—the cause of all of them, being their agent, form, and end, and all the existents seek their end by their movement towards Him, and this movement by which they seek their end is the movement for the sake of which they are created, and in so far as this concerns all existents, this movement exists by nature, and in so far as this concerns man, it is voluntary.[6] And therefore man is of all beings the one charged with duty and obligation. And this is the meaning of the Divine Words: 'Verily, we offered the trust to the heavens and the earth and the mountains, but they refused to bear it and shrank from it; but man bore it: verily he is ever unjust and ignorant.'[7]

And the philosophers only assert that, although all these ruling principles proceed from the First Principle, it is only some of them that do so directly, whereas others, ascending gradually from the lower world to the higher, proceed mediately. For they discovered that certain parts of heaven exist for the sake of the movements of other parts, and they related them in each instance to a first principle, till they finally arrived at the absolutely First Principle; and so it was evident to them that there was one unique* order and one unique act in which they all participate. But to ascertain the order, which he who contemplates reality and aspires to the knowledge of the First Principle perceives, is difficult, and what human understanding can grasp of it is only its general principle.[1] What led the philosophers to believe in a gradation of these principles, in conformity with the spatial order of their spheres, is that they saw that the highest sphere seems in its action superior to what is under it, and that all the other spheres follow its movement.[2] And therefore they believed that what was said about their order was based on their spatial order. But one might perhaps object that the order in the spheres is perhaps only based on their activity, not on their spatial order; for since it seemed that the activities and movements of the planets exist because of the movement of the sun, perhaps their movers in setting them in motion follow the sun, and the movement of the sun derives perhaps directly from the First.[3] For this reason there are in this question no indubitable assertions, but only assertions more or less plausible and likely to be true. And since this is established, let us now return to our subject.

Ghazali says:

The second answer is: people say of the First Principle that it knows only itself, because they want to avoid the implication of plurality in it, for the statement that it knows another would imply a duality: its knowing itself and its knowing another. However, the same applies to the first effect: it must necessarily know only itself. If it knew another and not itself alone, there would have to be a different cause for its knowing another than that for its knowing itself, but there is no other cause than that for its knowing itself, namely the First Principle. So it can only know itself, and the plurality which arose in this way disappears.

If it is said that it follows from its existence and from its knowing itself that it must know its principle, we answer: Does this necessity arise from a cause or without a cause? If the former is the case, there is no other cause than the one first cause from which only one effect can proceed, and indeed has proceeded, namely this first effect itself; how, therefore, could this second effect proceed from it? In the latter case, then, let the existence of the First Principle imply a plurality of existents without a cause, and let the plurality follow from them! But if such a thing cannot be imagined, because the necessary existent can be only one, and anything added to it must be a possible, and the possible needs a cause, then the following conclusion must be drawn concerning the effect: if it is an existent necessary by itself, then what the philosophers say is untrue, that there is only one necessary existent; if it is a possible,[1] then it needs a cause; but it has no cause,[2] and therefore it cannot know the existence of its cause.

There is no special necessity for the first effect to have a possible existence; this is necessary for any effect. However, that the effect should know its cause is not necessary for its existence, just as the knowledge of its effect is not necessary for the existence of the cause; still, it seems more plausible that the cause should know its effect than that the effect should know its cause.[3] Therefore the plurality which would arise from its knowing its principle is impossible; there is no principle for this knowledge and it is not a necessary consequence of an effect that it should know its principle; and out of this there is no issue.

I say:

This is a proof of one who affirms that the First Principle must, besides knowing itself, know its effect; for, if not, its knowing itself would be imperfect.[4]

The meaning of Ghazali's objection is that the knowledge the effect has of its principle must either be based on a cause or be without a cause. In the former case, there must be a cause in the First Principle, but there is none; in the latter case, a plurality must follow from the First Principle, even if it does not know it; if, however, a plurality follows from it, it cannot be a necessary existent, for there can be only one necessary existent, and that from which there proceeds more than one is only a possible existent; but the possible existent needs a cause, and therefore their assertion that the First Principle is a necessary existent is false, even if it does not know* its effect. He says also that if it is not a necessity of its existence that the effect should have knowledge of its cause, it even seems more fitting that it is not a necessity of its existence that the cause should know its effect.

My answer to this is that all this is sophistical. If we assume that the cause is an intellect and knows its effect, it does not follow that this is an addition to the essence of the cause; on the contrary, it belongs to the essence itself, since the emergence of the effect is the consequence of its essence.[5] And it is not true that if the effect proceeds from the First Principle not because of a cause, but because of the essence of this principle, a plurality proceeds from it, for according to the thesis of the philosophers the emergence of the effect depends on the essence of the First Principle: if its essence is one, one proceeds from it; if many, many proceed from it. What he assumes in this discussion, namely, that every effect is a possible existent, is only true for the composite effect, for there cannot be a compound that is eternal, and everything that is of a possible existence is generated, according to the philosophers, as Aristotle has shown in different passages of his works;[1] and we shall prove this more fully later in our discussion of the necessary being. What Avicenna calls the possible existent has only its name in common with what is in reality the possible existent; it is, therefore, by no means clear that it needs an agent in the way it is clear that the possible existent needs an agent.[2]

Ghazali says:

The third objection is: Is the self-knowledge of the first effect identical with its essence or not? If the former*, this is impossible, for knower and known cannot be identical; if the latter, let the same apply to the First Principle, so that plurality will follow* from the First Principle. And if the self-knowledge of the effect is not identical* with the essence of the effect, there will not only be a triplicity in the effect, as they affirm, but a quadruplicity, to wit: its essence, its knowledge of itself, its knowledge of its principle, and its being a possible existent by itself, and to this it should perhaps be added that it is an existent necessary through another—and then it would be fivefold. From this you can see and measure the depth of their ignorance.

I say:

In this discussion of the intellects there are two points: first the question about what these intellects know or do not know (this question was fully treated by the ancients); secondly, the question of what proceeds from these intellects. What Ghazali mentions here as the theory of the philosophers is in fact the individual opinion of Avicenna on this latter problem. Ghazali exerts himself especially to refute him and his followers, in order to create the impression that he has refuted them all; and this is acting like one who is, as he puts it, in the depths of ignorance. But this theory is not found in the works of any of the ancients; and there is no proof of it except the supposition that from the one there can proceed only one. But this proposition does not apply in the same way to the agents which are forms in matter as to the agents which are forms separate from matter, and according to the philosophers an intellect which is an effect must necessarily know its principle, and there are here not two entities, i.e. the intellect and something additional to its essence, for, if so, it would be a compound, and the intellect, which is simple, cannot be composite. And the difference in the separate forms between cause and effect is that the First Cause exists by itself and the second cause exists through its relation with the First Cause, for the fact of its being an effect lies in its substance and is not an additional entity, in contrast with material effects; e.g. colour is an entity which exists by itself in a body, but it is the cause of sight, in so far as it is related, and sight has no existence except in this relation;[1] and in the same way* substances which are separate from matter are substances which are of the nature of relation. For this reason the cause and the effect are unified in the forms separated from matter,[2] and in the same way* sensible forms are of the nature of relation, as has been proved in the book on psychology.[3]

Ghazali says:

The fourth objection is that it can be said: Triplicity is not sufficient in the first effect, for the body of heaven which, according to the philosophers, proceeds from one entity out of the essence of its principle is composite, and this in three ways.

The first way is that it is composed of form and matter, as is body generally, according to the philosophers, and both must have a principle, since matter differs from form and they are, according to the philosophers, interdependent causes, so that the one cannot come into being by means of the other without the intervention of another cause.[4]

I say:

What he says here is that according to the philosophers the body of the heavens is composed of matter, form, and soul, and that therefore there must be in the second intellect,[5] from which the body of the heavens proceeds, four entities, namely, one from which the form proceeds, one from which the *hyle* proceeds—as both are interdependent, for matter is in one way a cause of form and form in one way a cause of matter[6]—one from which the soul proceeds, and one from which the mover of the second sphere proceeds.[7] But the view that the body of the heavens is composed of form and matter like other bodies is falsely ascribed by Avicenna to the Peripatetics. On the contrary, according to them the body of the heavens is a simple body; if it were composite, it would, according to them, suffer corruption, and therefore they say that it neither comes into being nor perishes, and does not possess the potency for contraries.[8] If it were as Avicenna says, it would be composite like a living being,[9] and if this were true, quadruplicity would be a necessary consequence for the man who asserted that from the one only one can proceed. And we have already stated that the way these forms are causes for each other, for the heavenly bodies, and for the sublunary world, and the way the First Cause is a cause for all of them, is quite different from all this.

Ghazali says:

The second way is that the highest sphere has a definite measure of size, and its determination by this special measure taken from among all other measures is an addition to the existence of its essence, since its essence might be smaller or bigger than it is; therefore, it must have a determinant for this measure, added to the simple entity which causes its existence. The same necessity does not exist for the existence of the intellect, which is pure existence and not specified by any measure taken from among other measures, and therefore may be said to need only a simple cause.

I say:

The meaning of this statement is that when the philosophers say that the body of the sphere proceeds as a third entity, which by itself is not simple (for it is a body possessing quantity), there are here in reality two entities, the one which provides the substantial corporeality, the other the definite quantity; therefore there must be in the intellect from which the body of the sphere proceeds more than one entity, and therefore the second cause is not triple but quadruple. But this is a false assumption, for the philosophers do not believe that body in its entirety[1] proceeds from the separate principles; if anything proceeds from them, according to the philosophers, it is only the substantial form, and according to them the measures of the bodily parts follow from the forms; this, however, refers only to the forms in matter, but the heavenly bodies, since they are simple, are not susceptible of measure.[2] Therefore, to assume that form and matter proceed from an abstract principle is by no means in conformity with philosophical principles, and is quite absurd. In reality, the agent in transitory things,[3] according to the philosophers, produces neither the form nor the matter; it only makes a compound out of matter and form. If the agent produced the form in matter, it would produce the form in something, not from something.[4] This is not philosophical theory, and there is no sense in refuting it, as if it were.

Ghazali says, on behalf of the philosophers:

It might be said: If the sphere were bigger than it is, this greater size would be superfluous for the order of the universe; if smaller, it would not suffice for the intended order.

I say:

He means by this statement that the philosophers do not believe that, for example, the body of the sphere could be bigger or smaller than it is, for in either case the order intended in the universe would not be realized, and the sphere would not set the world in motion according to its natural power, but either too strongly or too weakly, both of which would involve the corruption of the world. A greater size of the world would not be a superfluity, as Ghazali says; no, out of both, bigness and smallness, the corruption of the world would result.[1]

Ghazali says, to refute the philosophers:

We answer: Does the determination of the manner of this order suffice in itself for the existence of what possesses this order, or does it need a cause to effect it? If you believe it suffices, then you regard it as superfluous to assume causes at all, and you may well judge that from the order of these existents the existents themselves result without any additional cause; if, however, you believe it does not suffice, but a cause is necessary, this new cause will not suffice either for the specification of these measures, but will itself need a cause for its specifying*.[2]

I say:

The summary of this is that he makes the objection against them that in the body there are many things which cannot proceed from one agent, unless they admit that many acts can proceed out of one agent, or unless they believe that many accidents of the body result from the form of the body and that the form of the body results from the agent. For, according to such an opinion, the accidents resulting from the body which comes into being through the agent do not proceed from the agent directly but through the mediation of the form.[3] This is a conception permissible to the doctrines of the philosophers, but not to those of the theologians. However, I believe that the Mu'tazilites think as the philosophers do that there are things which do not directly proceed from the agent.[4] We have already explained how the Monad is the cause of the order, and of the existence of all things which support this order, and there is no sense in repeating ourselves.

Ghazali says:

The third way is that in the highest heavens there are marked out two points, the poles, which are immovable and do not leave their position, whereas the parts of the equator change their position. Now either all the parts of the highest sphere are similar (and then there will not be a special determination of two points amongst all the points to be poles), or the parts of the sphere are different and some have a special character which others have not. What, then, is the principle of these differences? For the body of the heavens proceeds from only one and the same simple entity and the simple can cause only that which is simple of shape, namely the sphere, and that which is homogeneous, that is, has no special distinguishable character. And out of this there is no issue.

I say:

'Simple' has two meanings: first, simplicity can be attributed to that which is not composed of many parts, although it is composed of form and matter, and in this way the four elements are called simple;[1] secondly, it can be attributed to that which is not composed of form and matter capable of changing its form,[2] namely to the heavenly bodies; further, simplicity can be attributed to the agglomerate which has the same definition for its whole and its part, even when it is composed of the four elements.[3] The simple character which is attributed to the heavenly bodies can very well possess parts which are differentiated by nature, as are the right and left sides of the sphere and the poles; for the globe, in so far as it is a globe, must have definite poles and a definite centre through which globes differ individually, and it does not follow from the fact that the globe has definite sides that it is not simple, for it is simple in so far as it is not composed of form and matter in which there is potency, and it is non-homogeneous in so far as the part which receives the place of the poles* cannot be any part of the globe, but is a part determined by nature in each globe individually. If this were not so, globes could not have centres by nature through which they were differentiated; thus they are heterogeneous—in this special meaning of the word 'heterogeneous'—but this does not imply that they are composed of bodies different by nature, nor that their agent is composed of many potencies, for every globe is one. Nor do the philosophers regard it as true that every point of whatever globe can be a centre and that only the agent specifies the points, for this is only true in artificial things, not in natural globes.[4] And from the assumption that every point of the globe can be a centre, and that it is the agent which specifies the points, it does not follow that the agent is a manifold unless one assumes that there is in the empirical world nothing that can proceed from a single agent; for in the empirical world things are composed of the ten categories and therefore anything whatever in the world would need ten agents. But all this, to which the view in question leads, which is very much like babbling in metaphysics, is stupid and senseless talk. The artificial product in the empirical world is produced, indeed, by only one agent, even if it possesses the ten categories. How untrue is this proposition that the one can produce only one, if it is understood in the way Avicenna and Farabi understand it, and Ghazali himself in his *Niche for Lights*, where he accepts their theory of the First Principle.[1]

Ghazali says:

One might say: 'Perhaps there are in the principle different kinds of plurality which do not result from its being a principle,[2] only three or four are manifest to us, and the rest we do not perceive, but our incapacity for observation[3] does not shake our belief that the principle of plurality is plurality and that from the one no manifold can proceed.'

I say:

If the philosophers made such a statement, they would have to believe that there is in the first effect an infinite plurality, and one would necessarily have to ask them whence plurality comes in the first effect. And since they say that from the one no manifold proceeds, they would have to concede that the manifold cannot proceed from the One, but their statement* that from the one only one proceeds contradicts their statement* that what proceeds from the First Monad possesses plurality, for from the One one must proceed. Of course they can say that each term in the plurality of the first effect is a first term, but then there must be a plurality of first terms. It is most astonishing how this could remain hidden from Farabi and Avicenna, for they were the first who made these silly statements, and many followed them and attributed these theories to the philosophers. For when Farabi, Avicenna, and their school say that the plurality in the second principle arises through its self-knowledge and its knowing another, it follows for them that its essence has two natures or two forms, and it would be interesting to know which form proceeds from the First Principle and which does not. And there is a similar difficulty in their statement that the second principle is possible by itself, but necessary by another, for its possible nature must necessarily be different from its necessary nature, which it acquires from the necessary being. But the possible nature cannot become necessary, unless the nature of the possible can become necessary. Therefore there is in necessary natures no possibility at all, be it a possibility necessary by itself or a possibility necessary by another.[4] All these are senseless statements and assertions, weaker than those of the theologians, extraneous to philosophy, and not congruous with its principles, and none of these affirmations reaches the level of rhetorical persuasion, to say nothing of dialectic persuasion.

THE THIRD DISCUSSION

And therefore what Ghazali says in different passages of his books is true, that the metaphysics of Farabi and Avicenna are conjectural.

Ghazali says:

We answer: If you regard this as possible, say then that all existing things in their multiplicity (and indeed their number reaches thousands) derive from the first effect and one need not limit this to the body of the extreme sphere[1] and its soul, but all souls, heavenly and human, and all earthly and heavenly bodies can proceed from it, with the many diversities, belonging to them, which nobody has ever seen. But then the first effect will suffice.

I say:

This conclusion is true, especially when they imagine that the first act proceeding from the First Principle is the unity through which the first effect becomes a unique existent, notwithstanding the plurality in it. And indeed, if they allow an undetermined plurality in the first effect, it must be less or more than the number of existents, or equal to it; if less, they must introduce a third principle unless there is a thing without cause, if equal or more, the plurality assumed* in it will be superfluous.[2]

Ghazali says:

And then it follows that the First Cause by itself will suffice too. For if one regards it as possible that a plurality should arise inevitably, although without a cause, and although there is no necessity for it in the existence of the first effect, this will be permissible also with reference to the First Cause, and the existence of all things will be without a cause, although it is said that they follow inevitably and their number is not known. And if their existence without a cause can be imagined with reference to the First Cause, it can also be imagined with reference to the second cause; indeed, there is no sense in speaking of a reference to the first or to the second cause, since there is no distinction between them in time and place[3] and neither the first nor the second cause can be characterized by its relation to things which do not differ from them in time and place and can exist without a cause.[4]

I say:

He says that if a plurality in the first effect is permissible without a cause, because out of the First Cause there does not follow a plurality, one may also suppose a plurality within the First Cause, and there is no need to assume a second cause and a first effect. And if the existence of something without cause within the First Cause is impossible, then it is also impossible within the second cause; indeed, our expression 'second cause' has no sense, since in fact they are one and the same thing, and the one is not different from the other either in time or in space, and if it is permissible that something should exist without a cause, neither the First Cause nor the second can be specially distinguished by this; it suffices that it refers to one of them and therefore it is not necessary to refer it to the second cause.

Ghazali says by way of an answer in the name of the philosophers:

It might be said: 'The entities have become so many that they exceed thousands, but it seems absurd that a plurality of that extent exists in the first effect and for this reason we have multiplied the intermediates.'

Then he says in refutation of this:

We answer, however: To say 'it seems absurd' is pure conjecture, and such a judgement should not be applied to intelligibles. But if one says that it is impossible, we ask: 'Why is it impossible, what will refute it, and where is the criterion?' For, once we exceed the one and believe that one, two, or three entities can arise in the first effect without a cause, what makes it impossible that there should be four, five, indeed, a thousand and many thousands*, and who could fix the limit? No, if unity is once exceeded, nothing can be rejected. This proof again is decisive.

I say:

If, however, Avicenna and these other philosophers had answered that the first effect possesses plurality, and that necessarily any plurality becomes one through a unity which requires that plurality should depend on unity, and that this unity through which plurality becomes one is a simple entity which proceeds from an individual simple Monad, then they would have saved themselves from these objections of Ghazali, and disengaged themselves from these false theories.[1] But since Ghazali secured his point by ascribing a false assumption to the philosophers, and did not find anyone to give him a correct answer, he made merry and multiplied the impossibilities which can be deduced from their theory, for anyone who lets his horse canter in an empty space can make merry.[2] But if he had known that he did not thereby refute the philosophers, he would not have been so delighted about it. The fundamental mistake of Avicenna and Farabi was that they made the statement that from the one only one can proceed, and then assumed a plurality in the one which proceeds. Therefore they were forced to regard this plurality as uncaused. And their assumption that this plurality was a definite plurality[3] which demanded the introduction of a third and fourth principle was a supposition not enforced by any proof. And generally, this assumption is not a legitimate assumption for a first and second principle, for they might be asked, 'Why has only the second principle and not the first this special character of possessing a plurality?' All this is foolish and senseless talk. The fact is that Avicenna and Farabi did not know how the Monad was a cause in the system of Aristotle and the Peripatetics. Aristotle, in the twelfth book of his *Metaphysics*, expresses pride in his solution,[1] and says that none of his predecessors could say anything about this problem.[2] In the sense in which we have expounded the Aristotelian doctrine, this statement that out of the one only one can proceed is true, and the statement that out of the one a plurality proceeds is equally true.

Ghazali says:

Further, we affirm that the statement that out of the one only one can proceed is false in respect of the second effect, for out of it there emanates the sphere of the fixed stars, in which there are a thousand and twenty-odd stars*,[3] different in magnitude,[4] shape, position, colour,[5] and influence, be it of ill omen or auspicious, some in the shape of a ram, a bull, or a lion, others in the shape of a man;[6] they influence one and the same place of the sublunary world differently in conferment of cold and warmth, fortune and misfortune,[7] and their own measures are variable.[8] On account of their differences it cannot be said that they are all of one kind; for if this could be said, it might also be said that all the bodies of the world were of one and the same kind of corporeal nature, and that one cause sufficed for them all. But just as the differences in qualities, substances, and natures of the bodies of the sublunary world show that they themselves are different, in the same way the stars, no doubt, are shown to differ, and each of them will need a cause for its form, a cause for its matter, a cause for the special function in its nature, to bring warmth or cold or happiness or calamity, a cause for its being in the definite place it occupies, then again a cause for its special tendency to group itself with others in the shapes of different animals. And if this plurality can be imagined to be known in the second intellect, it can also be imagined in the first intellect; and then this first intellect will suffice.

I say:

He had already exhausted this difficulty which is of a type he uses abundantly in this book, and if the answer we have given in defence of the philosophers is valid, none of these impossibilities need follow. But if by this expression one understands that, from the simple numerically one, only one simple one—not something numerically one in one way, but plural in another—can proceed, and that its unity is the cause of the existence of plurality, then one can never escape from these doubts. And again, things only become many, according to the philosophers, through substantial differences, and differences through accidents—be they quantitative, qualitative, or in whichsoever of the nine categories of the accident—do not cause, according to them, differentiations in the substance,[1] and the heavenly bodies, as we said, are not composed of matter and form and are not specifically different, since they have, according to the philosophers, no common genus (for, if so, they would be composite, not simple).[2] But we have treated of this already, and there is no sense in repeating ourselves.

Ghazali says:

The fifth objection is to say: If we concede these inept assumptions and these erroneous judgements, how is it then that they are not ashamed to say that from the fact that the first effect is of a possible existence, there results the existence of the highest sphere, and that from its knowledge of itself there follows the existence of the soul of the sphere and from its knowledge of the First Principle there follows the existence of an intellect? What is the difference between this and the statement that the existence of an unknown man is necessary*, and that he is of a possible existence and knows himself and his Creator and then that from the fact that he is of a possible existence there follows the existence of a sphere? But it will be objected: What is the relation between his having a possible existence and the existence of a sphere following from him? And the same holds for the fact that from his knowing himself and his Creator there follow two other entities. But it would be ridiculous to say such a thing about a man or any other existent whatever, for the possibility of existence is a concept which does not change through the changing of the possible object, be it a man or an angel or a sphere.[3] I do not know how any madman could content himself with any of these assertions, let alone the learned who split hairs in their discussions about intelligibles.

I say:

These are all theories of Avicenna and his followers, which are not true and are not built on the foundations of the philosophers; still they are not so inept as this man says they are, nor does he represent them in a true light. For the man whom he supposed to be of a possible existence through himself and necessary through another, knowing himself and his agent, is only a true representation of the second cause, when it is assumed in addition that through his essence and through his knowledge he is the agent of the existents, in the way this is assumed by Avicenna and his school of the second principle, and in the way all philosophers must admit it of the First Principle, God, glory be to Him. If this is admitted, it follows that from this man two things proceed: one in so far as he knows himself, the other,

THE THIRD DISCUSSION

in so far as he knows his Creator, for he is supposed to act only because of his knowledge, and it is not absurd, if he is supposed to act because of his essence, to say that what proceeds from him, in so far as he has a possible existence, is different from what proceeds from him in so far as he has a necessary existence, since both these attributes exist in his nature. This theory, therefore, is not so ignominious as this man tries to represent it to be through this comparison, in order to cast odium on the theories of the philosophers and to make them despicable in the eyes of students.[1]

There is no difference between Ghazali's comparison and a person who said: If you assume a being living through life, willing through will, knowing through knowledge, hearing, seeing, and speaking through audition, sight, and speech, and the whole world proceeds from him,[2] it is possible* that from man, living, knowing, hearing, seeing, speaking, the whole world proceeds, for if these attributes by themselves determine the existence of the world, it cannot make any difference in the effect through whichever being possessing these attributes they produce it.[3] If this man Ghazali sought to speak the truth in this and erred, he might be forgiven; if, however, he understood how to deceive in these things and tried that, and if there were no necessity for him to do so, there is no excuse for him. And if he only wanted to show that he possessed no proof by which he could provide an answer to the question whence plurality proceeds, as might be inferred from what he says below, he speaks the truth, for Ghazali had not reached the degree of knowledge necessary for comprehending this problem, as will be seen from what he says later; and the reason is that he studied only the books of Avicenna, and through this the deficiency in his knowledge arose.

Ghazali says:

But if one should say to us: 'Certainly, you have refuted their theory, but what do you say yourself? Do you affirm that from one thing two different things can in any way proceed? In that case you offend reason. Or will you say that in the First Principle there is plurality? In that case you abandon the doctrine of God's unity. Or will you say that there is no plurality in the world? In that case you contradict the evidence of the senses. Or will you say that plurality occurs through intermediates? In that case you are forced to acknowledge the theory of your opponents.' We answer: 'We have not made a deep inquiry in this book; our aim—which we have attained—was only to disturb the claims of our opponents.' To this we may add that the claim that the thesis that two proceed from one is an affront to reason, and the claim that the attribution of eternal attributes to the First Principle contradicts the doctrine of God's unity—both these claims, we say, are vain and possess no proof. The impossibility that two should proceed from one is not known in the way the impossibility of one single person's being in two places is known; in short, it is known neither by intuitive necessity nor by deduction. What is the objection against saying: 'The First Principle is provided with knowledge, power, will; He acts as He wants, He judges as He wants, He creates the dissimilar and the similar as He wants and in the way He wants?' The impossibility of this is known neither by immediate necessity nor by deduction. But the prophets have brought us this truth, justifying it through their miracles, and we must accept it.[1] To inquire, however, how God's act proceeds from Him through His Will is vain and an illusory pursuit. Those who have sought to represent and understand this have arrived as a result of their inquiry at a first effect from which as a possible existent there proceeds a sphere, and from which, so far as it knows itself, there proceeds the soul of the sphere. But this is nonsense and is by no means an appropriate explanation. Let us therefore accept the principles of these things from the prophets, and let us believe in this, since the intellect does not regard it as impossible. And let us abandon the inquiry about quality, quantity, and quiddity,[2] for the human powers do not suffice for this. And therefore the master of the Divine Law has said: Think about God's creation, but do not think about God's essence.[3]

I say:

His statement is true, that we have to refer to the Law of God everything which the human mind is unable to grasp. For the knowledge which results from revelation comes only as a perfection of the sciences of the intellect; that is, any knowledge which the weakness of the human mind is unable to grasp is bestowed upon man by God through revelation. This inability to comprehend things the knowledge of which is, however, necessary in the life and existence of man, is either absolute—i.e. it is not in the nature of the intellect, in so far as it is intellect, to comprehend such a thing—or it is not in the nature of a certain class of men, and this kind of weakness is either a fundamental character of his disposition or something accidental through a lack of education. Revelation is a mercy bestowed on all these classes of men.[4]

And as to Ghazali's words:

Our aim—which we have attained—was only to disturb our opponents; this aim is not a proper one for him and is censurable in a learned man, for the intention of the learned, in so far as they are learned, must be to seek the truth, not to sow doubts and perplex minds.

And as to his words:

THE THIRD DISCUSSION

the impossibility that two should proceed from one is not known in the way the impossibility a single person's being in two places is known; although these two propositions are not of the same degree of assent, still the proposition that from the simple unit there proceeds only one single unit keeps its evidence inside the empirical world. Propositions which are evident differ in their degree of evidence, as has been shown in the *Posterior Analytics*,[1] and the reason for this is that when evident propositions are supported by imagination they receive a stronger degree of assent, and unsupported by imagination their assent is weakened; but only the masses rely on imagination, and he who is well trained in intellectual thought and renounces imagination accepts both propositions with the same degree of assent.

The strongest degree of evidence pertains to this proposition when a man makes an induction from transitory existents and sees that they only change their names and definitions through their acts and that, if any existent whatever could arise from any act and any agent whatever, the essences and definitions would become mixed and knowledge would be annihilated.[2] The soul, for instance, distinguishes itself from the inorganic only through its special acts which proceed from it, and inorganic things are only distinguished from one another through the acts that are proper to them; and the same applies to souls.[3] And if many acts were to proceed from a single potency, in the way that many acts proceed from composite potencies, there would be no difference between the simple and the composite essence and they would be indistinguishable for us. And again, if many acts could proceed from one single essence, an act without an agent would be possible, for an existent comes to be through an existent, not through a non-existent, and therefore the non-existent cannot come to be by itself; and if it is true that the mover of the privation and the transposer of its potency into act transposes it only through the actuality it possesses itself, of necessity the actuality it possesses must be of the same kind as the act it transposes.[4] If any effect whatever could proceed from any agent whatever, it would not be impossible that the effects should be actualized by themselves without an agent. And if many kinds of potency could be actualized through one and the same agent, this agent would itself have to possess these kinds or related kinds, for if it possessed only one of these kinds, all the other kinds would have to be actualized by themselves without a cause. It is not permissible to say: The only condition for the agent is that it exists as acting with an absolute action, not with a specified kind of action; for, in that case, any existent whatever would be able to perform any act whatever and what exists would be mixed;[1] besides, the absolute, that is the universal, existent stands nearer to non-existence than the real individual existent.[2] So those who denied the theory of universals denied the belief in a universal existent and in a universal becoming*,[3] whereas the champions of this theory regarded them as something midway between being and non-being; but if this were the case, it would follow that the universals could be a cause of existents. The proposition that from the one only one act can proceed is more evident for the empirical than for the divine world. For knowledge multiplies through the multiplying of the objects of thought in the world, since the intellect knows these objects in the way that they exist in the world, and they are the cause of its knowledge.[4] It is not possible for many objects of thought to be known through one act of thought, nor can one act of thought produce many effects in the empirical world, e.g. the knowledge of the artisan which produces, for example, a cupboard is different from the knowledge which produces a chair. But eternal wisdom and the eternal agent differ in this matter from temporal knowledge and the temporal agent.

If I were asked 'What is your own point of view in this question? You have denied Avicenna's theory of the cause of plurality, but what do you say yourself? For it has been pointed out that the different schools of philosophy have three different answers to this question; that the plurality comes only through matter; that the plurality comes only through instruments; that the plurality comes through mediators.[5] And it is said of the Peripatetics that they accept the theory which makes mediation the cause of plurality'—I cannot give in this book an answer to this question supported by a demonstrative proof. We find, however, neither in Aristotle nor in any of the known Peripatetics this theory which is ascribed to them, with the exception of Porphyry, the Tyrian, the author of the *Introduction to Logic*, and he is not among the most subtle of philosophers.[6] My opinion is that according to the principles of the Peripatetics the cause of plurality is a combination of three factors, the intermediates, the dispositions, and the instruments; and we have already explained how all these depend on the Monad and refer to it, for each of them exists through an absolute unity which is the cause of plurality. For it seems that the cause of the plurality of the separate intellects is the difference in their natures, by which they receive the knowledge they gain of the

THE THIRD DISCUSSION

First Principle and which acquire from the First Principle a unity which by itself is one single act, but which becomes many through the plurality of the recipients, just as there are many deputies under the power of a king and many arts under one art. This we shall examine in another place, and if some part of it becomes clear it will suffice; otherwise we must take refuge in revelation. In so far as the differences depend on differences between the four causes, the question is clear. For the differentiation of the spheres arises from the differences of their movers, of their forms, of their matter, supposing they have matter,[1] and of their acts which serve a special end in the world, even if the philosophers did not believe that these spheres exist for the sake of these acts.[2] As to the differences which arise primarily in the sublunary world in the elements, as for instance the differences between fire and earth, and in short the opposites, they are based on the differentiation of matter and on their varying distances from their movers,[3] which are the heavenly bodies. As to the difference between the two supreme movements,[4] one of which is the agent of generation and the other the agent of corruption, they depend on the differentiation of the heavenly bodies and their motions, as is proved in the book *On Generation and Corruption*. For the difference which arises from the heavenly bodies resembles the difference which arises from the difference in the instruments. To sum up: the factors for the origination of plurality from the one Agent are three, according to Aristotle, and he refers to the One in the sense mentioned above, namely, that the One is the cause of the plurality. In the sublunary world the differences arise from the four causes, that is to say, the difference of the agents, the matter, the instruments, and the intermediaries which transmit the acts of the First Agent without its direct interference, and those intermediaries are very similar to the instruments. And an example of the differentiation which arises through the difference of the recipients, and out of the fact that certain differentiated things cause others, is colour. For the colour which arises in the air differs from the colour in the body, and the colour in the faculty of sight, i.e. in the eye, from the colour in the air, and the colour in the common internal sense from the colour in the eye, and the colour in the imagination from the colour in the common internal sense, and the colour in the memorative and retentive faculty from the colour in the imagination; and all this has been explained in the book of psychology.[5]

THE FOURTH DISCUSSION
Showing that they are unable to prove the existence of a creator of the world

Ghazali says:

We say: Mankind is divided into two categories; one, the men of truth who have acknowledged that the world has become and know by necessity that what has become does not become by itself but needs a creator, and the reasonableness of their view lies in their affirmation of a creator; the other, the materialists, believe the world, in the state in which it exists,[1] to be eternal and do not attribute a creator to it, and their doctrine is intelligible, although their proof shows its inanity. But as to the philosophers, they believe the world to be eternal and still attribute a creator to it. This theory is self-contradictory and needs no refutation.[2]

I say:

The theory of the philosophers is, because of the factual evidence,[3] more intelligible than both the other theories together. There are two kinds of agent: (1) the agent to which the object which proceeds from it is only attached during the process of its becoming; once this process is finished, the object is not any more in need of it—for instance, the coming into existence of a house through the builder; (2) the agent from which nothing proceeds but an act which has no other existence than its dependence on it.[4] The distinctive mark of this act is that it is convertible with the existence of its object, i.e. when the act does not exist the object does not exist, and when the act exists the object exists—they are inseparable. This kind of agent is superior to the former and is more truly an agent, for this agent brings its object to being and conserves it, whereas the other agent only brings its objects to being, but requires another agent for its further conservation. The mover is such a superior agent in relation to the moved and to the things whose existence consists only in their movement. The philosophers, believing that movement is the act of a mover and that the existence of the world is only perfected through motion, say that the agent of motion is the agent of the world, and if the agent refrained for only one moment from its action, the world would be annihilated.[5] They use the following syllogism: The world is an act, or a thing whose existence is consequent upon this act. Each act by its existence implies the existence of an agent. Therefore the world has an agent existing by reason of its existence. The man who regards it as necessary that the act which proceeds from the agent of the world should have begun in time says: The world is temporal through an eternal agent. But the man for whom the act of the Eternal is eternal says: The world has come into being[1] from an eternal agent having an eternal act, i.e. an act without beginning or end; which does, however, not mean that the world is eternal by itself, as people who call the world eternal imagine it to be.

Ghazali says, on behalf of the philosophers:

The philosophers might answer: When we affirm that the world has a creator, we do not understand thereby a voluntary agent who acts after not having acted, as we observe in the various kinds of agents, like tailors, weavers, and builders, but we mean the cause of the world, and we call it the First Principle, understanding by this that there is no cause for its existence, but that it is a cause of the existence of other things; and if we call this principle the Creator, it is in this sense. It is easy to establish by a strict proof an existent for the existence of which there is no cause. For we say that the world and its existents either have a cause or have not. If it has a cause, this cause itself either has or has not a cause, and the same can be said about the latter cause, and either we go on *ad infinitum* in this way, and this is absurd, or we arrive at a last term, and this end is the First Cause, which has no cause for its existence and which we call First Principle. And if the world existed by itself without cause, then it would be clear what the First Principle is, for we only mean by it an existent without a cause and which is necessarily eternal. However, it is not possible that the First Principle should be the heavens, for there are many of these and the proof of unity contradicts this, and its impossibility is shown on examination of the attribute of the principle.[2] Nor can it be said that one single heaven, or one single body, the sun or any other body, can be the First Principle; for all these are bodies, and body is composed of matter and form, and the First Principle cannot be composite, as is clear on a second examination. Our intention is to show that an existent which has no cause is eternal by necessity and by universal consent, and only about its qualities is there a divergence of opinion. And this is what we mean by a first principle.

I say:

This argument carries a certain conviction, but still it is not true. For the term 'cause' is attributed equivocally to the four causes—agent, form, matter, and end. Therefore if this were the answer of the philosophers, it would be defective. For if they were asked which cause they mean by their statement that the world has a first cause, and if they answered, 'That agent whose act is uncreated and everlasting, and whose object is identical with its act', their answer would be true according to their doctrine; for against this conception, in the way we expounded it, there is no objection. But if they answered

'The formal cause', the objection would be raised* whether they supposed the form of the world to subsist by itself in the world, and if they answered, 'We mean a form separate from matter', their statement would be in harmony with their theory; but if they answered, 'We mean a form in matter', this would imply that the First Principle was not something incorporeal; and this does not accord with philosophical doctrine. Further, if they said, 'It is a cause which acts for an end', this again would agree with the philosophical doctrine. As you see, this statement is capable of many interpretations, and how can it be represented there as an answer of the philosophers?

And as to Ghazali's words:

We call it the First Principle, understanding by this that there is no cause for its existence, but that it is a cause for the existence of other things.

this again is a defective statement, for this might be said also of the first sphere, or of heaven in its entirety, or generally of any kind of existents which could be supposed to exist without a cause; and between this and the materialistic theory[1] there is no difference.

And as to Ghazali's words:

It is easy to establish by a strict proof an existent for the existence of which there is no cause.

this again is a defective statement, for the causes must be specified, and it must be shown that each kind has an initial term without cause—that is, that the agents lead upwards to a first agent, the formal causes to a first form, the material causes to a first matter, and the final causes to a first end.[2] And then it must still be shown that these four ultimate causes lead to a first cause. This is not clear from the statement as he expresses it here.

And in the same way the statement in which he brings a proof for the existence of a first cause is defective, i.e. his statement:

For we say that the world and its existents either have a cause or have not....

For the term 'cause' is used in an equivocal way. And similarly the infinite regress of causes is according to philosophical doctrine in one way impossible, in another way necessary; impossible when this regress is essential and in a straight line and the prior cause is a condition of the existence of the posterior, not impossible when this regress is accidental and circular, when the prior is not a condition for the posterior and when there exists an essential first cause—for instance, the origin of rain from a cloud, the origin of a cloud from vapour, the origin of vapour from rain. And this is according to the philosophers an eternal circular process, which of necessity, however, presupposes a first cause.[1] And similarly the coming into existence of one man from another is an eternal process, for in such cases the existence of the prior is not a condition for the existence of the posterior; indeed, the destruction of some of them is often a necessary condition. This kind of cause leads upwards to an eternal first cause which acts in each individual member of the series of causes at the moment of the becoming of its final effect; for instance, when Socrates engenders Plato, the ultimate mover, according to the philosophers, is the highest sphere, or the soul, or the intellect,[2] or all together, or God the Creator. And therefore Aristotle says that a man and the sun together engender a man,[3] and it is clear that the sun leads upwards to its mover and its mover to the First Principle. Therefore the past man is not a condition for the existence of the future man. Similarly, when an artisan produces successively a series of products of craftsmanship with different instruments, and produces these instruments through instruments and the latter again through other instruments,[4] the becoming of these instruments one from another is something accidental, and none of these instruments is a condition for the existence of the product of craftsmanship except the first[5] instrument which is in immediate contact with the work produced.[6] Now the father is necessary for the coming into existence of the son in the same way as the instrument which comes into immediate contact with the product of craftsmanship is necessary for its coming into existence. And the instrument with which this instrument is produced will be necessary for the production of this instrument, but will not be necessary for the production of the product of craftsmanship unless accidentally. Therefore sometimes, when the posterior instrument is produced from the matter of the anterior, the destruction of the anterior is a condition for the existence of the posterior, for instance, when a man comes into being from a man who has perished, through the latter becoming first a plant, then sperm or menstrual blood.[7] And we have already discussed this problem. Those, however, who regard an infinite series of essential causes as possible are materialists, and he who concedes this does not understand the efficient cause. And about the efficient cause there is no divergence of opinion among philosophers.

And as to Ghazali's words:

And if the world existed by itself without cause, then it would be clear what the First Principle is.

he means that the materialists as well as others acknowledge a first cause which has no cause, and their difference of opinion concerns only this principle, for the materialists say that it is the highest sphere and the others that it is a principle beyond the sphere and that the sphere is an effect; but these others are divided into two parties, those who say that the sphere is an act that has a beginning and those who say that it is an eternal act. And having declared that the acknowledgement of a first cause is common to the materialists as well as to others, Ghazali says:

However, it is not possible that the First Principle should be the heavens, for there are many of these and the proof of unity contradicts this;

meaning that from the order of the universe it is evident that its directing principle is one, just as it appears from the order in an army that its leader is one, namely, the commander of the army. And all this is true.

And as to Ghazali's words:

Nor can it be said that one single heaven or one single body, the sun or any other body, can be the First Principle; for all these are bodies, and body is composed of matter and form, and the first body cannot be composite.

I say:

The statement that each body is composed of matter and form does not accord with the theory of the philosophers (with the exception of Avicenna) about the heavenly body, unless one uses 'matter' here equivocally.[1] For according to the philosophers everything composed of matter and form has a beginning, like the coming into existence of a house and a cupboard; and the heavens, according to them, have not come into existence in this sense, and so they called them eternal, because their existence is coeternal with the First Principle. For since according to them the cause of corruption is matter, that which is incorruptible could not possess matter, but must be a simple entity. If generation and corruption were not found in sublunary bodies, we should not draw the conclusion that they were composed of matter and form, for the fundamental principle is that body is a single essence not less in its existence than in perception,[2] and if there were no corruption of sublunary bodies, we should judge that they were simple and that matter was body. But the fact that the body of the heavens does not suffer corruption shows that its matter is actual corporeality. And the soul which exists in this body does not exist in it because this body requires, as the bodies of animals do, the soul for its continuance, nor because it is necessary for the existence of this body to be animated, but only because the superior must of necessity exist in the condition of the superior and the animate is superior to the inanimate.[1] According to the philosophers there is no change* in the heavenly bodies, for they do not possess a potency in their substance. They therefore need not have matter in the way the generable bodies need this, but they are either, as Themistius affirms, forms,[2] or possess matter in an equivocal sense of the word. And I say that either the matters of the heavenly bodies are identical with their souls, or these matters are essentially alive, not alive through a life bestowed on them.[3]

Ghazali says:

To this there are two answers. The first is that it can be said: Since it follows from the tenets of your school that the bodies of the world are eternal, it must follow too that they have no cause, and your statement that on a second examination such a conclusion must be rejected will itself be rejected when we discuss God's unity and afterwards the denial of attributes to God.

I say:

Ghazali means that since they cannot prove the unity of the First Principle, and since they cannot prove either that the One cannot be body—for since they cannot deny the attributes, the First Principle must, according to them, be an essence endowed with attributes, and such an essence must be a body or a potency in a body[4]—it follows that the First Principle which has no cause is the celestial bodies. And this conclusion is valid against those who might argue in the way he says the philosophers argue. The philosophers, however, do not argue thus, and do not say that they are unable to prove the unity and incorporeality of the First Principle. But this question will be discussed later.

Ghazali says:

The second answer, and it is the answer proper to this question, is to say: it is established as a possibility that these existents can have a cause, but perhaps for this cause there is another cause, and so on *ad infinitum*. And you have no right to assert* that to admit an infinite series of causes is impossible, for we ask you, 'Do you know this by immediate necessary intuition or through a middle term?' Any claim to intuition is excluded, and any method of deductive proof is forbidden to you, since you admit celestial revolutions without an initial term; and if you permit a coming into existence for what is without end,[5] it is not impossible that the series should consist of causal relations and have as a final term an effect which has no further effect, although in the other direction the series does not end in a cause which has no anterior cause,[1] just as the past has a final term, namely the everchanging present, but no first term. If you protest that the past occurrences do not exist together at one moment or at certain moments, and that what does not exist cannot be described as finite or infinite, you are forced to admit this simultaneous existence for human souls in abstraction from their bodies; for they do not perish, according to you, and the number of souls in abstraction from their bodies is infinite, since the series of becoming from sperma to man and from man to sperma is infinite, and every man dies, but his soul remains and is numerically different from the soul of any man who dies before, simultaneously, or afterwards, although all these souls are one in species. Therefore at any moment there is an infinite number of souls in existence.

If you object that souls are not joined to each other, and that they have no order, either by nature or by position, and that you regard only those infinite existents as impossible which have order in space, like bodies which have a spatial order of higher and lower, or have a natural order like cause and effect, and that this is not the case with souls; we answer: 'This theory about position does not follow any more than its contrary;[2] you cannot regard one of the two cases as impossible without involving the other, for where is your proof for the distinction? And you cannot deny that this infinite number of souls must have an order, as some are prior to others and the past days and nights are infinite. If we suppose the birth of only one soul every day and night, the sum of souls, born in sequence one after the other, amounts at the present moment to infinity.

The utmost you can say about the cause is that its priority to the effect exists by nature, in the way that its superiority to the effect is a matter of essence and not of space. But if you do not regard an infinite sequence as impossible for real temporal priority, it cannot be impossible for natural essential priority either. But what can the philosophers mean when they deny the possibility of an infinite spatial superposition of bodies, but affirm the possibility of an infinite temporal sequence? Is this theory not really an inept theory without any foundation?

I say: As to Ghazali's words:

But perhaps for this cause there is another cause and so on *ad infinitum* ... and any method of deductive proof is forbidden to you, since you admit celestial revolutions without an initial term:

To this difficulty an answer was given above, when we said that the philosophers do not allow an infinite causal series, because this would lead to an effect without a cause, but assert that there is such a series accidentally from an eternal cause—not, however, in a

THE FOURTH DISCUSSION

straight line, nor simultaneously, nor in infinite matters, but only as a circular process.

What he says here about Avicenna, that he regarded an infinite number of souls as possible and that infinity is only impossible in what has a position, is not true[1] and no philosopher has said it; indeed, its impossibility is apparent from their general proof which we mentioned, and no conclusion can be drawn against them from this assumption of an actual infinity of souls. Indeed, those who believed that the souls are of a certain number through the number of bodies and that they are individually immortal profess to avoid this assumption through the doctrine of the transmigration of souls.[2]

And as to Ghazali's words:

But what can the philosophers mean when they deny the possibility of an infinite spatial superposition of bodies, but affirm the possibility of an infinite temporal sequence?

I say:

The difference between these two cases is very clear to the philosophers, for from the assumption of infinite bodies existing simultaneously there follows an infinite totality and an actual infinite, and this is impossible. But time has no position, and from the existence of an infinite temporal series of bodies no actual infinite follows.

Ghazali says on behalf of the philosophers:

The philosophers might say: The strict proof of the impossibility of an infinite causal series is as follows: each single cause of a series is either possible in itself or necessary; if it is necessary, it needs no cause, and if it is possible, then the whole series needs a cause additional to its essence, a cause standing outside the series.[3]

I say:

The first man to bring into philosophy the proof which Ghazali gives here as a philosophical one, was Avicenna, who regarded this proof as superior to those given by the ancients, since he claimed it to be based on the essence of the existent, whereas the older proofs are based on accidents consequent on the First Principle.[4] This proof Avicenna took from the theologians, who regarded the dichotomy of existence into possible and necessary as self-evident, and assumed that the possible needs an agent and that the world in its totality, as being possible, needs an agent of a necessary existence. This was a theory of the Mu'tazilites before the Ash'arites,[5] and it is excellent, and the only flaw in it is their assumption that the world in its totality is possible, for this is not self-evident. Avicenna wanted to give a general sense to this statement, and he gave to the 'possible' the meaning of 'what has a cause',[1] as Ghazali relates.[2] And even if this designation can be conceded, it does not effect the division which he had in view. For a primary division of existence into what has a cause and what has no cause is by no means self-evident. Further, what has a cause can be divided into what is possible and what is necessary.[3] If we understand by 'possible' the truly possible[4] we arrive at the necessary-possible[5] and not at the necessary which has no cause; and if we understand by 'possible' that which has a cause and is also necessary, there only follows from this that what has a cause has a cause and we may assume that this cause has a cause and so *ad infinitum*.[6] We do not therefore arrive at an existent without cause—for this is the meaning of the expression 'entity of a necessary existence'—unless by the possible which Avicenna assumes as the opposite of what has no cause we understand the truly possible, for in these possibles there cannot exist an infinite series of causes.[7] But if by 'possible' is meant those necessary things which have a cause, it has not yet been proved that their infinite number is impossible, in the way it is evident of the truly possible existents, and it is not yet proved that there is a necessary existent which needs a cause, so that from this assumption one can arrive at a necessary entity existing without a cause. Indeed, one has to prove that what applies to the total causal series of possible entities applies also to the total causal series of necessary existents.[8]

Ghazali says:

The terms 'possible' and 'necessary' are obscure, unless one understands by 'necessary' that which has no cause for its existence and by 'possible' that which has a cause for its existence;[9] then, by applying the terms as defined to the statement, we say: Each member of a causal series is possible in this sense of 'possible', namely, that it has a cause additional to its essence, but the series as a whole is not possible in this sense of 'possible'.[10] And if anything else is meant by 'possible', it is obscure. If it is objected that this makes the necessary existent consist of possible existents and this is impossible, we answer: By defining 'necessary' and 'possible' as we have done, you have all that is needed and we do not concede that it is impossible. To say that it is impossible would be like saying that it is impossible that what is eternal should be made up of what is temporal, for time according to you philosophers is eternal, but the individual circular movements are temporal and have initial terms, though collectively they have no initial term; therefore, that which has no initial term consists of entities having initial terms, and it is true of the single units that they have a beginning, but not true of them collectively. In the same way it can be said of each term of the causal series that it has a cause, but not of the series as a whole. And so not everything that is true of single units is true of their collectivity, for it is true of each single unit that it is one and a portion and a part, but not true of their collectivity; and any place on the earth which we choose is illuminated by the sun by day and is dark by night, and according to the philosophers each unit has begun, but not the whole. Through this it is proved that the man who admits temporal entities without a beginning, namely, the forms of the four elements,[1] cannot at the same time deny an infinity of causes, and we conclude from this that because of this difficulty there is no way in which they can prove the First Principle, and their dichotomy is purely arbitrary.[2]

I say:
The assumption of infinite possible causes implies the assumption of a possible without an agent, but the assumption of infinite necessary entities having causes implies only that what was assumed to have a cause has none, and this argument is true with the restriction that the impossibility of infinite entities which are of a possible nature does not involve the impossibility of infinite necessary entities.[3] If one wanted to give a demonstrative form to the argument used by Avicenna one should say: Possible existents must of necessity have causes which precede them, and if these causes again are possible it follows that they have causes and that there is an infinite regress; and if there is an infinite regress there is no cause, and the possible will exist without a cause, and this is impossible. Therefore the series must end in a necessary cause, and in this case this necessary cause must be necessary through a cause or without a cause, and if through a cause, this cause must have a cause and so on infinitely; and if we have an infinite regress here, it follows that what was assumed to have a cause has no cause, and this is impossible. Therefore the series must end in a cause necessary without a cause, i.e. necessary by itself, and this necessarily is the necessary existent. And when these distinctions are indicated, the proof becomes valid.[4] But if this argument is given in the form in which Avicenna gives it, it is invalid for many reasons, one of which is that the term 'possible' used in it is an equivocal one and that in this argument the primary dichotomy of all existents into what is possible and what is not possible, i.e. this division comprising the existent *qua* existent, is not true.

And as to Ghazali's words in his refutation of the philosophers:

We say: Each member of a causal series is possible in this sense of 'possible', namely, that it has a cause additional to its essence, but the whole series is not possible in this sense of 'possible'.

I say:

Ghazali means that when the philosophers concede that they understand by 'possible existent' that which has a cause and by 'necessary existent' that which has no cause, it can be said to them: 'According to your own principles the existence of an infinite causal series is not impossible, and the series in its totality will be a necessary existent,' for according to their own principles the philosophers admit that different judgements apply to the part and to the whole collectively. This statement is erroneous for many reasons, one of which is that the philosophers, as was mentioned before, do not allow an infinite series of essential causes, whether causes and effects of a possible[1] or of a necessary nature, as we have shown. The objection which can be directed against Avicenna is that when you divide existence into possible and necessary and identify the possible existent with that which has a cause and the necessary existent with that which has none, you can no longer prove the impossibility of the existence of an infinite causal series, for from its infinite character it follows that it is to be classed with existents which have no cause and it must therefore be of the nature of the necessary existent, especially as, according to him and his* school, eternity can consist of an infinite series of causes each of which is temporal.[2] The fault in Avicenna's argument arises only from his division of the existent into that which has a cause and that which has none. If he had made his division in the way we have done, none of these objections could be directed against him. And Ghazali's statement that the ancients, since they admit an infinite number of circular movements, make the eternal consist of an infinite number of entities, is false. For the term 'eternal', when it is attributed both to this infinite series and to the one eternal being, is used equivocally.[3]

And as to the words of Ghazali:

If it is objected that this makes the necessary existent consist of possible existents, and this is impossible, we answer: By defining 'necessary' and 'possible' as we have done you have all that is needed, and we do not concede that it is impossible.

I say:

Ghazali means that the philosophers understand by 'necessary' that which has no cause and by 'possible' that which has a cause, and that he, Ghazali, does not regard it as impossible that what has

THE FOURTH DISCUSSION

no cause should consist of an infinite number of causes, because, if he conceded that this was impossible, he would be denying the possibility of an infinity of causes, whereas he only wants to show that the philosophers' deduction of a necessary being is a *petitio principii*.[1]

Then Ghazali says:

To say that it is impossible would be like saying that it is impossible that what is eternal should be made up of what is temporal, for time, according to you philosophers, is eternal, but the individual circular movements are temporal and have initial terms; therefore that which has no initial term consists of entities having initial terms, and it is true of the single units that they have a beginning, but not true of them collectively. In the same way it can be said of each term of the causal series that it has a cause, but not of the series as a whole. And so not everything that is true of single units is true of their collectivity, for it is true of each single unit that it is one and a portion and a part, but not true of their collectivity.

I say:

Ghazali means that it is not impossible that what has no cause should consist of infinite effects in the way the eternal, according to the philosophers, consists of temporal entities, which are infinite in number. For time, according to the philosophers, is eternal, and consists of limited temporal parts, and likewise the movement of heaven is eternal according to the philosophers, and the circular movements of which it consists are infinite. And the answer is that the existence of an eternal consisting of temporal parts, in so far as they are infinite in number, is not a philosophical principle; on the contrary they deny it most strongly, and only the materialists affirm it. For the sum must consist either of a finite number of transitory members or of an infinite number. If the former is the case, it is generally admitted that the members must also be generically transitory.[2] For the latter case there are two theories. The materialists believe that the totality is of a possible nature and that the collectivity must be eternal and without a cause.[3] The philosophers admit this infinity and believe that such genera, because they consist of possible transitory constituents, must necessarily have an external cause, lasting and eternal, from which they acquire their eternity.[4] It is not true either, as Ghazali seems to imply, that the philosophers believe that the impossibility of an infinite series of causes depends on the impossibility that the eternal should consist of an infinity of constituents.[5] They affirm that the eternity of these generically different movements must lead to one single movement, and that the reason why there exist genera* which are transitory in their individuals, but eternal as a whole, is that there is an existent, eternal partly and totally, and this is the body of the heavens. The infinite movements are generically infinite only because of the one single continuous eternal movement of the body of the heavens. And only for the mind does the movement of heaven seem composed of many circular movements.[1] And the movement of the body of the heavens acquires its eternity—even if its particular movements are transitory—through a mover which must always move and through a body which also must always be moved and cannot stop in its motion, as happens with things which are moved in the sublunary world.

About genera there are three theories, that of those who say that all genera are transitory, because the individuals in them are finite, and that of those who say that there are genera which are eternal and have no first or last term, because they appear by their nature to have infinite individuals; the latter are divided into two groups: those, namely the philosophers, who say that such genera can only be truly said to be everlasting, because of one and the same necessary cause, without which they would perish on innumerable occasions in infinite time; and those, namely the materialists, who believe that the existence of the individuals of these genera is sufficient to make them eternal. It is important to take note of these three theories, for the whole controversy about the eternity or non-eternity of the world, and whether the world has an agent or not, is based on these fundamental propositions. The theologians and those who believe in a temporal creation of the world are at one extreme, the materialists at the other, while the philosophers hold an intermediate position.

If all this is once established, you will see that the proposition that the man who allows the existence of an infinite series of causes cannot admit a first cause is false, and that on the contrary the opposite is evident, namely, that the man who does not acknowledge infinite causes cannot prove the existence of an eternal first cause, since it is the existence of infinite effects which demands the necessity of an eternal cause from which the infinite causes acquire their existence; for if not, the genera, all of whose individuals are temporal, would be necessarily finite.[2] And in this and no other way can the eternal become the cause of temporal existents, and the existence of infinite temporal existents renders the existence of a single eternal first principle necessary, and there is no God but He.

Ghazali, answering this objection in the name of the philosophers, says:

The philosophers might say: The circular movements and the forms of the elements do not exist at the present moment; there actually exists only one single form of them, and what does not exist can be called neither finite nor infinite, unless one supposes them to exist in the imagination, and things which are only suppositions in the mind cannot be regarded as impossible, even if certain of these suppositions are supposed to be causes of other suppositions;[1] for man assumes this only in his imagination, and the discussion refers only to things in reality, not to things in the mind.[2] The only difficulty concerns the souls of the dead and, indeed, some philosophers[3] have arrived at the theory that there is only one eternal soul before it is united with bodies, and that after its separation from the bodies it becomes one again, so that it has no numerical quantity and can certainly not be called infinite. Other philosophers have thought that the soul follows from the constitution of the body, that death is nothing but the annihilation of the soul, and that the soul cannot subsist by itself without the body. In that case souls have no existence except in respect of the living, and the living are beings limited in number, and their finitude is not denied, and those that have ceased to exist cannot be qualified at all, either by finitude or by infinity, except when they are supposed to exist in imagination.

Then Ghazali says:

We answer: This difficulty about the souls has come to us from Avicenna and Farabi and the most acknowledged philosophers, since they concluded that the soul was a substance subsistent by itself; and this is also the view taken by Aristotle and by the commentators on the ancient philosophers. And to those philosophers who turn aside from this doctrine[4] we say: Can you imagine that at each moment something comes into being which will last for ever? A negative answer is impossible, and if they admit this possibility, we say: If you imagine that every day some new thing comes into being and continues to exist, then up to the present moment there will have been an infinite collection of existents and, even if the circular movement itself comes to an end, the lasting and endless existence of what has come into being during its revolution is not impossible. In this way this difficulty is firmly established, and it is quite irrelevant whether this survival concerns the soul of a man or a Jinni, the soul of a devil or an angel, or of any being whatever. And this is a necessary consequence of every philosophical theory which admits an infinity of circular movements.

I say:

The answer which he gives in the name of the philosophers, that the past revolutions and the past forms of the elements which have come from each other[5] are non-existent, and that the non-existent can be called neither finite nor infinite, is not a true one. And as to the difficulty he raises against them as to their theory about souls, no such theory is held by any philosophers, and the transference of one problem to another is a sophistical artifice.

THE FIFTH DISCUSSION

To show their incapacity to prove God's unity and the impossibility of two necessary existents both without a cause

Ghazali says:

The philosophers have two proofs of this. The first is to say, 'If there were two necessary existents, the species of necessary existence would be attributed to them both.[1] But what is said to be a necessary existent must either be so through itself, and cannot be imagined to be so through another, or it must be so through a cause, and the essence of the necessary existent will be an effect; and its cause then determines its necessity of existence.' 'But', say the philosophers, 'we understand by "necessary existent" only an entity whose existence has no connexion with a cause.'[2] And the philosophers affirm that the species 'man' is asserted of Zaid and of Amr and that Zaid is not a man through himself—for in that case Amr would not be a man—but through a cause which makes both him and Amr a man; and the plurality of men arises from the plurality of matter in which humanity inheres, and its inherence in matter is an effect which does not lie in the essence of humanity.[3] The same is the case with necessary existence in respect to the necessary existent: if it is through itself a necessary existent, it must possess this qualification exclusively, and if it exists because of a cause, it is an effect and cannot be a necessary existent. And from this it is clear that the necessary existent must needs be one.

To this Ghazali objects and says:

We say: Your statement that the species of necessary existence must belong to the necessary existent either through the necessary existent itself or through a cause is a self-contradictory disjunction, for we have already shown that the expression 'necessary existence' is obscure, unless we mean by it the denial of a cause, and so let us rather use* the term which is really meant by it and say: To admit two existents without a cause, and without the one's being a cause of the other, is not impossible. And your statement that what has no cause has none, either because of its own essence or through some cause, is a faulty disjunction, for one does not ask for the cause of a thing which is said to have no cause and to need no cause for its existence. And what sense is there in the statement that what has no cause has no cause either because of its own essence or through a cause? For to say 'no cause' is an absolute negation, and an absolute non-entity has no cause, and cannot be said to exist either by its own essence or not by its own essence. But if you mean by 'necessary existence' a positive qualification of the necessary existent, besides its being an existent without a cause for its existence, it is quite obscure what this meaning is. But the genuine meaning of this word is the negation of a cause for its existence, and this is an absolute negation about which it cannot be said that it is due to its essence or to a cause, such that the intended proof might be based on the supposition of this disjunction. To regard this as a proof is senseless and has no foundation whatever. On the contrary, we say that the meaning of its necessity is that it has no cause for its existence and no cause for its coming into existence, without there being any cause whatever for this; its being without a cause is, again, not caused by its essence; no, the fact that there is no cause for its existence and no cause for its being, has itself no cause whatsoever. This disjunction cannot be applied even to positive qualities, not to speak of that which is really equivalent to a negation. For suppose one were to say: 'Black is a colour because of its essence or through a cause, and if it is a colour because of its essence, then red cannot be a colour, and then the species of colouredness can exist only because of the essence of black; if, however, black is a colour because of a cause which has made it a colour, then black can be thought of as being without a colour, i.e. as not having been made a colour by a cause, for a determination added to an essence through a cause* can be represented in the imagination as absent, even if it exists in reality.'[1] 'But', it will be objected, 'this disjunction is false in itself, for one cannot say of black that it is a colour because of its essence, meaning by this that it cannot be through anything but its essence, and in the same way one cannot say that this existent is necessary because of its essence, i.e. that it has no cause because of its own essence, meaning by this that it cannot exist through anything but its essence.'

I say:

This method of proving the unity of God is peculiar to Avicenna, and is not found in any of the ancient philosophers; its premisses are common-sense premisses, and the terms are used in a more or less equivocal way. For this reason many objections can be urged against it. Still, when those terms and the aim they intend are properly analysed, this statement comes near to being a proof.

That this primary disjunction is faulty, as Ghazali asserts, is not true. He says that the meaning of 'necessary existent' is 'that which has no cause', and that the statement 'that what has no cause, has no cause, either because of its own essence or through another cause', and similarly the statement 'that the necessary existent is a necessary existent, either because of its own essence or through another cause' are meaningless statements. But this is by no means the case. For the meaning of this disjunction is only whether the necessary existent is such, because of a nature which characterizes it, in so far as it is numerically one,[1] or because of a nature which it has in common with others—for instance, when we say that Amr is a man because he is Amr, or because of a nature he has in common with Khalid. If he is a man because he is Amr, then humanity does not exist in anyone else, and if he is a man because of a general nature, then he is composed of two natures, a general one and a special one and the compound is an effect; but the necessary existent has no cause, and therefore the necessary existent is unique. And when Avicenna's statement is given in this form it is true.

And Ghazali's words:

and an absolute non-entity has no cause and it cannot be said to exist either by its own essence or not by its own essence

form a statement which is not true either. For there are two kinds of negation, the negation of a particular quality, proper to something (and this kind of negation must be understood in respect of the words 'by its own essence' used in this statement), and the negation of a quality, not particular to something (and this kind of negation must be understood here in respect of the term 'cause').[2] Ghazali affirms that this disjunction is not even true of positive qualities and therefore certainly not of negative and he objects to this disjunction by giving as an example black and colouredness. And he means that when we say of black that it is a colour, either because of its essence or through a cause, neither alternative can be true, and both are false. For if black were a cause, because of its essence, red could not be a colour, just as if Amr were a man because of his essence, Khalid could not be a man; on the other hand, if black were a colour through a cause, colour would have to be an addition to its essence, and an essence which receives an addition can be represented without this addition, and therefore this assumption would imply that black could be represented without colouredness, and this is absurd. But this argument of Ghazali is erroneous and sophistical, because of the equivocation in the terms 'essence' and 'cause'. For if by 'by its essence' is understood the opposite of 'by accident', our statement that black is a colour because of its essence is true, and at the same time it is not impossible that other things, red for instance, should be colours. And if by 'cause', in the expression that black is a colour through a cause, is understood something additional to its essence, i.e. that it is a colour through a cause external to black, it does not follow that black can be represented without colouredness. For the genus is an addition to the specific quality and the species, and the species or the specific quality cannot be represented without the genus, and only an accidental additional quality—not the essential additional quality—can be represented without the genus. And therefore our statement that black is a colour either because of its essence or through a cause is a disjunction of which, indeed, one of the alternatives must be true, i.e. black must be a colour either by black itself or through an entity additional to black. And this is what Avicenna meant by his assertion that the necessary existent must be a necessary existent, either through its own special character or through an addition which is not peculiar to it; if through the former, there cannot be two existents which are both necessary existents; if through the latter, both existents must be composed of a universal and of a peculiar entity, and the compound is not a necessary existent through itself. And if this is true, the words of Ghazali: 'What prevents us from representing two existents which should both be of a necessary existence?' are absurd.

And if it is objected, 'You have said that this statement comes near being a proof, but it seems to be a proper proof', we answer: We said this only because this proof seems to imply that the difference between those two assumed necessary existents must lie either in their particularity, and then they participate in their specific quality, or in their species, and then they participate in their generic quality, and both these differences are found only in compounds, and the insufficiency of this proof lies in this, that it has been demonstrated that there are existents which are differentiated, although they are simple and differ neither in species nor individually, namely, the separate intellects.[1] However, it appears from their nature that there must be in their existence a priority and posteriority of rank, for no other differentiation can be imagined in them. Avicenna's proof about the necessary existent must be therefore completed in this way: If there were two necessary existents, the difference between them must consist either in a numerical difference, or in a specific difference, or in rank.[2] In the first case they would agree in species; in the second case in genus, and in both cases the necessary existent would have to be composite. In the third case, however, the necessary existent will have to be one, and will be the cause of all the separate existents. And this is the truth, and the necessary existent is therefore one. For there is only this tripartite disjunction, two members of which are false, and therefore the third case, which necessitates the absolute uniqueness of the necessary existent, is the true one.[1]

Ghazali says:

The second proof of the philosophers[2] is that they say: If we assumed two necessary existents, they would have to be similar in every way or different. If they were similar in every way, they could not be thought to be a plurality or a duality, since two blacks can have only a duality, when they are in two places, or in one place at different times, for black and movement can only exist in one place and be two at the same time, because they differ essentially. When the two essences, like the two blacks, do not differ and at the same time are simultaneous and in one place, they cannot be thought to be a plurality; if one could speak of two simultaneous blacks as being in the same place, any individual could be said to be two, although not the slightest difference could be perceived between the two. Since they cannot be absolutely similar, they must* be different, but they cannot differ in time or in place, and they can therefore only differ in essence. But two things which differ in something must either participate in something or not participate in anything. The latter is impossible, for it would mean that they would participate neither in existence,[3] nor in the necessity of existence, nor in being subsistent in themselves and not inhering in a substratum. But if they agree in something and differ in something, that in which they agree must be different from that through which they differ; there will therefore be composition in them, and it will be possible to analyse them in thought. But there is no composition in the necessary existent, and just as it cannot be divided quantitatively, so it cannot be analysed by thought either, for its essence is not composed of elements which intellectual analysis could enumerate.[4] The words 'animal' and 'rational', for instance, mean that which constitutes the essence of man, namely, animal and rational, and what is meant by the word 'animal' when one speaks of a man is different from what is meant by 'rational', and therefore man is composed of parts which are ordered in the definition by words which indicate these parts, and the term 'man' is applied to the whole of them*.[5] This composition, however, cannot be imagined in the necessary existent, while duality cannot be imagined except in this way.

The answer is that we concede that duality can only be imagined where there is a differentiation, and that in two things, similar in every way, no difference can be imagined. But your statement that this kind of composition is impossible in the First Principle is a mere presumption, and where is your proof of it?

Let us now treat this problem in detail. It belongs to their well-known theories that the First Principle can as little be analysed intellectually as divided quantitatively, and on this fundamental truth, according to the philosophers, the uniqueness of God must be based.

I say:

Ghazali does not know the mistake which is in this second proof, and he begins to discuss with the philosophers the question to which they give a negative answer, namely, if one may introduce a plurality into the definition of the necessary existent. He wants* to consider this problem in detail, since the Ash'arites allow a plurality in God, regarding Him as an essence with attributes.[1] The mistake in this second proof is that two different things can be essentially different and have nothing in common but their name, in the case where they have no common genus, either proximate or remote, for instance, the term 'body', attributed by the philosophers to both the body of the heavens and the transitory body, and the term 'intellect' attributed to the intellect of man and the separate intellects, and the term 'existent' attributed to transitory things and to eternal. Such terms must be regarded as equivocal rather than as univocal, and therefore it does not follow that things which are differentiated must be composite.[2] And since Ghazali, in his answer to this proof of the philosophers, limits himself in the way he has indicated, he begins first by stating their theory of God's unity and then tries to refute the philosophers.

Ghazali, expounding the philosophical theory, says:

For the philosophers assert that God's unity can only be perfected by establishing the singleness of God's essence in every way, and by the denial of any possible plurality in Him. Now plurality can belong to things in five ways.[3]

First, to what can undergo division actually or in imagination, and therefore the single body is not absolutely one—it is one through the continuity which exists in it, which can suffer a decrease and can be quantitatively divided in imagination. This is impossible in the First Principle.

Secondly: a thing may be divided by thought, not quantitatively, into two different concepts, as for instance the division of body into matter and form, for although neither matter nor form can subsist separately, they are two different things in definition and in reality, and it is by their composition that a unity results, namely body. This also must be denied of God, for God cannot be a form or a matter* in a body, or be the compound of both. There are two reasons why God cannot be their compound, first because this compound can be divided into quantitative parts, actually or in imagination, secondly, because this compound can be divided conceptually into form and matter, and God cannot be matter, because matter needs a form, and the necessary existent is self-sufficient in every respect and its existence cannot be conjoined with the condition of something else besides it, and God cannot be form, because form needs matter.

Thirdly: the plurality through attributes implied in knowledge, power, and will;[1] if these attributes had a necessary existence, the essence and these attributes would participate in necessary existence and the necessary existent must be a plurality, and its uniqueness would be denied.

Fourthly: the rational plurality which results from the composition of genus and species. For black is black and colour, and blackness is not colouredness for the intellect, but colouredness is a genus, and blackness a specific difference, and therefore black is composed of genus and species; and animality is for the mind something different from humanity, for man is a rational animal, animal is a genus and rational a specific difference, and man is composed of genus and species, and this is a kind of plurality, and the philosophers affirmed that this kind also must be denied of the First Principle.

Fifthly: the plurality which results from the duality of a quiddity and the existence of this quiddity; for man before his existence has a quiddity, and existence occurs to it and enters into relation with it, and in this way the triangle has a quiddity, namely, it is a figure surrounded by three sides, and existence is not a component of this quiddity, and therefore the intellect can perceive the quiddity of man and the quiddity of a triangle without knowing whether they exist in the external world or not.[2] If existence were a component of the quiddity to which it is added, the fixation of this quiddity in the mind before its existence could not be imagined. Existence stands in a relation to quiddity, whether in a necessary inseparable relation, for instance, heaven, or in an accidental relation occurring after a thing's non-existence, like the quiddity of man in respect of Zaid or Amr and the quiddity of accidents and forms which occur.[3] And the philosophers affirm that this kind of plurality also must be denied of the First Principle. They say that the First Principle has no quiddity to which existence is joined, but existence is necessary to it, as is quiddity to the other entities.[4] Therefore necessary existence is at once a quiddity, a universal reality and a real nature, in the same way as a man, a tree, and heaven are quiddities.[5] For if the necessary existent needed a quiddity for its existence, it would be consequent on this essence and would not constitute it, and the consequent is something secondary and an effect, so that the necessary existent would be an effect, and that would be in opposition to its being necessary.

I say:

These are the theories of the philosophers which Ghazali mentions on the subject of their denial of plurality in the Monad. Then he begins to show how they contradict themselves on this question. We must now first examine these statements which he ascribes to them, and explain the degree of consent they reach; we shall then investigate* the contradictions of the philosophers which he mentions, and his methods of opposing them on this problem.

The first kind of division which, according to Ghazali, the philosophers deny of the First Principle, is the quantitative division, either in supposition or in reality. Everyone who believes that the First Principle is not a body, whether he believes that a body is composed of atoms or not, agrees about this. The proof of this is that the First Principle is not a body, and its discussion will follow.

The second kind is the qualitative division, like the division of body into matter and form, and this according to the doctrine of those, namely, the philosophers, who believe that body is composed of matter and form and this is not the place to discuss the truth of either of these theories. This division also is denied of the First Principle by everyone who believes that the First Principle is not body. As to the denial of the corporeality of the First Principle in so far as it is essentially a necessary existent, the discussion of this will follow later, when we give a complete account of the whole argument used in this matter. For as to Ghazali's words that the necessary existent does not need another, i.e. it does not consist of anything else, but that body consists of form and matter and neither of them are necessary existents, for form cannot dispense with matter and matter cannot dispense with form—there is here a problem; for according to the philosophers the body of the heavens is not composed of matter and form, but is simple, and it has sometimes been thought that it is a necessary existent by its own essence; but this problem will be treated later, and I do not know of any philosopher who has believed that the body of the heavens is composed of matter and form, with the sole exception of Avicenna. We have already spoken on this question in another place,[1] and shall discuss it still later on.

The third kind is the denial of the plurality of attributes in the necessary existent, for if these attributes were of a necessary existence, the necessary existent would be more than one, since the essence also is a necessary existent. And if the attributes were caused by the essence, they could not be necessary existents, and attributes of the necessary existent would not be necessary existents, otherwise the term 'necessary existent' would comprise the necessary existent and that which is not a necessary existent, and this is impossible and absurd. And this is a proof which comes very near to being an absolute truth, when it is conceded that the 'necessary existent' must indicate an immaterial existent, and in such existents, which subsist by themselves without being bodies, there cannot be imagined essential attributes of which their essence is constituted, not to speak of attributes which are additional to their essence, that is, the so-called accidents, for when accidents are imagined to be removed, the essence remains, which is not the case with the essential attributes. And therefore it is right to attribute essential attributes to their subject, since they constitute its identity,[1] but it is not right to attribute non-essential attributes to it, except through derivative words,[2] for we do not say of a man that he is knowledge, but we only say that he is an animal and that he is knowing;[3] however, the existence of such attributes in what is incorporeal is impossible, since the nature of these attributes is extraneous to their subject, and for this reason they are called accidents and are distinct from what is attributed essentially to the subject, be it a subject in the soul or in the external world. If it is objected that the philosophers believe that there are such attributes in the soul, since they believe that the soul can perceive, will, and move, although at the same time they hold that the soul is incorporeal, we answer that they do not mean that these attributes are additional to the essence, but that they are essential attributes, and it is of the nature of essential attributes not to multiply the substratum which actually supports them; they are a plurality only in the sense that the thing defined becomes a plurality through the parts of the definitions, that is, they are only a subjective plurality in the mind according to the philosophers, not an actual plurality outside the soul. For instance, the definition of man is 'rational animal', but reason and life are not actually distinguishable from each other outside the soul in the way colour and shape are. And therefore he who concedes that matter is not a condition for the existence of the soul must concede that in the separate existences there is a real oneness existing outside the soul, although this oneness becomes a plurality through definition.[4] This is the doctrine of the Christians concerning the three hypostases in the divine Nature. They do not believe that they are attributes additional to the essence, but according to them they are only a plurality in the definition—they are a potential, not an actual, plurality. Therefore they say that the three are one, i.e. one in act and three in potency.[5] We shall enumerate later the repre-

THE FIFTH DISCUSSION

hensible consequences and absurdities which arise from the doctrine that the First Principle possesses attributes additional to His essence.

The fourth kind of plurality is that which occurs to a thing because of its genus and specific difference; this plurality comes very near to that which belongs to a thing because of its matter and form, for there are only definitions for that which is composed of matter and form, and not for simple, non-compound things, and nobody need disagree about denying a plurality through definition to the First Principle.

The fifth kind of plurality is the plurality of essence and existence. Existence in the nature of things is a logical concept which affirms the conformity of a thing outside the soul with what is inside the soul.[1] Its meaning is synonymous with the true, and it is this that is meant by the copula in categorical propositions.[2] The term 'existence' is used in two senses; the first synonymous with the true, when we ask, for instance, if something exists or not, or whether a certain thing has such and such a quality or not.[3] The second sense stands in relation to the existing things as their genus, in the way the existent is divided into the ten categories, and into substance and accident.[4] When by existent is understood the true, there is no plurality outside the soul:[5] when by existent is understood what is understood by entity and thing,[6] the term 'existent' is attributed essentially to God and analogically to all other things in the way warmth is attributed to fire and to all warm things.[7] This is the theory of the philosophers.

But Ghazali based his discussion on the doctrine of Avicenna, and this is a false doctrine, for Avicenna believed that existence is something additional to the essence outside the soul and is like an accident of the essence. And if existence were a condition for the being of the essence and a condition for the essence of the necessary existent, the necessary existent would be composed of the conditioning and the conditioned and it would be of a possible existence. Avicenna affirms also that what exists as an addition to its essence has a cause. Now, existence for Avicenna is an accident which supervenes on the essence,[8] and to this Ghazali refers when he says:

For man before his existence has a quiddity and existence occurs to it and enters into relation with it, and in this way the triangle has a quiddity, namely, it is a figure surrounded by three sides, and existence is not a component of this quiddity, and therefore the intellect can perceive the quiddity of man and the quiddity of a triangle without knowing whether they exist in the exterior world or not.

This shows that the term 'existence' which he uses here is not the term which signifies the most universal genus of all entities, nor the term which indicates that a thing exists outside the soul. For the term 'existence' is used in two meanings, the former signifies the true and the latter the opposite of non-existence, and in this latter sense it is that which is divided into the ten categories and is like their genus. This essential sense which refers to the things which exist in the real world outside the soul is prior to the sense it has in the existents of second intention,[1] and it is this sense which is predicated of the ten categories analogically, and it is in this sense that we say of the substance that it exists by itself and of the accident that it exists through its existing in the existent which subsists by itself. As to the existent which has the meaning of the 'true', all the categories participate in it in the same way,[2] and the existent which has the meaning of the 'true' is something in the mind, namely that a thing is outside the soul in conformity with what it is inside the soul,[3] and the knowledge of this is prior to the knowledge of its quiddity; that is, knowledge of the quiddity of a thing cannot be asked for, unless it is known that it exists.[4] And as to those quiddities which precede in our minds the knowledge of their existence, they are not really quiddities, but only nominal definitions, and only when it is known that their meaning exists outside the soul does it become known that they are quiddities and definitions. And in this sense it is said in the book of the *Categories* that the intelligible universals of things become existent through their particulars, and that the particulars become intelligible through their universals.[5] And it is said in the *De Anima* that the faculty by which it is perceived that a thing is a definite particular and exists is another faculty than the faculty by which the quiddity of the definite particular is perceived,[6] and it is in this way that it is said that particulars exist in the external world and universals in the mind.[7] And there is no difference in the meaning of the 'true', whether it concerns material existents or separate existents. The theory that existence is an addition to the quiddity and that the existent in its essence does not subsist by it[8]—and this is the theory of Avicenna—is a most erroneous theory, for this would imply that the term 'existence' signified an accident outside the soul common to the ten categories. And then it can be asked about this accident when it is said to exist, if 'exist' is taken here in the meaning of the 'true' or whether it is meant that an accident exists in this accident, and so on *ad infinitum*, which is absurd, as we have shown

THE FIFTH DISCUSSION

elsewhere.¹ I believe that it is this meaning of 'existence' which Ghazali tried to deny of the First Principle, and indeed in this sense it must be denied of all existents and *a fortiori* of the First Principle, since it is a false theory.

Having mentioned this sense of unity in the statements of the philosophers, Ghazali now proceeds to describe the ways in which they contradict themselves in his opinion, and he says:

Now notwithstanding all this, the philosophers affirm of God that He is the First and a principle, an existent, a substance, a monad, that He is eternal, everlasting, knowledge and knower and known, an agent and a creator, that He is endowed with will and power and life, that He is the lover and the beloved, the enjoyer and the enjoyed, that He is generous, and the absolute good, and they believe that all this is meant by the term 'one', and does not imply any plurality. And this indeed is something very wonderful.

Now we must first state their theory clearly in order to understand it well, and then we shall occupy ourselves with its refutation, for it is an absurd undertaking to refute a theory before it is well understood. Now the central point for the understanding of their doctrine is that they say that the essence of the Principle is one, and the plurality of terms arises only through bringing something in relation to it or through bringing it in relation to something, or through denying something of it; for the negation of something does not cause a plurality in that of which it is denied, nor does the establishment of a relation produce a plurality.² Therefore they do not deny the plurality of the negations and the relations, and it is thus their task to refer all the qualities mentioned to negation and relation.

They say that when God is said to be the First this means a relation to all the existents after Him. When He is said to be a principle, it signifies that the existence of everything else depends on Him and is caused by Him; it means therefore a relation to an effect. And when He is said to exist, it means that He is apprehended,³ and when He is said to be a substance it means that He is the being of which it is denied that it inheres in a substratum and this is a negation.⁴ When He is said to be eternal, it means that His non-existence in the past is denied; and when He is said to be everlasting, it means that His non-existence in the future is denied, and the terms 'eternal' and 'everlasting' are reduced to an existence not preceded nor followed by a non-existence. When He is said to be a necessary existent, it means that there is no cause for His existence and that He is the cause of everything else, and this is a combination of negation and relation: the denial of a cause for His existence is a negation, and making Him the cause of everything else is a relation.

When He is said to be intellect, this means that He is free from matter and everything free from matter is intellect, i.e. thinks its own substance, is self-conscious, and knows everything else, and the essence of God is such:

He is free from matter and therefore—for these two expressions have the same meaning—He is an intellect.[1] When He is said to be knowing, it means that His essence which is intellect has an object of thought, namely His essence, for He is self-conscious and knows His own self, and His essence is the known and the knower for all that is one, since He is the known in so far as He is a quiddity, abstract from matter, not hidden from His essence which is intellect in the sense that it is a quiddity abstract from matter, from which nothing is hidden; and because He thinks His own self, He is knowing, and because He is His own object of thought, He is an object known, and since He thinks through* His own essence, not through something additional to His own essence, He is intellect, and it is not impossible that the knower and the thing known should be one, for the knower, when he knows that he knows, knows it because he is a knower,[2] so that knower and known are in a way the same; although our intellect is in this respect different from the intellect of the First Principle, for the intellect of the First Principle is eternally in act, whereas our intellect is sometimes in potency, sometimes in act.[3] And when He is said to be a creator, an agent and an originator and to have the other attributes of action, it means that His existence is eminent, from which the existence of the universe emanates in a necessary emanation, and that the existence of everything derives from Him and is consequent on His existence in the way that light is consequent on the sun and heat consequent on fire. But the relation of the world to God resembles the relation of light to the sun only in this, that both are effects, and not in any other way, for the sun is not aware of the emanation of light from it, nor fire of the emanation of heat from it; for this is mere nature.[4] But the First is conscious of Himself and is aware that His essence is the principle of everything else, and the emanation of everything which emanates from Him is known to Him, and He is not inattentive to anything that proceeds from Him. Nor can He be compared to one of us who puts himself between a sick man and the sun, for then it is the case that because of him, but not through his choice (although he does it consciously and not unwillingly either), the sick man is protected against the sun's heat, and it is his body which causes the shadow, but it is his soul, not his body, which knows that the shadow is falling and is pleased about it. But this does not apply to the First: in Him the agent is at the same time the knower and the one that is pleased; that is, He is not unwilling, and He is conscious that His perfection consists in the emanation proceeding from Him.[5] Yes, even if it were possible to assume that the man's body causing the shadow were identical with the knower of the shadow, who is pleased with it, even then he would not be similar to the First. For the First is both knower and agent, and His knowledge is the principle of His act; and His consciousness of Himself as the principle of the universe is the cause of the emanation of the universe and the existing order; and the existing order is the consequence of the order thought of, in the sense that it occurs through Him and that

He is the agent of the universe without there being an addition to His knowledge of the universe, since His knowledge of the universe is the cause of the emanation of the universe from Him, and His knowledge of the universe does not add anything to His self-consciousness, for He could not be self-conscious if He did not know that He is the principle of the universe, the object of His knowledge is in first intention His own essence, and the universe is the object of His knowledge in second intention,[1] and this is the meaning of His being an agent. And when it is said that He has power, nothing is meant but that He is an agent in the way we have stated, namely, that His existence is the existence from which the powers emanate through the emanation of which the arrangement of the world is ordered in the most perfect way possible in accomplishment and beauty.[2] And when it is said that He is willing, nothing is meant but that He is not inattentive to what emanates from Him and that He is not opposed to it; no, He knows that in the emanation of the universe His own perfection is attained, and it is permissible to say in this sense that He is satisfied, and it is permissible to say of the satisfied that He is willing; and His will is nothing but His very power and His power is nothing but His very knowledge and His knowledge nothing but His very essence, so that everything is reduced to His very essence. For His knowledge of things is not derived from things, for otherwise He would acquire His quality and perfection through another, and this is impossible in the necessary existent. But our knowledge is twofold: partly knowledge of a thing which results from its form like our knowledge of the form of heaven and earth, partly knowledge of our own invention, when we represent in ourselves the form of a thing we do not see and then produce it; in this case the existence of the form is derived from the knowledge and not the knowledge from the existence.[3] Now the knowledge the First has is of the second category, for the representation of the order in Himself is the cause of the emanation of the order from Him.[4] Indeed, if the mere presence of the form of a picture or of writing in our souls were sufficient for the occurrence of this form, then our knowledge would be identical with our power and our will;[5] but through our deficiency our representation does not suffice to produce the form, but we need besides a new act of will which results from our appetitive faculty, so that through these two the power which moves our muscles and our nerves in our organs can enter into motion, and through the movement of our muscles and nerves our hand or any other member can move, and through its movement the pen or any other external instrument can come into motion and through the movement of the pen the matter, e.g. the ink, can move, and so the form is realized which we represented in our souls. Therefore the very existence of this form in our souls is not a power and an act of will; no, in us power lies in the principle which moves our muscles and this form moves the mover which is the principle of the power.[6] But this is not the case with the necessary existent, for He is not composed of bodies from which the powers in His extremities originate, and so His power, His will, His knowledge, and His essence are all one.

When it is said that He is living,[1] nothing is meant but that He is conscious of the knowledge through which the existent which is called His act emanates from Him. For the living is the doer, the perceiver, and the meaning of the term is His essence in relation to His acts in the way we have described, not at all like our life, which can be only perfected through two different faculties from which perception and action result. But His life again is His very essence.

And when it is said that He is generous, what is meant is that the universe emanates from Him, but not for an end which refers to Himself,[2] for generosity is perfected by two conditions: first that the receiver of the benefit has profit of what is given to him, for* the giving of something to one who is not in need of it is not called generosity; secondly, that the benefactor is not himself in need of generosity, so that he himself becomes a benefactor through a need he experiences himself, and anyone who is generous out of a desire for praise and approbation or to avoid blame seeks a reward and is not generous.[3] But true generosity belongs to God alone, for He does not seek to avoid blame, nor does He desire a perfection acquired through praise, and the term 'generosity' indicates His existence in relation to His act and with the denial of an end, and this does not imply a plurality in His essence.

When He is said to be the absolute good, it means that His existence is free from any imperfection and from any possibility of non-existence, for badness has no essence, but refers to the non-existence of an essence or to the absence of the goodness of the essence.[4] For existence itself, in so far as it is existence, is good, and therefore this term refers* to the negation of the possibility of non-existence and of badness. Sometimes 'good' means that which is the cause of the order in things, and the First is the principle of the order of everything and therefore He is good;[5] and in this case the term signifies existence in a certain kind of relation.

When He is said to be a necessary existent, this existence is meant with the denial of a cause for His existence and the impossibility of a cause for His non-existence, in the beginning and at the end.

When it is said that He is the lover and the beloved,[6] the enjoyer and the enjoyed,[7] it means that He is every beauty and splendour and perfection, and that He is beloved and desired by the possessor of this perfection and the only meaning of 'enjoyment' is the perception of appropriate perfection. If it could be imagined of a single man that he knew his own perfection in comprehending all intelligibles, if he could comprehend them, that he knew the beauty of his own form, the perfection of his power, the strength of his limbs, in short if he perceived in himself the presence of all perfection of which he was capable, he would love his perfection and enjoy it, and his enjoyment would only be incomplete through the possibility of its loss and its diminution, for the joy which refers to the transitory, or to what is feared to be transitory, is not perfect.¹ But the First possesses the most perfect splendour and the most complete beauty, since all perfection is possible to Him and present in Him, and He perceives this beauty, secure against the possibility of its diminution and loss, and the perfection He possesses is superior to all perfection, and His love and His enjoyment of this perfection are superior to all love and to all enjoyment, and His enjoyment cannot be compared in any way to our enjoyment and is too glorious to be called enjoyment, joy, and delight, for we have no expressions for such concepts, and using these terms metaphorically for Him, we must be conscious of the great difference, just as when we apply to Him metaphorically our terms, 'willing', choosing', 'acting', we are convinced of the great distance between His will, power, and knowledge, from our will, power, and knowledge, and it is not impossible that this term 'enjoyment' should be regarded as improper and that another term should be used.² What we want to express is that His state is more glorious than the conditions of the angels, and more desirable, and the condition of the angels is more glorious than our condition; and if there were no other joy than in bodily desire and sex, the condition of the ass and the pig would be superior to the state of the angels, but the angels, who are separate from matter, have no other joy than the joy arising from the knowledge of their share in perfection and beauty, the cessation of which is not to be feared. But the joy of the First is superior to the joy of the angels, and the existence of the angels which are intellects separate from matter is possible in its essence and necessary of existence through another, and the possibility of non-existence is a kind of badness and imperfection, and nothing is absolutely free from badness except the First, and He is the absolute good and He possesses the utmost splendour and beauty; further, He is the beloved, whether anyone else loves Him or not, as He is the knower and the known, whether anyone else knows Him or not. And all these concepts refer to His essence and to His perception and to His knowledge of His essence, and the knowledge of His essence is His very essence, for He is pure intellect, and all this leads back to one single notion.

This is the way to set forth their doctrine, and these things can be divided into that which may be believed (but we shall show that according to their own principles they must regard it as untrue) and into that which may not be believed (and we shall show its falsehood). We shall now return to the five classes of plurality and to their claim to deny them, and shall show their inability to establish their proof, and shall treat each question separately.

I say:

The greater part of what he mentions in his description of the philosophical theories about God as being one, notwithstanding the plurality of attributes ascribed to Him, he has stated accurately, and we shall not argue with him about it, with the exception of his statement that to Him the designation of 'intellect' is a negation;[1] for this is not true—on the contrary it is the most special appellation for His essence according to the Peripatetics, in contrast to Plato's opinion that the intellect is not the First Principle and that intellect cannot be attributed to the First Principle.[2] Nor is his statement that in the separate intellects there is potency, non-existence, and badness a philosophical theory. But we shall now return to his refutations in these five questions.

THE SIXTH DISCUSSION
To refute their denial of attributes

Ghazali says:

The philosophers agree—exactly as do the Mu'tazilites—that it is impossible to ascribe to the First Principle knowledge, power, and will, and they affirm that we have received these terms through the Divine Law, and that they may be used as verbal expressions, but that they refer to one essence as we have explained previously, and that it is not permissible to accept an attribute additional to its essence in the way we may consider, as regards ourselves, our knowledge, power, and will, as attributes of ourselves, additional to our essence. And they affirm that this causes a plurality, because if these attributes are supposed to occur to us in the course of our development, we know that they are additional to our essence, because they constitute new facts*; on the other hand, if they are supposed to be simultaneous with our existence without any time-lag, their simultaneity does not prevent them from being an addition to our essence.[3] For when one thing is added to another and it is known that they are not identical, it is thought, even if they are simultaneous, that they are two. Therefore the fact that these qualities would be simultaneous with the essence of the First does not prevent them from being extraneous to its essence, and this causes a plurality in the necessary existent, and this is impossible; and therefore they all agree in the denial of the attributes.

I say:

The difficulty for the man who denies a plurality of attributes consists in this: that different attributes are reduced to one essence, so that for instance knowledge, will, and power would mean one and the same thing and signify one single essence, and that also knowledge and knower, power and possessing power, will and willer would have one and the same meaning. The difficulty for the man, however, who affirms that there exist both an essence and attributes additional to the essence, consists in this: that the essence becomes a condition for the existence of the attributes and the attributes a condition for the perfection of the essence, and that their combination would be a necessary existent, that is, one single existent in which there is neither cause nor effect. And this latter difficulty cannot be really solved when it is assumed that there exists an essentially necessary existent, for this implies that it must be one in every way and can in no way be composed of the condition and the conditioned and of cause and effect, for such a composition would have to be either necessary or possible; (1) if necessary, it would be necessary through another, not through itself, since it is difficult to assume an eternal compound as existing through itself, i.e. as not having a cause for its composition, and this is especially difficult for the man who believes that every accident is temporal,[1] since the fact of being a compound would be an eternal accident; (2) if possible, a cause would be needed to join together the effect and the cause. Now, according to philosophical principles it is quite impossible that there should be a compound existing by itself, having eternal attributes, since the composition would be a condition of its existence; and its parts could not be agents for the composition, for the composition would have to be a condition for their existence. Therefore, when the parts of any natural compound are disjoined, their original name can be only applied to them equivocally, e.g. the term 'hand', used of the hand which is a part of the living man and the hand which has been cut off; and every compound is for Aristotle transitory and *a fortiori* cannot be without a cause.[2]

But as to the system of Avicenna, with its division of the necessary existent from the possible existent, it does not lead to the denial of an eternal compound; for when we assume that the possible ends in a necessary cause and that the necessary cause must either have a cause or not, and in the former case must end in a necessary existent which has no cause, this reasoning leads through the impossibility of an infinite regress to a necessary existence which has no efficient cause—not, however, to an existent which has no cause at all, for this existent might have a formal or a material cause, unless it is assumed that everything which has matter and form, or in short every compound, must have an external cause; but this needs a proof which the demonstration based on the principle of the necessary existent does not contain, even if we do not consider the mistake in it we have already mentioned. And for exactly the same reason the proof of the Ash'arites that every temporal occurrence needs a cause does not lead to an eternal First Principle which is not composite, but only to a First Principle which is not temporal.

As to the fact that knower and knowledge are one, it is not impossible, but necessary, that such pairs of things lead up to the unity of their concepts; e.g. if the knower knows through knowledge, that through which he becomes a knower is more apt to be a knower, for the quality which any thing acquires from another is in itself more apt to possess the concept which is acquired, e.g. if the living bodies in our sublunary world are not alive by themselves, but through a life which inheres in them, then necessarily this life through which the non-living acquires life is alive by itself, or there would be an infinite regress; and the same is the case with knowledge and the other attributes.[1]

Now, it cannot be denied that one essence can have many attributes related, negative, or imaginary, in different ways without this implying a plurality in the essence, e.g. that a thing is an existent and one and possible or* necessary,[2] for when the one identical entity is viewed in so far as something else proceeds from it, it is called capable and acting, and in so far as it is viewed as differentiating between two opposite acts, it is called willing, and in so far as it is viewed as perceiving its object, knowing, and in so far as it* is viewed as perceiving and as a cause of motion, it is called living, since the living is the perceiving and the self-moving.[3] What is impossible is only a single simple existence with a plurality of attributes, existing by themselves, and especially if these attributes should be essential and exist in act, and as to these attributes existing in potency, it is not impossible, according to the philosophers, that something should be one in act and a plurality in potency, and this is the case according to them, with the parts of the definition in their relation to the thing defined.[4]

And as to Ghazali's words:

And they affirm that this causes a plurality ... that they are two.

he means by them that the fact that these attributes are simultaneous with the essence does not prevent them from being necessarily a plurality by themselves, just as, if their existence were posterior to the essence, or if some of them were posterior to others, mind would not conceive them as being one.

THE SIXTH DISCUSSION

After stating the view of the philosophers, Ghazali says:

But it must be said to the philosophers: How do you know the impossibility of plurality of this kind? for you are in opposition to all the Muslims, the Mu'tazilites excepted, and what is your proof of it? If someone says: 'Plurality is impossible, since the fact that the essence is regarded as one is equivalent to the impossibility of its having a plurality of attributes' this is just the point under discussion, and the impossibility is not self-evident, and a proof is needed. They have indeed two proofs. The first is that they say that, when subject and attribute are not identical, either both, subject and attribute, can exist independently of the other, or each will need the other, or only one of them will depend on the other. In the first case they will both be necessary existents, and this implies an absolute duality and is impossible. In the second case neither of them will be a necessary existent, because the meaning of a necessary existent is that it exists by itself and does not depend in any way on anything else, and when a thing requires something else, that other is its cause, since, if this other were annulled, its existence would be impossible and it would therefore exist not by itself but through another. In the third case the one which was dependent would be an effect and the necessary existent would be the other, on which it would be dependent, and that which was an effect would need a cause, and therefore this would necessarily involve connecting the essence of the necessary existent with a cause.[1]

I say:

When their opponents concede to the philosophers that there is an existent necessary by itself and that the meaning of the necessary existent is that it has no cause at all, neither in its essence through which it subsists, or through something external, they cannot escape the conclusion which the philosophers forced upon them: that if the attributes existed through the essence, the essence would be an existent necessary through itself, and the attributes would be necessary through something different from themselves, and the essence of the necessary existent would exist by itself, but the attributes would be necessary through something different from themselves, and essence and attributes together would form a compound.[2] But the Ash'arites do not concede to the philosophers that the existence of a necessary existent, subsisting by itself, implies that it has no cause whatsoever, for their argument leads only to the denial of an efficient cause additional to the essence.[3]

Ghazali says:

The objection against this is to say: The case to be accepted is the last, but we have shown in the fifth discussion that you have no proof for your denial of the first case, that of absolute duality; what is affirmed by you in the fifth discussion can only be justified by basing it upon your denial of plurality in this and the following discussions: how can you therefore base this discussion upon what* is itself the upshot of this discussion?[1] But the correct solution is to say: 'The essence does not need the attributes for its subsistence, whereas the attributes need a subject, as is the case with us ourselves.' There remains their statement that what is in need of something else is not a necessary existent.

One may ask them: Why do you make such a statement, if you understand by 'necessary existent' only that which has no efficient cause, and why is it impossible to say that, just as there is no agent for the essence of the necessary existent, which is eternal, there is no agent for its attributes, which are equally eternal? If, however, you understand by 'necessary existent' that which has no receptive cause, we answer that that is not implied in this conception of the necessary existent, which, according to this conception is all the same eternal and has no agent; and what is wrong with this conception?

If it is answered that the absolute necessary existent is that which has no efficient cause and no receptive cause,[2] for if a receptive cause for it were conceded, it would be conceded that it was an effect—we say: To call the receptive essence a receptive cause[3] is one of your technical terms, and there is no proof of the real existence of a necessary existent corresponding to your terminology; all that is proved is that there must be a final term to the series of causes and effects, and no more, and this series can end in a unit with eternal attributes which have no more an agent than the essence itself, and are supposed to be in the essence itself. But let us put aside this term 'necessary existent', which is full of possible confusion. The proof indeed only demonstrates the end of the series and nothing more, and your further claims are pure presumption.

If it is said: In the same way as the series of efficient causes must have an end, the series of receptive causes must have an end, since if every existent needed a substratum to inhere in it and this substratum again needed a substratum, this would imply an infinite series, just as this would be the case if every existent needed a cause and this cause again another cause—we answer: You are perfectly right and for this very reason we say that the series has an end and that the attribute exists in its essence and that this essence does not exist in something else, just as our knowledge exists in our essence and our essence is its substratum, but does not exist itself in a substratum. The series of efficient causes comes to an end for the attribute at the same time as for the essence, since the attribute has an agent no more than the essence has, still the essence provided with this attribute does not cease to exist, although neither itself nor its attribute has a cause. As to the receptive causes, its series can only end in the essence, for how could the negation of a cause imply the negation of a substratum?[4] The proof does not demonstrate anything but the termination of the series, and every method by which this termination can be explained is sufficient

THE SIXTH DISCUSSION

to establish the proof which demands the existence of the necessary existent. But if by 'necessary existent' is understood something besides the existent which has no efficient cause and which brings the causal series to an end, we do not by any means concede that this is necessary. And whenever the mind regards it as possible to acknowledge an eternal existent which has no cause for its existence, it regards it as possible to acknowledge an eternal subject for which there is no cause, either for its essence or for its attribute.

As to Ghazali's words:

We have shown in the fifth discussion that you have no proof for your denial of the first case, that of absolute duality; what is affirmed by you in the fifth discussion can only be justified by basing it upon your denial of plurality.

I say:

Ghazali means the philosophers' denial that subject and attribute are both subsistent by themselves, for from this it follows that they are independent of each other and that both are independent gods, which is a dualistic theory, since there is no connexion through which attribute and subject could become a unity. And since the philosophers used as an argument for the denial of this kind of plurality the fact that it has dualism as its consequence,[1] and a demonstration ought to proceed in the opposite sense, namely, that dualism would have to be denied, because of the impossibility of plurality, he says that their proof is circular and that they proved the principle by the conclusion.

Their objection, however, was not based upon the facts themselves, but on the theory of their opponents who deny dualism. And you have learned in another place that there are two kinds of refutation, one based on the objective facts, the other based on the statement of the opponent, and although the former is the true kind of refutation, the second type may also be used.[2]

As to Ghazali's words:

But the correct solution is to say: 'The essence does not need the attributes for its subsistence, whereas the attributes need a subject, as is the case with us ourselves.' There remains their statement that what is in need of another is not a necessary existent.

I say:

Ghazali means that, when this tripartite division which they use to deny plurality is submitted to them, the facts lead them to establish that (1) the necessary existent cannot be a compound of attribute

5 and subject; (2) the essence cannot be a plurality of attributes, for they cannot accept these things according to their principles. Then he starts to show that the impossibility which they strive to deduce from this division is not strict.

As to Ghazali's words:

One may ask them: Why do you make such a statement, if you understand by 'necessary existent' only that which has no efficient cause, and why is it impossible to say that, just as there is no agent for the essence of the necessary existent, which is eternal, there is no agent for its attributes, which are equally eternal?

I say:

All this is an objection to Avicenna's method of denying the attributes by establishing the necessary existent which exists by itself, but in this question the most convincing method of showing the necessity of unity and forcing it as a consequence upon the Ash'arites is the method of the Mu'tazilites. For the latter understand by 'possible existence' the truly possible,[1] and they believe that everything below the First Principle is such. Their opponents, the Ash'arites, accept this, and believe also that every possible has an agent, and that the series comes to an end through what is not possible in itself. The Mu'tazilites concede this to them, but they believe that from this concession it follows that the First, which is the final term of the series of possibility, is not a possible, and that this implies its absolute simplicity. The Ash'arites, however, say that the denial of true possibility does not imply simplicity, but only eternity and the absence of an efficient cause, and therefore there is among the Ash'arites no proof of the simplicity of the First through the proof based on the necessary existent.[2]

And Ghazali says:

If it is answered that the absolute necessary existent is that which has no efficient cause and no receptive cause, for if a receptive cause for it were conceded, it would be conceded that it was an effect.

I say:

Ghazali means that, if the philosophers say that the proof has led to a necessary existent which has no efficient cause, it has, according to them, no receptive cause either, and that according to the philosophers the assumption of essence and attributes implies the assumption of a receptive cause.

Then Ghazali, answering this, says:

THE SIXTH DISCUSSION

We say: To call the receptive essence a receptive cause is one of your technical terms, and there is no proof for the real existence of a necessary existent corresponding to your terminology; all that is proved is that there must be a final term to the series of causes and effects.

I say:

Ghazali means that the Ash'arites do not concede that this essence in which the attributes inhere is a receptive cause,[1] so as to be forced to admit an efficient cause for it. He says that the proof of the philosophers does not lead to an existent which has no receptive cause, let alone proving the existence of what has no essence and no attributes. It only proves that it has no efficient cause. This objection is a necessary consequence of their own proof. Even if the Ash'arites had accepted the philosophical theory that what has no efficient cause has no receptive cause, their own statement would not have been overthrown, for the essence which they assume only receives attributes which do not belong to the First, since they assume that the attributes are additional to the essence of the First, and they do not admit essential attributes in the way the Christians do.[2]

And as to Ghazali's words:

If it is said: In the same way as the series of efficient causes must have an end, the series of receptive causes must have an end, since if every existent needed a substratum to inhere in it and this substratum again needed a substratum, this would imply an infinite series, just as this would be the case if every existent needed a cause and this cause again another cause—we answer: You are perfectly right and for this very reason we say that the series has an end and that the attribute exists in its essence and that this essence does not exist in something else, just as our knowledge exists in our essence and our essence is its substratum, but does not exist itself in a substratum.

I say:

This statement has no connexion with this discussion either with respect to the philosophical theories he mentions or with respect to the answers he gives, and it is a kind of sophism, for there exists no relation between the question, whether the receptive causes must or must not have an end, and the problem which is under discussion, namely whether it is a condition of the First Agent that it should have a receptive cause.[3] For the inquiry about the finiteness of receptive causes differs from the inquiry about the finiteness of efficient causes, since he who admits the existence of receptive causes admits necessarily that their series must end in a primary receptive cause which is necessarily external to the First Agent, just as he admits the existence of a First Agent external to the receptive matter. For if the First Agent possessed matter, this matter would not exist numerically and individually either in the first recipient or in the inferior recipients of other things;[1] no, if the First Agent possessed matter, this matter would have to be a matter peculiar to it, and in short it would belong to it; that is, either it would be its primary matter or we should arrive at a first recipient, and this recipient would not be of the genus which is the condition for the existence of all the other existents proceeding from the First Agent.[2] But if matter were the condition for the existence of the First Agent, it would be a condition for the existence of all agents in their actions, and matter would not only be a condition for the existence of the agent's act—since every agent acts only on a recipient —but it would be a condition for the existence of the agent itself, and therefore every agent would be a body.[3]

All this the Ash'arites neither admit nor deny. But when the philosophers tell them that an essence to which such an attribute is ascribed must be a body, they answer: 'Such an attribute is ascribed by you to the soul and yet, according to you, the soul is not a body.'[4] This is the limit to which dialectical arguments in this question can be carried. But the demonstrations are in the works of the ancients which they wrote about this science, and especially in the books of Aristotle, not in the statements of Avicenna about this problem and of other thinkers belonging to Islam, if anything is to be found in them on this question. For their metaphysical theories are pure presumptions, since they proceed from common, not particular, notions, i.e. notions which are extraneous to the nature of the inquiry.

And as to Ghazali's words:

> The series of efficient causes comes to an end for the attribute at the same time as for the essence, since the attribute has an agent no more than the essence has, still the essence provided with this attribute does not cease to exist, although neither itself nor its attribute has a cause.

I say:

This is a statement which is not accepted by their opponents, the philosophers; on the contrary, they affirm that it is a condition of the First Agent that it should not receive an attribute, because reception indicates matter and it is therefore not possible to assume as the final term of the causal series an agent of any description whatsoever, but only an agent which has absolutely no agent, and to which no attribute—from which it would follow that it had an agent—can be ascribed. For the assumption of the existence of an attribute of the First Agent existing in a receptive cause which would be a condition for its existence is thought by the philosophers to be impossible. Indeed, anything for the existence of which there is a condition can only be connected with this condition through an external cause, for a thing cannot itself be the cause of its connexion with the condition of its existence, just as it cannot be the cause of its own existence. For the conditioned, if it were not connected with its condition, would have to exist by itself, and it needs an efficient cause to connect the condition with it, since a thing cannot be the cause of the existence of the condition of its own existence; but all these are common notions. And in general one cannot imagine that it is possible to arrive by this method, as applied to this problem, at something near evidence, because of the equivocation in the term 'existent necessary by itself', and in the term 'possible by itself, necessary through another', and the other preliminary notions which are added to them.

Ghazali says:

The second proof of the philosophers is that they say that the knowledge and the power in us do not enter the quiddity of our essence, but are accidental, and when these attributes are asserted of the First, they too do not enter the quiddity of its essence, but are accidental in their relation to it, even if they are lasting; for frequently an accident does not separate itself from its quiddity and is a necessary attribute of it, but still it does not therefore become a constituent of its essence. And if it is an accident, it is consequent on the essence and the essence is its cause, and it becomes an effect, and how can it then be a necessary existent?[1]

Then Ghazali says, refuting this:

This proof is identical with the first, notwithstanding the change of expression. For we say: If you mean by its being consequent on the essence, and by the essence's being its cause, that the essence is its efficient cause, and that it is the effect of the essence, this is not true, for this is not valid of our knowledge in relation to our essence, since our essence is not an efficient cause of our knowledge. If you mean that the essence is a substratum and that the attribute does not subsist by itself without being in a substratum, this is conceded, and why should it be impossible? For if you call this 'consequent' or 'accident' or 'effect' or whatever name you want to give it, its meaning does not change, since its meaning is nothing but 'existing in the essence in the way attributes exist in their subjects'. And it is by no means impossible that it should exist in the essence, and be all the same eternal and without an agent. All the proofs of the philosophers amount to nothing but the production of a shock by the use of a depreciating expression: 'possible', 'permissible', 'consequent', 'connected', 'effect'—but all this may be ignored. For it must be answered: If by this you mean that it has an agent, it is not true, and if only it is meant that it has no agent, but that it has a substratum in which it exists, then let this meaning be indicated by any expression you want, and still it will not become impossible.

I say:

This is using many words for one idea. But in this question the difference between the opponents consists in one point, namely: 'Can a thing which has a receptive cause be without an agent or not?' Now it belongs to the principles of the theologians that the connexion of condition and conditioned appertains to the domain of the permissible[1] and that whatever is permissible needs for its realization and actualization an agent which actualizes it and connects the condition with the conditioned, and that* the connexion is a condition for the existence of the conditioned and that it is possible neither that a thing should be the cause of the condition of its existence, nor that the condition should be the efficient cause of the existence of the conditioned, for our essence is not the efficient cause of the existence of the knowledge which exists in it, but our essence is a condition for the existence of the knowledge existing in it. And because of all these principles it is absolutely necessary that there should exist an efficient cause which brings about the connexion of condition and conditioned, and this is the case with every conjunction of a condition and a conditioned. But all these principles are annulled[2] by the philosophical theory that heaven is eternal, although it possesses essence and attributes, for the philosophers do not give it an agent of the kind which exists in the empirical world, as would be the consequence of these principles; they only assume that there is a proof which leads to an eternal connexion through an eternal connecting principle, and this is another kind of connexion, differing from that which exists in transitory things.[3] But all these are problems which need a serious examination. And the assumption of the philosophers[4] that these attributes do not constitute the essence is not true, for every essence is perfected by attributes through which it becomes more complete and illustrious, and, indeed, it is constituted by these attributes, since through knowledge, power, and will we become superior to those existents which do not possess knowledge, and the essence in which these attributes exist is common to us and to inorganic things. How therefore could such attributes be accidents consequent on our essence? All these are statements of people who have not studied well the psychological and accidental attributes.

THE SIXTH DISCUSSION

Ghazali says:

And often they shock by the use of a depreciating expression in another way, and they say: This leads to ascribing to the First a need for these attributes, so that it would not be self-sufficient absolutely, since the absolutely self-sufficient is not in need of anything else.[1]

Then Ghazali says, refuting this:

This is an extremely weak verbal* argument, for the attributes of perfection do not differ from the essence of the perfect being in such a way that he should be in need of anything else. And if he is eternally perfect through knowledge, power, and life, how could he be in need of anything, or how could his being attached to perfection be described as his being in need? It would be like saying that the perfect needs no perfection and that he who is in need of the attributes of perfection for his essence is imperfect; the answer is that perfection cannot mean anything but the existence of perfection in his essence, and likewise being self-sufficient does not mean anything but the existence of attributes that exclude every need in his essence. How therefore can the attributes of perfection through which divinity is perfected be denied through such purely verbal arguments?

I say:

There are two kinds of perfection: perfection through a thing's own self and perfection through attributes which give their subject its perfection, and these attributes must be in themselves perfect, for if they were perfect through perfect attributes, we should have to ask whether these attributes were perfect through themselves or through attributes, and we should have therefore to arrive at that which is perfect by itself as a final term. Now the perfect through another will necessarily need, according to the above principles if they are accepted, a bestower of the attributes of perfection; otherwise it would be imperfect. But that which is perfect by itself is like that which is existent by itself, and how true it is that the existent by itself is perfect by itself![2] If therefore there exists an existent by itself, it must be perfect by itself and self-sufficient by itself; otherwise it would be composed of an imperfect essence and attributes perfecting this essence. If this is true, the attribute and its subject are one and the same, and the acts which are ascribed to this subject as proceeding necessarily from different attributes exist only in a relative way.

Ghazali says, answering the philosophers:

And if it is said by the philosophers: When you admit an essence and an attribute and the inherence of an attribute in the essence, you admit a composition, and every compound needs a principle which composes it, and just because a body is composed, God cannot be a body—we answer:

Saying that every compound needs a composing principle is like saying that every existent needs a cause for its existence, and it may be answered: The First is eternal and exists without a cause and without a principle for its existence, and so it may be said that it is a subject, eternal, without a cause for its essence, for its attribute and for the existence of its attribute in its essence; indeed all this is eternal without a cause. But the First cannot be a body, because body is a temporal thing which cannot be free from what is temporal[1]: however, he who does not allow that body has a beginning must be forced to admit that the first cause can be a body, and we shall try later to force this consequence on the philosophers.

I say:

Composition is not like existence, because composition is like being set in motion*, namely, a passive quality, additional to the essence of things which receive the composition,[2] but existence is a quality which is the essence itself, and whoever says otherwise is mistaken indeed. Further, the compound cannot be divided into that which is compound by itself and that which is compound through another, so that one would finally come to an eternal compound in the way one arrives, where existents are concerned, at an eternal existent, and we have treated this problem in another place.[3] And again: If it is true, as we have said, that composition is something additional to existence, then one may say, if there exists a compound by itself, then there must exist also something moved by itself, and if there exists something moved by itself, then also a privation will come into existence by itself, for the existence of a privation is the actualization of a potency,[4] and the same applies to motion and the thing moved. But this is not the case with existence, for existence is not an attribute additional to the essence, and every existent which does not exist sometimes in potency and sometimes in act is an existent by itself, whereas the existence of a thing as moved occurs only when there is a moving power, and every moved thing therefore needs a mover.[5]

The distinctive point in this problem is that the two parts* in any compound must be either (1) mutually a condition for each other's existence, as is, according to the Peripatetics, the case with those which are composed of matters and forms,[6] or (2) neither of them a condition for the existence of the other, or (3) exclusively one the condition for the other.

In the first case the compound cannot be eternal, because the compound itself is a condition for the existence of the parts and the parts cannot be the cause of the compound, nor the compound its own cause, for otherwise a thing might be its own cause, and this kind of compound, therefore, is transitory and needs an agent for its actualization.[1]

In the second case—and for these compounds it is not in the nature of either of their parts that it implies the other—there is no composition possible without a composing factor, external to the parts, since the composition is not of their own nature so that their essence might exist through their nature or be a consequence of their nature; and if their nature determined the composition and they were both in themselves eternal, their composition would be eternal, but would need a cause which would give it unity, since no eternal thing can possess unity accidentally.

In the third case, and this is the case of the non-essential attribute and its subject, if the subject were eternal and were such as never to be without this attribute, the compound would be eternal. But if this were so, and if an eternal compound were admitted, the Ash'arite proof that all accidents are temporal would not be true, since if there were an eternal compound there would be eternal accidents, one of which would be the composition, whereas the principle on which the Ash'arites base their proof of the temporality of accidents is the fact that the parts of which a body, according to them, is composed must exist first separately; if, therefore, they allowed an eternal compound, it would be possible that there should be a composition not preceded by a separation, and a movement, not preceded by a rest, and if this were permissible, it would be possible that a body possessing eternal accidents should exist, and it would no longer be true for them that what cannot exist without the temporal is temporal. And further, it has already been said that every compound is only one because of a oneness existing in it, and this oneness exists only in it through something which is one through itself. And if this is so, then the one, in so far as it is one, precedes every compound, and the act of this one agent—if this agent is eternal—through which it gives all single existents which exist through it their oneness, is everlasting and without a beginning, not intermittent; for the agent whose act is attached to its object at the time of its actualization is temporal and its object is necessarily temporal, but the attachment of the First Agent to its object is everlasting and its power is everlastingly mixed with its object. And it is in this way that one must understand the relation of the First, God, praise be to Him, to all existents. But since it is not possible to prove these things here, let us turn away from them, since our sole aim was to show that this book of Ghazali does not contain any proofs, but mostly sophisms and at best dialectical arguments. But proofs are very rare, and they stand in relation to other arguments as unalloyed gold to the other minerals and the pure pearl to the other jewels.[1] And now let us revert to our subject.

Ghazali says:

All their proofs where this problem is concerned are imaginary. Further, they are not able to reduce all the qualities which they admit to the essence itself, for they assert, that it is knowing, and so they are forced to admit that this is something additional to its mere existence, and then one can ask them: 'Do you concede that the First knows something besides its essence?' Some of them concede this, whereas others affirm that it only knows its own self. The former position is that taken by Avicenna, for he affirms that the First knows all things in a universal timeless way, but that it does not know individuals, because to comprehend their continual becoming would imply a change in the essence of the knower.[2] But, we ask, is the knowledge which the First has of all the infinite number of species and genera identical with its self-knowledge or not? If you answer in the negative, you have affirmed a plurality and have contradicted your own principle; if you answer in the affirmative, you are like a man claiming that man's knowledge of other things is identical with his self-knowledge and with his own essence, and such a statement is mere stupidity.

And it may be argued: 'The definition of an identical thing is that its negation and affirmation cannot be imagined at the same time, and the knowledge of an identical thing, when it is an identical thing, cannot at the same time be imagined as existing and not existing. And since it is not impossible to imagine a man's self-knowledge without imagining his knowledge of something else, it may be said that his knowledge of something else is different from his self-knowledge, since, if they were the same, the affirmation or negation of the one would imply the affirmation or negation of the other. For it is impossible that Zaid should be at one and the same time both existing and not existing, but the existence of self-knowledge simultaneously with the non-existence of the knowledge of something else is not impossible, nor is this impossible with the self-knowledge of the First and its knowledge of something else, for the existence of the one can be imagined without the other and they are therefore two things, whereas the existence of its essence without the existence of its essence cannot be imagined, and if the knowledge of all things formed a unity, it would be impossible to imagine this duality. Therefore* all those philosophers who acknowledge that the First knows something besides its own essence have undoubtedly at the same time acknowledged a plurality.

I say:

The summary of this objection to the proposition that the First knows both itself and something else is that knowing one's self is different from knowing something else. But Ghazali falls here into confusion. For this can be understood in two ways: first, that Zaid's knowledge of his own individuality is identical with his knowledge of other things, and this is not true; secondly, that man's knowledge of other things, namely of existents, is identical with the knowledge of his own essence, and this is true.[1] And the proof is that his essence is nothing but his knowledge of the existents.[2] For if man like all other beings knows only the quiddity which characterizes him, and if his quiddity is the knowledge of things, then man's self-knowledge is necessarily the knowledge of all other things, for if they were different his essence would be different from his knowledge of things. This is clear in the case of the artisan, for his essence, through which he is called an artisan, is nothing but his knowledge of the products of art.[3] And as to Ghazali's words, that if his self-knowledge were identical with his knowledge of other things, then the negation of the one would be the negation of the other and the affirmation of the one the affirmation of the other, he means that if the self-consciousness of man were identical with his knowledge of other things, he could not know his own self without knowing the other things; that is, if he were ignorant of other things, he would not know his own self, and this proposition is in part true, in part false. For the quiddity of man is knowledge, and knowledge is the thing known in one respect and is something different in another. And if he is ignorant of a certain object of knowledge, he is ignorant of a part of his essence, and if he is ignorant of all knowables, he is ignorant of his essence; and to deny man this knowledge is absolutely the same as to deny man's self-consciousness, for if the thing known is denied to the knower in so far as the thing known and knowledge are one, man's self-consciousness itself is denied. But in so far as the thing known is not knowledge, it is not man, and to deny man this knowledge does not imply the denial of man's self-consciousness. And the same applies to individual men. For Zaid's knowledge of Amr is not Zaid himself, and therefore Zaid can know his own self, while being ignorant of Amr.

Ghazali says:

If it is said: 'The First does not know other things in first intention. No, it knows its own essence as the principle of the universe, and from this its knowledge of the universe follows in second intention,[4] since it cannot know its essence except as a principle, for this is the true sense of its essence, and it cannot know its essence as a principle for other things, without the other things entering into its knowledge by way of implication and consequence;

it is not impossible that from its essence consequences should follow, and this does not imply a plurality in its essence, and only a plurality in its essence is impossible'—there are different ways of answering this. First your assertion that it knows its essence to be a principle is a presumption; it suffices that it knows the existence of its essence, and the knowledge that it is a principle is an addition to its knowledge of its essence, since being a principle is a relation to the essence and it is possible that it should know its essence and not this relation, and if this being-a-principle were not a relation, its essence would be manifold and it would have existence and be a principle, and this forms a duality. And just as a man can know his essence without knowing that he is an effect, for his being an effect is a relation to his cause, so the fact that the First is a cause is a relation between itself and its object. This consequence is implied in the mere statement of the philosophers that it knows that it is a principle, since this comprises the knowledge of its essence and of its being a principle, and this is a relation, and the relation is not the essence, and the knowledge of the relation is not the knowledge of the essence and we have already given the proof of this, namely that we can imagine knowledge of the essence, without the knowledge of its being a principle, but knowledge of the essence without the knowledge of the essence cannot be imagined, since the essence is an identical unity.

I say:

The proposition which the philosophers defend against Ghazali in this question is based on philosophical principles which must be discussed first. For if the principles they have assumed and the deductions to which, according to them, their demonstration leads, are conceded, none of the consequences which Ghazali holds against them follows. The philosophers hold, namely, that the incorporeal existent is in its essence nothing but knowledge, for they believe that the forms[1] have no knowledge for the sole reason that they are in matter; but if a thing does not exist in matter, it is known to be knowing, and this is known because they found that when forms which are in matter are abstracted in the soul from matter they become knowledge and intellect, for intellect is nothing but the forms abstracted from matter,[2] and if this is true for things which by the principle of their nature are not abstracted, then it is still more appropriate for things which by the principle of their nature are abstracted to be knowledge and intellect. And since what is intelligible in things is their innermost reality, and since intellect is nothing but the perception of the intelligibles, our own intellect is the intelligible by itself, in so far as it is an intelligible, and so there is no difference between the intellect and the intelligible, except in so far

THE SIXTH DISCUSSION

as the intelligibles are intelligibles of things in the nature of which there is no intellect and which only become intellect because the intellect abstracts their forms from their matters, and through this our intellect is not the intelligible in every respect. But if there is a thing which does not exist in matter, then to conceive it by intellect is identical with its intelligible in every respect, and this is the case with the intellectual conception of the intelligibles. And no doubt* the intellect is nothing but the perception of the order and arrangement of existing things, but it is necessary for the separate intellect that it should not depend on the existing things in its intellectual conception of the existing things and of their order, and that its intelligible should not be posterior to them, for every other intellect is such that it follows the order which exists in the existents and perfects itself through it, and necessarily falls short in its intellectual conception of the things, and our intellect, therefore, cannot adequately fulfil the demands of the natures of existing things in respect of their order and arrangement. But if the natures of existing things follow the law of the intellect and our intellect is inadequate to perceive the natures of existent things, there must necessarily exist a knowledge of the arrangement and order which is the cause of the arrangement, order and wisdom which exist in every single being, and it is necessary that this intellect should be the harmony which is the cause of the harmony which exists in the existents, and that it should be impossible to ascribe to its perception knowledge of universals, let alone knowledge of individuals,[1] because universals are intelligibles which are consequent on and posterior to existents,[2] whereas on the contrary the existents are consequent on this intellect. And this intellect necessarily conceives existents by conceiving the harmony and order which exist in the existents through its essence, not by conceiving anything outside its essence, for in that case it would be the effect, not the cause, of the existent it conceives, and it would be inadequate.

And if you have understood this philosophical theory, you will have understood that the knowledge of things through a universal knowledge is inadequate, for it knows them in potency,[3] and that the separate intellect only conceives its own essence, and that by conceiving its own essence it conceives all existents, since its intellect is nothing but the harmony and order which exist in all beings, and this order and harmony is received by the active powers which possess order and harmony and exist in all beings and are called natures by the philosophers.[4] For it seems that in every being there are acts which follow the arrangement and order of the intellect, and this cannot happen by accident, nor can it happen through an intellect which resembles our intellect; no, this can only occur through an intellect more exalted than all beings, and this intellect is neither a universal nor an individual. And if you have understood this philosophical theory, all the difficulties which Ghazali raises here against the philosophers are solved; but if you assume that yonder intellect resembles our own, the difficulties mentioned follow. For the intellect which is in us is numerable and possesses plurality, but this is not the case with yonder intellect, for it is free from the plurality which belongs to our intelligibles and one cannot imagine a difference in it between the perceiver and the perceived, whereas to the intellect which is in us the perception of a thing is different from the perception that it is a principle of a thing, and likewise its perception of another is different in a certain way from the perception of itself. Still, our intellect has a resemblance to yonder intellect, and it is yonder intellect which gives our intellect this resemblance, for the intelligibles which are in yonder intellect are free from the imperfections which are in our intellect: for instance, our intellect only becomes the intelligible in so far as it is an intelligible, because there exists an intellect which is the intelligible in every respect. The reason for this is that everything which possesses an imperfect attribute possesses this attribute necessarily through a being which possesses it in a perfect way. For instance, that which possesses an insufficient warmth possesses this through a thing which possesses a perfect warmth, and likewise that which possesses an insufficient life or an imperfect intellect possesses this through a thing which possesses a perfect life or a perfect intellect.[1] And in the same way a thing which possesses a perfect rational act receives this act from a perfect intellect, and if the acts of all beings, although they do not possess intellects, are perfect rational acts, then there exists an intellect through which the acts of all beings become rational acts.

It is weak thinkers who, not having understood this, ask whether the First Principle thinks its own essence or if it thinks something outside its essence. But to assume that it thinks something outside its essence would imply that it is perfected by another thing, and to assume that it does not think something outside its essence would imply that it is ignorant of existents. One can only wonder at these people who remove from the attributes which are common to the Creator and the created, all the imperfections which they possess in

THE SIXTH DISCUSSION

the created, and who still make our intellect like His intellect, whereas nothing is more truly free from all imperfection than His intellect. This suffices for the present chapter, but now let us relate the other arguments of Ghazali in this chapter and call attention to the mistakes in them.

Ghazali says:

The second way to answer this assertion is to say that their expression that everything is known to it in second intention is without sense, for as soon as its knowledge comprehends a thing different from itself, in the way it comprehends its own essence, this First Principle will have two different objects of knowledge and it will know them both, for the plurality and the difference of the object known imply a plurality in the knowledge, since each of the two objects known receives in the imagination the discrimination which distinguishes it from the other. And therefore the knowledge of the one cannot be identical with the knowledge of the other, for in that case it would be impossible to suppose the existence of the one without the other, and indeed there could not be an other at all, since they would both form an identical whole, and using for it the expression 'second intention' does not make any difference. Further, I should be pleased to know how he who says that not even the weight of an atom, either in heaven or earth, escapes God's knowledge,[1] intends to deny the plurality, unless by saying that God knows the universe in a universal way. However, the universals which form the objects of His knowledge would be infinite,[2] and still His knowledge which is attached to them would remain one in every respect, notwithstanding their plurality and their differentiation.

I say:

The summary of this is found in two questions. The first is, 'How can its knowledge of its own self be identical with its knowledge of another?' The answer to this has already been given, namely that there is something analogous in the human mind which has led us to believe in the necessity of its being in the First Intellect.

The second question is whether its knowledge is multiplied through the plurality of its objects known and whether it comprehends all finite and infinite knowables in a way which makes it possible that its knowledge should comprehend the infinite. The answer to this question is that it is not impossible that there should exist in the First Knowledge, notwithstanding its unity, a distinction between the objects known, and it is not impossible, according to the philosophers, that it should know a thing, different from itself, and its own essence, through a knowledge which differs in such a way that there should exist a plurality of knowledge. The only thing which is absolutely impossible according to them is that the First Intellect should be perfected through the intelligible and caused by it, and if the First Intellect thought things different from itself in the way we do, it would be an effect of the existent known, not its cause, and it has been definitely proved that it is the cause of the existent. The plurality which the philosophers deny does not consist in its knowing through its own essence, but in its knowing through a knowledge which is additional to its essence; the denial, however, of this plurality in God does not imply the denial of a plurality of things known, except through dialectics, and Ghazali's transference of the problem of the plurality which is in the knowledge, according to the philosophers, to the problem of plurality which is in the things known themselves, is an act of sophistry, because it supposes that the philosophers deny the plurality which is in the knowledge through the things known, in the way they deny the plurality which arises through the duality of substratum and inherent.

But the truth in this question is that there is not a plurality of things known in the Eternal Knowledge like their numerical plurality in human knowledge. For the numerical plurality of things known in human knowledge arises from two sources: first the representations, and this resembles spatial plurality;[1] secondly the plurality of what is known in our intellect, namely the plurality which occurs in the first genus—which we may call being[2]—through its division into all the species which are subsumed under it, for our intellect is one[3] with respect to the universal genus which comprises all species existing in the world, whereas it becomes manifold through the plurality of the species. And it is clear that when we withhold the idea of the universal from the Eternal Knowledge, this plurality is in fact abandoned and there only remains in the Divine a plurality the perception of which is denied to our intellect, for otherwise our knowledge would be identical with this eternal knowledge, and this is impossible. And therefore what the philosophers say is true, that for the human understanding there is a limit, where it comes to a stand, and beyond which it cannot trespass, and this is our inability to understand the nature of this knowledge. And again, our intellect is knowledge of the existents in potency, not knowledge in act, and knowledge in potency is less perfect than knowledge in act; and the more our knowledge is universal, the more it comes under the heading of potential knowledge and the more its knowledge becomes imperfect.[4] But it is not true of the Eternal Knowledge that it is imperfect in any way, and in it there is no knowledge in potency, for knowledge in potency is knowledge in matter. Therefore the philosophers believe that the First Knowledge requires that there should be a knowledge in act and that there should be in the divine world no universal at all and no plurality which arises out of potency, like the plurality of the species which results from the genus. And for this reason alone we are unable to perceive the actually infinite, that the things known to us are separated from each other, and if there exists a knowledge in which the things known are unified, then with respect to it the finite and the infinite are equivalent.

The philosophers assert that there are definite proofs for all these statements, and if we understand by 'plurality in knowledge' only this plurality and this plurality is denied of the Divine, then the knowledge of God is a unity in act, but the nature of this unity and the representation of its reality are impossible for the human understanding, for if man could perceive the unity, his intellect would be identical with the intellect of the Creator, and this is impossible. And since knowledge of the individual is for us knowledge in act, we know that God's knowledge is more like knowledge of the individual than knowledge of the universal, although it is neither the one nor the other. And he who has understood this understands the Divine Words: 'Nor shall there escape from it the weight of an atom, either in the heavens or in the earth', and other similar verses which refer to this idea.

Ghazali says:

Avicenna, however, has put himself in opposition to all the other philosophers who, in order not to commit themselves to the consequence of plurality, took the view that the First only knows itself; how, then, can he share with them the denial of plurality? Still he distinguished himself from them by admitting its knowledge of other things, since he was ashamed to say that God is absolutely ignorant of this world and the next and knows only His own self—whereas all others know Him, and know also their own selves and other things, and are therefore superior to Him in knowledge—and he abandoned that blasphemous philosophical theory, refusing to accept it. Still he was not ashamed of persisting in the denial of this plurality in every respect, and he affirmed that God's knowledge of Himself and of other things, yes, of the totality of things, is identical with His essence without this implying any contradiction, and this is the very contradiction which the other philosophers were ashamed to accept, because of its obviousness. And thus no party among the philosophers could rid itself of a blasphemous doctrine, and it is in this manner that God acts towards the man who strays from His path and who believes that he has the power through his speculation and imagination to fathom the innermost nature of the Divine.

I say:

The answer to all this is clear from what we have said already, namely that the philosophers only deny that the First Principle knows other things than its own self in so far as these other things are of an inferior existence, so that the effect should not become a cause, nor the superior existence the inferior; for knowledge is identical with the thing known. They do not, however, deny it, in so far as it knows these other things by a knowledge, superior in being to the knowledge by which we know other things; on the contrary, it is necessary that it should know them in this way, because it is in this way that the other things proceed from the First Agent. As to the inquiry about the possibility of a plurality of things known in the Eternal Knowledge, that is a second question, and we have mentioned it, and it is not because of this that the philosophers sought refuge in the theory that the First knows only its own self, as Ghazali wrongly supposes; no, only because in short—as we have declared already—its knowledge should not be like our knowledge which differs from it in the extreme. And Avicenna wanted only to combine these two statements, that it knows only its own essence and that it knows other things by a knowledge superior to man's knowledge of them, since this knowledge constitutes its essence, and this is clear from Avicenna's words that it knows its own self and other things besides itself, and indeed all things which constitute its essence, although Avicenna does not explain this, as we have done. And, therefore, these words of his are not a real contradiction, nor are the other philosophers ashamed of them; no, this is a statement about which, explicitly or implicitly, they all agree. And if you have grasped this well, you will have understood Ghazali's bad faith in his attack on the philosophers, although he agrees with them in the greater part of their opinions.

Ghazali says, on behalf of the philosophers:

It may be said that if it is asserted that the First knows its own self as a principle by way of relation, the knowledge of two correlatives is one and the same, for the man who knows the son knows him through one single knowledge in which the knowledge of the father, of fatherhood, and sonhood are comprised, so that the objects of knowledge are manifold, but the knowledge is one.[1] And in the same way the First knows its essence as a principle for the other things besides itself and so the knowledge is one, although what is known is manifold. Further, if the First thinks this relation in reference to one single effect and its own relation towards it, and this does not imply a plurality, then a plurality is not implied by an addition of things which generically do not imply a plurality.[1] And likewise he who knows a thing and knows his knowing this thing, knows this thing through this knowledge, and therefore all knowledge is self-knowledge connected with the knowledge of the thing known,[2] and the known is manifold, but knowledge forms a unity.[3] An indication of this is also that you theologians believe that the things known to God are infinite, but His knowledge is one, and you do not attribute to God an infinite number of cognitions; if, indeed, the manifoldness of the known implied a plurality in the knowledge itself, well, let there then be an infinite number of cognitions in the essence of God. But this is absurd.

Then Ghazali says, answering the philosophers:

We say: Whenever knowledge is one in every respect, it cannot be imagined that it should be attached to two things known; on the contrary, this determines a certain plurality, according to the assumption and tenet of the philosophers themselves about the meaning of 'plurality', so that they even make the excessive claim that if the First had a quiddity to which existence were attributed, this would imply a plurality. And they do not think that to a single unity possessing reality existence also can be attributed; no, they assert that the existence is brought in relation to the reality and differs from it and determines a plurality, and on this assumption it is not possible that knowledge should attach itself to two objects of knowledge without this implying a greater and more important kind of plurality than that which is intended in the assumption of an existence, brought in relation to a quiddity. And as to the knowledge of a son and similarly of other relative concepts, there is in it a plurality, since there must necessarily be knowledge of the son himself and the father himself, and this is a dual knowledge, and there must be a third knowledge, and this is the relation; indeed, this third knowledge is implied in the dual knowledge which precedes it, as they are its necessary condition, for as long as the terms of relation are not known previously, the relation itself cannot be known, and there is thus a plurality of knowledge of which one part is conditioned through another. Likewise when the First knows itself as related to the other genera and species by being their principle, it needs the knowledge of its own essence and of the single genera and it must further know that there exists between itself and those genera and species the relation of being a principle, for otherwise the existence of this relation could not be supposed to be known to it. And as to their statement that he who knows something knows that he is knowing through this knowledge itself, so that the thing known can be manifold, but the knowledge remains one, this is not true; on the contrary, he knows that he knows through another knowledge, and this ends in a knowledge to which he does not pay attention and of which he is no longer conscious, and we do not say that there is an infinite regress, but there is a final term of knowledge attached to the thing known, and he is unconscious of the existence of the knowledge, but not of the existence of the known, like a man who knows the colour black and whose soul at the moment of his knowing it is plunged in the object of his knowledge, the colour black, and who is unconscious of his knowing this colour black and whose attention is not centred on it, for if it were, he would need another knowledge till his attention came to a stand.[1] And as to the affirmation of the philosophers that this can be turned against the theologians concerning the things known by God, for they are infinite, whereas God's knowledge according to the theologians is one, we answer, 'We have not plunged ourselves into this book to set right, but to destroy and to refute, and for this reason we have called this book "The Incoherence of the Philosophers", not "The Establishment of the Truth", and this argument against us is not conclusive.'

And if the philosophers say: 'We do not draw this conclusion against you theologians in so far as you hold the doctrine of a definite sect, but in so far as this problem is applied to the totality of mankind, and the difficulty for all human understanding is the same, and you have no right to claim it against us in particular, for it can be turned against you also, and there is no way out of it for any party'—we answer: 'No, but our aim is to make you desist from your claim to possess knowledge of the essential realities through strict proofs, and to make you doubt. And when your impotence becomes evident, we say that there are men who hold that the divine realities cannot be attained through rational inquiry, for it is not in human power to apprehend them and it was for this reason that Muhammed, the Lord of the Law, said "Ponder over God's creation, but do not ponder over God's essence".[2] Why then do you oppose this group of men who believe in the truth of the prophet through the proof of his miracles,[3] who confine the judgement of the intellect to a belief in God, the Sender of the Prophets, who guard themselves against any rational speculation about the attributes, who follow the Lord of the Law in his revelations about God's attributes, who accept his authority for the use of the terms "the knowing", "the willer", "the powerful", "the living", who refuse to acknowledge those meanings which are forbidden and who recognize our impotence to reach the Divine Intellect? You only refute these men in so far as they are ignorant of the methods of demonstration and of the arrangement of premisses according to the figures of the syllogisms, and you claim that you know these things by rational methods; but now your impotence, the breakdown of your methods, the shamelessness of your claim to knowledge, have come to light, and this is the intention of our criticism. And where is the man who would dare to claim that theological proofs have the strictness of geometrical proofs?'[4]

I say:

THE SIXTH DISCUSSION

All this prolix talk has only a rhetorical and dialectical value. And the arguments which he gives in favour of the philosophers about the doctrine of the unity of God's knowledge are two, the conclusion of which is that in our concepts there are conditions which do not through their plurality bring plurality into the concepts themselves, just as there appear in the existents conditions which do not bring plurality into their essences, for instance that a thing should be one and exist and be necessary or possible. And all this, if it is true, is a proof of a unique knowledge comprising a multitude, indeed an infinite number, of sciences.

The first argument which he uses in this section refers to those mental processes which occur to the concept in the soul and which resemble the conditions in the existents with respect to the relations and negations[1] which exist in them; for it appears from the nature of the relation which occurs in the concepts that it is a condition through which no plurality arises in the concepts,[2] and it is now argued that the relation which presents itself in the related things belongs to this class of conditions. Ghazali objects to this that the relation and the terms of the relation form a plurality of knowledge, and that for instance our knowledge of fatherhood is different from our knowledge of the father and the son. Now the truth is that the relation is an attribute additional to the terms of the relation outside the soul in the existents, but as to the relation which exists in the concepts, it is better suited to be a condition than an attribute additional to the terms of the relation;[3] however, all this is a comparison of man's knowledge with the Eternal Knowledge, and this is the very cause of the mistake. Everyone who concerns himself with doubt about the Eternal Knowledge and tries to solve it by what occurs in human knowledge does indeed transfer the knowledge from the empirical to the Divine concerning two existents which differ in an extreme degree, not existents which participate in their species or genus, but which are totally unlike.

The second proof is that we know a thing through a single knowledge and that we know that we know by a knowledge which is a condition in the first knowledge, not an attribute additional to it, and the proof of this is that otherwise there would arise an infinite series.[4] Now Ghazali's answer, that this knowledge is a second knowledge and that there is no infinite series here, is devoid of sense, for it is self-evident that this implies such a series, and it does not follow from the fact that when a man knows a thing but is not conscious that he knows the fact that he knows, that in the case when he knows that he knows, this second knowledge is an additional knowledge to the first; no, the second knowledge is one of the conditions of the first knowledge and its infinite regress is therefore not impossible; if, however, it were a knowledge existing by itself and additional to the first knowledge, an infinite series could not occur.[1]

As to the conclusion which the philosophers force upon the theologians, that all the theologians recognize that God's knowledge is infinite and that at the same time it is one, this is an *argumentum ad hominem*, not an objective argument based on the facts themselves. And from this there is no escape for the theologians, unless they assume that the knowledge of the Creator differs in this respect from the knowledge of the creature, and indeed there is no one more ignorant than the man who believes that the knowledge of God differs only quantitatively from the knowledge of the creature, that is that He only possesses more knowledge. All these are dialectical arguments, but one may be convinced of the fact that God's knowledge is one and that it is not an effect of the things known; no, it is their cause,[2] and a thing that has numerous causes is indeed manifold itself, whereas a thing that has numerous effects need not be manifold in the way that the effects form a plurality. And there is no doubt that the plurality which exists in the knowledge of the creature must be denied of God's knowledge, just as any change through the change of the objects known must be denied of Him, and the theologians assume this by one of their fundamental principles.[3] But the arguments which have been given here are all dialectical arguments.

And as to his statement that his aim here is not to reach knowledge of the truth but only to refute the theories of the philosophers and to reveal the inanity of their claims, this is not worthy of him—but rather of very bad men. And how could it be otherwise? For the greater part of the subtlety this man acquired—and he surpassed ordinary people through the subtlety he put in the books he composed—he only acquired from the books of the philosophers and from their teaching. And even supposing they erred in something, he ought not to have denied their merit in speculative thought and in those ideas through which they trained our understanding. Nay more, if they had only invented logic, he and anyone else who understands the importance of this science ought to thank them for it, and he himself was conscious of the value of logic and urged its study and wrote treatises about it,[4] and he says that there is no other way to learn the truth than through this science, and he had even such an exaggerated view of logic that he extracted it from the book of God, the holy Koran.¹ And is it allowed to one who is indebted to their books and to their teaching to such an extent that he excelled his contemporaries and that his fame in Islam became immense, is it really allowed to such a man to speak in this way of them, and to censure them so openly, so absolutely, and condemn their sciences? And suppose they erred in certain theological questions, we can only argue against their mistakes by the rules they have taught us in the logical sciences, and we are convinced that they will not blame us when we show them a mistake which might be found in their opinions. And indeed their aim was only the acquisition of truth, and if their only merit consisted in this, it would suffice for their praise, although nobody has said anything about theological problems that can be absolutely relied upon and nobody is guaranteed against mistakes but those whom God protects in a divine, superhuman way, namely the prophets, and I do not know what led this man to this attack against such statements; may God protect me against failings in word and in deed and forgive me if I fail!

And what he says of the belief held by those who follow the Divine Law in these things is in agreement with what is said by the renowned philosophers, for when it is said that God's knowledge and attributes cannot be described by, or compared to, the attributes of the creature, so that it cannot even be asserted that they are essence or an addition to the essence, this expresses the thought of genuine philosophers and other true thinkers, and God is the Saviour, the Leader.

Ghazali says:

It may be said, 'This difficulty applies only to Avicenna in so far as he says that the First knows other things, but the acknowledged philosophers are in agreement that it does not know anything besides itself, and this difficulty is therefore set aside.'

But we answer, 'What a terrible blasphemy is this doctrine! Verily, had it not had this extreme weakness, later philosophers would not have scorned it, but we shall draw attention to its reprehensible character, for this theory rates God's effects higher than Himself, since angel and man and every rational being knows himself and his principle and knows also of other beings, but the First knows only its own self and is therefore inferior to individual men, not to speak of the angels; indeed, the animals besides their awareness of themselves know other things, and without doubt knowledge is something noble and the lack of it is an imperfection. And what becomes of their statement that God, because He is the most perfect splendour and the utmost beauty, is the lover and the beloved? But what beauty can there be in mere existence which has no quiddity, no essence, which observes neither what occurs in the world nor what is a consequence or proceeds from its own essence? And what deficiency in God's whole world could be greater? And an intelligent man may well marvel at a group of men who according to their statement speculate deeply about the intelligibles, but whose inquiry culminates in a Lord of Lords and Cause of causes who does not possess any knowledge about anything that happens in the world. What difference is there then between Him and the dead, except that He has self-consciousness? And what perfection is there in His self-knowledge, if He is ignorant of everything else? And the blasphemy of this doctrine releases us from the use of many words and explanations.

Further, there may be said to them: 'Although you plunge yourselves in these shameful doctrines, you cannot free yourselves from plurality, for we ask: "Is the knowledge He has of His essence identical with His essence or not?" If you say, "No", you introduce plurality, and if you say they are identical, what then is the difference between you and a man who said that a man's knowledge of his essence was identical with his essence, which is pure foolishness? For the existence of this man's essence can be conceived, while he gives no attention to his essence,[1] whereas when afterwards his attention returns, he becomes aware of his essence. Therefore his awareness of his essence differs from his essence.'

If it is argued: 'Certainly a man can be without knowledge of his essence, but when this knowledge occurs to him, he becomes a different being', we answer: 'Non-identity cannot be understood through an accident and conjunction, for the identical thing cannot through an accident become another thing[2] and that other thing, conjoined with this, does not become identical with it, but keeps its individual otherness.[3] And the fact that God is eternally self-conscious does not prove that His knowledge of His essence is identical with His essence, for His essence can be imagined separately and the occurrence of His awareness afterwards, and if they were identical this could not be imagined.'[4]

And if it be said: 'His essence is intellect and knowledge, and He has not an essence in which afterwards knowledge exists', we answer: 'The foolishness of this is evident, for knowledge is an attribute and an accident which demands a subject, and to say, "He is in His essence intellect and knowledge" is like saying, "He is power and will, and power and will exist by themselves", and this again is like saying of black and white, quantity, fourness and threeness and all other accidents that they exist by themselves. And in exactly the same way as it is impossible that the attributes of bodies should exist by themselves without a body which itself is different from the attributes, it is known to be impossible that attributes like the knowledge, life, power, and will of living beings should exist by themselves, for they exist only in an essence. For life exists in an essence which receives life through it, and the same is the case with the other attributes. And therefore they do not simply content themselves

THE SIXTH DISCUSSION

with denying to the First all qualities (and not merely its real essence and quiddity); no, they deny to it also its very existence by itself[1] and reduce it to the entities of accidents and attributes which have no existence by themselves; and besides we shall show later in a special chapter their incapacity to prove that it is conscious either of itself or of other things.'

I say:

The problem concerning the knowledge of the Creator of Himself and of other things is one of those questions which it is forbidden to discuss in a dialectical way, let alone put them down in a book, for the understanding of the masses does not suffice to understand such subtleties, and when one embarks on such problems with them the meaning of divinity becomes void for them and therefore it is forbidden to them to occupy themselves with this knowledge, since it suffices for their blessedness to understand what is within their grasp. The Holy Law, the first intention of which is the instruction of the masses,[2] does not confine itself to the explanation of these things in the Creator by making them understood through their existence in human beings, for instance by the Divine Words: 'Why dost thou worship what can neither hear nor see nor avail thee aught?',[3] but enforces the real understanding of these entities in the Creator by comparing them even to the human limbs, for instance in the Divine Words: 'Or have they not seen that we have created for them of what our hands have made for them, cattle and they are owners thereof?'[4] and the Divine Words, 'I have created with my two hands'.[5] This problem indeed is reserved for the men versed in profound knowledge to whom God has permitted the sight of the true realities, and therefore it must not be mentioned in any books except those that are composed according to a strictly rational pattern, that is, such books as must be read in a rational order and after the acquisition of other sciences the study of which according to a demonstrative method is too difficult for most men, even for those who possess by nature a sound understanding, although such men are very scarce. But to discuss these questions with the masses is like bringing poisons to the bodies of many animals, for which they are real poisons. Poisons, however, are relative, and what is poison for one animal is nourishment for another. The same applies to ideas in relation to men; that is, there are ideas which are poison for one type of men, but which are nourishment for another type. And the man who regards all ideas as fit for all types of men is like one who gives all things as nourishment for all people; the man, however, who forbids free inquiry to the mature is like one who regards all nourishment as poison for everyone. But this is not correct, for there are things which are poison for one type of man and nourishment for another type.¹ And the man who brings poison to him for whom it is really poison merits punishment, although it may be nourishment for another, and similarly the man who forbids poison to a man for whom it is really nourishment so that this man may die without it, he too must be punished. And it is in this way that the question must be understood. But when the wicked and ignorant transgress and bring poison to the man for whom it is really poison, as if it were nourishment, then there is need of a physician² who through his science will exert himself to heal that man, and for this reason we have allowed ourselves to discuss this problem in such a book as this, and in any other case we should not regard this as permissible to us; on the contrary, it would be one of the greatest crimes, or a deed of the greatest wickedness on earth, and the punishment of the wicked is a fact well known in the Holy Law. And since it is impossible to avoid the discussion of this problem, let us treat it in such a way as is possible in this place for those who do not possess the preparation and mental training needed before entering upon speculation about it.

So we say that the philosophers, when they observed all perceptible things, found that they fell into two classes, the one a class perceptible by the senses, namely the individual bodies existing by themselves and the individual accidents in these bodies, and the other a class perceptible by the mind, namely, the quiddities and natures of these substances and accidents. And they found that in these bodies there are quiddities which exist essentially in them, and I understand by the 'quiddities' of bodies attributes existing in them, through which these bodies become existent in act and specified by the act which proceeds from them;³ and according to the philosophers these quiddities differ from the accidental attributes, because they found that the accidents were additions to the individual substance which exists by itself and that these accidents were in need of the substances for their existence*, whereas the substances do not need the accidents for their own existence. And they found also that those attributes which were not accidents were not additional to the essence, but that they were the genuine essence of the individual which exists by itself, so that if one imagined these attributes annulled, the essence itself would be annulled. Now, they discovered these qualities in individual bodies through the acts which characterize each of them; for instance they perceived the attributes through which plants by their particular action become plants[1] and the attributes through which animals by their particular actions become animals,[2] and in the same way they found in the minerals forms of this kind which are proper to them, through the particular actions of minerals.[3] Then, when they had investigated these attributes, they learned that they were in a substratum of this essence and this substratum became differentiated for them, because of the changing of the individual existents from one species into another species and from one genus into another genus through the change and alteration of these attributes;[4] for instance the change of the nature of fire into air by the cessation of the attribute from which the actuality of fire, through which fire is called fire, proceeds, and its change into the attribute from which the actuality peculiar to air, through which air is called air, proceeds. They also proved the existence of this substratum through the capacity of the individual essence to receive an actuality from another, just as they proved by the actuality the existence of form, for it could not be imagined that action and passivity proceed from one and the same nature.[5] They believed therefore that all active and passive bodies are composed of two natures, one active and the other passive, and they called the active nature form, quiddity, and substance, and the passive part subject, ultimate basis of existence[6] and matter. And from this it became clear to them that the perceptible bodies are not simple bodies as they appear to be to the senses, nor compounded of simple bodies, since they are compounded of action and passivity; and they found that what the senses perceive are these individual bodies, which are compounded of these two things which they called form and matter and that what the mind perceives of these bodies are these forms which only become concepts and intellect when the intellect abstracts them from the things existing by themselves, i.e. what the philosophers call substratum and matter.[7] And they found that the accidents also are divided in the intellect in a way similar to those two natures,[8] although their substratum in which they exist in reality is the bodies compounded of these two natures. And when they had distinguished the intelligibles from the sensibles and it had become clear to them that in sensible things there are two natures, potency and act, they inquired which of these two natures was prior to the other and found that the act was prior to the potency, because the agent was prior to its object,[1] and they investigated also causes and effects, which led them to a primary cause which by its act is the first cause of all causes, and it followed that this cause is pure act and that in it there is no potency at all, since if there were potency in it, it would be in part an effect, in part a cause, and could not be a primary cause. And since in everything composed of attribute and subject there is potency and act, it was a necessary implication for them that the First could not be composed of attribute and subject, and since everything free from matter was according to them intellect, it was necessary for them that the First should be intellect.

This in summary is the method of the philosophers, and if you are one of those whose mind is sufficiently trained to receive the sciences, and you are steadfast and have leisure, it is your duty* to look into the books and the sciences of the philosophers, so that you may discover in their works certain truths (or perhaps the reverse); but if you lack one of these three qualities, it is your duty* to keep yourself to the words of the Divine Law, and you should not look for these new conceptions in Islam; for if you do so, you will be neither a rationalist nor a traditionalist.[2]

Such was the philosophers' reason for their belief that the essence which they found to be the principle of the world was simple and that it was knowledge and intellect. And finding that the order which reigns in the world and its parts proceeds from a knowledge prior to it, they judged that this intellect and this knowledge was the principle of the world, which gave the world existence and made it intelligible. This is a theory very remote from the primitive ideas of mankind and from common notions, so that it is not permitted to divulge it to the masses or even to many people; indeed, the man who has proved its evidence is forbidden to reveal it to the man who has no power to discover its truth, for he would be like his murderer. And as to the term 'substance' which the philosophers give to that which is separate from matter, the First has the highest claim on the term 'substance', the terms 'existent', 'knowing', 'living',[3] and all the terms for the qualities it bestows on the existents and especially those attributes which belong to perfection, for the philosophers found that the proper definition of substance was what existed by itself and the First was the cause of everything that existed by itself.

To all the other reproofs which he levels against this doctrine no attention need be paid, except in front of the masses and the ordinary man, to whom, however, this discussion is forbidden.

THE SIXTH DISCUSSION

And as to Ghazali's words:

What beauty can there be in mere existence which has no quiddity, no essence, which observes neither what occurs in the world nor what is a consequence or proceeds from its own essence? . . .

—this whole statement is worthless, for if the philosophers assume a quiddity free from a substratum it is also void of attributes, and it cannot be a substratum for attributes except by being itself in a substratum and being composed of the nature of potency and the nature of act. The First possesses a quiddity that exists absolutely, and all other existents receive their quiddity only from it, and this First Principle is the existent which knows existents absolutely, because existents become existent and intelligible only through the knowledge this principle has of itself; for since this First Principle is the cause of the existence and intelligibility of existents, of their existence through its quiddity and of their intelligibility through its knowledge, it is the cause of the existence and intelligibility of their quiddities. The philosophers only denied that its knowledge of existents could take place in the same way as human knowledge which is their effect, whereas for God's knowledge the reverse is the case. For they had established this superhuman knowledge by proof. According to the Ash'arites, however, God possesses neither quiddity nor essence at all but* the existence of an entity neither possessing nor being a quiddity cannot be understood,[1] although some Ash'arites believed that God has a special quiddity by which He differs from all other existents,[2] and according to the Sufis it is this quiddity which is meant by the highest name of God.[3]

And as to Ghazali's words:

Further, there may be said to them: 'Although you plunge yourself in these shameful doctrines, you cannot free yourselves from plurality, for we ask: "Is the knowledge He has of His essence identical with His essence or not?" If you say, "No", you introduce plurality, and if you say, "they are identical", what then is the difference between you and a man who said that a man's knowledge of his essence was identical with his essence?'

I say:

This is an extremely weak statement, and a man who speaks like this deserves best to be put to shame and dishonoured. For the consequence he draws amounts to saying that the perfect one, who is free from the attributes of becoming and change and imperfection, might have the attribute of a being possessing imperfection and change. For a man indeed it is necessary, in so far as he is composed of a substratum and knowledge, which exists in this substratum, that his knowledge should differ from his essence in such a way as has been described before, since the substratum is the cause of change in the knowledge and the essence. And since man is man and the most noble of all sentient beings only through the intellect which is conjoined to his essence, but not by being essentially intellect, it is necessary that that which is intellect by its essence should be the most noble of all existents and that it should be free from the imperfections which exist in the human intellect.[1]

And as to Ghazali's words:

And if it be said: His essence is intellect and knowledge and He has not an essence in which afterwards knowledge exists, we answer: 'The foolishness of this is evident, for knowledge is an attribute and an accident which demands a subject, and to say "He is in His essence intellect and knowledge" is like saying "He is power and will, and power and will exist by themselves", and this again is like saying of black and white, fourness and threeness, and all other accidents that they exist by themselves.'

I say:

The error and confusion in his statement is very evident, for it has been proved that there is among attributes one that has a greater claim to the term 'substantiality' than the substance existing by itself, and this is the attribute through which the substance existing by itself becomes existing by itself. For it has been proved that the substratum for this attribute is something neither existing by itself nor existing in actuality; no, its existing by itself and its actual existence derive from this attribute, and this attribute in its existence is like that which receives the accidents, although certain of these attributes, as is evident from their nature, need a substratum in the changeable things, since it is the fundamental law of the accidents, that they exist in something else, whereas the fundamental law of the quiddities is that they exist by themselves, except when, in the sublunary world, these quiddities need a substratum through being in transitory things. But this attribute is at the greatest distance from the nature of an accident, and to compare this transcendent knowledge to sublunary accidents is extremely foolish, indeed more foolish than to consider the soul an accident like threeness and fourness.

And this suffices to show the incoherence and the foolishness of this whole argument, and let us rather call this book simply 'The Incoherence', not 'The Incoherence of the Philosophers'. And what is further from the nature of an accident than the nature of knowledge, and especially the knowledge of the First? And since it is at the greatest distance from the nature of an accident, it is at the greatest distance from having a necessity for a substratum.

THE SEVENTH DISCUSSION

To refute their claim that nothing can share with the First its genus, and be differentiated from it through a specific difference, and that with respect to its intellect the division into genus and specific difference cannot be applied to it[1]

Ghazali says:

Indeed, they are all of this opinion, and they deduce from this that, since nothing can share its genus, it cannot be differentiated through a specific difference and cannot have a definition, since a definition is constructed out of genus and specific difference and what has no composition cannot have a definition, for a definition is a kind of composition.[2] And they affirm that, since the First is said to resemble the first effect in being an existent and a substance and a cause for other things, and to differ from it in other respects, this certainly does not imply sharing in its genus; no, it is nothing but a sharing in a common necessary attribute. The difference between genus and necessary attribute consists in their content, not in universality, according to logical theory, for the genus, namely, the essential universal, is the answer to the question what the thing is, and is subsumed under the quiddity of the thing defined, and constitutes its essence: a man's being alive is subsumed under the quiddity of man, i.e. his animality, and is his genus, but his being born and created are his necessary attributes, and, although they are universals which can never be separated from him, are not subsumed under his quiddity, according to logical theory, about which there can be no misgiving.[3] And the philosophers affirm that existence is never subsumed under the quiddity of things, but stands in a relation to the quiddity, either necessarily and inseparably, like its relation to heaven, or subsequently, after their non-existence, like its relation to temporary things, and that the sharing of existence does not imply a sharing in genus.[4] And as to its sharing in 'being a cause to other things' with all the other causes, this is a necessary relation which likewise cannot be subsumed under the quiddity,[5] for neither the fact of being a principle nor existence constitutes the essence, but they are necessary attributes of the essence, consequent upon the constitution of the essence out of the parts of its quiddity, and this community is only the sharing of a necessary common attribute consecutive to the essence, not a community of genus. Things therefore are only defined by their constituents, and if they are defined by the necessary attributes this is only a description[1] to differentiate them, not to define their essential forms; for the triangle is not defined by the fact that its angles are equal to two right angles, although this is a necessary and common attribute of all triangles, but it is defined as a figure bounded by three sides. And the same applies to its being a substance, and the meaning of its being a substance is that it is an existent which does not exist in a substratum.[2] And the existent is not a genus, since, as it is related to a negation, namely not being in a substratum, it cannot become a constituent genus; indeed, even if it could be brought into a relation to something positive and it could be said that it existed in a substratum, it could not become a genus in the accident.[3] And the reason is that the man who knows substance by its definition, which is rather its description, namely that it is an existent which does not exist in a substratum, does not know whether it exists, and *a fortiori* does not know whether it exists in a substratum or not; no, the meaning of the description of substance is that it is the existent which does not exist in a substratum, i.e. that it is a certain reality which, when it does exist, does not exist in a substratum, but we do not mean that it actually exists at the time of the definition,[4] and its community is not the community of the genus, for only the constituents of the quiddity form the community of the genus which needs also a specific difference.[5] But the First has no other quiddity, except necessary existence, and necessary existence is its real nature and its own quiddity*, exclusively confined to it, and since necessary existence is exclusively confined to the First, it cannot be shared by others, it cannot have a specific difference, and it cannot have a definition.[6]

I say:

Here ends what Ghazali says of the philosophical views about this question, and it is partly true, partly false. As to his statement that no other thing can share with the First its genus and be distinguished from it through a specific difference, if he means by this the genus and the difference that are predicated univocally, it is true, for anything of this description is composed of a common form and a specific form, and such things possess a definition. But if by 'genus' is meant what is predicated analogically, I mean *per prius et posterius*,[7] then it can have a genus, e.g. existent, or thing, or identity, or essence, and it can have a kind of definition, and this kind of definition is used in the sciences—for instance, when it is said of the soul that it is the entelechy of the natural organic body,[8] and when it is said of the substance that it is the existent which does not exist in a substratum —but these definitions do not suffice for knowledge of the thing, and they are only given to indicate through it the different individuals

THE SEVENTH DISCUSSION

which fall under such definitions and to represent their peculiarities. But as to his statement that according to the philosophers the term 'existence' only indicates a necessary attribute of the essences of things, this is not true, and we have already explained this in another place and none of the philosophers has said this but Avicenna. Having denied that existence is a genus, predicted either univocally or equivocally, Avicenna affirmed that it was a term which signified a common necessary attribute of things. But the difficulty he found in regarding existence as an essence can be held up against him when it is regarded as a necessary attribute, for if it were a necessary attribute, this necessary attribute could not be given as an answer to the question what a thing is.[1] And further, if 'existence' really signifies a necessary attribute in things, does it signify this necessary attribute univocally, or equivocally, or in some other mode of attribution? And if it has a univocal meaning, how can there be an accident univocally predicated of things essentially different (I believe that Avicenna regarded this as possible)?[2] It is, however, impossible, because from different things the congruous and identical can only derive, when these different things agree in one nature, since necessarily a single necessary attribute must come from one nature, just as a single act* can proceed only from one nature. And since this is impossible, the term 'existence' indicates essences which have analogical meanings, essences some of which are more perfect than others; and therefore there exists in the things which have such an existence a principle which is the cause of that which exists in all the other things of this genus, just as our term 'warm' is a term which is predicated *per prius et posterius* of fire and all other warm things, and that of which it is asserted first, i.e. fire, is the cause of the existence of warmth in all other things, and the same is the case with substance, intellect, and principle and such terms (most metaphysical terms are of this kind), and such terms can indicate both substances and accidents.

And what he says of the description of substance is devoid of sense, but existence is the genus of substance and is included in its definition in the way the genera of the sublunary things are included in their definitions, and Farabi proved this in his book about demonstration, and this is the commonest view amongst philosophers.[3] Avicenna erred in this only because, since he thought that the 'existent' means the 'true' in the Arabic language, and that what indicates the true indicates an accident[4]—the true, however, really indicates* one of the second predicates, i.e. a predicable[1]—he believed that when the translator used the word 'existent' it meant only the 'true'. This, however, is not so, for the translators meant only to indicate what is also meant by 'entity' and 'thing'. Farabi explains this in his *Book of the Letters*[2] and he shows that one of the reasons for the occurrence of this mistake is that the term 'existent' in Arabic is a derivative in form and that a derivative signifies an accident, and in fact an accident is linguistically a derivative.[3] But since the translators did not find in Arabic a term which signified that concept which the ancient philosophers subdivided into substance and accident, potency and act, a term namely which should be a primitive symbol,[4] some translators signified that concept by the term 'existent', not to be understood as having a derivative meaning and signifying therefore an accident, but as having the same meaning as 'essence'. It is thus a technical term, not an idiomatic word. Some translators, because of the difficulty attached to it, decided to use for the concept, which the Greek language tried to express by deriving it from the pronoun which joins the predicate and the subject, the term which expresses this, because they thought that this word comes nearer to expressing this meaning, and they used instead of the term 'existent' the term 'haeceitas', but the fact that its grammatical form is not found in Arabic hindered its use, and the other party therefore preferred the term 'existent'.[5] And the term 'existent' which signifies the true does not signify the quiddity, and therefore one may often know the quiddity without knowing the existence,[6] and this meaning of 'existent' of necessity does not signify the quiddity in the compound substance, but is in the simple substance identical with the quiddity;[7] and this meaning is not what the translators intended by 'existence', for they meant the quiddity itself, and when we say of the existent that it is in part substance, in part accident, the sense meant by the translators must be understood, and this is the sense which is predicated analogically of different essences of things. When we say, however, that substance exists, it must be understood in the sense of the true. And therefore* if we have understood the well-known discussion of the ancient philosophers, whether the existent is one or more than one, which is found in the first book of Aristotle's *Physics* where he conducts a discussion with the ancient philosophers Parmenides and Melissus,[8] we need only understand by 'existent' that which signifies the essence. And if the 'existent' meant an accident in a substratum, then the statement that the existent was one would be self-contradictory.[1] And all this is clear for the man who is well grounded in the books of the philosophers.

And having stated the views of the philosophers, Ghazali begins to refute them, and says:

This is the sense of the doctrine of the philosophers. And the discussion with them consists of two parts: a question and a refutation. The question is: This is the simple narration of your doctrine, but how do you know the impossibility of this with respect to God, so as to build on it the refutation of dualism, since you say that a second God would have to participate in something and differ from the first in something, and that which partly possesses something in common with another, partly is different from it, is compound, whereas that He should be compound is absurd?

I say:

I have already said that this is only valid for something which possesses a common feature through a genus which is predicated univocally, not analogically. For if, by the assumption of a second God, a God were assumed of the same rank of divinity as the first, then the name of God would be predicated univocally, and He would be a genus, and the two Gods would have to be separated by a specific distinction and both would be compounded of a genus and a specific distinction, and the philosophers do not allow a genus to an eternal being;[2] but if the term 'existence' is predicated *per prius et posterius*, the prior will be the cause of the posterior.

Ghazali says, refuting the philosophers:

But we say: How do you know the impossibility of this kind of composition? For there is no proof except your denial of the attributes, which has been mentioned, namely that the compound of genus and species is an aggregate of parts; thus if it is possible for one or for a collection of the parts to exist without the others, this single one will be the necessary existent and the others will not be necessary; and if it is possible neither for the parts to exist without the totality, nor for the totality to exist without the parts, then the whole is an effect needing something else as its cause. We have already discussed this in the case of the attributes, and have shown that their plurality is not impossible, since an end of the causal series is admitted and all that is proved is that there is an end of the causal series. For those enormous difficulties which the philosophers have invented concerning the inherence of attributes in the necessary existent there is no proof whatever. If the necessary existent is what the philosophers describe it to be, namely to possess no plurality and not to need anything else for its existence, then there is no proof of the existence of this necessary existent; the only thing proved is that there is an end of the causal series, and we have exhausted this subject in our discussion of attributes. And for this kind of plurality it is still more obvious, for the division of a thing into genus and specific difference is not like the division of the subject into essence and attribute, since, indeed, the attribute is not the essence and the essence is not the attribute, but the species is not in every way different from the genus, for whenever we mention the species, we mention the genus with an addition, and when we speak of a man we only mention animal with the addition of reason.[1] And to ask whether humanity can be free from animality is like asking whether humanity can be without itself, when something is added to it. And indeed genus and species are more distant from plurality than attribute and subject.[2] And why should it be impossible that the causal series should end in two causes, one the cause of the heavens and the other the cause of the elements, or one the cause of the intellects and the other the cause of all bodies, and that there should be between those two causes a conceptual difference and separation as between redness and warmth when they exist in one and the same place? For they differ in content without our being obliged to assume in the redness a compound of genus and specific difference through which this difference is established; indeed, if it possesses a plurality, this kind of plurality does not impair the singleness of its essence, and why should this be impossible with respect to the causes? Through this there is shown the weakness of their refutation of the existence of two Gods.

I say:

Composition out of genus and specific difference is exactly the same as the composition of a thing in potency and a thing in act, for the nature which is indicated by the genus does not actually exist at any time without the presence of the nature which is called specific difference and form.[3] And everything which is composed of these two natures is, according to the philosophers, transitory, and possesses an agent, for the specific difference is one of the conditions for the existence of the genus in so far as the genus is in potency and does not exist without the specific difference. And the conjunction of either with its partner is in a certain way a condition for the existence of the other. And as a thing cannot itself be a cause of the condition of its existence, it necessarily possesses a cause which provides it with existence by conjoining the condition and the conditioned. Also, according to the philosophers the recipient is in reality something which possesses only potency, and if it is actually, then only accidentally; and what is received is actuality, and if it is potency, then only accidentally; for the recipient and the thing it receives are only distinguished by the fact that one of them is potentially something else, whereas actually it is the thing received[4] and whatever is potentially another thing must necessarily receive this other thing and lose the thing it actually is.¹ Therefore, if there should exist a recipient in actuality and a thing received in actuality, both would exist by themselves, but the recipient is necessarily body, for only body, or what is in a body, possesses receptivity primarily, and receptivity cannot be attributed to accidents and forms,² nor to the plane, the line, and the point,³ nor in general to what cannot be divided. As regards an incorporeal agent, this has been already proved,⁴ and as to an incorporeal recipient, or a recipient not embedded in matter, such a recipient is impossible, although there is a problem for the philosophers about the potential intellect.⁵ And indeed, if the compound has a subject and an attribute* which is not additional to its essence,⁶ it is transitory and necessarily a body, and if it has a subject and an attribute additional to its essence, without its having any potency in its substance even in respect of this attribute, as is the case according to the ancients with the body of the heavens,⁷ it possesses quantity of necessity and is a body. For, if from such an essence, supporting the attribute, bodiliness were taken away, it would no longer be a perceptible recipient, and equally the sensory perception of its attribute would be annulled and its attribute and subject would both become intellect, and they would be reduced to one single simple entity, for from the nature of the intellect and the intelligible it is evident that they are both one and the same thing, since plurality exists in them accidentally, namely through the substratum.⁸ And in short, when the philosophers assume an essence and attributes additional to the essence, this amounts to their assuming an eternal body with accidents inherent in it, and they do not doubt that* if they took away the quantity which is corporeity, the perceptible element in it would be annulled, and neither substratum nor inherent would exist any more; but if, on the other hand, they regarded the substratum and the inherent as abstracted from matter and body, the substratum and inherent would of necessity be both intellect and intelligible; but this is the Unique, the Uncompounded, God, the Truth.

As to his statement that the whole mistake of the philosophers consists in their calling the First the 'necessary existent', and that if instead they called it 'the causeless'', the conclusion which they draw about the First, concerning the necessary attributes of the necessary existent, would not follow—this statement is not true. For since they assume an existent which has no cause, it follows necessarily that it is in itself a necessary existent, just as, when a necessary existent existing by itself is assumed, it follows necessarily that it has no cause, and if it has no cause it is more appropriate that it should not be divided into two things, cause and effect. The assumption of the theologians that the First is composed of an attribute and a subject implies that it has an efficient cause,[1] and that therefore it is neither a first cause nor a necessary existent, and this is in contradiction to their assumption that it is one of those existents of which the attribute and the subject are reduced to one single simple entity; but there is no sense in repeating this and expatiating on it.

And as to his statement that it is not impossible of God, the First, that He should be composed of a substratum and an attribute additional to the substratum, and that therefore *a fortiori* it is not impossible that He should be composed of a substratum and an attribute which is identical with its substratum, we have already explained the way in which this is not impossible, namely when both are abstract from matter.

And as to his statement that their refutation of dualism does not prevent the possibility of the existence of two Gods, one of whom would be, for instance, the cause of heaven and the other the cause of the earth, or one the cause of the intelligible and the other the cause of the sensible in the bodies, and that their differentiation and distinction need not determine a contradiction, as there is no contradiction in redness and warmth which exist in one place—this statement is not true. For if the production and creation of the existent is assumed to be the effect of one nature and of one essence, not of two different natures, it would necessarily follow that if a second thing of this nature were assumed, similar in nature and intellect to the first, they would share in one attribute and differ in another. And their difference would come about either through the kind of differentiation which exists between individuals or through the kind of differentiation which exists between species. In the latter case the term 'God' would be predicated of them equivocally, and this is in contradiction with their assumption, for the species which participate in the genus are either contraries or stand between contraries, and this is wholly impossible.[2] And if they were individually differentiated, they would both be in matter, and this is in opposition to what is agreed about them. But if it is assumed that one of these natures is superior to the other and that this nature is predicated of them *per prius et posterius*, then the first nature will be superior to the second and the second will be necessarily its effect, so that for instance the creator of heaven will be the creator of the cause which creates the elements; and this is the theory of the philosophers. And both theories lead to the acceptance of a first cause; that of those who believe that the First acts through the mediation of many causes, and that of those who believe that the First is directly the cause of all other things without mediation. But according to the philosophers this latter theory cannot be true. For it is evident that the worlds exist through cause and effect, and it is inquiry concerning these causes which leads us to a first cause for everything. And if some of these different principles were wholly independent of others—that is, if some were not the cause of others—then the world could not be a single well-connected whole, and to the impossibility of this the Divine Words refer, 'Were there in both heaven and earth Gods beside God, both surely would have been corrupted'.¹

Ghazali says:

It may be said: This is impossible so far as the difference which exists between these two essences is either a condition for their necessary existence (and in that case it will exist in both the necessary existents, and then they will not differ anyhow), or neither the one nor the other specific difference is a condition (and since the necessary existence is able to exist without the things that are not a condition for it, the necessary existence will be perfected by something else).²

But we reply: This is exactly the same answer as you gave concerning the attributes and we have already discussed it,³ and the source of confusion throughout this problem is the expression 'necessary existent'; let us therefore get rid of this term; and indeed, we do not accept that demonstration proves a necessary existent, if anything else is meant by it but an eternal existent which has no cause, and if this is meant by it, let us abandon the term 'necessary existent' and let it be proved that an existent which has no cause and no agents cannot have a plurality and a distinctive mark, but indeed there is no proof of it. There remains therefore your question whether this specific difference is a condition of the causeless character of this causeless existent, and this is nonsense. For we have shown that there is no cause for its being without a cause, so as to make it possible to ask for its condition. It would be like asking whether blackness is a condition for the colour's becoming a colour, and if it is a condition, why redness is then a colour. And the answer is: as to the essential nature of colour, i.e. in so far as the essence of colouredness is asserted in the intellect, neither of them is a condition,⁴ and as to its existence, each of them is a condition for its existence, but not individually, since* a genus cannot exist in reality without a specific difference.⁵ And likewise the man who accepts two causes as starting-points of the series must say that they are differentiated through a specific difference, and both differences are a condition for their existence, no doubt, though not through their individuality.

I say:

The summary of what he says here of the proof of the philosophers is that they say that the specific difference through which the duality in the necessary existent occurs is either a condition or not a condition for necessary existence. If the specific difference through which they are distinguished is a condition for both the necessary existents, they will no longer be separated in their necessary existence and the necessary existent will be of necessity one and the same, just as, if black were to be a condition for the necessity of colour and white a condition for colouredness, they could not differ in colouredness. If, on the other hand, the specific difference does not enter into the essence of necessary existence, then both these necessary existents will have necessary existence only by accident, and their duality will not be based on their both being necessary existents. This, however, is not true, for the species are a condition for the existence of the genus, and both colours are a condition for the existence of the genus, though not individually (for in this case they could not exist together in the existence of the colour).[1]

Ghazali opposes this statement with two arguments. The first is that this can only happen in so far as 'necessary existent' means a special nature; according to the theologians, however, this is not the case, for they understand by 'necessary existent' only something negative, namely something which has no cause, and since negative things are not caused, how can, for the denial of the causeless, an argument like the following be used: 'That which distinguishes one causeless entity from another causeless entity is either a condition of its being causeless or not; if it is a condition, there cannot be any plurality or differentiation; and if it is not a condition, it cannot occasion a plurality in the causeless, which therefore will be one.' However, the erroneous part in Ghazali's reasoning is that he regards the causeless as a mere negation, and, as a negation has no cause, he asks how it could possess a condition which is the cause of its existence. But this is a fallacy, for particular negations, which are like infinite terms and which are used for distinguishing between existents,[2] have causes and conditions which determine this negation in them, just as they have causes and conditions which determine their positive qualities; and in this sense there is no difference between positive and negative attributes, and the necessity of the necessary existent is a necessary attribute of the causeless and there is no difference between saying 'the necessary existent' or 'the causeless'.

And the nonsense comes from those who talk like Ghazali, not from his opponents.

And the summary of Ghazali's second objection is that to say, as the philosophers do, that the specific difference through which the necessary existent is distinguished is either a condition or not, that in the former case the one necessary existent cannot be distinguished from the other in so far as they are necessarily existent and that therefore the necessary existent is one, and that in the latter case the necessary existent has no specific difference through which it can be divided: that to speak like this is like saying that if there exist more colours than one of the genus colour, the difference through which one colour is distinguished from another is either a condition for the existence of colour or not; that in the former case the one cannot be distinguished from the other in so far as they are colour, and colour is therefore one single nature; that in the latter case, if neither of them is a condition for the existence of colouredness, one colour has no specific difference through which it can be distinguished from another, and this is not true.[1]

Ghazali says, answering this problem on behalf of the philosophers:

It may be said perhaps: This is possible in the case of colour, for it has an existence related to the quiddity and additional to the quiddity, but it is not possible for the necessary existent, for it possesses only necessary existence, and there is therefore no quiddity to which its existence might be related, and just as the specific differences of black and red are not conditions for colouredness being colouredness, but only a condition for the actual realization of colour through a cause,[2] in the same way the specific difference cannot be a condition for necessary existence, for necessary existence is in relation to the First what colouredness is in relation to the colour, and not like the existence brought in relation to colouredness.[3]

But we reply, we do not accept this; on the contrary, the necessary existent has a real essence to which existence is attributed, as we shall show in the next discussion, and their statement that the First is an existence without quiddity is incomprehensible. The trend of their argument is, in short, that they base their denial of dualism on the denial that the First is composed of the generic and the specific, then they base the denial of this on their denial that there is a quiddity behind the existence. Therefore as soon as we have refuted this last proposition, which is their fundamental principle, their whole structure (which is a very shaky fabrication, just like a spider's web) tumbles down.

I say:

Ghazali builds the answer he gives here in the name of the philosophers on their statement that existence is an accident in the existent, i.e. the quiddity, and he objects against them that the existence in everything is something different from the essence, and he affirms that their whole argument is built only on this.[1] But the distinction which the philosophers make here does not save them from the implication held against them about colouredness and its specific differences, in whatever way they may turn the question. Indeed, nobody doubts that the specific differences of the genus are the cause of the genus, whether it is assumed that the existence of the genus is different from its essence, or that the essence and existence of the genus are identical; for if the specific differences were differences in the existence, and the existence of the colour were different from the quiddity of the colour, it would follow that the specific differences by which the colour is divided are not differences in the quiddity of the colour, but differences in one of its accidents,[2] and this is an absurd assumption.[3] Therefore the truth is to say, 'When we divide colour by its specific differences, the existence of the colour in so far as it is colour is only actual, either because it is white, or because it is black or any other colour. Thus we do not divide an accident of the colour, but we divide only the essence of the colour.[4] Through this solution the statement that existence is an accident in the existent is seen to be false, and the argument and his answer are unsound.

As to Ghazali's words:

They base their denial of dualism on the denial that the First is composed of the generic and the specific, then they base the denial of this on the denial that there is a quiddity behind the existence. Therefore as soon as we have refuted this last proposition, which is their fundamental principle, their whole structure tumbles down.

I say:

This argument is not sound, for their structure, the denial of individual duality attributed to simple things univocally, is self-evident, for if we assume a duality and two simple things possessing a common trait, the simple becomes a compound.[5] And the summary of the philosophical proof for this is that the nature called 'necessary existent', i.e. the cause which has no cause and which is a cause for other things, must be either numerically one or many; if many, it must be many through its form, one through the genus predicated univocally of it, or one through a relation, or one through the term only.[6] If it is like Zaid and Amr individually differentiated and specifically one, then it necessarily possesses *hyle*, and this is impossible. If it is differentiated through its form, but one through the genus predicated univocally of it, then it is necessarily composite. If it is one in its genus, predicated by analogy to one thing, there is no objection, and one part of it will be the cause of another and the series will end in a first cause, and this is what happens with the forms abstracted from matter, according to the philosophers. If it is only common through the term, then there is no objection to its being more than one, and this is the case with the four primary causes, i.e. the first agent, the ultimate form, the ultimate end, the ultimate matter.[1] Therefore, no strict proof is attained through this method, and one does not arrive at the First Principle as Avicenna thought, nor to its being necessarily one.

Ghazali says:

The second way is the drawing of the consequence, and we say: If existence, substantiality and being a principle are not a genus, because they do not give an answer to the question 'What is it?', then according to you the First is pure intellect just like the other intellects which are the principles of existence, called angels,[2] according to the philosophers, and which are the effects of the First, are intellects separate from matter. And this abstract reality comprises the First and the first effect. This First, further, is according to the philosophers simple, and there is no compound in its essence except through its necessary attributes, and both the First Cause and the first effect participate in being intellect without matter. This, however, is a generic reality. Nor is intellectuality, separate from matter, a necessary attribute, for it is indeed a quiddity, and this quiddity is common to the First and all the other intellects. Therefore, if they do not differ in anything else, you have necessarily conceived a duality without a further difference; and if they do differ, what then is this distinction apart from their intellectuality, which they have in common?* For what they have in common is participation in this abstract reality. For indeed the First is conscious of its own self and of others, according to those who believe that it is in its essence intellect separate from matter; and also the first effect, which is the first intellect which God has created without a mediator, participates in this characteristic. This proves that the intellects which are effects are different species, that they only participate in intellectuality and are besides this distinguished by specific differences, and that likewise the First participates with all the other intellects in this intellectuality. The philosophers, therefore, are either in plain contradiction to their own fundamental thesis, or* have to affirm that intellectuality does not constitute God's essence. And both positions are absurd according to them.

I say:

If you have understood what we have said before this, that there are things which have a term in common not univocally or equivocally, but by the universality of terms analogically related to one thing, and that the characteristic of these things is that they lead upwards to a first term in this genus which is the first cause of everything to which this word refers, like warmth, which is predicated of fire and all other warm things, and like the term 'existent' which is predicated of the substance and all other accidents, and like the term 'movement' predicated of motion in space* and all the other movements, you will not have to occupy yourself with the mistakes in this reasoning. For the term 'intellect' is predicated analogically of the separate intellects according to the philosophers, and there is among them a first intellect which is the cause of all the other intellects, and the same thing is true of substance. And the proof that they have not one nature in common is that some of them are the causes of others and the cause of a thing is prior to the effect, and the nature of cause and effect cannot be one in genus except in the individual causes, and this kind of community is contradictory to genuine generic community, for things which participate in genus have no first principle which is the cause of all the others—they are all of the same rank, and there is no simple principle in them—whereas the things which participate in something predicated of them analogically must have a simple first principle. And in this First no duality can be imagined, for if a second were assumed, it must be of the same level of existence and of the same nature as the First, and they would have one nature in common in which they would participate by generic participation and would have to be distinguished through specific differences, additional to the genus, and both would be composed of genus and specific difference, and everything which is of this description is temporal; and lastly that which is of the extreme perfection of existence must be unique, for if it were not unique, it could not be of the extreme perfection of existence, for that which is in the extreme degree cannot participate with anything else, for in the same way as one single line cannot have two extreme points at the same end, things extended in existence and differentiated through increase and decrease have not two extremes at the same side. And since Avicenna was not aware of this nature, which stands midway between the nature of that which is univocally predicated and those natures which participate only through the equivocation of the term or in a distant, accidental way, this objection was valid against him.

THE EIGHTH DISCUSSION

To refute their theory that the existence of the First is simple, namely that it is pure existence and that its existence stands in relation to no quiddity and to no essence, but stands to necessary existence as do other beings to their quiddity

Ghazali says:

There are two ways of attacking this theory. The first is to demand a proof and to ask how you know this, through the necessity of the intellect, or through speculation and not by immediate necessity; and in any case you must tell us your method of reasoning.

If it is said that, if the First had a quiddity, its existence would be related to it, and would be consequent[1] on this quiddity and would be its necessary attribute, and the consequent is an effect and therefore necessary existence would be an effect, and this is a contradiction, we answer: This is to revert to the source of the confusion in the application of the term 'necessary existence', for we call this entity 'reality' or 'quiddity' and this reality exists, i.e. it is not non-existent and is not denied, but its existence is brought into a relation with it, and if you like to call this 'consequent' and 'necessary attribute', we shall not quibble about words, if you have once acknowledged that it has no agent for its existence and that this existence has not ceased to be eternal and to have no efficient cause; if, however, you understand by 'consequent' and 'effect' that it has an efficient cause, this is not true. But if you mean something else, this is conceded, for it is not impossible,[2] since the demonstration proves only the end of a causal series and its ending in an existent reality; a positive quiddity, therefore, is possible, and there is no need to deny the quiddity.

If it is said: Then the quiddity becomes a cause for the existence which is consequent on it, and the existence becomes an effect and an object of the act, we answer: The quiddity in temporal things is not a cause of their existence, and why should it therefore be the case in the eternal, if you mean by 'cause' the agent? But if you mean something else by it, namely that without which it could not be, let that be accepted, for there is nothing impossible in it; the impossibility lies only in the infinite causal series, and if this series only comes to a final term, then the impossibility is cancelled; impossibility can be understood only on this point, therefore you must give a proof of its impossibility.[3]

All the proofs of the philosophers are nothing but presumptions that the term has a sense from which certain consequences follow, and nothing but the supposition that demonstration has in fact proved a necessary existent with the meaning the philosophers ascribed to it. We have, however, shown previously that this is not true. In short, this proof of the philosophers comes down to the proof of the denial of attributes and of the division into genus and specific difference; only this proof is still more ambiguous and weak, for this plurality is purely verbal, for the intellect does allow the acceptance of one single existent quiddity. The philosophers, however, say that every existent quiddity is a plurality, for it contains quiddity and existence, and this is an extreme confusion; for the meaning of a single existent is perfectly understandable—nothing exists which has no essence, and the existence of an essence does not annul its singleness.

I say:

Ghazali does not relate Avicenna's doctrine literally as he did in his book *The Aims of the Philosophers*.[1] For since Avicenna believed that the existence of a thing indicated an attribute additional to its essence, he could no longer admit that its essence was the agent of its existence out of the possibles, for then the thing would be the cause of its own existence and it would not have an agent. It follows from this, according to Avicenna, that everything which has an existence additional to its essence has an efficient cause, and since according to Avicenna the First has no agent, it follows necessarily that its existence is identical with its essence.[2] And therefore Ghazali's objection that Avicenna assimilates existence to a necessary attribute of the essence is not true, because the essence of a thing is the cause of its necessary attribute and it is not possible that a thing should be the cause of its own existence, because the existence of a thing is prior to its quiddity.[3] To identify the quiddity and the existence of a thing is not to do away with its quiddity, as Ghazali asserts, but is only the affirmation of the unity of quiddity and existence. If we regard existence as an accidental attribute of the existent, and it is the agent which gives possible things their existence, necessarily that which has no agent either cannot have an existence (and this is absurd), or its existence must be identical with its essence.

But the whole of this discussion is built on the mistake that the existence of a thing is one of its attributes. For the existence which in our knowledge is prior to the quiddity of a thing is that which signifies the true.[4] Therefore the question whether a thing exists, either (1) refers to that which has a cause that determines its existence, and in that case its potential meaning is to ask whether this thing has a cause or not, according to Aristotle at the beginning of the second chapter of the *Posterior Analytics*;[5] or (2) it refers to that which has no cause, and then its meaning is to ask whether a thing possesses a necessary attribute which determines its

THE EIGHTH DISCUSSION

existence.[1] And when by 'existent' is meant what is understood by 'thing' and 'entity',[2] it follows the rule of the genus which is predicated analogically,[3] and whatever it is in this sense is attributed in the same way to that which has a cause and to that which has none, and it does not signify anything but the concept of the existent, and by this is meant 'the true', and if it means something additional to the essence, it is only in a subjective sense which does not exist outside the soul except potentially, as is also the case with the universal.[4] And this is the way in which the ancient philosophers considered the First Principle, and they regarded it as a simple existent. As to the later philosophers in Islam, they stated that, in their speculation about the nature of the existent *qua* existent, they were led to accept a simple existent of this description.

The best method to follow, in my opinion, and the nearest to strict proof, is to say that the actualization of existents which have in their substance a possible existence necessarily occurs only through an actualizer which is in act, i.e. acting, and moves them and draws them out of potency into act. And if this actualizer itself is also of the nature of the possible, i.e. possible in its substance, there will have to be another actualizer for it, necessary in its substance and not possible, so that this sublunary world may be conserved, and the nature of the possible causes may remain everlastingly, proceeding without end. And if these causes exist without end, as appears from their nature, and each of them is possible, necessarily their cause, i.e. that which determines their permanence, must be something necessary in its substance, and if there were a moment in which nothing was moved at all, there would be no possibility of an origination of movement.[5] The nexus between temporal existence and eternal can only take place without a change affecting the First through that movement which is partly eternal, partly temporal.[6] And the thing moved by this movement is what Avicenna calls 'the existence necessary through another', and this 'necessary through another' must be a body everlastingly moved, and in this way it is possible that the essentially temporal and corruptible should exist in dependence on the eternal, and this through approach to something and through recession from it, as you observe it happen to transitory existents in relation to the heavenly bodies.[7] And since this moved body is necessary in its substance, possible in its local movement, it is necessary that the process should terminate in an absolutely necessary existent in which there is no potency at all, either in its substance, or locally or in any of the other forms of movement; and that which is of this description is necessarily simple, because if it were a compound, it would be possible, not necessary, and it would require a necessary existent. And this method of proving it is in my opinion sufficient, and it is true.

However, what Avicenna adds to this proof by saying that the possible existent must terminate either in an existent necessary through another or in an existent necessary through itself, and in the former case that the necessary through another should be a consequence of the existent necessary through itself, for he affirms that the existent necessary through another is in itself a possible existent and what is possible needs something necessary—this addition, is to my mind superfluous and erroneous, for in the necessary, in whatever way you suppose it, there is no possibility whatsoever and there exists nothing of a single nature of which it can be said that it is in one way possible and in another way necessary in its existence.[1] For the philosophers have proved that there is no possible whatsoever in the necessary; for the possible is the opposite of the necessary, and the only thing that can happen is that a thing should be in one way necessary, in another way possible, as they believed for instance to be the case with the heavenly body or what is above the body of the heavens, namely that it was necessary through its substance and possible in its movement and in space. What led Avicenna to this division was that he believed that the body of the heavens was essentially necessary through another, possible by itself, and we have shown in another place that this is not true. And the proof which Avicenna uses in dealing with the necessary existent, when this distinction and this indication are not made, is of the type of common dialectical notions; when, however, the distinction is made, it is of the type of demonstrative proof.

You must know further that the becoming of which the Holy Law speaks is of the kind of empirical becoming in this world, and this occurs in the forms of the existents which the Ash'arites call mental qualities[2] and the philosophers call forms, and this becoming occurs only through another thing and in time, and the Holy Words: 'Have not those who have disbelieved considered that the heavens and the earth were coherent, and we have rent them . . .'[3] and the Divine Words 'then he straightened himself up to the sky which was smoke . . .',[4] refer to this. But as to the relation which exists between the nature of the possible existent and the necessary existent, about this the Holy Law is silent, because it is too much above the understanding of the common man and knowledge of it is not necessary for his blessedness. When the Ash'arites affirm that the nature of the possible[1] is created and has come into existence in time out of nothing (a notion which all the philosophers oppose, whether they believe in the temporal beginning of the world or not), they do not say this, if you consider the question rightly, on the authority of the law of Islam, and there is no proof for it. What appears from the Holy Law is the commandment to abstain from investigating that about which the Holy Law is silent, and therefore it is said in the Traditions: 'The people did not cease thinking till they said: God has created this, but who has created God? And the Prophet said: When one of you finds this, this is an act of pure faith', and in another version: 'When one of you finds this, let him read the verse of the Koran: Say, He, God is one. And know that for the masses to turn to such a question comes from the whisperings of Satan and therefore the prophet said: This is an act of pure faith.'[2]

Ghazali says:

The second way is to say that an existence without quiddity or essence cannot be conceived, and just as mere non-existence, without a relation to an existent the non-existence of which can be supposed,[3] cannot be conceived, in the same way existence can be only conceived in relation to a definite essence, especially when it is defined as a single essence; for how could it be defined as single, conceptually differentiated from others, if it had not a real essence? For to deny the quiddity is to deny the real essence, and when you deny the real essence of the existent, the existent can no longer be understood. It is as if the philosophers affirmed at the same time existence and a non-existent, which is contradictory.[4] This is shown by the fact that, if it were conceivable, it would be also possible in the effects that there should be an existence without an essence, participating with the First in not having a real essence and a quiddity, differing from it in having a cause, whereas the First is causeless. And why should such an effect not be imagined? And is there any other reason for this than that it is inconceivable in itself? But what is inconceivable in itself does not become conceivable by the denial of its cause, nor does what is conceivable become inconceivable because it is supposed to have a cause. Such an extreme negation is the most obscure of their theories, although they believe indeed that they have proved what they say. Their doctrine ends in absolute negation, and indeed the denial of the quiddity is the denial of the real essence, and through the denial of this reality nothing remains but the word 'existence', which has no object at all when it is not related to a quiddity.[5]

398 And if it is said: 'Its real essence is that it is the necessary, and the necessary is its quiddity', we answer: 'The only sense of "necessary" is "causeless", and this is a negation which does not constitute a real essence; and the denial of a cause for the real essence presupposes the real essence, and therefore let the essence be conceivable, so that it can be described as being causeless; but the essence cannot be represented as non-existent, since "necessity" has no other meaning than "being causeless".[1] Besides, if the necessity were added to the existence, this would form a plurality; and if it is not added, how then could it be the quiddity? For the existence is not the quiddity, and thus what is not added to the existence cannot be the quiddity either.'

I say:

This whole paragraph is sophistry. For the philosophers do not assume that the First has an existence without a quiddity and a quiddity without an existence. They believe only that the existence in the compound is an additional attribute to its essence and it only acquires this attribute through the agent, and they believe that in that which is simple and causeless this attribute is not additional to the quiddity and that it has no quiddity differentiated from its existence; but they do not say that it has absolutely no quiddity, as he assumes in his objection against them.[2]

Having assumed that they deny the quiddity—which is false—Ghazali begins now to charge them with reprehensible theories and says:

If this were conceivable it would also be possible in the effects that there should be an existence without an essence, participating with the First in not having a real essence.

I say:

399 But the philosophers do not assume an existent absolutely without a quiddity: they only assume that it has not a quiddity like the quiddities of the other existents; and this is one of the sophistical fallacies, for the term 'quiddity' is ambiguous, and this assumption, and everything built upon it, is a sophistical argument, for the non-existent cannot be described either by denying or by affirming something of it. And Ghazali, by fallacies of the kind perpetrated in this book, is not exempt from wickedness or from ignorance, and he seems nearer to wickedness than to ignorance—or should we say that there is a necessity which obliged him to do this?

And as to his remark, that the meaning of 'necessary existent' is 'causeless', this is not true, but our expression that it is a necessary existent has a positive meaning, consequent on a nature which has absolutely no cause, no exterior agent, and no agent which is part of it.

And as to Ghazali's words:

If the necessity were added to the existence, this would form a plurality; and if it is not added, how then could it be the quiddity? For existence is not the quiddity, and thus what is not added to the existence cannot be the quiddity either.

I say:

According to the philosophers necessity is not an attribute added to the essence, and it is predicated of the essence in the same way as we say of it that it is inevitable and eternal.[1] And likewise if we understand by 'existence' a mental attribute, it is not an addition to the essence, but if we understand it as being an accident, in the way Avicenna regards it in the composite existent, then it becomes difficult to explain how the uncompounded can be the quiddity itself, although one might say perhaps: 'In the way the knowledge in the uncompounded becomes the knower himself.' If, however, one regards the existent as the true, all these doubts lose their meaning, and likewise, if one understands 'existent' as having the same sense as 'entity', and according to this it is true that the existence in the uncompounded is the quiddity itself.

THE NINTH DISCUSSION

To refute their proof that the First is incorporeal

Ghazali says:

There is a proof only for him who believes that body is only temporal, because it cannot be exempt from what is temporal and everything that is temporal needs a creator.[2] But you, when you admit an eternal body which has no beginning for its existence, although it is not exempt from temporal occurrences, why do you regard it as impossible that the First should be a body, either the sun, or the extreme heaven, or something else?

If the answer is made 'Because body must be composite and divisible into parts quantitatively, and into matter and form conceptually, and into qualities which characterize it necessarily so that it can be differentiated from other bodies (for otherwise all bodies in being body would be similar) and the necessary existent is one and cannot be divided in any of these ways' we answer: 'We have already refuted you in this, and have shown that you have no proof for it except that a collection is an effect, since some of its parts require others, and we have argued against it and have shown that when it is not impossible to suppose an existent without a creator, it is not impossible to suppose a compound without a composing principle and to suppose many existents without a creator, since you have based your denial of plurality and duality on the denial of composition and your denial of composition on the denial of a quiddity distinct from existence, and with respect to the last principle we have asked for its foundation and we have shown that it is a mere presumption.'

402 And if it is said: 'If a body has no soul, it cannot be an agent, and when it has a soul, well, then its soul is its cause, and then body cannot be the First', we answer: 'Our soul is not the cause of the existence of our body, nor is the soul of the sphere in itself a cause of its body, according to you, but they are two, having a distinct cause; and if they can be eternal, it is 5 possible that they have no cause.'

And if the question is asked, 'How can the conjunction of soul and body come about?', we answer, 'One might as well ask how the existence of the First comes about; the answer is that such a question may be asked about what is temporal, but about what is eternally existent one cannot ask how it has come about, and therefore* since body and its soul are both eternally existent, it is not impossible that their compound should be a creator.'

I say:

When a man has no other proof that the First is not body than 10 that he believes that all bodies are temporal, how weak is his proof, and how far distant from the nature of what has to be proved!—since it has been shown previously that the proofs on which the theologians build their statement that all bodies are temporal are conflicting; and what is more appropriate than to regard an eternal composite as possible, as I said in this book when speaking of the Ash'arites, i.e. in saying that according to them an eternal body is possible, since in the accidents there is some eternal element, according to their own theory, for instance, the characteristic of forming a compound; and therefore their proof that all bodies are temporal is not valid, because they base it exclusively on the temporal becoming of the accidents.[1] The ancient philosophers do not allow for the existence of a body eternal through itself, but only of one eternal through another, and 403 therefore according to them there must be an existent eternal through itself through which the eternal body becomes eternal. But if we expound their theories here, they have only a dialectical value, and you should therefore instead ask for their proofs in their proper place.

And as to Ghazali's refutation of this, and his words:

We answer: 'We have already refuted you in this, and we have shown that you have no proof for this except that a collection is an effect, since some of its parts require others.

I say:

He means that he has discussed this already previously, and he says that the philosophers cannot prove that the existent necessary through itself is not a body, since the meaning of 'existent necessary through itself' is 'that which has no efficient cause', and why should they regard an eternal body which has no efficient cause as impossible—and especially when it should be supposed to be a simple body, indivisible quantitatively or qualitatively, and in short an eternal composite[1] without a composing principle? This is a sound argument from which they cannot escape except through dialectical arguments.[2] But all the arguments which Ghazali gives in this book either against or on behalf of the philosophers or against Avicenna are dialectical through the equivocation of the terms used, and therefore it is not necessary to expatiate on this.

And as to his answer on behalf of the Ash'arites that what is eternal through itself does not need a cause for its eternity, and that when the theologians assume something eternal through itself and assume its essence as the cause of its attributes,[3] this essence does not become eternal because of something else,

I say:

It is a necessary consequence to be held up against Ghazali that the Eternal will be composed of a cause and an effect, and that the attributes will be eternal through their cause, i.e. the essence. And since the effect is not a condition for its own existence, the Eternal is the cause. And let us say that the essence which exists by itself is God and that the attributes are effects; then it can be argued against the theologians that they assume one thing eternal by itself and a plurality of things eternal through another, and that the combination of all these is God. But this is exactly their objection against those who say that God is eternal through Himself and the world eternal through another, namely God. Besides, they say that the Eternal is one, and all this is extremely contradictory.

And as to Ghazali's statement that to assume a compound without the factor which composes it, is not different from assuming an existent without a creator, and that the assumption either of a single existent of this description or of a plurality is not an impossible supposition for the mind, all this is erroneous. For composition does not demand a composing factor which again itself is composed, but there must be a series leading up to a composing factor composing by itself, just as, when the cause is an effect, there must finally be a cause which is not an effect. Nor is it possible, by means of an argument which leads to an existent without a creator, to prove the oneness of this existent.[1]

And as to his assertion that the denial of the quiddity implies the denial of the composition, and that this implies the assertion of composition in the First,[2] this is not true. And indeed the philosophers do not deny the quiddity of the First, but only deny that it has the kind of quiddity which is in the effects, and all this is a dialectical and doubtful argument. And already previously in this book we have given convincing arguments, according to the principles of the philosophers, to prove that the First is incorporeal, namely that the possible leads to a necessary existent and that the possible does not proceed from the necessary except through the mediation of an existent which is partly necessary, partly possible, and that this is the body of the heavens and its circular motion; and the most satisfactory way of expressing this according to the principles of the philosophers is to say that all bodies are finite in power, and that they only acquire their power of infinite movement through an incorporeal being.[3]

Ghazali answering the objection which infers that according to the philosophers the agent is nothing but the sphere, composed of soul and body, says:

If it is answered: 'This cannot be so, because body in so far as it is body does not create anything else and the soul which is attached to the body does not act except through the mediation of the body, but the body is not a means for the soul in the latter's creating bodies or in causing the existence of souls and of things which are not related to bodies', we answer: 'And why is it not possible that there should be amongst the souls a soul which has the characteristic of being so disposed that both bodies and incorporeals are produced through it? The impossibility of this is not a thing known necessarily, nor is there a proof for it, except that we do not experience this in the bodies we observe; but the absence of experience does not demonstrate its impossibility, and indeed the philosophers often ascribe things to the First Existent which are not generally ascribed to existents, and are not experienced in any other existent, and the absence of its being observed in other things is not a proof of its impossibility in reference to the First Existent, and the same holds concerning the body and its soul.'

THE NINTH DISCUSSION

I say:

As to his assertion that bodies do not create bodies, if by 'creating' is understood producing, the reverse is true, for a body in the empirical world can only come into being through a body,[1] and an animated body only through an animated body,[2] but the absolute body does not come into being at all, for, if it did, it would come into being *from* non-existence, not *after* non-existence.[3] Individual bodies only come into being out of individual bodies and through individual bodies,[4] and this through the body's being transferred from one name to another and from one definition to another, so that for instance the body of water changes into the body of fire, because out of the body of water is transformed the attribute through the transformation of which the name and definition of water is transferred to the name and definition of fire, and this happens necessarily through a body which is the agent, participating with the becoming body specifically or generically in either a univocal or an analogical way;[5] and whether the individual special corporeality in the water is transformed into the individual special corporeality of the fire is a problem to be studied.[6]

And as to Ghazali's words:

But the body is not a means for the soul in the latter's creating bodies or in causing the existence of souls,

I say:

This is an argument which he builds on an opinion some of the philosophers hold, that the bestower of forms on inanimate bodies and of souls is a separate substance, either intellect or a separate soul, and that it is not possible that either an animated body or an inanimate body should supply this. And if this opinion is held and at the same time it is assumed that heaven is an animated body, it is no longer possible for heaven to supply any of the transitory forms, either the soul or any other of these forms. For the soul which is in the body only acts through the mediation of the body, and that which acts through the mediation of the body can produce neither form nor soul, since it is not of the nature of the body to produce a substantial form, either a soul or any other substantial form. And this theory resembles that of Plato about forms separate from matter, and is the theory of Avicenna and others among the Muslim philosophers; their proof is that the body produces in the body only warmth or cold or moisture or dryness,[7] and only these are acts of the heavenly bodies according to them. But that which produces the substantial forms, and especially those which are animated, is a separate substance which they call the giver of forms.[1] But there are philosophers[2] who believe the contrary and affirm that what produces the forms in the bodies is bodies possessing forms similar to them either specifically or generically, those similar specifically being the living bodies which produce the living bodies of the empirical world, like the animals which are generated from other animals, whereas those forms produced by forms generically similar, and which are not produced from a male or a female, receive their lives according to the philosophers from the heavenly bodies, since these are alive. And these philosophers have non-empirical proofs which, however, need not be mentioned here.[3]

And therefore Ghazali argues against them in this way:

And why is it not possible that there should be among the souls a soul which has the characteristic of being so disposed that both bodies and incorporeals are produced through it?

I say:

He means: 'Why should it not be possible that there should be among the souls in bodies souls which have the characteristic of generating other animate and inanimate forms?' And how strange it is that Ghazali assumes that the production of body out of body does not happen in the empirical world, whereas nothing else is ever observed.

But you must understand that when the statements of the philosophers are abstracted from the demonstrative sciences they certainly become dialectical, whether they are generally acknowledged, or, if not, denied and regarded as strange. The reason is that demonstrative statements are only distinguished from statements which are not demonstrative, by being considered in the genus of science which is under investigation.[4] Those statements which can be subsumed under the definition of this genus of science, or which comprise in their definition this genus of science, are demonstrative, and those statements which do not seem to fulfil these conditions are not demonstrative. Demonstration is only possible when the nature of this genus of science under investigation is defined, and the sense in which its essential predicates exist is distinguished from the sense in which they do not, and when this is retained in mind by keeping to that sense in every statement adopted in this science, and by having the identical meaning always present in the mind. And when the soul is convinced that the statement is essential to this genus or a necessary consequence of its essence, the statement is true; but when this relation does not enter into the mind, or when it is only weakly established, the statement is only an opinion, and is not evident. And therefore the difference between proof and convincing opinion is more delicate than the appearance of a hair and more completely hidden than the exact limit between darkness and light, especially in theological* questions which are laid before the common people, because of the confusion between what is essential and what is accidental. Therefore we see that Ghazali, by relating the theories of the philosophers in this and others of his books and by showing them to people who have not studied their works with the necessary preparation the philosophers demand, changes the nature of the truth which exists in their theories or drives most people away from all their views. And by so doing he does more harm than good to the cause of truth. And God knows that I should not have related a single one of their views, or regarded this as permissible, but for the harm which results from Ghazali's doings to the cause of wisdom; and I understand by 'wisdom' speculation about things according to the rules of the nature of proof.

Ghazali says, on behalf of the philosophers:

If it is said that the highest sphere, or the sun, or whatever body you may imagine, possesses a special size which may be increased or decreased, and this possible size needs for its differentiation a differentiating principle and can therefore not be the First,[1] we answer: By what argument will you refute the man who says that this body must have the size it possesses* for the sake of the order of the universe, and this order could not exist if this body were smaller or larger—since you philosophers yourselves affirm that the first effect[2] determines the size of the highest sphere because all sizes are equivalent in relation to the essence of the first effect, but certain sizes are determined for the sake of the order which depends on them and therefore the actual size is necessary and no other is possible; and all this holds just as well when no effect is assumed.[3] Indeed, if the philosophers had established in the first effect, which is according to the philosophers the cause of the highest sphere, a specifying principle, as for instance the will, a further question might be put, since it might be asked why this principle willed this actual size rather than another, in the way the philosophers argued against the Muslims about their theory of the relation between the temporal world and the Eternal Will,[4] an argument which we turned against them with respect to the problems of the determination of the direction of the heavenly movement and of the determination of the points of the poles. And if it is clear that they are forced to admit that a thing is differentiated from a similar one and that this happens through a cause, it is unessential whether this differentiation be regarded as possible without a cause or through a cause, for it is indifferent whether one puts the question about the thing itself and asks why it has such-and-such a size, or whether one puts the question about the cause, and asks why it gave this thing this special size; and if the question about the cause may be answered by saying that this special measure is not like any other, because the order depends on it exclusively, the same answer may be made about the thing itself, and it will not need a cause. And there is no escape from this. For if the actual size which has been determined and has been realized were equivalent to the size which has not been realized, one might ask how one thing comes to be differentiated from a similar one, especially according to the principle of the philosophers who do not admit a differentiating will. If, however, there is no similar size, no possibility exists, and one must answer: 'This has been so from all eternity, and in the same way therefore as, according to the philosophers, the eternal cause exists.'[1] And let the man who studies this question seek help from what we said about their asking about the eternal will, a question which we turned against them with respect to the points of the poles and the direction of the movement of the sphere. It is therefore clear that the man who does not believe in the temporal creation of the bodies cannot establish a proof that the First is incorporeal.

I say:

This indeed is a very strange argument of Ghazali's. For he argues that they cannot prove another creator than the heavenly body, since they would have to give an answer by a principle in which they do not believe. For only the theologians accept this principle, since they say that heaven receives the determinate size it has, to the exclusion of other sizes it might have, from a differentiating cause, and that the differentiating principle must be eternal. He either attempted to deceive in this matter or was himself deceived. For the differentiation which the philosophers infer is different from that which the Ash'arites intend, for the Ash'arites understand by 'differentiation' the distinguishing of one thing either from a similar one or from an opposite one without this being determined by any wisdom in the thing itself which makes it necessary to differentiate one of the two opposite things. The philosophers, on the other hand, understand here by the differentiating principle only that which is determined by the wisdom in the product itself, namely the final cause, for according to them there is no quantity or quality in any being that has not an end based on wisdom, an end which must either be a necessity in the nature of the act of this being or exist in it, based on the principle of

THE SEVENTH DISCUSSION

superiority.[1] For if, so the philosophers believe, there were in created things a quantity or quality not determined by wisdom, they would have attributed to the First Maker and Creator an attitude in relation to His work which may be only attributed to the artisans among His creatures, with the intention of blaming them.[2] For when one has observed a work with respect to its quantity and quality, and asked why the maker of this work chose this quantity or this quality to the exclusion of all other possible quantities and qualities, there is no worse mistake than to answer 'Not because of the intrinsic wisdom and thoughtfulness in the product itself, but because he willed it,' since according to this view all quantities and qualities are similar with respect to the end of this product, which in fact the maker produced for its own sake, namely for the sake of the act for whose purpose it exists. For indeed every product is produced in view of something in it which would not proceed from it, if this product had no definite quantity, quality and nature*, although in some products an equivalent is possible. If any product whatever could determine any act whatever, there would exist no wisdom at all in any product, and there would be no art at all, and the quantities and qualities of the products would depend on the whim of the artisan and every man would be an artisan.[3] Or should we rather say that wisdom exists only in the product of the creature, not in the act of the Creator? But God forbid that we should believe such a thing of the First Creator; on the contrary, we believe that everything in the world is wisdom, although in many things our understanding of it is very imperfect and although we understand the wisdom of the Creator only through the wisdom of nature. And if the world is one single product of extreme wisdom, there is one wise principle whose existence the heavens and the earth and everything* in them need.[4] Indeed, nobody can regard the product of such wonderful wisdom as caused by itself, and the theologians in their wish to elevate the Creator have denied Him wisdom and withheld from Him the noblest of His qualities.

THE TENTH DISCUSSION

To prove their incapacity to demonstrate that the world has a creator and a cause, and that in fact they are forced to admit atheism

Ghazali says:

Their statement that body needs a creator and a cause can be understood from the theory of those[1] who argue that all bodies are temporal, because they cannot exist without what is temporal. But what keeps you philosophers from the doctrine of the materialists, namely that the world is eternal in the condition in which it actually is, and that it has no cause and no creator, that there is only a cause for temporal events and that no body comes into existence and no body is annihilated, and that only forms and accidents come into existence, for the bodies are the heavens (which are eternal) and the four elements, which are the stuff of the sublunary world, and their bodies and matters are eternal too, and there is only a change of forms in them through mixtures and alterations;[2] and that the souls of men and animals and plants come into existence, that all the causes of these temporal events terminate in the circular movement, and that the circular movement is eternal and its source the eternal soul of the sphere. Therefore there is no cause for the world and no creator for its bodies, but since the world, as it is, is eternal, there is no cause for it, i.e. no cause for its bodies. For indeed, what sense is there in the doctrine of the philosophers that these bodies exist through a cause, although they are eternal?

I say:

The philosophers assert that the man who says that all bodies have been produced (and by 'produced' must be understood creation *ex nihilo*) gives a meaning to the term 'produced' which is never found in the empirical world, and his statement surely stands in need of a proof. As to his attacks on the philosophers in this passage, so that he even forces on them the implication of atheism, we have already answered them previously and there is no sense in repeating ourselves, but, in short, the philosophers hold that body, be it temporal or eternal, cannot be independent in existence through itself; and this principle is, according to the philosophers, binding for the eternal body in the same way as for the temporal, although imagination does not help to explain how this is the case with the eternal body in the way it is with the temporal body.[3] Aristotle therefore, in the second book of *De caelo et mundo*,[4] when he wanted to explain the fact that the earth was circular by nature*, first assumed it to have come

THE TENTH DISCUSSION

into being in time so that the intellect might imagine its cause, and then transferred its existence to eternity.

Having forced on the philosophers these reprehensible deductions, Ghazali now gives an answer in defence of them and objects then to their answer.

Ghazali says:

And if the philosophers say: 'Everything that has no cause is of a necessary existence, and we philosophers have already mentioned the qualities of the necessary existent through which it is proved that body cannot be the necessary existent,' we answer: We have shown the mistake in your claim about the attributes of the necessary existent, and that your proof does not demonstrate anything but the termination of a causal series, and this termination also exists for the materialists at the beginning of things,[1] for they say that there is no cause for the bodies, and the forms and accidents are causes for each other and terminate in the circular movement part of which is the cause of another part in the same way as it takes place according to the doctrine of the philosophers, and this causal series[2] ends in this circular movement.

And the man who observes what we have related will understand the inability of those who believe in the eternity of bodies to claim at the same time that they have a cause, and the consequence of their theory is atheism and apostasy, which one party has clearly admitted, those namely who rely solely on the determinations of the intellect.

I say:

All this has been already answered, and its degree of truth has been stated, and there is no reason to repeat ourselves. And as to the materialists, they rely only on the senses, and when according to them the movements had terminated in the heavenly body and through this the causal series was ended, they thought that where sensation had come to a limit, the intellect also had come to a limit; but this is not true. But the philosophers considered the causes till they ended in the heavenly body, then they considered the intelligible causes and arrived at an existent which cannot be perceived and which is the principle of perceptible being, and this is the meaning of the words: 'Thus did we show Abraham the Kingdom of Heaven and of the earth. . . .'[3] The Ash'arites, however, rejected sensible causes; that is, they denied that certain sensible things are the causes of other sensible things, and they made the cause of sensible being a non-sensible being by a way of becoming which is neither experienced nor perceived, and they denied causes and effects; and this is a kind of view which is inconsistent with the nature of man in so far as he is man.[4]

Ghazali says, objecting to the argument of the philosophers:

If it is said that the proof that body is not a necessary existent is that, if it were a necessary existent, it would have neither an external nor an internal cause, but if it has a cause for its being composed, it will be possible in respect of its essence, and every possible needs a necessary existent, we answer: The terms 'necessary existent' and 'possible existent' are devoid of sense, and your whole confusion lies in these terms; but let us revert to their plain sense, which is the denial and the affirmation of a cause, for then your words amount to nothing else but saying that bodies either have a cause or not, and the materialists affirm the latter,[1] and why should you deny it? And when this is understood by 'possibility' and 'necessity', we say body is necessary and not possible, and your statement that body cannot be necessary is pure presumption without any foundation.

I say:

We have already said that if by 'necessary existent' is understood the causeless and by 'possible existent' is understood that which has a cause, the division of being into these two sections is not acknowledged, and opponents might say that this division is not true, but that, indeed, all existents are causeless. But when by 'necessary existent' is understood absolute necessary being and by 'possible' the genuinely possible, then we must arrive at a being which has no cause, for we can say that every being is either possible or necessary; if possible, it has a cause, and if this cause is of the nature of the possible, we have a series which ends in a necessary cause. Then, concerning this necessary cause it may be asked again whether some necessary beings might have a cause and other necessary beings none, and if a cause is ascribed to the nature of the necessary being which can have a cause, there will follow a series which ends in a necessary being which has no cause. Avicenna wanted by this division only to conform to the opinion of the philosophers concerning existents, for all philosophers agree that the body of the heavens is necessary through something else; whether, however, this thing necessary through another is possible by itself is a problem which has to be studied.[2] And this argument is therefore faulty when this method is followed, and this method is of necessity faulty, because being is not primarily divided into the genuinely possible and the necessary, for this is a division which is only known through the nature of existing things.[3]

Then Ghazali answers the philosophers' statement that body cannot be a necessary existent by itself, because it has parts which are its cause.

THE TENTH DISCUSSION 253

If it is said: 'It cannot be denied that body has parts, and that the whole is only constituted through the parts, and that the parts in a thing are prior to the whole,' we answer: 'Let it be so; certainly, the whole is constituted by the parts and their aggregation, but there is no cause for the parts nor for their aggregation, which on the contrary are eternally in the condition in which they are without an efficient cause.' And the philosophers cannot refute this, except by the argument of theirs which we have mentioned, which is based on the denial of plurality in the First; we have shown its futility, and apart from it there is no other method. It is therefore clear that for the man who does not believe in the temporal creation of bodies there is no foundation for believing in a creator at all.

I say:

This argument is, without doubt, binding for the man who follows the method of a necessary existent to prove the existence of an incorporeal being, but this is not the method followed by the ancient philosophers, and the first, so far as we know, who used it was Avicenna. He said that it was superior to the proof of the ancients, because the ancients arrived only at an immaterial being, the principle of the universe, through derivative things, namely motion and time; whereas this proof, according to Avicenna, arrives at the assertion of such a principle as the ancients established, through the investigation of the nature of the existent in so far as it is an existent. If indeed it did arrive at such an affirmation, what Avicenna says would be true; however, it does not.[1] For the most that could be affirmed of the existent necessarily existing by itself would be that it is not composed of matter and form, and generally speaking that it has no definition. But if it is supposed to exist as composed of eternal parts which are continuous by nature, as is the case with the world and its parts, it may indeed be said of the world with its parts that it is a necessary existent,[2] it being of course understood that there is a necessary existent. And we have already said that the method Avicenna followed to establish an existent of this description is not demonstrative and does not by nature lead to it, except in the way we have stated. The utmost consequence of this argument—and this constitutes its weakness—is the theory of those, namely the Peripatetics, who assume that there exists a simple body not composed of matter and form. For the man who assumes an eternal compound of actual parts must necessarily acknowledge that it is essentially one, and every oneness in a compound is one through an essential unity, namely a simple, and through this unity the world becomes one, and therefore Alexander of Aphrodisias says that there must exist a spiritual force which is diffused in all the parts of the universe in the same way as there is a force in all the parts of a single animal which binds them together, and the difference between the two forces is that the binding force in the world is eternal, because the conjoining principle is eternal, whereas the conjunction between the parts of the sublunary animal is individually transitory—although, through the eternal conjunction, not specifically transitory[1]—since it cannot be individually imperishable like the world.[2] And through this theory the Creator will be deprived of that very kind of perfection which nothing else can equal, as Aristotle says in his book *De animalibus*.[3] And we see nowadays that many of Avicenna's followers because of this aporia ascribe this opinion to him, and they say that he does not believe that there exists a separate existence, and they assert that this can be seen from what he says about the necessary existent in many passages, and that this is the view which he has laid down in his *Oriental Philosophy*, and they say that he only called this book *Oriental Philosophy*[4] because it is the doctrine of the Orientals; for they believed that according to the Orientals divinity is located in the heavenly bodies, as Avicenna himself had come to believe. However, notwithstanding this they accept* Aristotle's argument to prove the First Principle through movement.

And as for ourselves, we have discussed this argument at other times and have shown in what sense it can be regarded as evident, and we have solved all the doubts concerning it; we have also discussed Alexander's argument on this question, namely the one he uses in his book called *On the principles*.[5] For Alexander imagined that he was turning from Aristotle's argument to another; his argument, however, is taken from the principles which Aristotle proved, and both arguments are sound, though the more usual* is Aristotle's.

And when the argument for a necessary existent is verified, it is true according to me in the way I shall describe it, although it is used too generally and its different senses must be distinguished. It must, namely, be preceded by knowledge of the different kinds of possible existents in substance and the different kinds of necessary existents in substance. And then this argument takes this form: The possible existent in bodily substance must be preceded by the necessary existent in bodily substance, and the necessary existent in bodily substance must be preceded by the absolute necessary existent which does not possess any potency whatsoever, either in its substance or in any other of the different kinds of movements, and such an entity is not a body. For instance, it appears from the nature of the body of the heavens that it is a necessary existent in its bodily substance,[1] for otherwise there would have to be a body prior to it, and it appears also from its nature that it is a possible existent in its local movement; it is therefore necessary that its mover should be a necessary existent in its substance, and that there should be in it no potency whatsoever, either as regards movement or in any other respect, and that neither movement nor rest could be ascribed to it nor any other kind of change, and such an entity is absolutely without body and without any potency in a body. But the eternal parts of the world are only necessary existents in their substance, either universally like the four elements, or individually like the heavenly bodies.[2]

THE ELEVENTH DISCUSSION

To show the incapacity of those philosophers who believe that the First knows other things beside its own self and that it knows the genera and the species in a universal way, to prove that this is so

Ghazali says:

Since for the Muslims existence is confined to the temporal and the eternal, and there is for them nothing eternal except God and His attributes, and everything besides Him is temporally created by Him through His will, according to them the existent of necessity exists previously in His knowledge, for the object willed must be known by the willer. They deduced from this that the universe is known to Him, for the universe was willed by Him and produced by Him, and nothing comes into existence but what is produced through His will, and nothing is everlasting but His essence alone. And when once it was established that God wills and knows what He wills, He must be necessarily living,[3] and every living being is conscious of its own self,[4] and He is the most capable of knowing Himself. Therefore the whole universe is known to God, and they understood this through this argument, since they had found that He willed everything that happens in the world.

I say:

He says this only as an introduction and preparation for the comparison between his theory and that of the philosophers about eternal knowledge, because his theory seems at first sight more satisfactory than that of the philosophers. But when the theory of the theologians is tested, and shown up to him for whom such an exposure is necessary, it becomes clear that they only made God an eternal man,[1] for they compared the world with the products of art wrought by the will and knowledge and power of man. And when it was objected against them that He must then have a body, they answered that He is eternal and that all bodies are temporal. They were therefore forced to admit an immaterial man who produces all existents. But this theory is nothing but a metaphor and a poetical expression; and metaphorical expressions are certainly very convincing, till they are explored, but then their deficiency becomes evident. For indeed there is no nature more distant from that of the transitory than that of the eternal. And if this is true, it cannot be that there should exist one single species which is differentiated by eternity and non-eternity[2] as one single genus is differentiated through the various differences into which it is divided. For the distance between the eternal and the temporal is far greater than that between the different species which participate in temporality. And if the distance between eternity and non-eternity is greater than that between the various species, how then is it possible to apply a judgement about the empirical world to the invisible: for those two are opposite extremes? And when you have understood the sense of the attributes which exist in the visible world and those which exist in the invisible world, it will be clear to you that through the ambiguity of the terms they are so equivocal that they do not permit a transference from the visible to the invisible.

Life, for instance, added to the intellect of man only applies to the potentiality of motion in space through will and sense-perception,[3] but senses are impossible for the Creator and still more impossible for Him is motion in space. But the theologians ascribe to the Creator the faculty of sense-perception* without sense-organs, and deny His movement absolutely. Therefore either they do not ascribe life to the Creator in the sense it has in the animal and which is a condition for the existence of knowledge in man, or they identify it with perception in the way the philosophers say that perception and knowledge in the First are identical with life. Further, the meaning of 'will'[4] in man and in animal is a desire which rouses movement and which happens in animal and man to perfect a deficiency in their essence, and it is impossible that there should be in the Creator a desire because of an imperfection in His essence, which could be a cause of movement and action either in Himself or in something different from Himself. And how could an eternal will be imagined which should be the cause of an act occurring without an increase of the desire at the time of the act,[1] or how could a will and a desire be imagined which would be before, during, and after the act in the same state without any change occurring to them? And again, desire (in so far as it is the cause of movement) and movement are only found in body, and desire is only found in the animate body. Therefore according to the philosophers the meaning of 'will' in God is nothing but that every act proceeds from Him through knowledge, and knowledge in so far as it is knowledge is the knowledge of opposites, either of which can proceed from Him. And the Knower is called excellent by the fact that there always proceeds from Him the better of the opposites to the exclusion of the worse. Therefore the philosophers say that three attributes are most appropriate to the Creator, namely that He has knowledge, excellence, and power. And they say that His power is not inferior to His will, as is the case with man.

All this is the theory of the philosophers on this problem and in the way we have stated it here with its proofs, it is a persuasive not a demonstrative statement. It is for you to inquire about these questions in the places where they are treated in the books of demonstration, if you are one of the people of perfect eudaemonia, and if you are one of those who learn the arts the function of which is proof. For the demonstrative arts are very much like the practical; for just as a man who is not a craftsman cannot perform the function of craftsmanship, in the same way it is not possible for him who has not learned the arts of demonstration to perform the function of demonstration which is demonstration itself: indeed this is still more necessary for this art than for any other—and this is not generally acknowledged in the case of this practice only because it is a mere act[2]—and therefore such a demonstration can proceed only from one who has learned the art. The kinds of statement, however, are many, some demonstrative, others not, and since non-demonstrative statements can be adduced without knowledge of the art, it was thought that this might be also the case with demonstrative statements; but this is a great error. And therefore in the spheres of the demonstrative arts, no other statement is possible but a technical statement which only the student of this art can bring, just as is the case with the art of geometry. Nothing therefore of what we have said in this book is a technical demonstrative proof; they are all non-technical statements, some of them having greater persuasion than others, and it is in this spirit that what we have written here must be understood. So this book of Ghazali might be best given the name of the 'Incoherence of both parties together'.

All this in my opinion is in excess of the Holy Law, and an inquiry into something not ordered by a religious law because human power does not suffice for it. For not all knowledge about which the Holy Law is silent needs to be explored and explained to the masses as being, according to speculative thought, part of the dogmas of religion; for from this the greatest confusion arises. One must not speak about those things concerning which the Holy Law is silent; the masses must learn that human understanding is not sufficient to treat these problems, and must not go beyond what the teaching of the Holy Law explains in its texts, since this is teaching in which all can participate and which suffices for the attainment of their happiness. And just as the physician investigates the measure of health which agrees most with the healthy for the preservation of their health, and with the sick for the curing of their illness, so the Lord of the Holy Law instructs the masses only in so far as is needed for their acquisition of happiness. And the same thing holds in respect of the facts of human behaviour, only the investigation of these facts in so far as the Holy Law is silent about them is more legitimate, especially when they are of the same genus as those about which the Law pronounces judgement. For this reason the lawyers disagree about this kind of facts; some of them, the Zahirites, deny the use of analogy, whereas others, the analogists, admit it,[1] and this is absolutely the same thing as happens in the sphere of knowledge, only perhaps the Zahirites are happier in the purely intellectual sphere than in the practical.

And anyone amongst the two opposing parties who inquires after these questions must either belong to the followers of proof, i.e. the rationalists, or not; in the former case he will speak about them and base his statements on demonstration, he will know that this way of discussion is limited to the followers of proof, and he will know the places in which the Holy Law gives to the people who possess this kind of knowledge a hint about the conclusions to which demonstration leads; in the latter case he will be either a believer or an unbeliever: if he is a believer he will know that to discuss those questions is forbidden by the Holy Law, and if he is an unbeliever, it is not difficult for the followers of proof to refute him with the stringent proofs they possess. The rationalist must act in this way in every religion, but especially in our Divine Revelation, which although it is silent on certain intellectual problems nevertheless hints at the conclusions about them to which demonstration leads, without, however, mentioning these problems in its instruction of the masses.

Since this is established, we shall revert now to our subject, which is forced upon us by necessity—for otherwise, by God, the Knower, the Witness, the Revealer, we should not think it permissible to discuss such questions in this way. And Ghazali, having described the arguments through which the theologians prove the attribute of knowledge and other attributes, and shown that they are very evident because they are generally admitted and extremely easy to accept, begins to compare these arguments with those of the philosophers about these attributes, and this is an act of rhetoric.[1]

Ghazali says, addressing the philosophers: 431

And you, philosophers, when you affirm that the world is eternal and not produced by God's will, how do you know that He knows something beside His essence, for you require a proof of this?

Then Ghazali says:

And the summary of what Avicenna says to prove this in the course of his argument can be reduced to two heads: First, that the First does not exist in matter, and everything which does not exist in matter is pure intellect and all the intelligibles are revealed to it, for the obstacle to perceiving all things is attachment to matter and being occupied with matter, and the human soul is occupied by directing matter, i.e. its body, and when this occupation is terminated and it is not any longer defiled by the bodily passions and the despicable conditions which affect it through the things of nature, all the realities of the intelligibles are revealed to it[2] and therefore is it asserted that all the angels know all the intelligibles without exception, for they too are pure immaterial intellects.

And having related their theory, Ghazali argues against them:

But we say: If by your assertion that the First does not exist in matter, you mean that it is not a body, nor impressed on a body, but exists by itself not comprised by space nor locally specified by a direction, this is admitted by us. There remains then your answer to the question what its attribute is, namely that it is pure intellect—and what do you understand by 'intellect'? If you mean by it that which thinks all the other things, this is just what we are trying to find out and the point under discussion, and how, therefore, can you take it as the premiss of a syllogism which must prove it? And if you mean by it something else, namely that it thinks its own self—and some of your fellow-philosophers may concede this to you, but this amounts again to your saying that what thinks its own self thinks other things also—the answer to be made is 'Why do you claim this? For this is not known by necessity, and only Avicenna of all the philosophers affirmed it; and how can you claim this as necessary knowledge, or, if you know it by deduction, what is your proof?'

And if the assertion is made: 'Because what prevents the perception of things is matter, and the First is not matter', we answer: We concede that matter is an impediment, but we do not admit that it is the only impediment; and let them arrange their syllogism in the figure of the hypothetical syllogism and say: 'If this First is in matter it cannot think things, but it is not in matter, therefore it thinks things'.[1] And this is the assumption as a minor premiss of the opposite of the antecedent, but such an assumption does not lead to a conclusion in all cases, for it is like saying: 'If this is a man, it is an animal, but it is not a man, therefore it is not an animal'.[2] But this is not a necessary conclusion, for although not a man, it might be a horse, and therefore an animal. The assumption as a minor premiss of the opposite of the antecedent is valid only conditionally, as we have shown in our logic—namely, when the consequent is universally convertible with the antecedent, as when the logicians say: 'If the sun has risen, it is day, but the sun has not risen, therefore it is not day', for the only cause of its being day is the fact that the sun has risen—an example in which antecedent and consequent are convertible with each other—and the explanation of these theories and terms can be understood from our book 'The Touchstone of Knowledge'*, which we have written as an appendix to this book.[3] If, however, they say 'We claim that antecedent and consequent are here convertible, and that the one and only obstacle to thinking is being in matter', we answer: 'This is a pure presumption; where is your proof?'

I say:

The first mistake he makes here is that, in relating the theory and the proof, he regards the premisses he mentions as first principles, whereas for the philosophers they are conclusions from many premisses. For the philosophers had seen that every sensible existent is composed of matter and form, and that the form is the entity through which the existent becomes existent[4] and that it is the form which is designated by the name and the definition,[5] and that the specific act proceeds from the form in every existent, and it is this act which shows the existence of the forms in the existent.[6] For they had found that in substances there are active potencies, particular to every single existent, and passive potencies, either particular or common,[7] and that a thing cannot be passive by reason of the same thing as it is active; for activity is the opposite of passivity, and opposites do not admit each other, and it is only their substratum which admits them successively, e.g. hotness does not accept coldness, it is simply the hot body that accepts coldness by divesting itself of hotness and accepting coldness, and vice versa. Now when the philosophers found that this was the case with activity and passivity, they understood that all existents of this description were composed of two substances, a substance which is the act and a substance which is the potency, and they realized that the substance in act is the perfection of the substance in potency and that the substance in act stands in relation to the substance in potency as if it were the end of its actualization, for there is no actual difference between them.[1] Then, when they looked through all the different forms of existents, they found that all these substances must necessarily lead up to a substance in act which is absolutely devoid of matter, and this substance must necessarily be active and cannot have any passivity and cannot be subject to exhaustion, weariness, and decay; for such things occur to the substance in act only because it is the perfection of the substance in potency, not because it is pure act. For since the substance in potency only goes forth into act through a substance in act, the series of substances which are at the same time both active and passive must terminate in a substance which is pure act, and the series must terminate in that substance. And the proof of the existence of this substance, in so far as it is a mover and agent, through essential particular premisses, can be found in the eighth book of Aristotle's *Physics*.

Having established the existence of this substance by special and general arguments according to what is known in their books, the philosophers now investigated the nature of the forms in matter which produce motion, and they found some of them nearer to actuality and farther from potency because they are less than others involved in passivity, which is the special sign of the matter which exists in them. And they realized that that which among these forms is most destitute of matter is the soul, and especially the intellect, so that they started to doubt whether the intellect belongs to the forms which are in matter or not.[2] But when they investigated the perceiving forms amongst the forms of the soul and found that they were free from matter, they understood that the cause of perception consists in freedom from matter,[3] and since they discovered that the intellect is without passivity they understood that the reason why one form is inorganic and another perceptive consists in the fact that when it is the perfection of a potency it is inorganic or not percipient,[1] and when it is pure perfection with which no potency is mixed it is intellect.[2] All this they proved in a demonstrative order and by natural deductions which cannot be reproduced here in this demonstrative sequence, for this would involve collecting in one place what by its nature is treated in many different books, and anyone who has the slightest experience of the science of logic will acknowledge that this is an impossibility. Through arguments of this kind they came to realize that what has no passivity whatever is intellect and not body, for what is passive is body which exists in matter according to them.

An objection against the philosophers in these questions ought to be made only against the first principles they use in the proof of these conclusions, not against those conclusions themselves, as it is made by Ghazali. Through this they came to understand that there exists here an existent which is pure intellect, and when they saw further that the order which reigns in nature and in the act of nature follows an intellectual plan very much like the plan of the craftsman, they realized that there must exist an intellect which causes these natural potencies to act in an intellectual way, and through these two points they received the conviction that this existent which is pure intellect is that which bestows on the existents the order and arrangement in their acts. And they understood from all this that its thinking its own self is identical with its thinking all existents, and that this existent is not such that its thinking its own self is something different from the thought by which it thinks other things, as is the case with the human intellect. And about this intellect the disjunction assumed as a premiss, that every intellect either thinks its own self or thinks something else or thinks both together, is not valid. For when this disjunction is admitted, what is said is: 'If it thinks other things, it is self-evident that it must think its own self; however, if it thinks its own self, it is not at all necessary that it should think other things.' And we have discussed this previously.

And all the things which he says about the hypothetical syllogism which he formed in the figure he explained are not true. For the hypothetical syllogism is only valid when the minor and the legitimacy of the inference[3] are proved through one or more categorical syllogisms. For correct hypothetical inference in this question is: 'If what does not think is in matter, then what is not in matter thinks.' But, of course, first the truth of this conjunction and disjunction must

THE ELEVENTH DISCUSSION

be proved.[1] And these are the premises of which we said that they are according to the philosophers conclusions, whereas Ghazali pretends they are first principles for them, or nearly so. And when it is explained as we have done, it is a syllogism of a legitimate figure and of true premises. As to its legitimate form, the minor is the opposite of the consequent and the conclusion is the opposite of the antecedent, not as Ghazali believed, the minor the opposite of the antecedent and the conclusion the opposite of the consequent.[2] But since they are not first principles, nor generally acknowledged, nor evident at first sight, they are regarded, no doubt, by those who have never heard anything of these things as very much open to objection. But indeed Ghazali confused the sciences in a most terrible way, and he uprooted science from its foundation and its method.

Ghazali says:

The second argument is that the philosophers say: 'Although we assert neither that the First wills temporal production nor that it produces the world in time by secondary* intention, we nevertheless affirm that the First has made the world and that indeed the world has its existence through the First only, the First never losing its character as an agent and never ceasing to act; our theory only distinguishes itself from others in this point, in no way however with respect to the principle of the act. And since the agent must have knowledge in conformity with its act, the universe, according to us, exists through its act.'

But there are two ways to answer this, of which the first is: 'There are two kinds of action: voluntary, like the action of animal and man; and involuntary, like the action of the sun in producing light, of fire in producing heat, of water in producing cold. Now knowledge of the act is only necessary in voluntary acts, as in the human products of art, not in the acts of nature. But according to you philosophers, God has made the world consequent on His essence by nature and by necessity, not through will and choice; indeed, the universe is consequent on His essence, as light is on the sun, and just as the sun has no power to check its light, nor fire to repress its producing heat, so the First cannot check its acts. Now this kind of occurrence, although it may be called an act, does not imply knowledge at all.' And if it is answered that there is a difference between the two things, in that the procession of the universe from God's essence occurs through His knowledge of the universe and His representing the universal order in the course of the emamation of the universe, and He has no other cause than His knowledge of the universe, and His knowledge of the universe is identical with His essence, and if He had not this knowledge of the universe, the universe would not exist through Him, which is not the case with light in relation to the sun, we answer: 'In this you are in contradiction to your fellow-philosophers, for they say that His essence is the essence from which the existence of the universe in its order follows naturally and necessarily, and it is not because He knows this.[1] And what is wrong with this conception, once you agree with them in denying His will? And since the sun's knowledge of its light is no condition for its light, but its light is necessarily consequent on the sun, so let us accept this also in the case of the First; and nothing prevents this.'

I say:

In this section Ghazali begins by saying something reprehensible about the philosophers, namely that the Creator possesses a will neither with respect to the things produced nor with respect to the universe as a whole, because His act proceeds from His essence necessarily like the procession of light from the sun. Then he says of them that they say that through His acting He must have knowledge. The philosophers, however, do not deny the will of God, nor do they admit that He has a human will, for the human will implies a deficiency in the willer and a being affected by the object willed, and when the object is attained, the deficiency is completed and the passivity, which is called will, ceases. The philosophers only attribute a will to God in the sense that the acts which proceed from Him proceed through knowledge, and everything which proceeds through knowledge and wisdom proceeds through the will of the agent, not, however, necessarily and naturally, since the nature of knowledge does not imply (as he falsely affirms of the philosophers) the proceeding of the act. For if the nature of knowledge did imply this, then, when we say that God knows the opposites, it would be necessary that the opposites should proceed from Him together, and this is absurd. The fact that only one of the opposites proceeds from Him shows that there is another attribute present beside knowledge, namely will, and it is in this way that the affirmation of will in the First must be understood according to the philosophers.[2] For God, according to the philosophers, necessarily knows and wills through His knowledge. As to Ghazali's assertion that the act can be subdivided into two, into a natural act and a voluntary act, this is false. God's act according to the philosophers is in a certain way not natural, nor is it absolutely voluntary; it is voluntary without having the deficiency which is attached to the human will. Therefore the term 'will' is attributed to the Divine Will and the human in an equivocal way, just as the term 'knowledge' is attributed equivocally to eternal knowledge and to temporal. For the will in animals and man is a passivity which occurs to them through the object of desire and is caused by it. This is the meaning of 'will' in the case of the human will, but the Creator is too exalted to possess an attribute which should be an effect. Therefore by 'will' in God only the procession of the act joined to knowledge can be understood. And 'knowledge', as we said, refers to the two opposites, and in the knowledge of God there is knowledge of the opposites in a certain way, and His performing only the one shows that there exists in Him another attribute which is called 'will'.

Ghazali says:

The second way of answering is to concede that the procession of a thing from the agent implies knowledge of the thing which proceeds. Now, according to them, the act of God is one, namely the effect which is pure intellect, and God can only know this effect. The first effect again will only know what proceeds from it. For the universe does not proceed from God immediately, but through mediators and derivation and a series of consequences. For that which proceeds from what proceeds from Him need not be known to Him, and from Him Himself only one thing proceeds. And how should He know everything that proceeds mediately from Him? For this is not even necessary in voluntary acts, and how could it be necessary in natural acts? For the movement of a stone from the top of a mountain can occur through a voluntary propulsion which implies knowledge of the principle of motion, but does not imply knowledge of all the consequences which may occur through its knocking and breaking something.[1] And to this again the philosophers have no answer.

I answer:

The answer to this is that the Agent whose knowledge is of the highest perfection knows everything which proceeds from Him and which proceeds from that which proceeds from Him, and so from the first term to the last. And if the knowledge of the First is of the highest perfection, the First must know everything that proceeds from it either mediately or immediately, and its knowledge need not be of the same kind as our knowledge, for our knowledge is imperfect and posterior to the thing known.

Then Ghazali says, answering the objection he brought forward against the philosophers:

If, however, the philosophers should say: 'If we declared that the First only knows its own self, this would be a very reprehensible doctrine, for all other beings know themselves and know the First, and would therefore be superior to it; and how can the effect be superior to the cause?

I say:

This is an insufficient answer, for it opposes a rational argument with a moral one.

Then Ghazali answers this and says:

> We should answer: 'This reprehensible doctrine is a necessary consequence for those who follow* the philosophers in denying the Divine Will and the production of the world, and one must either adhere to it as the other philosophers do, or abandon the philosophers and acknowledge that the world is produced through will.'

I say:

Ghazali means that if they belong to those who affirm that God knows His work, only to avoid the reprehensible doctrine that He does not know anything but His own self, they are forced to acknowledge this reprehensible doctrine just as well, since they affirmed another reprehensible doctrine, namely the eternity of the world and the denial of the Will.[1] However, the philosophers do not deny the Will, and only deny that part of it which implies a deficiency.

Then Ghazali says:

How will you refute those philosophers who say that this knowledge does not add to God's dignity, since other beings need knowledge only in order to acquire perfection (for in their essence there is a deficiency) and man receives dignity through the intelligibles either that he may see his advantage in the coming events of this world and the next, or that his obscure and insufficient essence may be perfected, and likewise all the other creatures, but that the essence of God does not stand in need of perfection: nay, if a knowledge could be imagined through which He would be perfected, His essence, in so far as it is His essence, would be imperfect?

This is just the same kind of remark as your assertions, Avicenna, concerning His hearing and seeing and His knowing the particular beings which fall under the concept of time, for you agree with all the other philosophers in saying that God is too exalted for that, and that the changes which fall under the concept of time and which are divided into past and future events are not known to the First, since this would imply a change in its essence and a being influenced, and the denial of this does not imply an imperfection, but rather a perfection, and there is only an imperfection in the senses and the need for them.[2] If there were not this human imperfection, man would not be in need of the senses to guard himself against any change which might affect him. And in the same way you affirm that the knowledge of particular events is an imperfection. And if it is true that we can know all particular events and perceive all sensible things, whereas the First cannot know anything of the particulars nor perceive anything of sensible things without this implying any imperfection in the First, it may also be permitted to ascribe to others knowledge of the intelligible universals but to deny it of the First without this implying any imperfection in the First. There is no way out of this.

I say:

This is the proof of those who say that the First knows only itself, and we have already spoken of the theory of those who combine the doctrine that the First knows only itself with the theory that it knows all existents; and for this reason some of the best known philosophers affirm that God the Creator is Himself all existents and that He grants them in His benevolence, and there is no sense in repeating ourselves. The premisses used in this section are common dialectical propositions, since they all belong to those which compare the Divine to the empirical, although no common genus unites these two spheres and they do not possess any common factor at all. In general his discussion in this section, when he argues with Avicenna, who adduces the argument of those philosophers who believe that God in knowing Himself must know other things, since He must necessarily know what proceeds from Himself, and all the other assertions of Avicenna to prove this, which he relates, and which he uses himself again to refute Avicenna, are all taken from human conditions which he tries to refer to the Creator; and this is false, since the terms of these two types of knowledge are predicated equivocally.

Avicenna's assertion that any intelligent being from whom an act proceeds knows this act is a true proposition; not, however, in the sense in which the word 'knowledge' is used of the human intellect, when it understands a thing, for the human intellect is perfected by what it perceives and knows, and is affected by it, and the cause of action in man is the representation he forms in his intellect.[1] And Ghazali argues against this kind of proposition by saying that when a man acts and there follows from his act another act and from the second act a third and from the third a fourth, it is not necessary that the conscious agent should know all the consequences which follow from his first act; and Ghazali says to his opponent this is a fact which concerns voluntary acts, but how is it when one assumes an agent whose acts are not voluntary? And he only says this because he means that the affirmation of God's knowledge implies the affirmation of God's will.[2]

And therefore Ghazali says:

To this again the philosophers have no answer*.

I say:

Ghazali means that it does not follow that the First according to Avicenna thinks anything but the act which proceeds from it primarily, and this act is the second cause and the first effect. Neither is there an answer to the other difficulty which he states that if the First thinks only itself and nothing else, man would be more noble than it. And the reason why Ghazali's words carry a certain conviction is that if one imagines two men, one of whom thinks only his own self, whereas the other thinks his own self and other things besides, the latter intellect is regarded as superior to the former. However, as the term 'intellect' is applied to the human intellect and to this Divine Intellect in a purely equivocal way, since the latter is an agent and not a patient and the former a patient and not an agent, this analogy does not hold any longer.

Having given as Avicenna's argument the maxim which Avicenna applies to every intelligent being,[1] that the more knowledge an intellect possesses the nobler it is, and having affirmed that, according to him (Ghazali), it is just the philosophers' denial of God's will and of temporal creation which forces them to deny to God a knowledge of anything but Himself, since the conscious agent knows his effect only in so far as it differs from himself by being an object of his will, he says that this reprehensible assertion, i.e. the assertion that the effect which is man must be nobler than the cause which is the Creator, is a consequence for the philosophers only, since as the philosophers deny the coming into being of the world, they deny the Divine Will, as he affirms, and as they deny the Divine Will, they deny that God knows what proceeds from Him.[2] But all this, namely the denial of God's will, has been shown previously not to be true; for they deny only His temporal will. And having repeated Avicenna's arguments, which he regarded as being applicable both to the knowledge of the temporal and the knowledge of the eternal,[3] he begins to argue against him, showing the distinction which the philosophers established on this point between these two sciences, and indeed this consequence is incumbent on Avicenna.

And Ghazali says:

How will you refute those philosophers who say that this knowledge does not add to God's dignity, for only other beings need knowledge...?

I say:

The summary of this is that, if all these perceptions exist only because of man's imperfection, then God is too exalted for them; and therefore Ghazali says to Avicenna: 'Just as you acknowledge with your fellow-philosophers that God's not perceiving individual things is not a consequence of an imperfection in Him, for you have proved that the perception of individuals rests on an imperfection in the perceiver, in the same way the perception of other things than Himself need not derive from an imperfection in Him, since the perception of these other things depends on the imperfection of the perceiver.'

The answer to all this is that God's knowledge cannot be divided into the opposites of true and false in which human knowledge is divided; for instance, it may be said of a man that either he knows or he does not know other things, because these two propositions are contradictory, and when the one is true the other is false; but in the case of God both propositions, that He knows what He knows and that He does not know it*, are true, for He does not know it through a knowledge which determines an imperfection, namely human knowledge, but knows it through a knowledge which does not carry with it any imperfection, and this is a knowledge the quality of which nobody but God Himself can understand. And concerning both universals and individuals it is true of Him that He knows them and does not know them. This is the conclusion to which the principles of the ancient philosophers led; but those who make a distinction, and say that God knows universals but does not know particulars have not fully grasped their theory, and this is not a consequence of their principles. For all human sciences are passivities and impressions from the existents, and the existents operate on them. But the knowledge of the Creator operates on existents, and the existents receive the activities of His knowledge.

Once this is established, the whole quarrel between Ghazali and the philosophers comes to an end in regard to this chapter as well as the next two. We shall, however*, give an account of these chapters and mention in them both what is particular to them and those arguments which have been already discussed above.

THE TWELFTH DISCUSSION

About the impotence of the philosophers to prove that God knows Himself

Ghazali says:

We say that when the Muslims understood that the world was created through the will of God, they proved His knowledge from His will, then

His life from His will and His knowledge together,[1] then from His life, according to the principle that every living being knows itself,[2] they proved that He too must know His own essence, since He is alive. And this is a rational procedure of extreme force. For you philosophers, however, since you deny the divine will and the world's coming into existence, and since you affirm that what proceeds from Him proceeds in a necessary and natural sequence, why should it be impossible that His essence should be of such a nature that only the first effect proceeded from it, and that then the second effect followed the first till the whole order of existents was completed, but, notwithstanding this, the First would not know itself, just as neither fire from which heat proceeds, nor the sun from which light proceeds, know themselves or anything else? For only that which knows itself knows what proceeds from itself, and therefore knows other things besides itself. And we have already shown that, according to the theory of the philosophers the First does not know other things, and we have forced those who do not agree with them on this point to acknowledge this consequence which follows from their assumption. And if it does not know others, it is not absurd to suppose that it does not know its own self.

If they say: 'Everyone who does not know himself is dead, and how could the First be dead?'—we answer: 'This is indeed a conclusion which follows from your theory, since there is no difference between you and those who say that every one who does not act through will, power and choice, who neither hears nor sees, is dead, and he who does not know other things is dead. And if it is possible that the First is destitute of all these attributes, what need has it of knowing itself?' And if they return to the doctrine that everything which is free from matter is intellect by itself and therefore thinks itself, we have shown that this is an arbitrary judgement without any proof.

And if they say: 'The proof is that what is existent is divided into what is alive and what is dead, and what is alive is prior and superior to what is dead, and the First is prior and superior: therefore let it be alive; and every living being knows itself, since it is impossible that the living should be amongst its effects and should not itself be alive',[3] we answer: 'All this is pure presumption, for we affirm that it is not impossible that that which knows itself should follow from that which does not, either through many intermediaries or without mediation. And if the reason for its impossibility is that in that case the effect would be superior to the cause, well, it is not impossible that the effect should be superior to the cause, for the superiority of the cause to the effect is not a fundamental principle. Further, how can you refute the view that its superiority might consist not in its knowledge but in the fact that the existence of the universe* is a consequence of its essence? For the proof is that, whereas the First neither sees nor hears, there are many other beings who know other things than themselves and who do see and hear.'

And if it were said, 'Existents are divided into the seeing and the blind, the knowing and the ignorant', we answer: 'Well, let the seeing then be superior and let the First see and have knowledge of things!'[1] But the philosophers deny this, and say that its excellence does not consist in seeing and knowing things, but in not being in need of sight and knowledge and being the essence from which there proceeds the universe in which the knowing and the seeing beings exist. And in the same way it may be said that this essence does not possess excellence because it has knowledge itself, but because it is the principle of essences which possess knowledge, and this is an excellence which is peculiar to it.

The philosophers are therefore forced to deny also that the First knows itself, for nothing proves such a knowledge but will, and nothing proves will except the temporal beginning of the world, and if this principle is destroyed, all these things are destroyed which are accepted through the speculation of the mind alone. For they do not possess a proof for any thing they affirm or deny concerning the attributes of the First, but they make only such guesses and conjectures as lawyers would despise in their suppositions. However, no wonder that the intellect should be perplexed about the divine attributes; one should wonder only at the wonderful self-complacency of the philosophers, at their satisfaction with their proofs and their belief that they know those things through evident proofs, notwithstanding the mistakes and the errors in them.

I say:

The most wonderful thing is the claim of the theologians that the temporal becoming of the world implies that it has been willed by a will, for we find that temporal things occur through nature, through will, and by chance.[2] Those that occur through will are the products of art, and those that occur through nature are natural things, and if temporal things occurred only through will, will would have to be included in the definition of the temporal, whereas it is well known that the definition of temporal becoming is 'existence succeeding non-existence'. If indeed the world had come into being temporally, it would be more appropriate that it should have come into being, in so far as it was a natural existent, from principles appropriate to natural things, rather than from principles appropriate to artificial things, i.e. the will. Since, however, it is established that the world exists through a First Agent which preferred its existence to its non-existence, it is necessary that this agent should be a willer, and if this First Agent does not cease to prefer the world's existence to its non-existence, and the willer—as Ghazali says—must have knowledge, the philosophers are in complete agreement with the theologians about this fundamental point. The whole theological argument, however, which he gives has only persuasive power, because it compares natural things to artificial.

As to what he says of the philosophers, that they believe that what proceeds from the Creator proceeds in a natural way, this is a wrong imputation. What they really believe is that existents proceed from Him in a way superior to nature and to the human will, for both these ways are subject to an imperfection, but they are not the only possible ways, since it has been proved that the act of God can proceed from Him neither in a natural way nor in a voluntary, in the sense in which this is understood in the sublunary world. For will in an animal is the principle of movement, and if the Creator is devoid of movement, He is devoid of the principle of movement in the way a voluntary agent in the empirical world moves.[1] What proceeds from God proceeds in a nobler way than the voluntary, a way which nobody can understand but God Himself. And the proof that He wills is that He knows the opposites, and if He were an agent in absolutely the same way as He is a knower, He would carry out the two contrary acts together, and this is impossible; and therefore it is necessary that He should perform one of the two contraries through choice.[2]

The error of the theologians with regard to this question is that they say that every act is either natural or voluntary, but do not understand the meaning of either of these words. For nature, according to the philosophers, has different meanings, the primary being the ascending of fire and the descending of earth,[3] and an existent only has this movement when something has prevented it from being* in its natural place, and there was therefore something that constrained it; but the Creator is too high for this kind of nature. The philosophers also apply the term 'nature' to every potency from which an intellectual act proceeds, in the same way as the acts which proceed from the arts,[4] and some of the philosophers ascribe intellect to this nature, and some say that this nature does not possess intellect but acts only by nature.[5] And they say that this nature proceeds from an intellect, because they compare it to artificial things which move themselves and from which orderly well-arranged acts proceed.[6] And therefore their master Aristotle asserts that it is manifest that the nature of intellect rules the universe.[7] And how far is this belief from what Ghazali ascribes to them!

Who, however, assumes as a universal maxim that he who knows himself must know other things which proceed from him, must conclude that he who does not know other things cannot know himself.

THE TWELFTH DISCUSSION

And having refuted Avicenna's theory that God knows other things, by the arguments of the philosophers on this point which he adduces against him,[1] he concludes against him that the First does not know itself; and this conclusion is valid.[2]

And as to what he relates of the argument of the philosophers on this point, namely that they say that he who does not know himself is dead and the First cannot be dead, this is a persuasive argument composed of common propositions, for he who is not alive is not dead unless it is in his nature to receive life[3]—or one must mean by 'dead' what is meant by 'inanimate' and 'inorganic', and then this is a true dichotomy, for every existent is either alive or inorganic, provided we understand by 'life' a term which is equivocally used of the eternal and the corruptible.

And as to Ghazali's words:

And if they return to the doctrine that everything which is free from matter is intellect by itself and therefore thinks itself, we have shown that this is an arbitrary judgement without any proof.

I say:

We have already shown the manner in which this proof of the philosophers must be taken, in so far as this proof preserves its power by being given in this book—I mean its power is diminished, as is necessary when a thing is removed from its natural context. And as to what he says of their arguing on this point against the philosophers that the existent is either alive or dead, and that which is alive is more noble than that which is dead, and that the principle is nobler than that which is alive and that it is therefore necessarily alive, if by 'dead' is understood the inanimate, these propositions are common and true.

His assertion, however, that life can proceed from the lifeless and knowledge from what does not possess knowledge, and that the dignity of the First consists only in its being the principle of the universe, is false. For if life could proceed from the lifeless, then the existent might proceed from the non-existent, and then anything whatever might proceed from anything whatever, and there would be no congruity between causes and effects, either in the genus predicated analogically or in the species.[4]

As to his assertion that, when the philosophers say that what is nobler than life must be alive, it is like saying that that which is nobler than what has hearing and seeing must have hearing and seeing: the philosophers do not say so, for they deny that the First Principle can hear and see. And Ghazali's argument that, since, according to the philosophers, that which is superior to what hears and sees need not hear and see, then also what is superior to the living and the knowing need not itself be alive and possessed of knowledge and that, just as according to the philosophers that which possesses sight can proceed from what has no sight, so it is possible that knowledge should proceed from what has no knowledge: this is a very sophistical and false argument.

For according to the philosophers that which has no hearing or seeing is not absolutely superior to that which has hearing and seeing, but only because it has a perception superior to seeing and hearing, namely knowledge.[1] But, since there is nothing superior to knowledge, it is not possible that that which does not possess knowledge should be superior to that which does, be it a principle or not. For since some of the principles possess knowledge, others not, it is not permissible that those which do not know should be superior to those that do, just as little as this is possible in regard to effects which do and do not possess knowledge. And the nobility of being a principle cannot surpass the nobility of knowledge, unless the nobility of a principle that does not possess knowledge could surpass the nobility of a principle that does. And the excellence of being a principle cannot surpass the excellence of knowledge. And therefore it is necessary that the principle which has the utmost nobility should possess the utmost excellence, which is knowledge. The philosophers only avoid ascribing to the First hearing and seeing, because this would imply its possessing a soul. The Holy Law ascribes hearing and seeing to God to remind us that God is not deprived of any kind of knowledge and understanding, and the masses cannot be made to grasp this meaning except by the use of the terms 'hearing' and 'seeing', and for this reason this exegesis is limited to the learned, and therefore cannot be taken as one of the dogmas of the Holy Law common to the masses. And the same is the case with many questions the solutions of which the Holy Law leaves to science.

Everything this chapter contains is the confusion and the incoherence of Ghazali himself. But, we appeal to God on account of the mistakes the learned have made, and that He may pardon them because of their wish to glorify His name in all such questions, and we pray God that He may not place us among those who are excluded from the next world through their faults in this, or from the highest through their desire for the lowest, and that He may bestow on us final blessedness!

THE THIRTEENTH DISCUSSION

To refute those who affirm that God is ignorant of the individual things which are divided in time into present, past, and future

Ghazali says:
About this theory they all agree; for as to those who believe that God only knows Himself, this is implied in their belief; and as to those who believe that He knows things besides Himself (and this is the theory which Avicenna has chosen) they believe that God knows other things in a universal knowledge which does not fall under the concept of time and which is not differentiated through past, future, and present although, nevertheless, Avicenna affirms that not the weight of a grain escapes God's knowledge either on earth or in the heavens, since He knows individual things in a universal way.[1]

Now we must first understand this theory, and then occupy ourselves with refuting it. We shall explain this through an example, namely that the sun, for example, suffers an eclipse,[2] after not having been eclipsed, and afterwards recovers its light. There are therefore in an eclipse three moments: the moment when there was not yet an eclipse but the eclipse was expected in the future, the time when the eclipse was actually there, its being, and thirdly, the moment the eclipse had ceased but had been. Now we have in regard to these three conditions* a threefold knowledge: we know first that there is not yet an eclipse, but that there will be one, secondly that it is now there, and thirdly, that it has been present but is no longer present. This threefold knowledge is numerically distinguishable and differentiated and its sequence implies a change in the knowing essence, for if this knowing essence thought after the cessation of the eclipse that the eclipse was present as before, this would be ignorance, not knowledge, and if it thought during its presence that it was absent, this again would be ignorance, and the one knowledge cannot take the place of the other.

The philosophers affirm now that the condition of God is not differentiated by means of these three moments, for this would imply a change, and that He whose condition does not change cannot be imagined to know these things, for knowledge follows the object of knowledge, and when the object of knowledge changes, the knowledge changes, and when the knowledge changes, without doubt the knower changes too; but change in God is impossible. However, notwithstanding this, the philosophers affirm that God knows the eclipse and all its attributes and accidents, but through a knowledge which is attributed to Him in an eternal attribution and is unchangeable: God knows for instance that the sun exists and that the moon exists, and that they have emanated from God Himself through the medium of angels whom the philosophers in their technical terminology call 'separate intellects', and God knows that the sun and moon move in circles and that between their orbits there is an intersection at two points, the ascending and the descending node,[1] and that at certain times the sun and moon are together in these nodes and that then the sun is eclipsed— i.e. the body of the moon comes between the sun and the eyes of the observer, and the sun is concealed from his eyes, and that when the sun has passed a certain distance beyond this node, say a year, it is eclipsed again, and that this eclipse is either total or for a third or for a half, and that it will last an hour or two hours, and God knows equally all other time determinations and all other accidents of the eclipse; and nothing of this escapes God's knowledge. However, God's knowledge before, during, and after the eclipse is all of one kind without any differentiation and without any implication of a change in His essence. And such is His knowledge of all temporal occurrences which take place through causes which have other causes terminating finally in the circular movement of the heavens, and the cause of this movement is the soul of the heavens, and the cause of the soul's movement is its desire to assimilate itself to God and to the angels near Him.[2] And the whole universe is known to Him, that is, it is manifested to Him in one single congruous manifestation which is not influenced by time. Still, at the time of the eclipse it cannot be said that He knows that the eclipse is taking place now, nor does He know when it has passed that it has passed now, for He cannot be imagined to know anything which for its definition needs a relation to time, since this implies a change. This is their solution in so far as it concerns a division in time.[3]

And as concerns their theory about what is divided in matter and space, like individual men and animals, they say that God does not know the accidents of Zaid, Amr, and Khalid and that He knows only man in general, through a universal knowledge, and that He knows the accidents and properties of man in general, namely that he must have a body composed of limbs, some to grasp with, some to walk with, some to perceive with, some of which form a pair while some are single, and that the bodily faculties must be dispersed in all parts of the body. And the same applies to all the qualities which are inside and outside man's body and all its accidents, attributes, and consequences, so that there is nothing that is hidden from God in His knowledge of the universal. But the individual Zaid can only be distinguished from Amr through the senses, not through the intellect, and this distinction is based on pointing to a special direction, whereas the intellect can only understand direction and space absolutely as universals. And when we say 'this' and 'that'*, this is a case of pointing to a special relation of a sensible thing to the observer as being near to him or far from him, or in a definite place, and this is impossible where God is concerned.[4]

This then is the principle in which they believe, and through it they uproot the Divine Laws absolutely, for this principle implies that God cannot know whether Zaid obeys or disobeys Him, since God cannot know any new occurrences that happen to Zaid, as He does not know the individual Zaid; for the individual and his acts come into existence after non-existence, and as God does not know the individual, He cannot know his conditions and his acts—indeed, He cannot know that Zaid becomes a heretic or a true believer, for He can know only the unbelief and the belief of man in general, not as it is specified in individuals. Yes, God cannot know Muhammed's proclaiming himself a prophet at the time he did, nor can God know this of any definite prophet; He can only know that some people proclaim themselves prophets and that they have such-and-such qualities, but any individual prophet He cannot know, for he can only be known by sense-perception. Nor can He know the acts which proceed from the prophets, since they are divided as acts of a definite man through the division of time, and their perception with their diversity implies a change in the observer.

This is what we wanted to do first, namely to expound their view, then to render it intelligible, thirdly to show the perversities implied in it.

We shall now pass on to relate the artfulness* of their theory and the point where it fails. Their artfulness lies in the fact that they say: 'There are here three different moments, and a sequence of different things in one single subject no doubt implies a change in it. For if at the moment of the eclipse God thought that what was happening* was like what had been before, He would be ignorant; if, on the other hand, He knew that it was happening and knew previously that it was not happening, but would happen, His knowledge and His condition would have become different, and this would imply a change, for "change" means only a difference in the knowledge and a difference in the knowledge implies a difference in the knower, for he who did not know a thing and then knows it, has changed; previously he had no knowledge that it was happening, and then his knowledge was realized: therefore he changed.'

And they have elaborated this by saying that there are three kinds of conditions;[1] first a condition which is a mere relation*, as when we say right and left, for this does not refer to an essential attribute, but is a mere relation; for if you change a thing from your right to your left, your relation to it changes, but the condition of your essence does not change, for the relation changes with respect to the essence, but the essence does not change. The second kind of condition is of the same type, i.e. when you have the capacity to move bodies in front of you, and those bodies or part of them disappear, your innate power and your capacity does not change, for your capacity is first the capacity to move body in general and secondly to move a definite body in so far as it is a body; and the relation of the capacity to the definite body is not an essential attribute, but a mere relation, and the disappearance of the body determines the cessation of the relation, but not a change in the condition of the one who possesses this capacity. The third* kind of condition, however, is a change in the essence, for when one who had no knowledge acquires knowledge and one who had no power becomes powerful there is indeed a change.[1]

And the change in the object known causes a change in the knowledge, for the relation to the definite object known enters into the essence of the knowledge itself, since the essence of the definite knowledge is attached to the definite object known as it exists in reality, and when the knowledge attaches itself to it in another relation, it becomes necessarily another knowledge and this succession implies a differentiation in the essence* of the knowledge. And it cannot be said that God has one single knowledge which, having been knowledge of the future event, could become knowledge of the present event, and having been knowledge of the present event, could become knowledge of the past event, for although the knowledge would be one and the same and have similar conditions, there would be a change of relation to Him and the change of relation would enter into the essence of the knowledge; and this change would imply a change in the essence of the knowledge, and from this there would result a change (which is impossible) in God.

The objection to this is twofold.

First one can say: How will you refute one who says that God has one single knowledge of the eclipse, for instance, at a definite time, and that this knowledge before the occurrence of the eclipse is the knowledge that the eclipse will occur, and during the eclipse is identical with the knowledge that it is occurring, and after the eclipse identical with the knowledge that it has ceased, and that these differences refer to relations which imply neither a change in the essence of the knowledge nor a change in the essence of the knower, and that this is exactly like a mere relation?[2] For one single person can be at your right and then turn in front of you and go to your left, and there is a succession of relations with respect to you; but that which is changing is the person who takes up different positions, and God's knowledge must be understood in this way, for indeed we admit that God comprehends things in one single knowledge in everlasting eternity, and that His condition does not change; with their intention, the denial of His change, we do agree, but their assertion that it is necessary to regard the knowledge of an actual becoming and its cessation as a change, we refuse to accept. For how do you know this? Indeed, suppose God had created in us a knowledge that Zaid will arrive tomorrow at daybreak, and had made this knowledge permanent without creating for us another knowledge or the forgetfulness of this knowledge; then, by the mere previous knowledge, we should know at daybreak that at present Zaid is arriving and afterwards that he had arrived, and this one permanent knowledge would suffice to comprehend these three moments.[3]

There still remains their assertion that the relation to a definite object known enters into the essence of the knowledge of this object, and that whenever the relation becomes different the thing which has this essential

THE THIRTEENTH DISCUSSION

relation becomes different, and that whenever this differentiation and this sequence arise, there is a change.[1]

We say: If this is true, then rather follow the path of your fellow-philosophers when they say that God knows only Himself and that knowing Himself is identical with His essence, for if He knew man and animal and the inorganic in general (and these are undoubtedly different things), His relation to them would undoubtedly be different too; and one single knowledge cannot be a knowledge of different things, since the object related is differentiated, and the relation is differentiated, and the relation to the object known is essential to the knowledge, and this implies a multiplicity and a differentiation—not a mere multiplicity with a similarity, for similar things are things which can be substituted for each other, but the knowledge of an animal cannot be substituted for the knowledge of the inorganic, nor the knowledge of white for the knowledge of black, for they are two different things.[2] Besides, these species and genera and universal accidents are infinite[3] and they are different, and how can different sciences fall under one science? Again, this knowledge is the essence of the knower without any addition, and I should like to know how an intelligent man can regard the unity of the knowledge of one and the same thing, when this knowledge is divided through its relations with the past, the future, and the present, as impossible, and uphold the unity of the knowledge which is attached to all genera and all different species![4] For the diversity and the distance between the genera and the remote species is far greater than the difference which occurs in the conditions of one thing which is divided through the division of time; and if the former does not imply a plurality and differentiation, why then does the latter? And as soon as it is proved that the diversity of times is less important than the diversity of genera and species, and that the latter does not imply a plurality and a diversity, the former also will not imply this. And if this does not imply a diversity, then it will be possible that the whole universe should be comprehended in one everlasting knowledge in everlasting time, and that this should not imply a change in the essence of the knower.

I say:

This sophistry is based on the assimilation of Divine Knowledge to human and the comparison of the one knowledge with the other, for man perceives the individual through his senses, and universal existents through his intellect, and the cause of his perception is the thing perceived itself, and there is no doubt that the perception changes through the change in the things perceived and that their plurality implies its plurality.

As to his answer that it is possible that there should exist a knowledge the relation of which to the objects known is that kind of relation which does not enter into the essence of the thing related, like the relation of right and left, to that which has a right and a left—this is an answer which cannot be understood from the nature of human knowledge.[1] And his second objection, that those philosophers who affirm that God knows universals must, by admitting in His knowledge a plurality of species, conclude that a plurality of individuals and a plurality of conditions of one and the same individual is permissible for His knowledge, is a sophistical objection. For the knowledge of individuals is sensation or imagination, and the knowledge of universals is intellect,[2] and the new occurrence of individuals or conditions of individuals causes two things, a change and a plurality in the perception; whereas knowledge of species and genera does not imply a change, since the knowledge of them is invariable and they are unified in the knowledge which comprehends them, and universality and individuality only agree in their forming a plurality.

And his statement that those philosophers who assume one simple knowledge, which comprehends genera and species without there existing in it a plurality and diversity which the differentiation and diversity of the species and genera would imply, will have also to admit one simple knowledge which will comprehend different individuals and different conditions of one and the same individual, is like saying that if there is an intellect which comprehends species and genera, and this intellect is one, there must be one simple genus which comprehends different individuals; and this is a sophism, since the term 'knowledge' is predicated equivocally of divine and human knowledge of the universal and the individual.[3] But his remark that the plurality of species and genera causes a plurality in the knowledge is true, and the most competent philosophers therefore do not call God's knowledge of existents either universal or individual, for knowledge which implies the concepts of universal and individual is a passive intellect and an effect,[4] whereas the First Intellect is pure act and a cause, and His knowledge cannot be compared to human knowledge; for in so far as God does not think other things as being other than Himself His essence is not passive knowledge, and in so far as He thinks them as being identical with His essence, His essence is active knowledge.[5]

And the summary of their doctrine is that, since they ascertained by proofs that God thinks only Himself, His essence must of necessity be intellect. And as intellect, in so far as it is intellect, can only be attached to what exists, not to what does not exist, and it had been proved that there is no existent but those existents which we think, it was necessary that His intellect should be attached to them, since it was not possible that it should be attached to non-existence and there is no other kind of existent to which it might be attached.[1] And since it was necessary that it should be attached to the existents, it had to be attached either in the way our knowledge is attached to it, or in a superior way, and since the former is impossible, this knowledge must be attached in a superior way and according to a more perfect existence of existents than the existence of the existents to which our intellect is attached. For true knowledge is conformity with the existent,[2] and if His knowledge is superior to ours and His knowledge is attached to the existent in a way superior to our attachment to the existent, then there must be two kinds of existence, a superior and an inferior, and the superior existence must be the cause of the inferior.

And this is the meaning of the ancient philosophers, when they say that God is the totality of the existents which He bestows on us in His bounty and of which He is the agent. And therefore the chiefs of the Sufis say: there is no reality besides Him.[3] But all this is the knowledge of those who are steadfast in their knowledge, and this must not be written down and it must not be made an obligation of faith, and therefore it is not taught by the Divine Law. And one who mentions this truth where it should not be mentioned sins, and one who withholds it from those to whom it should be told sins too. And that one single thing can have different degrees of existence can be learned from the different degrees of existence of the soul.[4]

Ghazali says:

The second refutation is: 'What prevents you, according to your doctrine, from affirming God's knowledge of individuals, even if this implies His changing, for why do you not believe that this kind of change is not impossible in God, just as Jahm, one of the Mu'tazilites, says that His knowledge of temporals is temporal[5] and the later Karramites say that God is the substratum of the temporals?[6] The true believers refute these theories only by arguing that what changes cannot be without change, and what cannot be without change and without temporal occurrences is itself temporal and not eternal.[7] For you, however, according to your doctrine the world is eternal but not without change, and if you acknowledge an eternal which changes, nothing prevents you from accepting this theory.'

If you replied: We only regard this as impossible, because the temporal knowledge in His essence must either derive from Himself or from something else; that it should derive from Himself is impossible, for we have shown that from the eternal no temporal can proceed and that God cannot become active after having been at rest, for this would imply a change, and we have established this in treating the question of the temporal becoming of the world; and if it were to arise in His essence from something else, how could something else influence and change Him so that His conditions changed as if under the power and necessity of something different from Him?—we answer: Neither of these alternatives is impossible, according to your doctrine. As to your assertion that it is impossible that from the eternal a temporal being should proceed, we refuted this sufficiently when we treated this problem. According to you it is impossible that from the eternal there should proceed a temporal being which is the first of a series of temporal beings and it is only impossible that there should be a first temporal being.[1] However, these temporal beings have no infinite number of temporal causes, but by means of the circular movement they terminate in something eternal which is the soul and life of the sphere; and the soul of the sphere is eternal and the circular movement arises temporally from it and each part of this movement begins and ends, and that which follows it is surely a new occurrence.[2] Therefore, according to you the temporal beings arise from the eternal.[3] However, since the conditions of the eternal are uniform, the emanation of temporal occurrences from Him will be eternally uniform, just as the conditions of the movement are uniform, since they proceed from an eternal being whose conditions are uniform; and all the philosophical sects acknowledge that from an eternal being a temporal being can proceed, when this happens in a proportionate way and eternally. Therefore let the different types of His knowledge proceed from Him in this way.[4]

And as to the other alternative, that His knowledge should proceed from another, we answer: Why is that impossible according to you? There are here only three difficulties. The first is the changing, but we have already shown that this is a consequence of your theory.

The second difficulty, that one thing should be the cause of a change in another, is not impossible according to you; for let the occurrence of the thing be the cause of the occurrence of its being known, just as you say that the appearance of a coloured[5] figure in front of the pupil of the eye is the cause of the impression of the image of this figure on the vitreous humour of the pupil through the medium of the transparent air between the pupil and the figure seen;[6] and if therefore an inanimate object can be the cause of the impression of the form on the pupil—and this is the meaning of sight—why should it be impossible that the occurrence of temporal beings should cause the First to acquire its knowledge of them*? And just as the potency of seeing is disposed to perceive, and the appearance of the coloured figure, when the obstacles are removed, is the cause of the actualization of the perception, so let according to you the essence of the First Principle be disposed to receive knowledge and emerge from potency

THE THIRTEENTH DISCUSSION

into act through the existence of this temporal being. And if this implies a change in the eternal, a changing eternal is not impossible according to you. And if you protest that this is impossible in the necessary existent, you have no other proof for establishing the necessary existent than the necessity of a termination to the series of causes and effects, as has been shown previously, and we have proved that to end this series with an eternal being which can change is not impossible.

The third difficulty in the problem is that if the Eternal could change through another, this would be like subjection and the control of another over Him.

But one may say: Why is this impossible according to you? For it only means that the Eternal is the cause of the occurrence of the temporal beings through intermediaries, and that afterwards the occurrence of these temporal beings becomes the cause of the knowledge which the Eternal has of them. It is therefore as if He were Himself the cause of this knowledge reaching Him, although it reaches Him through intermediaries. And if you say that this is like subjection, let it be so, for this conforms to your doctrine, since you say that what proceeds from God proceeds in the way of necessity and nature, and that He has no power not to do it, and this too resembles a kind of bondage, and indicates that He is as it were under necessity as to that which proceeds from Him. And if it is said that this is no constraint, since His entelechy consists in the fact that He makes everything proceed from Himself, and that this is no subjection, then we answer that His entelechy consists in knowing everything, and if it is true to say that the knowledge which we receive in conjunction with everything that happens is a perfection for us,[1] not an imperfection or subjection, let the same be the case with respect to God.

I say:

The summary of this first objection against the philosophers, which is a refutation of their theories, not of the fact itself, is that 'according to your principles, philosophers, there exists an eternal being in which temporal beings inhere, namely the sphere; how can you therefore deny that the First Eternal is a subject in which temporal beings inhere?' The Ash'arites deny this only because of their theory that any subject in which temporal beings inhere is itself a temporal being. And this objection is dialectical,[2] for there are temporal beings which do not inhere in the eternal, namely the temporal beings which change the substance in which they inhere; and there are temporal beings which inhere in the eternal, namely the temporal beings which do not change the substance of their substratum, like the local movement of the moving body and transparency and illumination;[3] and further there is an eternal in which no movements and no changes inhere at all, namely the incorporeal eternal; and there is an eternal in which only some movements inhere, namely the eternal which is a body like the heavenly bodies, and when this distinction, which the philosophers require, is made, this objection becomes futile, for the discussion is only concerned with the incorporeal eternal.

Having made this objection against the philosophers, he gives the answer of the philosophers about this question, and the summary is that they are only prevented from admitting temporal knowledge in the First, because temporal knowledge must arise through itself or through another; and in the former case there would proceed from the eternal a temporal being, and according to the principles of the philosophers no temporal being can proceed from the eternal. Then he argues against this assertion that from the eternal no temporal being can proceed, by showing that they assume that the sphere is eternal and that they assume that temporal beings proceed from it.

But their justification of this is that the temporal cannot proceed from an absolutely eternal being, but only from an eternal being which is eternal in its substance, but temporal in its movements, namely the celestial body; and therefore the celestial body is according to them like an intermediary between the absolutely eternal and the absolutely temporal, for it is in one way eternal, in another way temporal, and this intermediary is the celestial circular movement according to the philosophers, and this movement is according to them eternal in its species, temporal in its parts. And so far as it is eternal, it proceeds from an eternal, and in so far as its parts are temporal, there proceed from them infinite temporal beings. And the only reason that prevented the philosophers from accepting an existence of temporal beings in the First was that the First is incorporeal and temporal beings only exist in body, for only in body, according to them, there is receptivity, and that which is free from matter has no receptivity.

And Ghazali's objection to the second part of the argument of the philosophers, namely that the First Cause cannot be an effect, is that it is possible that God's knowledge should be like the knowledge of man, that is that the things known should be the cause of His knowledge and their occurrence the cause of the fact that He knows them, just as the objects of sight are the cause of visual perception and the intelligible the cause of intellectual apprehension; so that in this way God's producing and creating existents would be the cause of His apprehending them, and it would not be His knowledge that would be the cause of His creating them.

But it is impossible, according to the philosophers, that God's knowledge should be analogous to ours, for our knowledge is the effect of the existents, whereas God's knowledge is their cause, and it is not true that eternal knowledge is of the same form as temporal. He who believes this makes God an eternal man[1] and man a mortal God,[2] and in short, it has previously been shown that God's knowledge stands in opposition to man's, for it is His knowledge which produces the existents, and it is not the existents which produce His knowledge.

THE FOURTEENTH DISCUSSION

To refute their proof that heaven is an animal moving in a circle in obedience to God

Ghazali says:

The philosophers say also that heaven is an animal and possesses a soul which has the same relation to the body of heaven as our souls to our bodies, and just as our bodies move by will to their ends through the moving power of the soul, heaven acts. And the aim of the heavens in their essential movement is to serve the Lord of the world in a way we shall relate.

Their doctrine in this question is something that cannot be refuted, and we shall not declare that it is impossible; for God has the power of creating life in any body, and neither the size of a body nor its circular shape is a hindrance to its being animated, for the condition of the existence of life is not limited to a particular shape, since animals, notwithstanding their different shapes, all participate in the reception of life.[3] But we claim their incapacity to reach this knowledge by rational proof, even if it is true, and only the prophets through divine revelation or inspiration could apprehend such a knowledge, but rational argument does not prove it; indeed, we do not even assert that it is impossible that such a thing should be known by proof, if there is a proof and this proof is valid, but we must say that what they have given as a proof has only the value of a conjecture, but lacks all strictness.

Their device* is that they say that heaven is moved, and this is a premiss given by perception.[4] And every body moved has a mover, which is a premiss established by reason, since if body were moved merely by being body, every body would be in motion.¹ Every mover receives its impulse either from the moved itself, like the nature in the stone which falls and the will in the movement of the animal conjoined with its power to move, or from an external mover which moves through constraint, as when a stone is flung upwards. Everything that is moved by something existing in itself is either unconscious of its movement (and we call this nature), like the falling of the stone, or conscious (and we call this voluntary or animated). This disjunction, that a movement is either constrained or natural or voluntary, comprises all the cases completely, so that if a movement does not fall under two of these divisions it must be of the third type. Now the movement of heaven cannot be constrained, because the mover of a movement by constraint is either (1) another body which is moved by constraint or by will, and in this case we must finally no doubt arrive at a will as mover, and when in the heavenly bodies a body moved through will is established, then our aim is reached, for what use is it to assume movements through constraint when finally we must admit a will?² or (2) God is the mover of its movement by constraint without intermediary, and this is impossible; for if it moves through Him in so far as it is a body and in so far as He is its creator, then necessarily every body ought to be moved.³

This movement, therefore, must be distinguished by a quality which marks this body off from all other bodies; and this quality will be its proximate mover, either by will or by nature. And it cannot be said that God moves it through His will, because His will has the same relation to all bodies, and why should this body be specially disposed so that God should move it rather than another? One cannot suppose this; for it is impossible, as has been shown in the question about the temporal beginning of the world. When it is therefore established that this body needs as a principle of movement a special qualification, the first division, that of the movement through constraint, is ruled out.

So there remains the possibility that this movement occurs by nature. But this is not possible, for nature by itself is not the cause of motion, because the meaning of 'motion' is the withdrawal from one place to another place; and a body does not move from the place in which it is when that place is its proper place. For this reason a bladder full of air on the surface of the water does not move, but when it is immersed it moves towards the surface of the water, and then it has found its proper place and has come to rest and its nature is stabilized; when, however, it is transferred to a place which is not its proper one, it withdraws to its proper place, just as it withdraws from mid-water to the border of the air.⁴ Now it cannot be imagined that the circular movement is natural, since it returns to every position and place which it would be supposed to abandon, and it is not by nature that a body seeks the place which it abandons, and therefore the bladder of air does not seek the interior of the water, nor the stone when

THE FOURTEENTH DISCUSSION

it has come to rest on the earth the air. Thus only the third division remains, that of movement by will.[1]

I say:

What he lays down in this section, that every thing moved either is moved by itself or through a body from outside and that it is this which is called constraint, is self-evident. But that for every thing which is moved by itself there is no mover but the moved[2] is not a self-evident proposition; it is only a common notion, and the philosophers indeed try to prove that every thing moved by itself has an interior mover different from it, through the use of other premises which are self-evident, and of premises which are the conclusions of other proofs, and this is something which may be ascertained in their books. And likewise it is not self-evident that every thing moved by an exterior mover must finally terminate in a thing moved by itself: what is posed here as a set of self-evident premises is, as a matter of fact, a mixture of the two kinds of assertions; that is to say they are partly conclusions and partly self-evident. Indeed, that what is moved by itself and not by an external body is moved either by its substance and nature or by an interior principle, and that it cannot be moved by something which cannot be seen or touched and which is connected with it from the outside (or in other words by an incorporeal entity) is self-evident.[3] You can claim* to have a proof for this, namely by saying that if this were not so*, upward movement would not be proper to fire rather than to earth; but it is, indeed, evident in itself.[4] And as to that which* does not move by its own substance and nature, this is evident in the things which are sometimes in motion and sometimes at rest, since that which is by nature cannot perform both of two opposites;[5] for those things, however, which are perceived to move continually, a proof is necessary.[6]

Again, as to his assertion that what is moved by itself is moved through a principle in itself, either a principle called 'nature' or a principle called 'soul' and 'choice', this is true, when previously it has been proved that nothing exists which is moved by itself. As concerns his affirmation that the principle called nature does not move by itself in space, except when it is not its proper place (for then it moves to its proper place and stays there), this is true. And his further remark that what moves in a circle has neither an improper nor a proper place, so that it could move from the one to the other either totally or partially, this is nearly self-evident and easy to uphold, and he has in this section mentioned something of its

473 explanation and proof; and therefore, when we understand 'nature' in the sense he has established here, circular movement cannot move by nature.

And as to his further remark that, when it does not move by nature, it moves through soul or through a potency which resembles the soul, it appears that the term 'soul' is predicated only equivocally of the soul in the celestial bodies,[1] and the learned for the most part apply the term 'nature' to every potency which performs a rational act, namely an act which conforms to the order and arrangement which exist in rational things;[2] but they exclude heaven from this kind of potency, because according to them it is heaven which provides this directing power for all existents.[3]

However, the argument of the ancients he relates here has only dialectical value, partly because much in it which is in reality a conclusion of a proof is assumed to be self-evident and partly because things are opposed in it which are not really in opposition. It is also dialectical because its premisses are probable and common notions. This was Avicenna's method of proving that the heavenly body was an animated body, but for this the ancients have a more efficient and clearer proof.

Ghazali says:

The objection is that we can assume* besides your theory three hypo-
474 theses which cannot be proved to be untrue. The first is that we assume the movement of heaven to take place through constraint by another body which desires its movement and makes it turn eternally, and that this body which sets it in motion is neither a sphere nor a circumference nor a heaven; their assertion is therefore false that the movement of heaven is voluntary and that heaven is animated, and what we have said is possible, and it cannot be denied except by a presumption of impossibility.

I say:

This is false, for the philosophers have proved that outside heaven there is no other body, and it cannot be inside heaven; besides, were this body to set it in motion, it would necessarily have to be moved itself, and we should have an infinite regress.[4]

Ghazali says:

The second hypothesis is to say: 'The movement occurs by constraint and its principle is the will of God, and indeed we say that the downward movement of a body also occurs by constraint, through God's creating this movement in this body; and the same can be said of all the other movements of those bodies which are not living.'

There still remains the fact that the philosophers regard this as impossible, because they ask why the will should have distinguished just this body, whereas all other bodies participate in bodiliness. But we have already explained that it is of the nature of the eternal Will to differentiate one thing from a similar one, and that the philosophers are forced to admit such a quality for the determination of the direction of the circular movement and for the determination of the place of the poles and their points, and we shall not repeat this; but our argument is, in short, that when they deny that a body can be differentiated for the attachment of the will to it without a distinctive attribute, this can be turned against them in regard to this distinctive attribute, for we ask them: 'Why is the body of heaven distinguished by this attribute, which sets it apart from all other bodies, although all other bodies are also bodies; and how can anything occur to it which does not occur to other bodies?' If this is caused by another attribute, we must repeat the same question about this other attribute, and in this way we should get an infinite series, and they would be forced in the end to acknowledge an arbitrary judgement of the will and the fact that in the principles there is something that distinguishes one thing from a similar one.

I say:

That a stone moves downwards through a quality which has been created in it, and fire upwards, and that these qualities are opposed —this is a self-evident fact, and to contradict it is pure folly. But it is still more foolish to say that the eternal Will causes the movement in these things everlastingly—without any act He deliberately chose[1]— and that this movement is not implanted in the nature of the thing, and that this is called constraint; for if this were true, things would have no nature, no real essence, no definition at all. For it is self-evident that the natures and definitions of things only differ through the difference of their acts, just as it is self-evident that every movement forced on a body comes from a body outside it. And this argument has no sense whatever.

And as to his affirmation 'that to assume that the act which proceeds from an existent requires a special attribute makes it necessary to ask about this attribute also why it characterizes this existent rather than any other of its kind', this is like saying that one ought to ask a man who asserted that earth and fire, which participate in bodiliness, were distinguished only by an attribute added to their bodiliness, why the attribute of fire characterizes fire and the attribute of earth, earth, and not rather the reverse. These, indeed, are the words of a man who does not assume for the attributes themselves a particular subject, but on the contrary believes that any attribute can be in any subject.[1] He who speaks like this denies also the definition and the differentiation of subjects, and their characterization through special attributes, which is the first cause of the specification of existents through particular attributes, and this assumption belongs to the principles of the Ash'arites who tried thereby to annul both religious and rational wisdom and, in short, reason itself.[2]

Ghazali says:

The third hypothesis is to admit that heaven is differentiated by an attribute and that this attribute is the principle of the movement, in the way they believe this of the downward movement, although in this case it is not known, as it is known in the case of the stone.[3]

And their assertion that a thing cannot by its nature abandon the place sought by its nature rests on a confusion.[4] For according to them there is here no numerical difference; on the contrary, the body is one and the circular movement is one, and neither the body nor the movement has an actual part; they are only divided by imagination, and this movement is not there to seek its place or to abandon it—indeed, it may well be that God creates a body in the essence of which there is something which determines a circular movement. The movement itself will then be determined by this attribute, not, however, the aiming at the place, for that would imply that arrival at the place would be the aim of the movement. And if your assertion that every movement takes place in seeking a place or abandoning it is a necessary principle, it is as if you made the seeking of the place the goal of nature, not the movement itself which will in this case only be a means.[5] But we say it is not absurd that the movement, not the seeking of a place, should be the goal itself; and why should that be impossible? And it is clear that, simply because they regard their hypothesis as the most plausible, we are not obliged to deny any other hypothesis absolutely; for to assert absolutely that heaven is a living being is pure presumption, for which there is no support.

I say:

The assertion of the philosophers that this movement is not a natural potency resembling the natural movement in earth and fire is true. And this is clear from their saying that this potency desires the place suitable to the body which possesses existence through this potency, and that the heavenly body, since all space is suitable to it, is not moved through such a potency, and the learned do not call this potency heavy or light.[6] Whether this potency depends on perception or not, and if so which kind of perception, is shown by other arguments.[7]

And the summary of this is to say: The inanity of the first hypothesis, namely that the mover of heaven might be another body which is not heaven, is self-evident or nearly so. For this body cannot set the heavenly body in a circular movement without being moved by itself, as if one were to say that a man or an angel turned the heavens from east to west.[1] And if this were true, this animated body would have to be either outside the world or inside it; and it is impossible that it should be outside the world, since outside the world there is neither place nor emptiness, as has been shown in many passages, and it would also be necessary that when this body set it in motion it should rest upon a body supporting it*, and this latter body again upon another, and so *ad infinitum*.[2] But that it should be inside the world is also impossible, for then it ought to be perceived by the senses, since any body inside the world can be perceived,[3] and this body, besides needing a body which would make it turn, would also need a body to carry it* or perhaps the body conveying it and the body setting it in motion might be identical, and the conveying body would need a body to convey it, and the number of animated bodies which set things in motion would have to be equal to the number of heavenly bodies. And one would also have to ask about these bodies whether they were composed of the four elements, in which case they would be transitory,[4] or whether they might be simple; and, if they were simple, what their nature was. All this is impossible, especially for one who has ascertained the natures of the simple bodies and learned their number and the species of bodies composed of them, and there is no sense in occupying ourselves with this matter here, for it has been proved in another place that this movement does not take place by constraint, since it is the principle of all movements, and through its intermediary, not only movements, but life[5] is distributed to all beings.

As to the second hypothesis, that God moves the heavens without having created a potency in them through which they move, this also is a very reprehensible doctrine, far from man's understanding. It would mean that God touches[6]* and moves everything which is in this sublunary world, and that the causes and effects which are perceived are all without meaning, and that man might be man through another quality than the quality God has created in him and that the same would be true for all other things. But such a denial would amount to a denial of the intelligibles, for the intellect perceives things only through their causes. This theory resembles the theory of those ancient philosophers, the Stoics,[7] who say that God exists in everything; and we shall engage in a discussion with them[1] when we treat the question of the denial of causes and effects.

The third objection which assumes a natural movement is to suppose that the movement of heaven is caused by a natural potency in it and through an essential attribute, not through a soul. It says that the argument of the philosophers in denying this is false, in so far as they build their proof on the following argument. The philosophers, that is, say that if the movement of heaven occurred by nature, the place sought by its natural movement would be identical with the place which it abandoned, because every part of heaven moves to places from which it has moved, since its movement is circular. The place, however, from which natural local movement retires is different from the place it aims at, for the place from which it moves is an accidental place,[2] while the place to which it moves is its natural place, in which it will come to rest. But, says Ghazali, this is a false assumption of the philosophers, for although they assume that the parts of heaven have many movements through many movers, this cannot be correct according to their own principles, for they affirm that the circular movement is unique, and that the body moved by it is unique, and therefore heaven is not in search of a place through its circular movement, and it is thus possible that in heaven there should be something through which it aims at the movement itself.

But the justification of the philosophers is that they only say this to such people as believe that the stars change their place through a natural movement, similar to the change of place found in things moved by nature. And the true assumption of the philosophers is that through the circular movement the thing moved is not in search of a place, but only seeks the circular movement itself, and that things which behave in this way have of necessity as their mover a soul and not nature. Movement, that is to say, has existence only in the intellect, since outside the soul there exists only the thing moved and in it there is only a particular movement without any lasting existence.[3] But what is moved towards movement in so far as it is movement must of necessity desire this movement, and what desires movement must of necessity represent it.[4]

And this is one of the arguments through which it is evident that the heavenly bodies are provided with intellect and desire; and this is clear also from various other arguments, one of which is that we find that circular bodies move with two contrary movements at the same time, towards the east and towards the west; and this cannot happen through nature, for that which moves through nature moves in one movement alone.¹

And we have already spoken of what caused the philosophers to believe that heaven possesses intellect, and their plainest proof is that, having understood that the mover of heaven is free from matter, they concluded that it can only move through being an object of thought and representation, and therefore the thing moved must be capable of thought and representation. And this is clear also from the fact that the movement of the heavens is a condition of the existence and preservation of the existents in the sublunary world, which cannot take place by accident. But these things can only be explained here in an informative and persuasive fashion.

THE FIFTEENTH DISCUSSION

To refute the theory of the philosophers about the aim which moves heaven²

Ghazali says:

The philosophers have also affirmed that heaven is an animal which obeys God by movement and by drawing near Him; for every voluntary movement arises for the sake of an end, since one cannot imagine that an act and a movement can proceed from an animal which does not prefer the act to its omission—indeed, if the act and its omission were to be equipollent, no act could be imagined.

Further, approach to God does not mean seeking His grace and guarding oneself from His wrath, since God is too exalted for wrath and grace; similar words can only be applied to Him metaphorically, and they are used in a metaphorical way when one speaks of His will to punish or to reward.³ Approach cannot mean the seeking of an approach to Him in space, for this is impossible; the only meaning it can have is of an approach in qualities, for God's existence is the most perfect and every other existence is imperfect in relation to His, and in this imperfection there are degrees and distinctions. The angels are nearest to Him in quality, not in place; and this is the meaning of the term 'the angels in His proximity' —namely, the intellectual substances which neither change nor alter nor pass away, and which know things as they really are.⁴ And the nearer man comes to the angels in qualities the nearer he comes to God, and the end of man's nature lies in assimilation to the angels.

And when it is established that this is the meaning of 'approach to

God', and that it refers to seeking approach to Him in qualities, then* this consists for man in knowledge of the realities of the existents and in his remaining eternally in the most perfect condition possible to him; for indeed permanence in the utmost perfection is God.

As to the angels in His proximity, any perfection that is possible for them is actual with them in their existence, since there is no potency in them which could emerge into act,[1] and therefore they are in the utmost perfection in regard to everything but God. And by 'heavenly angels' is meant the souls which move the heavens, and in them there is potency, and their perfections are divided into what is actual, like their circular shape and their appearance, which exists always, and what is potential, namely their appearance in a definite position and place; for any definite position is possible to them, but they are not actually in all positions, for to be in all of them at once is impossible.[2] And since they cannot be at all times in all particular positions at once, they try to exhaust all these particular positions by being in them specifically,[3] so that they do not cease to aim at one position and one place after another; and this potentiality is never ending, nor do these movements ever end.

But their one aim is to assimilate themselves to the First Principle, in the acquisition of the utmost perfection within the bounds of possibility with respect to Him, and this is the meaning of the obedience of the heavenly angels to God. And their assimilation is acquired in two ways. First, in completing every position specifically possible, and this is aimed at by first intention; secondly, by the order proceeding from their movement through the diversity of their configuration in trine and quartile, in conjunction and opposition, and through the diversity in the ascendant in relation to the earth, so that the good which is in the sublunary world can emanate from it, and all that happens arise from it. And every soul is intellective and longs for the perfection of its essence.

I say:

Everything he says here about the philosophers is a philosophical doctrine, or its consequence, or can be regarded as a philosophical doctrine, with one exception, when he says that heaven seeks by its movement the particular positions which are infinite; however, what is infinite cannot be sought, since it cannot be attained.[4] Nobody has held this doctrine but Avicenna, and Ghazali's objection to it, which we will mention later, is sufficient, and according to the philosophers it is the movement itself in so far as it is movement which is aimed at by heaven.[5] For the perfection of an animal, in so far as it is an animal, is movement; in this sublunary world rest occurs to the transitory animal only by accident, that is through the necessity of matter, for lassitude and fatigue touch the animal only because it is in matter.[6] The whole life and perfection of those animals which are

THE FIFTEENTH DISCUSSION

not affected by tiredness and languor must of necessity lie in their movement; and their assimilation to their Creator consists in this, that by their movement they impart life to what exists in this sublunary world.

This movement, however, does not occur according to the philosophers in first intention for the sake of this sublunary world; that is, the heavenly body is not in first intention created for the sake of this sublunary world. For indeed this movement is the special act for the sake of which heaven is created, and if this movement occurred in first intention for the sake of the sublunary world, the body of the heavens would be created only for the sake of this sublunary world, and it is impossible, according to the philosophers, that the superior should be created for the sake of the inferior; on the contrary, out of the superior there follows the existence of the inferior, just as the perfection of the ruler in relation to his subject does not lie in his being a ruler, but his being a ruler is only the consequence of his perfection. In the same way the providence which prevails in this world is like the care of the ruler for his subjects, who have no salvation and no existence except in him, and especially in the ruler who for his most perfect and noble existence does not need to be a ruler, let alone that he should need his subjects' existence.[1]

Ghazali says:

The objection to this is that in the premises of this argument there are controversial points. We shall not, however, pay any attention to them, but shall revert at once to the final intention the philosophers had in view and refute it from two standpoints.

The first is to say: 'To seek perfection through being in all possible places may be foolishness rather than obedience; is it not in some degree like a man, who has no occupation and who has adequate means to satisfy his wishes and needs, and who gets up and walks round in a country or in a house, and declares that by doing so he approaches God and that he perfects himself by arriving at all possible places, and says that it is possible for him to be in these places, but not possible for him to unite all the places numerically, and that therefore he fulfils this task specifically and that in this there is perfection and an approach to God? Indeed, it is his foolishness which makes him do such a stupid thing, and it may be said that to change positions and pass from place to place is not a perfection which has any value or which may be an object of desire.[2]

And there is no difference between what they say and this.

I say:

It might be thought that the silliness of such an argument either comes from a very ignorant or from a very wicked man. Ghazali, however, has neither of these dispositions. But sometimes unwise words come by way of exception from a man who is not ignorant, and wicked talk from a man who is not wicked, and it shows the imperfection of people that such conceits can be addressed to them.

But if we concede to Avicenna that the sphere aims through its movement at a change of positions, that this change of positions is what conserves the beings of this sublunary world after giving them their existence, and that this action is everlasting, can there then exist an obedience more complete than this? For instance, if a man exerted himself in guarding a city against the enemy, going round the city day and night, should we not regard this as a most important act of approach to God? But if we assumed that he moved round the town for the end which Ghazali attributes to Avicenna, namely that he only sought to perfect himself through trying to be in an infinite number of places, he would be declared mad.[1] And this is the meaning of the Divine Words: 'Verily thou canst not cleave the earth, and thou shalt not reach the mountains in height.'[2]

And his assertion that, since heaven cannot complete the individual numerical positions or join them, it has to complete them specifically, is a faulty, incomprehensible expression, unless he means that its movement has to last in its totality since it cannot be lasting in its parts. For there are movements which are lasting neither in their parts nor in their totality, namely the movements of the transitory; and there are movements which are lasting in their totality, transitory in their parts, but notwithstanding this such a movement is said to be one in ways which are distinguished in many passages of the books of the philosophers.[3] And his assertion that, since heaven cannot complete them numerically, it completes them specifically, is erroneous, since the movement of heaven is numerically one, and one can only apply such an expression to the transitory movements in the sublunary world; for these movements, since they cannot be numerically one, are specifically one and lasting through the movement which is numerically one.[4]

Ghazali says:

The second is to say: What you assert of the aim can be realized through the movement from west to east. Why, then, is the first movement from east to west, and why are not all the movements of the universe in the same direction? And if there is an intention in their diversity, why are they not different in an opposite way, so that the movement from the east should become the movement from the west, and the reverse? Everything you have mentioned of the occurrence of events like trine and sextile and others through the diversity of movements would happen just the same through the reverse. Also, what you have mentioned of the completion of the positions and places would happen just the same if the movement were in the opposite direction. Why then, since the reverse movement is possible for them, do they not move sometimes in one direction, sometimes in another, to complete all their possibilities, if it is in the completion of all their possibilities that their perfection lies? It is therefore shown that all these things are phantasms without any substance; for the secrets of the heavenly kingdom cannot be attained through such phantasms. God alone can manifest them to His prophets and saints through revelation, not through proof, and therefore the later philosophers are unable to give the reason for the direction of the movement of the heavenly bodies and why they have chosen it.

I say:

This objection is sophistical, for the transference from one question to another is an act of sophistry. Why does there follow, from their inability to assign the reason of the diversity in the directions of the movements of heaven, their inability to give the reason for the movement of heaven or to say that there is no reason at all for this movement? But this whole argument is extremely weak and feeble. However, how happy the theologians are about this problem! They believe that they have refuted the philosophers over it, since they are ignorant of the different arguments by which the philosophers have arrived at their reasons and of the many reasons that are required and must be assigned to every existent, since the causes differ through the variety in the natures of the existents. For simple existents have no other cause for what proceeds from them than their own natures and their forms,[1] but in composite things there are found, beside their forms, efficient causes which produce their composition and the conjunction of their parts. The earth, for instance, has no other cause for its downward movement than its attribute of earthiness, and fire has no other cause for its upward movement than its own nature and its form, and through this nature it is said to be the opposite of earth. Likewise, for up and down there are no reasons why the one direction should be higher and the other lower, but this is determined by their nature. And since the differentiation of directions is determined through the directions themselves, and the differentiation of the movements through the differentiation of the directions, no other reason can be assigned for the variation in the movements than the variation in the directions of the things moved, and the variation in their natures depends on the variation of their natures; i.e. some are nobler than others.

For instance, when a man sees that animals in walking place one leg in front of their body before the other and not the reverse, and asks why the animal does this, there is no sufficient answer except to say that an animal in its movement must have one leg to put forward and one to support itself on, and therefore an animal must have two sides, right and left, and the right is the one which is always* put forward first because of its special potency and the left the one which always, or mostly*, follows, because of its special potency; and it cannot be the reverse, so that the left side became the right, since the natures of the animal determine this, either through a determination in a majority of cases, or through a constant determination.[1]

The same is the case with the heavenly bodies since, if a person asks why heaven moves in a particular direction, the answer is that it is because it has a right and a left, and especially because it is evident from its nature that it is a living being, only it has the peculiarity that the right side in a part of it is the left side in another part,[2] and that although it has only this one organ of locomotion[3] it moves in opposite directions like a left foot which can also do the work of a right.[4] And just as the answer to the question whether the animal would not be more perfect if its right were its left, and why the right has been differentiated to be the right, and the left to be the left, is that the only reason for this is that the nature of the side called right has been determined by its essence to be the right and not the left, and that the left side has been determined by its essence to be the left and not the right, and the noblest has been attributed to the noblest; in the same way, when it is asked why the right side has been differentiated for the movement of the highest sphere to be the right and the left side to be the left (for the reverse was also possible as the case of the planets shows), the only answer is that the noblest direction has been attributed to the noblest body, as upward movement has been attributed to fire, downward movement to earth. As to the fact that the other heavens move in two contrary movements[5] besides the diurnal, this happens because of the necessity of this opposition of movements for the sublunary world, namely the movement of generation and corruption,[6] and it is not of the nature of the human intellect that it should apprehend more in such discussions and in this place than what we have mentioned.

Having made this objection against the philosophers and asserted that they have no answer to it, he mentions an answer which some of the philosophers give.

Ghazali says:

Some philosophers say that since the perfection occurs through movement, from whatever side it may be, and the order of events on earth requires a diversity of movements and a determination of directions, the motive concerning them of the principle of movement lies in the approach to God[1] and the motive of the direction of movement in the diffusion of good over the sublunary world. But we answer: 'This is false for two reasons. The first is: if one may imagine such a thing, let us declare that the nature of heaven demands rest, and must avoid movement and change, for this is in truth assimilation to God; for God is too exalted to change, and movement is a change, although God chose movement for the diffusion of His grace. For through it He is useful to others and it does not weigh on Him nor tire Him—so what is the objection to such a supposition?

'The second is that events are based on the diversity of the relations which result from the diversity in the directions of the movements. Now let the first movement be a movement from the west, and let the others move from the east, then the same diversity will arise as is needed for the diversity of the relations. Why then has one direction been specially chosen, since these varieties require only the principle of variety and in this sense one direction by itself is not superior to its contrary?'

I say:

This theologian wants to indicate the cause of this from the point of view of the final cause, not of the efficient, and none of the philosophers doubts that there is here a final cause in second intention, which is necessary for the existence of everything in the sublunary world. And although this cause has not yet been ascertained in detail, nobody doubts that every movement, every progression or regression of the stars, has an influence on sublunary existence, so that, if these movements differed, the sublunary world would become disorganized. But many of these causes are either still completely unknown or become known after a long time and a long experience,[2] as it is said that Aristotle asserted in his book *On Astrological Theorems*.[3]

As to the general questions, it is easier to discover them, and the astrologers have indeed come to know many of them and in our own time many of these things have been apprehended which ancient nations, like the Chaldaeans[4] and others, had already discovered.

And for this reason one cannot doubt that there is a wisdom in the existents, since it has become clear through induction that everything which appears in heaven is there through provident wisdom and through a final cause. And if there are final causes in animals, it is still more appropriate that there should be final causes in the heavenly bodies.[1] For in the case of man and animal about ten thousand signs of providence[2] have become known in a period of a thousand years, and it seems not impossible that in the infinite course of years much of the purpose of the heavenly bodies will come to light.[3] And we find that about these things the ancients give some mysterious indications which the initiated, that is the most highly reputed of the philosophers, know how to interpret.[4]

As to the two reasons in Ghazali's argument, the first, that assimilation to God would determine heaven to be at rest, since God is too exalted for movement, but that God has chosen movement because through it His grace can be diffused over transitory things—this is a faulty argument, since God is neither at rest nor moving,[5] and the motion of body is nobler for it than rest, and when an existent assimilates itself to God it assimilates itself to Him by being in the noblest of its states, which is movement. As to Ghazali's second point, it has been answered previously.

THE SIXTEENTH DISCUSSION

To refute their theory that the souls of the heavens observe all the particular events of this world, and that the meaning of 'the indelible tablet'[6] is the souls of the heavens, and that the inscription of the particular events of the world on the tablet resembles the delineation of the facts remembered on the faculty of memory contained in the brain of man,[7] and that this is not a broad hard body[8] on which things are written as things are written on a slate by children; since the quantity of this writing demands a large surface of material on which it is written, and if this writing is infinite, the material on which it is written must be infinite too, and one cannot imagine an infinite body, nor infinite lines on a

THE SIXTEENTH DISCUSSION

body, nor can an unlimited number of things be determined by a finite number of lines

Ghazali says:

And they assert that the heavenly angels are the souls of the heavens, and that the cherubim which are in the proximity of God are the separate intellects, which are substances subsisting by themselves which do not fill space and do not employ bodies, and that from them the individual forms emanate in the heavenly souls, and that those separate intellects are superior to the heavenly angels, because the former bestow and the latter acquire, and bestowing is superior to acquiring, and therefore the highest is symbolized by the pen[1] and it is said that God knows through the pen, because He is like the engraver who bestows as does the pen and the recipient is compared to the tablet.[2] And this is their doctrine. And the discussion of this question differs from the preceding one in so far as that what we mentioned previously is not impossible, because its conclusion was that heaven is an animal moving for a purpose, and this is possible; but this doctrine amounts to the assertion that the created can know the infinite particulars, which is often regarded as impossible, and in any case, has to be proved, since by itself it is a mere presumption.

I say:

What he mentions here is, to my knowledge, not said by any philosophers except Avicenna, namely that the heavenly bodies have representations, not to speak of the fact that these representations should be infinite, and Alexander of Aphrodisias explains in his book called *The Principles of the Universe* that these bodies have no representations, because representations exist only in animals because of their conservation, and these bodies do not fear corruption, and with respect to them representations would be valueless (and likewise sensations).[3] If they had representations they would also have sensations, since sensations are the condition for representations and every being which has representations necessarily has sensations, although the reverse is not true.[4] Therefore to interpret the indelible tablet in the way Ghazali says that they do is not correct, and the only possible interpretation of the separate intellects which move the different spheres by means of subordination is that they are the angels in the proximity of God,[5] if one wants to harmonize the conclusions of reason with the statements of the Holy Law.

Ghazali says:

And they prove this by saying that the circular movement is voluntary and that the will follows the thing willed,[6] and that a universal thing willed can only be intended by a universal will, and that from the universal will nothing proceeds.¹ For—so they say—every actual existent is determined and individual, and the relation of the universal will to the individual units is one and the same, and no individual thing proceeds from it. Therefore an individual will is needed for a definite movement. For every particular movement from every definite point to another definite point the sphere has a will, and this sphere no doubt has a representation of this particular movement through a bodily potency, since individuals only perceive through bodily potencies and every will must of necessity represent the thing willed, i.e. must know it, be it an individual or a universal. And if the sphere has a representation and a comprehension of the particular movements, it must of necessity also comprehend what follows from them through the diversity of their relations to the earth, because some of the individuals of the sphere are rising, some setting, some in the middle of the sky for some people and under the earth for others.*

And likewise it must know the consequences of the diversity of those relations which always arise anew through the movement, like trine and sextile, opposition and conjunction, to other such heavenly occurrences; and all earthly occurrences depend on heavenly occurrences either directly, or through one intermediary, or through many; and in short every event has a cause, occurring in a concatenation which terminates in the eternal heavenly movement, some parts of which are the causes of others.

Thus the causes and effects ascend in their concatenation to the particular heavenly movements, and the sphere representing the movements represents their consequences and the consequences of their consequences, so as to reach the end of the series.² And therefore the sphere observes everything that occurs and everything that will occur, and its occurrence is necessary through its cause, and whenever the cause is realized, the effect is realized. We only do not know the future events because all their causes are not known to us; for if we knew all the causes, we should know all the effects, for when we know, for instance, that fire will come into contact with cotton at a certain moment, we know that the cotton will burn, and when we know that a man will eat, we know that his appetite will be satisfied, and when we know that a man will walk over a certain spot lightly covered where a treasure is buried, and his feet will accidentally touch the treasure and he will perceive it,³ we know that he will be rich because of this treasure. Only as a matter of fact we do not know these causes. Sometimes we know part of the causes, and then we guess what may happen, and when we know the more important or the greater part of them, we have a sound opinion about the occurrence of these events; but if we knew all the causes, then we should know all the effects.⁴ However, the heavenly occurrences are many and, besides, they are mixed up with earthly events and it is not in human power to observe the causality of all these. But the souls of the heavens perceive it through

THE SIXTEENTH DISCUSSION 303

their perception of the First Cause and through the observation of their consequences and the consequences of their consequences, to the end of their concatenation.[1]

And therefore they say that the man who dreams sees in his dream what will happen in the future through being in contact with the indelible tablet and observing it.[2] And when he observes a thing it remains often in his memory as it really was, but sometimes his imagination hastens to symbolize it, for it is of the nature of this faculty to represent things through things which, in some way or another, are related to them, or to transfer things to their opposites; and the thing that was perceived is then effaced in his memory, but the image belonging to his imagination remains there. Then it is necessary to interpret what his imagination symbolizes, e.g. a man by means of a tree, a woman by means of a shoe, a servant by means of some household vessels, and a man who observes the paying of the legal alms and the poor-tax by means of linseed oil, for the linseed in the lamp is the cause of the illumination; it is on this principle that the interpretation of dreams is based.[3]

And they assert that contact with these souls takes place in a state of languor*, since then there is no obstacle; for when we are awake we are occupied with what the senses and our passions convey to us, and occupation with those sensual things keeps us away from this contact, but when in sleep some of these occupations are obliterated, the disposition for this contact appears. And they assert that the prophet Muhammed perceived the hidden universe in this way; however, the spiritual faculty of a prophet has such power that it cannot be overwhelmed by the external senses, and therefore he sees in a waking condition what other people perceive in their sleep.[4] But *his* imagination also pictures to him what he sees, and although sometimes the thing he sees remains in his memory exactly as it was, sometimes only its representation remains, and such an inspiration is just as much in need of interpretation as such dreams are. And if all events were not eternally inscribed on the indelible tablet, the prophets would not know the hidden world either awake or asleep; but the pen has indelibly fixed what shall be till the day of resurrection, and the meaning of this we have explained. And this we wanted to impart to make their doctrine understood.

I say:

We have already said that we do not know of anyone who holds this theory but Avicenna. And the proof which Ghazali relates rests on very weak premisses, although it is persuasive and dialectical. For it is assumed that every particular effect proceeds from an animate being through the particular representation of this effect and of the particular movements through which this effect is realized. To this major premiss a minor premiss is joined, that heaven is an animate being from which particular acts proceed. From these premises it is concluded that the particular effects, and the particular acts which proceed from heaven, occur through a particular representation which is called imagination; and that this is not only apparent from the different sciences, but also from many animals which perform particular acts, like the bees and the spider.[1]

But the objection to these premises is that no particular act proceeds from beings endowed with intellect, except when this act* is represented through a universal representation, and then endless individual things proceed from it—for instance the form of a cupboard proceeds from a carpenter only through a universal representation which does not distinguish one particular cupboard from another.[2] And the same thing happens when the works of animals proceed by nature[3] from them.[4] And these representations are an intermediary between the universal and the particular perceptions; that is, they are an intermediary between the definition of a thing[5] and its particular representation.[6] But if the heavenly bodies have representations, then they must have representations that are of the nature of the universal, not of the nature of the particular representation which is acquired through the senses. And it is not possible that our acts should proceed from particular representations, and therefore the philosophers believe that the represented forms from which the definite acts of animals proceed are like an intermediary between the intelligibles and the individual forms represented, e.g. the form by reason of which non-carnivorous birds flee from birds of prey, and the form by reason of which bees build their cells.[7] The only artisan who needs an individual sensible image is the one who does not possess this universal representation, which is necessary for the origination of the individual things.[8]

It is this universal image which is the motive power for the universal will which does not aim at a particular individual; and it is the individual will which aims at a particular individual of one and the same species—this, however, does not happen in the heavenly bodies.

And that a universal will should exist for a universal thing in so far as it is universal is impossible, since the universal does not exist outside the soul and has no transitory existence. And his primary division of will into a universal and an individual will is, indeed, not correct; otherwise one must say that the heavenly bodies move towards the definite limits of things without the definite limit being

THE SIXTEENTH DISCUSSION

accompanied by the representation of an individual existent, in contrast to what happens with us. And his assertion that no individual is realized through the universal will is false, if by 'universal will' is understood that which does not distinguish one individual from another, but represents it universally, as is the case with a king who arranges his armies for battle.[1] If, however, there is understood by 'will' its being attached to a universal entity itself, then it must be said that such an attachment is not a will at all, and there does not exist such a will except in the way we have explained.[2]

And if it followed from the nature of the heavenly bodies that they think sublunary things by way of imagination, they must do this through universal imaginations which are the results of definition, not through particular imaginations which are the results of sense-impressions. And it seems quite clear that they cannot think sublunary things through individual representations especially when it is said that what proceeds from them proceeds from them by second intention. However, the doctrine of the philosophers is that the heavenly bodies think themselves and think the sublunary world, and whether they think the sublunary world as something different from themselves is a problem that must be examined in places specially reserved for this problem; and in general, if the heavens know, the term 'knowledge' is attributed to our knowledge and theirs in an equivocal way.

As to the theory he gives here about the cause of revelation and dreams, this is the theory of Avicenna alone, and the opinions of the ancient philosophers differ from his. For the existence of a knowledge of individuals actually infinite, in so far as it is an individual knowledge, is impossible, and I understand by individual knowledge that kind of apprehension which is called representation. But there is no reason to introduce here the question of dreams and revelation, for this leads to much controversy, and such an act is an act of sophistry, not of dialectics. My statement, however, that the imaginations of the heavenly bodies are imaginations intermediary between individual and universal representations is a dialectical argument; for what results from the principle of the philosophers is that the heavenly bodies have no imagination whatever, for these imaginations, as we have said already, whether they are universal or particular, aim only at conservation and protection; and they are also a condition for our intellectual representation, which therefore is transitory, but the intellectual representation of the heavenly bodies, since it is not transitory, cannot be accompanied by imagination, for otherwise it would depend in one way or another on imagination. Therefore their apprehension is neither universal nor individual, but these two kinds of knowledge, universal and individual, are here unified, and because of this they can only be distinguished by their matters. And in this way knowledge of the occult and of dreams and the like can be acquired, and this will be explained perfectly in its proper place.

Ghazali says:

And the answer is for us to ask: How will you refute those who say that the prophet knows the occult through God, who shows it to him by way of revelation*, and the same is the case with the man who has visions in his sleep, which he only sees because God or an angel inspires them in him? We do not need any of the things you have related, and you have not the slightest proof for introducing the Holy Law by mentioning the Tablet and the Pen; for true believers do not in the least understand by 'the Tablet' and 'the Pen' what you have mentioned, and the way to embrace the religious dogmas is not to refuse to admit them in the way they must be understood.[1] And, although the possibility of what you have said is granted, so long as you cannot indicate why you deny the correctness of the sense in which these religious terms are understood, the reality of what you say cannot be known or verified. Indeed, the only way to arrive at knowledge of such things is through the Holy Law, not by reason. The rational proof of what you have said is primarily based on many premises, the refutation of which need not detain us, but we shall limit ourselves to the discussion of three propositions.

The first proposition is that you say that the movement of heaven is voluntary, and we have already settled this problem and shown the futility of your claim.

If, however, to oblige you we grant you this voluntary movement, the second proposition is your saying that heaven needs a particular representation for each particular movement, and this we do not concede. For according to you there are no parts in the sphere, which is one single thing and is only divided in imagination; nor are there particular movements, for there is only one continuous movement, and in order to complete all the places possible for it, it is sufficient for the sphere to desire this one movement, as you have indicated yourselves, and it will only need universal representation and a universal will.

Let us give an example of the universal and the particular will to make the intention of the philosophers clear. When, for instance, a man has a universal aim to make the pilgrimage to Mecca, from this universal will no movement follows,[2] for the movement occurs as a particular movement, in a particular direction, and of a particular extent, and the man does not cease, in directing himself to Mecca, to form new representations of the place one after another, where he will go and the direction he will take, and every particular representation will be followed by a particular will to move from the place which he has reached by his movement. And this is what they understood by a particular movement which follows a particular will; and this is granted, for the directions, when he takes the road to Mecca, are many, and the distance is undetermined, and he must determine place after place and direction after direction, passing from one particular will to another.

But the heavenly movement has only one direction, for it is a sphere and moves on its axis in its own space, going neither beyond its own space nor beyond the movement willed. There is therefore only one direction and one impulse and one aim*, like the downward movement of the stone, which tends towards the earth in the shortest way, and the shortest way is the straight line, and the straight line is determined,[1] and therefore this movement needs no new cause besides the universal nature which tends to the centre of the earth while it changes its distance from the earth, and arrives at and departs from one definite place after another. In the same way the universal will suffices for this movement, and nothing else is required, and the assumption of this proposition is a mere presumption.

I say:
As to Ghazali's words:

And the answer is for us to ask: How will you refute those who say. . . . We do not need any of the things you have related.

this answer is based on tradition, not on reason, and there is no sense in introducing it in this book. The philosophers examine everything there is in the Holy Law, and, if it is found to agree with reason, we arrive at a more perfect knowledge; if, however, reason does not perceive its truth, it becomes known that human reason cannot attain it, and that only the Holy Law perceives it.[2] Ghazali's argument against the philosophers about the interpretation of the Tablet and the Pen does not belong to the problem under discussion, and there is therefore no sense in introducing it here. And this interpretation of knowledge of the occult, according to Avicenna, has no sense.

The rational objection he adduces against Avicenna over this problem is well founded. For there are for heaven no particular motions of particular distances that would require imagination. The animate being which moves through particular motions in particular spaces* imagines, no doubt, these spaces towards which* it moves, and these movements, when it cannot visually perceive these distances; the circular, however, as Ghazali says, moves *qua* circular in one single movement, although from this one movement there follow many different particular motions in the existents below it. These spheres, however, are not concerned with those particular movements, but their only intention is to conserve the species of which these particulars are the particulars, not to conserve the existence of any of these particulars in so far as they are particulars, for, if so, heaven would surely possess imagination.

The question that still needs to be examined is whether the temporal particulars which proceed from the heavenly movement are intended for their own sake or only for the preservation of the species.[1] This question cannot be treated here, but it certainly seems that there exists a providence as concerns individuals, as appears from true dreams and the like, e.g. the prognostication of the future; however, in reality this is a providence concerning the species.[2]

Ghazali says:

The third proposition—and this indeed is a very bold presumption—is that they say that, when heaven represents particular movements, it also represents their results and consequences. This is pure nonsense, like saying that, when a man moves himself and knows his movement, he must also know the consequences of his movement vertically and horizontally (that is, the bodies which are above and under him and at his side), and when he moves in the sun he must know the places upon which his shadow falls and does not fall, and what happens through the coolness of his shadow because of the interruption of the rays of the sun there, and what happens through the compression of the particles of earth under his foot, and what happens through the separation of these particles, and what happens to the humours inside him by their changing through his movement into warmth, and which parts of him are changed into sweat, and so on, till he knows all the occurrences inside and outside his body of which the movement is the cause or the condition or the disposition or the aptitude. And this is nonsense which no intelligent man can believe, and by which none but the ignorant can be beguiled. And this is what this presumption amounts to.

Besides, we may ask: 'Are these different particulars which are known to the soul of the sphere the events which are occurring at the present moment or are future events also brought in relation to it?' If you limit its knowledge to present events you deny its perception of the occult and the apprehension of future events through it, by the prophets in the state of wakefulness, by others in their sleep; and then the point of this proof disappears. For it is indeed presumption to say that he who knows a thing knows its consequences and results, so that if we knew all causes we should also know all future events. For, indeed, the causes of all events are to be found at present in the heavenly movement, but it determines the effect either through one intermediary or through many. And if this knowledge covers the future also, it will not have an end, and how can the

THE SIXTEENTH DISCUSSION

distinction between particulars in the infinite future be known, and how can many different particular objects of knowledge, of an infinite number and without an end to their units, be collected in a created soul, at one and the same moment without any sequence?[1] He whose intellect does not perceive the impossibility of this may well despair of his intellect.

And if they reverse this against us with respect to God's knowledge, God's knowledge is not attached to its object in its correspondence with the things known, in the way this attachment exists in the case of things known by created beings, but as soon as the soul of the sphere moves round like the soul of man,[2] it belongs to the same kind as the soul of man, and also it participates with the soul of man in the perception of individuals through an intermediary.[3] And although no absolute knowledge can be had about this, it is most probable that the soul of the sphere is of the same kind as the human soul; and if this is not most probable, it is possible, and the possibility destroys the claim to absolute knowledge they put forward.

And if it is said, 'It is also proper to the human soul in its essence to perceive all things, but its preoccupation with the consequences of passion, anger, greed, resentment, envy, hunger, pain, and in short the accidents of the body and what the sensations convey to the body, is so great that, when the human soul is occupied with one of these things, it neglects everything else; but the souls of the spheres are free from these attributes, and nothing occupies them, and neither care nor pain nor perception overwhelms them, and therefore they know everything'—we answer: 'How do you know that nothing occupies them? Does not their service of the First and their longing for Him submerge them and keep them from the representation of particular things? And what makes it impossible to suppose other impediments than anger and passion? For these are sensual hindrances, and how do you know that these hindrances are limited in the way we experience them? For there are occupations for the learned through the excellence of their interests and the desire for leadership which children are unable to imagine, and which they cannot believe to be occupations and hindrances.[4] And how do you know that analogous things are impossible for the souls of the spheres?'

This is what we wanted to mention about those sciences to which they give the name of metaphysical.

I say:

As to his regarding it as impossible that there should exist an immaterial intellect which thinks things with their consequences, comprising them all, neither the impossibility nor the necessity of its existence is a self-evident fact, but the philosophers affirm that they have a proof of its existence. As to the existence of infinite representations, this cannot be imagined in any individual, but the philosophers affirm that they have a proof of the existence of the infinite in the eternal knowledge and an answer to the question how man can attain knowledge of particular events in the future through the eternal knowledge, namely that of these things the soul thinks only the universal which is in the intellect, not the particular* which is particularized in the soul*. For individuals are known* to the soul because it is potentially all existents, and what is in potency emerges into act either through the sensible things or through the nature of the intellect, which is prior to sensible things in reality (I mean the intellect through which sensible things become stable intelligibles, not, however, in such a way that in this knowledge there are representations of an infinite number of individuals).[1] In short, the philosophers assert that these two kinds of knowledge, the universal and the particular, are unified in the knowledge which is separated from matter; and when this knowledge emanates in the sublunary world it divides itself into universal and particular, although this knowledge itself is neither the one nor the other.[2] But the proof of this or its contrary cannot be given here. And the discussion here about these questions is like the assumption of geometrical propositions which are not well enough known to meet with immediate assent and which are not convincing at first sight. And Ghazali mixes one part with another, i.e. he starts objecting to one part of the theory through another, and this is the worst method of discussion, because in this way assent neither by proof nor by persuasion can be obtained.[3]

Likewise the problems about the differences between the souls of the heavenly bodies and the soul of man are all very obscure, and when such things are discussed in a place not proper to them the discussion becomes either irrelevant or dialectical and superficial; that is to say, the conclusions are drawn from possible premisses, like their assertion that the irascible and the concupiscible soul hinder the human soul in the perception of what is proper to it.[4] It appears from the nature of these and similar sayings that they are possible and are in need of proofs, and that they open the way to many conflicting possibilities.

And this closes what we decided to mention of the different assertions which this book contains about theological problems; this is the most important part of our book. We shall now speak on physical problems.

ABOUT THE NATURAL SCIENCES

Ghazali says:

The so-called natural sciences are many, and we shall enumerate their parts, in order to make it known that the Holy Law does not ask one to contest and refute them, except in certain points we shall mention.[1] They are divided into principal classes and subdivisions.[2] The principal classes are eight. In the first class are treated the divisibility, movement, and change which affect body in so far as it is body, and the relations and consequences of movement* like time, space, and void,[3] and all this is contained in Aristotle's *Physics*. The second treats of the disposition of the parts of the elements of the world, namely heaven and the four elements which are within the sphere of the moon, and their natures and the cause of the disposition of each of them in a definite place; and this is contained in Aristotle's *De coelo*. The third treats of the conditions of generation and corruption, of equivocal generation and of sexual generation, of growth and decay, of transmutations, and how the species are conserved, whereas the individuals perish through the two heavenly movements (westwards and eastwards), and this is contained in *De generatione et corruptione*. The fourth treats of the conditions which are found in the four elements through their mixture, by which there occur meteorological phenomena like clouds and rain and thunder, lightning, the halo round the moon, the rainbow, thunderbolts, winds, and earthquakes. The fifth treats of mineralogy, the sixth of botany. The seventh treats of zoology, which is contained in the book *Historia animalium*. The eighth treats of the soul of animals and the perceptive faculties, and says that the soul of man does not die through the death of his body but that it is a spiritual substance for which annihilation is impossible.

The subdivisions are seven: The first is medicine, whose end is the knowledge of the principles of the human body and its conditions of health and illness, their causes and symptoms, so that illness may be expelled and health preserved.[4] The second, judicial astrology, which conjectures from the aspects and configuration of the stars the conditions which will be found in the world and in the State and the consequences of dates of births and of years. The third is physiognomy, which infers character from the external appearance.[5] The fourth is dream-interpretation, which infers what the soul has witnessed of the world of the occult from dream images, for the imaginative faculty imagines this symbolically. The fifth is the telesmatical art, that is the combination of celestial virtues with some earthly so as to constitute a power which can perform marvellous acts in the earthly world.[6] The sixth is the art of incantation, which is the mixing of the virtues of earthly substances to produce marvellous things from them.[7] The seventh is alchemy, whose aim is to change the properties of minerals so that finally gold and silver are produced by a kind of magic.[1] And there is no need to be opposed to any of these sciences by reason of the Divine Law; we dissent from the philosophers in all these sciences in regard to four points only.

I say:

As to his enumeration of the eight kinds of physical science, this is exact according to the doctrine of Aristotle. But his enumeration of the subdivisions is not correct. Medicine is not one of the natural sciences, but is a practical science which takes its principles from physical science; for physical science is theoretical and medicine is practical, and when we study a problem common to theoretical science and practical we can regard it from two points of view; for instance, in our study of health and illness the student of physics observes health and nature as kinds of natural existents, whereas the physician studies them with the intention of preserving the one, health, and keeping down the other, illness. Neither does judicial astrology belong to physical science; it is only a prognostication of future events, and is of the same type as augury and vatication. Physiognomy is also of the same kind, except that its object is occult things in the present, not in the future.[2] The interpretation of dreams too is a prognosticating science, and this type belongs neither to the theoretical nor to the practical sciences, although it is reputed to have a practical value. The telesmatical art is vain, for if we assume the positions of the spheres to exert a power on artificial products, this power will remain inside the product and not pass on to things outside it. As to conjuring, this is the type of thing that produces wonder, but it is certainly not a theoretical science. Whether alchemy really exists is very dubious; if it exists, its artificial product cannot be identical with the product of nature; art can at most become similar to nature but cannot attain nature itself in reality.[3] As to the question whether it can produce anything which resembles the natural product generically, we do not possess sufficient data to assert categorically its impossibility or possibility, but only prolonged experiments over a lengthy period can procure the necessary evidence. We shall treat the four points Ghazali mentions one after the other.

Ghazali says:

The first point is their assertion that this connexion observed between causes and effects is of logical necessity, and that the existence of the cause without the effect or the effect without the cause is not within the realm of the contingent and possible. The second point is their assertion that human souls are substances existing by themselves,[1] not imprinted on the body, and that the meaning of death is the end of their attachment to the body and the end of their direction of the body; and that otherwise the soul would exist at any time by itself. They affirm that this is known by demonstrative proof. The third point is their assertion that these souls cannot cease to exist, but that when they exist they are eternal and their annihilation cannot be conceived.[2] The fourth point is their assertion that these souls cannot return to their bodies.[3]

As to the first point, it is necessary to contest it, for on its negation depends the possibility of affirming the existence of miracles which interrupt the usual course of nature,[4] like the changing of the rod into a serpent[5] or the resurrection of the dead or the cleavage of the moon,[6] and those who consider the ordinary course of nature a logical necessity regard all this as impossible. They interpret the resurrection of the dead in the Koran by saying that the cessation of the death of ignorance is to be understood by it, and the rod which conceived the arch-deceiver, the serpent, by saying that it means the clear divine proof in the hands of Moses to refute the false doctrines of the heretics; and as to the cleavage of the moon they often deny that it took place and assert that it does not rest on a sound tradition; and the philosophers accept miracles that interrupt the usual course of nature only in three cases.[7]

First: in respect to the imaginative faculty they say that when this faculty becomes predominant and strong, and the senses and perceptions do not submerge it, it observes the Indelible Tablet, and the forms of particular events which will happen in the future become imprinted on it; and that this happens to the prophets in a waking condition and to other people in sleep, and that this is a peculiar quality of the imaginative faculty in prophecy.[8]

Secondly: in respect of a property of the rational speculative faculty i.e. intellectual acuteness,[9] that is rapidity in passing from one known thing to another; for often when a problem which has been proved is mentioned to a keen-sighted man he is at once aware of its proof, and when the proof is mentioned to him he understands what is proved by himself, and in general when the middle term occurs to him he is at once aware of the conclusion, and when the two terms* of the conclusion are present in his mind the middle term which connects the two terms of the conclusion occurs to him. And in this matter people are different; there are those who understand by themselves, those who understand when the slightest hint is given to them, and those who, being instructed, understand only after much trouble; and while on the one hand it may be assumed that incapacity to understand can reach such a degree that a man does not understand anything at all and has, although instructed, no disposition whatever to grasp the intelligibles, it may on the other hand be assumed that his capacity and proficiency may be so great as to arrive at a comprehension of all the intelligibles or the majority of them in the shortest and quickest time. And this difference exists quantitatively over all or certain problems, and qualitatively so that there is an excellence in quickness and easiness, and the understanding of a holy and pure soul may reach through its acuteness all intelligibles in the shortest time possible; and this is the soul of a prophet, who possesses a miraculous speculative faculty and so far as the intelligibles are concerned is not in need of a teacher*; but it is as if he learned by himself, and he it is who is described by the words 'the oil of which would well-nigh give light though no fire were in contact with it, light upon light'.[1]

Thirdly: in respect to a practical psychological faculty which can reach such a pitch as to influence and subject the things of nature: for instance, when our soul imagines something the limbs and the potencies in these limbs obey it and move in the required direction which we imagine, so that when a man imagines something sweet of taste the corners of his mouth begin to water, and the potency which brings forth the saliva from the places where it is springs into action, and when coitus is imagined the copulative potency springs into action, and the penis extends;[2] indeed, when a man walks on a plank between two walls over an empty space, his imagination is stirred by the possibility of falling and his body is impressed by this imagination and in fact he falls, but when this plank is on the earth, he walks over it without falling.[3] This happens because the body and the bodily faculties are created to be subservient and subordinate to the soul, and there is a difference here according to the purity and the power of the souls. And it is not impossible that the power of the soul should reach such a degree that also the natural power of things outside a man's body obeys it*, since the soul of man is not impressed on his body although there is created in man's nature a certain impulse and desire to govern his body.[4] And if it is possible that the limbs* of his body should obey him, it is not impossible that other things besides his body should obey him and that his soul should control the blasts of the wind or the downpour of rain, or the striking of a thunderbolt or the trembling of the earth, which causes a land to be swallowed up* with its inhabitants.[5] The same is the case with his influence in producing cold or warmth or a movement in the air; this warmth or cold comes about through his soul,[6] all these things occur without any apparent physical cause, and such a thing will be a miracle brought about by a prophet. But this only happens in matters disposed* to receive it, and cannot attain such a scale that wood could be changed into an animal or that the moon, which cannot undergo cleavage, could be cloven. This is their theory of miracles, and we do not deny anything they have mentioned, and that such things happen to prophets; we are only opposed to their limiting themselves to this, and to their denial of the possibility that a stick might change into a serpent, and of the resurrection of the dead and other things. We must occupy ourselves with this question in order to be able to assert the existence of miracles and for still another reason, namely to give effective support to the doctrine on which the Muslims base their belief that God can do anything. And let us now fulfil our intention.

I say:
The ancient philosophers did not discuss the problem of miracles, since according to them such things must not be examined and questioned; for they are the principles of the religions, and the man who inquires into them and doubts them merits punishment, like the man who examines the other general religious principles, such as whether God exists or blessedness or the virtues. For the existence of all these cannot be doubted, and the mode of their existence is something divine which human apprehension cannot attain. The reason for this is that these are the principles of the acts through which man becomes virtuous, and that one can only attain knowledge after the attainment of virtue.[1] One must not investigate the principles which cause virtue before the attainment of virtue, and since the theoretical sciences can only be perfected through assumptions and axioms which the learner* accepts in the first place, this must be still more the case with the practical sciences.

As to what Ghazali relates of the causes of this as they are according to the philosophers, I do not know anyone who asserts this but Avicenna. And if such facts are verified and it is possible that a body could be changed qualitatively* through something which is neither a body nor a bodily potency,[2] then the reasons he mentions for this are possible; but not everything which in its nature is possible[3] can be done by man, for what is possible to man is well known. Most things which are possible in themselves are impossible for man, and what is true of the prophet, that he can interrupt the ordinary course of nature, is impossible for man, but possible in itself; and because of this one need not assume that things logically impossible are possible for the prophets, and if you observe those miracles whose existence is confirmed, you will find that they are of this kind.[4] The clearest of miracles is the Venerable Book of Allah,[5] the existence of which is not an interruption of the course of nature assumed by tradition, like the changing of a rod into a serpent, but its miraculous nature is established by way of perception and consideration for every man who has been or who will be till the day of resurrection. And so this miracle* is far superior to all others.

Let this suffice for the man who is not satisfied with passing this problem over in silence, and may he understand that the argument on which the learned base their belief in the prophets is another, to which Ghazali himself has drawn attention in another place,[6] namely the act which proceeds from that quality through which the prophet is called prophet, that is the act of making known the mysterious and establishing religious laws which are in accordance with the truth and which bring about acts that will determine the happiness of the totality of mankind. I do not know anyone but Avicenna who has held the theory about dreams Ghazali mentions. The ancient philosophers assert about revelation and dreams only that they proceed from God through the intermediation of a spiritual incorporeal being which is according to them the bestower of the human intellect, and which is called by the best authors* the active intellect and in the Holy Law angel. We shall now return to Ghazali's four points.

THE FIRST DISCUSSION

517 Ghazali says:

According to us the connexion between what is usually believed to be a cause and what is believed to be an effect is not a necessary connexion; each of two things has its own individuality and is not the other,[1] and neither the affirmation nor the negation, neither the existence nor the non-existence of the one is implied in the affirmation, negation, existence, and non-existence of the other—e.g. the satisfaction of thirst does not imply drinking, nor satiety eating, nor burning contact with fire, nor light sunrise, nor decapitation death, nor recovery the drinking of medicine, nor evacuation the taking of a purgative, and so on for all the empirical connexions existing in medicine, astronomy, the sciences, and the crafts.[2] For the connexion in these things is based on a prior power of God to create them in a successive order, though not because this connexion is necessary in itself and cannot be disjoined*—on the contrary, it is in God's power to create satiety without eating, and death without decapitation, and to let life persist notwithstanding the decapitation, and so on with respect to all connexions. The philosophers, however, deny this possibility and claim that that is impossible. To investigate all these innumerable connexions would take us too long, and so we shall choose one single example, namely the burning of cotton through contact with fire; for we regard it as possible that the contact might occur without the burning taking place, and also that the cotton might be changed into ashes without any contact with fire, although the philosophers deny this possibility. The discussion of this matter has three points.

The first is that our opponent claims that the agent of the burning is the fire exclusively;[3] this is a natural, not a voluntary agent, and cannot abstain from what is in its nature when it is brought into contact with a receptive substratum. This we deny, saying: The agent of the burning is God, through His creating the black in the cotton and the disconnexion of its parts, and it is God who made the cotton burn and made it ashes either through the intermediation of angels or without intermediation. For fire is a dead body which has no action, and what is the proof that it is the agent? Indeed, the philosophers have no other proof than the observation of the occurrence of the burning, when there is contact with fire, but observation proves only a simultaneity,[1] not a causation, and, in reality, there is no other cause but God.[2] For there is unanimity of opinion about the fact that the union of the spirit with the perceptive and moving faculties in the sperm of animals does not originate in the natures contained in warmth, cold, moistness, and dryness, and that the father is neither the agent of the embryo through introducing the sperm into the uterus, nor the agent of its life, its sight and hearing, and all its other faculties. And although it is well known that the same faculties exist in the father, still nobody thinks that these faculties exist through him; no, their existence is produced by the First either directly or through the intermediation of the angels who are in charge of these events.[3] Of this fact the philosophers who believe in a creator are quite convinced, but it is precisely with them that we are in dispute.

It has been shown that coexistence does not indicate causation. We shall make this still more clear through an example. Suppose that a man blind from birth, whose eyes are veiled by a membrane and who has never heard people talk of the difference between night and day, has the membrane removed from his eyes by day and sees visible things, he will surely think then that the actual perception in his eyes of the forms of visible things is caused by the opening of his eyelids, and that as long as his sight is sound and in function, the hindrance removed and the object in front of him visible, he will, without doubt, be able to see, and he will never think that he will not see, till, at the moment when the sun sets and the air darkens, he will understand that it was the light of the sun which impressed the visible forms on his sight.[4] And for what other reason do our opponents believe that in the principles of existence[5] there are causes and influences from which the events which coincide with them proceed, than that they are constant, do not disappear, and are not moving bodies which vanish from sight? For if they disappeared or vanished we should observe the disjunction and understand then that behind our perceptions there exists a cause. And out of this there is no issue, according to the very conclusions of the philosophers themselves.

The true philosophers[6] were therefore unanimously of the opinion that these accidents and events which occur when there is a contact of bodies, or in general a change in their positions, proceed from the bestower of forms who is an angel or a plurality of angels, so that they even said that the impression of the visible forms on the eye occurs through the bestower of forms, and that the rising of the sun, the soundness of the pupil, and the existence of the visible object are only the preparations and dispositions which enable the substratum to receive the forms; and this theory they applied to all events. And this refutes the claim of those who profess that fire is the agent of burning, bread the agent of satiety, medicine the agent of health, and so on.

I say:

To deny the existence of efficient causes which are observed in sensible things is sophistry, and he who defends this doctrine either denies with his tongue what is present in his mind or is carried away by a sophistical doubt which occurs to him concerning this question. For he who denies this can no longer acknowledge that every act must have an agent. The question whether these causes by themselves are sufficient to perform the acts which proceed from them, or need an external cause for the perfection of their act, whether separate or not, is not self-evident and requires much investigation and research. And if the theologians had doubts about the efficient causes which are perceived to cause each other, because there are also effects whose cause is not perceived, this is illogical. Those things whose causes are not perceived are still unknown and must be investigated, precisely because their causes are not perceived; and since everything whose causes are not perceived is still unknown by nature and must be investigated, it follows necessarily that what is not unknown has causes which are perceived.[1] The man who reasons like the theologians does not distinguish between what is self-evident and what is unknown,[2] and everything Ghazali says in this passage is sophistical.

And further, what do the theologians say about the essential causes, the understanding of which alone can make a thing understood? For it is self-evident that things have essences and attributes which determine the special functions of each thing and through which the essences and names of things are differentiated. If a thing had not its specific nature, it would not have a special name nor a definition, and all things would be one—indeed, not even one;[3] for it might be asked whether this one has one special act or one special passivity or not, and if it had a special act, then there would indeed exist special acts proceeding from special natures, but if it had no single special act, then the one would not be one.[4] But if the nature of oneness is denied, the nature of being is denied, and the consequence of the denial of being is nothingness.[5]

Further, are the acts which proceed from all things absolutely necessary for those in whose nature it lies to perform them, or are they only performed in most cases or in half the cases?[1] This is a question which must be investigated, since one single action-and-passivity between two existent things occurs only through one relation out of an infinite number, and it happens often that one relation hinders* another. Therefore it is not absolutely certain that fire acts when it is brought near a sensitive body,[2] for surely it is not improbable that there should be something which stands in such a relation to the sensitive thing as to hinder the action of the fire, as is asserted of talc and other things. But one need not therefore deny fire its burning power so long as fire keeps its name and definition.

Further, it is self-evident that all events have four causes, agent, form, matter, and end, and that they are necessary for the existence of the effects—especially those causes which form a part of the effect, namely that which is called by the philosophers matter, by the theologians condition and substratum,[3] and that which is called by the philosophers form, by the theologians psychological quality.[4] The theologians acknowledge that there exist conditions which are necessary to the conditioned, as when they say that life is a condition of knowledge; and they equally recognize that things have realities and definitions, and that these are necessary for the existence of the existent, and therefore they here judge the visible and the invisible according to one and the same scheme.[5] And they adopt the same attitude towards the consequences of a thing's essence, namely what they call 'sign',[6] as for instance when they say that the harmony* in the world indicates that its agent possesses mind and that the existence of a world having a design indicates that its agent knows this world.[7] Now intelligence is nothing but the perception* of things with their causes, and in this it distinguishes itself from all the other faculties of apprehension, and he who denies causes must deny the intellect. Logic implies the existence of causes and effects, and knowledge of these effects can only be rendered perfect through knowledge of their causes. Denial of cause implies the denial of knowledge, and denial of knowledge implies that nothing in this world can be really known, and that what is supposed to be known is nothing but opinion, that neither proof nor definition exist, and that the essential attributes which compose definitions are void. The man who denies the necessity of any item of knowledge must admit that even this, his own affirmation, is not necessary knowledge.[8]

As to those who admit that there exists, besides necessary know-

523 ledge, knowledge which is not necessary, about which the soul forms a judgement on slight evidence and imagines it to be necessary, whereas it is not necessary, the philosophers do not deny this. And if they call such a fact 'habit' this may be granted, but otherwise I do not know what they understand by the term 'habit'—whether they mean that it is the habit of the agent, the habit of the existing things, or our habit to form a judgement about such things?[1] It is, however, impossible that God should have a habit, for a habit is a custom which the agent acquires and from which a frequent repetition of his act follows, whereas God says in the Holy Book: 'Thou shalt not find any alteration in the course of God, and they shall not find any change in the course of God.'[2] If they mean a habit in existing things, habit can only exist in the animated;[3] if it exists in something else, it is really a nature, and it is not possible that a thing should have a nature which determined it either necessarily or in most cases.[4] If they mean our habit of forming judgements about things, such a habit is nothing but an act of the soul which is determined by its nature and through which the intellect becomes intellect. The philosophers do not deny such a habit; but 'habit' is an ambiguous term, and if it is analysed it means only a hypothetical act; as when we say 'So-and-so has the habit of acting in such-and-such a way', meaning that he will act in that way most of the time. If this were true, everything would be the case only by supposition, and there would be no wisdom in the world from which it might be inferred that its agent was wise.

And, as we said, we need not doubt that some of these existents cause each other and act through each other, and that in themselves they do not suffice for their act, but that they are in need of an external agent whose act is a condition of their act, and not only of their act but even of their existence. However, about the essence of this agent or of these agents the philosophers differ in one way, although in another they agree. They all agree in this, that the First Agent is immaterial and that its act is the condition of the existence and acts of existents, and that the act of their agent reaches these existents through the intermediation of an effect* of this agent, which is different from these existents and which, according to some of them, is exclusively the heavenly sphere, whereas others assume besides this sphere another immaterial existent which they call the bestower of forms.

But this is not the place to investigate these theories, and the highest part of their inquiry is this; and if you are one of those who desire these truths, then follow the right road which leads to them. The reason why the philosophers differed about the origin of the essential forms and especially of the forms of the soul is that they could not relate them to the warm, cold, moist, and dry, which are the causes of all natural things which come into being and pass away,[1] whereas the materialists related everything which does not seem to have an apparent cause to the warm, cold, moist, and dry, affirming that these things originated through certain mixtures of those elements, just as colours and other accidents come into existence.[2] And the philosophers tried to refute them.

Ghazali says:

Our second point is concerned with those who acknowledge that these events proceed from their principles, but say that the disposition to receive the forms arises from their observed and apparent causes. However, according to them also the events proceed from these principles not by deliberation and will, but by necessity and nature, as light does from the sun, and the substrata differ for their reception only through the differentiations in their disposition. For instance, a polished body receives the rays of the sun, reflects them and illuminates another spot with them, whereas an opaque body does not receive them; the air does not hinder the penetration of the sun's light, but a stone does; certain things become soft through the sun, others hard;[3] certain things, like the garments which the fuller bleaches, become white through the sun, others like the fuller's face become black:[4] the principle is, however, one and the same, although the effects differ through the differences of disposition in the substratum. Thus there is no hindrance or incapacity in the emanation of what emanates from the principles of existence; the insufficiency lies only in the receiving substrata. If this is true, and we assume a fire that has the quality it has, and two similar pieces of cotton in the same contact with it, how can it be imagined that only one and not the other will be burned, as there is here no voluntary act? And from this point of view they deny that Abraham could fall into the fire and not be burned notwithstanding the fact that the fire remained fire, and they affirm that this could only be possible through abstracting the warmth from the fire (through which it would, however, cease to be fire) or through changing the essence of Abraham and making him a stone or something on which fire has no influence, and neither the one nor the other is possible.

I say:

Those philosophers who say that these perceptible existents do not act on each other, and that their agent is exclusively an external principle, cannot affirm that their apparent action on each other is totally illusory, but would say that this action is limited to preparing the disposition to accept the forms from the external principle. However, I do not know any philosopher who affirms this absolutely; they assert this only of the essential forms, not of the forms of accidents. They all agree that warmth causes warmth, and that all the four qualities act likewise, but in such a way that through it the elemental fire[1] and the warmth which proceeds from the heavenly bodies are conserved. The theory which Ghazali ascribes to the philosophers, that the separate principles act by nature, not by choice, is not held by any important philosophers;[2] on the contrary, the philosophers affirm that that which possesses knowledge must act by choice. However, according to the philosophers, in view of the excellence which exists in the world, there can proceed out of two contraries only the better, and their choice is not made to perfect their essences—since there is no imperfection in their essence—but in order that through it those existents which have an imperfection in their nature may be perfected.

As to the objection which Ghazali ascribes to the philosophers over the miracle of Abraham, such things are only asserted by heretical Muslims. The learned among the philosophers do not permit discussion or disputation about the principles of religion, and he who does such a thing needs, according to them, a severe lesson. For whereas every science has its principles, and every student of this science must concede its principles and may not interfere with them by denying them, this is still more obligatory in the practical science of religion, for to walk on the path of the religious virtues is necessary for man's existence, according to them, not in so far as he is a man, but in so far as he has knowledge; and therefore it is necessary for every man to concede the principles of religion and invest with authority the man who lays them down. The denial and discussion of these principles denies human existence, and therefore heretics must be killed. Of religious principles it must be said that they are divine things which surpass human understanding, but must be acknowledged although their causes are unknown.

Therefore we do not find that any of the ancient philosophers discusses miracles, although they were known and had appeared all over the world, for they are the principles on which religion is based and religion is the principle of the virtues; nor did they discuss any of the things which are said to happen after death. For if a man grows up according to the religious virtues he becomes absolutely virtuous, and if time and felicity are granted to him, so that he becomes one of the deeply learned thinkers and it happens that he can explain one of the principles of religion, it is enjoined upon him that he should not divulge this explanation and should say 'all these are the terms of religion and the wise', conforming himself to the Divine Words, 'but those who are deeply versed in knowledge say: we believe in it, it is all from our Lord'.[1]

Ghazali says:

There are two answers to this theory. The first is to say: 'We do not accept the assertion that the principles do not act in a voluntary way and that God does not act through His will, and we have already refuted their claim in treating of the question of the temporal creation of the world. If it is established that the Agent creates the burning through His will when the piece of cotton is brought in contact with the fire, He can equally well omit to create it when the contact takes place.

I say:

Ghazali, to confuse his opponent, here regards as established what his opponent refuses to admit, and says that his opponent has no proof for his refusal. He says that the First Agent causes the burning without an intermediary He might have created in order that the burning might take place* through the fire. But such a claim abolishes any perception of the existence of causes and effects. No philosopher doubts that, for instance, the fire is the cause of the burning which occurs in the cotton through the fire—not, however, absolutely, but by an external principle which is the condition of the existence of fire, not to speak of its burning. The philosophers differ only about the quiddity of this principle—whether it is a separate principle, or an intermediary between the event and the separate principle besides the fire.

Ghazali says, on behalf of the philosophers:

But it may be said that such a conception involves reprehensible impossibilities. For if you deny the necessary dependence of effects or their causes and relate them to the will of their Creator, and do not allow even in the will a particular definite pattern, but regard it as possible that it may vary and change in type, then it may happen to any of us that there should be in his presence beasts of prey and flaming fires and immovable mountains and enemies equipped with arms, without his seeing them, because God had not created in him the faculty of seeing them. And a man who had left a book at home might find it on his return changed into a youth, handsome, intelligent, and efficient, or into an animal; or if he left a youth at home, he might find him turned into a dog; or he might leave ashes and find them changed into musk; or a stone changed into gold, and gold changed into stone. And if he were asked about any of these things, he would answer: 'I do not know what there is at present in my house; I only know that I left a book in my house, but perhaps by now it is a horse which has soiled the library with its urine and excrement, and I left in my house a piece of bread which has perhaps changed into an apple-tree.' For God is able to do all these things, and it does not belong to the necessity of a horse that it should be created from a sperm, nor is it of the necessity of a tree that it should be created from a seed; no, there is no necessity that it should be created out of anything at all. And perhaps God creates things which never existed before; indeed, when one sees a man one never saw before and is asked whether this man has been generated, one should answer hesitantly: 'It may be that he was one of the fruits in the market which has been changed into a man, and that this is that man.' For God can do any possible thing, and this is possible, and one cannot avoid being perplexed by it; and to this kind of fancy one may yield *ad infinitum*, but these examples will do.[1]

But the answer is to say: If it were true that the existence of the possible implied that there could not be created in man any knowledge of the non-occurrence of a possible, all these consequences would follow necessarily. But we are not at a loss over any of the examples which you have brought forward. For God has created in us the knowledge that He will not do all these possible things, and we only profess that these things are not necessary, but that they are possible and may or may not happen, and protracted habit time after time fixes their occurrence in our minds according to the past habit in a fixed impression. Yes, it is possible that a prophet should know in such ways as the philosophers have explained that a certain man will not come tomorrow from a journey, and although his coming is possible the prophet knows that this possibility will not be realized.[2] And often you may observe even ordinary men of whom you know that they are not aware of anything occult, and can know the intelligible only through instruction, and still it cannot be denied that nevertheless their soul and conjecturing power[3] can acquire sufficient strength to apprehend what the prophets apprehend in so far as they know the possibility of an event, but know that it will not happen. And if God interrupts the habitual course by causing this unusual event to happen this knowledge of the habitual is at the time of the interruption removed from their hearts and He no longer creates it. There is, therefore, no objection to admitting that a thing may be possible for God, but that He had the previous knowledge that although He might have done so He would not carry it out during a certain time, and that He has created in us the knowledge that He would not do it during that time.[4]

I say:

When the theologians admit that the opposite of everything existing is equally possible, and that it is such in regard to the Agent, and that only one of these opposites can be differentiated through the will of the Agent, there is no fixed standard for His will either constantly or for most cases, according to which things must happen. For this reason the theologians are open to all the scandalous implications with which they are charged. For true knowledge* is the knowledge of a thing as it is in reality.[1] And if in reality there only existed, in regard both to the substratum and to the Agent,[2] the possibility of the two opposites,[3] there would no longer, even for the twinkling of an eye, be any permanent knowledge of anything, since we suppose such an agent to rule existents like a tyrannical prince who has the highest power*, for whom nobody in his dominion can deputize*, of whom no standard or custom is known to which reference might be made.[4] Indeed, the acts of such a prince will undoubtedly be unknown by nature, and if an act of his comes into existence the continuance of its existence at any moment will be unknown by nature.

Ghazali's defence against these difficulties that God created in us the knowledge that these possibilities would be realized only at special times, such as at the time of the miracle, is not a true one. For the knowledge created[5] in us is always in conformity with the nature of the real thing, since the definition of truth is that a thing is believed to be such as it is in reality.[6] If therefore there is knowledge of these possibles, there must be in the real possibles a condition to which our knowledge refers, either through these possibles themselves or through the agent, or for both reasons—a condition which the theologians call habit.[7] And since the existence of this condition which is called habit is impossible in the First Agent, this condition can only be found in the existents, and this, as we said, is what the philosophers call nature.[8]

The same congruity exists between God's knowledge and the existents, although God's knowledge of existents is their cause, and these existents are the consequence of God's knowledge, and therefore reality conforms to God's knowledge.[9] If, for instance, knowledge of Zaid's coming reaches the prophet through a communication of God, the reason why the actual happening is congruous with the knowledge is nothing but the fact that the nature of the actually existent[10] is a consequence of the eternal knowledge, for knowledge *qua* knowledge can only refer to something which has an actualized nature.[11] The knowledge of the Creator is the reason why this nature becomes actual in the existent which is attached to it.[1] Our ignorance of these possibles is brought about through our ignorance of the nature which determines the being or non-being of a thing.[2] If the opposites in existents were in a condition of equilibrium, both in themselves[3] and through their efficient causes, it would follow that they neither existed nor did not exist, or that they existed and did not exist at the same time, and one of the opposites must therefore have a preponderance in existence. And it is the knowledge of the existence of this nature which causes the actualization of one of the opposites. And the knowledge attached to this nature is either a knowledge prior to it, and this is the knowledge of which this nature is the effect, namely eternal knowledge, or the knowledge which is consequent on this nature, namely non-eternal knowledge. The attainment of the occult is nothing but the vision of this nature, and our acquisition of this knowledge not preceded by any proof is what is called in ordinary human beings a dream, and in prophets inspiration. The eternal will and eternal knowledge are the causes of this nature in existents. And this is the meaning of the Divine Words: 'Say that none in the heavens or on the earth know the occult but God alone.'[4] This nature is sometimes necessary and sometimes what happens in most cases.[5] Dreams and inspiration are only, as we said, the announcement of this nature in possible things, and the sciences which claim the prognostication of future events possess only rare traces of the influences of this nature or constitution or whatever you wish to call it, namely that which is actualized in itself and to which the knowledge attaches itself.

Ghazali says:

The second answer—and in it is to be found deliverance from these reprehensible consequences[6]—is to agree that in fire there is created a nature which burns two similar pieces of cotton which are brought into contact with it and does not differentiate between them, when they are alike in every respect.[7] But still we regard it as possible that a prophet should be thrown into the fire and not burn, either through a change in the quality of the fire or through a change in the quality of the prophet, and that either through God or through the angels there should arise a quality in the fire which limited its heat to its own body, so that it did not go beyond it, but remained confined to it, keeping, however, to the form and reality of the fire, without its heat and influence extending beyond it; or that there should arise in the body of the person an attribute, which did not stop* the body from being flesh and bone, but still defended* it against the action of the fire. For we can see a man rub himself with talc and sit down in a lighted oven and not suffer from it; and if one had not seen it, one would deny it, and the denial of our opponents that it lies in God's power to confer on the fire or to the body an attribute which prevents it from being burnt is like the denial of one who has not seen the talc and its effect.[1] For strange and marvellous things are in the power of God, many of which we have not seen, and why should we deny their possibility and regard them as impossible?

And also the bringing back to life of the dead and the changing of a stick into a serpent are possible in the following way: matter can receive any form, and therefore earth and the other elements can be changed into a plant,[2] and a plant, when an animal eats it, can be changed into blood,[3] then blood can be changed into sperm,[4] and then sperm can be thrown into the womb and take the character of an animal.[5] This, in the habitual course of nature, takes place over a long space of time, but why does our opponent declare it impossible that matter should pass through these different phases in a shorter period than is usual, and when once a shorter period is allowed there is no limit to its being shorter and shorter, so that these potencies can always become quicker in their action and eventually arrive at the stage of being a miracle of a prophet.[6]

And if it is asked: 'Does this arise through the soul of the prophet or through another principle at the instigation of the prophet?'—we answer: 'Does what you acknowledge may happen through the power of the prophet's soul, like the downpour of rain or the falling of a thunderbolt or earthquakes—does that occur through him or through another principle? What we say about the facts which we have mentioned is like what you say about those facts which you regard as possible. And the best method according to both you and us is to relate these things to God, either immediately or through the intermediation of the angels. But at the time these occurrences become real, the attention of the prophet turns to such facts, and the order of the good determines its appearance to ensure the duration of the order of religion, and this gives a preponderance to the side of existence. The fact in itself is possible, and the principle in God is His magnanimity; but such a fact only emanates from Him when necessity gives a preponderance to its existence and the good determines it, and the good only determines it when a prophet needs it to establish his prophetic office for the promulgation of the good.'[7]

And all this is in accordance with the theory of the philosophers and follows from it for them, since they allow to the prophet a particular characteristic which distinguishes him from common people. There is no intellectual criterion for the extent of its possibility, but there is no need to declare it false when it rests on a good tradition and the religious law states it to be true. Now, in general, it is only the sperm which accepts the form of animals—and it receives its animal potencies only from the angels, who according to the philosophers, are the principles of existents—and only a man can be created from the sperm of a man, and only a horse from the sperm of a horse, in so far as the actualization of the sperm through the horse determines the preponderance of the analogous form of a horse over all other forms, and it accepts only the form to which in this way the preponderance is given, and therefore barley never grows from wheat or an apple from a pear.[1] Further, we see that certain kinds of animal are only produced by spontaneous generation from earth and never are generated by procreation—e.g. worms, and some which are produced both spontaneously and by procreation like the mouse, the serpent, and the scorpion, for their generation can come also from earth.[2] Their disposition to accept forms varies through causes unknown to us, and it is not in human power to ascertain them, since those forms do not, according to the philosophers, emanate from the angels by their good pleasure or haphazard,[3] but in every substratum only in such a way that a form arises for whose acceptance it is specially determined through its own disposition. These dispositions differ, and their principles are, according to the philosophers, the aspects of the stars and the different relative positions of the heavenly bodies in their movements. And through this the possibility is open that there may be in the principles of these dispositions wonderful and marvellous things, so that those who understand talismans through their knowledge of the particular qualities of minerals and of the stars succeed in combining the heavenly potencies with those mineral peculiarities, and make shapes of these earthly substances, and seek a special virtue for them and produce marvellous things in the world through them. And often they drive serpents and scorpions from a country, and sometimes bugs, and they do other things which are known to belong to the science of talismans.

And since there is no fixed criterion for the principles of these dispositions, and we cannot ascertain their essence or limit them, how can we know that it is impossible that in certain bodies dispositions occur to change their phases at a quicker rhythm, so that such a body would be disposed to accept a form for the acceptance of which it was not prepared before, which is claimed to be a miracle? There is no denying this, except through a lack of understanding and an unfamiliarity with higher things and oblivion of the secrets of God in the created world and in nature. And he who has examined the many wonders of the sciences does not consider in any way impossible for God's power what is told of the wonders of the prophets.[4]

Our opponents may say: 'We agree with you that everything possible is in the power of God, and you theologians agree with us that the impossible cannot be done and that there are things whose impossibility is known and things which are known to be possible, and that there are also things about which the understanding is undecided and which it does not hold to be either impossible or possible. Now what according to you is the limit of the impossible? If the impossible includes nothing but the simultaneous affirmation and negation of the same thing, then say that of

ABOUT THE NATURAL SCIENCES

two things the one is not the other, and that the existence of the one does not demand the existence of the other. And say then that God can create will without knowledge of the thing willed, and knowledge without life,[1] and that He can move the hand of a dead man and make him sit and write volumes with his hand and engage himself in sciences while he has his eye open and his looks are fixed on his work, although he does not see and there is no life in him and he has no power, and it is God alone who creates all these ordered actions with the moving of the dead man's hand, and the movement comes from God. But by regarding this as possible the difference between voluntary action and a reflex action like shivering* is destroyed, and a judicious act will no longer indicate that the agent possesses knowledge or power.[2] It will then be necessary that God should be able to change genera and transform the substance into an accident and knowledge into power and black into white and a voice into an odour, just as He is able to change the inorganic into an animal and a stone into gold, and it will then follow that God can also bring about other unlimited impossibilities.'

The answer to this is to say that the impossible cannot be done by God, and the impossible consists in the simultaneous affirmation and negation of a thing, or the affirmation of the more particular with the negation of the more general, or the affirmation of two things with the negation of one of them, and what does not refer to this is not impossible and what is not impossible can be done. The identification of black and white is impossible, because by the affirmation of the form of black in the substratum the negation of the form of white and of the existence of white is implied; and since the negation of white is implied by the affirmation of black, the simultaneous affirmation and negation of white is impossible.[3] And the existence of a person in two places at once is only impossible[4] because we imply by his being in the house that he cannot be in another place, and it cannot be understood from the denial that he is in another place that he can be simultaneously both in another place and in the house. And in the same way by will is implied the seeking of something that can be known, and if we assume a seeking without knowledge there cannot be a will and we would then deny what we had implied. And it is impossible that in the inorganic knowledge should be created, because we understand by inorganic that which does not perceive, and if in the organic perception was created it would become impossible to call it inorganic in the sense in which this word is understood.

As to the transformation of one genus into another, some theologians affirm that it is in the power of God,[5] but we say that for one thing to become another is irrational; for, if for instance, the black could be transformed into power, the black would either remain or not, and if it does not exist any more, it is not changed but simply does not exist any more and something else exists; and if it remains existent together with power, it is not changed, but something else is brought in relation to it, and if the black remains and power does not exist, then it does not change, but remains as it was before. And when we say that blood changes into sperm, we mean by it that this identical matter is divested of one form and invested with another; and it amounts to this, that one form becomes non-existent and another form comes into existence while the matter remains, and that two forms succeed one another in it. And when we say that water becomes air through being heated, we mean by it that the matter which had received the form of the water is deprived of this form and takes another, and the matter is common to them but the attribute changes. And it is the same when we say that the stick is changed into a serpent or earth into an animal. But there is no matter common to the accident and the substance, nor to black and to power, nor to the other categories, and it is impossible for this reason that they should be changed into each other.

As to God's moving the hand of a dead man, and raising this man up in the form of a living one who sits and writes, so that through the movement of his hand a well-ordered script is written, this in itself is not impossible as long as we refer events to the will of a voluntary being, and it is only to be denied because the habitual course of nature is in opposition to it. And your affirmation, philosophers, that, if this is so, the judiciousness of an act no longer indicates that the agent possesses knowledge is false, for the agent in this case is God; He determines the act and He performs it. And as to your assertion that if this is so there is no longer any difference between shivering and voluntary motion, we answer that we know this difference only because we experience in ourselves the difference between these two conditions, and we find thereby that the differentiating factor is power,[1] and know that of the two classes of the possible the one happens at one time, the other at another; that is to say, we produce movement with the power to produce it at one time, and a movement without this power at another. Now, when we observe other movements than ours and see many well-ordered movements, we attain knowledge of the power behind them,[2] and God creates in us all these different kinds of knowledge through the habitual course of events, through which one of the two classes of possibility becomes known, though the impossibility of the second class is not proved thereby.

I say:

When Ghazali saw that the theory that things have no particular qualities and forms from which particular acts follow, for every thing is very objectionable, and contrary to common sense, he conceded this in this last section and replaced it by the denial of two points: first that a thing can have these qualities but that they need not act on a thing in the way they usually act on it, e.g. fire can have its warmth but need not burn something that is brought near to it,

ABOUT THE NATURAL SCIENCES

even if it is usually burnt when fire is brought near to it; secondly that the particular forms have not a particular matter in every object.

The first point can be accepted by the philosophers, for because of external causes the procession of acts from agents may not be necessary,[1] and it is not impossible that for instance fire may sometimes be brought near cotton without burning it, when something is placed with the cotton that makes it non-inflammable, as Ghazali says in his instance of talc and a living being.

As to the point that matter is one of the conditions for material things, this cannot be denied by the theologians,[2] for, as Ghazali says, there is no difference between our simultaneous negation and affirmation of a thing and our simultaneous denial of part of it and affirmation of the whole. And since things consist of two qualities, a general and a particular—and this is what the philosophers mean by the term 'definition', a definition being composed according to them of a genus and a specific difference—it is indifferent for the denial of an existent which of its two qualities is denied. For instance, since man consists of two qualities, one being a general quality, viz. animality, and the second a particular, viz. rationality, man remains man just as little when we take away his animality as when we take away his rationality, for animality is a condition of rationality and when the condition is removed the conditioned is removed equally.

On this question the theologians and the philosophers agree, except that the philosophers believe that for particular things the general qualities are just as much a condition as the particular, and this the theologians do not believe; for the philosophers, for instance, warmth and moisture are a condition of life in the transient,[3] because they are more general than life, just as life is a condition of rationality.[4] But the theologians do not believe this, and so you hear them say: 'For us dryness* and moisture are not a condition of life.' For the philosophers shape, too, is one of the particular conditions of life in an organic being; if not, one of two following cases might arise: either the special shape of the animal might exist without exercising any function, or this special shape might not exist at all.[5] For instance, for the philosophers the hand is the organ of the intellect, and by means of it man performs his rational acts, like writing and the carrying on of the other arts; now if intelligence were possible in the inorganic, it would be possible that intellect might exist without performing its function, and it would be as if warmth could exist without warming the things that are normally warmed by it.[6] Also, according to the philosophers, every existent has a definite quantity and a definite quality, and also the time when it comes into existence and during which it persists are determined, although in all these determinations there is, according to the philosophers, a certain latitude.[1]

Theologians and philosophers agree that the matter of existents which participate in one and the same matter sometimes accepts one of two forms and sometimes its opposite, as happens, according to them, with the forms of the four elements, fire, air, water, and earth. Only in regard to the things which have no common matter or which have different matters do they disagree whether some of them can accept the forms of others—for instance, whether something which is not known by experience to accept a certain form except through many intermediaries can also accept this ultimate form without intermediaries. For instance, the plant comes into existence through composition out of the elements; it becomes blood and sperm through being eaten by an animal and from sperm and blood comes the animal, as is said in the Divine Words: 'We created man from an extract of clay, then We made him a clot in a sure depository'[2] and so on till His words 'and blessed be God, the best of creators'. The theologians affirm that the soul of man can inhere in earth without the intermediaries known by experience,[3] whereas the philosophers deny this and say that, if this were possible, wisdom would consist in the creation of man without such intermediaries, and a creator who created in such a way would be the best and most powerful of creators; both parties claim that what they say is self-evident, and neither has any proof for its theory. And you, reader, consult your heart; it is your duty to believe what it announces, and this is what God—who may make us and you into men of truth and evidence—has ordained for you.

But some of the Muslims have even affirmed that there can be attributed to God the power to combine the two opposites, and their dubious proof is that the judgement of our intellect that this is impossible is something which has been impressed on the intellect, whereas if there had been impressed on it the judgement that this is possible, it would not deny this possibility, but admit it.[4] For such people it follows as a consequence that neither intellect nor existents have a well-defined nature, and that the truth which exists in the intellect does not correspond to the existence of existing things. The theologians themselves are ashamed of such a theory, but if they held it, it would be more consistent with their point of view than the contradictions in which their opponents involve them on this point. For their opponents try to find out where the difference lies between what as a matter of fact the theologians affirm on this point and what they deny, and it is very difficult for them to make this out—indeed they do not find anything but vague words. We find, therefore, that those most expert in the art of theological discussion take refuge in denying the necessary connexion between condition and conditioned, between a thing and its definition, between a thing and its cause and between a thing and its sign. All this is full of sophistry and is without sense, and the theologian who did this was Abu-l-Ma'ali.[1] The general argument which solves these difficulties is that existents are divided into opposites and correlates, and if the latter could be separated, the former might be united, but opposites are not united and correlates therefore cannot be separated. And this is the wisdom of God and God's course in created things, and you will never find in God's course any alteration.[2] And it is through the perception of this wisdom that the intellect of man becomes intellect, and the existence of such wisdom in the eternal intellect is the cause of its existence in reality. The intellect therefore is not a possible entity which might have been created with other qualities, as Ibn Hazm imagined.[3]

THE SECOND DISCUSSION

Their impotence to show by demonstrative proof that the human soul is a spiritual substance which exists by itself and does not fill space, is neither body nor impressed on a body, is neither continuous with the body nor separated from the body,[4] just as neither God nor the angels according to them is outside or inside the world

Ghazali says:

The discussion of this question demands the exposition of their theory about the animal and human faculties.[5] The animal faculties are divided according to them into motive and apprehensive, and the apprehensive are of two classes, the external and the internal. The external are the five senses, and these faculties are entities impressed on the bodies.[6] The internal are three in number.[7] The first is the representative faculty in the foremost part of the brain behind the faculty of sight;[8] in it the forms of the things seen remain after the closing of the eye, and in this faculty there is impressed and collected* what the five senses bring to it, and it is therefore called the common sense. If it did not exist, a man who saw white honey and perceives its sweetness by taste could not, when he saw it a second time, apprehend its sweetness as long as he had not tasted it as he did the first time, but in the common sense there is something which judges that this white is the sweetness, and there is in it, no doubt, a judging element for which both these things, colour and sweetness, are brought together and which determines then that when the one is present the other must be there too.[1]

The second is the estimative faculty,[2] which is that which apprehends the intentions[3] whereas the first apprehends the forms;[4] and the meaning of 'forms' is 'that which cannot be without matter, i.e. body', whereas the meaning of 'intentions' is 'that which does not require a body for its existence, although it can happen that it occurs in a body'—like enmity and concord. The sheep perceives the colour, shape, and appearance of the wolf, which are only found in body, but it perceives also that the wolf is its enemy, and the lamb perceives the shape and colour of its mother and then perceives its love and tenderness, and for this reason it flees from the wolf while it walks behind the mother. Discord and concord need not be in bodies like colour and shape, but it sometimes happens that they occur in bodies. This faculty differs from the first*, and is located in the posterior ventricle of the brain.[5]

The third faculty is called in animals the imaginative and in man the cogitative,[6] and its nature is to combine the sensible forms and to compose the intentions with the forms:[7] it is located in the middle ventricle between the place where the forms are kept and that where the intentions are retained.[8] Because of this man can imagine a horse that flies and a being with the head of a man and the body of a horse, and other combinations, although he has never seen such things. It is more appropriate, as will be shown, to join this faculty with the motive faculties than with the apprehensive.[9] The places where these faculties are located are known only through medicine, for if a lesion occurs to one of these ventricles the faculties become defective.[10]

Further, the philosophers affirm that the faculty on which the forms of sensible things are impressed through the five senses retains these forms so that they do not disappear after their reception, for one thing does not retain another through the faculty by which it receives it, for water receives without retaining, while wax receives through its wetness and retains through its dryness, by contrast with water.[11] Through this consideration that which retains is different from that which receives, and this is called the retentive faculty. And in the same way intentions are impressed on the estimative faculty, and a faculty retains them, which is called the memorative.[12] Through this consideration, these internal perceptions, when the imaginative faculty is joined to them, become five in number, like the external faculties.

The motive faculties[1] form two classes, in so far as they are only stimulating motion or executing motion and acting; the stimulating motive faculty is the impulsive and appetitive faculty; this is the faculty which stimulates the acting motive power to move when, in the representative faculty which we have mentioned,[2] there is inscribed the form of something to be sought or avoided. The stimulating faculty has two branches, one called concupiscent which excites to a movement, through which there is an approach to the things represented as necessary or useful in a search for pleasure, and the irascible which excites to a movement through which the thing represented as injurious or mischievous is removed as one seeks to master it. Through this faculty the complete determination to act is effected, which is called will.[3]

The motive faculty which itself executes movement is a faculty which is diffused in the nerves and muscles and has the function of contracting the muscles and drawing the tendons and ligaments which are in contact with the limbs in the direction where this faculty resides, or of relaxing and extending them so that the ligaments and tendons move in the opposite direction.[4] These are the animal faculties of the soul as described in a summary way, without the details.

And as regards the soul which thinks things and is called the rational or discursive soul by the philosophers (and by 'discursive'[5] is meant 'rational', because discourse is the most typical external operation of reason and therefore the intellective soul takes its name from it), it has two faculties, a knowing and an acting, and both are called intellect, though equivocally.[6] And the acting faculty is one which is a principle moving man's body towards the well-ordered human arts, whose order derives from the deliberation proper to man. The knowing faculty, which is called the speculative, is one which has the function of perceiving the real natures of the intelligibles in abstraction from matter, place, and position; and these are the universal concepts which the theologians call sometimes conditions and sometimes modes,[7] and which the philosophers call abstract universals.

The soul has therefore two faculties on two sides: the speculative faculty on the side of the angels, since through it it receives from the angels knowledge of realities (and this faculty must always be receptive for the things coming from above); and the practical faculty on the inferior side, which is the side of the body which it directs and whose morals it improves. This faculty must rule over all the other bodily faculties, and all the others must be trained by it and subjected to it. It must not itself be affected or influenced by them, but they must be influenced by it, in such a way that there will not through the bodily attributes occur in the soul subservient dispositions, called vices, but that this faculty may remain predominant and arouse in the soul dispositions called virtues.[8]

This is a summary of the human vital faculties, which they distinguished and about which they spoke at great length, and we have omitted the vegetative faculties, since there is no need to mention them as they are not connected with our subject. Nothing of what we have mentioned need be denied on religious grounds, for all these things are observable facts whose habitual course has been provided by God. We only want now to refute their claim that the soul being an essence subsistent by itself[1] can be known by demonstrative rational proofs, and we do not seek to refute those who say that it is impossible that this knowledge should derive from God's power or who believe that the religious law is opposed to this; for perhaps it will be clear at the dividing on the Day of Judgement that the Holy Law regards it as true. However, we reject their claim that this can be known by mere reason and that the religious law is not necessary for its knowledge, and we shall ask them to produce their proofs and indeed they have many.

I say:

All this is nothing but an account of the theory of the philosophers about these faculties and his conception of them; only he followed Avicenna, who distinguished himself from the rest of the philosophers by assuming in the animal another faculty than the imaginative,[2] which he calls the estimative faculty and which replaces the cogitative faculty in man, and he says that the ancients applied the term 'imaginative faculty' to the estimative, and when they do this then the imaginative faculty in the animal is a substitute for the cogitative faculty in man and will be located in the middle ventricle of the brain.[3] And when the term 'imaginative' is applied to the faculty which apprehends* shape,[4] this is said to reside in the foremost part of the brain. There is no contradiction in the fact that the retentive and memorative faculties should both be in the posterior part of the brain, for retaining and memory are two in function, but one in their substratum. And what appears from the theory of the ancients is that the imaginative faculty in the animal is that which determines that the wolf should be an enemy of the sheep and that the sheep should be a friend of the lamb, for the imaginative faculty is a perceptive one[5] and it necessarily possesses judgement, and there is no need to introduce another faculty. What Avicenna says would only be possible if the imaginative faculty were not perceptive; and there is no sense in adding another faculty to the imaginative in the animal, especially in an animal which possesses many arts by nature, for its representations are not derived from the senses[6] and seem to be perceptions intermediary between the intellectual and the sensible* forms, and the question of these forms* is concisely treated in *De sensu et sensato*,[7] and we shall leave this subject here and return to Ghazali's objections against the philosophers.

Ghazali says:

The first proof is that they say that intellectual cognitions inhere in human souls, and are limited and have units which cannot be divided, and therefore their substratum must also be indivisible and every body is divisible, and this proves that the substratum of the cognitions is something incorporeal*.[1] One can put this into a logical form according to the figures of logic, but the easiest way is to say that if the substratum of knowledge is a divisible body, then the knowledge which inheres in it must be divisible too; but the inherent knowledge is not divisible, and therefore the substratum is not a body: and this is a mixed hypothetical syllogism in which the consequent is denied, from which there follows the denial of the antecedent in all cases; and there is no doubt about the validity of this figure of the syllogism, nor again about its premisses, for the major is that everything inherent in something divisible is necessarily divisible, the divisibility of its substratum being assumed, and this is a major about which one cannot have any doubt. The minor is that knowledge as a unity inheres in man and is not divided, for its infinite division is impossible, and if it is limited, then it comprises no doubt units which cannot be divided; and in short, when we know a thing, we cannot assume that a part can cease and a part remain, because it has no parts.

The objection rests on two points. It may be said:

'How will you refute those who say that the substratum of knowledge is an atom in space which cannot be divided, as is known from the theory of the theologians?'[2] And then there remains nothing to be said against it but to question its possibility, and to ask how all that is known can exist in one atom, whereas all the atoms which surround this one are deprived of it although they are near to it. But to question its possibility has no value, as one can also turn it against the doctrine of the philosophers, by asking how the soul can be one single thing which is not in space or outside the body, either continuous with it or separated from it. However, we should not stress this first point, for the discussion of the problem of the atom is lengthy,[3] and the philosophers have geometrical proofs against it whose discussion is intricate, and one of their many arguments is to ask: 'Does one of the sides of an atom between two atoms touch the identical spot the other side touches or not?' The former is impossible, because its consequence would be that the two sides coincided, whereas a thing that is in contact with another is in contact, and the latter implies the affirmation of a plurality and divisibility,[4] and the solution of this difficulty is long and we need not go deeper into it and will now turn to the other point.

Your affirmation that everything which inheres in a body must be divisible is contradicted by what you say of the estimative faculty of the sheep where the hostility of the wolf is concerned, for in the judgement of one single thing no division can be imagined, since hostility has no part, so that one part of it might be perceived and another neglected. Still, according to you this perception takes place in a bodily faculty, and the souls of animals are impressed on their bodies and do not survive death, and all the philosophers agree about this. And if it is possible for you to regard as divisible that which is perceived by the five senses, by the common sense and by the faculty which retains the forms, this is not possible for you in the case of those intentions which are not supposed to be in matter.

And if it be said: 'Absolute hostility, abstracted from matter, is not perceived by the sheep, but only the hostility of the definite individual wolf connected with its bodily individuality and shape, and only the rational faculty perceives universal realities abstracted from matter'—we answer that the sheep perceives, indeed, the colour and shape of the wolf and then its hostility, and if the colour is impressed on the faculty of sight and the same happens to the shape, and it is divided through the division of the substratum of sight, I ask, 'through what does the sheep perceive the hostility? If through a body, hostility is divided, and I should like to know what this perception is when it is divided, whether it is a perception of a part of the hostility—and how can it have a part?—or whether every part is a perception of the hostility and the hostility is known many times as its perception is fixed in every part of the substratum.'[1] And thus this problem is a difficulty for their proof and must be solved.

And if it is said: 'This is an argument against the intelligibles, but the intelligibles cannot be denied,[2] and as long as you cannot call in question the premisses that knowledge cannot be divided and that what cannot be divided cannot be in a divisible body, you can have no doubt about the consequence'—the answer is: 'We have only written this book to show the incoherence and contradictions in the doctrine of the philosophers, and such a contradiction arises over this question, since through it either your theory about the rational soul is refuted or your theory about the estimative faculty.'

Further we say that this contradiction shows that they are not conscious of the point, which confounds* their syllogism, and it may well be that the origin of their confusion lies in their statement that knowledge is impressed on a body in the way colour is impressed on a coloured thing, the colour being divided with the division of the coloured thing, so that knowledge must be divided by the division of its substratum.[3] The mistake lies in the term 'impression', since it may well be that the relation of knowledge to its substratum is not like that of colour to the coloured object so that it could be regarded as being spread over it, diffused over its sides and divisible with it; knowledge might well be related to its substratum in another way which would not allow its divisibility although its substratum was divisible; yes, its relation to it might be like that of perception of the hostility to the body,[4] and the relations of the attributes to their substrata do not all follow the same pattern and they are not all known to us with all their details so that we could rely on our knowledge, and to judge such a question without a perfect comprehension of all the details of the relation is an unreliable judgement. In short, we do not deny that what the philosophers say gives reasonable and predominant reasons for belief, but we deny that it is known by an evidence which excludes error and doubt. And it is in this way that a doubt about it may be raised.

I say:

When the premises which the philosophers use are taken in an indefinite way the consequence Ghazali draws is valid. For our assertion that every attribute inhering in a body which is divisible is divisible through the divisibility of the body can be understood in two ways. First it may be meant that the definition of every part of this attribute which inheres in the particular body is identical with the definition of the whole: for instance the white inhering in the white body, for every part of whiteness which inheres in the individual body has one and the same definition as the whole of whiteness in this body.[1] Secondly, it may be meant that the attribute is attached to the body without a specific shape,[2] and this attribute again is divided through the division of the body not in such a way that the intension of the definition of the whole is identical with the intension of the definition of every part—for instance, the faculty of sight which exists in one who sees—but in such a way that it is subject to a difference in intensity according to the greater and lesser receptivity of the substratum, and therefore the power of sight is stronger in the healthy and the young than in the sick and the old.[3] What is common to those two classes* is that they are composed of individuals, i.e. that they are divided by quantity and not by quiddity, i.e. that either the uniqueness of the definition and the quiddity remains or that they are annulled.[4] Those which can be divided quantitatively into any particular part are one by definition and quiddity* and those which cannot be divided* into any individual part whatever[5] only differ from the first class in a degree of intensity, for the action of the part which has vanished is not identical with that of the part which remains, since the action of the part which has vanished in weak sight does not act in the same way as the weak sight.[6] Those two classes have it in common that colour also cannot be divided by the division of its substratum into any particular part whatever and keep its definition absolutely intact, but the division terminates in a particular part in which the colour, when it is distributed to it, disappears.[7] The only thing which keeps its distribution always intact is the nature of the continuous in so far as it is continuous, i.e. the form of continuity.[8]

When this premiss is assumed in this way, namely by holding that everything which is divisible in either of these two classes has a body as its substratum, it is self-evident, and the converse, that everything which is in a body is divisible according to one of these two classes, is evident too; and when this is verified, then the converse of its opposite is true also, namely that what is not divisible according to one of these two classes cannot be in a body. If to these premisses there is added further what is evident in the case of the universal intelligibles, namely that they are not divisible in either of the two ways, since they are not individual forms, it is clear that there follows from this that neither is the substratum of these intelligibles a body, nor is the faculty which has the power to produce them a faculty in a body; and it follows that their substratum is a spiritual faculty which perceives itself and other things.

But Ghazali took first the one of these two classes and denied that the universal intelligibles belong to it, and then made his objection by means of the second class, which exists in the faculty of sight and in the imaginative faculty, and in doing this he committed a sophism; but the science of the soul is too profound and too elevated to be apprehended by dialectics.[1]

Besides, Ghazali has not adduced the argument in the manner in which Avicenna brought it out,[2] for Avicenna built his argument only on the following: If the intelligibles inhered in a body, they would have to be either in an indivisible part of it, or in a divisible part. Then he refuted the possibility of their being in an indivisible part of the body, and after this refutation he denied that, if the intellect inhered in a body, it could inhere in an indivisible part of it. Then he denied that it could inhere in a divisible part of it and so he denied that it could inhere in body at all.

And when Ghazali denied one of these two divisions he said it was not impossible that there might be another form of relation between the intellect and the body than this, but it is quite clear that if the intellect is related to the body there can exist only two kinds of relation, either to a divisible or to an indivisible substratum.

This proof can be completed[3] by saying that the intellect is not attached to any animal faculty in the way the form is attached to its substratum, for the denial of its being attached to the body implies necessarily the denial of its being attached to any animal faculty which is attached to the body. For, if the intellect were attached to any of the animal faculties, it would as Aristotle says be unable to act except through this faculty, but then this faculty would not

ABOUT THE NATURAL SCIENCES 341

perceive the intellect. This is the argument on which Aristotle himself bases his proof that the intellect is separate.[1]

We shall now mention the second objection which Ghazali raises against the second proof of the philosophers, but we must first observe that their proofs, when they are taken out of their context in those sciences to which they belong, can have at the most the value of dialectical arguments. The only aim of this book of ours is therefore to ascertain the value of the arguments in it which are ascribed to the two parties, and to show to which of the two disputants the terms 'incoherence' and 'contradiction' would be applied with greater justification.

Ghazali says:

554

The second proof is that the philosophers say:

'If the knowledge of one single intellectual notion, i.e. a notion abstracted from matter, were impressed on matter as accidents are impressed on bodily substances, their division would necessarily follow the division of the body, as has been shown before. And if it is not impressed on matter nor spread out over it, and the term 'impression' is rejected, let us then use another term and say, 'Is there a relation between knowledge and the knower?'

It is absurd to deny the relation, for if there did not exist a relation, why would it be better to know something than not to know it*? And if there is a relation, this relation can take place in three ways; either there will be a relation to every part of the substratum, or to some parts to the exclusion of others, or to no part whatever. It is false to say that the notion has no relation to any individual part of the substratum; for if there is no relation to the units, there can be no relation to the aggregate, since a collection of disconnected units is not an aggregate, but itself disconnected. It is false to say that there might be a relation to some part, for the part that was not related would have nothing to do with this notion and therefore would not come into the present discussion. And it is false to say that every part of the substratum might be related to it, for if it were related in all its parts to this notion in its totality, then each single part of the substratum would possess not a part of the notion but the notion in its totality, and this notion would therefore be repeated infinitely in act; on the other hand, if every part were related to this notion in a special way, different from the relation of another part, then this notion would be divided in its content; and we have shown that the content of a notion, one and the same in every respect, is indivisible; if the relation, however, of each part were related to another part of the notion, then this notion would clearly be divided, and this is impossible.[2] And from this it is clear that the things perceived which are in the five senses are only images of the particular divided forms, and that the meaning of perception is the arrival of the image of the thing perceived in the soul of the perceiver, so that every part of the image of the thing perceived is related to a part of the bodily organ.

And the objection against this is what has been said before. For by replacing the term 'impression' by 'relation' the difficulty is not removed which arises over the question what of the hostility of the wolf is impressed on the estimative faculty of the sheep, as we have mentioned; for the perception is no doubt related to it, and with this relation there must occur what you have said, and hostility is not a measurable thing possessing a measurable quantity, so that its image could be impressed on a measurable body and its parts related to the parts of that body, and the fact that the shape of the wolf is measurable does not remove the difficulty, for the sheep perceives something else as well as the shape, namely the adversity, opposition, and hostility, and this hostility, added to the shape through the hostility, has no magnitude, and still the sheep perceives it through a body having magnitude; and that is necessarily a difficulty in this proof as well as in the first.

And if someone says: 'Do you not refute these proofs by asserting that knowledge inheres in a spatial indivisible body, namely the atom?' we answer: 'No, for* the discussion of the atom is connected with geometrical questions the solution and discussion of which is long and arduous. Further, such a theory would not remove the difficulty, for the power and the will ought then also to be in this atom. For man acts, and this acting cannot be imagined without power and will, which would also be in this atom; and the power to write resides in the hand and the fingers, but knowledge of it does not reside in the hand, for it does not cease when the hand is cut off; nor is the will in the hand, for often a man wants to write, when his hand has withered and he is not able to do so, not because his will has gone, but because his power has.'[1]

I say:

This discussion is not an independent one, but only a complement to the first, for in the first discussion it was merely assumed that knowledge is not divided by the division of its substratum, and here an attempt is made to prove this by making use of a division into three categories. And he repeats the same objection, which presented itself to him because he did not carry out the division of matter in the two senses in which it can be taken. For when the philosophers denied that the intellect could be divided through the division of its substratum in the way in which accidents are divided through the division of their substratum, and there exists another way of division in body which must be applied to the bodily functions of perception, they had a doubt about these faculties. The proof is only completed by denying that the intellect can be divided in either of these ways, and by showing that everything which exists in a body is necessarily divisible in one of them.

For of those things in the body which are divided in this second way, i.e. which are not by definition divisible through the division of their substratum[1] it was sometimes doubted whether they are separable from their substratum or not.[2] For we see it happen that most parts of the substratum decay and still this kind of existence, i.e. the individual perception, does not decay; and it was thought that it might happen that, just as the form does not disappear through the disappearance of one or more parts of its substratum, in the same way the form might not disappear when the whole was destroyed, and that the decay of the act of the form through its substratum was similar to the decay of the act of the artisan through the deterioration of his tools. And therefore Aristotle says that if an old man had the eye of a young man, he would see as well as the young one, meaning that it is thought that the decrepitude which occurs to the sight of the old man does not happen because of the decay of the faculty but because of the decay of the organs.[3] And he tries to prove this by the inactivity of the organ or the greater part of it in sleep, fainting, drunkenness, and the illnesses through which the perceptions of the senses decay, whereas it is quite certain that the faculties are not destroyed in these conditions.[4] And this is still more evident in those animals which live when they are cut in two; and most plants have this peculiarity, although they do not possess the faculty of perception.[5]

But the discussion of the soul is very obscure, and therefore God has only given knowledge of it to those who are deeply learned; and therefore God, answering the question of the masses about this problem, says that this kind of question is not their concern, saying: 'They will ask thee of the spirit. Say: "The spirit comes at the bidding of my Lord, and ye are given but a little knowledge thereof." '[6] And the comparison of death with sleep in this question is an evident proof that the soul survives, since the activity of the soul ceases in sleep through the inactivity of its organ, but the existence of the soul does not cease, and therefore it is necessary that its condition in death should be like its condition in sleep, for the parts follow the same rule.[7] And this is a proof which all can understand and which is suitable to be believed by the masses, and will show the learned the way in which the survival of the soul is ascertained. And this is evident from the Divine Words: 'God takes to Himself souls at the time of their death; and those who do not die in their sleep.'[8]

Ghazali says:

The third proof is that they say that, if knowledge resided in a part of the body, the knower would be this part to the exclusion of all the other parts of man, but it is said of man that it is he who knows, and knowledge is an attribute of man in his totality without reference to any specified place.[1] But this is nonsense, for he is spoken of as seeing and hearing and tasting, and the animals also are described in this way; but this does not mean that the perception of the senses is not in the body, it is only a metaphorical expression like the expression that someone is in Baghdad, although he is in a part of the whole of Baghdad, not in the whole of Baghdad, the reference however being made to the whole.

I say:

When it is conceded that the intellect is not related to one of man's organs—and this has already been proved, since it is not self-evident—it follows that its substratum is not a body, and that our assertion that man knows is not analogous to our assertion that he sees.[2] For since it is self-evident that he sees through a particular organ, it is clear that when we refer sight to man absolutely, the expression is allowed according to the custom of the Arabs and other people.[3] And since there is no particular organ for the intellect, it is clear that, when we say of him that he knows, this does not mean that a part of him knows. However, how he knows is not clear by itself, for it does not appear that there is an organ or a special place in an organ which possesses this special faculty, as is the case with the imaginative faculty and the cogitative and memorative faculties, the localization of which in parts of the brain is known.

Ghazali says:

The fourth proof is that, if knowledge inhered for instance in a part of the heart or the brain, then necessarily ignorance, its opposite, might reside in another part of the heart or the brain, and it would then be possible that a man should both know and not know one and the same thing at the same time. And since this is impossible, it is proved that the place of ignorance and the place of knowledge are identical, and that this place is one single place in which it is impossible to bring opposites together. But if this place were divisible, it would not be impossible that ignorance should reside in one part of it and knowledge in another, for a thing's being in one place is not contradicted by its opposite's being in another, just as there may be piebaldness in one and the same horse, and black and white in a single eye, but in two spots. This, however, does not follow for the senses, as there is no opposite to their perception; but sometimes they perceive and sometimes not, and there exists between them the sole opposition of being and not-being, and we can surely say that someone perceives through some parts, for instance the eye and the ear, and not through the other parts of his body; and there is no contradiction in this. And you cannot evade this difficulty by saying that knowing is the opposite of not-knowing, and that judgement is something common to the whole body; for it is impossible that the judgement should be in any other place but in the place of its cause, and the knower is the place in which the knowledge resides; and if the term is applied to the whole, this is a metaphor, as when we say that a man is in Baghdad, although he is in a part of it, and when we say that a man sees although we know with certainty that the judgement of his sight[1] does not reside in his foot and hand but is peculiar to his eye. The judgements are opposed to each other in the same way as their causes, and the judgements are limited to the place where the causes reside. And one cannot evade the difficulty by saying that the place disposed to receive the knowledge and the ignorance of man is one single place in which they can oppose each other, for according to you theologians every body which possesses life can receive knowledge and ignorance, and no other condition but life is imposed, and all the parts of the body are according to you equivalent so far as the reception of knowledge is concerned.[2]

The objection to this is that it can be turned against you philosophers in the matter of desire, longing, and will; these things exist in animals as well as in men, and are things impressed on the body, but it is impossible that one should flee from the object one longs for and that repugnance and craving in regard to one and the same thing should exist in him together, the desire being in one place and the repugnance in another. Still, that does not prove that they do not inhere in bodies, for these potencies, although they are many and distributed over different organs, have one thing that joins them together, namely the soul,[3] which is common both to animal and to man; and since this cohesive entity forms a unity, the mutually contradictory relations enter into relation with it in turns. This does not prove that the soul is not impressed upon the body, as is quite clear in the case of animals.

I say:

The only logical consequence of what he says here in the name of the philosophers is that knowledge does not inhere in the body in the way colour and in general all accidents do; it does not, however, follow that it does not inhere in body at all. For the impossibility that the place of knowledge should receive the knowledge and want of knowledge of a thing necessarily demonstrates its identity, since opposites cannot inhere in one and the same place, and this kind of impossibility is common to all attributes, whether perceptive or nonperceptive. But what is peculiar to the receptivity of knowledge is that it can perceive opposites together; and this can only happen through an indivisible apprehension in an indivisible substratum, for he who judges is of necessity one, and therefore it is said that knowledge of opposites is one and the same.[1] And this kind of receptivity is of necessity proper to the soul alone. What is indeed proved by the philosophers is that this is the condition of the common sense when it exercises its judgement over the five senses, and this common sense is according to the philosophers something bodily.[2] And therefore there is in this argument no proof that the intellect does not inhere in a body, for we have already said that there are two kinds of inherence, the inherence of non-perceptive attributes and that of perceptive.

And the objection Ghazali makes here is true, namely that the appetitive soul does not tend to opposites at the same time although it resides in the body. I do not know of any philosopher who has used this argument[3] to establish the survival of the soul, unless he paid no attention to the philosophical doctrine* that it is the characteristic of every perceptive faculty that in its perception two opposites cannot be joined,[4] just as it is the peculiarity of contraries outside the soul that they cannot be together in one and the same substratum; and this is what the perceptive potencies have in common with the non-perceptive. It is proper to the perceptive faculties to judge co-existing contraries, one of them being known through knowledge of the other,[5] and it is proper to non-psychical potencies to be divided through the division of the body so that contraries can be in one body at the same time, though not in the same part. And since the soul is a substratum that cannot be divided in this way, contraries cannot be in it together, i.e. in two parts of the substratum.

Such arguments are all arguments of people who have not grasped the views of the philosophers about this problem. How little does a man understand, who gives it as a proof of the soul's survival that it does not judge two opposites at the same time, for from this it follows only that the substratum of the soul is one, and not divided in the way the substratum of the accidents is divided; and it does not follow from the proof that the substratum is not divided in the way the substratum of the accidents is divided that the substratum is not divided at all.

Ghazali says:

The fifth proof is: If the intellect perceived the intelligibles through a bodily organ, it would not know its own self.[6] But the consequent is impossible; therefore it knows its own self and the antecedent is impossible. We answer: It is conceded that from the exclusion of the contrary of the consequent the contrary of the antecedent follows,[1] but only when the consequence of the antecedent has been previously established, and we say we do not concede the necessity of the consequence; and what is your proof?

And if it is said that the proof is that, because sight is in the body, sight does not attach itself to sight, and the seeing is not seen nor the hearing heard, and so on with respect to the other senses; and if the intellect, too, could only perceive through body it could not perceive itself, but the intellect thinks itself just as it thinks other things, and it thinks that it thinks itself and that it thinks other things—we answer: What you assert is wrong on two points. The first is that according to us sight could be attached to itself, just as one and the same knowledge can be knowledge of other things and of itself, only in the usual course of events this does not happen; but according to us the interruption of the usual course of events is possible. The second, and this is the stronger argument, is for us to say that we concede this for the senses; but why, if this is impossible for some senses, is it impossible for others, and why is it impossible that there should be a difference in the behaviour of the senses with respect to perception although they are all in the body?—just as sight differs from touch through the fact that touch, like taste, can only come to perceive by being in contact with the object touched, whereas separation from the object is a condition of sight, so that when the eyelids cover the eye it does not see the colour of the eyelid,[2] not being at a distance from it.[3] But this difference does not necessitate that they should differ in their need to be in a body, and it is not impossible that there should be among the senses something called intellect that differs from the others in that it perceives itself.

I say:

The first objection, that the usual course of events might be interrupted so that sight might see itself, is an argument of the utmost sophistry and imposture, and we have discussed it already. As to the second objection, that it is not impossible that a bodily perception should perceive itself, this has a certain plausibility, but when the motive is known which led the philosophers to their assertion, then the impossibility of this supposition becomes clear, for perception is something which exists between the agent and the patient, and it consists of the perceiver and the perceived. It is impossible that a sense should be in one and the same respect its own agent and patient, and the duality of agent and patient in sense arises, as concerns its act, from the side of the form and, as concerns its passivity, from the side of the matter.[4] But no composite can think itself, because if this were so, its essence would be different from that by which it thinks, for it would think only with a part of its essence; and since intellect and intelligible are identical,[1] if the composite thought its essence, the composite would become a simple, and the whole the part, and all this is impossible. When this is established here in this way, it is only a dialectical proof; but in the proper demonstrative order, i.e. preceded by the conclusions which ought to precede it, it can become a necessary one.

Ghazali says:

The sixth proof is that they say that, if the intellect perceived through a bodily organ like sight, it would be just as incapable of perceiving its own organ as the other senses; but it perceives the brain and the heart and what is claimed to be its organ, so that it is proved that it has no organ or substratum, for otherwise it would not perceive the brain and the heart*.[2]

We have the same kind of objection against this as against the preceding proof. We say it is not inconceivable that sight should perceive its subject, for that it does not perceive it is only what happens in the usual course of events. Or* shall we rather say it is not impossible that the senses should differ individually in this respect, although it is common to them all to be impressed on bodies, as has been said before? And why do you say that what exists in a body cannot perceive the body, and how do you know its impossibility in all cases, since to make an infinite generalization from a finite number of individual cases has no logical validity? In logic it is stated, as an example of an inference made from one particular cause or many particular causes to all causes, that when we say, after learning it by induction through observing all the animals, 'all animals move the lower jaw in masticating', the crocodile has been neglected, since it moves the upper.[3] The philosophers have only made the induction from the five senses, and found this known common feature in them and then judged that all the senses must be like this. But perhaps the intellect is another type of sense which stands in regard to the other senses as the crocodile stands to the other animals, and in this case there would be some senses which could perceive their substratum although they were corporeal and divisible, and other senses which could not do this; just as the senses can be divided into those which perceive the thing perceived without contact, like sight, and those which cannot perceive without contact, like taste and touch. Although, therefore, what the philosophers affirm creates a certain presumption, it does not afford reliable evidence.

But it may be said by the philosophers:[4] We do not merely point to the enumeration of the senses but lay stress on a proof, and say that if the heart or the brain were the soul of man, he could never be unaware of them, and never for a moment not think of them, just as he is never unconscious of himself; for nobody's self is ever unaware of itself, but it is always affirming itself in its soul, but as long as man has not heard any one speaking about the heart and the brain or has not observed them through the dissection of another man, he does not perceive them and does not believe in their existence. But if the intellect inhered in the body, it would necessarily either think or not think of this body continually; neither the one nor the other is the case, but it sometimes thinks of its body* and sometimes does not*. This can be proved by the fact that the perception which inheres in the substratum perceives that substratum either because of a relation between itself and the substratum—and one cannot imagine another relation between them than that of inherence—and then the perception must perceive its substratum continually, or this relation will not suffice; and in this case the perception can never perceive its substratum, since there can never occur another relation between them; just as because of the fact that it thinks itself, it thinks itself always and is not sometimes aware, sometimes unaware of itself.

But we answer: As long as a man is conscious of himself and aware of his soul, he is also aware of his body; indeed, the name, form, and shape of the heart are not well defined for him, but he regards his soul and self as a body to such an extent that he regards even his clothes and his house as belonging to his self,[1] but the soul or the self which the philosophers mention has no relation to the house or the clothes. This primary attribution of the soul to the body is necessary for man, and his unconsciousness of the form and name of his soul is like his unconsciousness of the seat of smell, which is two excrescences in the foremost part of the brain resembling the nipples of the breast;[2] still, everyone knows that he perceives smell with his body, but he does not represent the shape of the seat of this perception, nor does he define this seat, although he perceives that it is nearer to his head than to his heels, and, in relation to the whole of his head, nearer to the inside of his nose than to the inside of his ear. Man knows his soul in the same way, and he knows that the essence through which the soul exists is nearer to his heart and breast than to his foot, and he supposes that his soul will persist when he loses his foot, but he does not regard it as possible that his soul should persist when his heart is taken away. But what the philosophers say about his being sometimes aware of his body*, sometimes not*, is not true.

I say:

As to his objection against the assertion that a body or a bodily faculty cannot know itself, because the senses are perceptive faculties in bodies and do not know themselves, this assertion indeed is based on induction, and induction does not provide absolute evidence.[3] As to Ghazali's comparison of this to the induction which establishes that all animals move their lower jaw, this comparison is only valid in part. For the induction that all animals move their lower jaw is an imperfect one, because not all animals have been enumerated; whereas the man who assumes that no sense perceives itself has certainly made a complete induction, for there are no other senses than the five.[1] But the judgement based on the observation of the senses that no perceptive faculty is in a body resembles the induction by which it is judged that all animals move their lower jaw; for, just as in the latter case not all the animals, in the former not all the perceptive faculties are enumerated.[2]

As to his saying in the name of the philosophers that if the intellect were in the body, it would, when it perceives, perceive the body in which it is, this is a silly and inane assertion which is not made by the philosophers. It would only follow if everyone who perceived a thing had to perceive it together with its definition; but that is not so, for we perceive the soul and many other things without perceiving their definition. If, indeed, we perceived the definition of the soul together with its existence, we should of necessity know through its definition* that it was in the body or that it was incorporeal; for, if it were in the body, the body would be necessarily included in its definition, and if it were not in the body, the body would not be included in the definition. And this is what one must believe about this problem.

As for Ghazali's objection, that a man knows of his soul that it is in his body although he cannot specify in which part—this indeed is true, for the ancients had different opinions about its seat, but our knowledge that the soul is in the body does not mean that we know that it receives its existence through being in the body; this is not self-evident, and is a question about which the philosophers ancient as well as modern differ, for if the body serves as an instrument for the soul, the soul does not receive its existence through the body; but if the body is like a substratum for its accident, then the soul can only exist through the body.

Ghazali says:

The seventh proof. The philosophers say that the faculties which perceive through the bodily organs become tired through the long-continued performance of the act of perception, since the continuation of their action destroys the mixture of their elements and tires them, and in the same way excessive stimulation of the perceptive faculties makes them weak and often even corrupts them, so that afterwards they are not able to perceive something lighter and more delicate; so for instance a loud voice and a strong light hinder or corrupt the perception of a low voice and delicate objects of sight afterwards; and in fact the man who tastes something extremely sweet does not afterwards taste something less sweet. But the intellectual faculty behaves in the opposite way; a long observation of intelligibles does not tire it, and the perception of important necessary truths gives it strength for the perception of easy observations and does not weaken it, and if sometimes tiredness may befall it, this happens because it makes use of and gets assistance from the imaginative faculty, so that the organ of the imaginative faculty becomes weary and no longer serves the intellect.[1]

Our objection to this follows the same line as before, and we say that it may well be that the bodily senses differ in this; and what is true for some of them need not be true for others—yes, it may be that the bodies themselves may differ and that some of them may grow weak through a certain type of movement, whereas others may grow strong through a certain type of movement, not weak, and that when this type of movement has made an impression on them, it causes a renewal of strength in them so that they do not perceive any new impression made on them. And all this is possible, since a judgement valid for some is not valid for all.

I say:

This is an old proof of the philosophers, and it amounts to this: that when the intellect perceives a strong intelligible and afterwards turns to the perception of a slighter, it perceives it more easily, and this shows that it does not perceive through the body, since we find that the bodily perceptive faculties are impressed by strong sensations in a way which lessens their power of perception, so that after strong sensations they cannot perceive things of slight intensity. The reason is that through every form which inheres in a body the body receives an impression, because this form is necessarily mixed* with it; for otherwise this form would not be a form in a body. Now since the philosophers found that the receptacle of the intelligibles was not impressed by the intelligibles, they decided that this receptacle was not a body.

And against this there is no objection. For every substratum which is impressed congruously or incongruously by the inherence of the form in it, be it little or much, is necessarily corporeal, and the reverse is also true, namely that everything corporeal is impressed by the form which is realized in it, and the magnitude of the impression depends on the magnitude of the mixing of the form and the body. And the cause of this is that every becoming is the consequence of a change, and if a form could inhere in a body without a change it might happen that there could be a form whose realization did not impress its substratum.

Ghazali says:

The eighth proof is that the philosophers say: 'All the faculties of parts of the body become weaker, when they have reached the end of their growth at forty years and later; so sight and hearing and the other faculties become weaker, but the intellectual faculty becomes strong in most cases only after this age.[1] And the loss of insight in the intelligibles, through illness in the body and through dotage in old age, does not argue against this, for as long as it is proved that at certain times the intellect is strong notwithstanding the weakness of the body, it is clear that it exists by itself, and its decline at the time of the declining of the body does not imply that it exists through the body, for from a negative consequent alternating with a positive consequent there is no inference.[2] For we say that, if the intellectual faculty exists through the body, then the weakness of the body will weaken it at all times, but the consequent is false and therefore the antecedent is false; but, when we say the consequent is true, sometimes it does not follow that the antecedent is true. Further, the cause of this is that the soul has an activity through itself, when nothing hinders it and it is not preoccupied with something. For the soul has two kinds of action, one in relation to the body, namely to govern and rule it, and one in relation to its principles and essence, and this is to perceive the intelligibles, and these two kinds of action hinder each other and are opposed to each other, and when it is occupied with the one action, it turns away from the other and it cannot combine both. And its occupations through the body are sense-perception and imagination and the passions, anger, fear, grief, and pain, but when it sets out to think the intelligible it neglects all these other things. Yes, sense-perception by itself sometimes hinders the apprehension and contemplation of the intellect without the occurrence of any damage to the organ of the intellect or to the intellect itself, and the reason for this is that the soul is prevented from one action through being occupied with another, and therefore during pain, disease, and fear—for this also is a disease of the brain[3]—intellectual speculation leaves off. And why should it be impossible that through this difference in these two kinds of action in the soul they should hinder each other, since even two acts of the same kind may impede each other, for fear is stunned by pain and desire by anger and the observation of one intelligible by that of another? And a sign that the illness which enters the body does not occur in the substratum of the sciences is that, when the sick man recovers, he does not need to learn the sciences anew, but the disposition of his soul becomes the same as it was before, and those sciences come back to him exactly as they were without any new learning.

The objection is that we say that there may be innumerable causes for the increase and the decrease of the faculties, for some of the faculties increase in power at the beginning of life, some in middle life, some at the end, and the same is the case with the intellect and only a topical proof can be claimed. And it is not impossible that smell and sight should differ in this, that smell becomes stronger after forty years and sight weaker, although they both inhere in the body, just as those faculties differ in animals; for in some animals smell is stronger, in others hearing and sight because of the difference in their temperaments, and it is not possible to ascertain these facts absolutely. Nor is it impossible that the temperament of the organs also should differ with individual persons and conditions. One of the reasons why the decay of sight is earlier than the decay of the intellect is that sight is earlier, for a man sees when he is first created, whereas his intellect is not mature before fifteen years or more,[1] according to the different opinions we find people to have about this problem; and it is even said that greyness comes earlier to the hair on the head than to that on the beard, because the hair on the head grows earlier. If one goes deeper into these causes and does not simply refer them to the usual course of nature, one cannot base any sure knowledge thereon, because the possibilities for certain faculties to become stronger and others weaker are unlimited, and nothing evident results from this.

I say:

When it is assumed that the substratum of the perceptive faculties is the natural heat, and that natural heat suffers diminution after forty years, then intellect must behave in the same way in this respect; that is, if its substratum is natural heat,[2] then it is necessary that the intellect should become old as the natural heat becomes old. If, however, it is thought that the substrata for the intellect and the senses are different, then it is not necessary that both should be similar in their lifetimes.

Ghazali says:

The ninth proof is that the philosophers say: How can man be attributed to body with its accidents, for those bodies are continually in dissolution, and nutrition replaces what is dissolved, so that when we see a child after its separation from its mother's womb fall ill a few times and become thin and then fat again and grow up, we may safely say that after forty years no particle remains of what was there when his mother was delivered of it. Indeed, the child began its existence out of the parts of the sperm alone, but nothing of the particles of the sperm remains in it; no, all this is dissolved and has changed into something else, and then this body has become another.[3] Still we say that the identical man remains and his notions remain with him from the beginning of his youth, although all the bodily parts have changed. And this shows that the soul has an existence outside the body and that the body is its organ.[4]

The objection is that this is contradicted by what happens to animals and plants, for when the condition of their being small is compared to the condition of their being big, their identity is asserted equally with the identity of man; still, it does not prove that they have an incorporeal existence.[5] And what is said about knowledge is refuted by the retention of imaginative forms, for they remain in the boy from youth to old age, although the particles of his brain change.

I say:

None of the ancient philosophers used this proof for the survival of the soul; they only used it to show that in individuals there is an essence which remains from birth to death and that things are not in an eternal flux, as was believed by many ancients who denied necessary knowledge, so that Plato was forced to introduce the forms. There is no sense in occupying ourselves with this, and the objection of Ghazali against this proof is valid.

Ghazali says:

The tenth proof is that they say that the intellectual faculty perceives the general intellectual universals which the theologians call modes, so that man in general is apprehended (whereas the senses perceive the individuality of a definite man), and this universal differs from the man who is perceived by the senses, for what is perceived by the senses is in a particular place, and his colour, size, and position are particular, but the intelligible absolute man is abstracted from all these things; however, in him there is everything to which the term 'man' is applied, although he has not the colour, size, position, or place, of the man perceived by the senses, and even a man who may exist in the future is subsumed under him; indeed, if man disappeared there would remain this reality of man in the intellect, in abstraction from all these particular things.

And in this way, from everything perceived by the senses as an individual, there results for the intellect a reality, universal and abstracted from matters and from positions, so that its attributes can be divided into what is essential (as, for example, corporeity for plants and animals, and animality for man) and into what is accidental (like whiteness and length for man), and this reality is judged as being essential or accidental for the genus of man and plant and of everything not apprehended as an individual perceived by the senses, and so it is shown that the universal, in abstraction from sensible attachments, is intelligible and invariable in the mind of man.

This intelligible universal cannot be pointed at,[1] nor has it a position or size, and in its abstraction from position and matter it is either related to its object (which is impossible, for its object has position and place and size) or to its subject (which is the rational soul), and therefore the soul cannot have a position or be pointed at or have a size, for if it had all these things what inheres in it would also possess them.[2]

And the objection is that the idea of a universal which you philosophers assume as existing in the intellect is not accepted by us.[3] According to us nothing inheres in the intellect but what inheres in the senses, only it inheres in the senses as an aggregate which they cannot separate, whereas the intellect is able to do so. Further, when it is separated, the single part separated from its attachments is just as much an individual in the intellect as the aggregate with its attachments, only this invariable part[1] in the mind is related to the thing thought of[2] and to similar things by one single relation, and in this way it is said to be a universal. For there is in the intellect the form[3] of the individual thing thought of which is first perceived by the senses, and the relation of this form to all the individuals of this genus which the senses perceive is one and the same. If, after seeing one man, someone sees another, no new form occurs to him, as happens when he sees a horse after seeing a man, for then two different forms occur in him. A similar thing happens to the senses themselves, for when a man sees water, one form occurs in his imagination, and if he sees blood afterwards, another form occurs, but if he sees another water, no other form occurs, but the form of the water which is impressed on his imagination is an image for all individual stretches of water, and for this reason it is often thought to be a universal.

And in the same way, when for instance he sees a hand, there occurs in his imagination and in his intellect the natural position of its parts, namely the surface of the hand and the division of the fingers in it and the ending of the fingers in the nails, and besides this there occur to him the smallness or bigness of the hand and its colour, and if he sees another hand which resembles the first in everything, no other new form occurs to him; no, this second observation, when a new thing occurs, does not produce an impression on his imagination, just as, when he sees the water after having previously seen it in one and the same vessel and in the same quantity, no new impression is produced. And he may see another hand, different in colour and size, and then there occurs to him another colour and another size, but there does not happen to him a new form of hand, for the small black hand has in common with the big white hand the position of its parts, differing from it in colour, and of that in which the second hand agrees with the first no new form is produced, since both forms are identical, but the form of the things in which they differ is renewed. And this is the meaning of the universal both in sensation and in intellect, for when the intellect apprehends the form of the body of an animal, then it does not acquire a new form of corporeity from a plant, just as in imagination the form of two stretches of water perceived at two different times need not be renewed; and the same happens with all things that have something in common.

But this does not permit one to assert the existence of a universal which has no position whatever, although the intellect can judge that there exists something that cannot be pointed at and has no spatial position; for instance, it can assert the existence of the creator of the universe, with the understanding, however, that such a creator cannot be imagined to exist in matter, and in this kind of reality the abstraction from matter is in the intelligible itself and is not caused by the intellect and by thinking.[4] But as to the forms acquired from material things, this happens in the way we have mentioned.

573 I say:

The meaning of the philosophical theory he relates is that the intellect apprehends, in relation to the individuals which have a common species, a single entity, in which they participate and which is the quiddity of this species without this entity's being divided into the things in which the individuals *qua* individuals are divided, like space and position and the matters through which they receive their plurality. This entity must be ingenerable and incorruptible[1] and is not destroyed by the disappearance of one of the individuals in which it exists, and the sciences therefore are eternal and not corruptible except by accident, that is to say by their connexion with Zaid and Amr; that is, only through this connexion are they corruptible, and not in themselves, since if they were transitory in themselves this connexion would exist in their essence and they could not constitute an identity.[2] And the philosophers say that, if this is established for the intellect and the intellect is in the soul, it is necessary that the soul should not be divisible in the way in which individuals are divisible, and that the soul in Amr and in Zaid should be one single entity.[3] And this proof is strong in the case of the intellect, because in the intellect there is no individuality whatever; the soul, however, although it is free from the matters* through which the individuals receive their plurality, is said by the most famous philosophers not to abandon the nature of the individual, although it is an apprehending entity.[4] This is a point which has to be considered.

As for Ghazali's objection, it amounts to saying that the intellect is something individual and that universality is an accident of it, and therefore Ghazali compares the way in which the intellect observes a common feature in individuals to the way in which the senses perceive the same thing many times, since for Ghazali the intelligible is a unity, but not something universal, and for him the animality of Zaid is numerically identical with the animality which he observes in Khalid.[5] And this is false, and if it were true, there would be no difference between sense-perception and the apprehension of the intellect.

The Third Discussion

576 And after this Ghazali says that the philosophers have two proofs to demonstrate that the soul after once existing cannot perish.[6] The first is that if the soul perished this could only be imagined in one of these three ways: either (1) it perishes simultaneously with the body,

or (2) through an opposite which is found in it, or (3) through the power of God, the powerful. It is false that it can perish through the corruption of the body, for it is separated from the body. It is false that it can have an opposite, for a separate substance has no opposite.[1] And it is false, as has been shown before, that the power of God can attach itself to non-being.[2]

Now, Ghazali objecting to the philosophers answers: 'We theologians do not admit that the soul is external to the body; besides, it is the special theory of Avicenna that the souls are numerically differentiated through the differentiation of the bodies, for that there should be one single soul in every respect and in all people brings about many impossibilities, for instance that when Zaid knows something Amr should know it too, and when Amr does not know something Zaid should not know it either; and many other impossibilities follow from this assumption.'[3] And Ghazali adduces against Avicenna the argument that when it is assumed that the souls are numerically differentiated through the differentiation of the bodies, then they are attached to the bodies and must necessarily perish with their decay.

The philosophers, however, can answer that it is by no means necessary that, when there exists between two things a relation of attachment and love, for instance the relation between the lover and the beloved and the relation between iron and the magnet, the destruction of the one should cause the destruction of the other. But Avicenna's opponents may ask his partisans through what the individuation and numerical plurality of souls takes place, when they are separated from their matters, for the numerical plurality of individuals arises only through matter. He who claims the survival and the numerical plurality of souls should say that they are in a subtle matter, namely the animal warmth which emanates from the heavenly bodies, and this is a warmth which is not fire and in which there is not a principle of fire; in this warmth there are the souls which create the sublunary bodies and those which inhere in these bodies.[4] And none of the philosophers is opposed to the theory that in the elements there is heavenly warmth and that this is the substratum for the potencies which produce animals and plants, but some of the philosophers call this potency a natural heavenly potency, whereas Galen calls it the forming power and sometimes the demiurge, saying that it seems that there exists a wise maker of the living being who has created it and that this is apparent from anatomy, but where this maker is and what His substance is is too lofty a problem for human understanding.[1] From this Plato proves that the soul is separated from the body, for the soul creates and forms the body, and if the body were the condition for the existence of the soul, the soul would not have created it or formed it.[2] This creative soul is most apparent in the animals which do not procreate, but it is also evident in the animals which do. And just as we know that the soul is something added to the natural warmth, since it is not of the nature of warmth *qua* warmth to produce well-ordered intelligible acts, so we know that the warmth which is in the seeds does not suffice to create and to form. And the philosophers do not disagree about the fact that there are in the elements souls creating each species of animals, plants, and minerals that exists, and that each of them needs a directing principle and preserving powers for it to come into existence and remain. And these souls are either like intermediaries between the souls of the heavenly bodies and the souls in the sensible bodies of the sublunary world, and then no doubt they have absolute dominion over these latter souls and these bodies, and from here arises the belief in the Jinn,[3] or these souls themselves are attached to the bodies which they create according to a resemblance which exists between them, and when the bodies decay they return to their spiritual matter and to the subtle imperceptible bodies.

And there are none of the old philosophers who do not acknowledge these souls, and they only disagree as to whether they are identical with the souls in our bodies or of another kind. And as to those who accept a bestower of forms,[4] they regard these powers as a separate intellect; but this theory is not found in any of the old philosophers, but only in some philosophers of Islam, because it belongs to their principles that the separate principles do not change their matters by transformation in respect of substance and primarily, for the cause of change is the opposite of the thing changed.[5] This question is one of the most difficult in philosophy, and the best explanation that can be given of this problem is that the material intellect thinks an infinite number of things in one single intelligible, and that it judges these things in a universal judgement, and that that which forms its essence is absolutely immaterial.[6] Therefore Aristotle praises Anaxagoras[7] for having made intellect, namely an immaterial form, the prime mover, and for this reason it does not suffer any action from anything, for the cause of passivity is matter and in this respect the passive potencies are in the same position as the active, for it is the passive potencies possessing matters which accept definite things.

The Fourth Discussion

Having finished this question Ghazali begins to say that the philosophers deny bodily resurrection.[1] This is a problem which is not found in any of the older philosophers, although resurrection has been mentioned in different religions for at least a thousand years and the philosophers whose theories have come to us are of a more recent date. The first to mention bodily resurrection were the prophets of Israel after Moses, as is evident from the Psalms and many books attributed to the Israelites.[2] Bodily resurrection is also affirmed in the New Testament and attributed by tradition to Jesus. It is a theory of the Sabaeans, whose religion is according to Ibn Hazm the oldest.[3]

But the philosophers in particular, as is only natural, regard this doctrine as most important and believe in it most, and the reason is that it is conducive to an order amongst men on which man's being, as man, depends and through which he can attain the greatest happiness proper to him,[4] for it is a necessity for the existence of the moral and speculative virtues[5] and of the practical sciences in men. They hold namely that man cannot live in this world without the practical sciences, nor in this and the next world without the speculative virtues, and that neither of these categories is perfected or completed without the practical virtues,[6] and that the practical virtues can only become strong through the knowledge and adoration of God by the services prescribed by the laws of the different religions, like offerings and prayers and supplications and other such utterances by which praise is rendered to God, the angels, and the prophets.

In short, the philosophers believe that religious laws are necessary political arts, the principles of which are taken from natural reason and inspiration,[7] especially in what is common to all religions, although religions differ here more or less. The philosophers further hold that one must not object either through a positive or through a negative statement to any of the general religious principles, for instance whether it is obligatory to serve God or not, and still more whether God does or does not exist, and they affirm this also concerning the other religious principles, for instance bliss in the beyond and its possibility; for all religions agree in the acceptance of another existence after death, although they differ in the description of this existence, just as they agree about the knowledge, attributes, and acts of God, although they differ more or less in their utterances about the essence and the acts of the Principle. All religions agree also about the acts conducive to bliss in the next world, although they differ about the determination of these acts.

In short, the religions are, according to the philosophers, obligatory,[1] since they lead towards wisdom in a way universal to all human beings, for philosophy only leads a certain number of intelligent people to the knowledge of happiness, and they therefore have to learn wisdom, whereas religions seek the instruction of the masses generally. Notwithstanding this, we do not find any religion which is not attentive to the special needs of the learned, although it is primarily concerned with the things in which the masses participate. And since the existence of the learned class is only perfected and its full happiness attained by participation with the class of the masses,[2] the general doctrine is also obligatory for the existence and life of this special class, both at the time of their youth and growth (and nobody doubts this), and when they pass on to attain the excellence which is their distinguishing characteristic. For it belongs to the necessary excellence of a man of learning that he should not despise the doctrines in which he has been brought up, and that he should explain them in the fairest way, and that he should understand that the aim of these doctrines lies in their universal character, not in their particularity, and that, if he expresses a doubt concerning the religious principles in which he has been brought up, or explains them in a way contradictory to the prophets and turns away from their path, he merits more than anyone else that the term unbeliever should be applied to him, and he is liable to the penalty for unbelief in the religion in which he has been brought up.

Further, he is under obligation to choose the best religion of his period, even when they are all equally true for him, and he must believe that the best will be abrogated by the introduction of a still better. Therefore the learned who were instructing the people in Alexandria became Muhammedans when Islam reached them, and the learned in the Roman Empire became Christians when the religion of Jesus was introduced there. And nobody doubts that among the Israelites there were many learned men, and this is apparent from the books which are found amongst the Israelites and

ABOUT THE NATURAL SCIENCES

which are attributed to Solomon. And never has wisdom ceased among the inspired, i.e. the prophets, and therefore it is the truest of all sayings that every prophet is a sage,[1] but not every sage a prophet; the learned, however, are those of whom it is said that they are the heirs of the prophets.[2]

And since in the principles of the demonstrative sciences there are postulates and axioms which are assumed, this must still more be the case for the religions which take their origin in inspiration and reason. Every religion exists through inspiration and is blended with reason. And he who holds that it is possible that there should exist a natural religion based on reason alone must admit that this religion must be less perfect than those which spring from reason and inspiration. And all philosophers agree that the principles of action must be taken on authority, for there is no demonstration for the necessity of action except through the existence of virtues which are realized through moral actions and through practice.

And it is clear from this that all the learned hold about religions the opinion that the principles of the actions and regulations prescribed in every religion are received from the prophets and lawgivers, who regard those necessary principles as praiseworthy which most incite the masses to the performance of virtuous acts; and so nobody doubts that those who are brought up on those principles are of a more perfect virtue than those who are brought up on others, for instance that the prayers in our religion hold men back from ignominy and wickedness, as God's word certifies, and that the prayer ordained in our religion fulfils this purpose more truly than the prayers ordained in others, and this by the conditions imposed on it of number, time, recitation, purity, and desistance from acts and words harmful to it. And the same may be said of the doctrine of the beyond in our religion, which is more conducive to virtuous actions than what is said in others. Thus to represent the beyond in material images is more appropriate than purely spiritual representation, as is said in the Divine Words: 'The likeness of the Paradise which those who fear God are promised, beneath it rivers flow.'[3] And the Prophet has said: 'In it there is what no eye has seen, no ear has heard, nor ever entered the mind of man.'[4] And Ibn Abbas said: 'There is no relation in the other world to this world but the names.'[5] And he meant by this that the beyond is another creation of a higher order than this world, and another phase superior to our earthly. He need not deny this who believes that we see one single thing developing itself from one phase to another, for instance the transformation of the inorganic into beings conscious of their own essences, i.e. the intellectual forms. Those who are in doubt about this and object to it and try to explain it are those who seek to destroy the religious prescriptions and to undo the virtues. They are, as everyone knows, the heretics and those who believe that the end of man consists only in sensual enjoyment. When such people have really the power to destroy religious belief both theologians and philosophers will no doubt kill them, but when they have no actual power the best arguments that can be brought against them are those that are contained in the Holy Book. What Ghazali says against them is right, and in refuting them it must be admitted that the soul is immortal, as is proved by rational and religious proofs, and it must be assumed that what arises from the dead is simulacra[1] of these earthly bodies, not these bodies themselves, for that which has perished does not return individually and a thing can only return as an image of that which has perished, not as a being identical with what has perished, as Ghazali declares. Therefore the doctrine of resurrection of those theologians who believe that the soul is an accident and that the bodies which arise are identical with those that perished cannot be true. For what perished and became anew can only be specifically, not numerically, one, and this argument is especially valid against those theologians who hold that an accident does not last two moments.

Ghazali accused the philosophers of heresy on three points. One concerns this question, and we have already shown what opinion the philosophers hold about this, and that according to them it is a speculative problem. The second point is the theory attributed to the philosophers that God does not know individuals, but here again we have shown that they do not say this. The third point is their theory of the eternity of the world, but again we have shown that what they understand by this term has not the meaning for which they are accused of heresy by the theologians. Ghazali asserts in this book that no Muslim believes in a purely spiritual resurrection, and in another book he says that the Sufis hold it.[2] According to this latter assertion those who believe in a spiritual but not in a perceptible resurrection are not declared heretics by universal consent,[3] and this permits belief in a spiritual resurrection. But again in another book he repeats his accusation of heresy as if it rested on universal consent.[4] And all this, as you see, is confusing. And no doubt this man erred in religious questions as he erred in rational problems. God is the succourer for the finding of what is true, and He invests with the truth whomever He chooses.

I have decided to break off my inquiry about these things here, and I ask pardon for their discussion, and if it were not an obligation to seek the truth for those who are entitled to it—and those are, as Galen says, one in a thousand[1]—and to prevent from discussion those who have no claim to it, I would not have treated all this. And God knows every single letter, and perhaps God will accept my excuse and forgive my stumbling in His bounty, generosity, munificence and excellence—there is no God but He!

APPENDIX

Page	Bouyges's text	My readings
4. 3	ثلاثة	اربعة
4. 6	ممكنا عنه	ممكنا
11. 5	العرفي	العرضي
13. 9	ذكروه	ذكرتموه
14. 12	قولهم	قولكم
16. 8	يستحق	يشحن
18. 12	مذ وقعت	قد وقعت
18. 13	الحركة	الحركة الاولى
21. 9	للآلة	لآلاته
22. 13, 14	بمراتب	بمرتبة
25. 5	تعين	يعين
25. 9	ممن	من
26. 10	يدّعى	ندّعى
28. 10	وكمية	بكمية
31. 11	سنين	سنتين
32. 14	الزمكم	الزموكم
33. 4	بعدد	تعدد
33. 12	انكروا على	انكر
33. 13	تراخى	الا يتراخى
34. 2	عليها	عليه
37. 13	المتشوف	المتشوق
39. 8	لا لان	لا ان
40. 10	تميز	تمييز
40. 11	ترجيح	ترجيح
50. 15	قلنا هو	قلنا

Page	Bouyges's text	My readings
52. 7	الهيئات	الاحيان
55. 15	الازمنة	الازمنة المتخالفة
56. 14	الفاسد	الواحد
59. 13	قبل محرك	قبل متحرك
60. 14	ترجيح	ترجح
66. 9	طبيعة	طبيعته
68. 12	حجتهم	حججهم
69. 9	فتقدمه	قد تقدمه
69. 12	لموسى	لعيسى
71. 10	تمثل	يمثل
72. 6	افتراق	اقتران
75. 13	حركة	حركات
78. 4	للفوق	الفوق
80. 10	تجدد	تحدد
82. 3	ترى	يرون
88. 1	طرفه	طرفيه
89. 7	ولذلك	وكذلك
93. 7 (95. 6)	يضيف	يضيفه
93. 7 (95. 6)	اشياء	باشياء
101. 4	فى غير موضوع	غير موضوع
111. 14	يغلط	يغالط
112. 7	ابتناء	ابتناؤه
113. 14	الحادث	الحوادث
114. 3	الموضوعين	الموضوعين
114. 4	ان وضعوا	وضعوا
115. 11	وجه	وجوه
116. 2	قواعد العقائد	الاقتصاد فى الاعتقاد

APPENDIX

Page	Bouyges's text	My readings
129. 7	تتحلك	تستحيل
130. 8	يزيد	نزيد
131. 14	أما	إما
131. 15	أما	إما
133. 2	عدما	معدوما
134. 5	فينعدم	فيعدم
135. 8	محل الحوادث	محل للحوادث
140. 11	الكائن	الكائن الفاسد
140. 14	بدنه	بذاته
142. 7	وكذلك	ولذلك
150. 10	غير منفصل من	منفصل عن
154. 12	رطب	حار
159. 2	من	ما
163 (5th line from below)	وسبق	فسبق
163 (5th line from below)	فكونه	وكونه
166. 2	بالموجود	بالموجَد
166. 4	جوهر الموجود	جوهر الموجد
167. 5	لان	ان
169. 6	معها	قبلها
169. 6	معلوله	معلولها
169. 11	موجودا	موجود
171. 9	يقر على موكله	يقرر موكله
176. 2	فتأتي المقدمة	فنأتي بالمقدمة
178. 2	لها	له
191. 2	يتحرك	تحرك
194. 13	هذا	هزأ

Page	Bouyges's text	My readings
196. 7	تقدير	تقرير
196. 8	الوجود الممكن	الموجود الممكن
200. 13	اعنى الاجسام الغير الكائنة الفاسدة	I omit these words which I regard as a gloss.
200. 15	بل اتحادا من جميع الوجوه	I omit these words which seem superfluous.
209. 10	على حال	على كل حال
212. 1	الاجرام	الاجرام السماوية
214. 6	الهيولى	ووجود الهيولى
214. 15	بما	ما
225. 16	وسيأتى	وعن بعضها سيأتى
228. 1	ذاته	من ذاته
228. 4	النفس	اللون
229. 8	وموجودا	موجودا
233. 7	آخر	احد
235. 15	يعلم	لم يعلم
237. 2	فان كان غيره	فان كان عينه فهو محال لان العلم غير المعلوم وان كان غيره
237. 2	ويلزم	فيلزم
237. 2	ليس غيره	ليس عينه فاذاً
238. 7	لذلك	كذلك
238. 9	لذلك	كذلك
242. 1	التركيب	التخصيص
243. 16	النقطتين	القطبين
245. 10	فقولكم	فقولهم
245. 10	قولكم	قولهم

APPENDIX

Page	Bouyges's text	My readings
247. 9	الواردة	الموضوعة
249. 3	الف والا	الف وآلاف
250. 14	مئتا كوكب	عشرون كوكبا
252. 7	عرف	وجب
253. 15	لزم ان	ان
258. 10	ولون	وكون
266. 8	لكان ايضا	لكان
271. 12	خلاف	اختلاف
273. 3	قولهم	قولكم
280. 12	عندكم	عندهم
283. 1	اجساما	اجناسا
288. 6	فلتستعمل	فلنستعمل
289. 3	لعلة	بعلة
294. 3	ولا بد	فلا بد
294. 12	لمجموعه	لمجموعها
295. 3	رأى	رام
296. 9	ولا مادة فى هيولى	ولا مادة
298. 1	نشير	نسير
306. 15	لذاته	بذاته
308. 11	فلعل	فان
308. 18	فترجع هذه الاسماء	فيرجع هذا الاسم
311. 6	تجردت	تجددت
315. 1	وواجبا	او واجبا
315. 4	العلم	الشىء
317. 9	عليها	عليه
328. 3	ولان	وان
329. 6	وعظى	لفظى

Page	Bouyges's text	My readings
331. 4	التحريك	التحرك
331. 17	جزئيه او اجزائه	جزئيه
335. 12	وكل	فكل
339. 1	ولان	وان
359. 5	القائمة بها	فى قوامها
361. 12	فعرضتك	ففرضك
361. 14	فعرضتك	ففرضك
364. 2	لان	لكن
368. 16	جقيقية وماهية	حقيقته وماهيته
370. 10	العقل	الفعل
371. 11	بل	يدل
373. 3	وكذلك	ولذلك
377. 2	صفة وبوصوف	موصوف وصفة
377. 13	يشعرون لانهم	يشكّون انهم
381. 6	اى	اذ
387. 5	المشاركة والعقلية	المشاركة العقلية
387. 10	والمصير	او المصير
388. 2	الموضع	الوضع
402. 7	وكذلك	ولذلك
409. 16	الامور المادية	الامور الالهية
410. 12	غاية	عليه
413. 2-3	..	Transpose the words وكيفية محدودة وطبيعة محدودة after بكمية محدودة
413. 13	ومن	وما
415. 10	بطبائعها	بطبيعتها
421. 10	يضعفون	يضعون
422. 1	الطبيعة	الطريقة

APPENDIX

Page	Bouyges's text	My readings
426. 4	حياة	حواسا
432. 12	مدارك العقول	معيار العلم
437. 5	ثاسا	ثانيا
441. 2	مقاد	منقاد
443. 11	فهذا لازم لا جواب عنه	فهذا ايضا لا جواب عنه
445. 14 (bis)	نعلمه	يعلمه
446. 11	على حال	على كل حال
448. 10	الوجود الكلى	وجود الكل
450. 15	تكون	ان يكون
456. 1	الثلاثة انحاء من الوجوه	الاحوال الثلاثة
457. 10	وهذا	وذلك
458. 5	خيالهم	حيالهم
458. 7	سيكون	يكون
458. 11		شخصية omit
458. 17	والثانى	والثالث
459. 3	حال	ذات
470. 4	خيالهم	حيالهم
472. 2	قد رام	قدرتم
472. 2	لو كان	لولا
472. 4	انه	الذى
473. 15	نقرر	نقدر
478. 3	ساكن	ساند
478. 6	يحملها	يحمله
479. 3	الملابس	الملابس
483. 3	وذلك	فذلك
489. 9	ابتداءً	ابدا
489. 9-10	ابتداء فى	ابدا او فى
496. 9	تحت قوم	تحت قدم قوم

Page	Bouyges's text	My readings
497. 12	مبذول	ممذول
498. 10	ذلك المعنى	ذلك الفعل
501. 13	الابتداء	الابداء
502. 20	جسم	صوب
504. 1	جزئية له	جزئية
504. 2	عليها	اليها
506. 15	من الجزئي	المعنى الجزئي
506. 16	وقتها	فيها
506. 16	المعروفة	معروفة
509 (1), l. 4	يتبعه	يتبعها
513. 1	حد	حدا
513. 8	تعلم	معلم
513. 17	تخدمه	تخدمها
513. 18	اجسام	اعضاء
513. 20	تنخسف	لتخسف
514. 2	هواء مستعد	مواد مستعدة
515. 1	المعلم	المتعلم
515. 5	بغير استحالة	بتغير استحالة
516. 1	هذه المعجزات	هذه المعجزة
516. 10	الحدث	الحذق
517. 9	للفوت	للفرق
521. 7	تابعة	عائقة
522. 5	اتقان	اتفاق
522. 7	ادراكه	ادراك
524. 8	معقول	مفعول
528. 12	لتكون	ليكون
531. 2	اليقيني	الحقيقي
531. 5	المثل الاعلى	الملك الاعلى

APPENDIX

Page	Bouyges's text	My readings
531. 5	يعتاص	يعتاض
533. 17	يخرجه	تخرجه
533. 17	فيدفع	فتدفع
535. 25	الرعدة	الرعشة
539. 4	الهيئة	اليبوسة
543. 12	فتجتمع	فيجتمع
544. 11	الثانية	الاولى
547. 4	تخص	تحصل
547. 13	المتخيلة	المحسوسة
547. 14	الصورة	الصور
548. 4	محله شىء لا ينقسم	محلها شىء لا بجسم
550. 1	يلتبس	تلبيس
551. 3	هاتين القوتين	هذين النوعين
551. 5	وهى	فهى
551. 6	ولا تنقسم ... وهذه	والتى لا تنقسم ... فهذه
554. 7	كون غيره به عالما	كون غير عالم به
555. 10	لان	لا لان
561. 5	بقوله	بقولهم
564. 6	ادركه	ادركها
564. 8	اذ	او
565. 6	يعقل	يعقله
565. 6	لا يعقل	لا يعقله
565. 19	يغفل عن الجسم	يعقل الجسم
565. 19	لا يغفل عنه	لا يعقله
566. 16	من وجودها	من حدها
568. 15	مخالفة	مخالطة له
574. 11	الاعراض	المواد

INDEX OF PROPER NAMES

ibn 'Abbās, 585, 8.
Abraham, 52, 2. 52, 3. 191, 11. 193, 3. 416, 16. 527, 2.
Alexander of Aphrodisias, 420, 12. 421, 13. 495, 7.
Anaxagoras, 177, 12. 579, 11.
Aristotle, 21, 12. 49, 14. 79, 9. 14. 88, 12. 171, 12, 14. 172, 2. 176, 3. 180, 3, 8. 181, 8. 187, 9. 206, 2. 236, 10. 250, 7. 259, 11, 14. 261, 10. 268, 12. 313, 8. 373, 5. 392, 12. 415, 9. 421, 3, 10, 14, 15. 422, 1. 451, 4. 510, 2. 553, 7, 9. 556, 14. 579, 11.
Ash'arites, 8, 8. 12, 8. 13, 2. 14, 2. 15, 10. 17, 9–10. 25, 6. 89, 8. 90, 2. 92, 10. 93, 8. 94, 7. 117, 6. 124, 9. 133, 15. 136, 9. 137–139. 158, 9. 169, 15. 172, 14. 205, 10. 218, 12–15. 219, 10. 223, 16. 225, 11. 276, 8. 295, 4. 314, 4. 317, 3. 320, 13. 321, 1, 6. 322, 5, 9. 324, 12. 333, 5. 364, 1–3. 396, 3, 10. 402, 13. 403, 14. 412, 2. 416, 16. 466, 4. 476, 6.
Avicenna, 27, 7, 11. 54, 13. 86, 10. 92, 1. 107, 8. 141, 1. 163, 8. 166, 9, 11. 167, 13. 168, 6. 179, 9. 182, 5. 184, 6. 186, 5. 197, 15. 198, 1. 199, 4. 236, 11. 237, 8. 239, 8, 10. 245, 1, 14. 249, 5. 252, 14. 253, 5. 254, 10. 259, 7. 270, 13. 274, 15. 276, 2, 4. 10. 278, 15. 279, 9. 280, 7. 289, 7. 290, 7. 292, 1. 293, 1. 299, 5. 302, 13. 303, 2. 304, 16. 313, 9. 320, 11. 325, 2. 347, 5. 370, 1, 7. 371, 10. 386, 11, 13. 389, 5. 391, 14. 394, 6. 395, 1, 16. 400, 3. 403, 12. 407, 11. 418, 9. 419, 10. 421, 4–5. 442, 13, 15. 443, 1. 444, 5, 14. 445, 5. 451, 8. 473, 13. 484, 5. 486, 3, 10. 495, 5. 497, 21. 500, 13. 503, 12, 14. 515, 3. 516, 3, 7. 546, 15. 547, 10. 552, 12. 576, 8.

Chaldaeans, 492, 8.
Christians, 301, 5. 322, 13.

Dahriyya, 20, 7. 266, 17. 269, 12, 16. 270, 1, 4. 282, 6, 9. 283, 17. 284, 4. 416, 10. 525, 2.

al-Fārābī (abū Naṣr), 54, 13. 179, 9. 184, 6. 245, 1, 14. 371, 9, 15.

Galen, 127, 11. 155, 4. 212, 16. 577, 15. 588, 3.

al-Ghazālī, *passim*.

ibn Ḥazm, 208, 10. 542, 9. 580, 8.
Hippocrates, 140, 13.
abū'l Hudhail, 119, 14. 121, 2.

Israelites, 580, 5. 583, 11, 12.

Jesus, 69, 12. 580, 7. 583, 10.
al-Juwainī (abū'l Ma'ālī), 542, 12.

Karrāmites, 6, 9. 135, 11. 136, 7.

Materialists, cf. Dahriyya.
Melissus, 373, 5.
Moses, 69, 12. 580, 15.
Mutakallimūn, 21, 10. 22, 7, 10, 12. 25, 10. 35, 6. 37, 3. 51, 9. 54, 15. 69, 1. 72, 4. 78, 12. 99, 6. 132, 4. 188, 1. 193, 14. 210, 5. 218, 11. 223, 16. 225, 16. 226, 6. 227, 5. 242, 8. 246, 10. 276, 4. 284, 3. 295, 3. 295, 3. 328, 1. 351, 15. 352, 1. 352, 11. 378, 7. 411, 16. 425, 1. 426, 4. 430, 10. 449, 13. 521, 16. 530, 18. 531, 1. 538, 5, 13, 15. 539, 3. 540, 12. 541, 10. 542, 2. 586, 8. 587, 6.
Mu'tazilites, 105, 5. 106, 11. 134, 8. 218, 12, 16. 222, 14. 225, 7. 242, 8. 276, 8. 320, 13.

Parmenides, 373, 5.
Peripatetics, 178, 6. 206, 2. 239, 8. 250, 8. 259, 14. 310, 3. 332, 3. 420, 8.
Plato, 25, 6. 29, 7. 171, 12. 172, 1. 177, 15. 187, 10. 268, 10. 310, 7. 407, 10. 572, 2. 578, 2.
Porphyry, 260, 1.
Pythagoras, 177, 12. 579, 11.

Sabaeans, 580, 8.
ibn Sīnā, cf. Avicenna.
Socrates, 268, 10.
'Sophists', 542, 1, 11.
Stoics, 479, 8.
Ṣūfīs, 364, 4. 463, 11. 587, 7.

Themistius, 271, 14.

Ẓāhirites, 12, 13. 429, 10.
Zanādiqa (heretical Muslims), 527, 2, 11. 585, 14.

VOLUME II

CONTENTS
(VOLUME II)

NOTES	1
Index of Proper Names mentioned in the Introduction and in the Notes	207
Index of Subjects mentioned in the Notes	211
Some contradictions in Aristotle's System	215
Arabic–Greek Index to the Notes	216
Greek–Arabic Index to the Notes	218

NOTES

μόνοι φιλοσοφῆσαι Ἕλληνες δύνανται
Only Greeks philosophize, EPICURUS
(CLEM. ALEX. *Strom.* i. 15; DIOG. LAERT. X. 117)

> One must know that everything the Moslems, Mu'tazilites as well as Ash'arites, have professed concerning these subjects, has been borrowed from the Greeks and Syrians who applied themselves to the criticism of the philosophers.
> (MAIMONIDES, *Guide of the Perplexed*, i. 71)

p. 1. 1. According to Aristotelian logic, demonstrative proof which affords necessary, absolute truth must be distinguished from dialectical and rhetorical proofs which only yield probability. The term تصديق is a translation of the Stoic term συγκατάθεσις, assent, and synonymous with تحقيق, but whereas for the Stoics assent may be given to the single representation, for the Aristotelian logicians in Islam assent refers always to a proposition. The Arabs divide Logic into two parts, the one treating of concepts, تصور, the other of judgements in so far as they refer to the exterior world, تصديق (cf. e.g. Avicenna, *Salvation*, ed. H. 1331, p. 3).

p. 1. 2. The general term for eternity is قدم (Greek ἀϊδιότης), but Aristotle distinguishes the eternal *a parte ante*, the ungenerated, ἀγένητον, ازلی, from the eternal *a parte post*, the indestructible, ἄφθαρτον, ابدی. There is also the term αἰών, دهر ('timeless eternity'), in scholastic philosophy *aevum*, used by Plato (*Tim.* 39 d) and Aristotle (*De caelo* A 9. 279^{a}22), which becomes especially important in Neoplatonism.

p. 1. 3. The basic ideas of this proof, which presumes an eternal agent, are to be found in Aristotle, who regards himself as the first thinker to affirm that the world is ungenerated (*De caelo* A 10. 279^{b}12): that the world cannot have had an origin, because there could be no new decision in the mind of God for its beginning (cf. the passage of Aristotle—probably from the *De philosophia* fr. 22 Rose—quoted by Cicero, *Acad. pr.* ii. 38 'neque enim ortum esse unquam mundum, quod nulla fuerit *novo consilio* inito tam praeclari operis inceptio'); that in all change there is potentiality (e.g. *Phys.* Γ 2); that the potential needs an actualizer which already exists actually (*Met.* Θ 8. 1049^{b}24).

The argument itself follows closely Proclus' third argument in John Philoponus' *De aeternitate mundi*, Rabe, p. 42, which I here give in summary: The demiurge will be either always in act or sometimes in potency. If he is always in act, then his work (δημιουργούμενον) also will be always in act; if he is sometimes in potency, there must be an actualizer of this potency. Therefore either we shall have an infinite regress, always seeking a new cause for the actualization of this potency, or we shall have to admit a cause always in act. In the argument given by Ghazali we find the term مرجّح ('determining principle', or more literally 'what causes to incline'; the Greek word is τὸ ἐπικλῖνον—see for this word below, note 19.1.), which is used by the Muslim theologians in their proof (inspired by Aristotle) for the existence of God: the possible existence of the world needs for its actual existence a مرجّح, a determining principle which cannot have itself a cause, as an infinite series of causes is impossible. The argument given by Ghazali is found in substance, for example, in Avicenna's *Salvation*, pp. 415-17.

Shahrastani, a younger contemporary of Ghazali, gives in his book *Religious and Philosophical Sects* (ed. Cureton, p. 338) a short and somewhat imperfect enumeration of eight of Proclus' eighteen arguments (that mentioned above is the second). Shahrastani says that all these arguments have a logical flaw, that they were used by Avicenna, but that he himself has composed a special book to refute them logically (على قوانين منطقية).

p. 1. 4. As an Aristotelian, Averroës ought to have accepted this argument, and as a matter of fact he ultimately does so. In his objection, which corresponds to that of Philoponus, he seems moved by a certain *esprit de contradiction* against his Moslem fellow-philosophers. Averroës argues like Philoponus that both the 'potential' and the 'actual' are homonymous terms. Philoponus (op. cit., p. 46) distinguishes a potency which is a natural aptitude, φυσικὴ ἐπιτηδειότης εἴς τι, and a potency *in habitu*, καθ' ἕξιν. According to Philoponus, a man having a natural aptitude to become a teacher needs an external cause to become a teacher; being once a teacher *in habitu*, i.e. having sufficient knowledge, he no longer needs an external cause. But the question of the internality or externality of the cause is not relevant to Proclus' argument.

p. 1. 5. Common notions; common, عامة = مشهورة, i.e. κοινόν = ἔνδοξον = τὰ δοκοῦντα πᾶσιν ἢ τοῖς πλείστοις, the domain of probability (*Top. A* 1. 100ᵇ22). That proofs are concerned with things proper to the same genus: *Anal. Post. A* 7.

p. 1. 6. The different meanings of the possible, Aristotle, *Met. Δ* 12; ἐπὶ τὸ πολύ, الاكثرى; ἐπ' ἔλαττον, الاقلّ; ἐπ' ἴσον, على التساوى.

p. 2. 1. For the ἐπὶ τὸ πολύ does not happen by chance; cf. *Met. Δ* 30. 1025ᵃ15 and *De caelo A* 12. 283ᵃ32.

p. 2. 2. The natural has its principle of movement in itself, the artificial is moved from the outside; *Phys. B* 1. 192ᵇ13.

p. 2. 3. The soul has its principle of movement in itself; *De an. B* 1. 412ᵇ16.

p. 2. 4. The four types of change: e.g. *Phys. E* 1. 225ᵃ3.

p. 2. 5. i.e. the eternal unmoved mover and the eternally moved; cf. *Met. Λ* 6.

NOTES

p. 2. 6. A sect named after Muhammed ibn Karram of Khorasan (ninth century). They say that God is a substratum for new accidents, and that nothing comes into existence in the world without being preceded by new accidents in God, e.g. new volitions (cf. e.g. Baghdadi, *The Differences between the Sects*, p. 202).

p. 2. 7. Matter is the principle of all generation and corruption, e.g. *Met. H* 5. 1044^{b}27; matter is eternal, e.g. *Met. B* 4. 999^{b}5.

p. 2. 8. This is the νοῦς παθητικός, called in Arabic (in accordance with Alexander of Aphrodisias, *De an.* 82. 20 sqq. Bruns) also العقل الهيولاني, νοῦς ὑλικός, mentioned in Aristotle, *De an. Γ* 5, where he distinguishes an active and a passive intellect, the intellect which 'does' and the intellect which 'becomes everything'. Greek and Arab commentators elaborated Aristotle's scanty and rather obscure remarks about the intellect and made a number of new distinctions. This potential intellect is regarded by Averroës (and by Thomas Aquinas) as eternal, in opposition to Aristotle, *De an. Γ* 5. 430^{a}23: τοῦτο (i.e. τὸ ποιοῦν) μόνον ἀθάνατον καὶ ἀΐδιον (see also below, note 14. 4).

p. 2. 9. The non-rational faculties only produce the effect proper to them, whereas the rational are able to produce contrary effects, e.g. *Met. Θ* 5. 1048^{a}8.

p. 3. 1. This is the fallacy τὸ ἁπλῶς ἢ μὴ ἁπλῶς, *fallacia a dicto secundum quid ad dictum simpliciter*.

p. 3. 2. Cf. Aristotle, *De caelo A* 5. 271^{b}8: εἴπερ καὶ τὸ μικρὸν παραβῆναι τῆς ἀληθείας ἀφισταμένοις γίνεται πόρρω μυριοπλάσιον, a small deviation from the truth at the beginning multiplies itself later ten thousandfold.

p. 3. 3. This is the Ash'arite theory, which is in conformity with that of Philoponus in his sixteenth argument. One must distinguish, says Philoponus (op. cit., pp. 567–8), between God's eternally willing something and God's willing it to be eternal, between God's eternal will and the eternity of the object of His will. It was not in the nature of Socrates to be created before Sophroniscus; but before Sophroniscus became, God had willed that Socrates should be, not absolutely, not always, but when it should be possible. Therefore God willed what He had ordained to be before it became, and He willed it to be at the time when its becoming should be possible.

This agrees with the teaching of St. Augustine, who, using Cicero's expression *novum consilium*, denies expressly that there could be in God a *novum consilium* (*De civ. dei*, Kalb., xii. 15). However, St. Augustine is well aware of the difficulty of his theory and he says (loc. cit.): 'valde quippe altum est et semper fuisse et hominem, quem nunquam fecerat, ex aliquo tempore primum facere voluisse nec consilium voluntatemque mutasse' (that God has always existed and that after a certain time He created man whom He had not wanted to create before, without having changed His mind and will—this, indeed, is very deep for us).

p. 3. 4. i.e. a change in the agent.

p. 3. 5. It is not clear why he regards this as difficult to prove, since the proof follows immediately. Probably he means that the whole problem of God's relation to the world is a difficult one.

p. 3. 6. The word حال which I translate here by 'disposition' is a most ambiguous one. I take it here to be the translation of the Aristotelian term διάθεσις ('disposition') which is opposed to ἕξις, ملكة ('habitude'), the former denoting a temporary, the latter a more lasting condition. But Averroës, I think, uses this word here, too, in reference to its theological meaning. The systems of the Muslim theologians (called in Arabic Mutakallimun, a translation of the Greek διαλεκτικοί) are largely dependent on Stoicism, and their term حال is a translation of the Stoic term πὼς ἔχον. This term does not signify a thing, a material reality, but a fact or event, either a state, e.g. the fact that a body is in space, or a result of a cause, e.g. the fact that I will, which is the result of the will in me, a living being. These states and events are regarded by the Stoics and those Muslim theologians who accept this theory as something either intermediate between reality and unreality or as not real; they are meanings (in a more or less objective sense), λεκτά, معان; thoughts (in a more or less objective sense), νοήματα, احكام (both these Arabic words are very ambiguous: معنى, for example, can also mean 'idea' in the Platonic sense). The theologians accepted also from the Stoics the term τί, شيء, the 'something' which is defined as هو ما يجوز ان يخبر عنه, everything of which something can be said, and which includes the real and the unreal.

The term حال applied by the theologians to the attributes of God gives them a certain unreality so as not to impair God's unity. Amongst the Muslim theologians there are never-ending discussions about the حال (Sextus Empiricus, *Adv. log.* viii. 262, speaks of the ἀνήνυτος μάχη among the Stoics about the existence of the λεκτά). About the use of the term حال for the universal by the Ash'arites see below (for the Stoic theory see v. Arnim, *Stoicorum Veterum Fragmenta*, ii. 48–49, 118–22, 131–3, and E. Bréhier, *La Théorie des incorporels dans l'ancien Stoicisme*, deuxième éd., Paris, 1928; for the Muslim theory Shahrastani, *The Utmost Proficiency in Theology*, ed. Guillaume, pp. 131 sqq.).

It may perhaps be noted that the Stoics introduced into philosophy the concepts of meaning and of event or fact. The Stoics distinguish the sentence, i.e. the words, from the judgement and from the fact meant; e.g. 'it is raining' is at the same time a sentence, a judgement, and the objective fact, meant or expressed by these words. The Stoics, too, saw that the realm of meaning, i.e. of the things meant, which includes the past, the future, the universal, the possible, the impossible, the imaginary, the false and illusory, is infinitely vaster than the universe of actual reality. The Muslim theologians use the Stoic theory of meaning to define the words of God as meanings without the concomitance of physical speech (cf. op. cit., especially p. 289), and the theory of the 'something' to explain God's knowledge of the non-existent possible world before its actual existence (see op. cit., pp. 150 sqq.).

The paradox of the reality of non-being, that there are things which do not exist, was foreshadowed by Plato, *Soph.* 240 B. It is a characteristic of the undefinable act of meaning that its object need not exist. Indeed, all our planning concerns the not yet existing future just as our memories refer to the no more existing past. This is an ultimate fact which cannot be explained, i.e. reduced to another fact, nor represented, nor described by any material image.

p. 3. 7. That this new disposition may be in the effect and not in the agent—in the creature, not in the creator—seems rather astonishing, but refers to the theological theory that the acts of God do not affect God's essence, but are only related to the object (for this theory see Al-Ash'ari, *The Dogmas of the Muslim Theologians*, ed. Ritter, p. 176). This conforms to Plotinus' theory (*Enneads* vi. 9. 3) that to speak of God's causation is not to attribute something to Him but to us, and to Christian dogma, e.g. St. Augustine, *De trinitate* v. 16: concerning the unchangeable substance of God we must admit that something may be so predicated relatively in respect to the creature that although it begins to be so predicated in time, yet nothing shall be understood to have happened to the substance of God itself, but only to the creature in respect of which it is predicated; *De civ. dei* xxii. 2. 2 'cum deus mutare dicitur voluntatem, homines potius quam ipse mutantur'.

p. 4. 1. i.e. the act of creation depends on a new disposition, and this new disposition will be either caused by another God or by God Himself. If by God Himself, there will be an act of God prior to the creation which we regarded as God's first act.

The problem is set out by Aristotle, *Phys.* Θ 1. 251^{b}30: if the moving had existed without moving, a cause would have been necessary for the change, one would then have had a change anterior to the first.

p. 4. 2. At haphazard and by themselves من تلقاء هﺎ, ἀπὸ ταὐτομάτου.

p. 4. 3. The older philosophers concerned themselves only with material principles: see Aristotle, *Met.* A 3–5.

p. 4. 4. That desire (ὄρεξις) and purpose or will (προαίρεσις) are able to produce contrary effects: *Met.* Θ 5. 1048^{a}4.

p. 4. 5. νῦν δὲ ὁ μὲν νοῦς οὐ φαίνεται κινῶν ἄνευ ὀρέξεως· ἡ γὰρ βούλησις ὄρεξις, for intellect does not seem to move without desire, and will is desire (*De an.* Γ 10. 433^{a}22).

p. 4. 6. This is much the same conception as in Plotinus, who denies that God has the power to do one of two contraries which is the property of those who can abstain from always doing the best (vi. 8. 21); regards God as Free Will itself, αὐτὸ ἐφ' ἑαυτῷ (vi. 8. 8); affirms that God's will does not differ from His essence and that everything in Him is will πᾶν ἄρα βούλησις ἦν (vi. 8. 21); but still regards the world as produced by natural necessity (iii. 2. 2).

Averroës's criticism is justified in so far as the idea of will implies a choice of the unrealized and a possible realization of it in time; an eternal will is a contradiction in terms, and Averroës's own theory that God's action is intermediate between voluntary and involuntary action is untenable, because there is no such intermediate; his analogy with an existence neither outside nor inside the world is defective, for to the non-spatial neither 'outside' nor 'inside' can be applied (according to Arist. *De caelo* A 9. 279^{a}18, God is not in space).

It is one of the difficulties of the Aristotelian system that it is frankly teleological and at the same time refuses to ascribe will to God; but, since every organism tends to an end, the difficulty of a teleological conception touches us all. Averroës's theory enables him both to affirm and to deny that God has a will.

p. 5. 1. Convention وضع, θέσις, as opposed to طبع, φύσις, nature.

p. 5. 2. The divorce becomes irrevocable when the sentence of divorce has been pronounced by the husband three times. The wife cannot then return to him until she has been married and divorced by another husband.

p. 5. 3. Up to this point everything agrees with Aristotle's theory of the will, *Met.* Θ 5.

p. 5. 4. The point raised here cannot be met by the Aristotelian theory of the will, for Aristotle, like Plato, does not regard the will as something *sui generis*. Aristotle either identifies the will with the decision (ἡ προαίρεσις) out of which the act follows of necessity, when the object of desire presents itself (*Met.* Θ 5. 1048^{a}11), or he regards the will as a reasonable desire (*De an.* Γ 10. 433^{a}24) and the impulse to motion is given by a φαντασία λογιστική (433^{b}29); his theory, however, remains obscure.

p. 6. 1. i.e. the divorce is void, because it is not the immediate effect of the pronouncement. The validity of the conditionally pronounced divorce is a point of discussion in the legal schools of Islam. The 'Literalists' are a school of law which keeps to a literal interpretation of the religious texts.

p. 6. 2. All proof depends ultimately on immediately known first principles (ἄμεσα) (*Anal. post.* A 21).

p. 6. 3. For the most certain principle must be also the best known, γνωριμωτάτη (*Met.* Γ 3. 1005^{b}11).

p. 7. 1. Common notions do not by themselves imply absolute truth, but belong to the domain of the probable (see note 1. 5). Compare, however, the preceding note. What is indeed according to Aristotle the criterion for the objective truth of the first principles but their universal acknowledgement?

p. 7. 2. According to the Muslim Aristotelians who combine in their theology Aristotelian with Neoplatonic elements, God knows Himself, but, knowing Himself, He knows all the universals without this plurality's preventing His unity: the knower, the knowledge, and the known are one.

p. 8. 1. Assertions whose contrary is equally false are those in which the predicate does not apply to the subject (*Top. B* 8. 114ª4), e.g. the colourless is neither black nor white. Ghazali's assertion that there may be a proof of the opposite of a necessary truth can neither be proved nor refuted, since, being in opposition to the principle of contradiction, it annuls the idea of proof.

p. 8. 2. For οὐ πᾶν τὸ φαινόμενον ἀληθές (*Met. Γ* 5. 1010ᵇ1).

p. 8. 3. Sound understanding فِطْرَة فَائِقَة, ὀρθὸς λόγος, *ratio recta*; about the ὀρθὸς λόγος as a criterion amongst the older Stoics see Diog. Laert. vii. 54 (*Stoic. Vet. Fr.* i. 142. 15). The word فطرة in the sense of *lumen naturale* is much used by the theologians, and we find it already in this sense in an old tradition: 'Every child is born in the *lumen naturale* (i.e. of Islam); it is his parents who make of him a Jew or a Christian or a Parsee' (cf. Tertullian's *anima naturaliter christiana*)—which shows how early Stoic influence is felt in Islam. The theologians often use بالفطرة (φύσει, by nature) where the philosophers would prefer بالطبع. Sometimes ὀρθὸς λόγος is translated simply by عقل, as, for instance, in the translation of the Stoic definition ὀρθὸς λόγος προστακτικὸς μὲν ὧν ποιητέον, ἀπαγορευτικὸς δὲ ὧν οὐ ποιητέον: right reason commands what is to be done and forbids what is not to be done, a definition which the Muʿtazilites took over (see e.g. the definitions of عقل in Farabi, *De intellectu*, ad init.; Massignon, *Passion d'al-Hallaj*, pp. 543–4; Lane, *Arabic-English Dictionary*).

p. 9. 1. This argument concerned with the impossibility of an infinite number is the first given by John Philoponus. The impossibility of an infinite number of revolutions of the different planets is a favourite argument in Muhammadan theology (e.g. Shahrastani, *The Utmost Proficiency*, p. 29; Ibn ʿUthman al-Khayyat, *The Book of Triumph*, Nyberg, p. 35.; and Ibn Hazm, *On Religious and Philosophical Sects*, ed. H. 1317, i, p. 16) for the creation of the world. It is not found in Philoponus in this connexion, but it derives from him (from his lost Refutation of Aristotle's doctrine of the eternity of the world), for it is given as a quotation from him by Simplicius in his commentary on *Phys. Θ* 1 (Diels, 1179. 15–27). Philoponus says in his first argument that if the world were eternal, there would be not only an infinite number of men, but also of horses and dogs; infinity therefore would be triplicated, which is absurd, because nothing can be greater than infinity.

p. 10. 1. i.e. the movements of, for example, Saturn will have the same proportion to the movements, for example, of the sun in one year as in ten years.

p. 10. 2. This sentence is in fact contradictory: a potential infinite cannot be an infinite whole. For Aristotle the infinite can only be potential (λείπεται οὖν δυνάμει εἶναι τὸ ἄπειρον, *Phys.* Γ 6. 206ᵃ18), by which he means that time can be infinitely, endlessly, increased or divided, number infinitely increased, space infinitely divided, but that there cannot be an actual infinite magnitude (ibid. 206ᵃ16), where the word 'infinite' does not simply mean a negation, but something positive, a magnitude that contains the whole of a non-ending series. What is possible is to increase or to divide endlessly (for which the term 'potential infinity' is very badly chosen); the existence of an infinite whole is neither actual nor possible, according to Aristotelian principles, but totally impossible.

That what has no beginning can have no end, and what has a beginning must have an end, is proved in *De caelo* A 12 (282ᵇ2 εἰ φθαρτόν, γενητόν ... , εἰ δὲ ἀγένητον, ἄφθαρτον ὑπόκειται). This is often regarded as more or less axiomatic, cf. e.g. Cicero, *De nat. deor.* 8.20: 'hunc censes primis, ut dicitur, labris gustasse physiologiam, id est naturae rationem, qui quicquam quod ortum sit putet aeternum esse posse?' (Do you think that one who believes that anything that has come into being can be eternal, can have the slightest notion of natural philosophy?). See also Origen, *Contra Celsum* iii. 43.

p. 10. 3. A shorter time bears a relation to a longer only if both are finite (*De caelo* A 6. 274ᵃ8).

p. 10. 4. This means that if there existed things actually infinite there would exist a proportion between them (for—this I suppose is Averroës's assumption—the actual infinite would have the same character as the actual finite). There is, however, nothing actually infinite. Nor, in a strict sense, is there any actual finite time. For actual, in a strict sense, means present. The present, the 'now', however is, according to Aristotle, a limit of time, not time itself. In Averroës actual time is in fact synonymous with finite time and it is therefore not difficult for him to prove that all actual time is finite.

p. 10. 5. This argument (which is found, e.g., in Abu Zaid al-Balkhi—or rather al-Mutahhar al-Maqdisi—*The Book of Creation and History*, Huart, i, p. 121, and in Ibn Hazm, op. cit. i, p. 18) is exactly Kant's proof for the thesis in his first antinomy. Kant says: 'For if we assumed that the world had no beginning in time, then an eternity must have elapsed up to any given point of time, and therefore an infinite series of successive states of things must have occurred in the world. The infinity of a series, however, consists in this, that it never can be completed by means of a successive synthesis'.

This argument is found in Philoponus' first proof (op. cit., p. 10).: εἰ οὖν τὸ ἄπειρον ἀδιεξίτητον, καθ' ἕκαστον δὲ ἄτομον προϊοῦσα ἡ τοῦ γένους διαδοχὴ διὰ ἀπείρων ἀτόμων μέχρι τῶν νῦν ὄντων κατήντησεν, διεξιτητὸν ἄρα τὸ ἄπειρον γέγονεν· ὅπερ ἐστὶν ἀδύνατον, if, therefore, the infinite cannot be traversed and the succession, which in each genus progresses along the different individuals, arrives at the actual present through an infinite number of individuals, the infinite has been traversed, which is impossible.

p. 10. 6. This is a *petitio principii* and presupposes—according to Aristotelian theory—that there cannot be an infinite series of causes (*Met.* α 2) and that all movement must end in a prime unmoved mover (*Phys.* Θ 5).

p. 11. 1. Aristotle's theory of a first cause and a prime mover seems to me one of the more disputable points of his philosophy, and the Muslim theologians fully saw its difficulty.

For Aristotle the world is eternal and uncreated; time and movement are both eternal and there is an eternal series of movements (it must be added that the Muslim Aristotelians, who combine Neoplatonic with Aristotelian elements, speak of a creation of the world, an eternal creation; the world emanates eternally out of God, but this does not change the problem essentially, since both an eternal cause for an eternally identical effect, and an eternal creation, are contradictory conceptions, cause and creation both implying change). If, therefore, cause is regarded as antecedent to effect (and it is often regarded by Aristotle as an antecedent in time: man is produced from a prior man, cf. *Met.* Θ 8. 1049ᵇ24), there cannot be a first cause, since there is no first moment. But according to Aristotle (see above) there must be an unmoved principle of all movement. If we accept this, the world in its totality is passive, cause and effect are simultaneous, and God is not the first cause, but in fact the only cause. However, even this does not solve the difficulty, for if we regard uniform motion (the prime mover is the cause of uniform, συνεχής, movement, *Phys.* Θ 5. 259ᵃ16) as an identical state, as we moderns do, who acknowledge the principle of inertia, no cause at all is needed; if, on the other hand, we regard uniform motion as spatial change, a change in the effect presupposes a change in the cause and in this way changes in God would be introduced, in opposition to Aristotelian doctrine, which holds the contradictory view that an unchanging God can be the cause of a changing world (compare note 33. 1).

p. 11. 2. The acts of God derive immediately from Him; there is therefore no causal nexus between these, and we have no infinite causal series.

p. 11. 3. Man, when he produces man, does not produce him essentially, but only accidentally (whatever this means); the real cause is God, the real essential relation between the prior and the posterior man is a time-relation. This is not Aristotelian doctrine, but Averroës's exegesis. Aristotle (*Phys.* Θ 5 ad init.) distinguishes the immediate action of an agent from his acting through some instrumentality, a stick, for example, which he uses as a lever. You can say both that the last of a series of instruments is the mover and that the first mover (the man, e.g., who moves his hand which moves the stick) is the mover, but you will agree, according to Aristotle, that the first mover is the real mover, for without the first the last would not move anything, whereas the last does not move the first. Aristotle, however, tries to prove that there cannot be an infinite series of intermediates, although he regards the production of man out of man as eternal. Here lies the real difficulty.

p. 11. 4. i.e. God acts immediately, without instrument, as the mover of the world; where He needs an instrument, as in the production of man, for which He needs a prior man as an instrument, He has no first instrument; i.e. there is no first man, but the series of men is infinite.

p. 11. 5. οὐκ ἔστι κινήσεως κίνησις (Phys. E 2. 225^{b}15; Met. K 12. 1068^{a}15); ἀδύνατον τὴν ἀρχὴν ἕτερόν τι οὖσαν εἶναι ἀρχήν (Met. N 1. 1087^{a}33; Phys. A 6. 189^{a}30).

p. 12. 1. Averroës in his answer ignores the difficulty of how in the present a past infinite can have come to an end. Aristotle does not seem to have felt the contradiction between his thesis 'that what has no beginning can have no end, and that what has a beginning must have an end' and his description of the present, the 'now' (τὸ νῦν, الآن) as a kind of intermediate (μεσότης τις) containing both an end and a beginning—the end of an infinite past, the beginning of an infinite future (Phys. Θ 1. 251^{b}21). If it is said there is here no end, for the end is also a beginning, what in that case will be the definition of an end?

p. 12. 2. The unreality or subjectivity of an object of thought does not change its characterization; a hundred real thalers, said Kant, do not contain the least coin more than a hundred possible thalers.

The text has a variant: 'Therefore, when we imagine a number of horses . . . .' This may perhaps be the correct reading; horses is a favourite example with Aristotle when speaking of numbers (e.g. Phys. Δ 12. 220^{b}11; 11. 220^{a}24; 14. 223^{b}5).

p. 12. 3. For Aristotle possible existence does not mean only possible existence in the sense of my belief that a thing may possibly exist, but also the existence of a hypostatized possibility, an existing reality which is the source of an actual existent. For Aristotle all becoming is nothing but the change from a state of possible existence (in this second meaning) to a state of actual existence, and in contradiction to his own *principium tertii exclusi* (i.e. that there is no *tertium quid* between existence and its opposite, non-existence), he regards this potential existence as something intermediate between existence and non-existence (De gen. et corr. A 3. 317^{b}23). However, a potential existent ought to always have the possibility of becoming an actual existent, but here Averroës posits a potential existent, i.e. an infinite whole,

NOTES

which can never be an actual existent (cf. note 10. 2). That he regards potentiality as belonging to the domain of non-existence (in a certain sense) is in accordance with Aristotelian terminology (see *Met. N* 2. 1089ª28). Certainly all this is very confusing, and the ambiguity of Aristotle's terminology is not only a source of confusion but itself the consequence of a confusion of thought.

p. 12. 4. According to Aristotle the existence of time might be regarded as dubious, for the past exists no longer, the future is not yet, and the present is only a limit (*Phys. Δ* 10. 217ᵇ32). That only the present exists (ὑπάρχειν), whereas the past and future merely subsist (ὑφεστηκέναι) is maintained by Chrysippus (*Stoic. Vet. Fr.* ii. 164. 26; 165. 34). See also Augustine, *Confess.* xii. 15: 'praeteritum enim iam non est et futurum nondum est'; (ibid. 16) 'praeterita vero quae iam non sunt, aut futura quae nondum sunt, quis metiri potest, nisi forte audebit quis dicere metiri posse quod non est?'

p. 13. 1. Here he seems to regard time as exclusively in the soul. This subjective conception of time is found already in Aristotle (ἀδύνατον εἶναι χρόνον ψυχῆς μὴ οὔσης, *Phys. Δ* 14. 223ª26). Throughout the whole history of philosophy there is confusion of the subjective with the non-existent, and time is regarded as incorporeal, i.e. subjective or non-existent, by the Stoics, who in their materialism and sensationalism deny the reality of everything which is not apprehended by the senses—they even make the self-contradictory assertion (which might be regarded as a definition of Kant's system) that it is we who put the relations into things (*Stoic. Vet. Fr.* ii. 133. 22: πρός τι ἐστὶ τὸ πρὸς ἑτέρῳ νοούμενον), an assertion which, if taken seriously, would destroy the whole world, ourselves and our problems included, but in which, as we shall see, they are followed by the Muslim theologians. However, in these questions they show no consistency, and it would be a mistake to regard Ghazali's conceptions as especially subjectivist—as has been done—, this kind of subjectivism (of which we shall find many examples in Averroës too) being characteristic of Hellenistic philosophy generally (see note 41.2).

p. 13. 2. This does not seem very consistent. First, representation or imagination is given as the reason why we falsely regard the objective infinite as finite; now it is given as the reason why the future is rightly believed to be infinite.

p. 13. 3. Time has begun according to Plato, but may be infinite. 'Time has come into being together with Heaven in order that they may be dissolved together, if ever they have to be dissolved' (*Tim.* 38 b).

p. 13. 4. True to their principle, since according to Aristotle a beginning implies an end. For the incorruptibility of the world see below (Chapter II).

p. 14. 1. See note 8.1.

p. 14. 2. The word I translate by 'immediate intuitive apprehension' is ذوق, γεῦσις, 'taste', a word which belongs to the mystical terminology of the Sufis and which means the immediate mystical apprehension of the Divine. Plotinus says (*Enn.* v. 1. 7) that the purest Intellect (ὁ νοῦς ὁ καθαρώτατος) devours or swallows (καταπίνειν) the intelligible gods and in i. 6. 7 he speaks of the ἀπόλαυσις θεοῦ, *fruitio dei*, which becomes thence an accepted mystical term (the metaphor is obviously connected with certain rites of mystical religion). A definition of γεῦσις is given by Origen (*Comm. in Ioan.* xx. 33; Migne, xiv. 671) as the power of the soul to taste and to apprehend the quality of intelligible food (ψυχῆς δύναμις γευστικὴ καὶ ἀντιληπτικὴ τῆς ποιότητος τῶν νοητῶν τροφῶν), and Tauler (*Predigt* 26) says: 'Das Höchste, was der Mensch empfangen kann, ist die sechste und siebente Gabe des Geistes: Verständnis und *schmeckende* Weisheit für Gott, für die göttliche Süße, die süßer ist als Honig und Honigseim.' There is a close resemblance between fourteenth-century German mysticism and Sufism, both being derived from the same sources, Neoplatonism and Gnosticism.

p. 14. 3. The philosophers. This is only true if by 'philosophers' is meant Aristotle and his more strictly Peripatetic commentators like Alexander of Aphrodisias (according to Aristotle only the νοῦς which comes from outside, θύραθεν, is immortal, which seems to imply that my individual personality does not survive; however, the question as to what my individual personality consists in, was never asked by Aristotle or any other Greek thinker; see next note); it is not true either for Plato or for the Neoplatonists, including those commentators of Aristotle who have a Neoplatonic bias—e.g. all the Muslim predecessors of Averroës who deny with Aristotle (see *De an.* A 3. 407^{b}13 and 414^{a}21) the pre-existence of the soul and metempsychosis, and together with the Platonists accept the idea of personal immortality, although their pronouncements are various and are not always determined by purely philosophical considerations. At an earlier date Ibn Tufail in his philosophical novel had complained about Al-Farabi's inconsistency on this question.

p. 14. 4. ἀλλ' ὅσα ἀριθμῷ πολλά, ὕλην ἔχει (*Met.* Λ 8. 1074^{a}33). Callias and Socrates differ only in their bodies, but are one in their form, i.e. in their soul (Z 8. 1034^{a}5), and Socrates is unique only through his matter (1074^{a}35) (Aristotle, however, is not consistent, and declares (*De an.* A 3. 407^{b}26 and B 2. 414^{a}21) that each soul is fitted only to its own special body). This theory identifies my spiritual identity with my bodily identity and implies a denial of a spiritual Ego. Nevertheless it was Aristotle who introduced into philosophy (*De an.* Γ 2 ad init.) the idea of selfconsciousness, i.e. my consciousness of being the subject of my acts of sensation; but this consciousness concerns only acts of sensation and is itself a sensitive principle, the common sense (τὸ κοινὸν αἰσθητήριον), situated in the heart. The Stoics took over this idea from Aristotle, giving this consciousness a special term, συνείδησις, 'my knowledge of my own state', translated by Cicero, *De fin.* iii. 5. 16 as *sensus sui*, originating in the ἡγεμονικόν, القوة المدبرة, in the heart; Plotinus (iv. 3. 26) has four other terms for selfconsciousness: σύνεσις, συναίσθησις, παρακολούθησις, σύνθεσις, all of which may be of Stoic origin. But the connexion of the purely rational faculties, which according to Aristotle have no localization in the body, with the sensual faculties remains obscure. Avicenna in his *Recovery*, following Plotinus, *Enn*. iv. 7. 10—posits an immediate (بلا وسط) awareness (i.e. one not mediated by any sensual faculty) of my individual spiritual identity, which is incorruptible. For Avicenna, as for Plotinus (and for Plato), my soul is the link between the Divine and the animal; as belonging to the Divine world, it is identical with, or a part of, the Intellect and the World-Soul (both may be said, see note 15. 1) and this is my true nature; as connected with the animal it is aware of the things of the body which it directs. The Intellect and the World-Soul stand in Plotinus' system in the relation of Aristotle's active and passive intellect; it is through his Neoplatonic interpretation that Averroës can regard the passive intellect as incorruptible. We live in two worlds and have in fact two souls, each of us possesses a double Ego (διττὸν οὖν τὸ ἡμεῖς, *Enn*. i. 1. 10), and the awareness of my individual spiritual identity in pure thought, which is mentioned by Avicenna, is but the awareness of the identity of my higher Ego with the universal Reason. The consequence would seem to be that everything that characterizes the individual, since it is connected with the body, is doomed to annihilation with the body. This, however, is a consequence which neither Plato nor Plotinus nor Avicenna seems willing to accept: the individual Socrates is immortal.

p. 14. 5. This was not the opinion of Plotinus, who at *Enn*. v. 7. 2 (last sentence) accepts from the Stoics the *principium identitatis indiscernibilium*, known in modern philosophy through Leibniz: not two hairs, not two grains are alike (Cic. *Acad. pr.* ii. 26. 85; Seneca, *Ep. ad Luc.* 113. 16). This principle is known also in Islam (see e.g. Ibn Hazm, op. cit. i, p. 93, l. 1); the theologian Hisham al-Futi says, just as Leibniz does, that God cannot create two exactly similar things, since they would then be identical (Ibn Hazm, op. cit. iv, p. 196).

p. 14. 6. According to Avicenna—e.g. *Salvation*, p. 203—entities which have no fixed order in space or nature, ما لا ترتيبه فى الوضع والطبع, like certain angels and devils, may form a simultaneous numerical infinity. For Avicenna there cannot be a pre-existence of souls (see e.g. his *Salvation*, pp. 300–2), because before their entrance into bodies they would have to be one or many; they cannot be many, because in an immaterial essence there is no *principium individuationis* for a plurality; they cannot be one, because this one soul would have to be divided amongst the bodies, whereas the immaterial cannot be divided. They can, however, exist after separation from their bodies, because then they are distinct through the bodies in which they have been, through the times in which they were created, and through the distinctions in their own forms according to the different conditions of their former bodies. Plotinus (*Enn.* v. 7. 3), in order to avoid an actual infinity of spiritual entities (λόγοι), accepts the Stoic theory of different world-cycles. This is also Origen's solution of the difficulty of the actual infinite (cf. *De princip.* ii. 9. 1 and iii. 5. 3). Marcus Aurelius, as a materialist, asks (iv. 21; ed. Stich, p. 37): 'If souls endure, how will the air hold them all from eternity?'

p. 14. 7. This is the argument given by Aristotle against an actual infinity; *Phys.* Γ 5. 204^{a}21.

p. 15. 1. It is important to distinguish three theories which are confused by the Arabic commentators.

(1) The Platonic theory that the individual soul stands in relation to the soul of the universe as the individual part to the individual whole (Plot. iv. 3. 1): ἐκ τῆς τοῦ παντὸς ψυχῆς καὶ τὰς ἡμετέρας εἶναι. Plato says in the *Philebus* (30 a) that, as our body is a part of the universe, so our soul is a part of the soul of the universe, and this idea finds its mythical expression in *Timaeus* 41 d: the demiurge creates the individual souls out of the same material as he had created the universal soul, although less pure. The same conception of the individual soul as a real part (μέρος) of the World-Soul is found in Stoicism: see Marcus Aurelius ii. 4, v. 27.

(2) The Plotinian theory of substantial identity: πᾶσαι αἱ ψυχαὶ τοίνυν μία (*Enn.* vi. 5. 9). Plotinus, who quotes both passages of Plato (iv. 3. 1 and iv. 3. 7), regards the individual soul and the soul of the universe as ultimately identical; he denies that this identity can be explained in any materialistic way (this, according to him, was not intended by Plato), and he remarks (vi. 4. 12) that this identity is like the identical noise that is heard by different persons or the identical object which they see, showing by this profound remark that he is aware that the perception of one object by many percipients is an irreducible fact which cannot be described or represented by any material image. Greek psychology on the whole does not distinguish clearly between the percipient, the perceiving, and the object perceived, or between the thinker, the thinking, and the object of thought; subject and object are identified, and the theory of the oneness of all souls expresses the truth that the many can perceive one common object, just as Aristotle's theory of the uniqueness of the active intellect expresses the truth that the many can think one identical thought, but the uniqueness of the object is transferred to the subject.

(3) The Aristotelian theory of the identity of the universal. Callias and Socrates are one through their form; this means that although individually two, they are one in their universal essence, their soul. The universal is the same in a number of different individuals, and the same yellow may be in many individuals; the identity of the universal and the identity of the

NOTES

individual should not, however, be confused. The universal 'soul' is hypostatized by the Neoplatonic commentators as the soul of the universe.

p. 15. 2. Plotinus is fully aware of this obvious difficulty and discusses it unsuccessfully (*Enn.* iv. 3. 5); his spiritualism cannot explain man's individuality, man's privacy of vision and thought. But Ghazali's nominalism cannot explain man's membership of a common world of sense and thought, for the consequence of all nominalism is solipsism.

p. 15. 3. The different meanings of 'part' are discussed by Aristotle, *Met. Δ* 26, and Plotinus, *Enn.* iv. 3. 2.

p. 15. 4. This, of course, is a *petitio principii* and presupposes the Aristotelian doctrine that all unity is based on form, all plurality on matter.

p. 15. 5. After death all souls must be one.

p. 15. 6. For the meanings of 'identity' (ταὐτό) and 'different' (διάφορον) see Aristotle, *Met. Δ* 9.

p. 16. 1. For the divisible, διαιρετόν, i.e. the quantum, ποσόν, see *Met. Δ* 13, where the ποσὸν καθ᾿ ἑαυτό and the ποσὸν κατὰ συμβεβηκός are mentioned.

p. 16. 2. In *De anima* (Γ 5. 430^{a}15) Aristotle compares the active intellect to light, his third term in the comparison being the actualization of the potential: the active intellect actualizes the potential intellect as light actualizes the colours which exist already potentially. Averroës, however, uses the comparison as Plotinus does, for the soul generally, and he passes unawares from Aristotle's conception of the soul as a universal to Plotinus' conception of the substantial identity of the universal and the individual soul. For Plotinus' treatment see especially *Enn.* iv. 3. 22–23; it is interesting to observe how in this passage light is regarded at the same time as an image of the soul, ψυχὴ . . . ὡς τὸ φῶς (loc. cit. 22 ad init.) and as the reality of the soul, σῶμα πεφωτισμένον (loc. cit. 23 ad init.); all representation tends to materialization. The metaphor of light goes back to the passage in Plato, *Rep.* vi. 508 b, c, 509 b.

p. 16. 3. Philosophy distinguishes itself from sophistry through its ethos (Arist., *Met.* Γ 2. 1004^{b}24): ἡ φιλοσοφία διαφέρει τῆς σοφιστικῆς τοῦ βίου τῇ προαιρέσει.

p. 16. 4. In a tentative way, πειραστικός; dialectic is merely tentative, where philosophy claims to know (Arist., *Met.* Γ 2. 1004^{b}25): ἔστι δὲ ἡ διαλεκτικὴ πειραστικὴ περὶ ὧν ἡ φιλοσοφία γνωστική.

p. 16. 5. This kind of argument in defence of objective truth, which is very common in Islam amongst the theologians as well (cf. Baghdadi's arguments in Wensinck, *The Muslim Creed*, p. 251), goes back to Plato, *Theaet.* 170 c. It is asserted by Aristotle (*Met.* Γ 3. 6), in his elaborate discussion of the principle of contradiction, that all discussion rests ultimately on first principles, and that not to know of what things one should and should not ask for demonstration is the result of lack of education (δι' ἀπαιδευσίαν, Γ 4. 1006ᵃ6). The Stoics argue against the Sceptics that you cannot deny the possibility of proof without proving it, and that he who affirms that nothing can be known with surety must know at least that he knows this (cf. e.g. Sext. Emp. *Hyp. Pyrrh.* ii. 186; Cic. *Acad. Post.* ii. 9. 28); and Lucretius, too, says (*De rer. nat.* iv. 469–70 'denique nil sciri si quis putat, id quoque nescit, |an sciri possit, quoniam nil scire fatetur.' See also Cicero, *De fin.* ii. 13. 43 and Seneca, *Q. nat.* vii. 32. 2).

The argument is also found in the Christian Fathers; see especially Clement of Alexandria in his chapter against the Sceptics, *Strom.* viii. 35, St. Augustine, *De trinitate* ix. 10 '. . . si dubitat, scit se nescire . . .', and Eusebius, *Praep. evang.* xiv. 18. 760b . . . εἰ δὲ ἀγνοοῦσιν (the Sceptics) ὁποῖόν ἐστι τὸ δῆλον, οὐκ ἂν εἰδεῖεν οὐδὲ τί τὸ ἄδηλον.

It may perhaps be added here that the Muslim theologians regard the conviction of the existence, for example, of a country or of a town by reliable hearsay, i.e. traced back without interruption to an eyewitness (الخبر المتواتر) as unassailable (see Baghdadi, op. cit., pp. 312–14), here following the Greek empiricists, who also give the existence of a country or town (Crete, Sicily, Sardinia in Galen, *Subfig. Emp.* 52; Alexandria in Galen's *On Medical Experience*, Arabic version, xx. 5) by hearsay from an eyewitness (αὐτόπτης) as an example of reliable knowledge. In their rules for the reliability of a tradition the theologians seem to be influenced by the rules given by the empiricists (see Galen, *Subfig. Emp.* 51) for the reliability of traditional knowledge, ἱστορία (ἱστορία ἐστὶν ἀπαγγελία τῶν ἑωραμένων), and like the empiricists they emphasize the concord (συμφωνία, مواطأة), trustworthiness, and situation of the witnesses; however, whereas the theologians distinguish between traditions the evidence of which is immediate and necessary and those the evidence of which is acquired and valid only for practical purposes (عمل), for the empiricists, those forerunners of the pragmatists, all evidence is valid only in relation to our actions and the life of the community (ὁ βίος ὁ κοινός: see Sext. Emp. *Hyp. Pyrrh.* i. 237).

p. 16. 6. In these three last sentences Averroës is following Aristotle, *Met. K* 6. 1063ᵃ7. 16 and *Met. Γ* 5. 1009ᵃ16–22.

p. 17. 1. The introduction of the concept of possibility does not change the problem, and the difficulty remains the same, that of the completion of an infinite series. In what follows Averroës wants to eliminate the concept of time and to base the argument merely on the concept of possibility. It was, says Averroës, in God's unlimited power to choose one of an unlimited number of time-points for His creation of time. Averroës then transfers the unlimited possibility (of choice) in the subject, i.e. God, to the object, i.e. the time-points, and regards the possibility as a qualification of these points. The termination of this infinite series of possible time-points would be a condition for the beginning of finite time, which according to the supposition was created by God (this condition introduces, of course, the concept of time, which is, however, already implied in the concept of creation). Aristotle himself bases an argument for eternity on the idea of possibility. If time, so he says (*De caelo A* 12. 283ᵃ11 sqq.), had been generated, an infinite series of possible time-points (σημεῖα) would have existed before the generation of time. But an infinite series of possibilities is contradictory according to Aristotle, because the possible implies the possibility of existence and non-existence which, according to him, cannot coexist infinitely. The possible cannot be eternal.

p. 17. 2. See pp. 48 sqq.

p. 17. 3. i.e. the finite time supposed to have been created by God.

p. 17. 4. According to Aristotle, a quality can be attributed to something whether it possesses this quality potentially or actually; 'seeing' can mean both 'having the capacity of sight' and 'seeing actually' (*Met. Δ* 7. 1017ᵇ1). For the possible as disposition see *Met. Δ* 12. 1019ᵇ5. By a possibility which is simultaneous with a thing is meant a faculty, a capacity, an ability, a power. I shall discuss the difficult and ambiguous term 'possible' more in detail later.

p. 18. 1. For the argument which Averroës gives is double-edged; on the basis of God's omnipotence one might also prove an infinite number of possible spatial extensions; according to the Peripatetics, however, the spatial extension of the world is finite.

p. 18. 2. The possible, i.e. the actualized or realized possible, the created time. The identification of the possible with the actual is, as we shall see later, a Megarian Ashʿarite theory.

p. 18. 3. The passage which follows is somewhat confused, and does not render quite correctly the real objection of the philosophers, which is closely similar to Kant's argument for the eternity of the world in the antithesis of the first antinomy. The philosophical objection is that, since all time-points are similar, there is no difference in them which could determine God to choose a definite time-point as the moment for His creation (see e.g. Avicenna, *Salvation*, p. 418; the basic idea is in Arist. *De caelo A* 12. 283ᵃ11, cf. *Phys.* Θ 252ᵃ14, and already in Parmenides, Diels, *Fr. d. Vorsokr.* fr. 8). But the problem is not quite the same as that of the presence of black or white in certain things of nature, for black and white are not similar; the problem here is that of God's intention in choosing the one rather than the other. The confusion lies in the term مخصص ('differentiating principle'), which can mean as used by Ghazali (like مرجح *praeponderans*, determining principle or principle giving preponderance) (1) a principle which, determining or choosing without any motive one of two *similar objects*, establishes a distinction between them through this choice, (2) a principle which determines or chooses, without the motive being known, the existence of one of two opposites which seem *equally purposeful*, (3) the dissimilarity which is the motive for the choice. The conception of a 'differentiating principle' is of Stoic origin. Through God as the logos the world gradually develops through division (Diog. Laert. vii. 136); all things are set in opposition through the logos, e.g. the mortal and the immortal, the material and the immaterial (Plutarch, *De solert. an.* ii. 9); Lactantius says (*Stoic. Vet. Fr.* i. 42. 23) that Zeno called the logos *naturae dispositor*; Ps.-Arist. (*De mundo* 5. 397ᵃ17) has the word χωρίζειν (the natures of the different kinds of animals are separated); and Philo uses the expression (*Quis rer. div. her.* 26. 130) λόγος τομεύς, the specifying logos.

Ghazali probably borrowed his theory of a differentiating principle from his master Juwaini (for whose theory see Averroës, *Theology and Philosophy*, ed. Müller, p. 40).

Aristotle, although he is convinced that nature always does the best possible, ἡ φύσις ἀεὶ ποιεῖ τῶν ἐνδεχομένων τὸ βέλτιστον (*De caelo B* 5. 288ᵃ2) (which seems to imply that even for nature—or for God—not everything is possible, a problem much discussed in theology, since it denies one of its postulates, God's omnipotence), and that nothing in the eternal world can happen by chance and at random, 287ᵇ24, says (287ᵇ31) that to ask a reason for everything would seem to show an excessive simplicity (εὐήθεια) and zeal (προθυμία). The Aristotelian and Stoic principle that God does always τὸ βέλτιστον, الأصلح, is generally admitted by the Muslim theologians (cf. also Leibniz's *principium melioris*).

p. 18. 4. We should not inquire after the motives of the Eternal, according to the Koran, xii. 23: God is not to be questioned concerning what He does.

p. 19. 1. According to Plutarch (*De stoic. rep.* xxiii, *Stoic. Vet. Fr.* ii. 973) there were certain philosophers, ἔνιοι τῶν φιλοσόφων, who accepted a faculty in the soul which could determine the soul to choose without any external cause, when there is an *absolute equipoise of motives*, and Plutarch uses for this faculty (loc. cit.) the term τὸ ἐπικλῖνον, i.e. that which inclines, مرجح (Chrysippus denied the existence of such a faculty, which would imply the existence of the causeless, ἀναίτιον). This is the theory which, as we will see, Ghazali adopted for the human will. However, in the definition he gives here (and he seems to speak here of the will in general and not only of the Divine Will; but the whole passage is ambiguous) he regards the will in every act of will as an ἐπικλῖνον or a τομεύς, since he assumes in the agent for *every* voluntary act an *equal possibility* of acting or not acting. This is the Pelagian conception of the *liberum arbitrium*.

p. 19. 2. This would be rather an argument for the opposite of Ghazali's thesis, for will is a faculty, a power, which needs for its actualization a cause, a motive.

p. 19. 3. πᾶσα δύναμις ἅμα τῆς ἀντιφάσεώς ἐστιν, every potency is at one and the same time a potency of the opposite (*Met.* Θ 8. 1050^{b}8).

p. 19. 4. According to the Muslim theologians God has power to act and to will.

p. 19. 5. For the Divine Will also could only choose between things exhibiting a dissimilarity.

p. 19. 6. It is, however, the similarity, not the opposition of the time-points, which constitutes the philosophical objection; see pages 22, 25, and 32, and note 32. 4.

p. 20. 1. Differentiating principle, i.e. a dissimilarity; the term 'differentiating principle' has a different sense for Averroës from that which it has for Ghazali.

p. 20. 2. It would not contain the possibility of contrary effects; warmth —says Aristotle (*Met.* Θ 2. 1046^{b}5)—is capable only of heating, but the medical art can produce both disease and health.

p. 20. 3. i.e. they reject the idea of a Divine Will, at least in the theological sense.

p. 20. 4. نقل, μεταφορά; for transference as a form of sophistry, see *De soph. elench.* 18. 176^{b}20.

p. 21. 1. i.e. in the Koran will is attributed to God.

p. 21. 2. The original of this example is in Aristotle, *De caelo* B 13. 295^{b}32, where, discussing Plato's theory that the earth is sustained in heaven through the equivalence (ὁμοιότης) of the surrounding heaven (*Phaedo* 108 e), he speaks of the constraint of equivalence in a man who, at an equal distance from food and drink and equally starving and thirsting, must remain where he is. More or less the same example, *duo cibi aequaliter appetibiles*, is found in Thomas Aquinas, *Summa theol.* I. ii. 13. 6, and in Dante, *Par.* iv. 1–6, who adds, however, the much less paradoxical example of a lamb standing *egualmente temendo* between two hungry and fierce wolves. The paradox becomes known later as that of Buridan's ass (although in Buridan, who often gives asses as examples, this particular ass is not found), and the example of an ass dying with hunger between two similar bundles of straw at an equal distance is mentioned and discussed by such different authors as Montaigne, *Essais*, ii. 14; Spinoza, Scholion at the end of *Eth.* ii; Bayle in his *Dictionnaire*; and Schopenhauer, *Die beiden Grundprobleme der Ethik*, 2nd ed., p. 58.

p. 22. 1. According to Aristotle there are four classes of opposition: contradiction, privation, contrariety, relation; the first opposition is that of being and not-being, πρώτη ἐναντίωσις ἕξις καὶ στέρησις τελεία (absolute privation, i.e. non-being) (*Met.* I 4. 1055^{a}33).

p. 22. 2. i.e. it is only through our desires that we regard two similar things as different.

p. 22. 3. For the definition of will as desire of a good, ἡ βούλησις ὄρεξις ἀγαθοῦ, see *Top*. Z 8. 146ᵇ5.

p. 22. 4. 'The desires which belong to the essence of the things willed'. This contradictory sentence, which implies that the thing willed is the willer, refers to Aristotle's theory of God as the mover of the world through being desired and loved (κινεῖ ὡς ἐρώμενον), and is but a consequence of the profound contradiction in Aristotle's system in that God is both the supreme Agent and the supreme End. Not only does Aristotle ascribe the motion of the heavens to their love—'l'Amor che muove il sole e l'altre stelle'—but he attributes even to matter a desire for the divine, the good, and the desirable (*Phys. A* 9. 192ᵃ16). That to be is better than not to be, βέλτιον τὸ εἶναι τοῦ μὴ εἶναι (*De gen. et corr.* B 10. 336ᵇ28) is Aristotelian optimism.

p. 23. 1. Averroës misses the point here completely. Certainly the donkey will take one or the other of the two bundles rather than die, but the question is what determines its taking the one rather than the other. Obviously it will take the one that comes first to hand; only, when there is a complete equivalence of all conditions, this is impossible, and Spinoza says bluntly that the donkey will have to die. As a matter of fact, in such cases a complete equivalence of psychological and physical conditions is never reached; no living body even is strictly symmetrical, and if *per impossibile* such an equivalence could be momentarily reached, the world is changing, not static, and the donkey will move and not die.

p. 23. 2. What Averroës wants to express here, I believe, is not the *principium identitatis indiscernibilium*, but simply the fact that two individual things, even when completely similar, are not identical. Averroës, I think, confuses similarity with identity. By 'the quality exclusive to it' he means, probably, its spatial or temporal localization.

p. 23. 3. The impossible—like the necessary—is for Aristotle of two kinds, the logically impossible, the impossible through the necessity of thought, and the empirically impossible, not based on the necessity of thought (see Aristotle, *Met. Δ* 12. 1019ᵇ21). Since a logical impossibility is here in question, the impossibility is valid for all cases: divine, natural, and logical.

p. 24. 1. The sun, by moving on the ecliptic, approaches to and recedes from the different points of the earth, and is in this way the cause of change, of coming to be and passing away in the sublunary world (*De gen. et corr.* B 10). The theory of the eccentric sphere, κύκλος ἔκκεντρος, and the apogee, ἀπόγειον, belongs to Ptolemaic astronomy, see e.g. *Alm.* iii. 3 (according to Simplicius, *In Arist. libr. de caelo*, Heiberg, p. 507, the Pythagoreans were perhaps the first to introduce an eccentric sphere for the sun). The apogee is the point farthest from the earth on the orbit of a planet which has its centre outside the earth. All change in the sublunary world is conditioned by the positions and movements of the heavenly spheres, ταῖς ἄνω φοραῖς (*Meteor.* A 2. 339ᵃ21).

p. 24. 2. The problem why the heaven revolves in the one direction rather than the other is posed by Aristotle at *De caelo* B 5, and the problem why the planets have a movement different from that of the sphere of the fixed stars at *De caelo* B 3. According to Aristotle only two points on the sphere of heaven have a distinguishing mark (διαφορά) and they are the two poles through their immobility.

p. 24. 3. In Arabian astronomy the ninth sphere serves to communicate the diurnal motion to all the other spheres. The fineness of the simple body increases with its distance from the centre: see *De caelo* B 4. 287ᵇ20 and *Meteor.* A 3. 340ᵇ6.

p. 24. 4. These two spheres, i.e. (*a*) the ninth sphere; (*b*) all the other spheres together.

p. 24. 5. Ghazali means, evidently, that the ecliptic might have passed through the points which are in the actual world occupied by the poles; the actual poles would then have had to occupy other points; he cannot mean that the ecliptic might go through the poles, since the order of the world depends on the relation between the ecliptic and the poles. Ghazali's objection is not quite analogous to that of the philosophers, who argue against a creation which implies a pre-existence in time by saying that since all time-points are similar no definite time-point could cause a new volition in God. Ghazali's objection, that God could not choose individual points from among the homogeneous points of the world-globe to serve as poles, does not imply that God first created the globe and then chose the poles from amongst its homogeneous points; the implication is that any other two points which God might have chosen, while creating the world, would have been equally purposeful, so that the choice of the actual poles cannot depend on a choice made by God based on His conception of the best possible world. There is no answer to this objection, which is valid against a complete explanation of the world by final causes; one might as well ask why God created me and not someone similar in my stead (one cannot ask—says Plotinus, *Enn.* iii. 3. 3, why plants have no sensations and are not animals, or animals are not men; this would be like asking why men are not gods); all explanation in terms of final causes presupposes a number of primitive facts and laws which cannot themselves be explained by final causes. Theophrastus in his *Metaphysics* (see especially ad fin.) had already remarked that certain things do not seem to exist for the sake of an end, and that we must limit teleological explanation. The consequence of Ghazali's theory that God's will is not determined by any motive at all, however, would seem to be that there is no wisdom whatever in the world and that nothing has a purpose. But Stoics and Aristotelians, Muslim theologians and philosophers alike, believe in the principle of τὸ βέλτιστον, الاصلح, 'que tout est pour le mieux dans le meilleur des mondes possibles'.

p. 25. 1. A salience and a differentiation of the angles خروج زوايا وتفاوتها οὐδὲν γὰρ ἀπηρτημένον ἔχει οὐδὲ προέχον, ὥσπερ τὸ εὐθύγραμμιον (De caelo B 8. 290ᵇ6).

p. 26. 1. Possible, ἐνδεχόμενον, i.e. accidental, συμβεβηκός. The accidental, according to Aristotle, is what may or may not happen, and is not based on any inner necessity: συμβεβηκὸς δέ ἐστιν ... ὃ ἐνδέχεται ὑπάρχειν ὁτῳοῦν ἑνὶ καὶ τῷ αὐτῷ καὶ μὴ ὑπάρχειν (Top. A 5. 102ᵇ4). Averroës means that the position of the poles seems accidental, but is nevertheless based on necessity. In what follows Averroës reproduces the Aristotelian doctrine as found in the De caelo.

p. 26. 2. τὸ δὴ κύκλῳ σῶμα φερόμενον ἀδύνατον ἔχειν βάρος ἢ κουφότητα (De caelo A 3. 269ᵇ30).

p. 26. 3. The properties of the four elements in the matter of weight and lightness are treated by Aristotle, De caelo Δ 4; fire is absolutely light, because it rises higher than anything else; earth is absolutely heavy, because it sinks below everything else.

p. 26. 4. High, فوق, ἄνω, i.e. away from the centre; low, اسفل, κάτω, i.e. towards the centre (De caelo A 2. 268ᵇ21).

p. 27. 1. The sphere has only one surface, ἐπιφάνεια (De caelo B 4. 286ᵇ30), and is therefore the primary body, just as the circle is the primary figure; the spherical shape of heaven is proved by Aristotle at De caelo B 4.

p. 27. 2. Rectilinear bodies (τὰ εὐθύγραμμα) are not essentially finite, since an addition to a straight line is always possible (286ᵇ20).

p. 27. 3. The impossibility of there being any bodily mass or any empty space beyond heaven is demonstrated by Aristotle, De caelo A 9.

p. 27. 4. Since the heaven is alive (ὁ οὐρανὸς ἔμψυχος), it is clear—says Aristotle (De caelo B 2. 285ᵃ30)—that it must possess a right and a left; see also note 28. 4.

p. 27. 5. That all generation is effected through the movements of the heavenly bodies is shown by Aristotle, De caelo B 3. 286ᵇ1–9. For the theory that this continual production and corruption is based on the movements of the heavenly bodies, see De gen. et corr. B 10; cf. also note 24. 1.

p. 27. 6. Cf. Philo, De provid. ii. 74 (Stoic. Vet. Fr. ii. 332.3): 'Numerus autem planetarum prodest universo'. 'Mundum esse opus providentiae' is especially emphasized by the Stoics. According to Aristotle εἰσὶ δύο αἰτίαι, τό θ' οὗ ἕνεκα καὶ τὸ ἐξ ἀνάγκης (e.g. Phys. B 7. 198ᵇ17). See note 31. 1.

p. 28. 1. That each heavenly sphere has its own eternal principle of movement is stated in Aristotle, Met. Λ 8. 1073ᵃ33; that the heavens are composed of simple bodies moving through their own nature and not by force, having their definite natural movement, a circular one, which has no contrary as rectilinear movement has, since it turns, i.e. it moves at the same time in two directions, is stated in Aristotle, *De caelo A* 2. The sentence about the magnet is not found in Aristotle, nor, as far as I know, in any Greek commentator; it touches a very delicate point in the Aristotelian philosophy, for according to Aristotle the spheres move through an external principle, God, their final principle; they move in fact like iron which is attracted by the magnet (with the exception, as Averroës mentions, that the magnet can attract from any direction). One could say that the heaven either moves in virtue of its own nature (κατὰ τὴν ἑαυτοῦ φύσιν) or through an external principle which attracts it; Aristotelianism, however, wishes to have it both ways.

p. 28. 2. This passage is a commentary on Aristotle, *De caelo B* 2. 285ᵃ12 sqq. Aristotle has (285ᵃ15) the sentence that certain living beings differ only in power or faculty, whereas other living beings differ also in shape (τὰ μὲν γὰρ τῇ δυνάμει διαφέρει μόνον, τὰ δὲ καὶ τοῖς σχήμασι . . .). That the world needs for its spherical movement neither hands, legs, nor feet is laid down in *Timaeus* 34.

p. 28. 3. Aristotle proves (*Met. Λ* 8. 1074ᵃ31) that there can be but one heaven, since only through matter can there be plurality (man is one in species but numerically many because of his matter, e.g. Socrates, Callias). But the heavenly bodies are in a sense immaterial (*Met. H* 4. 1044ᵇ7) and yet they form a plurality and have a plurality of immaterial moving principles (the heavenly bodies and their movers are not always well distinguished). This plurality is explained by the Neoplatonic commentators as being not a plurality of individuals which would need matter, but as a plurality of universals. Every divine being, although it is unique (πάντα μοναδικὰ τὰ οὐράνια ζῷα, Simplic., *Comment. de caelo* 276. 32), forms a species in itself and is a universal (νοητόν). These beings are called angels by the theologians, both Muslim and Christian, and Thomas Aquinas affirms that there are as many species of angels as there are individual angels.

p. 28. 4. According to Aristotle heaven possesses τὸ ἄνω καὶ κάτω, τὸ δεξιὸν καὶ ἀριστερόν, τὸ ἔμπροσθεν καὶ ὄπισθεν (cf. *De caelo B* 2 and *B* 5). The diurnal revolution from East to West moves in the better direction (ἐπὶ τὸ τιμιώτερον) and is a forward movement. Aristotle regards the south pole as the more divine and the superior. If you imagine yourself standing with your feet to the north pole and your head to the south pole, you will see heaven turn in front of you in its diurnal movement from your left to your right (see *De caelo B* 2 ad fin., and *B* 5 ad fin.).

p. 29. 1. Koran x. 65.

p. 29. 2. Koran xxx. 29.

p. 29. 3. According to Aristotle the organ derives from its function (not the reverse), and he censures Anaxagoras for saying that man is the most intelligent being, because he has hands; whereas, according to Aristotle, he has hands because he is the most intelligent being. Nature, like an intelligent man, provides everything with the instrument it can use (*De part. an.* Δ 10. 687^{a}7 sqq.).

On the movement of the crab ($\kappa\alpha\rho\kappa\iota\nu\sigma$) see Aristotle, *De an. incess.* 14 712^{b}13.

p. 29. 4. According to Aristotle nature (or God) acts like the craftsman (see e.g. *Phys.* B 8 ad fin. and 9 ad fin.). That in every work of art, one must inquire for its intention ($\tau\epsilon\lambda\sigma$, اية غا) is a doctrine found, for example, in Aristotle, *Phys.* B 9, where as an example we find the saw, ὁ πρίων, المنشار (200^{a}10), as also below in the text, p. 54. See also note 31. 1.

p. 29. 5. Koran xviii. 103-4.

p. 30. 1. Koran vi. 75.

p. 30. 2. Heavenly bodies are in trine or sextile or conjunction, when, as viewed from the earth, they are respectively distant from each other a third of the zodiac (i.e. 120°) or a sixth or in close proximity.

p. 30. 3. Aristotle has an answer to this: the highest sphere has the greatest dignity and must therefore have the superior movement ($\tau\iota\mu\iota\omega\tau\epsilon\rho\sigma\nu$), which is the diurnal movement from East to West, whereas the other spheres move from West to East (see note 28. 4).

p. 31. 1. The whole of this passage is rather confused, but it is a consequence of Aristotle's dualistic conception of nature, i.e. of a necessary and a teleological element in nature. Aristotle introduced the conception of immanent teleology; nature itself strives towards an end (but in different places—see *De caelo* A 4, *De gen. et corr.* B 10, *Eth. Nic.* K 11, *Polit.* H 4— Aristotle identifies nature and God, which of course destroys the opposition of immanence and transcendence; the Muslim commentators often put the emphasis on God rather than on nature). But just as a craftsman cannot make a saw without iron, so nature is bound by the necessities of its material; in order to create, nature needs materials with specific qualities and inherent necessities. This conception would imply that certain materials having their own laws are presupposed by nature, and so are not nature itself; nowhere, however, does Aristotle indicate what these materials are, and indeed this whole conception is in opposition to his fundamental thesis that matter in itself, i.e. without having as yet received any form—and form and end are fundamentally identical for Aristotle—is absolutely undetermined. It may be added that the basic relation of matter and form is extremely obscure; both primary matter and form are ungenerated, non-spatial, non-individual, but yet it is said that the form enters into matter and that out of the combination of these ungenerated, non-individual entities the transitory individual comes into being. Besides, man as a universal form is eternal; as an individual man he is transitory. For Aristotle, only individuals exist; what then can it mean to say that the universal form is ungenerated? The Neoplatonic commentators explained this by saying that universals exist in the mind of God (a theory found already in the Middle Platonist Albinus), and the Muslim Aristotelians followed this tradition. It is God who is the source from which everything emanates, it is He who provides matter with its forms, (either directly, or indirectly as in Plotinus and Avicenna through the νοῦς, عقل, ὁ χορηγὸς τῶν λόγων *Enn.* V. 9. 3, واهب الصور, the *dator formarum*) and this is Averroës's conception also. Nevertheless we frequently find in Averroës the more naturalistic conception of matter as having its own qualities, its own potencies and necessities; and such a passage we have here. It may be—he says—that the existence of man cannot be explained by the potencies of his substratum alone, and that we must look for a final cause; but other actualities can be wholly explained by the potencies which are found in their substrata, and he gives as an example the seeing of the eye—probably referring to Aristotle, *Meteor.* Δ 12. 390ᵃ10, where it is said that the eye is an eye in full actuality when it sees. See also notes 31. 7 and 62. 6.

p. 31. 2. The word I translate by 'substratum' is القابل, which is a translation of τὸ πάσχον, τὸ πάθος. Like many Aristotelian terms this word is ambiguous; it is often synonymous with ὑποκείμενον, *substratum*, and as this is the sense it has a few lines farther on I take it so here; but πάθη, ἔργα, and πράξεις are sometimes synonymous and one might perhaps translate 'the effect of both is equivalent', which would seem more logical.

p. 31. 3. For example, a period of 5,000 years ago is not equivalent or similar to that of 6,000 years ago; these two times are equivalent only in so far as there is nothing in them which would determine God to choose the one rather than the other as the moment of creation.

p. 31. 4. Since a desirable result cannot be accomplished through any and every material, but needs materials that have the required nature. See note 31. 1.

p. 31. 5. However, possibility implies always two opposites. Averroës means the time of its production is different from the time of its corruption. For the underlying problem see below note 52. 6.

p. 31. 6. Time, says Aristotle (*Phys.* Δ 14. 222ᵇ30), is the condition for every change and for everything that moves: φανερὸν ὅτι πᾶσα μεταβολὴ καὶ ἅπαν τὸ κινούμενον ἐν χρόνῳ.

p. 31. 7. The proximate matter of things which have the principle of becoming in themselves—a grain, for example—develops by itself when there is no exterior obstacle; whereas out of wood a carpenter can make either a chair or a table; see *Met.* Θ 7. 1049ᵃ13.

p. 32. 1. This is not very clear. The source of the proof for God, based on contingency, i.e. that the possible must be actualized by a necessary existent, is certainly in Aristotle; it is only the term 'determining principle', مرجّح, which is taken from the theologians (see note 1. 3). The argument is found in Farabi, e.g. *The Book of the Gems* ad init., and Avicenna, *The Recovery* iv. 1. 6. For Aristotle, Farabi, and Avicenna God is the prime, indirect cause of all acts; for the Ash'arites God is the direct, indeed the only, agent.

p. 32. 2. τὸ πρότερον καὶ ὕστερον πῶς ἔσται χρόνου μὴ ὄντος; *Phys.* Θ 1. 251^{b}10.

p. 32. 3. The prior in the past is that which is farther away from the present moment (τὸ νῦν), the prior in the future that which is nearer to it; *Met.* Δ 11. 1018^{b}15 (see note 41. 2).

p. 32. 4. For why should the world be generated just at this particular moment, when for an infinite time it had not existed? *De caelo* A 12. 283^{a}13.

p. 32. 5. i.e. there is no analogy between the difference in moments of time and the difference in directions.

p. 32. 6. 'The second objection', compare p. 3.

p. 33. 1. For this argument compare note 11. 1. According to Aristotle, although movement is eternal, God is the first mover; according to the Muslim Aristotelians, although the world is eternal, God is its creator (Ghazali, as we shall see, rightly rejects the idea of eternal creation, as did John Philoponus, who asks, op. cit., p. 14, l. 14: τὸ γὰρ ἀεὶ ὂν πῶς ἂν εἰς τὸ εἶναι παράγοιτο; how could what always is be brought into being?). Aristotle himself tried to prove at *Met.* α 2 that there cannot be an infinite series of causes and that there must be a first cause. But if the world and time are eternal, and a cause precedes its effect both in nature and in art, says Philoponus (op. cit., p. 14, l. 19), there will be an infinite series of causes and effects, e.g. an infinite series of fathers and sons. If one denies such an infinite series, time must be finite and there must be a first cause for this finite temporal series. However, Aristotle does not deny, but admits, an infinite series of individuals in a sequence of causes and effects; what he denies (*Met.* α 2) is an infinite series of genera—that flesh may come from earth, earth from fire, fire from something else, and so on *ad infinitum*.

p. 33. 2. This whole passage seems to be a commentary on such passages as Aristotle, *Met.* α 2. 994^{a}30 sqq., where it is said that coming to be out of another thing, as water comes from air, implies the destruction of that other thing: the generation of the one is the destruction of the other, for there is no absolute becoming of substances, cf. *De gen. et corr.* A 3. 319^{a}20: καὶ ἔστιν ἡ θατέρου γένεσις ἀεὶ ἐπὶ τῶν οὐσιῶν ἄλλου φθορὰ καὶ ἡ ἄλλου φθορὰ ἄλλου γένεσις.

NOTES

p. 33. 3. See p. 11.

p. 33. 4. Of a circular nature (in Greek, ἀνακάμπτειν). This is clearer in the case in which water comes into existence out of air, and the process is reversible, than it is in the example of a man coming into existence from a man. However, the meaning is that there is no ascending series, either infinite or finite, to a first cause. And here is the difficulty of the whole conception, for if man can come into existence out of man eternally, in an eternal causal series, where is the need to posit a first cause at all? And if it is claimed that God is the *condicio sine qua non* of the existence and indeed of the possibility of this process, the relation between two eternally constant terms is not a causal one, since causation presupposes change.

p. 33. 5. *Phys.* Γ 5. 204ᵇ22.

p. 34. 1. This is a Neoplatonic rather than an Aristotelian conception; it is not the individual man, but man generically that proceeds from God, i.e. man generically emanates from the idea of man in God. Nothing, however, is more obscure than the Neoplatonic conception of emanation, which is not a flowing from a source, not a causal relation in time: the idea of man in God, and man generically, are simultaneous eternally; and even this, perhaps, is not true, since the idea in God exists in timeless eternity (see text below).

p. 34. 2. This means probably that if there were no eternal agent there could not be an infinite series.

p. 34. 3. μὴ κατ' οὐσίαν, Aristotle, *Met.* Λ 7. 1072ᵇ7.

p. 34. 4. As concerns its parts: The sphere of heaven, in its uniform and circular movement, always follows the same course and therefore does not change as a whole; it is simply that its parts change their place. However, the term جزء, 'part' (like the original Greek term μέρος—and μερικός—in late Greek use) is ambiguous and can mean also 'particular', and on the ambiguity of this term the plausibility of the argument depends in part: the movement of the heavenly sphere, since it does not change as a whole or generically is the cause of the eternal and generical, but in so far as it changes in its parts or particulars it is the cause of the particular and temporal (cf. note 35. 1). (The word كلّ, 'whole', is also ambiguous, and can mean 'universal'.)

p. 34. 5. Through the inclination of the ecliptic the sun is the cause of all generation and corruption; see Aristotle, *De gen. et corr.* B 10.

p. 34. 6. The four kinds of change: in substance, quality, quantity, locality. See note 2. 4.

p. 34. 7. φορὰ γὰρ ἡ πρώτη τῶν μεταβολῶν, Aristotle, *Met.* Λ 7. 1072ᵇ8. The whole passage is a comment, with a slight Neoplatonic bias, on Aristotle, *Met.* Λ 7. 1072ᵇ4–10.

p. 34. 8. Essentially and accidentally. As Averroës explains in the following passage, moving essentially means moving by a mover existing simultaneously with the thing moved, moving accidentally means moving by a mover preceding the thing moved; this distinction is not found in Aristotle and as a matter of fact annuls the proof, for it cannot be seen why an infinite series of accidentally moving movers should not suffice.

p. 34. 9. *Phys.* Θ 5. 256ᵃ17: ἀδύνατον γὰρ εἰς ἄπειρον ἰέναι τὸ κινοῦν καὶ κινούμενον ὑπ᾽ ἄλλου αὐτό· τῶν γὰρ ἀπείρων οὐκ ἔστιν οὐδὲν πρῶτον.

p. 34. 10. Preservation حفظ, σωτηρία. For God as preserver, σωτήρ, of the world, see Ps.-Arist. *De mundo* 6. 397ᵇ20.

p. 34. 11. 'Heaven and earth and all that is between them' is a Koranic expression, Sur. xx. 5.

p. 35. 1. See note 34. 4; جزئي, μερικός, means 'particular' or 'of the parts'; كلي, ὁλικός, 'universal' or 'of the whole'.

p. 35. 2. i.e. God. This is not very well expressed; no alternative should have been put forward. It is the movement of heaven, in which eternity and temporality are combined, which forms the link (σύνδεσμος, اتصال) between the eternal and the temporal.

p. 35. 3. Surely this strange theory, which seems both to deny and to imply a creation of the world in time, was not propounded by any philosopher. Ghazali seems to advance it only for the pleasure of refuting it.

p. 35. 4. i.e. how can new things arise in the world?

p. 36. 1. i.e. *qua* temporal.

p. 36. 2. i.e. Socrates as an individual depends on the transience in the movement of heaven; Socrates as a universal, as a human being, depends on the eternity of the First Mover (or—Averroës' position here shifts—on what is eternal in the movement of heaven). This conception is not Aristotelian.

p. 36. 3. Ghazali's argument is perfectly sound. The unchanging infinite eternal and the transient finite individual are incommensurable. No change can depend on the unchangeable, and to posit as a link an entity participating in both natures does not solve the difficulty but doubles it, for the relation of the primary terms to the intermediate term remains as obscure as the relation between the primary terms. The idea of the link, of mediation, goes back to Plato's conception, in *Tim.* 35, of the World-Soul which possesses the opposite qualities of the ταὐτόν and the θάτερον, of uniformity and change; it became in later Greek philosophy one of the chief devices to safeguard God's transcendence. And all transition is gradual: *natura non facit saltum* (Arist. *Hist. an.* Θ 1. 588ᵇ4), ما ترى فى خلق الله من تفاوت, 'you do not find any discontinuity in God's creation', as the Arabs have it. Cf. also Leibniz's *principium continui*.

p. 37. 1. The following argument, the substance of which is found in Avicenna (e.g. *Salvation*, p. 419), is based on Aristotle, *Phys.* Θ 1. 251 ^{b}10 (cf. *Met.* Λ 6. 1071^{b}8): How could there be any 'before' (πρότερον) or 'after' (ὕστερον) if there were no time, or how could time itself exist if there were no motion? Proclus in his fifth argument gives a variation not based on the term 'before' but on the term 'once' (ποτέ). He says in brief: When once there was no time, there was time, for 'once' implies time (τὸ γὰρ ποτὲ χρονικόν); and since time is the measure of the movement of heaven, heaven is coeternal with time. The same argument is found in Ps.-Philo, *De incorr. mundi* 53, p. 89, 8 Cohn-Reiter (notwithstanding Cumont's arguments I still regard this work as spurious, as does, for instance, von Arnim). See also Sextus Empiricus, *Adv. phys.* ii. 189.

p. 37. 2. Definitions of 'prior' (and 'posterior') are given by Aristotle, e.g. *Cat.* 12 and *Met.* Δ 11. 'Essential' and 'natural priority' are Aristotelian terms: πρότερον κατ' οὐσίαν (*Phys.* Θ 6. 260^{b}19) and πρότερον φύσει (9. 265^{a}22). The example of one and two is given in *Cat.* 12 and found also in Avicenna, loc. cit.

p. 37. 3. Aristotle gives it as an example of the simultaneity of cause and effect, where cause and effect are not reversible, that the intervention of the earth causes the eclipse of the moon (*Anal. Post. B* 16). This presupposes, of course, that light does not travel.

p. 37. 4. Since the effect always follows the cause.

p. 37. 5. The builder, however, is also prior to the wall in the order of causation.

p. 38. 1. Just as Averroës' objection to the first argument was inspired by John Philoponus, so in this objection he is influenced by Philoponus' objection to Proclus' fifth argument. Philoponus says that when, for example, it is said that God was before men knew God, 'was' cannot express time (ἦν is not a χρονικὸν πρόσρημα), since God is not in time, but in the αἰών, timeless eternity. Averroës also denies priority to God in the sense of causation. This is a necessary consequence of the denial of the simultaneity of God and of the world: since causation is in time, a time-relation is the necessary condition of any causal relation (neither Plato nor Aristotle, who also regard God as existing in timeless eternity, has seen this consequence). Philoponus does not treat of that problem in this argument, but Plotinus regards God as a *causa sui generis* (whatever this means) and declares, *Enn.* vi. 8. 8, that in one way God is an ἀρχή, in another way not; and this is also Averroës's theory here. But up to now the whole argument against the theologians has been built upon the idea that God is a cause and the world His effect, and Averroës's way of hunting with the hounds and running with the hare lands him, as we shall see, in the most flagrant contradiction.

p. 38. 2. Ghazali's originality lies in the example. In such sentences, says Philoponus (op. cit., p. 116, l. 10), 'existed' or 'was' ($\mathring{\eta}\nu$) expresses a mere existence, ψιλὴ ὕπαρξις (cf. Plato, *Tim.* 38 a). Philoponus also regards the φαντασία, which can represent the timeless only in time, as the cause of the error.

p. 39. 1. Here is the flagrant contradiction I mentioned, for here the relation between God and the world is, notwithstanding the denial immediately preceding, regarded as a causal relation in which the cause does not precede the effect, but is eternally simultaneous with it.

p. 39. 2. See *Cat.* 11. 14^{a}15: δῆλον δὲ ὅτι καὶ περὶ ταὐτὸν ἢ εἴδει ἢ γένει πέφυκε γίνεσθαι τὰ ἐναντία.

p. 39. 3. The difficulty exists only when the effect is axiomatically regarded as following the cause immediately in time; if the effect can be delayed, it must be in time; and if it is in time, the cause must be in time.

p. 39. 4. This proof is found in Aristotle, *Phys.* Θ 1. 251^{a}17–20.

p. 39. 5. That nothing can be in movement or at rest at an instant (τὸ νῦν, الآن) is proved by Aristotle, *Phys.* Z 3. 234^{a}24–^{b}9. According to Plato, *Parm.* 156 d, e, the transition from rest to movement takes place instantaneously (τὸ ἐξαίφνης) and for the Megarians movement takes place at an instant, discontinuously by jumps (see Arist. *Phys.* Z 1. 232^{a}6–10; ib. 9. 240^{b}30–241^{a}6; and Sext. Emp. *Adv. phys.* ii. 85). The discontinuous conception of movement is found also in Stoicism (ἔχει τὸ πάλιν καὶ πάλιν Simpl. *In Arist. Cat.*, see *Stoic. Vet. Fr.* ii. 161. 21). In Islam the idea of a jump (الطفرة) in movement is connected with the name of an-Nazzam, but as a matter of fact the conception of the discontinuity of reality, combined with the Megarian and Stoic denial of potentiality, is one of the basic ideas of Muslim theology.

p. 39. 6. That change (becoming or motion) is the actualization of what exists potentially, in so far as it exists potentially (ἡ τοῦ δυνάμει ὄντος ἐντελέχεια, ᾗ τοιοῦτον, κίνησίς ἐστιν), is proved by Aristotle, *Phys.* Γ 1. 200^{b}25–201^{a}29.

p. 40. 1. πάντα τὰ ἐν χρόνῳ ὄντα περιέχεσθαι ὑπὸ χρόνου, Aristotle, *Phys.* Δ 12. 221^{a}28.

p. 40. 2. I take this sentence to mean: God is not prior to Jesus in time, provided that you do not regard God as creating the world (and Jesus) in time and as preceding it. Jesus is only a posterior entity in so far as He is an effect—what Averroës calls here an accidental posteriority—of an infinite series of causes and effects. The duration of the world as a whole is not preceded by anything, since time is infinite; it is only particular parts of this duration that are preceded and followed by time.

p. 40. 3. This question is discussed by Philoponus, p. 116, l. 12, who answers it in the same way as Averroës does: It is permissible to say of the Timeless, He was when there was no time, and He will be when there will be no time, ἦν ὅτε οὐκ ἦν χρόνος καὶ ἔσται ὅτε οὐκ ἔσται. Philoponus adds that we must not mind the weakness of our expressions, but give our attention to their meaning.

p. 41. 1. 'God was indulgent and compassionate.' One might translate equally: 'God is indulgent'. The so-called perfect in Arabic can indicate a state either in the past or in the present. The example, however, given by Philoponus, who himself quotes Plato, *Tim.* 29 e, is: ἀγαθὸς ἦν, ἀγαθῷ δὲ οὐδεὶς περὶ οὐδενὸς οὐδέποτε ἐγγίγνεται φθόνος, God *was* good and the good can never have the slightest envy of anything (therefore God created the world).

p. 41. 2. In the following interesting, but slightly confused, passage Ghazali is no longer dependent on Philoponus. He begins by saying that future and past are relative to us (he ought to have said to the 'now' in which we are at present). The subjectivity of time, as I have remarked already (see note 13.1.), is often asserted in Hellenistic philosophy. In *de Ei apud Delphos*, Plutarch, in a passage quoted by Eusebius *Praepar. Evang.* xi. 11. 529a in which he expounds a Heraclitean view of nature which comes very near to the conceptions of the Muslim theologians, says: 'the terms of time, "afterwards", "before", "will be", "has been", are already by themselves a confession (ἐξομολόγησις) of the unreality of time'. Proclus in a passage of his commentary on Plato *Tim.* (*Stoic. Vet. Fr.* ii. 166. 4) says that the Stoics and many Peripatetics assert that time is κατ' ἐπίνοιαν ψιλήν, a mere product of thought. (Stobaeus, *Eclog. Phys.* 252, mentions by name the Peripatetics Antiphanes and Critolaus, as saying that time is a νόημα ἢ μέτρον, οὐ'χ ὑπόστασις, a concept or measure, not an existent.) Ghazali, however, does not develop this idea, but goes on arguing quite rightly that, if an extreme limit in time-extension is illusory, an extreme limit in spatial extension is illusory also. But, whereas we moderns regard such a limit as logically impossible, i.e. contradictory, Ghazali regards it as well founded and its denial an illusion of the imagination; for although denying the eternity of movement he seems to accept the Aristotelian conception of time and space as dependent on motion and body.

p. 41. 3. This argument would have been more convincing if Ghazali could have shown that the past may also become the future.

p. 41. 4. All this, i.e. the belief in the infinity of time.

p. 42. 1. This definition agrees with the conception of διάστημα, بعد, 'extension' or 'interval', as quoted by Simplicius (*Comm. in Arist. phys.* 571. 22): τὸ διάστημα τὸ μεταξὺ τῶν ἐσχάτων τοῦ περιέχοντος τὸν τόπον. This is, however, a conception of space which Aristotle himself rejects (*Phys. Δ* 4.

211ᵇ7), but which seems to have been adopted later by the Stoics, according to Simplicius (loc. cit.) and Themistius (*Stoic. Vet. Fr.* ii. 165. 11).

p. 42. 2. διάστημα, بعد, 'extension', can mean also 'dimension', for which Aristotle has also the term διάστασις; as space has three dimensions—μῆκος, πλάτος, βάθος (*Phys. Δ* 1. 209ᵃ4)—high and low are only one of the three relations into which extension can be divided.

p. 42. 3. By counting; the relation of the soul to time is treated by Aristotle, *Phys. Δ* 14. 223ᵃ16-29.

p. 42. 4. The necessary is eternal and unmovable; nothing compulsory or against its nature attaches to it (Arist. *Met. Δ* 5 ad fin.).

p. 43. 1. ᾧ γὰρ ἡ κίνησις ὑπάρχει, τούτου ἡ ἀκινησία ἠρεμία, Aristotle, *Phys. Γ* 2. 202ᵃ4.

p. 43. 2. Absolute becoming cannot be a movement, for, if it were, the non-existent in its becoming would have to move: Aristotle, *Phys. E* 1. 225ᵃ25. Absolute becoming would imply that the non-existent existed already, ibid. 28.

p. 43. 3. The Arabic text has only one word, عدم, στέρησις; both the Arabic word and the Greek can mean, according to the context, either absolute non-existence, τὸ μὴ ὄν, or privation; here, of course, relative non-existence, privation, is meant; becoming develops from contrary to contrary, the privation of health, for example, is sickness, of warmth, coldness, the sick man becomes healthy, the warm thing cold, but coldness and health, being forms, do not become or perish; they are eternal (see e.g. *Phys. B* 5. 205ᵃ6 and *Met. B* 4. 999ᵇ5).

p. 43. 4. A vacuum, emptiness, which according to Aristotle does not exist, would have the potentiality of extension, because a body could occupy it: κενὸν δ' εἶναί φασιν ἐν ᾧ μὴ ἐνυπάρχει σῶμα, δυνατὸν δ' ἐστὶ γενέσθαι, *De caelo A* 9. 279ᵃ13 (this is a definition accepted later by the Stoics, see Sext. Emp. *Hyp. Pyrrh.* iii. 124). In using the expression 'for instance' Averroës thinks probably of a matter, ὕλη, without extension which might be erroneously assumed to exist.

p. 43. 5. The paralogism Ghazali commits, according to Averroës, is that παρὰ τὴν ἔλλειψιν τοῦ λόγου, i.e. based on an insufficiency in the definition (*De soph. elench.* 5. 167ᵃ22).

p. 43. 6. Since time does not abide, says Aristotle, it cannot have position (θέσις), and one should rather say of it that it has order (τάξις), through its relations of prior and posterior (*Cat.* 6. 5ᵃ27-30).

p. 44. 1. τὸ νῦν τελευτὴ καὶ ἀρχὴ χρόνου. . . . τοῦ μὲν παρήκοντος τελευτή, ἀρχὴ δὲ τοῦ μέλλοντος, *Phys. Δ* 13. 222ᵃ33-ᵇ6.

p. 44. 2. Since it is impossible that time could exist or be conceived without the present, and since the present is a kind of middle combining beginning and end (ἀρχὴν καὶ τελευτὴν ἔχον ἅμα) . . ., time must be eternal and stretch away from it in two directions, *Phys.* Θ 1. 251ᵇ19–26.

p. 44. 3. ἡ στιγμὴ πέρας γραμμῆς e.g. *Top. Z* 4. 141ᵇ20–21.

p. 44. 4. ἡ στιγμὴ ἀρχὴ γραμμῆς e.g. *Top. A* 18. 108ᵇ30.

p. 44. 5. 'That its becoming is a vanishing'—this is one of the paradoxes of continuity. The past 'now' must have vanished before the present 'now', but it could not have vanished when it was itself the 'now', because then it would not have been, nor could it have vanished in another 'now' than itself (see Arist. *Phys.* Δ 9. 218ᵃ15–18).

p. 44. 6. It is clear, says Aristotle, that the 'now' is not a part of time any more than points are part of a line, *Phys.* Δ 11. 220ᵃ18.

p. 44. 7. Spatial quantity has position (θέσις); number and time have order, τάξις, *Cat.* 6. 5ᵃ15 (see note 43. 6).

p. 44. 8. i.e. of being a present and preceded by a past, for this is its definition.

p. 45. 1. So far as the infinite void is infinite, says Aristotle, it could not have a high (ἄνω) or low (κάτω), and so far as it is emptiness, no high nor low could be distinguished in it, any more than any distinctions can be made in the nothing; and emptiness is nothing positive, but a mere στέρησις, *Phys.* Δ 8. 215ᵃ8.

p. 45. 2. For how can there be any natural movement in the undifferentiated infinite vacuum? loc. cit. ᵃ6.

p. 45. 3. See note 27. 2.

p. 45. 4. On the whole Aristotle regards the accident as a universal (only in *Cat.* 2 does he draw an explicit distinction between the universal and the individual accident), in agreement with our common language, for when we say, 'This table is yellow', 'yellow' is a universal, and when we speak of 'this yellow' we mean this shade of yellow, a universal and not an individual yellow. The commentators, however, often regard the yellow of the table and the yellow of the chair as individually different, and as individualized and localized through their substratum, and this is what Averroës means here. He makes the true observation that the point is localized in the individual line and can be pointed at, it is a this, a τόδε τι, it is here or there; but the 'now' is everywhere, for it is everywhere now, or, as Aristotle expresses it, *Phys.* Δ 12. 220ᵇ5: 'everywhere the identical time is simultaneous'.

p. 45. 5. Time is not movement, says Aristotle, but that by which movement can be numerically expressed, οὐκ ἄρα κίνησις ὁ χρόνος ἀλλ' ᾗ ἀριθμὸν ἔχει ἡ κίνησις, *Phys.* Δ 11. 219ᵇ2.

p. 45. 6. The relation between movement, the 'now', time, and number in Aristotle's physics seems very obscure, ὁ χρόνος ἐστὶ τὸ ἀριθμούμενον καὶ οὐχ ᾧ ἀριθμοῦμεν, time is the thing numbered and *not* the numbers by which we count (219^{b}7) and it is the 'now' which counts according to *Phys.* 220^{a}22. Plotinus in his attack on Aristotle's definition of time, *Enn.* iii. 7. 8, says that there is no explanation given whether the time is the measure or the thing measured. Still, what Averroës says expresses at least one of the things Aristotle intended. The number 'ten' can be attributed to ten horses or any other group of ten, says Aristotle, 220^{a}23; and a hundred men and a hundred horses have the same number, but the horses numbered are different from the men numbered, 220^{b}10.

p. 45. 7. Aristotle does not speak of a cave in connexion with time (he has the simile of the cave, inspired by Plato, in *De philosophia* fr. 12 Rose—Cic. *De nat. deor.* 2. 37. 95), but he says, *Phys. Δ* 11. 219^{a}4, that even in the dark, and even if we had no perceptions through the body, we should know time through a movement in the soul.

p. 45. 8. That movements exist in time is clear, but how the things numbered can exist in number cannot be understood; it is rather number which exists in the things numbered. This shows the fallaciousness of the analogy.

p. 46. 1. ὁ χρόνος ἀριθμός ἐστι κινήσεως κατὰ τὸ πρότερον καὶ ὕστερον, e.g. *Phys. Δ* 11. 219^{b}1–2.

p. 46. 2. For it would be the individual accident of that individual movement.

p. 46. 3. i.e. the comparison of the temporal with the spatial limit.

p. 47. 1. The answer Ghazali here gives in the name of the philosophers is not one that can have been given by a philosopher of the school of Aristotle, for whom 'above' and 'below' not only have a real physical significance, but who distinguishes explicitly between an objective sense, by nature, φύσει, and a relative sense of the terms up, down, right, and left according to the position we take up (κατὰ τὴν θέσιν ὅπως ἂν στραφῶμεν, *Phys. Δ* 1. 208^{b}16). As a matter of fact the argument is based on a passage in *Tim.* 62 d–63 a, in which Plato says, to put it briefly, that, since the universe is in the form of a sphere and its circumference is everywhere at the same distance from the centre, the earth, which cannot be called anything else but centre, it would be irrational to call any part above or below. A man walking round the earth in a circle would often stand at the antipodes (ἀντίπους) of his former position and would then call the same direction above which formerly he had called below. This passage is summarized by Aristotle, *De caelo Δ* 1. 308^{a}18, in one sentence: some say that there is no above and below in the world, because all directions are equivalent and anyone walking round from anywhere will come to stand at his antipode. Aristotle then refutes this theory by saying that 'above' has a real physical sense and means 'nearest to the extreme, τὸ ἔσχατον, the circumference', and

NOTES

'below', 'nearest to the centre, the earth'. Ghazali seems on the whole to agree with the argument given in the name of the philosophers. He does not seem to be aware that it is in contradiction with two of the principles enunciated by himself: that time is relative to us (see p. 41), for time is regarded here as objective and irreversible; and that spatial extension is apprehended as divided through the relation of high and low (see p. 42).

p. 47. 2. For the answer is irrelevant, since the problem is: Why is there a final term to the *objective* spatial dimension?

p. 47. 3. φύσει.

p. 47. 4. See p. 27.

p. 47. 5. Ghazali will not really object that 'above' and 'below' form an infinite series because of experience based on imagination, since according to him 'above' and 'below' have no definite sense; he will now use the terms 'outside' and 'inside', which for Averroës, however, have the same meaning as 'above' and 'below'.

p. 47. 6. Aristotle does not distinguish space from place, i.e. the space actually occupied by a body. The consequence of this is his negation of the void. The space of the world is contained as in a vessel by its extreme surface. A body is in a place when it is surrounded by another body outside it; but if not, not (Arist. *Phys.* Δ 5. 212ª31).

p. 48. 1. To be consistent Ghazali ought to have said 'cannot be imagined'.

p. 48. 2. Imperceptible, غائب, ἀναίσθητον. Those who believe in the void, says Aristotle, believe it to be an extension not occupied by any perceptible body (*Phys.* Δ 6. 213ª27); and he says, *Phys.* Γ 5. ad init., that it is impossible that there should exist an infinite void separated from the perceptible.

p. 48 .3. Amongst the five reasons which Aristotle, *Phys.* Γ 4. 203ᵇ15, gives for the belief in something infinite, he reckons the imagination as the most important. Through imagination that which is outside heaven, τὸ ἔξω τοῦ οὐρανοῦ, seems to be unlimited, and this would imply also the infinitude of body.

p. 49. 1. The word I translate by 'measure', تقدير, is ambiguous and can mean also 'possibility'; either meaning would be appropriate here.

p. 49. 2. The whole of this passage is a variation on the argument given by Averroës, pp. 17-18, see also note 17. 1.

p. 49. 3. οὐ μόνον δὲ τὴν κίνησιν τῷ χρόνῳ μετροῦμεν, ἀλλὰ καὶ τῇ κινήσει τὸν χρόνον διὰ τὸ ὁρίζεσθαι ὑπ' ἀλλήλων: not only do we measure movement through time, but reciprocally time through movement, since they mutually determine each other, Aristotle, *Phys.* Δ 12. 220ᵇ14.

p. 50. 1. i.e. we can find that one movement is longer than another by measuring them with units they both have in common. Aristotle says, loc. cit. l. 18: 'when we call time much or little we measure it through units of motion, as we measure numbered things through the units of number—the number of horses, for example, by taking one horse as a unit'.

p. 50. 2. Every actuality is the actualization of a potentiality, and since movement is the actualization of the mobile as such ($\phi\alpha\mu\grave{\epsilon}\nu$ $\delta\grave{\eta}$ $\tau\grave{\eta}\nu$ $\kappa\acute{\iota}\nu\eta\sigma\iota\nu$ $\epsilon\tilde{\iota}\nu\alpha\iota$ $\grave{\epsilon}\nu\tau\epsilon\lambda\acute{\epsilon}\chi\epsilon\iota\alpha\nu$ $\tau o\tilde{\upsilon}$ $\kappa\iota\nu\eta\tau o\tilde{\upsilon}$ $\tilde{\mathring{\eta}}$ $\kappa\iota\nu\eta\tau\acute{o}\nu$ Phys. Θ 1. 251^{a}9), it presupposes the existence of a mobile. And since movement is measured by time, time also must be eternal.

p. 50. 3. This argument is found, for example, in Avicenna's *Salvation*, p. 189 and p. 421.

p. 50. 4. i.e. every potentiality will realize its actuality and every actuality is the consequence of its own potentiality; e.g. if God had created the world a thousand years ago, this would have been the actualization of the potentiality of creating the world a thousand years ago, and the world could not have been created eleven hundred years ago, because this was never realized and therefore was not possible. Averroës refers here to one of the problems most discussed in Islam, whether there can be possibles that are never realized. According to Aristotle, *Met.* Θ 4 ad init., you cannot say that a certain thing may possibly be but will never be, for this would destroy the definition of the impossible, since 'impossible' means what will never be (it is this conception of the possible which is meant by Aristotle when he declares that there cannot be an infinite possible time, since a possible cannot be infinitely unrealized; see note 17. 1 and below). Averroës himself often accepts this definition, but it is contrary to the basic idea of Aristotelian philosophy, the reality of a potentiality which may or may not happen; and by declaring that the possible must happen he reduces it to necessity. This conception of the possible—which is also maintained by Simplicius, *In Phys.* 1225. 32 $\delta \upsilon \nu \alpha \tau \tilde{\omega}$ $\grave{\alpha}\delta\acute{\upsilon}\nu\alpha\tau o\nu$ $o\mathring{\upsilon}\chi$ $\tilde{\epsilon}\pi\epsilon\tau\alpha\iota$—forms the basis of the argument given by the Megarian Diodorus Cronus, see my *Ep. d. Met. d. Av.*, p. 209.

p. 50. 5. i.e. since every possible movement in the world is in time, it may well be that any 'possible' is connected with time (the question, however, is: Are there any 'possibles' outside the world?).

p. 51. 1. There is certainly no difference.

p. 51. 2. The reasoning is: it is impossible to imagine the world smaller or bigger than it actually is (this is a *petitio principii*, for it needs to be proved that actually it is not infinite), but before the world existed and its possibility was actualized, the world might possibly have any size, since it was then not yet necessary that the world should have its actual size. This implies that the future is not yet determined, but that when a thing has once occurred it must necessarily be what it is. This conception is found in Aristotle, *De interpr.* 9. 19ᵃ23: that a thing is in the time in which it is, is indeed necessary (τὸ μὲν οὖν εἶναι τὸ ὂν ὅταν ᾖ ... ἀνάγκη), but it is not necessary that a naval battle will take place tomorrow, it is only necessary that either it will take place or not. In reference to the future there are therefore three natures: the possible, the impossible, and the necessary.

p. 52. 1. See note 27. 3.

p. 52. 2. i.e. it is based on reason, not on mere imagination.

p. 52. 3. That the generation of the world would imply a σύστασις, some formation out of which the change could take place, is laid down by Aristotle, *De caelo* A 10. 280ᵃ23, and he proves, ibid. Γ 2. 301ᵇ30–302ᵃ9, the impossibility of a generation *ex nihilo*, since it demands an empty space to hold previously non-existent bodies. Compare the Stoic argument (Ps.-Philo, *De incorrupt. mundi* 102, *Stoic. Vet. Fr.* ii. 188. 24) that there has to be empty space in which the world can dissolve itself at its conflagration.

p. 52. 4. This sentence expresses of course a certain contempt for the theologians. Maimonides in his *Guide of the Perplexed*, i, ch. 73, where he gives a summary of the system of the Muslim theologians, says only of the older Mutakallimun that they believed in the theory of the Void. Empty space is refuted by Ibn Hazm, op. cit. v. 70, 71 and i. 25 sqq.

p. 52. 5. By the Ashʿarites. Ghazali here gives in Ashʿarite terminology a theory of the Ashʿarites which he criticizes, although he accepts it ultimately. He pretends, however, that it is given by the philosophers, and indeed it may have been given by a philosopher for the reason stated in note 50. 4 (cf. also next note), but there is here some confusion in Ghazali's mind.

p. 52. 6. i.e. the world, having the size it has, could not have been created otherwise, for the possible is what will be some day realized; a difference in size was never realized, and it was therefore not possible and *could* not have been realized, i.e. it is impossible that reality should have been different from what it actually is (cf. Spinoza, *Eth.* i, prop. xxxiii: 'res nullo alio modo neque alio ordine a Deo produci potuerunt, quam productae sunt'). The theory of the Ashʿarites comes to the same as Aristotle's doctrine that the possible must always be realized, but neither Aristotle nor Averroës is aware of the implication of this doctrine, i.e. that it destroys their own theory of objective possibility—the possibility of opposite acts. The Ashʿarites in their doctrine of the possible are dependent on the Megarian and Stoic conception of the possible, just as in their whole conception of fate and will they depend on the Stoics. The Ashʿarite doctrine that there is no possible before the real, actual fact, that the possible is coexistent and coextensive with the actual, is the Megarian theory 'that a thing can act only when it is acting, and when it is not acting cannot act', criticized by Aristotle at *Met.*

Θ 3. 1046ᵇ29. The word مقدور, which I translate by 'can be done', corresponds in its original meaning to the Stoical term εἱμαρμένον, that which is decreed; but since for the Ashʿarites what is decreed is the real, and the real is the possible, and the possible is what can be done, the term takes the meaning which it has here, that of anything that can be done by a will, be it the eternal Will or the will of a transitory being (the same development had taken place in Stoic doctrine, where the εἱμαρμένη became identified with the ἐπιδεκτικὸν τοῦ γενέσθαι, i.e. fate is what is capable of becoming, see Plutarch, *De stoic. rep.* 46 and note 53. 1). We find in Shahrastani, *Religious and Philosophical Sects*, p. 69, 1, the following definition المكتسب هو المقدور بالقدرة الحادثة والحاصل تحت القدرة الحادثة which I would translate: 'acts in our power (المكتسب) corresponds to the Stoic term τὸ ἐφ' ἡμῖν) are those which have been decreed to be done, and therefore can be done, by the power of a transitory being, and can be realized by it'. This is the Stoic conception of the will of the creature as an instrument through which the predestined will of God can be realized. It seems to me embodied in such definitions as in Alexander of Aphrodisias, *De fato* 13, *Stoic. Vet. Fr.* ii. 285. 33 τὰς διὰ τῶν ζῴων ὑπὸ τῆς εἱμαρμένης γινομένας ἐπὶ τοῖς ζῴοις εἶναι: what is in the power of animals is what is realized by fate through them as its instrument; or in its Latin form in Chalcidius, *Commentary on the Timaeus*, *Stoic. Vet. Fr.* ii. 272. 4: 'quae in nostra potestate posita, omnia certe ex initio disposita atque decreta'.

The Ashʿarite denial of potentiality, i.e. the denial of the possible *in rerum natura*, taken from the Megarians, is founded on the law of thought, later formulated and violated by Aristotle—see note 12. 3—that a thing either is or is not, *tertium non datur*, whereas the potential, as what *may* be, *is* not yet, still seems to have some reality. From this law of thought, too, the Megarians and the Ashʿarites, as before them the Eleatics, had deduced that there can be no becoming (since what becomes neither is nor is not) nor transition in time, nor movement in space, for what passes in time *is* not in time, since it passes, and what moves would *be* nowhere, since it moves. Therefore the Megarians and the Muslim theologians conclude that what we call movement is the being (or illogically κινήματα, timeless jumps—illogically, for there is no identity in the atoms) of a material atom (ἀμερές) at the next time-atom in the next space-atom (that this is the theory of the Megarians can be seen from Arist., *Phys.* Z 10. 240ᵇ31, and Sext. Emp. *Adv. phys.* ii. 85). This implies the atomic structure of nature (see *Pyrrh. Hyp.* iii. 32; for the atomic view in Islam see, e.g., the extensive discussion in Ibn Hazm, op. cit. v. 92). This atomic structure of nature is not admitted by the Stoics, who believe in the infinite divisibility of matter, time, and space (the Muʿtazilite an-Nazzam, who is the Islamic thinker most influenced by Stoicism, also accepts this infinite divisibility); but from them the Muslim theologians take the idea of a passive material universe and the one active principle, God. In Islam, however, the immanent Stoic God, the agent of a unified universe, becomes the transcendent Allah, who discontinuously creates and re-creates His atomic world.

The problem of the existence of potentiality, i.e. objective possibility—capacities, faculties, tendencies, dispositions, powers, all the entities that imply the term 'can' (and every individual is a centre of such possibilities)—in which we all seem to believe when we are not philosophizing, was much discussed in later Greek and Roman philosophy (see e.g. Ps.-Plutarch *De fato*, Cicero *De fato*, and especially Alexander of Aphrodisias *De fato*, an important book which has never been properly translated) and even became a subject of polite banter (see Cicero, *Ad familiares* ix. 4, *Stoic. Vet. Fr.* ii. 93). The problem is very difficult, and I do not see how the Eleatic-Megarian argument can be refuted.

Aristotle argues against the Megarians (*Met.* Θ 3) that potentiality must necessarily precede actuality; before a man builds, he says—and it seems almost a truism, for it seems evident that it is through the knowledge which he has acquired and which lies dormant in his soul that the builder will practise his art—he must possess the art of building, i.e. he must be a potential builder; before a man actually sees or walks he must have the capacity to see or walk. However, there is here a difficulty—which the Megarian Diodorus Cronus saw in his κυριεύων λόγος, his 'master-proof' (for the problem compare Cicero, *De fato* 7.13 where the question is discussed whether a signet-ring, *gemma*, which never will be broken can be regarded as breakable): it is not possible for a man to see, i.e. he cannot see, before all the conditions of his seeing are fulfilled, e.g. when it is light and his eyes are uncovered; it is impossible that he should walk if he does not will to walk. But if all the conditions of his seeing and walking are fulfilled, so that he can see and walk, he will see and walk actually and his seeing and walking will be necessary, not possible. Indeed, we seem to hold the contrary propositions that we act because we have the power to act (because we can act), and that we act because we have to act. The difficulty is felt by Aristotle, where he says (*Met.* Θ 7. 1049^{a}8) that a house is potentially a house when there are no obstacles and when nothing has to be added or subtracted or altered. But in such a case the potential house is already the actual house, and there is no process, no becoming.

The idea of potentiality (and potentiality in Aristotle does not only mean 'capacity', 'power', i.e. 'can do', but also 'can be', 'can exist', 'can undergo') seems to express our belief in the fundamental identity of things, our belief that *ex nihilo nihil*, *que rien ne se crée, rien ne se perd*, that all change, all becoming is but a transformation of what existed previously under another form, is but a coming-to-be out of something, a development, an evolution (i.e. an unrolling; cf. Cicero, *De div.* i. 56. 127: the series of events in time is like the uncoiling of a rope, *quasi rudentis explicatio*), that tomorrow is contained in today, that *ciascuna cosa, qual ella è, diventa* (Dante, *Parad.* xx. 78). But the idea of potentiality leaves two things unexplained: (1) the status of potentiality, this mysterious state of dormancy between being and non-being; (2) the very process of actualization, of development, of evolution, for in the actualizing process either something is added to the potentiality and then we have a becoming out of nothing, or nothing is added and then there is no change. Aristotle tries to have it both ways. In the example of the house given above the potential house is already the actual house, there is no process, no becoming; in the example of wine turning sour (cf. note 61. 6), the actual sourness is the actualization of a potential sourness, but how this actualization takes place cannot be understood, as Aristotle himself admits, and the actual sourness, since it was not there before, arises out of nothing.

p. 52. 7. They have compromised themselves by accusing their opponents of charging God with impotence, since they themselves hold that it is impossible that the world should be bigger or smaller than it actually is.

p. 53. 1. The implication of this argument is that for God only the contradictory is impossible. Ghazali here makes the important distinction between logical impossibility or necessity and factual or hypothetical impossibility or necessity, τὸ ἀναγκαῖον ἁπλῶς and τὸ ἀναγκαῖον ἐξ ὑποθέσεως, found confusedly in Aristotle, *De part. an.* A 1. 639^{b}24 (cf. *Met.* Δ 5. 1015^{b}9 and *Met.* Λ 7. 1072^{b}12; see also note 23. 3). This distinction is known in modern philosophy through Leibniz's distinction of *vérités de fait* and *vérités de raison* (*Monad.* 33, *Nouv. Essais*, i. 1. 26). A *vérité de raison* is that A is not not-A; a *vérité de fait*, that fire burns. The distinction is, however, complicated by the fact that we believe that there are reasons why fire burns, as Leibniz acknowledges, *Monad.* 31–32, that in the apparent changing events there are underlying identities, and the aim of science is to find, in the *vérités de fait*, *vérités de raison*. The problem of possibility in relation to God was much discussed both in Eastern and Western scholasticism. Some, like Ibn Hazm, hold that God can do the impossible, whereas the Ashʿarites exclude the logically impossible or what they hold to be the logically impossible (see Ibn Hazm's criticism of them, op. cit. iv. 214, l. 1). Both Ghazali and the Ashʿarites hold the contradictory propositions that nothing is possible but what exists, and that for God everything is possible but the logically impossible. Plutarch, *De stoic. repugn.* c. 46, *Stoic. Vet. Fr.* ii. 64. 39, reproaches the Stoics with the same contradiction. In modern philosophy Descartes believed in God's omnipotence; Leibniz excluded the logically impossible.

p. 53. 2. i.e. the possibility that the world might be larger or smaller than it actually is.

p. 53. 3. Averroës does not express himself well, but what is implied is sound. He should have said: All logical inference is necessary; no inference

NOTES

about fact, however, is based solely on logical necessity, but needs as an initial premiss a fact, self-evident (*cogito*, e.g.) but not logically necessary; if, however, by false reasoning you assume a fact, contradictions will follow from this assumption whose exposition is called by Aristotle ἐκ (or διὰ) τοῦ ἀδυνάτου δεικνύναι (or ἀποδεῖξαι), e.g. *Anal. Pr. A* 17. 37ᵃ9, a *reductio ad absurdum*.

p. 53. 4. ὥστε οὔτε νῦν εἰσὶ πλείους οὐρανοὶ οὔτ᾽ ἐγένοντο οὔτ᾽ ἐνδέχεται γενέσθαι πλείους· ἀλλ᾽ εἷς καὶ μόνος καὶ τέλειος οὗτος οὐρανός ἐστιν, *De caelo A* 9. 279ᵃ9.

p. 53. 5. i.e. after the study of logic.

p. 53. 6. From the thesis that it is impossible that something which has not happened (or will not happen) might have happened, Ghazali concludes rightly that everything that happens is necessary (of course this implies a belief in natural law; if you deny natural law with the Ashʿarites, things are neither necessary nor possible, they simply are). This necessity is admitted by Averroës. Ghazali, using the double sense of 'necessity' in Aristotle, proceeds to conclude, from the fact that everything happens by necessity, that it will have no cause. Aristotle, as we saw, distinguishes logical necessity and factual necessity—a fact is necessary when it has happened through a cause; primary logical necessity is not conditioned, but is necessary by itself and eternal, i.e. it is eternally true or valid. Aristotle, who constantly confuses the individual and the universal, facts and propositions, regards God's existence as such an eternal truth and therefore unconditioned and necessary by itself (see especially the passage at *Met. Δ* 5. 1015ᵇ9 indicated above in note 53. 1).

p. 54. 1. This doctrine is not proper to Avicenna, but, as we have shown, is fundamentally Aristotelian. It is the correct answer, according to Aristotle, that God's existence is necessary through His own essence, whereas the existence of transitory beings needs an extraneous cause.

p. 54. 2. This example (see note 29. 4) is highly confused. He has to show that transitory existents which are necessary have a cause; what he shows is that there are necessities which cannot be attributed to existents because they express a relation between universals. The necessity he mentions here concerns the conditions for a saw being a saw, but does not refer to the existence of any particular saw.

p. 54. 3. There is no necessary connexion between the atoms of the Ashʿarite atomic universe, nor does God stand under any law or any constraint; on the contrary, He is the law, the Λόγος, the Νόμος (the Arabs have the word ناموس, *nāmūs*). The latter idea is Heraclitean and Stoic.

p. 54. 4. i.e. according to Ghazali: the opponent of the philosopher, i.e. the Ashʿarite.

p. 54. 5. The argument is not similar, but identical. The thesis is: the world is only possible during its existence. Convert this statement and you have: the world is impossible before its existence. This is the objection which Aristotle makes against the Megarians, Met. Θ 2. 1047ᵃ10: ἔτι εἰ ἀδύνατον τὸ ἐστερημένον δυνάμεως, τὸ μὴ γενόμενον ἀδύνατον ἔσται γενέσθαι; again, if that which has no possibility is impossible, that which is not happening cannot possibly happen, i.e. if the possible is what happens, that which does not happen ('that which has no possibility') is impossible; therefore, Aristotle concludes, before the possible thing happened it was impossible. Aristotle's argument rests on a *quaternio terminorum*: he takes 'possible' in its Megarian sense of 'happening' and 'impossible' in the usual sense of 'what cannot happen'. If he had given to the word 'impossible' the sense the Megarians intended, his argument would only have amounted to this: 'If that which is not, is not, that which is not happening is not happening.' Ghazali turns here completely round; he now makes the philosophers, using Aristotle's argument, attack the Ashʿarite thesis, which he pretended they held, and he defends the Ashʿarite thesis which he previously attacked himself.

p. 54. 6. If you take 'impossible' to mean, as it does for the Ashʿarites, 'non-existent' and 'possible' 'existent', this is certainly quite obvious.

p. 54. 7. Ghazali now reverts to his former argument based on the analogy of time and space; this sentence has no connexion with what immediately precedes.

p. 54. 8. i.e. the suppositions of different possibilities in time for the creation of the world as given in Avicenna's argument, pp. 48–49.

p. 54. 9. i.e. because all things are in time, imagination represents God as in time.

p. 55. 1. i.e. the possible implies the impossible, but the impossible is what necessarily cannot happen and therefore implies necessity.

p. 55. 2. This·refers to Aristotle, Met. Δ 12. 1019ᵇ23 and De caelo A 12. 281ᵇ27: to assume that what is impossible may exist, e.g. the fact that the diagonal of a square is commensurate with the side, is an impossible falsehood, because, according to Aristotle, its contrary is not only false, but also false of necessity; to assume that the possible may exist is a possible falsehood, because the contrary is not necessarily false; that a man should be seated is possible, says Aristotle, since it is not necessarily false that he is seated.

p. 55. 3. This is quite true. The Megarians and the Ashʿarites should not have said that the possible is coextensive with the actual; they should have said that 'possible' has no meaning at all.

p. 55. 4. If it is impossible before its existence, it cannot be true, as he has just said, that a thing should be possible before its existence.

p. 55. 5. Nothing absolutely incorruptible—says Aristotle, Met. Θ 1050ᵇ16—is absolutely potential: οὐδὲν ἄρα τῶν ἀφθάρτων ἁπλῶς δυνάμει ἐστὶν ἁπλῶς.

p. 55. 6. See notes 50. 4, 17. 1, and below.

p. 56. 1. This is one of the fundamental ideas of the Aristotelian philosophy and also one of its fundamental contradictions: in action (ἐνέργεια) فعل, lies the perfection (ἐντελέχεια) استكمال, of every being, and indeed these two terms are often used synonymously; on the other hand, the idea of action *presupposes* the idea of perfection, of an end; action is not an end in itself (this is denied by Arist. Met. Θ 6. 1048ᵇ18, at least for certain actions), but tends towards an end. We have here the old difficulty of change and becoming, concealed through the ambiguous use of the term ἐνέργεια. ἐνέργεια is the act, the actualizing, it is also the end of the process of actualizing, the *being* in actuality, the reality attained, and in fact it is synonymous with reality. Without realizing it Aristotle identifies becoming and being, the act, ἐνέργεια, towards the end becomes the end, ἐντελέχεια, and inversely the end, ἐντελέχεια, becomes the act, ἐνέργεια. There is a similar confusion in Aristotle's theory of movement which he defines Phys. Θ 5. 257ᵇ8 as an incomplete action, ἐντελέχεια ἀτελής. Now every activity is the actualization of a potency, i.e. a change, and every change for Aristotle is movement. However, in this definition Aristotle seems to mean by action not the process, the attaining of the end, but the end attained, whereas in the definition of movement as ἡ τοῦ δυνάμει ἐντελέχεια by entelechy the process is meant.

p. 57. 1. This proof is the same as that of Avicenna (pp. 48–49) and Averroës (p. 17), only here it is applied to the existence of the world. It is based on the idea that what is possible must at some time be realized, and that therefore nothing can be eternally possible; and it is a *petitio principii*, i.e. it assumes that the world is ungenerated (if you substitute the words 'existence of Socrates' for 'existence of the world' the argument will not prove the eternal existence of Socrates). The world is not eternal, because it could not not have been, but, because the world is eternal, it could not not be. The same *petitio principii* is found in Aristotle, De caelo A 10-12, which is the source of this argument, where, besides, Aristotle proves *in extenso* the two truisms (1) that what exists during an infinite time—and he implies by 'infinite', infinite *a parte ante* and *a parte post*—can neither become nor perish, since if it did, it would only be at some time; and (2) that what is both ungenerated and incorruptible cannot be of the nature of the possible (i.e. the changing), i.e. can neither be generated nor be destroyed.

p. 57. 2. 'Possible' in the sense of what 'has to be'.

p. 57. 3. i.e. is logically necessary; absurd, محال, ἄτοπος.

p. 57. 4. Cf. *De caelo A* 12. 281ᵇ20: if anything that exists for an infinite time is destructible (φθαρτόν), it must have the possibility of not being.

p. 57. 5. Or more exactly, Aristotle says, *Phys.* Γ 4. 203ᵇ30: ἐνδέχεσθαι ἢ εἶναι οὐδὲν διαφέρει ἐν τοῖς ἀϊδίοις, in eternal beings possibility (i.e. realization) and existence coincide.

p. 57. 6. This is in opposition to the Ash'arite doctrine that possibility conforms to reality, i.e. is coextensive with it.

p. 58. 1. This sentence agrees with the Ash'arite doctrine that the possible is what has become (i.e. that possibility is coextensive with reality); i.e. Ghazali first affirms in this passage, in opposition to the argument of the philosophers which implies that what becomes had necessarily to become, that there is objective possibility: the world could become at any time whatever, i.e. God could create at any moment, but did not do so; and then he denies this in the last sentence by saying that only what has been realized is possible. What he wants to say is this: the world might have been created at any time, but it has been in fact created (its creation was possible, in the Ash'arite sense) at a definite specified time. This is, of course, a *petitio principii*, since the problem is whether the world was created or is eternal.

p. 58. 2. The problem of an alternative generation and corruption, as asserted by Empedocles, the Atomists, and Heraclitus (the Stoics later renew the Heraclitean doctrine of the world as ἁπτόμενος μέτρα, ἀποσβεννύμενος μέτρα, inflamed and extinguished according to measures), is discussed by Aristotle, *De caelo* A 10. 280ᵃ11. He compares this to the evolution of a child into a man, and the production of a child out of a man, and says it must be an ordered, not a fortuitous process, and must be not an absolute generation and destruction of the world, but only a change in its dispositions (διαθέσεις).

p. 58. 3. The theologians believe in the corruptibility of the world, for which, as we will see in the next chapter, they give the main Stoic argument.

p. 58. 4. See, for example, Aristotle, *Met.* Z 7. 1032ᵃ20: δυνατὸν γὰρ καὶ εἶναι καὶ μὴ εἶναι ἕκαστον αὐτῶν, τοῦτο δ' ἐστὶν ἡ ἐν ἑκάστῳ ὕλη, for what in every thing has the potency to be or not to be, that is the matter in every thing.

p. 58. 5. This is not absolutely true; the forms do not become either—form is eternal like matter, and becoming is a change of form in matter. Aristotle, however, has also (*Phys.* A 9. 192ᵇ1) the term φυσικὰ καὶ φθαρτὰ εἰδή, natural and perishable forms. See note 31. 1.

p. 59. 1. e.g. *Met.* Θ 8. 1050ᵇ16: οὐθὲν ἄρα τῶν ἀφθάρτων ἁπλῶς δυνάμει ἐστὶν ὂν ἁπλῶς, nothing which is essentially incorruptible is essentially in potency (i.e. can be or not be).

p. 59. 2. This is not absolutely true; it is in contradiction to what Ghazali has just said, namely that matter itself *is* the essentially potential. It is, however, true that in Aristotelian philosophy potentiality is at the same time the substrate, the potentiality in the substrate, and the potentiality of the agent. See the text below and note 62. 6.

p. 59. 3. See note 11. 5.

p. 59. 4. i.e. that a man can do something is a consequence of his possessing the power to do it.

p. 59. 5. i.e. an objective reality, not something subjective.

p. 59. 6. i.e. matter.

p. 60. 1. For the circularity of this process see page 33 and note 33. 4.

p. 60. 2. Aristotle admits both an objective necessity and an objective possibility. The Stoics, who regard the world as a closed unique system in which everything that happens is the necessary consequence of an eternally determined concatenation of causes and effects, deny objective possibility (not quite consistently, as we have seen) and define possibility and chance in terms of our human ignorance of the laws of nature, αἰτία ἄδηλος ἀνθρωπίνῳ λογισμῷ (Alex. Aphr. *De fato* c. 8, p. 174. 2, *Stoic. Vet. Fr.* ii. 281. 35). It would seem that only the Eleatics and Megarians, who absolutely deny all becoming, could deny both objective necessity and objective possibility. However, the Stoics divide 'things' (see note 3. 6) into the corporeal and the incorporeal, relations belonging to the incorporeal. Necessity and possibility, being both relations and incorporeal, would have to be regarded by them as subjective. The Stoics seem to have committed the same inconsistency as many moderns who appear to believe in the objective necessity of cause and in the necessary character of objective laws of nature, but regard both possibility and necessity as expressing not the characteristics of things, but the conditions of our knowledge of them. That Ghazali may have taken his argument from some late Stoic source is indicated by the expression 'provided no obstacle presents itself'. Sextus Empiricus tells us in fact (*Adv. log.* i. 253) that the later Stoics regarded the apprehensive presentation τὴν καταληπτικὴν φαντασίαν as a criterion of truth, *provided that it has no obstacle*, τὸ μηδὲν ἔχουσαν ἔνστημα. The term καταληπτός, مفهوم, the apprehended, comprehended (*comprehendibile* in Cicero's translation, see *Stoic. Vet. Fr.* i. 18. 18), is frequently used in Muslim theology (see e.g. Massignon, op. cit., p. 56), and is often regarded by the theologians as synonymous with 'possible' ممكن. For the intermediate position of the apprehensive presentation see Cicero, loc. cit.: 'sed inter scientiam et inscientiam comprehensionem . . . collocabat (scilicet: Zeno), eamque neque in rectis neque in pravis numerabat, sed soli credendum esse dicebat'. Chrysippus' definition of the possible (Alex. Aphr. *De fato* c. 10, *Stoic. Vet. Fr.* ii, p. 279. 15) as that which is not prevented from happening by anything, although it may not happen (δυνατὸν εἶναι γενέσθαι τοῦτο ὃ ὑπ' οὐδενὸς κωλύεται γενέσθαι, κἂν μὴ γενήται) implies of course objective possibility (see also note 241. 1).

p. 60. 3. This, the most obvious definition of truth, is based on Aristotle, *De interpr.* 9. 19ᵃ33 ὁμοίως οἱ λόγοι ἀληθεῖς ὥσπερ τὰ πράγματα. The definition becomes somewhat problematic when one asks what in the mind conforms to reality; but when rightly interpreted it is undoubtedly true, since it expresses in the form of an image the tautology that a true judgement is a judgement which expresses a truth ('truth' which is assumed in all thought is indefinable and irreducible like all primary concepts). Aristotle has also in this form the definition *Met.* Γ 6. 1011ᵇ26: τὸ μὲν γὰρ λέγειν τὸ ὂν μὴ εἶναι ἢ τὸ μὴ ὂν εἶναι ψεῦδος, τὸ δὲ ὂν εἶναι καὶ τὸ μὴ ὂν μὴ εἶναι ἀληθές. Aristotle holds three views on truth: (1) the conformity of thought with reality; (2) a connexion between concepts (συμπλοκὴ νοημάτων) inside the judgement, *De an.* Γ 8. 432ᵃ11; (3) reality itself, *Met.* Θ 10. 1051ᵇ1.

p. 60. 4. It is an Aristotelian assumption that every logical concept has its counterpart in reality; thus the absence of a quality (privation, στέρησις) takes for Aristotle a positive meaning, and even of absolute privation, the non-existent, he says (*Met.* Γ 2. 1003ᵇ10) that it is something, namely the non-existent (see note 61. 7). The 'something' (τί, see note 3. 6) plays an important role in Stoicism, which distinguishes between meaning and existence: 'nothing' means something, but the 'something' it means does not exist. Averroës in his answer might have said that the impossible, like the non-existent, expresses a negation; neither the impossible nor the non-existent exists, and therefore they need no substratum, but the non-existence of the impossible does not imply the non-existence of the possible, and the problem Ghazali has touched upon does not concern the impossible only, the negation of the possible, but negation generally; however, he follows a more Aristotelian train of thought, and regards the privation of the possible as a reality.

p. 61. 1. Ghazali seems to hold that every concept has to be either necessary, impossible, or possible; modality, however, refers only to judgements. Ghazali's argument would have seemed more plausible, if he had given as an example that four *can* be divided by two, which is a purely rational judgement and does not refer to any definite time. Ghazali's argument may be an interpretation of the Stoic theory as, for example, expounded by Cicero (loc. cit.): 'visis non omnibus adiungebat [scilicet: Zeno] fidem, sed iis solum quae *propriam quandam* haberent declarationem earum rerum quae viderentur'. The apprehending presentation carries with itself its own evidence.

p. 61. 2. By the 'possible' as predicated of the recipient he means the at present existing and actualized matter which is changing, losing one attribute and taking the contrary; e.g. wine turning into vinegar. The opposite of this possible is the impossible, for the matter of the wine can never become non-existent. The opposite of the sweetness of the wine is the acidity of the vinegar, and this acidity is necessary because the wine, turning into vinegar, will necessarily become acid.

p. 61. 3. The sweetness (i.e. the potentiality to become acidity) loses its potentiality when the wine has become acid, i.e. the sweetness is not there any more (οὐκ ἐνυπάρχει, see *Phys. A* 8. 191ᵇ16).

p. 61. 4. It is the wine which is potentially vinegar, and which changes from potential vinegar into actual vinegar; in other words, becoming is not the change of a quality into another quality, of the sweetness into acidity; the substance, the substratum (the wine; the term 'substratum' is ambiguous, and I shall explain the difficulty below) becomes another substance through a change of quality. Something persists, says Aristotle, *Met. Λ* 2 ad init., but the opposite does not persist; there is, therefore, a third entity besides the opposites, namely matter, cf. *Phys. A* 7. 190ᵃ17.

p. 61. 5. So far as I know, this definition is not found in Aristotle in exactly this form, but it expresses his conception perfectly. Cf. such passages as *Met. N* 2. 1089ᵃ28: τὸ κατὰ δύναμιν (viz. μὴ ὄν) ἐκ τούτου ἡ γένεσίς ἐστιν, out of the possible (which is said not to be) generation follows, and *Met. Θ* 8. 1050ᵇ11: τὸ ἄρα δυνατὸν εἶναι ἐνδέχεται καὶ εἶναι καὶ μὴ εἶναι, that, then, which can possibly be can either be or not be.

p. 61. 6. The possible non-existent lies in the στέρησις of what may become; in our example, the sweetness is the στέρησις (i.e. it is the non-acidity) of the acidity. In this στέρησις, in this sweetness (the non-acidity), the acidity lies potentially hidden; this potency is a kind of intermediate between pure nothingness and full reality. It seems an astonishing and unbelievable paradox, Aristotle himself says (*Phys. A* 8. 191ᵇ16), that anything can become in this way out of the non-existent.

p. 61. 7. Indeed, the Muʿtazilite doctrine of the non-existent as a reality is based on Aristotle's doctrine of στέρησις as something positive (see also note 3. 6). There is an interesting parallel in early medieval Western philosophy: Fredegisus of Tours (an Englishman who was a pupil of Alcuin and who died in 819) says in his *Epistola de nihilo et tenebris* (ed. Migne, *Patr. L.* cv. 751): 'Omnis significatio est quod est. "Nihil" autem aliquid significat. Igitur "nihil" eius significatio est quid est, id est rei existentis.'

p. 62. 1. The actualized matter, wine *qua* wine, is in actuality; in the wine, however, there is an underlying substratum, matter, ὕλη, which is in potency. The last section of this passage is redundant and only repeats what I have tried to explain in notes 61. 2 to 61. 6.

p. 62. 2. The acidity of the vinegar is the outcome of the process of becoming; i.e. it belongs to the becoming in so far as it is actual, it exists in the product, whereas the non-acidity, the sweetness changing into it, has disappeared.

p. 62. 3. i.e. matter cannot be already actual, for becoming implies something that is not actual.

p. 62. 4. i.e. both Muʿtazilites and philosophers regard non-existence as something positive. The philosophers, however, believe that non-existence, which they call matter, never exists in reality without being connected with a form. The transition from blood to sperma and from sperma to the members of the embryo refers to Aristotle's theory, *De gen. an.* A 19. 726^{b}5, that sperma is concocted blood coming from all parts μόρια, اعضاء, of the animal and possessing potentially all the parts of the new animal.

p. 62. 5. i.e. it would be an independent reality, fully existent and actual in itself.

p. 62. 6. The whole of this passage is a faithful, although somewhat redundant, summary of Aristotle's theory of becoming, discussed in *Phys.* A 6–10. This theory is contradictory, for it is said that becoming is the transition of a στέρησις into a positive quality (e.g. non-acidity into acidity) and that in the στέρησις its opposite potentially lies, but it is also said, as I have explained in note 61. 4, that the sweetness, the στέρησις of acidity does *not* become acidity; it leaves the wine and is replaced by its opposite, the acidity, and therefore it is the substratum, the substance, the wine, which becomes acid, i.e. the potentiality lies in the wine, not in the sweetness. But even this latter thesis can only be maintained through an ambiguity in the term 'substratum' or 'substance'. For although the wine may be called a substance or substratum, according to Aristotle's definition (*Cat.* 5) that the substance is the individual, the real substratum of the whole process is not the wine but matter. For the wine is nothing but the combination of matter and form; when wine turns into vinegar some forms leave the substratum, matter, to be replaced by other forms; there is here no becoming, only a change of forms; the real substratum, unqualified matter, remains, and remains eternally. For matter is eternal, although according to Aristotle it is pure potentiality, and nothing potential, according to him, can be eternal, and in this eternal matter eternal forms alternatively appear and vanish eternally, for forms too are eternal. Eternal forms and eternal matter, indeed, are the basic principles of the whole system, and through the combination of these principles the transient world is said to arise. But how can such heterogeneous elements as matter and form combine; how can the transient individual arise out of the combination of these two eternal elements? Whence do these eternal forms come, and whither do they go? Concerning this last problem there are two attempts at solution: (1) the transcendent Middle Platonic and Neoplatonic solution that they lie eternally in the mind of a transcendent God; (2) the immanent Stoic solution that the individual forms (λόγοι) lie in germ (σπερματικῶς) hidden in the immanent divine logos which unfolds itself in the world fatally and inexorably. The theory of a germinal development, كمون, was known in Islam and is ascribed to an-Nazzam (cf. note 31. 1 and compare my *Epitome der Metaphysik des Averroes*, pp. 190–1).

NOTES

p. 62. 7. Although this is in verbal agreement with Avicenna it is scarcely true in fact, for according to the Muslim philosophers, who combine the Plotinian concept of the soul as a substance with the Aristotelian concept of the soul as a form, the human soul never subsists by itself; during life it is in need of the human body, and after death it is, in one way or another, part of the universal soul; see notes 15. 1 and 14. 4.

p. 62. 8. منطبع, 'impressed', is a translation of the Stoic term τυπούμενον or ἐνσφραγιζόμενον used of the presentation, φαντασία, as stamped on the material soul (see e.g. Sext. Emp. *Hyp. Pyrrh*. ii. 70; *Adv. log*. i. 228). The expressions τύπος and σφραγιζόμενοι are used earlier by Aristotle, *De memoria* 1. 450^{a}31–32; see also note 67. 1. That the soul is not impressed on the body is often maintained by Avicenna, e.g. *Book of Theorems and Notices*, ed. Forget, p. 219.

p. 63. 1. According to Aristotle the soul has its seat in warmth (θερμόν) or in spirit (πνεῦμα); see *De gen. an*. B 3. 736^{b}29, cf. note 64. 4.

p. 63. 2. i.e. becoming implies a relation to a pre-existent matter and to an agent, but the individual souls do not become out of anything, nor are they created (*ex nihilo*) by God. The mystery of the human personality, the uniqueness of my Ego, cannot be explained by science, which tries to rationalize events by seeking to find the underlying identities in the apparent changes. However much I may resemble my parents, however much the same universals may describe my physical and moral constitution, it is I, my unique Ego, *individuum ineffabile*, who becomes, lives, thinks, suffers, enjoys, and dies. Neither the traducianism of the rationalists, nor the creationism of the faithful, can explain the primary fact of my individual, personal existence.

p. 63. 3. i.e. God.

p. 63. 4. See note 14. 6.

p. 63. 5. Light, according to Plotinus (*Enn*. iv. 5. 7), is incorporeal; the image in the mirror is the act of the object reflected, and when the object disappears, the image vanishes; in the same way the individual soul reflects the light of the world-soul (cf. Leibniz's conception of the monad as 'un miroir vivant, représentatif de l'Univers selon son point de vue', *Œuvres*, Erdmann, p. 714). According to Aristotle, *Meteor*. Γ 2. 372^{a}33, there are in mirrors different possibilities of reflection, in some of which only shape is reflected, in others colour also.

p. 63. 6. 'Sound understanding', ὀρθὸς λόγος, see note 8. 3. Islam has no faith in the self-taught man (*autodidactus*): من لا معلم له الشيطان معلمه, 'Satan is the master of him who has no master', says an Arabic proverb.

p. 63. 7. This is an Arabic proverb. Maidani has it in this form: ان الجواد قد يعثر (Freytag, *Meid. Prov*. i, p. 11).

p. 64. 1. The distinction between knowing and the object known provides the conclusive argument against all subjectivism. If perception and thought had no object beyond themselves, we should dwell in timeless monads without windows or communication—timeless, for time would be subjective too. All knowledge is relational, related to an object of knowledge; if *percipere* and *cognoscere* were identical with their objects, there could be neither illusion nor falsehood, but everything would merely be. The Platonic Socrates in the *Theaetetus* realized this when he drew the consequence from Protagoras' doctrine (167 a): οὔτε γὰρ τὰ μὴ ὄντα δυνατὸν δοξάσαι οὔτε ἄλλα παρ' ἃ ἂν πάσχῃ, ταῦτα δὲ ἀεὶ ἀληθῆ, for no one can think anything but what he thinks, nor perceive anything but what he perceives, and this is always true. For all our thinking the existence of a unique, common, objective world is an unavoidable primary assumption. Cf. note 65. 3.

p. 64. 2. i.e. the Platonists and Neoplatonists.

p. 64. 3. Galen says, e.g. *Quod anim. mor. corp. temp. seq.* c. 3. 775 K., that if the soul is mortal (which seems problematic to Galen), all the forms and parts of the soul will have potentialities which foliow (διώκει, يتبع) the temperament (κρᾶσις, مزاج) of its matter.

p. 64. 4. 'The possibility prior to the becoming is relative to matter': this refers probably to Aristotle's theory that the seat of the soul is in warmth and spirit, by which he wishes to explain how the soul can be transferred through procreation from one being to another. The problem, however, is how and whence the new individual soul arises. This problem was not seen by Aristotle, for whom soul is a form, a universal, whereas Callias and Socrates are individuals only through their bodies; see notes 14. 4 and 67. 3.

p. 64. 5. According to Aristotle the soul is ἐντελέχεια ἡ πρώτη σώματος φυσικοῦ ὀργανικοῦ, the first entelechy of a natural, organic body ('organic', i.e. used as an instrument), *De an.* B i. 412^{b}5; the body is merely there to serve as an instrument for the soul, *De part. an.* A 1. 641^{a}29.

p. 64. 6. That they have objects seems in contradiction to Ghazali's theory, which appears to assert that concepts simply are. If they have objects, what, according to Ghazali, are these objects, and in what, according to Ghazali, does science consist?

p. 65. 1. Blackness and whiteness, black and white, however, are just as much universals as receptivity of colour.

p. 65. 2. i.e. if it is not impossible for other concepts to exist only in minds, not in the external world.

p. 65. 3. We have entered here upon the perennial problem of universals. Ghazali is justified in saying that one cannot assert the objectivity of necessity and possibility and deny the objectivity of universals. If we believe with the Aristotelians in the 'natures' of things, we have to admit the objectivity of universals, although we may be at a loss to explain the mode of their being and how these universals and 'natures' are related to the individuals. Ghazali's own nominalistic view is untenable; it is based on the common illusion of *representing* the spiritual, of regarding as representable what cannot be represented, and on the consequent representation, materialization, and localization of thought as imprints in the soul, as individual spiritual atoms *in* the mind. Material things, however, are subsistent by themselves—they merely *are*; but every perception, every thought, expresses a relation, and points beyond itself. We perceive things, we think about things, and every object of thought can become the object of thought for innumerable thinkers: the basic, unrepresentable fact of thought, inexplicable and indefinable—since it is assumed in all definition and explanation—, is that we can mean something objective, and that our meaning can be communicated to others and understood by them.

p. 65. 4. That knowledge is *not* knowledge of the universal concept is a view contrary to that of Aristotle, who says that knowledge is always of the universal, e.g. *Met. B* 6 ad fin. καθόλου ἡ ἐπιστήμη πάντων. This is the great and insoluble difficulty of his system, that for it all reality is individual, all knowledge universal. The second assertion, that the individuals are known in a universal way, γνωρίζονται τῷ καθόλου λόγῳ, agrees with Aristotle, *Met. Z* 10. 1036ª8.

p. 65. 5. i.e. although potentially things are universals, namely when they are known. This is, of course, a *petitio principii*, for the question is: How can, and why should, the mind think as a universal, what in reality is an individual?

p. 65. 6. The conception of the real as accidentally individual, essentially universal, is not found in Aristotle; it is not very clear what it means, and it seems rather a Platonizing conception of Aristotle. (It is true, of course, that according to Aristotle the individual consists of a universal form *plus* matter, but this rather adds to the difficulty, for how, out of these two heterogeneous and non-individual elements, can the individual arise?)

p. 66. 1. According to the Neoplatonic conception of the Muslim Aristotelians, universals, i.e. the ideas, exist permanently in the Mind of God.

p. 66. 2. e.g. blackness is impossible for a thing which eternally possesses the opposite of blackness, i.e. whiteness.

p. 67. 1. This sophistical argument seems to imply that words can mean only existents; now the impossible does not exist, and therefore the term 'impossible' cannot be applied to anything. The whole argument is a *reductio ad absurdum* of a materialistic and nominalistic conception of thought, of the conception that every thought is an individual imprint (τύπωσις) in the soul. This Stoic conception was definitely refuted by anticipation in Plato *Theaet.* 191 c sqq. (Plato already uses the terms ἀποτυποῦσθαι, *receive an impression*, and δακτυλίων σημεῖα, *seals of signet-rings*). The Muʿtazilites (and Aristotelians) affirm that, since 'non-existence' means something, the non-existent exists (in a way); Ghazali asserts that, since the non-existent does not exist, 'non-existence' does not mean anything. The difficulty was seen by Plato, who makes Socrates ask at *Theaet.* 189 a: 'Will not he who thinks of the non-existent (μὴ ὄν) think of nothing (οὐδέν)? And does he who thinks of nothing think at all?'

p. 67. 2. This seems in contradiction to Ghazali's own theory that there is no objective possibility.

p. 67. 3. See note 63. 2. For Aristotle the soul of the child is transmitted by the parents (both Aristotle and the Stoics are traducianists), or rather there is one soul, a universal in all human beings. The real crux of Platonism, Aristotelianism, and Neo-platonism is the relation of the universal to the individual.

p. 67. 4. A remote or secondary relation, since the soul in its essence or existence, at least according to the Neoplatonic commentators, is not dependent on the body, but is essentially a part of the World-Soul and comes from the outside into the body. It is not impressed on the body, but merely directs the body.

p. 67. 5. i.e. God, who can produce them *ex nihilo* by His will. Ghazali means that you might just as well say that the soul is potentially in God as that it is potentially in matter, since the soul is not extracted by God out of matter. The statue is not more potentially in the marble than in the sculptor, since the sculptor brings the form of the statue out of himself into the matter of the marble. And the relation of the soul to the body is still more 'remote' for the commentators than the relation of form to matter. For, says Plotinus (*Enn.* iv. 3. 20), the soul, which is not in the body as in a place, ἐν τόπῳ, or in a container, ἐν ἀγγείῳ, is not its form either, for the form which is involved in matter is not self-subsistent; if it is said that the soul is not engendered but self-subsistent, how can the self-subsistent soul be in the body?

p. 67. 6. See the Aristotelian definition of the soul quoted in note 64. 3.

p. 67. 7. The metaphor of the soul as a steersman or pilot is found in Plato, *Phaedr.* 247 c, where the rational part of the soul is called ψυχῆς κυβερνήτης (cf. Arist. *De an.* B 1. 413ᵃ9). At *Tim.* 41 e the demiurge is said to have placed the souls ὡς ἐς ὄχημα, as in a ship.

p. 68. 1. This refers to the Aristotelian doctrine of the triad which exists where there is motion, *Phys.* Θ 5. 256ᵇ13: the mover, the instrument of motion, τὸ ᾧ κινεῖ, and the object moved. The living being is a cause of motion, it moves itself: κινεῖται γὰρ τὸ ζῷον αὐτὸ ὑφ' αὑτοῦ, *Phys.* Θ 4. 254^{b}16, it is a mover and a thing moved. To set it in motion it needs an eternal mover which is not itself moved, for if everything in motion were moved, it would follow that whatever was capable of causing a change would be capable of suffering a change, *Phys.* Θ 5. 257^{a}15. I do not see how this theory settles the difficulty.

p. 68. 2. Averroës substitutes the word 'identical' for the word 'similar', which he used previously.

p. 68. 3. How could it be otherwise? Besides, according to Averroës, all judgements refer to something outside the soul.

p. 68. 4. This seems rather like the aporetic (ἀπορητική) or dubitative method of the Sceptics, see Sext. Emp. *Hyp. Pyrrh.* i. 3. 7.

p. 68. 5. The title given in the text is *The Foundation of Dogmatics*. There is no such work, although the second book of Ghazali's *Vivification of Theology* bears this name. Its third chapter contains a very short and popular summary of his *Golden Mean in Dogmatics* (written immediately after the present work) to which he himself refers the serious student. Probably through an error of the copyist the title of this book is given wrongly in the text, but Ghazali refers without doubt to his *The Golden Mean in Dogmatics* (which has been translated into Spanish by M. Asin Palacios, Madrid, 1924), in which he sets out to prove by reason the dogmas of religion according to the Ash'arites. In his introduction Ghazali says, for example, that theology, i.e. religion based on rational proof, is not incumbent on the faithful (and may even be dangerous for certain types of men), since Islam does not distinguish between faith based on (1) an act of faith and mere acceptance, on (2) tradition or authority, on (3) rational proof. The book has four parts: (i) God's existence and essence; (ii) the divine attributes and the properties of these attributes; (iii) the divine operations; (iv) demonstration of prophetic revelation. There is no full discussion in it of the problem of the temporal creation of the world, but he repeats in it some of the arguments given in the present book, e.g. the argument based on the revolutions of the different spheres.

p. 69. 1. Probably the correct title was not given in Averroës' copy of Ghazali's *Incoherence of the Philosophers*.

p. 69. 2. The same remark concerning the same book is made by Averroës in his *Theology and Philosophy*, ed. Mueller, p. 21. *The Niche for Lights* is a commentary, following the Neoplatonic mysticism of the Sufis, (1) on the verses of the Koran (Sur. xxiv. 35), which cry out for a mystical interpretation: 'Allah is the light of the heavens and of the earth. His light is like a niche wherein is a lamp, the lamp within a glass, the glass as if it were a glittering star. From a blessed tree it is lit, an olive-tree neither of the East, nor of the West, the oil whereof were well-nigh luminous, though no fire touched it. Light upon Light'; and (2) on the Tradition: 'Allah has seventy thousand veils of light and darkness; were He to withdraw this curtain, the splendour of His countenance would surely consume anyone who apprehended Him with his sight.' In this treatise Ghazali expresses his belief in God's absolute transcendence and utter ineffability, in a mediating principle between God and the world (see note 36. 3), and in mystical ecstasy.

p. 69. 3. i.e. as an ordered universe, κόσμος.

p. 70. 1. One would expect 'must conform to the possibility'; that it 'may or may not conform' is the theological view (see below, note 70. 4).

p. 70. 2. Abu Hudhail ibn al-Allaf of Basra, one of the earlier Mu'tazilites of the beginning of the ninth century, and a contemporary and adversary of an-Nazzam. He applied the theory that what has a first term must have a last term even to God's knowledge and power and, according to Ibn Hazm, op. cit. iv, pp. 192-3, he said that God, having arrived at the final term of His power, would not be any more able to create even an atom or to move a leaf or to resuscitate a dead mosquito.

p. 70. 3. Simultaneously, متلاحقا, ἅμα κατὰ χρόνον; successively متساوقا ἐφεξῆς; i.e. at any moment all the parts of the past are there in their totality.

p. 70. 4. According to the Koran, Sura xxxix. 67, on the Day of Judgement 'the whole earth shall be His handful and the heavens will be rolled up in His right hand'. That we can know only through the Divine Law that the world will end was held by certain Mu'tazilites. According to, for example, 'Abu Zaid al-Balkhi' (cf. above, note 10. 5), *The Book of Creation and History*, i, p. 125 (see also ii, p. 133), there is no rational proof of the annihilation of the world; the series of numbers needs a first term, but no final term, and a man may have eternal remorse, although his remorse must have a beginning. It became the orthodox view that the annihilation of the whole world (including the destruction of heaven and hell, which, however, will not happen, as is known by revelation) is possible, جائز, considered as something in God's power, see Baghdadi, op. cit., p. 319. Thomas Aquinas held that similarly the problem of the eternity of the world *a parte ante* cannot be solved by mere reason.

p. 70. 5. We have seen, however, p. 37, that Averroës himself regards God as not existing in eternal time, i.e. in an eternal sequence of past, present, and future, but in timeless eternity, i.e. αἰών, دهر. The conception of God as existing in timeless eternity severs all relation between God and the world; the conception of God as in eternal time implies in God an instability, a change, a passing, a past.

p. 70. 6. Averroës takes 'first term' in a chronological sense and 'the First' in the sense of the highest principle (in Arabic the expression 'the first' is used here in both cases).

p. 70. 7. Here 'first term' means God and 'its act' is the world, which according to the theologians has a beginning.

p. 71. 1. This is rather a difficult theory, for even if God and movement are eternal, the past states or acts of God and the past movements would seem to have ended.

p. 71. 2. It is not clear whether any definite philosopher is meant; of course many philosophers must have admitted that the past acts of the Eternal are past and ended. He may perhaps mean Plato, for whom the world has a beginning.

p. 71. 3. Incomprehensible غير معروف = غير معلوم, ἀκατάληπτος.

p. 71. 4. Compare Aristotle, *Phys. Δ* 12. 221ᵇ3: the eternal, τὰ ἀεὶ ὄντα, is not in time.

p. 71. 5. This, I believe, does not signify anything but the tautology that only the present or the present movement exists or takes place at present.

p. 72. 1. i.e. finite existence, since the infinite cannot be represented.

p. 72. 2. When the existence of a thing is perfect, i.e. when all the conditions of its existence are fulfilled, its action cannot be delayed.

p. 72. 3. *petitio principii*, مصادرة على المطلوب, ἅπτεσθαι τῆς ζητήσεως ἐξ ἀρχῆς.

p. 73. 1. Averroës wants to suggest that the philosophical view of an eternal creation is not in contradiction to the Koranic view and that the verb 'to produce', 'to cause to happen', which occurs in the Koran, Sura lxv. 1, does not necessarily imply a time-factor, and that therefore the Ash'arites gave a wrong interpretation of the true conception of the Koran. (The verb 'to produce', أحدث in Arabic is a causative form of the verb 'to become' which corresponds to the Greek γίγνεσθαι.)

p. 73. 2. Here he wants to suggest that the philosophical view is in fact the common view of Muslims, and that when they say that the world is not eternal, they really mean that the world has a cause, so that the difference is only verbal, لفظي, not factual, معنوي.

p. 73. 3. He is possibly alluding here to the Maturidites who—in opposition to the rival school of the Ash'arites—see, for example, Muhammad al-Murtada, *Commentary on Ghazali's Vivification of Theology*, ii, p. 8—regard God's attributes of action, صفات الفعل, and His creative production, تكوين, as coeternal with the attributes of His nature. Ibn Hazm, op. cit. iv, p. 212, speaks of even the Ash'arites as holding the heretical view that the world is eternal. For, according to him, the Ashʿarites affirm that God says eternally 'كن' 'let it be' to all things, whether they have been created or will be created, and this, according to Ibn Hazm, implies the eternity of the world. The theological distinctions are in any case very subtle.

p. 74. 1. This is an Aristotelian principle (*Top. A* 3) which Aristotle himself puts into practice.

p. 74. 2. This argument, as far as I know, is not found in those works of Galen which have come down to us, although there is a reference to our problem in *De plac. Hippocr. et Plat.*, Mueller, p. 783 (K. v, p. 760), where Galen says: It is not astonishing that more questions have not been settled in philosophy, since in philosophy one cannot base one's judgement on evident experience ($\pi\epsilon\hat{\iota}\rho\alpha$); and so some declare that the world has not come into being, others that it has. Most probably the argument was found in the fourth book of the lost work *De demonstratione*, $\Pi\epsilon\rho\hat{\iota}\ \dot{\alpha}\pi o\delta\epsilon\hat{\iota}\xi\epsilon\omega\varsigma$, في البرهان, a work of which, among other parts, the first half of Book IV was known to the Arabs. In this book Galen discussed those arguments which, since they are based on an imperfect experience, can only reach a certain degree of probability. Averroës in his commentary on *De caelo* (see I. Mueller, *Über Galens Werk vom wissenschaftlichen Beweis*, Abh. philos.-philolog. Kl. d. K. Bayr. Ak. d. W., Bd. xx) refers to Galen's arguments in *De demonstratione* about the eternity of the world and says: 'Galenus aestimat quod nullus potest scire mundum esse aeternum nisi per has propositiones quarum origo est a sensu et testimonio; dicit in suo libro quem composuit de eis quae credit, quod nihil certum habebat de mundo utrum esset novus aut antiquus, et manifestum est quod ipse non utitur in antiquitate mundi nisi talibus propositionibus ex verbis suis et in libro suo quem appellavit Demonstrationem.' Philoponus, *De aet. mundi* xviii, p. 599. 23 gives a long quotation out of Galen's *De demonstratione* in which Galen comes to the conclusion that 'ungenerated' implies 'indissoluble', but not the reverse, for what is indissoluble may be indissoluble not essentially but extrinsically, 'since it may have been provided with immortality', and Galen himself quotes *Tim.* 41 b, where the demiurge says to the gods he has created: 'since you are created, you are not altogether immortal and indissoluble, but you shall not be dissolved nor experience the fate of death'.

Galen's argument is directed against the Stoic syllogism to prove the corruptibility of the world (see Diog. Laert. *Vitae* vii. 141 and Ps.-Philo *De aetern. mundi* 124 (p. 110. 11 Reiter); the argument is found also in Philoponus, *De aet. mundi*, p. 502): 'That whose parts are corruptible is corruptible as a whole. Now the parts of the world are corruptible, and therefore the world is corruptible. Moreover, everything is corruptible, if it is capable of decay ($\dot{\epsilon}\pi\iota\delta\epsilon\kappa\tau\iota\kappa\dot{o}\nu\ \tau\hat{\eta}\varsigma\ \dot{\epsilon}\pi\hat{\iota}\ \tau\dot{o}\ \chi\epsilon\hat{\iota}\rho o\nu\ \mu\epsilon\tau\alpha\beta o\lambda\hat{\eta}\varsigma$).' The premiss of the Stoic argument seems to be assumed by Ghazali. The Ashʿarites accepted this Stoic argument, and say (see e.g. the Arabic text of our book, 466. 5): كل ما تحله الحوادث فهو محدث 'everything in which transient entities inhere is itself transient'. (This argument is refuted at length by Averroës, *Philosophy and Theology*, ed. Mueller, pp. 31 sqq.)

Galen's argument is based on *De caelo* A 3. 270^{b}11, where Aristotle says: the truth of the eternity of Heaven is clear from the evidence of the senses, at least so far as to warrant the assent of human faith, for we find in what has been handed down from generations no trace of a change in either the whole or the parts of the outermost heaven. According to Plato, *Tim.* 33 a, the world is ἀγήρων καὶ ἄνοσος, 'undecaying and free from sickness'.

That, if the heaven were destroyed, the sun, which according to the Stoics is a visible God, αἰσθητὸς θεός, would be destroyed, is argued by Ps.-Philo, op. cit. 46 (p. 87. 1 Reiter).

p. 74. 3. i.e. the ordinary hypothetical syllogism قياس شرطى متصل, συνημμένον ἀξίωμα, in opposition to the hypothetical disjunctive syllogism قياس شرطى منفصل, διεζευγμένον ἀξίωμα (for these terms and the ambiguity of the term διεζευγμένον ἀξίωμα see Galen, *Intr. dial.* 3, *Stoic. Vet. Fr.* ii. 71. 15).

p. 75. 1. That the transitory things of our sublunary world are of no significance in relation to the size of the universe is stated by Aristotle, *Met.* Γ 5. 1010^{a}28: ὁ γὰρ περὶ ἡμᾶς τοῦ αἰσθητοῦ τόπος ἐν φθορᾷ καὶ γενέσει διατελεῖ μόνος ὤν, ἀλλ' οὗτος οὐθὲν ὡς εἰπεῖν μόριον τοῦ παντός ἐστιν. Cf. *Meteor.* A 3. 339^{b}13–340^{a}18.

p. 75. 2. This all agrees with Aristotle, *De caelo* A 3. 270^{a}13–35; A 9. 278^{b}21.

p. 75. 3. In the *Posterior Analytics* Aristotle says (A 3) that everything cannot be proved, but there are immediately evident principles, ἀρχαὶ ἄμεσοι. These principles are of two classes, those common to all the sciences, and those proper to specific sciences, e.g. number and magnitude, *Anal. Post.* A 7 ad fin.

p. 75. 4. 'Abu Zaid al-Balkhi', op. cit. ii. 18, tells us that the generality of astronomers affirm that the sun is $166\frac{1}{32}$ times the size of the earth. Actually the surface of the sun exceeds that of the earth 11,900 times, while its volume is 1,306,000 times greater than that of the earth.

p. 77. 1. The difficulty mentioned in this section did not exist for the Greek philosophers, who admit neither a creation *ex nihilo* nor a destruction *in nihil*. Nobody is so naïve (εὐήθης)—says Ps.-Philo, op. cit. 5 (p. 74. 3. Reiter) as to ask whether the world can be absolutely annihilated, since absolute annihilation, ἡ ἐκ τοῦ ὄντος ἀναίρεσις, is a non-entity, ἀνύπαρκτον; the question is, rather, whether its order can be corrupted and dissolved; however, says Ps.-Philo 83 (p. 98. 16 Reiter) if there were, as the Stoics believe, a conflagration, ἐκπύρωσις, of the world, in what would God's activity, God's life, then consist, and would not His inactivity be in fact His death, since life is activity?

p. 77. 2. For temporal production implies annihilation.

p. 77. 3. For the performance of nothingness is doing nothing. The problem is a consequence of the failure to distinguish between the act and the end or intention of the act. It is another example of the identification of the process of the act and its end, mentioned in note 56. 1, which language itself does not always distinguish sharply: 'annihilation' can mean the act of annihilating or the result of this act. Non-existence, even my own non-existence, can be my intention, but my act of annihilating is something positive.

p. 78. 1. i.e. the theologians deny potential existence, they deny that there is a *tertium quid* between existence and non-existence, that there is a passage from the one to the other, i.e. becoming; they transfer the mystery of change to the agency of God, or rather, through the miraculous idea of creation they eliminate the idea of becoming: God said 'let it be' and the thing was, immediately, without any process.

p. 78. 2. i.e. either there is no agent or cause at all, or God's act must attach itself to the non-existent.

p. 78. 3. Contrary opposites (ἐναντία) that have middle terms can, according to Aristotle, only pass into each other through the middle terms; e.g. before arriving from white at black one has to pass grey (*Met.* 1. 7 and *Cat.* 10). The difficulty, however, of the problem of becoming lies precisely in the fact that there is no middle term between being and not-being; a thing either is or is not.

p. 78. 4. The simile is taken from Plato, *Rep.* vii. 514 sqq.: beings living in a cave and brought into light will, owing to the weakness of their eyes, believe that the shadows they formerly saw are truer than the objects which are now shown to them.

p. 78. 5. In this defence of the doctrine *rien ne se crée, rien ne se perd* there still is, besides the general problem of becoming, this difficulty: it may be said that I existed potentially before my actual existence, in so far as my existence was possible, but once gone I am gone for ever and have no potential existence any more, since 'potential' refers always to the future. Uptorn trees are not rooted again.

p. 78. 6. This is not quite correct; according to Aristotle neither matter nor form, both of which are eternal, is subsistent by itself. The only thing subsistent by itself is the combination of both, the individual, and this is transitory.

p. 79. 1. Since the theologians regard the act of God not as a process but as a static fact in which the intention, the result, and the act all coincide,

NOTES

they do not make the result of the annihilating act, namely the annihilation of the world, i.e. nothingness, directly dependent on Him, for this would mean that God intended and did nothing. The following rather naïve theories, which seem indeed to have been inspired by the criticism of the philosophers, have therefore the tendency to interpolate between God and the annihilation of the world a *tertium quid*, a quasi-positive entity which causes the annihilation. By doing this they of course introduce a process between this *tertium quid* and the annihilation.

p. 79. 2. This theory is ascribed by Baghdadi, op. cit., pp. 168 and 183, to Jubbai and his son Abu Hashim. Abu Hashim is regarded as the most important Muʿtazilite of his generation. According to this theory God cannot destroy an atom without involving the destruction of Heaven and Earth.

p. 79. 3. i.e. if extinction existed in a substratum, it could not be the opposite of existence, i.e. non-existence, since a non-existent existent is absurd.

p. 79. 4. According to Bagdhadi, op. cit., p. 319, most of the Karramites, however, regarded it as impossible for God to destroy the bodies in the Universe.

p. 80. 1. Condition, حال : for the theological sense see note 3. 6.

p. 80. 2. This is rather a strange conception. The Karramites assert that the act of God is an external relation and does not change the essence of the substratum, i.e. His essence, but inheres in the substratum. (A favourite example for both the philosophers and the theologians of an external relation is that of right and left; there is no difference in the objects themselves, whether I am at their right or their left, Aristotle argues, *De caelo* B 2. 285[a]1.) This is a contradiction, for if it inheres in the substrate, it is not merely an external relation. The obvious objection is that an act is not an external relation, since it assumes in the agent a change, a newness, like the change from whiteness to blackness. Averroës, however, moved perhaps by an *esprit de contradiction* against the Ashʿarites, takes just the opposite view, denying that an act does inhere and admitting that it is a purely external relation.

p. 80. 3. He evidently means temporal reality in the world, for there is a temporal reality in God, or in relation to God, produced by Him.

p. 80. 4. Since the temporal reality in God, or in relation to God, does not affect His essence.

p. 80. 5. This amounts to saying that an act is not an external relation, since it assumes in the agent a change, a newness.

p. 80. 6. اذا ابقى الموجود وقتا جاز ان يبقى وقتين, If the existent exists one instant, it is permissible that it should exist two instants, says Ibn

Hazm, op. cit. iv. 85, who also admits the logical possibility of an eternity *a parte post*.

p. 81. 1. We do not perceive identity, which is a rational concept. There is no place for identity (nor for similarity) in a nominalistic and sensationalistic system. Our judgement that we have an identical individual assumes (1) that there is an exterior world, (2) that every change is based on causation. Ghazali, who accepts the Ashʿarite principle that there is no natural causation, but that God is the only agent, has no right to assert the identity of individuals, since everything is continually changing and every change depends on a new creative act of God (besides, since hair grows, it is not unconditionally true that the hair on a man's head today is identical with the hair there was yesterday). In addition, we must distinguish between 'This white is the same as that white', which asserts an identity of universals, and 'This is the identical hair', which asserts the identity of an individual. Ibn Hazm, criticizing the Ashʿarites (v. 107), says there is no more extraordinary foolishness, لا عجب اعجب من حمق, than to say that the whiteness of snow, the blackness of tar, the greenness of grass are different now from what they were before.

p. 81. 2. Compare Aristotle's argument, *Met.* K 2. 1060ᵃ34: If there are perishable principles for perishable things, we need other perishable principles for them, and so shall have an infinite regress. The difficulty in an infinite regress exists for all relations. All duality implies infinity, since between any two terms there is a middle term, as the Eleatics saw. This had become a well-known argument with the Greek Sceptics and Neoplatonists and the Muslim theologians and Mystics for proving the subjectivity and unreality of relations. The question whether the creating act was different from, or identical with, the thing created was discussed in Islam. The opponents of their duality based themselves on the infinite regress this duality would involve (see Ibn Hazm, op. cit. v. 40). The Muʿtazilite Muʿammar was widely known in Islam for his acceptance of the infinity of relations (احوال). He regarded them, however, in the Stoic fashion as المعاني, τὰ λεκτά, something intermediate between being and not-being (see note 3. 6).

p. 81. 3. Flux, سيلان, τὸ ῥεῖν, cf. Aristotle, *De caelo* Γ 1. 298ᵇ29, πάντα γίγνεσθαι καὶ ῥεῖν ... ὅπερ ἐοίκασι βούλεσθαι λέγειν ἄλλοι τε πολλοὶ καὶ Ἡράκλειτος ὁ Ἐφέσιος. It is a curious fact that the two schools, the Heracliteans and the Megarians, who start from opposite premisses, the former that there is no being but only becoming, the latter that there is only being but no becoming, arrive at the same conclusion: that nothing is permanent. Both theories may be spoken of as theories of flux.

p. 81. 4. This is the theory of the famous Ashʿarite theologian Baqillani (end of the tenth century). Ibn Hazm, op. cit. iv. 222, gives a quotation from Baqillani's *Book about the Doctrines of the Qarmates*, where Baqillani says: 'Accidents cannot endure, and their annihilation is necessary in the second instant after their becoming, without an annihilating cause. The accidents annihilate the substances, since they annul the spatial relations and conditions without which the substances cannot exist.' Ibn Hazm adds that this implies the heretical doctrine that God is not the cause of their annihilation.

p. 82. 1. 'does not inhere in a substratum': i.e. the individual substance, e.g. this stone, according to the definition at the beginning of *Cat.* 5: οὐσία δέ ἐστιν . . . ἣ μήτε καθ' ὑποκειμένου τινὸς λέγεται μήτ' ἐν ὑποκειμένῳ τινί ἐστιν.

p. 82. 2. This is not quite correct; the individual substance is transient; what he means is that it does not become absolutely non-existent, since its matter and form are eternal.

p. 82. 3. This argument is based on Aristotle's argument against the Megarians, *Phys.* Z 10. 240^{b}17–30: a thing which is changing must be partially this and partially that, but in the indivisible instant there cannot be a change: it must be wholly this or that, wholly existent or wholly non-existent.

p. 82. 4. i.e. that the accidents should be made a condition for the persistence of the substance.

p. 83. 1. ἐγὼ δέ φημι, εἰ ἓν ἦν ὁ ἄνθρωπος οὐδέποτε ἂν ἤλγεεν· οὐδὲ γὰρ ἂν ἦν, ὑφ' ὅτου ἀλγήσειεν ἓν ἐών, I say: if man consisted of a unique substance, he would not suffer, for what would be for this simple existent the cause of his suffering? This sentence is a quotation from the second chapter of Ps.-Hippocrates Περὶ φύσιος ἀνθρώπου. In this little treatise, which starts by discussing the view that the human body consists of one unique substance, there is expounded the theory of the four bodily humours: the sanguine, the choleric, the phlegmatic, and the melancholic. Aristotle (*Hist. an.* Γ 3. 512^{b}12) gives a quotation from the second part of this work, which, however, he ascribes to Polybus. Galen, who regarded the book, or at least the first part of it, as genuine, wrote on it a still extant commentary which was in part translated and abbreviated by Hunain ibn Ishaq (see G. Bergsträsser, *H. ibn Ishaq und die Syr. und Arab. Galen-Übersetz.*, No. 102). The Arabic translation of *De natura hominis*, with Galen's commentary, is still extant in three copies, cf. H. Diels, *Handschriften der antiken Ärzte*, i, p. 101 and Aya Sofya 3632. This same quotation is found in Nemesius, *De natura hominis*, Migne, xl. 629.

p. 83. 2. See note 14. 6.

p. 83. 3. Ghazali's theory might be explained by saying that God wills the annihilation, and then the annihilation occurs. Of course the problem is: What is the relation between the object of His will and His will, in what does His act consist? But this relation is not more obscure for His annihilative than for His creative act, for when God wills 'let it be' and 'it is', why *is* it, why is *its being* the act of God? And since by God's power is meant the fact that He can do it, what does He do, besides willing it?

p. 84. 1. The same idea is very well expressed by 'Abu Zaid al-Balkhi', op. cit. ii. 135: 'If it is said that we cannot understand production out of nothing, for, for example, a ring must be made out of silver, it must be answered that the shape of the ring is something new which did not exist and its maker created it out of nothing. If the coming into existence of a new accident is possible, why not the coming into existence of a body out of nothing? The whole question is, do new things appear? well, we see them appear.'

p. 85. 1. The so-called answer of the philosophers is in fact a consequence of the Megarian theory, and Ghazali ought to agree with it. The Megarians are true to the principle that something either is or is not, *tertium non datur*; there is no becoming, since becoming is illogical, and there is no disappearing, which is just as irrational. At one time-atom there was black, at another time-atom there is white; nothing else can be affirmed. Reality is positive, but in becoming and disappearing a non-positive reality seems implied.

p. 85. 2. This answer comes dangerously near the Mu'tazilite proposition that the non-existent exists. It is true that the existence of white implies the non-existence of black; but the truth that the existence of white implies the non-existence of black does not imply the existence or reality of the non-existent black. What we consider as real is the event, the passage, the passing from black into white, the becoming of white, the disappearing of black, but this very passage is denied by the Megarians and Ash'arites. Becoming and disappearance imply time, whereas the laws of identity and contradiction do not imply time. For the laws of thought, as for the principles of mathematics, there is no such process as change; they are valid timelessly.

p. 85. 3. For even God cannot do the impossible; for another instance see, for example, my *Ep. d. Met. d. Av.*, p. 106. Aristotle himself at *Eth. Nic.* Z 2. 1139^{b}10 quotes Agathon's lines:

> For even God lacks this one thing alone,
> To make a deed that has been done, undone.

p. 86. 1. Cf. Aristotle, *Phys. A* 8. 191^{b}13 about στέρησις: nothing comes absolutely from not-being, οὐδὲν ἁπλῶς ἐκ μὴ ὄντος, but only from what is not-being *per accidens*, ἐκ μὴ ὄντος κατὰ συμβεβηκός.

p. 86. 2. Cf. Aristotle, *Phys. E* 6. 229^{b}25: ἁπλῶς ἐναντίον κίνησις κινήσει, ἀντίκειται δὲ καὶ ἠρεμία, στέρησις γάρ. Movements are contrary, when the one passes from this opposite to that, and the other from that to this.

p. 86. 3. i.e. not the opposition of two positives.

p. 86. 4. For the contradiction in Aristotle's theory of becoming and στέρησις see note 62. 6. The Aristotelians would answer that the movable potentially possesses movement and has therefore a positive στέρησις (of course when one speaks of a positive στέρησις the opposition of ἕξις and στέρησις, of possession and non-possession, is annulled).

p. 86. 5. The vitreous humour of the eye الرطوبة الجليدية من العين, τὸ ὑαλοειδὲς ὑγρὸν τοῦ ὀφθαλμοῦ. According to the Aristotelian theory of perception the sense-organ receives the form of the object perceived without its matter. According to De sensu 2. 438^{a}12 sqq. sight has its seat in the pupil, κόρη, which consists of water (cf. Hist. an. A 9. 491^{b}21: τὸ ὑγρὸν τοῦ ὀφθαλμοῦ ᾧ βλέπει, ἡ κόρη).

p. 86. 6. See note 58. 2.

p. 87. 1. There may be here an allusion to the title of one of Ghazali's books, *The Distinction between Faith and Heresy*.

p. 87. 2. Here, indeed, we have the fundamental difficulty of the Neoplatonic philosophy of emanation and of the theology of the Muslim philosophers. If we admit with the Eleatics that 'becoming' cannot mean anything but 'coming from', and that ultimate Reality is nothing but the absolute, simple monad, how then, from this highest principle, this absolutely simple monad, can the infinite variation of this world of multiple things derive, how can the One provide the plurality it does not possess itself (as Plotinus himself asks, Enn v. 3. 15: ἃ μὴ ἔχει πῶς παρέσχεν ;)? Plurality, if it exists, must consist of units, says Zeno the Eleatic (Diels, *Fr. d. Vors.*^{5} i, p. 252. 23 sqq.), and since there cannot be a plurality of units, there is only the One (cf. Arist. Met. B 4. 1001^{a}27). The Sceptics reaffirm this Eleatic doctrine, and Aenesidemus says (Sext. Emp. Adv. Phys. i. 220): οὔτε γὰρ τὸ ἓν γενέσθαι δύο δυνατόν ἐστι οὔτε τὰ δύο τρίτον ἀποτελεῖ, two cannot arise out of the one, nor can the two produce a third (Democritus too had said that one cannot come into existence from two nor two from one, a dictum which Aristotle approves, restricting it, however, to actual existence, see Met. Z 13. 1039^{a}9). The Muslim Aristotelians accept the principle that from the one only one can proceed, but use it illogically to explain the emanation of the many from the one according to the Neoplatonic principle of a gradual pluralization, laid down, for example, in Porphyry, *Sententiae* xi: αἱ ἀσώματοι ὑποστάσεις ὑποβαίνουσαι μὲν μερίζονται καὶ πληθύνονται . . . ὑπερβαίνουσαι δὲ ἑνίζονται (cf. Plotinus, Enn. v. 3. 16). Ghazali's criticism in the following chapter consists in showing the inconsistency of the philosophers in their surreptitiously introducing a plurality both into the One itself and into its emanation.

p. 88. 1. The conception of will as a passivity seems rather strange: one would imagine that it is the activity κατ' ἐξοχήν. However, according to Aristotle, the will is ultimately based on pleasure and pain (*De an.* B 2. 413^{b}23) and will is the sign (σημεῖον) of pains and pleasures (Arist. Rhet.

B 4. 1381ᵃ7). Sextus Empiricus says (*Adv. phys.* i. 146): 'Sensation is a kind of alteration. . . . If God, then, has a sensation, He is altered, if He is altered, He is capable of alteration and change . . . and if so, He is also perishable.'

p. 88. 2. i.e. will brings to perfection the qualities of the willer.

p. 89. 1. i.e. man is an agent and therefore a cause; the sun is a cause; therefore we may metaphorically (but not properly) call the sun an agent, the *tertium comparationis* between man and sun being that they are both causes.

p. 89. 2. In the proper sense.

p. 89. 3. There is some confusion in this paragraph. Ghazali reproaches the philosophers who, according to him, admit only a natural causal relation between God and the objects of His acts, with calling God an agent; only a voluntary agent is an agent according to him. At the same time he reproaches them with calling all natural causes agents. The consequence would seem to be that the philosophers do not distinguish between agent and cause. To ascribe an act to a non-living being would seem to Ghazali, to use a modern expression, a kind of animism or fetishism. Non-living beings do not act, according to him; between fire and burning there is only a constant time-sequence. This is also the theory of modern empiricists. However, for the modern empiricist, as well as for the Ashʿarite Ghazali, all causal relations (inclusive of voluntary acts) in the empirical world are reducible to a time-sequence. According to Hume, between my will and the movement of my arm there is no other relation than an empirically perceptible sequence in time, and the same is said by the Ashʿarites, who, as I shall show later, are dependent on Greek empiricism. (The Ashʿarites acknowledge one voluntary essential agent, God, who, however, is not of this world.) But why then speak of animism or fetishism, as the empiricist E. Mach does—e.g. *Die Mechanik*, p. 455—, or why this distinction between agent and cause which Ghazali establishes? Averroës is aware of the contradiction in Ghazali, and in the following passages he puts forward some forceful criticisms.

p. 89. 4. i.e. a voluntary act, like any potential act, is not inseparably conjoined with its agent, but heat cannot be separated from fire. This would imply, in contradiction to Aristotle's theory, a superiority of the potential to the actual; and besides, according to Aristotle, God's act is inseparable from Him—God is eternally in activity.

p. 90. 1. 'Separated' seems to be used equivocally; as used here of God it seems to have the meaning of transcendent.

p. 90. 2. Cf. below, notes 90. 4 and 90. 5.

p. 90. 3. For God's bounty as the motive of creation cf. Plato, *Tim.* 29 d, e and Plotinus, *Enn.* v. 4. 1.

p. 90. 4. This astonishing quotation—which as far as I know has never been discussed—is not found in any of the genuine or spurious works of Aristotle that have come to us. It seems a quotation from a Muslim religious writer rather than from a Greek philosopher. However, by creation *ex nihilo* is not meant here the orthodox conception of a temporal creation *ex nihilo*, but an eternal creation. An eternal creation, as I have tried to show, is a contradictory conception, and of course to regard such a creation as *ex nihilo* emphasizes the contradiction, since logically this can only mean that the creation was preceded by nothingness, although this is explicitly denied. This contradiction does not seem to have been felt by Averroës, but I do not think Aristotle can have expressed this contradiction so manifestly. On the other hand, it does not seem improbable to me that this quotation is in some way connected with Aristotle's dialogue *De philosophia*, the theology of which seems to have been, according to the Epicurean in Cicero's *De nat. deor.* i. 13. 33 (fr. 26 Rose), somewhat confused. In the dialogues Aristotle expresses himself in a more popular way and takes on the exposition of his own ideas (cf. Cicero, *Ad Att.* xiii. 19. 4). The passages of *De philosophia* quoted by Cicero (frr. 12, 22) show that Aristotle regarded the world as an eternal, divine work (*opus*); we find in *De philosophia* the proof for the existence of God, based on the degrees of being (fr. 16, from Simplicius, *De caelo* i. 9, p. 288. 28 Heiberg; this proof is developed by Cleanthes—see Sext. Emp. *Adv. phys.* i. 88–93—and is one of the proofs of Thomas Aquinas); the stars are regarded in this dialogue as having voluntary movements (fr. 24 from Cicero, *De nat. deor.* ii. 16. 44) and, according to a passage in Ps.-Philo, *De aetern. mundi* (fr. 18), Aristotle accused in it those who did not recognize the eternity of the world as guilty of a terrible atheism, δεινὴ ἀθεότης, since they compared the transitory works of man, χειρόκμητα, with such great visible gods, like the sun, the moon, and all the other divine stars.

p. 90. 5. Cf. Ps.-Aristotle, *De mundo* c. 6. 397^{b}9: God is the cause which holds the Universe together: ἡ τῶν ὅλων συνεκτικὴ αἰτία. No nature is sufficient by itself, so that it can be deprived of God's conserving power (οὐδεμία δὲ φύσις αὐτὴ καθ' ἑαυτήν ἐστιν αὐτάρκης ἐρημωθεῖσα τῆς ἐκ τούτου σωτηρίας 397^{b}15). Compare also Aristotle, *Met. Λ* 10 ad init.: order exists in the world as in an army, for the order of the army depends on the leader, whereas the leader does not depend on the army. See also Plotinus, *Enn.* iii. 2. 2 about the ἁρμονία and σύνταξις in the world. The ideal of ἁρμονία is originally Pythagorean. The term συνεκτικὴ αἰτία is of Stoic origin. According to Clement of Alexandria (*Stoic. Vet. Fr.* ii. 121. 25) a synectic cause is one in whose presence the effect remains, while on its being removed the effect is removed. See also note 137. 3 in my *Ep. d. Met. d. Av.*

p. 90. 6. i.e. the composition of matter and form is the *condicio sine qua non* of all individual existence.

p. 91. 1. In the expression 'living being-man' there is a redundancy, because in the definition of man 'living being' is included. For Aristotle there is a difficulty in such expressions as 'snubness ($\sigma\iota\mu\acute{o}\tau\eta s$) of the nose' which seem redundant, 'for snubness is only found in a nose, so that we must include in its definition the nose, since what is snub is a concave nose' (Met. K 7. 1064ᵃ23, cf. Z 5.1030ᵇ17).

p. 91. 2. In Avicenna's system there is a tripartite division of reality: the absolute necessary (or necessary by itself), i.e. God; the hypothetical necessary (or necessary through another), i.e. heaven, the absolute possible, i.e. matter. This division conforms to Aristotle's of the unmoved mover, i.e. the first, immaterial, mover; the moved and also moving, i.e. heaven; the moved but non-moving, i.e. matter (Met. Λ 7. 1072ᵃ24, Phys. Θ 5. 256ᵇ20; De an. Γ 10. 433ᵇ13). For Aristotle all reality is in the end based on the actuality of an eternal prime mover, existing of necessity: $\dot{\epsilon}\xi$ $\dot{a}\nu\acute{a}\gamma\kappa\eta s$ $\ddot{a}\rho a$ $\dot{\epsilon}\sigma\tau\grave{\iota}\nu$ $\ddot{o}\nu$ (Met. Λ 7. 1072ᵇ10). Cf. notes 164 .4 and 164. 5.

p. 91. 3. I suspect that the meaning of this somewhat obscure sentence is: if you mean by 'agent' a creator who gives existence, perhaps the world can be explained without such an eternal creator; only an eternal prime mover is necessary which brings out, by its setting in motion, potency into act. If this interpretation is correct, Averroës, in order to contradict Avicenna's theory of an eternal creation, which is, in fact, also his own, returns here to a strictly Aristotelian point of view.

p. 92. 1. The natural faculties of the living body are treated by Galen in a special work, *De facultatibus naturalibus*, in which he regards the three biological faculties of genesis, growth, and nutrition through which the animals are directed ($\delta\iota o\iota\kappa\epsilon\hat{\iota}\sigma\theta a\iota$) as acts ($\ddot{\epsilon}\rho\gamma a$) of nature, not of the soul. The animal has the faculty of nutrition to maintain itself as long as possible, $\ddot{o}\pi\omega s$ $\ddot{\epsilon}\omega s$ $\pi\lambda\epsilon\acute{\iota}\sigma\tau o\upsilon$ $\delta\iota a\phi\upsilon\lambda a\chi\theta\hat{\eta}$ (*De fac. nat.* i. 9).

p. 93. 1. Koran xviii. 76.

p. 94. 1. i.e. fire always gives heat, but the voluntary agent has a choice of opposites: e.g. Aristotle, Met. Θ 2. 1046ᵇ4.

p. 94. 2. i.e. since, according to the Ash'arites, God creates our acts in us, the action of the human will must, according to them, be an illusion; how can we therefore know that there is such a thing as voluntary action in the Divine World? (Compare note 89. 3.)

p. 95. 1. The first mover in the example given above would be the man who threw the other into the fire.

p. 95. 2. For this type of fallacy, $\tau\grave{o}$ $\dot{a}\pi\lambda\hat{\omega}s$ $\ddot{\eta}$ $\mu\grave{\eta}$ $\dot{a}\pi\lambda\hat{\omega}s$, see Aristotle, *De soph. elench.* 25.

p. 97. 1. For this argument, which is the logical outcome of the theory that the world is eternally existent, i.e. eternally in act, although it has a

NOTES

cause, compare Avicenna, *Salvation*, p. 346, where he defends the thesis that it is the existence, not the non-existence of the effect which is related to the agent: العدم للمفعول ليس من الفاعل بل الوجود (see also op. cit., p. 356 and Avicenna, *The Recovery, Met.* vi 1, p. 523, ed. Teheran, 1885). It is a significant fact, as showing that this argument destroys the idea of causation, that it forms part of the sceptical refutation of the concept of cause in general. Sextus Empiricus, having asserted (*Adv. phys.* i. 233) that the simultaneous cannot be the cause of the simultaneous, since so far as their existence is concerned both are equivalent, denies that the cause can be prior to the effect, since the effect does not yet exist and the cause cannot be related to something non-existent (cf. also Diog. Laert. ix. 98).

p. 97. 2. i.e. according to Averroës Avicenna neglects potential existence.

p. 98. 1. 'Bringing into existence'; here, of course, the intrinsic contradiction lies in that it brings into existence what already exists from eternity.

p. 98. 2. Averroës fails to solve the difficulty. The philosophical proof of the eternity of the world is, as we have seen, based on the argument that, if the world were in a state of potentiality, a new cause would be necessary to actualize it. Averroës' solution would therefore imply a continual change in the agent. Aristotle himself says, *Met.* Θ 8. 1050^{b}20, that there is no potentiality in the eternally moved (i.e. heaven), except in the matter of 'whence' and 'whither'. For the whole problem compare note 11. 1.

p. 98. 3. Aristotle himself distinguishes at *Met.* Θ 8. 1050^{a}30 between actuality in the product and in the agent. Where the product is something different from the action, the actuality is in the product, e.g. the act of building in the thing that is being built, but where there is no product besides the action, the actuality exists in the agents themselves, e.g. the act of seeing in the man who sees. This distinction rests on the ambiguity of the term 'actuality' (ἐνέργεια) which can mean both 'reality' and 'action'.

p. 98. 4. 'Cannot become an effect'; the Arabic is ambiguous and may also be translated 'can be an effect'. This ambiguity conceals the difficulty. An existent can be an effect, when by 'effect' is understood the result, not the process of becoming; but an existent cannot become an effect, i.e. it can no longer become what it is already.

p. 99. 1. This section refers to Avicenna's theory in *The Recovery, Met.* vi. 2, p. 525, where he defends the theory of the simultaneity of cause and effect, ان كل علة فهى مع معلولها, against the argument of the theologians that, for example, the building remains when the builder has disappeared. Of course, according to this conception of causation God cannot be regarded any longer as a creator, nor even as a cause of change, as a prime mover. The relation between God and the world is here conceived as static: God is merely ἡ τῶν ὅλων συνεκτικὴ αἰτία, the power which holds the universe together, as it is expressed in Ps.-Aristotle, *De mundo* 6. 397^{b}9 (see note 90. 5).

p. 99. 2. For this section compare the distinction made by Aristotle in the passage quoted in note 98. 3. Averroës means that there cannot be, for example, a thought (or thinking, for the Aristotelian philosophy does not usually distinguish between these two) without a thinker, for a thought as an effect consists in its relation to a thinker and where there is no thinker there cannot be a thought. But the building can exist when the builder exists no more, since its relation as an effect is not essential to it and it has an existence and a substance or matter of its own. Here we have one of those naturalistic conceptions in Averroës to which I referred in note 31. 1. It is directly opposite to the Neoplatonic idea of the world as an eternal emanation from God, and even to the conception of God as the αἰτία συνεκτική, the binding element without which the world would disintegrate. As regards the real problem, Averroës is not aware of the ambiguity of the term 'effect'. If by 'effect' is meant the process of change, it is true that *causa cessante cessat effectus*; if by 'effect' is meant the result of the process, the effect remains when the cause has ceased to act (we saw in note 56. 1 that the Aristotelian philosophy does not distinguish consistently between the process, ἐνέργεια, and the result, ἐντελέχεια).

p. 99. 3. The thoughts of the celestial bodies are, as pure ideas, reality itself, and have no other existence than as ideas, whereas the thoughts of human beings are, according to the Aristotelian psychology (*De an. Γ* 4), forms abstracted from the matters in which they exist in reality.

p. 100. 1. Aulus Gellius (*Noct. Att.* vii. 13) says that his master, the Platonist Taurus, used to discuss the problem whether—since a man is either dead or alive—he dies when he is alive or when he is dead. The same question is posed by St. Augustine, *De civ. dei* xiii. 11 (see also Sext. Emp. *Hyp. pyrrh.* iii. 111 and *Adv. Math.* i. 269 and ii. 346). There are three answers given to this question: (1) The Platonic answer (*Parmenides* 156 d, e), given by Taurus and St. Augustine, that time is discontinuous and that there is an intermediary between life and death, a timeless passage in the instant, in which a man is neither alive nor dead. (2) The Megarian answer, that time is discontinuous and that there is no passage—a man is either alive or dead, but does not die. (3) The Aristotelian answer, that time is continuous and that there is a process in time during which a man is neither alive nor dead, but dies. One would have expected Ghazali to give the Megarian answer, since according to his Ash'arite conception there is no process in nature, but every change is immediately the effect of God's creative act. But the fear of attaching God's will to the non-existent makes him choose the Aristotelian solution (according to this conception, however, dying is not an existent, although neither is it a non-existent). Ghazali does not realize that voluntary action is always related to the non-existent: in the realm of physics only the actually existing exercises an influence, but in the realm of the soul it is the hope and fear of a not yet existing future—

hope and fear which may even be based on an illusion—that determine its actions. Throughout this passage what is meant by 'effect' is not the result of the process but the process, the passing itself which is caused by the agent; the result is regarded as the consequence of the process, while the initial non-existence of the result is regarded as a necessary condition for causal action.

p. 100. 2. According to the definition that wind is a movement of air, ὁ ἄνεμος κίνησις ἀέρος Aristotle, Meteor. A 13. 349ᵃ19. The comparison is, of course, lame, for without movement the air remains, whereas, according to this passage, the world, deprived of movement, becomes non-existent.

p. 100. 3. e.g. thunder (βροντή, see Meteor. Γ 1) and lightning (ἀστραπή, see Meteor. B 9).

p. 100. 4. It is movement which is eternally 'in becoming'; here, however, Averroës identifies the world with movement, and regards the world as eternally becoming.

p. 101. 1. According to Cat. 8 there are four classes of quality: disposition, habitus, passive quality, and shape (figure and form).

p. 101. 2. The difference between Avicenna and Averroës, according to his opinion in this section, is very slight, if indeed there is any difference at all. Avicenna says, as does Averroës in many places, that without God's sustaining power the world would become non-existent. Averroës affirms here that, without God as a moving cause and the form bestowed by Him upon the world the world could no longer exist. Averroës seems here to regard the world as having its matter by itself, but as matter cannot exist without form the existence of the world depends entirely on God.

p. 101. 3. He seems to mean that if the water moved later than the hand, the water, when the hand moved, would have first to move out of the hand and then detach itself and start its own movement.

p. 101. 4. This is, of course, a *petitio principii*: the effect cannot be prior to the cause, because in that case it could not be an effect.

p. 101. 5. 'The stable existent' and 'that which exists without moving or resting by nature' i.e. the immaterial Intellects. They stand in another relation to God than the moving world: a timeless relation.

p. 101. 6. i.e. if something happens to it that impedes its action.

p. 102. 1. i.e. action implies change.

p. 102. 2. Ghazali, as his example shows, is here expressing a correct idea wrongly. What he really wants to say is that the causal relation implies time and change, but that the logical relation of ground and consequent is timeless; however, through the ambiguity of language which uses the term سبب for both ground and cause, he is only dimly aware of this fact, and tends

—as his expression shows—to regard the logical relation as also an ontological one (I might have translated, instead of 'cause', 'ground', but the next sentence shows clearly that he confuses ground and cause; of course what we call 'cause' is regarded in the Aristotelian philosophy as only one—the agent or efficient cause—amongst several causes, and in the Aristotelian philosophy there is no consistent distinction between the logical and the ontological).

p. 102. 3. He ought to have said: the consequence of a fact is not the effect of this fact, except metaphorically (the ontological term 'effect' has been substituted for the logical term 'consequence').

p. 102. 4. This sentence invalidates Ghazali's whole argument, according to which God is not only an agent but the sole agent, and stands in flagrant contradiction to what follows. Here, however, it is not the Ash'arite theologian Ghazali who speaks, but Ghazali the mystic, for whom every expression relating to God is but a symbol: 'Alles Vergängliche ist nur ein Gleichnis'.

p. 102. 5. i.e. it is a change; this is in fact the Aristotelian conception of God: an eternal mover.

p. 102. 6. This of course reduces all life to a puppet-show. But compare Sebastian Franck, *Paradoxon*, 264–8: 'Der Vogel singt und fliegt eigentlich nicht, sondern wird gesungen und in den Lüften dahingetragen, Gott ist es, der in ihm singt, lebt, webt und fliegt. Alle Kreaturen tun nur, was Gott will. Diesen Unterschied hat es aber mit dem Menschen, diesem hat er freien Willen gegeben und will ihn mit diesem führen und ziehen.'

p. 103. 1. i.e. that cause and effect are both existents of the same order, and that the relation of cause and effect does not imply an act of God.

p. 103. 2. This refers to Aristotle, *Met.* Λ 3. 1070ᵃ21: τὰ μὲν οὖν κινοῦντα αἴτια ὡς προγεγενημένα ὄντα, τὰ δ' ὡς ὁ λόγος ἅμα, the moving cause precedes, but the formal cause is simultaneous. The father, for example, precedes the son as his efficient cause. Averroës means that God as an efficient cause acts eternally, although this eternal action is not implied in the idea of an efficient cause.

p. 103. 3. e.g. according to Simplicius, Aristotle and Plato agree about the problem of creation: Aristotle only denies the coming into existence of the world in time from not-being into being (*Comm. in libr. De Caelo*, p. 103. 4–6). Simplicius says—*In Phys. libr.* 1363. 8–12—that his master Ammonius wrote a special book with many arguments, πίστεις, to show that according to Aristotle God is also the efficient cause (ποιητικὸν αἴτιον) of the Universe. This book was known to the Arabs, and is mentioned in the *Fihrist*, p. 253, under the title شرح مذاهب ارسطاطاليس فى الصانع, *Explanation of Aristotle's theories about the Creator*.

p. 103. 4. 'Has come to be', i.e. implies a change. All this is to some extent sophistical. It is true, of course, that movement implies a change, but the movement of the world is eternal and uniform and this uniformity does not change (compare note 11. 1). Throughout this passage Averroës identifies mover and creator.

p. 103. 5. According to Aristotle, however, matter and form, the constituents of the world, are eternal.

p. 104. 1. For this principle, *ex uno non fit nisi unum*, as it is expressed by the Schoolmen; see note 87. 2.

p. 104. 2. Here Averroës does not seem to acknowledge this principle. It is, however, acknowledged by him, e.g. in his *Epitome of Metaphysics* (see my translation, p. 135 and note 135. 1). The only criticism of this principle he allows himself is that, following Avicenna—*The Recovery*, *Met.* v. 6—he asserts that the principle cannot be reversed, i.e. it is true that from duality only duality can proceed, but it is not true that duality can only proceed from duality.

p. 104. 3. This comparison with the carpenter and his instruments, the axe and the saw, is found in Farabi, *The Ideal State* (Dieterici, p. 16. 17).

p. 104. 4. There is a slight confusion in this paragraph. He wants to reproduce the thesis of Farabi and Avicenna that from the One a plurality can only proceed through mediation (see e.g. Avicenna, *The Recovery*, *Met.* v. 6, where he tries to prove that there cannot be any plurality or matter in the First, and Farabi, loc. cit.), but in fact he reproduces the thesis that no plurality whatever can proceed from the One, even through mediation. Sextus Empiricus (*Adv. phys.* i. 244) says that it would be absurd to say that the cause of the syllable *di* could be only the *d* without the *i*, and he goes on to argue (247) that the plurality of the effect cannot be explained by one unique power in the cause, since the sun dries mud but melts wax, whitens clothes but blackens our faces, an example which Ghazali reproduces here (cf. also p. 321 text).

p. 105. 1. i.e. somewhere unity and plurality will have to meet.

p. 105. 2. i.e. *ex uno unum* is true, but referring to God it has only a symbolic meaning, just as will, when ascribed to God, is attributed to Him only by analogy with our human will. Of course this amounts in fact to a denial of the principle.

p. 106. 1. That the series of final, formal, and efficient causes ends in a supreme cause is proved by Aristotle, *Met.* α 2. For God as pure self-conscious thought, see *Met.* Λ 9.

p. 106. 2. See note 104. 2.

p. 106. 3. This refers to the passages in Aristotle, *Met.* A 4. 985^{a}2, where Aristotle discusses the theory of Empedocles that love is the cause of good things and strife of bad, and *Met. Λ* 10. 1075ᵃ25 sqq., where he shows the impossible or paradoxical consequences (ἀδύνατα ἢ ἄτοπα) of those who 'make all things out of opposites', and where, 1075ᵇ1, Empedocles' theory is discussed.

p. 106. 4. Both these comparisons are based on Aristotle, *Met. Λ* 10, where the order of the world is compared to the order of an army through its leader (see note 90. 5) and to the order in a state through its own ruler. This comparison of the world to a state—which is developed in Ps.-Aristotle, *De mundo*—is very frequent in later Greek–Roman philosophy and is found, for example, in Philo, Epictetus, Sextus Empiricus, Plotinus, Cicero, Seneca, Marcus Aurelius.

p. 106. 5. Koran xxi. 22. Even in the Koran a feeble echo is sometimes heard of the all-pervading voice of Greek philosophy. Here we have a vague reminiscence of the Greek (Heraclitean, Pythagorean, Aristotelian, Stoic, Neoplatonic) conception that a unity is needed to prevent the disintegration of opposite principles. That there cannot be two hostile Gods is stated by Plato, *Plt.* 269 e.

p. 106. 6. In an accidental way, κατὰ παρακολούθησιν, as the Stoic term is, i.e. as an accessory phenomenon, not intended but unavoidable. This is one of the principles of the Platonic–Stoic theodicy. The most complete exposition of these principles is found in Plotinus, *Enn.* iii. 2.

p. 106. 7. This is Stoic: the bad happens not uselessly (οὐκ ἀχρήστως) but with respect to the administration (οἰκονομία) of the whole, as in states (cf. Plutarch, *De Stoic. repugn.* 35).

p. 106. 8. According to the optimistic Aristotelian principle (*De gen. et corr. B* 10. 336ᵇ28: βέλτιον τὸ εἶναι ἢ τὸ μὴ εἶναι) that existence is better than non-existence.

p. 107. 1. Cf. Sext. Emp., *Adv. phys.* i. 6: Anaxagoras says, 'All things were together and Intellect came and ordered them'; he assumed that Intellect, which according to him is God, is the efficient cause, ἀρχὴ δραστήριος, and the mixture, πολυμιγία, of the homoeomeries, the material principle.

p. 107. 2. Cf. note 36. 3. It is a pity that Averroës does not tell us whom he intends by those who introduce plurality through instruments. I presume that the difference here between mediators and instruments is that the former are regarded as living beings—e.g. the created gods who are not essentially immortal, *Tim.* 41 a–d, and the eternal movers which, according to the Muhammadan commentators, emanate from the First—the latter not. In that case the instrument is τὸ ὑφ' οὗ, that by which things come to be, which is, according to Aristotle, *Met. Z* 7. 1032ᵃ24, their nature, their form.

p. 107. 3. About Averroës' contemporaries little is known. However, at the court of the Almohad Caliph Abu Ya'qub, the patron of Averroës, who favoured the arts and philosophy, who collected books from all parts, and who sought the company of the learned, there must have been a great interest in philosophical speculation. One of his favourites, his chief physician Ibn Tufail, in his well-known work *Hayy ibn Yaqzan*, although admitting the eternity of the world and its eternal emanation from God, does not treat the question which occupies us here, i.e. how this emanation takes place.

p. 107. 4. Averroës here denies explicitly a gradual emanation from God, but by making the immaterial principles ascend to God and form a causal series his theory is identical with the theory he wants to refute and which, indeed, he himself holds in his *Epitome of Metaphysics*. As a matter of fact the idea of a gradual emanation is the basic idea of Arabian Aristotelianism, and cannot be eliminated without destroying the system.

p. 107. 5. The forms in the four elements are the first forms that enter into, or are in, prime matter, matter not yet qualified.

p. 107. 6. This passage is contradictory. The problem is: Do the forms and the matters all emanate from God, or have some, and especially primary matter, an independent existence previously? Averroës affirms both at the same time. The problem is a crucial point even for the Aristotelian philosophy. How, in a monistic system in which everything derives from one supreme principle, can the perishable, the temporal, the finite, derive from the imperishable, the eternal, the infinite? Aristotle saw the difficulty clearly, when he discussed at *Met. Γ* 4. 1000ᵃ5 the *aporia* (problem) whether the principles for the eternal and the perishable can be the same or must be different (cf. note 36. 3, and my *Epitome*, p. xx).

p. 108. 1. It is, however, Averroës's own theory in his *Epitome of Metaphysics* (see my translation, pp. 131–2).

p. 108. 2. ὅλως δὲ ὁ νοῦς ἐστὶν ὁ κατ' ἐνέργειαν τὰ πράγματα ... (Aristotle, *De an. Γ* 6. 431ᵇ16), Intellect therefore cannot be the cause of any duality (for the problem of the unity in the νοῦς according to Aristotle see my *Epitome*, notes 47. 6 and 124. 1). According to Plotinus, however, Intellect implies a duality, for self-consciousness, as the word συν-αίσθησις indicates, implies a duality and the First is beyond Intellect (*Enn.* v. 3. 13). For the Arabic Aristotelians, who combine Aristotelian elements with others from Neoplatonism, the First, God, is a self-conscious Unit from whom the First Intellect, νοῦς, emanates.

p. 108. 3. i.e. for the agent in the empirical world *ex uno unum* is valid, i.e. each agent has its specific act (fire cannot but burn), but the divine agent is an agent *sui generis*. This, however, does not seem to be the opinion of Aristotle, who affirms at *Met. Λ* 8. 1073ᵃ28 that a single movement can be performed only by a single, eternal mover (τὴν μίαν κίνησιν ὑφ' ἑνός).

p. 108. 4. i.e. the active Intellect; the connexion with the preceding sentence is not very clear; it would almost seem that Averroës identifies God here with the active Intellect; this is, as a matter of fact, Alexander of Aphrodisias' conception (*De an.* 80. 16–92. 11; *Mantissa* 106. 19–113. 24), which is not accepted by Averroës.

p. 108. 5. This is not exact; see note 2. 8. The passive Intellect is the same as the potential or material Intellect.

p. 108. 6. Compare Plotinus, *Enn.* vi. 5. 1: τὸ ἓν καὶ ταὐτὸν ἀριθμῷ πανταχοῦ ἅμα ὅλον εἶναι κοινὴ μέν τις ἔννοιά φησιν . . ., that the identical one is wholly everywhere is a common human notion; instinctively we declare that the God who lives in us all is one and identical.

p. 108. 7. The idea (which became one of the principles of Neoplatonism —see e.g. Proclus, *Inst. Theol.*, prop. 7) that the cause possesses in the fullest measure that which it communicates to others, is, with this example taken from warmth, found in Aristotle's *Metaphysics* (α 1. 993^{b}24—ascribed in the ancient world to Pasicles): ἕκαστον δὲ μάλιστα αὐτὸ τῶν ἄλλων καθ' ὃ καὶ τοῖς ἄλλοις ὑπάρχει τὸ συνώνυμον, οἷον τὸ πῦρ θερμότατον.

p. 109. 1. This sentence shows up the *petitio principii* in the whole argument: 'since they are many'; but the problem is precisely, How can there be a many—how can the many proceed from the one?

p. 109. 2. i.e. the matter of the sublunary world.

p. 109. 3. The term 'First Intellect' is confusing. The 'First Intellect' corresponds to the νοῦς of the Neoplatonic system, according to which the absolute First, the Monad, does not think. But according to the Arabic philosophers God, the First, is Himself intellect—a theory found as early as Simplicius, *Comm. in Enchir. Epict.* c. 38, who asserts that the highest principle, the ἀρχὴ ἀρχῶν, the God of Gods, possesses the highest γνῶσις.

p. 109. 4. i.e. the sphere surrounding the world assumed by Ptolemy to explain the precession of the equinoxes (see my *Ep. d. Met. d. Av.*, note 112. 6).

p. 110. 1. i.e. these intellects are of a gradually diminishing unification and dignity. According to Proclus, *Inst. Theol.*, prop. 95, the more unified a power, the more capable it is of infinitude. πᾶσα δύναμις, ἑνικωτέρα οὖσα, τῆς πληθυνομένης ἀπειροτέρα.

p. 110. 2. For the degree of nobility compare Proclus, *Inst. Theol.*, prop. 129: All divine bodies are divine through the influence of a divine soul, all divine souls through a divine intellect, and all divine intellects through participation in a divine monad.

p. 110. 3. Or from a superior intellect, for this process repeats itself eight times, since there are nine spheres.

p. 110. 4. This sentence invalidates the whole theory; there is an admission here that there is something in the effect which is not found in the cause, that although the Monad is the ultimate Source of everything, the effect cannot be wholly deduced from the cause. The same contradiction is found in Proclus, who, notwithstanding his theory of gradual emanation, admits αὐθυπόστατα, self-subsistent entities (*Inst. Theol.*, prop. 40). Further, Aristotle's monism of a First Mover or a First Cause is contradicted by his pluralism, by his acceptance (*Met. Λ* 8. 1073^{a}33) of a number of unmoved movers for the planets.

p. 110. 5. This section contains a succinct exposition of the ingenious theory of emanation, as it is found amongst the Arabic philosophers (e.g. in Avicenna, *Recovery of the Soul, Met.* ix. 6 and *Salvation*, pp. 448 sqq., and especially p. 455; Farabi, *The Ideal State*, p. 19; and also in Averroës in his *Ep. d. Met. d. Av.*—see my translation, p. 131 —who seems there to accept the general principles of the theory he denies here). This theory combines Aristotle's astronomical theory with the Neoplatonic theory of emanation, and introduces into the Aristotelian framework Proclus' conception of the triadic process of emanation, μένειν, προιέναι, ἐπιστρέφειν (*Inst. Theol.*, prop. 35).

Although this theory is by no means consonant with the general naturalistic trend of Aristotle's system, there are two aspects of his philosophy in which it may be defended or from which it can be deduced. (1) In the closing chapters of his theology (*Met. Λ*) God is much more than a mere Prime Mover: the world hangs on God (ἤρτηται, 1072^{b}14), it is God who gives unity and order to the world, which without God would disintegrate and become non-existent. (2) Aristotle's idea of God as the Absolute First Cause implies the gradual ascent of a single series of causes to God, and the proposition mentioned in note 108. 7, that the cause contains the effect in a superior way, implies a gradual descent from God—a degradation, i.e. an emanation, from God. The thesis of, for example, Simplicius and Ammonius that God, according to Aristotle, is not only a Prime Mover, but the Eternal Creator of an eternal world, has therefore a certain plausibility (in strict logic the theory of an eternal creation or, what amounts to the same thing, the theory of emanation, implies the contradiction that the world proceeds eternally, i.e. timelessly from God, i.e. is eternally both inside and outside God).

I have not found the theory, described in the text, in any Greek philosopher; it seems to me, however, highly probable, both because of its plausibility and because of the absence of originality in the Arabic commentators, that it is not, as Averroës suggests, an invention of theirs, but must have been found in the later Alexandrian School of Neoplatonic commentators, i.e. the School of Ammonius Hermiae, which combined the exegesis of Aristotle's treatises with a moderate Neoplatonism. It may be remembered that the idea of the fundamental identity of Aristotle's system and Plato's was widely upheld among the Neoplatonists. We find amongst the works of Porphyry mentioned by Suidas a treatise Περὶ τοῦ μίαν εἶναι τὴν Πλάτωνος καὶ Ἀριστοτέλους αἵρεσιν, and there is a treatise, attributed to Farabi, and edited and translated by Dieterici, bearing the same title الجمع بين رايى الحكيمين افلاطون الالاهى وارسطوطاليس (in which the epithet, blasphemous in Muhammadan eyes, of الالهى, θεῖος, is given to Plato). In this latter treatise Ammonius and Themistius are mentioned and the *Theology of Aristotle* is referred to, to prove that Aristotle regarded God as the eternal creator of this eternal world, الصانع المبدع لهذا العالم.

p. 111. 1. One would have expected Averroës to say: rational animals ... moving themselves at the command of these principles. As a matter of fact the whole theory is confused: the principles of the heavenly bodies are their intellects and souls; these intellects and souls are regarded as commanding them, but the heavenly bodies themselves are rational beings, i.e. they include intellects and souls. The theory is based on the metaphors of Aristotle, who regards the relation of God to the celestial bodies as that of the beloved to the lover, κινεῖ ὡς ἐρώμενον, 1072ª3, and as the relation of the leader of an army, στρατηγός, 1075ª14, to the army; but these metaphors are not equivalent: according to the first, God is passive and only an object of desire (the term 'mover' is ambiguous in Aristotle and can mean both the final cause and the efficient cause of the movement), whereas according to the second, God has a certain activity. According to both, however, the movements of the celestial bodies have their source of movement, their moving cause, in themselves, their souls. The comparison of the world as a State in which the orders of the highest authority are transmitted by proxies is found in Ps.-Aristotle, *De mundo* 6. 398ª6. The conception of the world as a State is general in the Stoics; cf. *Stoic. Vet. Fr.* ii, pp. 327 sqq.: 'mundum esse urbem (vel domum) bene administratam'.

p. 111. 2. ἐπὶ τῶν ἄνευ ὕλης τὸ αὐτό ἐστι τὸ νοεῖν καὶ τὸ νοούμενον, Aristotle, *De an*. Γ 4. 430ª4. For this theory compare my *Ep. d. Met. d. Av.*, note 47. 6.

p. 111. 3. No fatigue or weariness; this is based on Aristotle, *De caelo* B 1. 284ª13, where the mover of the world is said to be ἄπονος: cf. also Ps.-Aristotle, *De mundo* 6. 400ᵇ10, where He is described as ἄλυπος, ἄπονος, πάσης κεχωρισμένος σωματικῆς ἀσθενείας, and Philo, *De providentia* ii. 74 (*Stoic. Vet. Fr.* ii. 201. 10): 'item sine labore et defatigatione est earum (scil. stellarum fixarum) circumactio'.

p. 111. 4. Koran xli. 11.

p. 112. 1. This is Stoic. Man as a reasonable being stands under the obligation of the universal divine law (see e.g. Cicero, *De leg.* i. 12. 33). It is his first duty to know and acknowledge God's power and majesty. Compare, for example, Seneca, *Epist.* 95. 50: 'primus est deorum cultus deos credere, deinde reddere illis maiestatem suam, reddere bonitatem, sine qua nulla maiestas est', and Epictetus' beautiful words (*Disc.* i. 16. 20): 'what else can I, an old cripple, do but sing for all others my hymns to God. If I were a nightingale, a swan, I would sing like the nightingale and the swan, but since I am a reasonable being, it is in the manner of a reasonable being that I have to sing my hymn to God.'

The term تكليف, 'divine command', 'imperative injunction', 'divine law', which corresponds to the Greek προστακτικόν and νόμος, is a technical term in Muslim theology (cf. Baghdadi, *The Roots of Religion*, Stambul, 1928, pp. 149, 205, 207 sqq., and *Dict. of Techn. Terms* under تكليف, p. 1255), and the important problem it involves, i.e. the problem of the autonomy of ethics, is much discussed in Islam under the influence of Greek philosophy. What is the foundation of moral obligation? What is the foundation of our obligation to know God? According to the Muʿtazilites it is reason; according to the Maturidites it is the command of God which, however, is known by reason; according to the Ashʿarites it is the fact that it is written in the Divine Book (see Goldziher, *Vorlesungen über den Islam*, p. 110). The first two conceptions are in accordance with the Stoic view. Right and wrong are autonomous, and exist by nature, φύσει, بالطبع, not by convention or tradition, θέσει, بالوضع, and it is the law of Nature, which is identical with the law of God, found by reason, which commands what is to be done and forbids what is to be avoided. According to Marcianus (see *Stoic. Vet. Fr.* iii. 77. 34) Chrysippus began his book Περὶ νόμου with the words: ὁ νόμος πάντων ἐστι βασιλεὺς θείων τε καὶ ἀνθρωπίνων πραγμάτων· δεῖ δὲ αὐτὸν προστάτην τε εἶναι τῶν καλῶν καὶ τῶν αἰσχρῶν καὶ ἄρχοντα καὶ ἡγεμόνα, καὶ κατὰ τοῦτο κανόνα τε εἶναι δικαίων καὶ ἀδίκων καὶ τῶν φύσει πολιτικῶν ζῴων προστακτικὸν μὲν ὧν ποιητέον, ἀπαγορευτικὸν δὲ ὧν οὐ ποιητέον. A thing is not good because God has ordained it, but God has ordained it because it is good. The relativist Carneades, for whom morals exist only in relation to society and who maintained that the terms 'right' and 'wrong' can therefore not be applied to God—see Cicero, *De nat. deor.* iii. 15. 38—had objected that if God had virtue by nature, He would stand under the power of the moral law—cf. Sext. Emp. *Adv. phys.* i. 176. The Muʿtazilites fully grant the inference, and admit that just as in the logical domain God's power is restricted, since even He cannot perform what is logically contradictory, He is also bound by the moral law, and it is of necessity that He has ordained what He has ordained and forbidden what He has forbidden; indeed, He stands under the double bondage of reason: that of pure reason and that of practical. The orthodox Muslim, however, denies that there is any necessity for God in the moral domain. It was possible, جائز, for God to impose other laws than those He has actually decreed.

p. 112. 2. Positions, i.e. they keep a certain order, τάξις, in Latin *ordo* (cf. Cicero, *De nat. deor.* ii. 16. 43).

p. 112. 3. Koran xxxvii. 164.

p. 112. 4. Connexion, ارتباط, i.e. their order and union, σύστασις, cf. Ps.-Aristotle *De mundo* 5. 396^{b}23: ἡ τῶν ὅλων σύστασις.

p. 112. 5. i.e. the systematic study of their works, beginning with logic, cf. Aristotle, *Met.* Γ 3. 1005^{b}2.

p. 112. 6. One may freely accept, says Aristotle, *Top.* A 10. 104^{a}11, that on which the wise agree, when it does not stand in opposition to the opinion of the many. This is contrary to Epicurus' aristocratic view, see Seneca, *Ep.* 29. 10: 'nunquam volui populo placere, nam quae ego scio, non probat populus; quae probat populus, ego nescio'.

p. 113. 1. Cf. e.g. Cicero, *De nat. deor.* ii. 16. 43: 'sensum autem astrorum atque intellegentiam maxume declarat ordo eorum et constantia; nihi lest enim quod ratione et numero moveri possit sine consilio, in quo nihil est temerarium, nihil varium, nihil fortuitum . . . .'

p. 113. 2. Conservation, حفظ, σωτηρία, cf. Ps.-Aristotle, *De mundo* 6. 400^{a}4.

p. 113. 3. It was Aristotle who first asserted—*De gen. et corr.* B 10. 336^{a}31—that it was the sun's movement on the ecliptic, ἡ φορὰ κατὰ τὸν λοξὸν κύκλον, which influenced all earthly change, all earthly becoming and decay. All that follows agrees with the traditional views of the Stoic theodicy, cf. e.g. Cicero, *De nat. deor.* ii. 19 and ii. 40.

p. 113. 4. Cf. Aristotle, *Meteor.* B 4. 361^{a}7.

p. 113. 5. Koran xiv. 37; xvi. 12.

p. 114. 1. The better being cannot fail to possess in the highest degree the best qualities, i.e. life and reason. The basic idea of this argument is Stoic, cf. Cicero, *De nat. deor.* ii. 14. 38: How can the world, which embraces all things, fail to possess that which is the best? But there is nothing better than intelligence and reason: the world therefore cannot be without them.

p. 114. 2. Koran xl. 59.

p. 114. 3. Cf. e.g. Cicero, *De nat. deor.* ii. 31. 79: if mankind possesses intellect, faith, virtue, whence can these have flowed down to the earth, if not from the gods?

p. 114. 4. For the gods—according to Plotinus (*Enn.* v. 8. 3)—are not concerned with human affairs, they contemplate only the Divine and the Intelligible: καὶ ἴσασι πάντα, καὶ γιγνώσκουσι οὐ τὰ ἀνθρώπεια, ἀλλὰ τὰ ἑαυτῶν, τὰ θεῖα καὶ ὅσα νοῦς ὁρᾷ.

p. 114. 5. Koran xli. 10.

p. 115. 1. Cf. e.g. Cicero, *De nat. deor.* ii. 5. 13: when a man goes into a house or a gymnasium or to the market place, and sees the method, the order, the discipline in all things that happen there, he cannot possibly suppose that all this comes about without a cause, but he understands that there is someone who commands and whose orders are obeyed.

p. 115. 2. Koran vi. 75.

p. 115. 3. According to Averroës' *Ep. d. Met.* (see my translation, p. 113) there are forty-five of these movers, if each of the seven planets has its own mover for its daily revolution. 'Seven or eight' seems rather strange; one would have expected 'eight or nine', i.e. one for the daily movement of the heaven of the fixed stars, seven for the daily movement of the planets, and a problematic one to explain the precession of the equinoxes ($\mu\epsilon\tau\dot{\alpha}\pi\tau\omega\sigma\iota\varsigma$). Compare for all this my *Ep. d. Met. d. Av.*, pp. 112–13 and notes.

p. 115. 4. Cf. Plotinus, *Enn.* v. 5. 3: ὁ δὲ ἐκεῖ βασιλεὺς οὐκ ἀλλοτρίων ἄρχων, ἀλλ' ἔχων τὴν δικαιοτάτην καὶ φύσει ἀρχὴν καὶ τὴν ἀληθῆ βασιλείαν, ἅτε τῆς ἀληθείας βασιλεύς καὶ ὢν κατὰ φύσιν κύριος τοῦ αὐτοῦ ἀθρόου γεννήματος .... In yonder world the king does not govern like a man governs aliens, He exercises the most just and the most natural government, the true kingdom, for He is the King of Truth and has by nature power over all those He has engendered Himself.

p. 115. 5. Koran xix. 94.

p. 116. 1. Koran vi. 75.

p. 116. 2. Probably Averroës thinks here of τῶν θαυμάτων ταὐτόματα, 'those marvellous things which move themselves', mentioned by Aristotle, *Met.* A 2. 983ᵃ14, at which people wonder who have not yet ascertained their causes.

p. 117. 1. The proof, of course, that it is necessary.

p. 117. 2. For then in the First also the necessity of existence would create a duality. Ghazali's argument is excellent and unassailable, and exposes clearly the surreptitious introduction of duality. The basic idea was put forward by Aenesidemus (Sext. Emp. *Adv. phys.* i. 219 sqq.) in his denial of causation: a cause can only act by either remaining by itself or joining with something else. In the first case, it cannot effect anything but its own nature, in the latter case the two together cannot produce a third; therefore nothing can come into being which did not exist previously.

p. 118. 1. A condition, حالة, πῶς ἔχον, something subjective, i.e. not something outside the soul, an external relation (for Averroës often regards all relations as subjective, as is frequent in post-Aristotelian philosophy, or even as negations).

p. 118. 2. i.e. the necessary is that which has no cause (or rather which needs no cause) for its existence; all other entities have (or need) causes for their existence. We shall discuss later this definition of the 'necessary'.

p. 118. 3. Averroës here raises incidentally the important problem of those notions, like 'one' and 'being', which are predicated of everything and are called by the schoolmen *notiones transcendentales* (the *aporia* of 'one' and 'being' is discussed by Aristotle, *Met. B* 3. 998^{b}14: they are not genera, because they have no species), and which Averroës seems here to regard as subjective (unity he regards, in fact, as negative, cf. Aristotle's definition of μονάς—*Met. Δ* 6. 1016^{b}24–25—as τὸ κατὰ τὸ ποσὸν ᾗ ποσὸν ἀδιαίρετον πάντῃ καὶ ἄθετον).

The whole discussion is irrelevant to Ghazali's argument and does not invalidate his dichotomy: if necessity and possibility do not add anything to existence, then neither the necessary existent nor the possible existent contains a plurality, and the emanation of a plurality out of the Monad remains unexplained.

p. 118. 4. The real possible, matter, is transitory; the first effect is eternal, i.e. necessary, although it is possible. The same contradiction exists for Aristotle: the material world is eternal, i.e. necessary, although matter is potential and nothing potential is eternal. The contradiction rests finally on the confusion between logical and ontological necessity. Cf. notes 53. 6 and 163. 4.

p. 118. 5. We are here involved in a circle: Averroës seems here to regard both 'necessary' and 'possible' as mere negations, 'necessary' being the negation of 'possible' and 'possible' the negation of 'necessary'.

p. 118. 6. He seems to mean that if, through the necessity in it, there were a duality in the necessary existent, the necessary existent would be necessary by itself and at the same time its necessity would be caused by the necessity in it; but then the necessary existent would not be necessary by itself.

p. 118. 7. Cf. Kant, *Krit. d. rein. Vernunft*, A 598, B 626: 'Sein ist kein reales Prädikat d. i. ein Begriff von irgend etwas, was zu dem Begriffe eines Dinges hinzukommen könne.'

p. 118. 8. When we say a thing exists, or a thing is one, 'exists' and 'one' are predicates and therefore, according to Avicenna, accidents (for the discussion of this theory see my *Ep. d. Met. d. Av.*, pp. 8 and 17 and notes).

p. 118. 9. This is not correct; the theory is originally Aristotelian, e.g. τῶν μὲν δὴ ἕτερον αἴτιον τοῦ ἀναγκαῖα εἶναι, τῶν δὲ οὐθέν, ἀλλὰ διὰ ταῦτα ἕτερά ἐστιν ἐξ ἀνάγκης, some things have an extraneous cause of their necessity, others not, but are themselves the cause of necessity in other things (*Met. Δ* 5. 1015^{b}10; for the discussion of this theory see my *Ep. d. Met. d. Av.*, p. 150).

p. 119. 1. For Aristotle this composition exists in the generated only: every individual is the synthesis of two things, matter and form, and it is its matter to which possibility is attributed, e.g. *De gen. et corr. B* 9. 335^{a}32: ὡς μὲν οὖν ὕλη τοῖς γεννητοῖς ἐστὶν αἴτιον τὸ δυνατὸν εἶναι καὶ μὴ εἶναι. Cf., however, note 141. 2.

NOTES

p. 119. 2. This is rather a curious way of putting it, since 'relation' is one of the ten categories. As we have seen, the Stoics, the Sceptics, and also the Muslim theologians regarded relations as subjective.

p. 119. 3. This does not seem to me to follow from the sentence he quotes.

p. 119. 4. This seems in absolute opposition to the view held by Aristotle, and by Averroës himself, that all becoming is but the transition of a pre-existent potentiality to actuality.

p. 120. 1. This is the very point Ghazali makes.

p. 120. 2. I think he means that every body has actually a unity, i.e. it is one, but is a synthesis of matter and form, and, since matter represents the potential, is a plurality potentially.

p. 120. 3. For, since it is pure form, it lacks matter—i.e. potency, the principle of plurality.

p. 120. 4. But a thing is either simple or composite—*tertium non datur*.

p. 120. 5. The theory seems something of a *petitio principii*. Ghazali asks: 'How, from the absolutely simple One, can a plurality proceed?' Averroës answers: 'The One is absolutely simple, but contains potentially a plurality, i.e. a plurality proceeds from it.'

p. 121. 1. This form, i.e. this second principle.

p. 121. 2. In the soul of an individual man there are, according to the Arabian Aristotelians, different intellects, e.g. the material and the active intellect, i.e. different forms having different definitions. The second principle would therefore be a composite intellect like the intellect of man.

p. 121. 3. Cf. Thomas Aquinas, *In Met.* lib. xii. 11: 'nec tamen sequitur quod omnia alia a se ei sunt ignota; nam intelligendo se intelligit omnia alia'.

p. 121. 4. Of course this is no answer to Ghazali's objection.

p. 122. 1. The thing known is the perfection of the knower: δυνάμει πώς ἐστι τὰ νοητὰ ὁ νοῦς, ἀλλ' ἐντελεχείᾳ οὐδέν, πρὶν ἂν νοῇ (Arist. *De an.* Γ 4. 429^{b}30; however, God's Intellect is eternally in act, eternally in perfection). Avicenna affirms (*Salvation*, p. 404) that God, knowing Himself and knowing that He is the principle of everything, knows everything that emanates from Him, but knows individual things only in a universal way. But Avicenna denies (op. cit., p. 403) that God knows things through the things themselves, for in this case His essence would depend on these things (i.e. if through my free will I perform an act and God knows this act, God's knowledge will depend on my action). The difference between Avicenna and Averroës here consists, therefore, only in the fact that Averroës denies that it is through God's knowledge that He is their principle, that He knows all things. For Averroës the essence of God consists in all things knowable in the noblest form of knowledge (according to the Aristotelian theory that the Intellect in act is identical with the things known).

p. 122. 2. But compare p. 120 and note 130. 4, and below: 'they need not all have the same degree of simplicity', and p. 123.

p. 123. 1. i.e. the intellect would not know the things as they are.

p. 123. 2. Cf. Aristotle, *Anal. Post. A* i. 71ᵃ1: πᾶσα διδασκαλία καὶ πᾶσα μάθησις διανοητικὴ ἐκ προϋπαρχούσης γίνεται γνώσεως.

p. 123. 3. Possibly he is here referring to Alexander of Aphrodisias, who admits that the natural and necessary consequences of God's causation are known to Him (*Quaest. nat.* ii. 21), i.e. that there is in God a πρόνοια, a providence for the sublunary world. At *De fato* xxx (see also the passage in Freudenthal, *Die durch Averroës erhaltenen Fragmente Alexanders*, p. 112) Alexander denies the Stoic theory that the gods know future events; for future events are not yet determined, contain a potential element, and are infinite, and are therefore unknowable before they come into actuality. It is unreasonable to attribute even to the gods knowledge of the unknowable; even for them the impossible keeps its character. Avicenna's theory, which I shall discuss later in more detail, seems an elaboration of Alexander's.

p. 124. 1. A similar objection is made by Aristotle (*De an. A* 5. 410ᵇ4 sqq., cf. *Met. B* 4. 1000ᵇ3) to Empedocles, whose theory, according to Aristotle, would imply that God is the most unintelligent, ἀφρονέστατος, of beings, since He alone cannot know what every mortal being knows.

p. 124. 2. Koran xviii. 49.

p. 124. 3. 'who think wicked thoughts about God': words used at Koran xlviii. 6.

p. 125. 1. Averroës is here referring probably to *Met. Λ* 8. 1074ᵇ9, where Aristotle says that the arts and sciences in fact *do* perish, and that in the first utterances of science there is something like a divine inspiration, θείως εἰρῆσθαι, according to the faulty Arabic rendering followed by Averroës (*Met.*, p. 1687 Bouyges): فسيظن ان ذلك القول الاهى. Human affairs turn in a circle, φασὶ γὰρ κύκλον εἶναι τὰ ἀνθρώπινα πράγματα, *Phys. Δ* 14. 223ᵇ24.

p. 125. 2. Ibn Hazm, op. cit. i. 72. The superhuman origin of the sciences and arts is current in Greek mythology. It is embodied, for example, in the myth of Prometheus (the 'Fore-Thinker'), Hephaestus, and Athena as told by Plato, *Plt.* 274 c. Ibn Hazm says, loc. cit., line 1: 'We know clearly that man could never have acquired sciences and arts guided solely by his own natural powers and without being taught.' He enumerates different sciences (e.g. medicine and astronomy) and arts, which man could never have acquired without divine assistance. One of the examples he gives is language 'which man could never have fixed by convention without using another language or by starting from another language' (according to Aristotle,

De interpr. c. 2. 16ª19, language, although not the psychological basis of language, is fixed by convention, θέσει, or κατὰ συνθήκην; Epicurus asserts that language exists by nature, φύσει, cf. Diog. Laert. x. 75).

p. 125. 3. The substance, الجوهر, here synonymous with the essence الذات, i.e. the substance or the essence κατ' ἐξοχήν: God.

p. 126. 1. God as the reckoner: Koran iv. 7 and xxxiii. 39.

p. 126. 2. According to Aristotle, however (*De an.* Γ 3. 427ᵇ11 and 428ᵃ11), perception, αἴσθησις, is always true; only through judgement and imagination are we liable to error. But Zeno affirmed (Cic. *Acad. post.* i. 14. 41) that one should not have faith in all sense-impressions (*visis, φαντασίαις*), but only in those that are trustworthy, i.e. φαντασίαι καταληπτικαί; against which Epicurus said (Cic. *De nat. deor.* i. 25. 70) that if one single sense-impression were false, none would be true.

p. 126. 3. In normal cases, like the generation of man from man, the father (the proximate agent, τὸ ἐγγύτατον αἴτιον, الفاعل القريب) and the son are identical in species (man), but in abnormal cases, like the generation of the mule from a horse and a donkey, they participate only in the genus next above them (cf. Arist. *Met.* Z 8. 1033ᵇ33).

p. 126. 4. He refers here possibly to Strato (see note 251. 1) or the naturalistic theory ascribed to Avicenna, in his *Oriental Philosophy*; see below, note 254. 4.

p. 127. 1. I think he means, by 'abstract principle, connected with the heavenly bodies', one or possibly more immaterial movers of heavenly bodies. A principle inferior to God would be, for example, the World-Soul or the First Intellect.

p. 127. 2. 'elements': the text has الاجرام البسيطة, τὰ ἁπλᾶ σώματα, i.e. τὰ στοιχεῖα, the elements. The mutual transition of the elements is caused by the movement of the celestial bodies; see Aristotle, *Meteor.* A 2. 339ᵃ21 and ibid. Δ 1, ad init.

p. 127. 3. 'the formative faculty', القوة المصوّرة, ἡ δύναμις ἡ διαπλαστικὴ ἥν δὴ καὶ τεχνικὴν εἶναι λέγομεν, through which everything has a purpose and nothing is in vain (ἀργόν) or superfluous (περιττόν), Galen, *De natur. facult.* i. 6. 15.

p. 127. 4. By 'abstract principle' he probably means here Avicenna's *dator formarum* which is the last intellect emanating from God and which is identified with Aristotle's active intellect.

p. 127. 5. i.e. the World-Soul of the Platonists.

p. 127. 6. ὁ τοῦ σώματος ἡμῶν δημιουργός, whose substance (οὐσία) is unknown to us and who is called by Hippocrates 'nature', φύσις (Galen, *De plac. Hipp. et Plat.*, Mueller, p. 809. 6).

p. 127. 7. Cf. my *Ep. d. Met. d. Av.*, p. 44 and note 44. 2.

p. 127. 8. Cf. Aristotle, *De caelo* A 10. 280^{a}24.

p. 127. 9. Description, رسم, ὑπογραφή, a term of Stoic logic. Through the ὑπογραφή we describe by their proper qualities those highest concepts which cannot be defined; cf. Simplicius, *In Cat.* 75. 30.

p. 128. 1. This refers to Aristotle, *De an.* A 3. 407^{a}9–20, where he criticizes Plato's theory of the World-Soul by saying that thought does not possess unity through magnitude, i.e. cannot be divided through the division of the body. For how will Mind think, if it be extended, and through which parts of the extension? (Cf. also 430^{b}15, where it is said that the Intellect thinks through an indivisible mental act, and *De sensu* 7. 449^{a}3.) The same criticism of a materialistic conception of thought is found in Plotinus, *Enn.* iv. 7. 8. The whole problem will be treated later *in extenso*.

p. 128. 2. Cf. Aristotle, *De gen. et corr.* A 4. 320^{a}2: ἔστι δὲ ὕλη μάλιστα μὲν καὶ κυρίως τὸ ὑποκείμενον γενέσεως καὶ φθορᾶς δεκτικόν.

p. 128. 3. Cf. Aristotle, *De caelo* A 10. 280^{a}24.

p. 128. 4. Perception is the reception in the soul of the form of the external thing perceived without the matter, Aristotle, *De an.* B 12. 424^{a}17; intellect is a form which knows or apprehends intelligible forms, Aristotle, *De an.* Γ 8. 431^{b}20–432^{a}3 (for this theory compare my *Ep. d. Met. d. Av.*, note 47. 6).

p. 128. 5. Cf. Aristotle, *Met.* Λ 7. 1072^{b}18: ἡ δὲ νόησις ἡ καθ' αὑτὴν τοῦ καθ' αὑτὸ ἀρίστου, καὶ ἡ μάλιστα τοῦ μάλιστα.

p. 128. 6. i.e. the relation of intellectual to sensible existence is like the relation of craftsmanship to its material (οἷον ἡ τέχνη πρὸς τὴν ὕλην, *De an.* Γ 5. 430^{a}12); the image (εἴδωλον) of the craftsmanship, says Plotinus (*Enn.* v. 9. 5), penetrates into the matter, but the craftsmanship itself remains in its identity outside the matter.

p. 129. 1. This is the important Plotinian theory of creative knowledge. If the First Intellect, says Plotinus (*Enn.* v. 9. 5), has to be the creative power of the Universe, it cannot think it, in creating it, as existing in that which does not yet exist. The intelligibles must therefore exist prior to the world, and cannot be an image of the sensible things; on the contrary they are their archetypes . . . . This theory was accepted by both Christian and Muhammadan theologians. *We* know the things because they are; they *are* because God knows them. St. Augustine says (*De trin.* xv. 22): 'with respect to all His creatures, both spiritual and corporeal, He does not know them, because they are, but they are because He knows them' ('non quia sunt, ideo novit, sed ideo sunt, quia novit'). And John Scotus Eriugena, *De div. nat.* Migne, cxxii. 596 B, says: '. . . divina siquidems cientiao mnium, quae sunt, causa est. Non enim ideo Deus scit ea, quae sunt, quia subsistunt, sed ideo subsistunt, quia Deus ea scit.' Compare St. Thomas Aquinas, *Summ. Theol.* i, qu. 14, art. 10. We shall see that this theory is accepted also by Ghazali (cf. too his analogous doctrine that God differentiates things through His choice, not that He chooses them because they are differentiated).

p. 129. 2. For this compare Ptolemaeus, *Hypotheses* (ex Arab. interpret. est L. Nix, Leipzig, 1907), p. 119, and note 115. 1 of my *Ep. d. Met. d. Av.*

p. 130. 1. For it is a basic principle of Neoplatonism that emanation implies a progressive degradation (ἐξίτηλον), e.g. *Enn.* iii. 8. 4: ὁμογενὲς γὰρ ἀεὶ δεῖ τὸ γεννώμενον εἶναι· ἀσθενέστερον μὲν τῷ ἐξίτηλον καταβαῖνον γίγνεσθαι.

p. 130. 2. In this rather obscure sentence there is of course a contradiction: if the First is the cause of everything, the inferior Intellects cannot create anything. Averroës means evidently that the First is only the first or supreme cause of everything and that the inferior Intellects are subordinate causes. By 'saying[6] each intellect is the cause of its own essence, i.e. the human intellect', I think Averroës means that all these separate (χωριστός, cf. *De an.* Γ 5. 430ᵃ17) Intellects are (or are the cause of) the Active Intellect (ὁ ποιητικὸς νοῦς) which exists in each human being from birth to death, whenever he thinks.

p. 130. 3. These are God's seven attributes, about which the Muhammadan theologians agree, although they disagree about their nature.

p. 130. 4. i.e. God is the unique efficient cause.

p. 130. 5. The Ash'arites, like the Stoics, ascribe to God knowledge of individual things. Against this the Peripatetics hold (see Alexander of Aphrodisias' argument in *Die durch Averroës erhaltenen Frgm. Alexanders*, p. 113 and my *Ep. d. Met. d. Av.*, p. 145) that the knowledge of individuals, since there is in infinite time an infinite number of them, would imply an infinite actual knowledge, and an actual infinite is impossible even for God.

p. 131. 1. i.e. they could not explain the relation.

p. 131. 2. Averroës refers here to the Stoic argument of the Ash'arites, that everything in the world is transitory and that which is transitory in its parts is transitory as a whole.

p. 131. 3. i.e. there is no objective necessity in them, since the things of this world have no 'natures', characters, dispositions, capacities.

p. 131. 4. This may mean either that there are no *vérités de raison* (the Ash'arites, however—but not orthodox theologians like Ibn Hazm— admitted that the contradictory is not possible even for God) or that the intellect cannot find any necessity in the world.

p. 131. 5. This is a true and profound remark: if there is no necessity in things, there can be no wisdom, no reason, in their maker. For wisdom implies necessity, since reason is the making of inferences, the finding of objective necessities. It may be added that to ascribe wisdom to God is to deny His omniscience, as was seen by Carneades, who said (Sext. Emp. *Adv. phys.* i. 167–8) that God cannot possess reason (φρόνησις) and cannot deliberate (βουλεύεσθαι), since one who reasons has not yet found. It is the prerogative of man to reason and to act, because he partly knows, partly does not know. All action implies a supposition and the knowledge of a necessary relation: I can act voluntarily when I know that, if I do *this*, *that* will happen. All reasoning implies an ignorance and the possible knowledge of a necessity: I reason when I want to find that, if, when I do *this*, *that* will happen.

p. 131. 6. This is very true; cf. note 89. 3.

p. 131. 7. i.e. we infer voluntary action in the Divine only by analogy with voluntary action in ourselves.

p. 132. 1. Namely God who possesses attributes.

p. 132. 2. i.e. they proved that the heavens are produced by admitting in them accidents, i.e. transitoriness, and by the argument that that which is transitory in its part is transitory as a whole.

p. 132. 3. i.e. they supposed that this creation had taken place *ex nihilo*.

p. 132. 4. i.e. *ex nihilo*.

p. 132. 5. Koran xxiii. 12–14.

p. 132. 6. Koran xxi. 31.

p. 132. 7. Koran xi. 9.

p. 132. 8. Koran xli. 10.

p. 132. 9. According to the Aristotelians the individuality of a thing is based on its being composed of matter and form; but every atom is an individual by itself, in its simplicity.

p. 133. 1. It is the non-cold (the warm, for *omnis determinatio est negatio*) which takes the place of the cold, when a thing becomes warm. Every negative is just as much an object of the mind as the positive, and possesses therefore a certain reality, according to Aristotle. The non-existent world was, according to the Muʻtazilites, an object of God's thought before the creation of the world. God creates the world by conferring on this object of His thought the attribute of existence (for existence is an attribute for the Muʻtazilites and for Avicenna, though not for the Ashʻarites and Averroës).

p. 133. 2. Cf. my *Ep. d. Met. d. Av.*, note 63. 2, for the inherence of corporeality in primary matter.

p. 133. 3. e.g. an individual man has individual transitory qualities, and therefore the individual man is transitory; but man as a universal is a rational being, this rationality which is one generically is eternal and has no first term; therefore, why should man in general be produced?

p. 133. 4. 'necessary', i.e. it is a necessary, evident proposition for the philosophers that *infinitum actu non datur*. But the philosophers and Ash'arites did not agree about the *infinitum actu*.

p. 134. 1. i.e. the father is the cause of the son, but the father is himself a son, i.e. the effect of another father; if therefore the power the father had to generate a son had to come to him from a father who had generated him, we should have an infinite regress. There must therefore be a power (an all-pervading power, δύναμις διὰ τῆς ὕλης πεφοιτηκυῖα, as the Stoics have it) which moves the matter in itself motionless (ὕλη καθ' αὑτήν ἀκίνητος) of the Universe, and this power will be God.

This Stoic argument (see Sext. Emp. *Adv. phys.* i. 75–77) is a logical correction and consequence of Aristotle's doctrine of the prime mover. According to Aristotle there is an infinite sequence of fathers and sons, of causes and effects. But all change derives ultimately from a prime mover, itself unmoved, not itself an effect. This prime mover, however, is not at the beginning of the causal series father–son–father, since this series is infinite, but, moving eternally, is so eternal with this series; the prime mover is therefore, in fact, the unique mover, the unique cause, and source of all change.

p. 134. 2. This is in agreement with Aristotle's theory of movement, e.g. *Phys.* Θ 4. 255ᵃ16: we must always distinguish the mover from the moved, just as we see this when a living agent moves a lifeless thing; and *Phys.* Θ 5. 257ᵇ9: the mover is already an actual existent, τὸ δὲ κινοῦν ἤδη ἐνεργείᾳ ἐστίν; but I do not see how this refutes the Ash'arite argument.

p. 134. 3. i.e. that there is no causation in the world.

p. 134. 4. 'end': this is just the point; the series father–son–father is infinite, and does not end in an agent which itself is not an effect, i.e. the prime mover, but the prime mover acts eternally and is coeternal with the series, which would not exist at all without this prime mover.

p. 134. 5. This is both Aristotelian and Neoplatonic. For Aristotle everything immaterial is indivisible, *Met.* Λ 9. 1075ᵃ7: ἀδιαίρετον πᾶν τὸ μὴ ἔχον ὕλην. In God the thinker and the thought are identical, and the divine thought is eternally indivisible. For Neoplatonism compare, for example, Proclus, *Instit. theol.* v, prop. 47: πᾶν τὸ αὐθυπόστατον ἀμερές ἐστι καὶ ἁπλοῦν, 'all that is self-subsistent is without parts and simple', and its proof; and especially Plotinus, *Enn.* v. 4. 1: τό τε μὴ ἁπλοῦν τῶν ἐν αὐτῷ ἁπλῶν δεόμενον ἵν' ᾖ ἐξ ἐκείνων, 'that which is not simple needs simple entities for its composition'. This doctrine has profoundly influenced monotheistic theology, Christian (see next note), Muhammadan, and Jewish. In Muhammadan theology the word توحيد, 'God's one-ness', i.e. 'the uniqueness of God', takes also the meaning of God's simplicity. This problem will be discussed later *in extenso*.

p. 134. 6. i.e. they are *termini transcendentales*. For this theory of the Muʿtazilites see, for example, Shahrastani, op. cit. ed. Cureton, i. 30, and Baghdadi, *The Different Sects*, p. 93. That there is no composition in God is also affirmed by the Alexandrian Fathers, e.g. St. Athanasius (Migne, xxvi. 1044 B): οὐ γὰρ σύνθετος ὁ θεὸς ὁ τὰ πάντα εἰς τὸ εἶναι συντεθεικώς . . .· ἁπλῆ γάρ ἐστιν οὐσία ἐν ᾗ οὐκ ἔνι ποιότης, God who has compounded everything is not Himself compounded . . . for a substance in which there is no attribute is simple.

p. 134. 7. The Ashʿarites assert that God's attributes are distinct from His essence.

p. 135. 1. Cf. e.g. Aristotle, *Met. B* 1. 995ᵇ2 and *Top. A* 2. 101ᵃ35.

p. 135. 2. 'God's essence exceeds even the understanding of the blessed in their mystical union with God' ('excedit ipsam copulationem intellectus beatorum, qui essentiam Dei vident per copulationem'), says Thomas Aquinas following Dionysius Areopagita, *De divin. nom.* v. 1.

p. 135. 3. Averroës refers here to the theory originally held by the Muʿtazilite Abu Hashim (cf. e.g. Fakhr ad-Din al-Razi, *Compendium of the Opinions of the Ancients*, Cairo, H. 1323, p. 111), that God possesses a positive quality which characterizes Him, i.e. His being God, His divinity (الإلٰهية), other theologians denied this (see Razi, loc. cit.) and applied to God the method of negation, تنزيه (literally 'removal'; the word is an exact translation of the term ἀφαίρεσις), i.e. they asserted that God had to be described by negation, and that there are negative qualities in Him, and that the positive qualities He possesses He does not possess in the way other beings possess them. Negative theology is a characteristic of Neoplatonism (see *Enn.* v. 3. 13, where the First is said to be ineffable, ἄρρητον) and, indeed, of all mysticism, since in its ultimate consequence the elimination or synthesis of opposites in the Absolute—as in the self-contradictory assertion of Dionysius Areopagita that nothing positive or negative can be asserted of that which is itself the cause of everything positive and negative, ἡ πάντων θέσις, ἡ πάντων ἀφαίρεσις, τὸ ὑπὲρ πᾶσαν καὶ θέσιν καὶ ἀφαίρεσιν—it is the total surrender of reason before the mystery of God. Negative theology is emphasized especially by the later Neoplatonists; e.g. for Damascius, *De principiis* (Kopp, pp. 5 sqq.), the First is neither a cause nor a non-cause, neither a principle nor not a principle, neither at the beginning of the Universe nor transcending it (ἐπέκεινα πάντων). Dionysius Areopagita, in his *Mystical Theology*, iv and v, enumerates more than fifty negations about God.

p. 135. 4. This is rather unusual, for according to the Arabic philosophers (Averroës included) the Platonic ideas, i.e. the universals, exist eternally in the mind of God (this synthesis of Plato and Aristotle is found already in Middle-Platonism, Neo-Pythagoreanism, and Philo Judaeus). But by 'universals' Averroës here evidently means the universals that have a transitory existence in the minds of men and are abstracted from individual things in the way described by Aristotle, *Anal. Post.* B 19. Averroës here employs both the method of theology *per negationem* and that of theology *per analogiam* or *per eminentiam* (ὑπεροχή). God has a thought superior to our thought, but none of the attributes of our thought is valid for God's thought. The obvious objection is to ask how God's thought can be regarded as thought at all. According to Dionysius Areopagita, there is a threefold way to the knowledge of God: by absolute negation, by absolute superiority, and by regarding Him as the absolute cause (ἐν τῇ πάντων ἀφαιρέσει καὶ ὑπεροχῇ καὶ ἐν τῇ πάντων αἰτίᾳ (*De div. nom.* viii. 3).

p. 135. 5. Cf., however, the argument of Alexander of Aphrodisias against God's knowledge of individuals (note 130. 5), an argument which Averroës copies in his *Epitome* (see my translation, p. 145).

p. 136. 1. The implication of this *petitio principii* would seem to be that the order of the Universe proves definitely the existence of a creative intellect.

p. 136. 2. That existence or being has different degrees is a basic idea of Aristotelian thought: τὸ δὲ ὂν λέγεται μὲν πολλαχῶς says Aristotle, e.g. at the beginning of Γ 2 of his *Metaphysics*; and at *Met.* Γ 2. 1003^{b}6 he says: some things are spoken of as being, because they are substances, others because they are affections of substance (πάθη οὐσίας), others because they lead towards substance . . . and therefore we say that even non-being *is* non-being.

p. 136. 3. A strange conception, but a consequence of a theory of perception without an 'ego'; cf. Aristotle, *De an.* Γ 2. 425^{b}22: ἔτι δὲ καὶ τὸ ὁρῶν ἔστιν ὡς κεχρωμάτισται· τὸ γὰρ αἰσθητήριον δεκτικὸν τοῦ αἰσθητοῦ ἄνευ τῆς ὕλης ἕκαστον, i.e. that which sees is, in the act of seeing, in a way coloured, for it receives without its matter the identical form which exists in the coloured object perceived.

p. 136. 4. Imagination, which according to Aristotle differs from sense-perception and is included in thought, is the faculty in virtue of which we say that an image presents itself to us, ἡ φαντασία καθ' ἣν λέγομεν φάντασμά τι ἡμῖν γίγνεσθαι (*De an.* Γ 3. 428^{a}1).

p. 136. 5. Memory is imagination consciously referring to an earlier perception of which the image is a copy, Aristotle, *De mem.* 1. 449^{b}24 sqq.

p. 136. 6. That the universe is a unified body, ἡνωμένον τι σῶμα, kept together through its one cohesive power, ἕξις, is a Stoic doctrine, cf. Sext. Emp. *Adv. phys.* i. 77–78.

p. 137. 1. That the first tendency of the animal is towards its own preservation (ἡ πρώτη ὁρμὴ ἐπὶ τὸ τηρεῖν ἑαυτό Diog. Laert. vii. 85, cf. v. Arnim, *Stoic. Vet. Fr.* iii. 43 sqq.) is a Stoic doctrine which is found, for example, in

St. Augustine (*De civ. dei* xi. 28), Thomas Aquinas (*Contr. gent.* iii. 65), Hobbes (*English Works*, Molesworth, iv. 83), and Spinoza ('una quaeque res, quantum in se est, in suo perseverare conatur', *Eth.* iii, prop. 6). According to the Stoic doctrine as exposed by Cicero (*De fin.* iii. 20) there is no conflict between self-love and the equally natural love of humanity: the theatre of the world is open to all, although every spectator has a right to his own seat. And Seneca says (*Ep.* 48. 2): 'alteri vivas oportet, si vis tibi vivere', you cannot but live for others, if you want to live for yourself.

p. 137. 2. i.e. πνεῦμα, *spiritus*, the Stoic life-spirit.

p. 137. 3. The analogy between the world, the macrocosm (the term 'macrocosm' is not found in classical Greek; Aristotle—see below—has μέγας κόσμος; it occurs for the first time in its Latin form in Higden, 14th century, but it may well be older, cf. *O.E.D.* s.v.), and the living being (especially man), the microcosm, was maintained by various Greek philosophers, e.g. Democritus (fr. 34 Diels), Plato, Aristotle (*Phys.* Θ 2. 252ᵇ24: εἰ δ' ἐν ζῴῳ τοῦτο δυνατὸν γενέσθαι, τί κωλύει τὸ αὐτὸ συμβῆναι καὶ κατὰ τὸ πᾶν; εἰ γὰρ ἐν μικρῷ κόσμῳ γίνεται, καὶ ἐν μεγάλῳ), and, especially in its Stoic form of a universal 'sympathy', συμπάθεια τῶν ὅλων, had a great influence, both in Orient and Occident, on mystical writings, on alchemy, chiromancy, astrology, magic, and also medicine (al-Kindi, Cardano, Paracelsus, R. Fludd) in the Middle Ages and the Renaissance. It finds its deepest poetical expression in Goethe's *Faust*.

p. 137. 4. That the universe is unified and connected by the all-permeating pneuma, τὸ πᾶν ἡνῶσθαί τε καὶ συνέχεσθαι πνεύματός τινος διὰ παντὸς διήκοντος αὐτοῦ is a Stoic doctrine which, however, is denied by Alexander of Aphrodisias, *De mixt.*, p. 223. 25 (*Stoic. Vet. Fr.* ii. 145. 16).

p. 137. 5. Koran xxxv. 39.

p. 137. 6. i.e. in the immaterial celestial world opposites coincide; the one can be many, the identical differentiated.

p. 138. 1. i.e. God.

p. 138. 2. Whether the daily movement of the heaven of the fixed stars and of the spheres of the planets proceeds from one mover, and all the spheres are connected (as would seem to be Aristotle's theory at *Met.* Λ 8. 1073ᵇ25), or whether every planet has its own mover for its daily movement (as would seem to be his theory at 1074ᵃ15), forms a point of discussion among the commentators (see my *Ep. d. Met. d. Av.*, p. 113).

p. 138. 3. 'On them'; but, indeed, those immaterial existents are themselves nothing but the forms.

p. 138. 4. According to Aristotle (*Phys.* B 7. 198ᵃ25) form and end are identical generally: τὸ μὲν γὰρ τί ἐστι καὶ τὸ οὗ ἕνεκα ἕν ἐστιν.

p. 138. 5. I have already discussed Aristotle's theory of God as the prime mover and supreme end (note 22. 4); the theory here exposed shows that in God the opposites coincide—He is the One who contains the Many, He is the form and the end He bestows on others, He is the prime mover and the supreme end—and substantiates Ghazali's accusation of the irrationality of this theology.

p. 138. 6. Through the introduction of the idea of creation Aristotle's conception of God as the ultimate passive end of desire is vitiated. The world tends towards God, but the ultimate motive lies in God's desire to be loved with a love—conscious and voluntary in man, unconscious in the animated (cf. August. *Sol.* i. 2: 'Deus quem amat omne quod potest amare, sive sciens, sive nesciens'), expressed in motion; cf. Bernard of Clairvaux, *Liber de dilig. deo* vii. 22: 'causa diligendi deum deus est ... nam et efficiens et finalis: ipse dat occasionem, ipse creat affectionem, desiderium ipse consummat'. Neoplatonism distinguishes three kinds of unifying and conjoining force, ἑνωτικὴ καὶ συγκρατικὴ δύναμις, three kinds of love in the created (for the Neoplatonic theory of love cf. Plotinus *Enn.* iii. 5 and Proclus, *Comm. in Platonis primum Alcibiadem,* ed. Cousin, vol. ii, pp. 78 sqq. and pp. 137 sqq.; for the terminology see also Dionys. Areop. *De div. nom.* iv. 15):

(1) ἔρως φυσικός, *amor naturalis,* love as the cosmic force of attraction and movement in all natural things (this is based on Eryximachus' speech in Plato's *Symposium* 186–9—cf. Empedocles fr. 17 Diels—and on the passage of Aristotle, *Phys.* A 9. 192^{a}16);

(2) ἔρως ψυχικός, *amor sensitivus,* in man and the living, 'earthly love', i.e. the principle of procreation, a desire for the eternity and duration of the species (the distinction between earthly and heavenly love is based on the distinction between an earthly and a heavenly Aphrodite in Plato's *Symposium* 180 c, d);

(3) ἔρως νοερός, *amor* (or *caritas*) *intellectivus* (or *rationalis,* or *intellectualis*) in man, 'heavenly love', the love for God, the love for the divine, immortal forms, which in its greatest intensity becomes ἔρως ἐκστατικός, in which the identity of the lover vanishes in the beloved (for the definition of ecstatic love see Dionys. Areop. *De div. nom.* iv. 13, ad init.).

This Neoplatonic conception of love is found in mystical theology both in East and West; in Islam, for example, in Avicenna's *Treatise on Love* رسالة فى العشق, and there are ideas connected with it in Ghazali's section on Love in the sixth book, fourth section, of his *Vivification of Theology* (for Ghazali primary natural love is self-love, i.e. the desire of everything for its own preservation—see note 137. 1; for Ghazali as for medieval theologians, like Bernard of Clairvaux and Thomas Aquinas, and Renaissance authors like Telesio and Campanella, there is a continuous gradation from self-love to love for God). In the fifteenth century, through the revival of

Neoplatonism it finds a new expression in such works as the *Commentary on the Symposium* of Marsiglio Ficino and the *Dialoghi d'Amore* of Leo Hebraeus (Judah Abravanel). R. Burton in his *Anatomy of Melancholy* (Part III, sec. 1, mem. i, subs. 2) mentions Leo's division of Love in his second dialogue into natural, sensible, and intellectual love. Spinoza took his idea of *amor intellectualis* from Leo Hebraeus. For the poetical expression of this idea compare Dante's sublime words (*Parad.* xxx. 40):

'Luce intellettual, piena d'amore;
Amor di vero ben, pien di letizia;
Letizia che trascende ogni dolzore.'

p. 138. 7. Koran xxxiii. 72.

p. 139. 1. Cf. my *Ep. d. Met. d. Av.*, note 112. 3; astronomical theories, according to the Greeks, are only concerned with phenomena and do not provide knowledge of the underlying reality.

p. 139. 2. The reasons why the action of the highest sphere seems superior are mentioned by Averroës in his *Epitome of the Metaphysics* (see my translation, p. 132 and note 132. 2); the most important are that the highest sphere gives motion to the greatest number of bodies (Arist. *De caelo B* 12. 292^{b}25) and that what is nearest to the mover must have the most rapid motion (Arist. *De caelo A* 9. 279^{a}16; *Phys.* Θ 10. 267^{b}6).

p. 139. 3. For this, compare my *Ep. d. Met. d. Av.*, note 122. 2: Stoic philosophy regarded the sun as the ἡγεμονικόν.

p. 140. 1. i.e. if the knowledge of its cause—which is a second effect, surreptitiously introduced—is possible.

p. 140. 2. It has no cause according to the latter alternative; Ghazali's argument is of course perfectly sound; from the One no plurality can be logically deduced.

p. 140. 3. Since according to the theory of emanation the superior includes the inferior (but in this case Ghazali would seem to accept the theory of emanation); or perhaps he only means that the Creator must know His creation.

p. 140. 4. i.e. a proof of one who does not think that knowledge of the effect in the knower implies a duality in the knower.

p. 140. 5. This is of course a *petitio principii*.

p. 141. 1. Cf. e.g. Aristotle, *Met. Δ* 5. 1015^{b}12: τὸ κυρίως ἀναγκαῖον τὸ ἁπλοῦν ('that which is absolutely necessary is the simple'), and *Met.* Θ 8. 1050^{b}6, 'The eternal is essentially prior to the generated (φθαρτά) and nothing eternal is potential'.

p. 141. 2. The fault lies not with Avicenna, whose conception of the necessary is in agreement with Aristotle's, but with the contradiction that there is here in Aristotle's system. According to Aristotle there are several unmoved, immaterial, eternal movers (this in itself contradicts the theory that matter is the *principium individuationis*). Since nothing eternal is potential, there cannot be any potentiality in these movers, and they seem therefore independent of the First Principle and in any case their relation to the First Principle is nowhere explained. On the other hand, the First Principle is the First Cause, and therefore everything must depend on it; and since these immaterial movers thus receive their necessity from an external cause (ἕτερον αἴτιον, *Met. Δ* 5. 1015ᵇ10), there must be an element of potentiality in them, and only their cause, the First Principle, can be κυρίως ἀναγκαῖον, absolutely necessary. There is a similar contradiction in Aristotle over the categories. He asserts (*Met. Z* 1. 1028ᵃ29) that substance is the cause (διὰ ταύτην) of the other categories, but also (*Met. Λ* 4. 1070ᵇ1) that the categories cannot be deduced from one another (παρὰ γὰρ τὴν οὐσίαν καὶ τἆλλα τὰ κατηγορούμενα οὐδέν ἐστι κοινόν). There are both monistic and pluralistic tendencies in Aristotle; the later commentators emphasized the monistic.

p. 142. 1. This refers probably to Aristotle, *De an . B* 7 ad init.: the 'object of sight is the visible ... and that which is visible in itself (καθ' αὑτό) is not visible by its essence (λόγῳ) but because it contains in itself the cause of visibility'. Averroës means that colour which exists by itself, i.e. which is something real in a body, is the cause of sight; still the colour does not change by being seen, but only enters into an external relation with the percipient. A cat may look at a king, but the king does not change by being the cause of the cat's seeing him.

p. 142. 2. This would be true only on the assumption (one often made in post-Aristotelian philosophy) that all relations are unreal, and indeed if all relations are unreal, only the One remains.

p. 142. 3. According to Aristotle (*De an. B* 12) perception is the reception of the sensible forms الصور الحسّيّة, τὰ αἰσθητὰ εἴδη, without their matter.

p. 142. 4. Ghazali here raises a delicate point in Aristotelian philosophy. Heaven seems to be a body. Now body is something material, but it is not simply matter, for matter is by definition the unqualified—Plotinus says explicitly (e.g. *Enn.* iii. 6. 7) that matter is ἀσώματος—and body possesses dimensions. Although Aristotle nowhere explains how matter can become body (for he seems mostly to have regarded matter as something corporeal) the commentators discuss the question of the form through which prime matter can become body (cf. my *Ep. d. Met. d. Av.*, note 63. 2; the problem has been posed by Plotinus, *Enn.* ii. 7. 3). Since matter and form always exist conjointly and in mutual dependence, there must be two principles for their existence, as Ghazali rightly remarks.

p. 142. 5. One would have expected, instead of 'the second intellect' 'the first intellect', i.e. the first effect; here, however, Averroës seems to regard God as the first intellect.

p. 142. 6. i.e. matter and form are conditions for each other's existence.

p. 142. 7. Here the process of emanation is described in a somewhat different manner from that mentioned above, p. 109.

p. 142. 8. If one understands by 'matter', as Averroës does here, following Aristotle's definition *De gen. et corr.* A 4. 320ᵃ2, the substratum of production and corruption, τὸ ὑποκείμενον γενέσεως καὶ φθορᾶς δεκτικόν, heaven does not possess matter (but it can in that case hardly be called body); if, however, by ὕλη is meant the substratum of locomotion (as, e.g., *Met.* Λ 2. 1069ᵇ25, where Aristotle says that what is eternal has matter, not a matter which admits of generation, but a matter which only allows motion from one place to another), then the heavenly substance (αἰθήρ) possesses or is matter.

p. 142. 9. As a matter of fact, according to Aristotle (*De caelo* B 12. 292ᵃ18), and Averroës himself, the heavens (or spheres or stars) are living beings.

p. 143. 1. 'body in its entirety', i.e. body as composed of matter and form; matter as the substratum and receptacle of forms (ὑποκείμενόν τι καὶ ὑποδοχὴ εἰδῶν, *Enn.* ii. 4. 1), does not emanate from the First.

p. 143. 2. This is a very strange conception; we have seen, however, that Averroës ascribes a definite measure to the sun, a heavenly body; but here Averroës follows Themistius (see note 161. 2).

p. 143. 3. Averroës here avoids the difficulty by passing from a supernatural agent to an agent in the empirical world.

p. 143. 4. For becoming is 'coming from' (see note 87. 2).

p. 144. 1. For our world is one and unique and perfect, εἷς καὶ μόνος καὶ τέλειος οὗτος οὐρανός ἐστιν (Arist. *De caelo* A. 9. 279ᵃ10).

p. 144. 2. i.e. the order, the measure of the world, must have been a cause, and this cause must have been determined or specified by an agent, God.

p. 144. 3. Averroës does not, and cannot, explain how this is possible, for how can the universal form of body contain the infinite variety of accidents of the individual bodies?

p. 144. 4. i.e. the Ash'arites believe that God is the only agent, the only cause of everything that happens; the philosophers believe that God is the primary cause, but that there are intermediate causes; the Muʻtazilites believe that at least human actions, since man acts spontaneously and his will is free, are not directly dependent on God, and the Muʻtazilite Muammar believed even (cf. Shahrastani, op. cit., ed. Cureton, p. 46) that God has created bodies alone and that accidents arise by natural necessity from the body.

p. 145. 1. The four elements, στοιχεῖα, are called by Aristotle τὰ ἁπλᾶ σώματα or τὰ ἁπλᾶ, e.g. *Met.* A 3. 984ᵃ6.

NOTES

p. 145. 2. See above, note 142. 8.

p. 145. 3. For the simple as synonymous with the unmixed, τὸ ἀμιγές (opp. τὸ κεκραμένον), i.e. the homogeneous, cf. e.g. Aristotle, *De sensu* 7. 447^{a}18.

p. 145. 4. For, according to both Aristotle (cf. *Phys.* B 8. 199^{b}26) and Plotinus (*Enn.* iii. 8. 2 ad fin.), Nature, although its acts tend towards an end, does not choose or deliberate.

p. 146. 1. For the *Niche for lights* compare note 69. 2. Ghazali's mediating principle is regarded by him as the mover of the ninth sphere, like Avicenna's First Intellect. The proposition 'ex uno non fit nisi unum' is not mentioned by Ghazali.

p. 146. 2. i.e. there are in the First Effect pluralities which cannot be deduced from the fact that it is a first effect, since as a first effect it ought to be simple.

p. 146. 3. Cf. the analogous argument, p. 24.

p. 146. 4. This seems true enough, but is more closely in agreement with the Stoic denial of possibility than with Aristotle (and with Averroës himself), for whom on the contrary the possible can become, or has to become, necessary through an external agent, and who distinguishes what is absolutely necessary from what is so hypothetically (cf. notes 141. 1 and 141. 2).

p. 147. 1. i.e. the outermost sphere. Ghazali wants to show in what follows that God is the immediate cause of everything, and that He cannot act through mediation, as is the Neoplatonic doctrine, and also his own in the *Niche for Lights*.

p. 147. 2. This amounts to saying that the First Cause and the First Effect are absolutely similar; they both have the same plurality, and notwithstanding their plurality they are both a unity; the opposites of plurality and unity coincide in them both. As Ghazali is going to remark, why then not say that the cause and the effect are identical? For what is their *principium individuationis*?

p. 147. 3. For these two principles are both eternal and immaterial, i.e. not in place; they have no *principium individuationis*.

p. 147. 4. 'things which do not differ from them in time and place', i.e. all heavenly and human souls and all earthly and heavenly bodies; but souls differ from them in time, for they are not eternal, and bodies differ from them in space, since *qua* bodies these bodies are in space. But perhaps one must understand that in the Divine Mind human souls in some incomprehensible way are eternal, and bodies immaterial.

p. 148. 1. Cf. p. 108.

p. 148. 2. For in the absence of a rival he cannot be overtaken; for this proverb see Maidani, ed. Freytag, i, p. 315, ch. xxi. 27.

p. 148. 3. i.e. three; from the First Effect three things emanate.

p. 149. 1. That there is one primary reality: the prime, eternal, immaterial, immovable mover.

p. 149. 2. Cf. Aristotle, Met. Λ 8. 1073ᵃ17: we must show that on the number of principles other thinkers have made no clear statement whatever, ὅτι περὶ πλήθους οὐθὲν εἰρήκασιν ὅ τι καὶ σαφὲς εἰπεῖν.

p. 149. 3. In the *Almagest* (ed. Halma, t. ii, p. 831) the number of stars, as established by Hipparchus, is given as 1,022, to which the three stars of the πλόκαμος, الضفيرة (Coma), which he has omitted, must be added. The number 1,025 was generally accepted by the Arabs, although Abd al-Rahman al-Sufi, *Description des étoiles fixes*, transl. Schjellerup, p. 40, says that there are many more stars which, however, are so faint that they cannot be counted.

p. 149. 4. The Greek astronomers divided the stars according to their apparent magnitude, i.e. their luminous intensity, into six classes, which were again subdivided by al-Sufi.

p. 149. 5. In the *Almagest* (7. 5) six stars are called reddish, ὑπόκιρρος (*subrufus*), amongst which is Sirius, which to us today appears white; cf. Schjellerup, op. cit., p. 25. For the statements of the Arabs concerning the colour of some stars compare Nallino, *al-Battani, Opus Astronomicum*, ii. 283-9.

p. 149. 6. As an example of stars in the shape of a man, صورة الانسان, al-Sufi gives, for example, Gemini, الجوزاء (op. cit., p. 40).

p. 149. 7. e.g. the pernicious influence of Sirius is mentioned as early as Homer, *Iliad* xxii. 30, and our expression 'dog-days' (κυνοκαύματα, *dies caniculares*) still testifies to the belief in the influence on the weather attributed to this star (Canicula, the dog-star).

p. 149. 8. For the differences between Hipparchus (in the *Almagest*) and al-Sufi over the luminous intensities of the stars compare the synoptic table in Schjellerup, op. cit., p. 5.

p. 150. 1. For this dangerous theory (for what remains of the τόδε τι, the individual substance, when the accidents are eliminated?) compare Aristotle, *Met. E* 2, where the accidental is said to be very near to the non-existent, τὸ συμβεβηκὸς ἐγγύς τι τοῦ μὴ ὄντος, and where it is affirmed that there can be no speculation about the accidental, περὶ τὸ κατὰ συμβεβηκὸς οὐδεμία ἐστὶ θεωρία.

p. 150. 2. This too is a somewhat dangerous theory; they are not individually different, because they have no matter, and for the same reason (for the genus represents the matter in the definition., cf. Arist. *Met. H* 6. 1045ᵃ34) they are not specifically different; how then can they differ at all?

p. 150. 3. i.e. possibility is only a formal logical concept and does not make a material change in what might possibly exist. As Kant has it

'Hundert wirkliche Taler enthalten nicht das Mindeste mehr als hundert mögliche.'

p. 151. 1. In this passage Averroës, although he affirms that Avicenna's theory is not true, seems to regard it as plausible, neglecting the objections he himself has made; and, indeed, it is the theory of mediation which he himself accepts, the theory of a supreme ruler who governs the world by proxy.

p. 151. 2. The terms 'living through life', 'willing through will', &c., are found in the Ash'arite formulation of God's attributes.

p. 151. 3. This is not the point Ghazali makes. Ghazali reproaches Avicenna with making categorical and, as he believes, absurd assertions about a purely hypothetical entity. Averroës ought to have shown that only from such an hypothesis can the observed facts be reasonably deduced.

p. 152. 1. Celsus (Orig. *Contra Cels.* i. 68) does not regard miracles as a justification of truth, they might equally well be the work of wicked men under the influence of an evil spirit. It may be remarked that Muhammad himself (see Koran xxix. 49, xiii. 27–30, xvii. 92–97) does not really claim to have performed any miracles (the Koranic word is آيات signs; cf. the Christian term σημεῖα), although the Muhammadans ascribe to him a number, the greatest of which is the Koran itself (as a proof of this Koran cxix. 48 is quoted). My great compatriot Hugo Grotius uses Muhammad's concession to refute Islam. Jesus wrought miracles—he says—but Muhammad declared that he was sent with arms, not with miracles, 'Mahumetis se missum ait non cum miraculis, sed cum armis' (*De vera religione christiana*, lib. vi).

p. 152. 2. i.e. let us not ask how it happened. بلا كيف 'without the "how" ', i.e. without inquiring how it happened, is the formula by which the Ash'arites express their ignorance of the right way to interpret the too anthropomorphic religious conceptions of the Divine, which, however, they refuse to abandon. Compare the dictum *credo quia absurdum* ascribed to Tertullian.

p. 152. 3. This tendentious saying, ascribed to the Prophet, which, as far as I know, is not found in the canonical Collections of Traditions, seems to recommend the acquisition of worldly knowledge. According to the orthodox conception, however, the religious Muslim ought to avoid all the worldly sciences of the ancients (علوم القدماء); and the equally tendentious tradition of the prayer of Muhammad is often quoted, that God might protect him from useless science (علم لا ينفع) (cf. Goldziher, *Stellung der alten islamischen Orthodoxie zu den antiken Wissenschaften*, Abh. d. K. Pr. Akad. d.

Wiss., Jahrg. 1915, phil.-hist. Kl., No. 8, p. 6; see also Goldziher, *Buch vom Wesen der Seele*, Abh. d. K. Gesellsch. d. Wiss. zu Göttingen, 1907, phil.-hist. Kl., No. 9, p. 60).

p. 152. 4. رحمة, the mercy of God, corresponds to the Hebrew conception of רַחֲמִים and the Christian conception of ἔλεος. That revelation rests on God's mercy is found in Christian theologians also; cf. e.g. Lactantius, *De divin. inst.* i. 1. 6: 'quod quia fieri non potuit, ut homini per seipsum ratio divina innotesceret, non est passus hominem Deus lumen sapientiae requirentem diutius errare . . ., aperuit oculos eius aliquando et notionem veritatem munus suum fecit.' Cf. Koran xxi. 107. It is the Stoics who base their proof of the reality of divination on the love shown by the gods. If there are gods, so it is said (Cic. *De div.* i. 38. 82), and they do not show to man in advance what is going to happen, they do not love man ('si sunt di neque ante declarant hominibus quae futura sunt . . .non diligunt homines').

This passage of Averroës is not in agreement with his usual purely rationalistic attitude; it must, however, be remembered that even his master Aristotle expresses, in *De philosophia*, fr. 10 Rose, his belief in divinely inspired dreams (cf. also the Aristotelic passage from Ps.-Arist., *Problems* Λ 1, in Cic. *De div.* i. 38. 81). It may be added here that the well-known Averroistic conception of religion as threefold, the religion of the masses, of the lawyers, and of the philosophers, is based on the theory of such Stoic and eclectic philosophers as Panaetius, Mucius Scaevola, and Varro; cf. St. Augustine, *De civ. dei* vi. 5: 'tria genera theologiae dicit (i.e. Varro) esse . . . eorumque unum mythicon, alterum physicon, tertium civile'. The first is, according to Varro, the theology of the poets (i.e. for Averroës, of the masses), the second of the philosophers, the third of the State (i.e. for Averroës of the lawyers). Compare also *De civ. dei* iv. 27: 'pontificem Scaevolam disputasse tria genera tradita deorum: unum a poetis, alterum a philosophis, tertium a principibus civitatis'. (There is an allusion to this passage in Gibbon, *Decline and Fall*, ch. ii, where he says: 'The various modes of worship which prevailed in the Roman world were all considered by the people as equally true, by the philosophers as equally false, and by the magistrates as equally useful.') This threefold division must have been widely accepted, for we find it also in Plutarch, *Amator.* 18. 10, where he says that we have received our religious views from three types of men: ποιηταί, νομοθέται, φιλόσοφοι. For Origen just as there is a threefold nature in man, body, soul, and spirit, so there is a threefold sense of Scripture, the literal, the moral, and the mystical (Orig. *De princ.* iv. 11: 'sicut ergo homo constare dicitur ex corpore et anima et spiritu, ita etiam sancta scriptura'). Compare the gnostic division of mankind into ὑλικοί, ψυχικοί, πνευματικοί. (As early as Aristotle, *Met.* α 3. 995^{a}6, three kinds of people are distinguished: those who accept only mathematical proof, those who accept proof by example, and those who accept proof by poetical quotation.)

NOTES

p. 153. 1. This refers, I think, to the passage (*Anal. Post.* A 10. 76ᵇ18) where Aristotle says that the certainty that number exists is not the same as the certainty that cold and warmth exist: οὐ γὰρ ὁμοίως δῆλον ὅτι ἀριθμός ἔστι καὶ ὅτι ψυχρὸν καὶ θερμόν.

p. 153. 2. i.e. everything has its own specific 'nature', its own specific 'powers', from which its own specific acts follow. If there were no cause, we read in Sext. Emp. *Adv. phys.* i. 202, everything might come from anything and at any place and time. Ghazali, as we shall see later, is well aware of this objection against the denial of cause.

p. 153. 3. The soul is the principle of the living, i.e. of that which has the faculty of self-movement which, in its most simple form, in plants, is limited to nutrition, growth, and decay, τροφή, αὔξησις, φθίσις (cf. Arist. *De an.* B 2. 413ᵃ20).

p. 153. 4. e.g. only man can beget man, only the physician can produce health through the concept of health he possesses (see e.g. Arist. *Met.* Λ 4 ad fin.).

p. 154. 1. i.e. if the One were regarded as a universal and if it were regarded as acting *qua* universal. Here Averroës turns against Plato's theory of ideas; however, the word he uses here in the text for universals, حال, is that used by the theologians (a translation of the term πῶς ἔχον of the Stoics); he seems therefore to have in mind here those theologians who regard universals not like the ideas of Platonists, which are ultimate realities, but more like the Stoic λεκτά, things intermediate between reality and unreality (see note 3. 6). The argument he gives, however, is based on that of Aristotle against the conception of Platonic ideas as causes (e.g. *Met.* A 9. 991ᵃ19 sqq.): How can the identical idea remain in itself and exist apart, and at the same time transfer itself to innumerable things? How can it be at the same time the model and the copy? But Aristotle's conception of becoming exhibits the same difficulty, and the relation of the universal to the individual remains obscure. For when John begets Peter, what John transfers to Peter is not his identity, but a universal form, i.e. humanity, the identical form which every father transfers to his son. But how can the many possess what is identical and transfer it, and how can the individual proceed from the universal?

p. 154. 2. According to the Aristotelian doctrine that what exists primarily and absolutely is the individual substance (cf. e.g. Arist. *Met.* Z 1. 1028ᵃ30).

p. 154. 3. i.e. in a becoming through universals.

p. 154. 4. According to the Aristotelian conception of truth (*Met.* Γ 6. 1011ᵇ26) as the correspondence between thought and reality.

p. 154. 5. See p. 107 and note 107. 2.

p. 154. 6. Avicenna shows in his *Theorems and Notices*, p. 180, the same lack of appreciation for Porphyry whose 'Ἀφορμαί he regards as utterly worthless (حَشْف). St. Augustine (*De civ. dei* xix. 22) shows a greater appreciation of Porphyry, whom he calls 'doctissimus philosophorum, quamvis Christianorum acerrimus inimicus'. But Eusebius, *Praep. Ev.* v. 14. 230a says that Porphyry, whom he calls, ironically, ὁ γενναῖος Ἑλλήνων φιλόσοφος, ὁ θαυμαστὸς θεολόγος, ὁ τῶν ἀπορρήτων μύστης, 'this noble philosopher, this marvellous theologian, this adept of the mysteries', tries through his quotation of oracular texts to give the impression that his philosophy—in fact inspired by a demoniac power—contains the secrets of the gods. (For further appreciations of Porphyry see Holstenius, *De vita et scriptis Porphyrii, philosophi*, Rome, 1630, p. 11.)

Averroës refers here probably to the theory of gradual emanation in Porphyry's Ἀφορμαὶ πρὸς τὰ νοητά (known to the Arabs under the title فى العقل والمعقول, cf. A. Mueller, *Die griechischen Philosophen in der arab. Überlieferung*, p. 25).

p. 155. 1. Cf. note 142. 8.

p. 155. 2. i.e. so far as these acts aim at the conservation of the sublunary world; for the less noble cannot be what the more noble aims at (see e.g. Porphyry, *Sententiae* 30).

p. 155. 3. i.e. their efficient causes, i.e. the third principle, ἡ τρίτη ἀρχή, (besides matter and form) of which Aristotle says (*De gen. et corr.* B 9. 335^{b}7) that none of his predecessors had been able to establish it, although they had some slight inkling of it.

p. 155. 4. δύο κινήσεις (*De gen. et corr.* B 10. 336^{a}34), the two motions of the sun along the ecliptic by which it approaches and recedes from any given point on the earth.

p. 155. 5. See the parallel passage (p. 136 and notes). The question of the common internal sense, *sensus communis*, αἴσθησις κοινή (see e.g. *De an.* Γ 1. 425^{a}27) I shall treat later.

p. 156. 1. The world, in the state it exists in, i.e. *our* world, the world as a cosmos, an ordered whole.

p. 156. 2. See note 33. 1; cf. also Ibn Hazm, op. cit. i. 24: becoming implies a prior non-existence, معنى المحدث هو ما لم يكن ثم كان. It may be added here that Zacharias of Mytilene, a contemporary of Philoponus, who in the same way as Philoponus tried to refute Proclus' arguments for the eternity of the world, attempted, in his dialogue *Ammonius seu de mundi opificio*, to rebut Ammonius Hermiae's arguments for this eternity, also asserts that an eternal creation is a contradiction in terms (op. cit., ed. Migne, lxxxv. 1093).

p. 156. 3. Because of the factual evidence, δι' ἐμπειρίαν.

p. 156. 4. Aristotle distinguishes, *Met.* Θ 8. 1050ᵃ30, the actuality which is in the product, e.g. the house which is being built, from the actuality which is in the exercise of the action itself, e.g. the act of seeing which is in the seeing subject.

p. 156. 5. Cf. pp. 98–99 and notes 98. 3 and 99. 2.

p. 157. 1. The Arabic word I translate by 'has come into being' is حادث. I have translated the same term one line above by 'temporal'; the speciousness of the argument lies in the ambiguity of this term.

p. 157. 2. Aristotle lays down as a condition for the First Principle that it must be itself unmoved, that it must be an unmoved mover, *Phys.* Θ 5. 257ᵃ31–257ᵇ13.

p. 158. 1. By 'materialistic theory' is meant not only the mechanistic and atomistic conception of nature held by Democritus and Epicurus (for the arguments against Democritus cf. Arist. *De gen. an.* E 8), but also such a system as that of Strato, who denies the need for an immaterial divine principle for the explanation of the universe (cf. Cic. *Acad. Pr.* ii. 38. 121 'Strato ... negat opere deorum se uti ad fabricandum universum').

p. 158. 2. Aristotle tries to prove (*Met.* α 2), for all four types of cause, that they cannot form an infinite series.

p. 159. 1. See p. 33 and note 33. 2. For the two ways of coming from another thing, the one in which the process is irreversible, the other in which it is reversible, cf. Aristotle, *Met.* α 2. 994ᵃ22 sqq. (see also Arist. *De gen. et corr.* B 11. 338ᵃ5 about rectilinear, εἰς εὐθύ, and circular, κύκλῳ, generation). The difficulty of the whole problem lies in this, that when the cause is regarded as prior in time to the effect and time is eternal, the causal series also has to be eternal.

p. 159. 2. The soul, i.e. the soul as totality, the Platonic or Neoplatonic World-Soul; the intellect, i.e. the νοῦς as a supramundane entity.

p. 159. 3. e.g. Aristotle, *Met.* Λ 5. 1071ᵃ13: ἀνθρώπου αἴτιον ... ὁ πατήρ, καὶ ... ὁ ἥλιος, ἄνθρωπος ἄνθρωπον γεννᾷ καὶ ἥλιος, *Phys.* B 2. 194ᵇ13.

p. 159. 4. This sentence seems to be tautological.

p. 159. 5. First, i.e. nearest to the product of art, but, in fact, last in the series of instruments.

p. 159. 6. This is completely arbitrary; all the instruments are conditions for the existence of the product (cf. also note 11. 3).

p. 159. 7. i.e. from the matter of the dead man a plant comes into being, which through nutrition becomes sperm or menstrual blood (cf. my *Ep. d. Met. d. Av.*, p. 73 and the note 73. 1).

p. 160. 1. See note 142. 8.

p. 160. 2. Body in itself is what is extended in any direction (Arist. *Phys.* Γ 5. 204ᵇ20: σῶμα μὲν γάρ ἐστι τὸ πάντῃ ἔχον διάστασιν) and is perceptible in place (Arist. *Phys.* Γ 5. 205ᵇ31 : πᾶν σῶμα αἰσθητὸν ἐν τόπῳ.

p. 161. 1. Cf. the dictum of Zeno of Citium (Sext. Emp. *Adv. phys.* i. 104): the rational is better than the non-rational and the animate better than the inanimate, but nothing is better than the cosmos, therefore the cosmos is rational and animate.

p. 161. 2. This refers, I think, to the passage in Themistius, *Paraphrasis in libr. Λ Metaphys.*, ed. Landauer, 5. 22: 'in omnibus vero, quae mutantur, id quod mutationem subit necessario corpus est quoddam; idcirco substantiae perpetuae [i.e. the heavenly movers which are identified with their bodies] quae generationem et corruptionem non subeunt, cum loco mutentur et ipsae, fieri non potest quin corpora sint.'

p. 161. 3. i.e. they *are* life in themselves; this seems to me, however, an impossible conception, for life or soul is defined by Aristotle in relation to a body which is moved by it; soul is the faculty of self-movement in a body, *De an.* B 1. 412ᵇ16: ἡ ψυχὴ λόγος σώματος φυσικοῦ τοιουδὶ ἔχοντος ἀρχὴν κινήσεως καὶ στάσεως ἐν ἑαυτῷ.

p. 161. 4. For that which can be attributed to a substance is its accidents, and the accidental—cf. e.g. Aristotle, *Met.* K 8. 1065ᵃ1—is what occurs, but neither necessarily nor for the most part; and what can or cannot occur possesses matter (cf. e.g. *Met.* Θ 7. 1032ᵃ20).

p. 161. 5. A first cause, according to Ghazali, implies a coming into existence, but a circular process is infinite *a parte post*.

p. 162. 1. i.e. the first cause.

p. 162. 2. That an infinite series of entities not having position is possible does not follow any more than that an infinite series of entities having a position should be impossible.

p. 163. 1. See, however, note 14. 6.

p. 163. 2. Cf. note 14. 6.

p. 163. 3. Leibniz, who, of the great philosophers since Descartes, is the one most strongly dependent on scholastic philosophy (in Spinoza the influence of Stoicism is overwhelming) has this argument in the following form in his *Monadology* (Erdmann, p. 708): The connexion of all contingent things leads us to conclude that outside this connexion there is a necessary Being who is their source and origin.

p. 163. 4. Avicenna, for the reason given by Averroës, places this argument at the beginning of the metaphysical part of his *Recovery* (i. 6–7). He is perfectly justified in ascribing this argument to the philosophers, for it is implied in Aristotle's whole system, and all the elements in it are found in Aristotle himself: the dichotomy of reality into the eternal and divine and the possible is asserted by Aristotle, *De gen. an.* B 1. 731ᵇ24; that everything absolutely necessary is eternal, *Eth. Nic.* Z 3. 1139ᵇ24 (absolutely, ἁπλῶς, as distinguished from the hypothetically, ἐξ ὑποθέσεως, necessary: see e.g. *Phys.* B 9. 199ᵇ34); that 'eternal' and 'necessary' are convertible, *De gen. et corr.* B 11. 338ᵃ1; that the eternal is essentially prior to the perishable, *Met.* Θ 8. 1050ᵇ7; that the actual is essentially prior to the potential, *Met.* Θ 8. 1050ᵃ4; that certain things owe their necessity to something other than themselves, others not, but are the cause of the necessity in others, *Met.* Δ 5. 1015ᵇ9; that nothing which exists necessarily can be potential, *Met.* Θ 8. 1050ᵇ18; that in its primary and absolute sense the necessary is the simple, *Met.* Δ 5. 1015ᵇ11; finally, the necessity of an eternal unmoved substance is proved *Met.* Λ 6, and it is affirmed at *Met.* Λ 7. 1072ᵇ10 that the first mover possesses its existence of necessity, ἐξ ἀνάγκης ἄρα ἐστὶν ὄν.

The argument is based on the confusion, deeply rooted in Aristotle's system, of the ontological with the logical—here of ontological necessity with logical necessity, of necessity in reality with necessary truth. That the angles of the triangle are equal to two right angles is a necessary universal truth; it is not valid at one time, invalid at another time (see Arist. *Met.* Θ 10. 1052ᵃ4), but its validity is eternal or rather timeless (this immutability of truth concerns not only the relations of universals but also all past events; for also the past is at rest, forever beyond the sway of time—it is eternally true that once there lived in Athens a man called Socrates; it is the trembling, ever-changing 'now' that alters today's truth into tomorrow's falsehood). This being-valid of truth is confused by Aristotle with ontological being, i.e. the existence of individuals in reality; and he says at *Met.* Θ 10. 1051ᵇ1 that being in the strictest sense is truth, τὸ δὲ κυριώτατα ὂν ἀληθές (about the threefold conception of truth in Aristotle see my *Ep. d. Met. d. Av.*, note 81. 3). So it comes about that the intrinsic necessity attributed to timeless universal truth is transferred to the eternal existence of an individual prime mover, i.e. God. This identification of God and Truth is found in both Christian and Muslim theology; 'te invoco, deus veritas, in quo et a quo et per quem vera sunt quae vera sunt omnia', says St. Augustine, *Soliloq.* i. 1. 3 and 'The Truth (الحق)' is an epithet applied to God by the Muslim theologians with the meaning of 'the necessarily-existing by His own essence' (see Lane, *Ar.-Engl. Dict.*).

p. 163. 5. The theory of the theologians that the possibles in God need for their actualization in time a necessary eternally existent, i.e. God, is nothing but the Jewish–Christian–Muslim conception of creation expressed in Aristotelian terminology.

p. 164. 1. e.g. in his *Recovery*, *Met.* i. 6: فنقول ان الواجب الوجود بذاته لا علة له وان الممكن بذاته له علة. The potential (i.e. matter) needs a cause for its actualization, and everything in the world except the prime mover has some degree of potentiality, since potentiality implies a capacity for change.

p. 164. 2. See below and note 164. 9.

p. 164. 3. Averroës here means, I think, by 'possible' the transitory, sublunary things, and by 'necessary' the separate Intellects, the eternal celestial bodies, or the world as a whole.

p. 164. 4. i.e. matter, or rather the transient individual.

p. 164. 5. i.e. everything eternal with the exception of God; in this argument there is implied a trichotomy of reality into the absolutely necessary (i.e. the prime mover), the necessary-possible or hypothetically necessary (i.e. everything eternal, with the exception of the prime mover), and the possible (i.e. actualized matter), which corresponds to the Aristotelian trichotomy of the absolute mover, the moving and moved, and the absolutely moved (cf. *De an.* $\varGamma$ 10. 433^{b}13; *Met.* $\varLambda$ 7. 1072^{a}24; *Phys.* $\varTheta$ 5. 256^{b}20).

p. 164. 6. But such an assumption would be false, as Averroës will show below, for there cannot be an infinite series of necessary causes.

p. 164. 7. For material causes cannot proceed from one another endlessly, e.g. flesh from earth, earth from air, air from fire, and so on (Arist. *Met.* α 2. 994^{a}3).

p. 164. 8. i.e. that the world, which is eternal as a whole, has a cause.

p. 164. 9. This formula shows clearly the confusion between the logical and the ontological, for 'cause' is a purely ontological concept and an event is necessary just when it *has* a cause.

p. 164. 10. Ghazali regards it as contradictory that every member of the series should have a cause, but that the whole series should have none. He accepts it, however, here for the sake of argument.

p. 165. 1. i.e. the elements are eternal.

p. 165. 2. Ghazali's argument is irrefutable. It is always the same question: How can an eternal world have a first cause?

p. 165. 3. Averroës means that by proving that the possible transient causes need an eternal necessary cause (heaven, for instance) it is not yet proved that the series of necessary agents is finite. The proof he gives is of course a *petitio principii*, for why should there be more than one eternal mover?

p. 165. 4. Averroës tries to avoid Ghazali's objection by dropping Avicenna's identification of the necessary and the causeless, but the objection remains valid and can be directed against Aristotle himself; for if eternity implies both a necessity and an actuality which need no actualizer, the world as a whole, being eternal, will be both necessary and causeless.

NOTES

p. 166. 1. i.e. the material causes, flesh, earth, and air are essential, and therefore cannot form an infinite series.

p. 166. 2. Cf. note 165. 4.

p. 166. 3. The eternity of the one eternal being is timeless eternity, αἰών, دهر; see, however, note 70. 5 and p. 37.

p. 167. 1. i.e. Ghazali, as frequently, does not want to make a positive assertion; he wants only to show the futility of the philosophers' arguments; نتيجة ما يرام (*petitio principii*) is a literal translation of the Greek τὸ ἐξ ἀρχῆς αἰτεῖσθαι.

p. 167. 2. i.e. the totality of a finite number of finites is finite (this is, of course, a tautology).

p. 167. 3. i.e. the materialists believe that every member of the series has a cause, but that the members are infinite in number and therefore there is no first cause; he ought really to have said, since he speaks here of a temporal, not a causal series, 'The materialists believe that every part has a beginning, but that the parts are infinite in number and that therefore the series has no beginning'; but since time is, in Aristotelian philosophy, a function of movement (for time is the number of movement in respect of before and after), the time-series and the series of movements are identified.

p. 167. 4. Here, too, Averroës speaks of a causal series, not of the time-series. Genera are eternal according to Aristotle, *De gen. an.* B 1. 731^{b}35: διὸ γένος ἀεὶ ἀνθρώπων καὶ ζῴων ἐστὶ καὶ φυτῶν, e.g. in the series father–son–father every individual is mortal, but the series is infinite and man as a genus is eternal; it is through reproduction and the eternity of their genus that animals participate in the eternal and the divine, cf. Aristotle, *De an.* B 414^{a}29 and Plato, *Symp.* 206 e and 207 a. Cf. also St. Augustine, *De civ. dei* vi. 4: 'alii namque, sicut de ipso mundo crediderunt, semper fuisse homines opinantur. unde ait et Apuleius, cum hoc animantium genus describant: *singillatim mortales, cuncti tamen universo genere perpetui*'.

p. 167. 5. i.e. the philosophers do not object to an infinite series of non-essential causes, but this series must depend on an eternal essential cause outside it.

p. 168. 1. This subjective conception would seem to imply that all finitude and particularity depend solely on our minds, and is in contradiction to p. 33—and also to the following sentence in the text—where the particularity in the heavenly movements serves to explain the particularity and transiency of sublunary affairs. The contradiction is based on the difficulty of, on the one side, guarding the eternal from all contamination with the transitory, and on the other, deriving the transient from the eternal.

p. 168. 2. This sentence is of course tautological: he who does not concede the infinity of a series of causes must admit that this series is finite.

p. 169. 1. i.e. even if some of these imaginary things are regarded as causes of other imaginary things.

p. 169. 2. Cf. p. 12.

p. 169. 3. Cf. p. 14.

p. 169. 4. i.e. of the one eternal soul subsisting by itself.

p. 169. 5. For the origination of the elements from each other see Aristotle, *De gen. et corr.* B 4.

p. 170. 1. i.e. they would be individually different, but would have the species of necessary existence in common. The argument given here by Ghazali is taken from Avicenna's *Salvation*, p. 374, where the author summarizes the argument he gives in *The Recovery* (*Met.* i. 7) by which he tries to prove that the necessary existent can be neither a genus nor a species, but must be the simple Monad. (That the absolute One, τὸ πάντως ἕν, cannot be predicated of anything, and therefore cannot be a genus, is proved by Plotinus, *Enn.* vi. 2. 9.) This argument, although its elements are to be found in Aristotle (see note 163. 4), does not occur in his works in this form. It rests on the Platonic, Aristotelian, and Neoplatonic confusion between the logical concept of species and specific difference, and the ontological concept of cause (the word εἶδος in Aristotle's philosophy means both the logical concept of species and the ontological concept of 'form', which is for Aristotle a kind of cause; Plato also gives his 'ideas' a dynamic sense—e.g. *Phaedo* 100 d): every plurality has a specific difference which must be caused by an entity, which, if it contained a plurality, would again need a cause. (There is a similar confusion in Aristotle's philosophy between the logical concept of genus and the ontological concept of matter; cf., for example, *Met.* Δ 28. 1024ᵇ9.)

p. 170. 2. Avicenna, *Recovery*, loc. cit., says: ليس حقيقة الواجب الوجود الا نفس تاكد الوجود, 'the nature of the necessary existent is simply the establishing of its existence through its essence'; cf. Spinoza, *Eth.* i, prop. iii: 'ad naturam substantiae pertinet existere—ipsius essentia involvit necessario existentiam'. I should agree with Ghazali that the only meaning one can give to this—as to Spinoza's related expression *causa sui*—is that it has no cause whatever. Plotinus also affirms that the existence of the First is identical with His essence: οὐκ ἄλλο μὲν αὐτό, ἄλλο δὲ ἡ οὐσία αὐτοῦ, *Enn.* vi. 8. 12.

p. 170. 3. Cf. Aristotle, *Met.* Λ 8. 1074ᵃ33: plurality is the consequence of matter, ὅσα ἀριθμῷ πολλὰ ὕλην ἔχει . . . humanity applies to many, e.g. to Socrates, &c. . . . but the primary essence has no matter, for it is perfect reality (ἐντελέχεια). That the Monad is prior to plurality (πᾶν πλῆθος δεύτερόν ἐστι τοῦ ἑνός) is one of the basic principles of Neoplatonism; for its proof, based on the confusion mentioned above, see, for example, Proclus, *Instit. Theol.*, prop. v.

p. 171. 1. i.e. if black is black through its essence and the essence of black is the species 'colouredness', then red will not be a colour; if, on the other hand, the essence of black is black itself, the species (or exterior cause) 'colouredness', which has made it a colour, will be added to it; in this case, however, black ought to be separable from colour in thought or imagination, for something added to an essence by a cause can be separated from it in thought (Ghazali here means, I presume, the non-essential characteristics of a thing, e.g. a man may be thought of as being without hands: cf. Averroës's discussion below), but black is not separable in thought or imagination from colour, and therefore cannot have been made a colour by a cause. The difficulty of the separation of black and colour in thought involved in this argument, in which there is a serious confusion between the logical and the ontological, rests on the common confusion between the meaning of the abstract universal and its representation: black in reality or as represented is indeed a colour, but the abstract term 'blackness' means only the characterization of a colour, not a colour itself, just as 'humanity' does not mean a man. Ghazali's argument seems to refer to the passage in Avicenna's *Salvation*, p. 378, where he raises the difficulty why colour cannot exist in reality without being black or white, although colouredness is not colouredness through either of them.

p. 172. 1. Averroës in his answer implies, of course, what Ghazali denies, that the assertion that the necessary existent exists through its essence has a positive meaning.

p. 172. 2. Averroës seems to mean that everything except the necessary existent needs a cause for its existence, and only the necessary existent has the property of existing through its essence; although the common term 'existing through a cause' cannot be applied to the necessary existent, this property is not denied. This answer implies what Ghazali denies, that the essence of the necessary existent has a positive property.

p. 173. 1. This sentence is of course self-contradictory, for how can existents be differentiated, when they differ neither in species nor individually? As we have seen, the existence of a number of immaterial, independent movers is one of the contradictions in Aristotle's philosophy, which bases all plurality on matter and makes all becoming dependent on one primary cause (cf. note 141. 2).

p. 173. 2. Difference in rank, however, presupposes both a numerical and a specific difference.

p. 174. 1. The tripartite disjunction is: two necessary existents differ (1) either numerically, (2) or in species, (3) or in rank. The third case is true, therefore the necessary existents are one. This is, of course, self-contradictory. What he means is that the third case is false too. There can be only one First.

p. 174. 2. This so-called second proof, that every duality implies a unity prior to it, is simply an elaboration of the first argument. Avicenna in his *Salvation* devotes three sections to proving the uniqueness of the necessary existent, in a passage in which is found the substance of what Ghazali says here: (1) a section entitled 'that the species of the necessary existent cannot be predicated of many', p. 374; (2) a section entitled 'that the necessary existent is one in every way', p. 375; (3) a section entitled 'that there cannot be two necessary existents', p. 375.

p. 174. 3. This implies that to the First not even existence can be attributed, and this, indeed, is asserted by Plotinus (*Enn.* vi. 7. 16), who affirms that even the copula ἔστι cannot be attributed to the First; for nothing at all can be attributed to Him, although we can possess Him, without being able to name Him, feeling as in divine enthusiasm that we possess something god-like in our bosom (cf. *Enn.* v. 3. 14). But this conception, which would logically imply the very negation of God, is identified with the view that God's being, like His unity, is something *sui generis*, that God's existence is a super-existence.

Aristotle had already affirmed (e.g. *Met.* Γ 2. 1003ᵃ33) that being is attributed analogically, i.e. in relation to one central point, to one single nature, πρὸς ἓν καὶ μίαν τινὰ φύσιν (this is the reason why the study of being belongs to one single science i.e. metaphysics), and since this central point is substance and substance in its highest form is pure eternal being, i.e. God, simply from this conception the Neoplatonic, the mystical view of reality, the dream-view of finite reality, may be deduced. It is only God, the Eternal, who in reality exists; it is we, the finite beings, whose very existence is already intermingled with not-being, whose stuff is made of dreams.

p. 174. 4. One should not ascribe to the First even a merely logical duality, says Plotinus, *Enn.* vi. 8. 13: οὐ ποιητέον οὐδ' ὡς εἰς ἐπίνοιαν δύο.

p. 174. 5. For the formula, of which the word is a sign, becomes the definition of the thing (ὁ γὰρ λόγος οὗ τὸ ὄνομα σημεῖον ὁρισμὸς ἔσται, Arist. *Met.* Γ 7. 1012ᵃ24).

p. 175. 1. i.e. they hold that the attributes of God are distinct from His essence.

p. 175. 2. What Averroës affirms here is in contradiction with the passage in Aristotle's *Metaphysics*, discussed in note 174. 3, where he asserts that being is attributed analogically and where he expressly denies that it is attributed equivocally (ὁμωνύμως, Γ 1. 1003ᵃ34).

p. 175. 3. In his *Salvation* (p. 375) Avicenna affirms that the First cannot be divided either quantitatively, or through constituent principles, or through the parts of the definition. Aristotle mentions these three types of division at *Met.* Δ 25, where he gives a fivefold definition of μέρος, part.

p. 176. 1. i.e. attributes which the theologians ascribe to God, but which are denied to Him by Plotinus, for whom God has neither will nor thought, nor even any action, ἐνέργεια, at all; cf. e.g. *Enn.* i. 7. 1 and vi. 9. 6: ὥστε τῷ ἑνὶ οὐδὲν ἀγαθόν ἐστιν, οὐδὲ βούλησις τοίνυν οὐδενός. However, we find in Plotinus the same contradiction as we have already found in Aristotle. For Plotinus, too, God, eternally at rest, ἐν ἡσύχῳ, is at the same time the eternally constant aim and passive object of desire to which everything tends, and the power of everything, δύναμις τῶν πάντων (iii. 8. 10 ad init.), essentially activity and eternal wakefulness, ἐγρήγορσις, (vi. 8. 16).

p. 176. 2. Quiddity, whatness, ماهية, τὸ τί ἐστιν or τὸ τί ἦν εἶναι (generally synonymous with ذات, οὐσία), is an ambiguous term which in this passage means both the definition of a thing and any universal concept.

p. 176. 3. i.e. the universal 'heaven' is eternally realized in the individually existent heaven, but the universal 'man' has a temporary existence in Zaid and 'Amr.

p. 176. 4. i.e. every 'this' is a 'what', a 'something', but God's 'whatness' is that He is.

p. 176. 5. Man, tree, heaven are only universals, but God is at the same time a universal, a Platonic idea, and an individual existent.

p. 177. 1. See p. 142 and note 142. 8.

p. 178. 1. Its identity or its individuality, i.e. what constitutes its true being, its very nature (cf. e.g. Arist. *Met.* Z 4).

p. 178. 2. Through derivative words, through derivation, باشتقاق الاسم, through paronomasia (cf. Arist. *Cat.* 1. 1ᵃ12): perhaps one might translate 'by analogy', for the meaning of the derivative word bears an analogy to that of the primitive (cf. Arist. *Met.* Γ 2).

p. 178. 3. i.e. we can say of man that he is an animal, for animal is part of his essence; we cannot say of him that he is knowledge, because knowledge is a non-essential attribute, although we can ascribe to him knowing (*which is a word derived from knowledge*) as an accident.

p. 178. 4. This subjectivist conception seems to stand in contradiction to what he has said before, viz. that in immaterial existents no essential attributes can be imagined of which their essence consists.

p. 178. 5. This interesting passage is a not illegitimate interpretation of the theory of certain Greek Fathers—Averroës refers here probably to St. John Damascene—who, to avoid the danger of Tritheism and to safeguard the Unity of God, seem sometimes to regard the distinction of the persons as a purely logical one. Post-Aristotelian philosophers (and the Arabs followed their example, as we have seen), in order to solve certain philosophical difficulties, often employ the argument of subjectivity and relativity, and the Greek Fathers made an abundant use both of it and of the term κατ' ἐπίνοιαν (according to thought, i.e. purely logical). According to St. John Damascene there exists between the three divine Persons a compenetration (which he calls περιχώρησις, circumincession); the divine Persons have but one will and one activity, and the son (*logos*) and the Spirit (*pneuma*) are faculties (δυνάμεις) of the Father, the distinction between Them resting only on reason, ἐπινοίᾳ δὲ τὸ διῃρημένον (*De fide orthod.*, Migne, xciv. 828).

p. 179. 1. Averroës identifies reality and truth, and here gives Aristotle's transeunt definition of truth, *Met.* Γ 7. 1011ᵇ26: τὸ μὲν γὰρ λέγειν τὸ ὂν μὴ εἶναι ἢ τὸ μὴ ὂν εἶναι ψεῦδος, τὸ δὲ τὸ ὂν εἶναι καὶ τὸ μὴ ὂν μὴ εἶναι ἀληθές, of which Thomas Aquinas (*Contra gent.* i. 59) gives the following interpretation: 'veritas intellectus est adaequatio intellectus et rei, secundum quod intellectus dicit esse quod est, vel non esse quod non est'.

p. 179. 2. This is scarcely correct, according to Aristotle. When he defines truth (*De an.* Γ 8. 432ᵃ11) as a συμπλοκὴ νοημάτων he regards it as a relation inside the mind, and has abandoned the transeunt conception.

p. 179. 3. He means: when we ask whether something exists or not, this 'something' must be an entity in the mind, since we are not yet sure that it exists in reality.

p. 179. 4. According to Aristotle (e.g. *Met. B* 3. 998ᵇ22) being is not really a genus; for 'being' as used with reference to the ten categories see, for example, Aristotle, *Met.* Θ 10. 1051ᵃ34 and *Met. Δ* 7. 1017ᵃ24.

p. 179. 5. I do not know whether Averroës here has in view the Neoplatonic mystical conception that the highest reality in itself is one, and that it is thought that originates multiplicity; it is through the dialectical process of the νοῦς (according to Plotinus, *Enn.* vi. 7. 13) that all differentiation comes into being; it is the nature of the νοῦς to differentiate universally, φύσιν ἄρα ἔχει ἐπὶ πᾶν ἑτεροιοῦσθαι. It may be, however, that Averroës means that by regarding existence solely as the true, another aspect of existence is neglected.

p. 179. 6. Entity, ذات, and thing, شيء, are translations of the Stoic term τί, the highest genus of all being, including the existent and the non-existent.

p. 179. 7. Cf. note 174. 3.

p. 179. 8. Aristotle does not clearly distinguish between 'being' ('that which is', τὸ ὄν) as a substantive and 'being' ('to be', τὸ εἶναι) as a verb. If one takes 'being' as a verb, it is plausible to regard existence as an accident, for in the sentence 'a thing is', 'is' as an attribute is an accident; taken, however, as a substantive, being, τὸ ὄν, is the equivalent of ἡ οὐσία, i.e. substance. Avicenna takes the former, Averroës the latter view. For Averroës

NOTES

existence is the existent thing itself or the genus of existing things (though, regarded as a genus, it can be predicated and is an accident). See also my *Ep. d. Met. d. Av.* pp. iv–v.

p. 180. 1. The existents of first intention (الوجه الاول, πρώτη θέσις, *prima intentio*, in scholastic terminology), i.e. first intention of the mind, are the individual things in the external world of which the ten categories or predicaments are the highest genera; the existents of second intention (الوجه الثاني, δευτέρα θέσις) are the concepts in the mind of which the five predicables, genus, species, differentia, property, and accident, are the highest genera. As early as Aristotle (*Cat.* 5. 2ª14) we find the term δεύτεραι οὐσίαι for the genera and species, which, however, are regarded in his philosophy as having some objective existence, although not an independent, separate (χωριστός) one.

p. 180. 2. Since the things in the mind are in conformity with the things outside the mind.

p. 180. 3. There is some confusion here; the 'true' means an existent in the mind, but this existent in the mind seems to be aware of an existent outside the mind and able to compare itself with it. The confusion is based on the common error of not distinguishing between thought, the thinking as an act, the meaning in an active sense, and thought—the object of thought, the thing meant. The former may be said (by a spatial metaphor) to be *in* the mind; to the latter there belongs everything thinkable, existing or non-existing, possible or impossible, false or true; it is neither in your mind nor in mine, for exactly the same thing may be meant by you and by me.

p. 180. 4. i.e. you cannot know *what* a thing is before you know *that* it is; cf. Aristotle *Anal. Post.* B 7. 92ᵇ4: ἀνάγκη γὰρ τὸν εἰδότα τὸ τί ἐστιν ἄνθρωπος ἢ ἄλλο ὁτιοῦν, εἰδέναι καὶ ὅτι ἔστιν.

p. 180. 5. This sentence is not found in the *Categories*. Averroës seems to take it as an interpretation of the beginning of *Cat.* cap. 5, where it is said that the individual cannot be predicated and that it is the universal which predicates the individual.

p. 180. 6. Cf. Aristotle, *De an.* B 5. 417ᵇ22: τῶν καθ' ἕκαστον ἡ κατ' ἐνέργειαν αἴσθησις, ἡ δὲ ἐπιστήμη τῶν καθόλου.

p. 180. 7. Aristotle does not say explicitly that the universal exists only in the mind (the forms existing in the individuals express a universality; cf. note 180. 1), although according to him knowledge refers always to the essential, the universal (cf. e.g. *Met.* Z 6. 1031ᵇ20: τὸ ἐπίστασθαι ἕκαστον τοῦτό ἐστι τὸ τί ἦν εἶναι ἐπίστασθαι); Averroës here follows an interpretation which is found as early as Alexander of Aphrodisias, *De an.* (Bruns), p. 90. 5: νοούμενα δὲ χωρὶς ὕλης κοινά τε καὶ καθόλου γίνεται, καὶ τότε ἐστὶ νοῦς, ὅταν νοῆται, εἰ δὲ μὴ νοοῖτο, οὐδὲ ἔστιν ἔτι, ὥστε χωρισθέντα τοῦ νοοῦντος αὐτὰ νοῦ φθείρεται. Of course this conception destroys the definition of truth as conformity between things inside the mind and things outside it.

p. 180. 8. 'by it': i.e. by its existence; existence is not an accident, but the essence itself, according to Averroës.

p. 181. 1. Cf. my *Ep. d. Met. d. Av.* pp. 8–9. Aristotle himself had seen this difficulty, and denied (cf. note 179. 4) that existence or being was a genus; however, his own conception that even the non-existent, since it *is* a non-existent, possesses being in a certain way, implies the same infinite regress, for if the non-existent is, then the non-existence of the non-existent is, and so on.

p. 181. 2. The theory here expounded, that the plurality of negations and relations attributed to God does not destroy His unity, is found in Avicenna, *Salvation*, pp. 408 sqq., and *Recovery*, Met. viii. 7–8. The basic principle, that all determination of God is either negative or relative, is found in Plotinus: negative, e.g. Enn. vi. 8. 11 (cf. v. 3. 14): ἐν ἀφαιρέσει πάντα τὰ περὶ τούτου λεγόμενα, relative, Enn. vi. 9. 3: ἐπεὶ καὶ τὸ αἴτιον λέγειν οὐ κατηγορεῖν ἐστι συμβεβηκός τι αὐτῷ, ἀλλ' ἡμῖν, ὅτι ἔχομέν τι παρ' αὐτοῦ ἐκείνου ὄντος ἐν αὐτῷ.

p. 181. 3. 'apprehended', معلوم, καταληπτός. We are able, says Plotinus (Enn. v. 3. 14), to apprehend Him without being able to name Him, ἔχειν δὲ οὐ κωλυόμεθα, κἂν μὴ λέγωμεν. This seems more closely in agreement with Averroës than with Avicenna, who seems to regard existence as a positive determination in God, whereas all the other attributes determine this existence either relatively or negatively; cf. *Salvation*, p. 410: الصفة الأولى للواجب انه ان وموجود ثم الصفات الاخرى يكون بعضها المتعين فيه هذا الوجود مع اضافة وبعضها هذا الوجود مع السلب, the first attribute of the necessary being is that it is (اِن) and exists; the other attributes determine this existence either relatively or negatively. Compare also Plotinus, Enn. vi. 7. 38, where it is said that 'is', ἐστί, cannot be predicated of God, but points to His essence, τὸ δέ ἐστιν οὐχ ὡς κατ' ἄλλου ἄλλο, ἀλλ' ὡς σημαῖνον ὃ ἔστι.

p. 181. 4. This is part of the Aristotelian definition of substance (the individual), *Cat.* 5. 2ᵃ11: οὐσία δέ ἐστιν ... ἣ μήτε καθ' ὑποκειμένου τινὸς λέγεται μήτ' ἐν ὑποκειμένῳ τινί ἐστιν. It is negative, since *individuum est ineffabile*; it is experienced, but beyond description.

p. 182. 1. To this negative definition of intellect Averroës objects, as we shall see on p. 186. It is, however, in agreement with Avicenna, op. cit. p. 410: واذا قيل عقل ... لم يعن بالحقيقة الا ان هذا الوجود مسلوبا عنه جواز مخالطة المادة وعلاقتها, when He is called intellect, this only means that His existence cannot be mixed with matter and its accompaniments.

p. 182. 2. Here there is a reference to the problem of self-consciousness as set forth by Aristotle (*De an.* Γ 2. 425^{b}12–25; Γ 4. 430^{a}2–9): if perception (or thought) needed another perception (or thought) to become conscious of itself, we should have an infinite regress. The difficulty had been seen already by Plato, *Charmides* 168 d, e. The problem is mentioned by Avicenna in his *Salvation*, pp. 399–400, in the chapter in which he sets out to prove that the necessary existent is in itself the thought, the thinker, and the object of thought.

p. 182. 3. According to Aristotle (*De an.* Γ 4. 430^{a}5) there is an intermission in the process of our thinking.

p. 182. 4. For Clemens Alexandrinus, *Strom.* vii. 7. 42, the mark which distinguishes God's action from the action of fire is will: God is not involuntarily good (ἄκων ἀγαθός) as the fire is involuntarily productive of warmth; in Him the imparting of good things is voluntary, ἑκούσιος.

p. 182. 5. This whole passage seems to refer to Plotinus, *Enn.* vi. 8. 12–13. The presence (παρουσία) of the good is not accidental in God, according to Plotinus, *Enn.* vi. 8. 13. His essence is not external to His will. The good in Him implies a will which does not destroy His unity. In addition God's act cannot be differentiated from His essence, εἰ μὲν οὖν ἐστί τις ἐνέργεια ἐν αὐτῷ, καὶ ἐν τῇ ἐνεργείᾳ αὐτὸν θησόμεθα, οὐδ' ἂν διὰ τοῦτο εἴη ἂν ἕτερον αὑτοῦ (*Enn.* vi. 8. 12). Each of us, through his body, is far distant from the Essence; through his soul he participates in the Essence, but he is not fundamentally essence (κυρίως οὐσία) and therefore not master of his essence (*Enn.* vi. 8. 12).

p. 183. 1. 'in second intention', κατὰ παρακολούθησιν, as a necessary consequence (the term is Stoic), for the Universe in itself is not an end, but a consequence. For the theory based on Plato that the visible world has not been created by intention, λογισμῷ, but by necessity, ἀνάγκῃ, see, for example, Plotinus, *Enn.* iii. 2. 2.

p. 183. 2. Cf. Plotinus, *Enn.* vi. 4. 3: God remains in Himself, and from Him all powers emanate to everything, δυνάμεις δὲ ἀπ' αὐτοῦ ἰέναι ἐπὶ πάντα.

p. 183. 3. This seems to be based on the Aristotelian distinction between the theoretical and the practical Intellect (e.g. *De an.* Γ 9. 432^{b}26) and the commentators' division of the Aristotelian philosophy into the theoretical and the practical.

p. 183. 4. Cf. the passage in Clemens Alexandrinus, *Protr.* c. iv, 63, Stählin, i. 48. 18, where he says that God creates merely through His will; the effect follows His mere willing immediately, ψιλῷ τῷ βούλεσθαι δημιουργεῖ καὶ τῷ μόνον ἐθελῆσαι αὐτὸν ἕπεται τὸ γεγενῆσθαι.

p. 183. 5. It seemed to me, says Plotinus (*Enn.* v. 8. 7), that if we ourselves were the archetypes, the essence, and the forms all together, and if the form which produces the sublunary things were our essence, we should create without exertion, ἐδόκει δέ μοι, ὅτι καί, εἰ ἡμεῖς ἀρχέτυπα καὶ οὐσία καὶ εἴδη ἅμα, καὶ τὸ εἶδος τὸ ποιοῦν ἐνταῦθα ἦν ἡμῶν οὐσία, ἐκράτησεν ἂν ἄνευ πόνων ἡ ἡμετέρα δημιουργία.

p. 183. 6. Cf. Aristotle, *De mot. an.* 7. 701ᵃ 35: ἡ ἐσχάτη αἰτία τοῦ κινεῖσθαι ὄρεξις, αὕτη δὲ γίνεται ἢ δι' αἰσθήσεως ἢ διὰ φαντασίας καὶ νοήσεως.

p. 184. 1. Life belongs also to God, says Aristotle (*Met.* Λ 7. 1072ᵇ26 καὶ ζωὴ δέ γε ὑπάρχει); we say therefore that God is a living being, eternal, perfectly good, so that life and timeless eternity, continuous and unending, belong to God; φαμὲν δὴ τὸν θεὸν εἶναι ζῷον ἀίδιον ἄριστον, ὥστε ζωὴ καὶ αἰὼν συνεχὴς καὶ ἀίδιος ὑπάρχει τῷ θεῷ. According to Plotinus, *Enn.* vi. 5. 12, an inexhaustible and infinite life-stream proceeds from God, whose nature is as it were boiling over with life, φύσιν ... ἐν αὐτῇ οἷον ὑπερζέουσαν ζωῇ.

p. 184. 2. 'not for an end which refers to Himself'; this is, as Avicenna says (*Salvation*, p. 411), a negative attribute. Cf. Plotinus, for example, *Enn.* vi. 9. 6: ἀλλ' ἔστιν ὑπεράγαθον καὶ αὐτὸ οὐχ ἑαυτῷ, τοῖς δ' ἄλλοις ἀγαθόν, εἴ τι αὐτοῦ δύναται μεταλαμβάνειν, He is the 'hypergood': He is the good not for Himself, but for the others who can participate in Him. The doctrine of God's generosity (ἀφθονία) goes back to the *Timaeus*-passage 29 d: He was good, and the good can never grudge anything to anything. And being generous, He desired that all things should be as like Himself as they could be.

p. 184. 3. Avicenna gives, for example, in his *Theorems and Notices*, Forget, p. 159, this definition of generosity: الجود افادة ما ينبغى لا لعوض. Generosity is giving in the right way, not for the sake of reward. In his *Recovery*, *Met.* vi. 5, he has a long passage about generosity.

p. 184. 4. For badness as a στέρησις or ἀπουσία (or ἔλλειψις) ἀγαθοῦ see Plotinus, *Enn.* i. 8. 3. The basic idea that the cause of badness lies in matter as non-being is to be found already in Plato, *Tim.* 46 c, 46 e, 48 a.

p. 184. 5. For the highest good as the order (τάξις) of the universe cf. Aristotle, *Met.* Λ 10. 1075ᵃ11.

p. 184. 6. 'the lover and the beloved'; cf. Plotinus, *Enn.* vi. 8. 15 (ad init.): καὶ ἐράσμιον καὶ ἔρως ὁ αὐτὸς καὶ αὐτοῦ ἔρως.

p. 184. 7. The doctrine of God's joy as based on His thought goes back to the passage of Aristotle, *Met.* Λ 7. 1072ᵇ14 sqq.

p. 185. 1. And if God is always in this happy condition in which we sometimes are, says Aristotle (*Met.* Λ 7. 1072ᵇ24), this is wonderful, and if in a still happier condition, this is still more wonderful.

p. 185. 2. That all the expressions used to describe God are only metaphorically used (οὐκ ὀρθῶς), since even for thought He is not a duality (οὐδ' ὡς εἰς ἐπίνοιαν δύο), is stated by Plotinus, *Enn.* vi. 8. 13.

p. 186. 1. Cf. note 182. 1.

p. 186. 2. i.e. Plato in the interpretation of Plotinus. God is anterior to thought, says Plotinus, *Enn.* vi. 9. 6: πρὸ γὰρ κινήσεως καὶ πρὸ νοήσεως.

p. 186. 3. The philosophers, however, do not say what this essence is, i.e. who or what the owner is of these attributes.

p. 187. 1. As, for instance, the Ash'arites believe.

p. 187. 2. The example of the hand is to be found in Aristotle, e.g. *De gen. an.* A 19. 726^{b}22: ἡ χεὶρ ἄνευ ψυχικῆς δυνάμεως οὐκ ἔστι χεὶρ ἀλλὰ μόνον ὁμώνυμον, without the faculty of the soul a hand is only a hand equivocally; another example is the finger, δάκτυλος (cf. especially *Met.* Z 10. 1035^{b}25) or the eye, ὀφθαλμός (*De gen. an.* B 1. 735^{a}8) and generally ὁ νεκρὸς ἄνθρωπος ὁμωνύμως, a corpse is a man equivocally (*Meteor.* Δ 12. 389^{b}31).

p. 188. 1. This principle that the cause contains the effect in a superior way is found already, with the example of fire, in Aristotle's *Metaphysics*, i.e. in Book α, which was ascribed by many among the ancients to Pasicles: ἕκαστον δὲ μάλιστα αὐτὸ τῶν ἄλλων, καθ' ὃ καὶ τοῖς ἄλλοις ὑπάρχει τὸ συνώνυμον, οἷον τὸ πῦρ θερμότατον (*Met.* α 1. 993^{b}24). This principle, which implies a gradual degradation in the causal process, in the process of becoming, or in emanation (in coming from), became one of the fundamental truths of Neoplatonism. It is the νοῦς ποιητικός, which is for Alexander of Aphrodisias identical with God, the κυρίως νοητόν, which is the cause of the intelligibility of everything else: τὸ μάλιστα δὴ καὶ τῇ αὑτοῦ φύσει νοητὸν εὐλόγως αἴτιον καὶ τῆς τῶν ἄλλων νοήσεως (Alex. Aphrod. *De an.*, Bruns, 89. 5).

p. 188. 2. Here he seems to have in view the so-called *notiones transcendentales*; in the following, however, he regards certain attributes as being constituted through relation.

p. 188. 3. Cf. Aristotle, *De An.* A 2. 403^{b}25: τὸ ἔμψυχον δὴ τοῦ ἀψύχου δυοῖν μάλιστα διαφέρειν δοκεῖ, κινήσει τε καὶ τῷ αἰσθάνεσθαι, the animate seems to differ from the inanimate through two things: motion and perception.

p. 188. 4. For this theory compare Aristotle, *Met.* H 6.

p. 189. 1. i.e. if the dependent one also were regarded as a necessary existent, this necessary existent would be causally related. Of course the whole argument in this paragraph is tautological. If the dependence of attribute on subject is identified with the dependence of effect on cause, every attribute will require a cause.

p. 189. 2. All this, of course, is a pure tautology.

p. 189. 3. i.e. they admit certain attributes in the Creator.

p. 190. 1. i.e. the denial of absolute duality in the proof given above by Ghazali is, according to him, a *petitio principii*; cf. p. 191.

p. 190. 2. The receptive cause τὸ δεκτικόν (cf. Arist. *Met. I* 4. 1055ᵃ29) is the matter in which the forms or attributes inhere. That the First cannot have a receptive cause seems to be understood in the sense that it cannot itself be receptive of attributes (cf. note 190. 4).

p. 190. 3. Or to call matter a material cause.

p. 190. 4. i.e. the impossibility of an infinite series of receptacles or receptive causes does not imply that the First cannot itself be a receptive cause, i.e. receptive or in possession of attributes.

p. 191. 1. i.e. their argument was an *argumentum ad hominem* (for the *argumentum ad hominem* cf. Arist. *Top. B* 5).

p. 191. 2. Cf. Aristotle, *Top. A* 1. 100ᵃ27 sqq.: Necessary proof depends on our knowledge of the real causes and principles of things; the dialectical syllogism—which Aristotle calls also ἐπιχείρημα—is deduction from opinions: ἀπόδειξις μὲν οὖν ἐστιν, ὅταν ἐξ ἀληθῶν καὶ πρώτων ὁ συλλογισμὸς ᾖ, ἢ ἐκ τοιούτων ἃ διά τινων πρώτων καὶ ἀληθῶν τῆς περὶ αὐτὰ γνώσεως τὴν ἀρχὴν εἴληφεν· διαλεκτικὸς δὲ συλλογισμὸς ὁ ἐξ ἐνδόξων συλλογιζόμενος.

p. 192. 1. i.e. that which has a cause.

p. 192. 2. i.e. the Muʻtazilites deny the existence of any eternal attributes as distinct from the nature or essence of God, whereas the Ashʻarites affirm them.

p. 193. 1. A receptive cause, i.e. matter. For the composition of the compound of matter and attributes an efficient cause is needed, according to the philosophers.

p. 193. 2. This seems to me nothing but a *petitio principii*: since the Ashʻarites admit exterior or additional attributes, their First Principle is not absolutely simple, whereas the First Principle has to be absolutely simple. The Christians, i.e. the Alexandrian and Cappadocian Fathers, do indeed regard God as of an ineffable simplicity. For Origen, e.g. *De principiis* i. 6, God is 'ex omni parte μονάς et ut ita dicam ἑνάς', He is a 'simplex intellectualis natura'. St. Augustine (*De civ. dei* viii. 6), praises the Platonists for having understood that God's attributes are identical with His essence: 'quia non aliud illi est esse, aliud vivere, quasi possit esse non vivens; nec aliud illi est vivere, aliud intellegere, quasi possit vivere non intellegens; nec aliud illi est intellegere, aliud beatum esse, quasi possit intellegere non beatus; sed quod est illi vivere, intellegere, beatum esse, hoc est illi esse.' This is the Aristotelian conception of God as an eternal, thinking, living, blessed existence, in *Met. Λ* 7.

p. 193. 3. i.e. whether the First Agent must have matter.

p. 194. 1. i.e. matter is the *principium individuationis*; cf. Aristotle, *Phys.* Α 7. 190ᵇ24: ὁ μὲν γὰρ ἄνθρωπος καὶ ὁ χρυσὸς καὶ ὅλως ἡ ὕλη ἀριθμητή· τόδε γάρ τι μᾶλλον, for man and gold and generally matter are numerable unities, and still more is the particular individual such, i.e. this man is numerically different from that man through his matter.

p. 194. 2. i.e. if the First Agent possessed matter, it would be a matter *sui generis*, not the matter which is common to all material things.

p. 194. 3. The argument seems to me rather confused: Averroës seems to imply that even this matter *sui generis* would have to be a body. In the theory that matter is the *principium individuationis* the bodily nature of matter is always assumed, for it is impossible to understand how matter as the absolutely undifferentiated can be the ground of individual differentiation. Of course such a theory can neither explain the individuality of my 'ego' nor of God's 'ego' which thinks itself. Aristotle, however, also regards the form as *principium individuationis*; cf. e.g. *Met.* Z 6. 1031ᵃ17.

p. 194. 4. Such an attribute: i.e. an attribute additional to its essence; the argument seems to me fairly plausible.

p. 195. 1. Aristotle (cf. e.g. *Met.* Δ 30. 1025ᵃ30) distinguishes (*a*) the essential attribute συμβεβηκὸς καθ' αὑτό, لازم, which, although it is not its essence, is possessed universally by a thing in virtue of itself, e.g. the possession by a triangle of angles equal to two right angles, from (*b*) the mere συμβεβηκός, لاحق, which happens to a thing only in certain particular cases, like the paleness of a musician. There is an ambiguity in the term συμβεβηκός which in συμβεβηκὸς καθ' αὑτό means quality generally, whereas used absolutely it can mean the accidental in opposition to the essential. But the verb συμβαίνειν, لحق (or also ὑπάρχειν), meaning 'supervene', implies a sequence.

p. 196. 1. Or possible or transitory; 'permissible', جائز, means originally the morally permissible, permissible according to the religious law. It is a curious and significant fact that the classification of actions into five groups in Islam was taken over from Stoicism. The dutiful, necessary act, واجب, فرض, corresponds to the Stoic κατόρθωμα, *recte factum*; the commendable act, مندوب, مستحب, to προηγμένον, *commodum*; the morally indifferent act, جائز, مباح, to ἀδιάφορον, *medium*; the unbecoming act, مكروه, to ἀποπρο- ηγμένον, *incommodum*; and the sinful act, حرام, to ἁμάρτημα, *peccatum*. It may be added that the long controversy in Islam whether there is or is not a middle term between belief and unbelief is inspired by Stoic thought. The Stoics originally believed that virtue can neither be increased nor decreased, οὔτε ἐπιτείνεσθαι οὔτε ἀνίεσθαι, that there is no intermediate term between virtue and sin, μηδὲν μέσον εἶναι ἀρετῆς καὶ κακίας (Diog. Laert. vii. 227), and that all sins are equal, ἴσα ἐστὶ τὰ ἁμαρτήματα; for whether a man is a hundred stadia from his aim or only one stadium, he is equally not there (cf. Sext. Emp. *Adv. log.* i. 422 and Diog. Laert. viii. 120); and those theologians who asserted that belief is based only on تصديق, assent (i.e. the Stoic συγκατάθεσις; for faith as a θεοσεβείας συγκατάθεσις see, for example, Clem. Alex. *Strom.* ii. 2. 8), held that faith can be neither increased nor diminished. The term جائز takes, then, also the meaning of the logically permissible, i.e. the non-contradictory, the logically possible, and in this way, since for them everything is possible but the logically impossible, it becomes synonymous for the theologians with ممكن, the possible.

p. 196. 2. For according to the theologians only God, the simple, unique immaterial efficient cause, who connects the condition and the conditioned in a transitory conjunction, is eternal.

p. 196. 3. i.e. the theologians regard God, the efficient cause, as acting in time through a prior knowledge and will, as we imagine empirical, rational beings to act, but the philosophers assume an eternal unique connexion between an eternal unifying principle and an eternal world.

p. 196. 4. 'the assumption of the philosophers': the text has 'their assumption', but I presume from the context that the philosophers are meant here. Here Averroës, in opposition to Avicenna, seems to regard these attributes in God as something positive. But according to Averroës's conception here—which, however, is quite in agreement with Aristotle, for whom, too, the essence is the end of the process of becoming, e.g. Met. Δ 4. 1015^{a}10: ἡ οὐσία ... ἐστὶ τὸ τέλος τῆς γενέσεως—an essence is not a subject of attributes, but is constituted by the attributes, and through this the Aristotelian opposition of essence and attributes is destroyed.

p. 197. 1. Both philosophers and theologians describe God as the self-sufficient, الغني, ὁ αὐτάρκης, cf., for example, Aristotle, *Met.* N 4. 1091^{b}18. The term الغني is an epithet given to God in several places in the Koran. I believe its meaning there is 'the rich one', the one, as Muhammad says, 'to whom belongs all that is in the heavens and on earth', but the word is later interpreted under the influence, I think, of Greek philosophy, as meaning 'self-sufficient'.

p. 197. 2. This seems in contradiction to the assertion on p. 196 that every essence is perfected by attributes.

p. 198. 1. i.e. according to the Asha'rite (Stoic) doctrine that what cannot be free from the temporal is itself temporal.

p. 198. 2. For this compare Aristotle, *Phys.* Γ 1. 200^{b}26: the mover is the active, τὸ ποιητικόν, and the moved the passive, τὸ παθητικόν, and the moved is moved through the action of the mover, τὸ κινητὸν κινητὸν ὑπὸ τοῦ κινητικοῦ.

p. 198. 3. For this compare Aristotle, *Phys.* E 2. 225^b 33, where it is proved that there is no absolute generation, no generation of the substance, i.e of the compound *qua* compound, no generation of generation, since absolute generation would imply an infinite regress and one could never arrive at a first compound. On the other hand, the series of possibles or moved movers ends in an eternal necessary existent or unmoved mover.

p. 198. 4. i.e. a cold thing, for example, cannot become warm—cold being potentially warm and the privation of warm—without an agent which actualizes the warmth, 'for from the potentially existing the actually existing is always produced by an actually existing...; there is always a first mover and the mover exists already actually' (cf. Arist. *Met.* Θ 8. 1049^{b}24).

p. 198. 5. ἅπαν τὸ κινούμενον ἀνάγκη ὑπό τινος κινεῖσθαι (Arist. *Phys.* H 1 ad init.).

p. 198. 6. i.e. the concrete substance (ἡ σύνολος οὐσία) composed of matter and form, cf., for example, *Met.* Z 11. 1037^{a}30.

p. 199. 1. Cf. Aristotle, *Met.* N 2. 1088^{b}14 sqq., where Aristotle asserts that what consists of elements must have matter, i.e. potentiality, and that the potential can either be actualized or not.

p. 200. 1. It may be remarked here that the Arabic word for 'substance' or 'essence' is جوهر, a word which by origin means 'jewel'. Averroës remarks in his *Ep. d. Met.* (see my translation, p. 11) that this name was given to substance because it is the most valuable of the categories.

p. 200. 2. This problem will be discussed more fully later. The whole problem of God's knowledge is clearly stated as early as Plato's *Parmenides*, 134: only God can know the universal, and nothing can be known to God but the perfect truth of ideas; there is an unbridgeable chasm between God and men; it is impossible for the divine and eternal to know the things of men, τὰ ἀνθρώπεια πράγματα, and equally for our fleeting human knowledge to reach the divine truth. Plotinus repeats this idea at *Enn.* v. 8. 3: the gods eternally possess their wisdom in an impassible, immutable, and pure intellect (ἐν ἀπαθεῖ τῷ νῷ καὶ στασίμῳ καὶ καθαρῷ); they know everything, however, not the things of men, τὰ ἀνθρώπεια, but the things divine. But to this Plotinus adds, *Enn.* v. 8. 4, the idea which so strongly influenced Leibniz: in the intelligible world everything comprises everything in itself and beholds everything in everything else, everything is everywhere, everything is everything, each thing is anything, and the splendour is infinite (cf. Leibniz: 'chaque monade est un miroir vivant, représentatif de l'Univers suivant son point de vue'). The idea of a difference in value between God's knowledge and man's is found also in Aristotle. Thinking in its purest form, i.e. God's thought, is concerned with the highest good, i.e. with itself (cf. *Met.* Λ 7. 1072^{b}18: ἡ δὲ νόησις ἡ καθ' αὑτὴν τοῦ καθ' αὑτὸ ἀρίστου, καὶ ἡ μάλιστα τοῦ μάλιστα). There is a parallelism between thinker and thought. However, it is one of the disturbing consequences of Aristotle's theory (or rather of one side of his theory) that, in fact, material, individual things cannot be the object of thought at all, since thought is only concerned with the universal, i.e. the unalterable, the eternal.

p. 201. 1. It seems true enough, indeed, that Zaid's knowledge of his own individuality is not identical with his knowledge of other things, but then it cannot be true that man's knowledge of other things is identical with the knowledge of his own essence, i.e. his individuality. This dilemma exists for all theories (Hume's as well as Aristotle's) which do not distinguish between the subject of thought, the Ego, and its object.

p. 201. 2. According to Aristotle's theory that thought and the object of thought are identical (ταὐτὸν νοῦς καὶ νοητόν), Aristotle even says (De an. Γ 6. 431^{b}16): ὅλως δὲ ὁ νοῦς ἐστιν ὁ κατ' ἐνέργειαν τὰ πράγματα νοῶν, the intellect when it thinks is the things. But the things exist also when the intellect does not think them, and the intellect does not add anything to the things by its thinking, since, when it thinks, it is identical with the things. Thought therefore is nothing. (Aristotle himself says, De an. Γ 4. 429^{a}22, that the intellect is nothing at all actually, before it thinks, ὁ νοῦς ... οὐδέν ἐστιν ἐνεργείᾳ τῶν ὄντων πρὶν νοεῖν.) The difficulty of conceiving the intellect without making it falsify reality by adding something to it through thinking caused Aristotle to adopt a theory which annuls thought itself (the same view was held by Plotinus even more emphatically, Enn. v. 3. 5: contemplation must be identical with the contemplated, the intellect with the intelligible; without this identity one cannot possess the truth, since instead of possessing realities, one would only have an impression, τύπος, of them which would be different from the realities and therefore not the truth). However, Aristotle also regards the intellect as an existent in which the concepts exist: the νοῦς is a δεκτικὸν τοῦ εἴδους. In some passages, too, Aristotle tries to express the character of thought as an act, and he conceives it then as a touching (θιγγάνειν) or a participation (μετάληψις): the thinker touches the object of thought, cf. Met. Θ 10. 1051^{b}24 and especially Met. Λ 7. 1072^{b}20, where this contact is mentioned in connexion with the identification of thought and its object: αὐτὸν δὲ νοεῖ ὁ νοῦς κατὰ μετάληψιν τοῦ νοητοῦ · νοητὸς γὰρ γίγνεται θιγγάνων καὶ νοῶν, ὥστε ταὐτὸν νοῦς καὶ νοητόν. These conceptions are complicated still more by the introduction of his obscure theory of an active and a passive intellect.

p. 201. 3. Cf. Aristotle, Met. Z 7. 1032^{b}22: artificial production starts from the knowledge in the soul of the artisan. That which produces and from which the movement starts in artificial production is the form in the soul, τὸ δὴ ποιοῦν καὶ ὅθεν ἄρχεται ἡ κίνησις ... ἐὰν μὲν ἀπὸ τέχνης, τὸ εἶδός ἐστι τὸ ἐν τῇ ψυχῇ.

p. 201. 4. In second intention, i.e. by way of implication and consequence (παρακολούθησις), i.e. not through deliberation (λογισμῷ), but through logical

NOTES

necessity (ἀνάγκῃ), just as, according to Plotinus, *Enn.* iii. 2. 2, the sensible world emanates from the intelligible.

p. 202. 1. i.e. the forms in matter, which are called by Alexander of Aphrodisias ἔνυλα εἴδη.

p. 202. 2. Cf. Aristotle, *De an.* Γ 4. 430ᵃ2: ἐπὶ μὲν γὰρ τῶν ἄνευ ὕλης τὸ αὐτό ἐστι τὸ νοοῦν καὶ τὸ νοούμενον.

p. 203. 1. For Avicenna God cannot know individuals (at least not as individuals), but His knowledge is limited to unalterable, eternal universals. (Porphyry, *Sentent.* xxiii, expressed the difference between the universal intellect and the particular in this way: in the universal intellect the particular existents also exist universally, whereas in the particular intellect both the universal and the individual exist individually.) Averroës goes beyond this: God knows through a knowledge which is neither the knowledge of universals nor the knowledge of individuals, and is superior to the knowledge of men and incomprehensible to them. This, of course, makes the term 'knowledge' as applied to God not only incomprehensible but meaningless.

p. 203. 2. Although Aristotle regards the individual existent alone as the truly real, from which through abstraction the universals are acquired, he asserts all the same that the universal, as form and essence of things, by its nature and absolutely, is prior to the individual (cf. e.g. *Anal. Post. A* 2. 17ᵇ33). Averroës here follows Alexander of Aphrodisias, for whom the universal is also by its nature posterior to the individual, since the existence of universals depends on the existence of the individuals; cf. Simplicius, *In Arist. Cat. Comm.*, Kalbfleisch, c. 5, p. 82, 1. 22: ὁ μέντοι Ἀλέξανδρος ἐνταῦθα καὶ τῇ φύσει ὕστερα τὰ καθόλου τῶν καθ' ἕκαστα εἶναι φιλονεικεῖ ... κοινοῦ γὰρ ὄντος, φησίν, ἀνάγκη καὶ ἄτομον εἶναι· ἐν γὰρ τοῖς κοινοῖς τὰ ἄτομα περιέχεται.

p. 203. 3. 'in potency'. This is a consequence of the conception that the universal is posterior by nature to the individual, and would imply something very different from what Aristotle maintained, namely that knowledge of the individual is superior to knowledge of the universal. However, even Aristotle regards the genus, the more universal, in the definition as representing the matter, i.e. the potential, whereas the *differentia specifica* represents the form: cf. Aristotle, *Met. H* 6. 1045ᵃ34.

p. 203. 4. 'the active powers which ... are called natures'; cf. Aristotle, *De gen. an. B* 4. 740ᵇ35: ἡ ποιοῦσα δύναμις ... ἡ φύσις ἡ ἑκάστου, ἐνυπάρχουσα καὶ ἐν φυτοῖς καὶ ἐν ζῴοις πᾶσιν.

p. 204. 1. Cf. Aristotle, *Met. α* 1. 993ᵇ24.

p. 205. 1. That not even the weight of an atom, either in heaven or on earth, escapes God is stated in the Koran, xxxiv. 3 (cf. note 275. 1).

p. 205. 2. That universals are infinite does not seem to be the opinion of Alexander of Aphrodisias, who in a passage transmitted by Averroës (see

Freudenthal, *Die durch Averroese rhaltenen Fragmente Alexanders*, p. 133. 5) argues against the Stoics, who assert that the divine Providence is concerned with individuals, saying that this would imply a knowledge of the infinite future, which is impossible, since the measure of the infinite is impossible, and what is impossible is impossible also for the gods (cf. also Alex. Aphr. *De fato*, Bruns, p. 200. 22). ('Infinite', however, is ambiguous and can mean 'eternal').

p. 206. 1. According to Aristotle (see *De An.* Γ 3. 428^{b}10 sqq.) the representation, φαντασία, does not occur apart from sensation, ἄνευ αἰσθήσεως, and is similar to sensation, and in sensation the common properties, like movement and size, are preserved. That is why Averroës can say that the plurality of representations resembles plurality in space.

p. 206. 2. 'which we may call being': Aristotle himself, as we have seen already—see note 179. 4—denies explicitly that being, τὸ ὄν, is a genus, but the older Stoics seem to regard being, since it has itself no genus, as the highest genus (cf. Diog. Laert. vii. 61); and in any case the Stoics include everything in one highest genus: ἐπὶ πάντων ἓν γένος λαμβάνουσιν (Plotinus, *Enn.* vi. 1. 35).

p. 206. 3. i.e. being.

p. 206. 4. Cf. note 203. 3.

p. 208. 1. According to Aristotle, *Met.* Δ 15. 1021^{a}23, the relation father-son is one of those which by their very essence are related to something else, τῷ ὅπερ ἐστὶν ἄλλου λέγεσθαι αὐτὸ ὅ ἐστιν. Cf. also the (tautological) Stoic definition of relation, Sext. Emp. *Adv. log.* ii. 162 : πρός τι δέ ἐστι τὰ κατὰ τὴν ὡς πρὸς ἕτερον σχέσιν νοούμενα καὶ οὐκέτι ἀπολελυμένως λαμβανόμενα, the relative is what is conceived in relation to another thing, neither of them being apprehended separately.

p. 209. 1. Since they all fall under the most universal genus of 'being' or of 'something' (τί, شَيْء).

p. 209. 2. Cf. the passage in Aristotle, *Met.* Λ 7. 1072^{b}20 quoted in note 201. 2: αὐτὸν δὲ νοεῖ ὁ νοῦς κατὰ μετάληψιν τοῦ νοητοῦ, 'the intellect thinks itself through partaking of the thing known'. 'Self-knowledge' is here ambiguous; it means both self-consciousness, the fact that in all *cogitare* an 'ego' is implied (cf. note 201. 2) and all the knowledge an individual 'self' has acquired. It is on this very ambiguity that the theory is built that God in knowing Himself knows all other things.

p. 209. 3. The logic of facts forces the Aristotelians to establish distinctions which—since in their system there is no subject, no 'ego', and they identify the things known with the knowledge of things—they are not entitled to make—i.e. the distinctions between (1) self-knowledge, (2) the knowledge the individual 'self' possesses, (3) the things known. By 'unity of knowledge' is here meant the unity of experience and knowledge in each of us through the unity and identity of his 'self'. Unity of knowledge, ἐπιστήμης ἑνότης, is affirmed by Aristotle in another sense, when he declares (*Met. Γ* 2. 1003ᵇ21) that the study of all species of being *qua* being belongs to a science which is generically one, whereas the study of the several species of being belongs to the specific parts of this science. But it is not true that knowledge, although the knower is a unity, need not possess plurality, when the things known form a plurality, for knowledge is dependent on the things known and has to conform to their nature. What is true, and seems to me a primary truth, although it is denied both by the idealist and by the relativist, is that the object of knowledge is not affected by the fact of being known. A cat may look at a king, and the king is not affected by the cat's awareness of him. All knowledge implies being, implies facts that can be known and that are independent of this knowledge. Being is prior to knowledge (and even the possibility of being which enables us to act through knowledge is prior to knowledge). If the object of knowledge were affected by its being known, nobody could twice perceive an identical thing, nor could the same object be perceived by many or the same thought be common to many; and however inexplicable it may be, we are aware of living in one unique common universe and of communicating our thoughts, and even the relativist and the idealist are forced to admit that at least their theories would be true, i.e. correspond to the facts, even if no one ever held them. God, therefore, is not affected by our loving Him or our knowing Him, but as to His knowledge, either God's knowledge is dependent on our decisions and acts in so far as it follows them; or God knows them from eternity, and then the human drama is but a puppet-show; or the eternal sequence of becoming and passing away is eternally beyond His ken.

p. 210. 1. i.e. if a man perceives a thing, he is either completely plunged in the contemplation of that thing and is unaware that he is the perceiver, or if he perceives that he perceives there is a limit to the series, i.e. there is not an infinite series of his perceiving that he perceives that he perceives . . . .

p. 210. 2. i.e. God, the Unknowable, the Ineffable, can be understood only by His works and His providence. This tendentious tradition is quite alien to primitive Islam and is inspired by the study of Greek and Christian philosophy. Cf. St. Theophilus, *Ad Autolyc.* (Migne, vi. 1032A): Just as the soul of man cannot be seen, but can be understood through the movement of his body, God cannot be seen by the eyes of man, but must be understood by His Providence and His works; and St. Gregory of Nyssa, *De an. et resurrect.* (Migne, xlvi. 28C): Just as, through observing the universe, the macrocosm, and the omnipotent wisdom (ἡ παντοδύναμος σοφία) which pervades it, we arrive at an intellect which is above sense-perception, ὑπὲρ αἴσθησιν, so in contemplating man, the microcosm, we can infer from the visible appearances the hidden and imperceptible intellect; and Maximus

Confessor, *Ambigua* (Migne, xci. 1285–7): Just as our human intellect, which is one and invisible in itself, yet manifests itself in words and deeds and expresses its thought in letters and figures, so the Divine Essence which is far above the reach of our intellect manifests itself in the created universe. Compare with this Wisdom of Solomon xiii. 5: 'For from the greatness of the beauty even of created things in like proportion does man form the image of their first maker', and Romans i. 20: 'For the invisible things of Him since the creation of the world are clearly seen, being understood by the things that are made, even His everlasting power and divinity', in both of which Stoic influence is unmistakable.

p. 210. 3. This is the orthodox conception. That miracles by themselves are not an absolute proof of the mission of the prophet is not only affirmed by the Mu'tazilites, but even by the Ash'arite Baqillani, who held that miracles might also be performed by a sorcerer or a saint (for the whole problem cf. Ibn Hazm, op. cit. v. 2–12). Already Celsus (Orig. *Contra Cels.* i. 68) had asked: 'Since sorcerers can perform the same feats as Jesus, must we admit that they too are "sons of God"?'

p. 210. 4. Compare with this the passage in St. Gregory of Nyssa, *De vita St. Greg. Thaumat.* (Migne, xlvi. 901), where he speaks of the internal discord, ἐμφύλιος πόλεμος, of the Greek philosophers over the Divine, and praises the stable word of faith, which in its simplicity is proclaimed to all equally and does not find its strength in some logical jugglery and artificial constructions of logic, λογικῇ τινι περιεργίᾳ καὶ τεχνικαῖς πλοκαῖς, since, indeed, the transcendent nature, ἡ ὑπερκειμένη φύσις, is inaccessible, ἀνεπίβατος, to human reason.

p. 211. 1. This seems to imply that even negations have a certain objective existence.

p. 211. 2. This is rather badly expressed, for if there are concepts, there is already a plurality. The meaning is: 'The terms of the relation constitute with the relation a unity, or the terms of the relation are nothing additional to the relation.'

p. 211. 3. This seems to mean that the father and the son have an existence in reality independent of their relation to each other, but that in our thoughts fatherhood implies sonhood and the thought fatherhood–sonhood constitutes a unity. However, we can think of the father without thinking of the son.

p. 211. 4. 'the first knowledge': i.e. my knowing a thing includes my consciousness of my knowing this thing. This seems to me a sound theory: in all perception and knowledge the consciousness of an 'ego' is included.

p. 212. 1. Averroës seems to mean that the series 'the knowledge that I know that I know' can be infinitely extended, and its infinity is implied in the idea of knowledge. This infinity, however, according to Averroës, is only a potential infinity (which is admissible), not an actual infinity (which is impossible).

p. 212. 2. i.e. God's knowledge does not depend on the reality of the things known; God does not know things because they exist, but God's knowledge is a creative knowledge, and the things exist because God knows them. Of course, if *esse = percipi*, even our human knowledge does not depend on the reality of things; and for Kant the mere possibility of knowledge implies a creative element—which, however, implies that my thought that thought is creative is itself creative.

p. 212. 3. i.e. by their doctrine of God's unalterable unity, توحيد.

p. 212. 4. Ghazali had written three treatises on Logic: *The Touchstone of Science in Logic*, معيار العلم فى فن المنطق, *The Touchstone of Speculation in Logic*, محك النظر فى المنطق, and *The Just Balance*, القسطاس المستقيم.

p. 213. 1. This refers to Ghazali's curious work, mentioned in the preceding note, *The Just Balance*, in which he extracts the principles of Logic from verses of the Koran, and where (p. 20, ed. Kabbani, Cairo, 1900) he bases his belief that the principles of Logic can be deduced from the Koran on the verses at the beginning of Sura lv, the Merciful, where it is said that God taught man demonstration (or articulate speech), البيان, and 'set the balance that in the balance ye should not transgress'.

p. 214. 1. i.e. when he is plunged in the contemplation of something else. For Ghazali, therefore, the inference *cogito ergo sum* would not be valid, since according to him thought or consciousness does not imply the self-consciousness of an 'ego'.

p. 214. 2. Since the addition of a non-essential accident does not change the individuality of a thing.

p. 214. 3. i.e. two individual entities keep their individuality even when they are conjoined. The conception of God's attributes as here expressed is in agreement with al-Ash'ari, cf. Shahrastani, *Relig. and Philos. Sects*, pp. 66–67.

p. 214. 4. This criticism is not altogether illegitimate. For Aristotle God is pure form, pure being, or pure thought, i.e. a universal existing independently and so individually; i.e. God is an individual universal or a universal individual.

p. 215. 1. Since only substances (in which attributes inhere) exist by themselves. St. Augustine, *De trinit.* vii. 5, just because he asserts that no attributes can inhere in God, declares that *in deo substantia abusive dicitur*. Only transient compound things are truly called substances. But since it is impious to say that goodness inheres in God instead of saying that God's essence is goodness, God can be in truth only called essence, not substance ('nefas est autem dicere ut subsistat et subsit Deus bonitate sua, atque illa bonitas non substantia sit vel potius essentia, neque ipse Deus sit bonitas sua, sed in illo sit tamquam in subiecto: unde manifestum est Deum abusive substantiam vocari').

p. 215. 2. That the religious texts of the past (i.e. Homer and Hesiod) address themselves to the masses in a language intelligible to them, the deeper sense of which, ὑπόνοια, can be understood by the philosopher only is one of the more general theses of the Greek age of enlightenment. Antisthenes, the father of Cynicism, had declared that Homer had only in part spoken the truth; in another part, however, κατὰ δόξαν, he had spoken in agreement with vulgar opinion, and therefore his words needed philosophical interpretation (cf. Dio Chrysost. *Orat.* liii). It was the Stoics who more than any others practised the principle of ἀλληγορία, allegorical exposition.

p. 215. 3. Koran xix. 43.

p. 215. 4. Koran xxxvi. 71.

p. 215. 5. Koran xxxviii. 75.

p. 216. 1. Cf. Themistius, *Orationes*, xxvi. 319 b: It was a special characteristic of Aristotle to believe that the same teachings were not suited for the masses and the philosophers, just as the same drugs (φάρμακα) or provisions are not suited both for the perfectly healthy and for those of a precarious health, but for the former the really wholesome and for the latter that which agrees with their actual bodily state. He therefore called some exoteric (θυραίους) and made them generally accessible (ἀνέτους ἐποιήσατο), and shut some within (εἴσω ἀπέκλεισε) and communicated them only to a few in security. We find an analogous conception in Averroës's great Jewish contemporary, Maimonides, who says (*Guide of the Perplexed*, i. 33) that the Scriptures, since they had to be understood by children, women, and the masses, could not be written in philosophical language; this would have been like rearing an infant on wheaten bread, meat, and wine, which would certainly kill it. Compare Spinoza, *Tract. theol. polit.* xii: 'primis Iudaeis religio tamquam lex scripta tradita est, nimirum quia tum temporis veluti infantes habebantur'. See also 1 Cor. iii. 1–2: 'And I, brethren, could not speak unto you as unto spiritual (πνευματικοῖς) but as unto carnal (σαρκίνοις) even as unto babes in Christ. I have fed you with milk and not with meat (βρῶμα, i.e. solid food), for hitherto ye were not able to bear it, neither yet now are ye able.' This metaphor is found already in Philo, *De agricult.* (Cohn), 9, p. 96, 26: ἐπεὶ δὲ νηπίοις μέν ἐστι γάλα τροφή, τελείοις δὲ τὰ ἐκ πυρῶν πέμματα, καὶ ψυχῆς γαλακτώδεις μὲν ἂν εἶεν τροφαὶ κατὰ τὴν παιδικὴν ἡλικίαν τὰ τῆς ἐγκυκλίου μουσικῆς προπαιδεύματα.

p. 216. 2. For Themistius also the physician is a favourite metaphor for the philosopher, see, for example, *Oration.* v. 63 b, xxiv. 302 *b*, and the metaphor is ascribed to Antisthenes (Diog. Laert. vi. 1. 4 and 6). In later Greek philosophy, and in Roman, the image of philosophy as a *medicina mentis* is a commonplace, e.g. Cicero, *Tusc.* iii. 6: 'est animi medicina (φάρμακον) philosophia', and it is found in Plutarch, Seneca, Epictetus, and Marcus Aurelius among others.

p. 216. 3. Cf. Aristotle, *Met. H* 3. 1043ᵇ1: τὸ γὰρ τί ἦν εἶναι τῷ εἴδει καὶ τῇ ἐνεργείᾳ ὑπάρχει, and *Met. Λ* 8. 1074ᵃ35: τὸ δὲ τί ἦν εἶναι . . . ἐντελέχεια.

p. 217. 1. i.e. nutrition and generation; cf. Aristotle, *De gen. an.* B 4. 740ᵇ34.

p. 217. 2. i.e. perception; cf. Aristotle, *De an.* B 2. 413ᵇ1.

p. 217. 3. For each substance (even the inorganic) is a kind of actuality and nature, ἐντελέχεια καὶ φύσις τις ἑκάστη (οὐσία): Aristotle, *Met. H* 3. 1044ᵃ9.

p. 217. 4. Cf. e.g. Aristotle, *Met. H* 1. 1042ᵃ32: ἐν πάσαις γὰρ ταῖς ἀντικειμέναις μεταβολαῖς ἐστί τι τὸ ὑποκείμενον.

p. 217. 5. Cf. Aristotle, *Met. Θ* 8. 1050ᵇ2: τὸ εἶδος ἐνέργειά ἐστιν, and Aristotle, *De gen. et corr.* A 4. 320ᵃ2: ἔστι δὲ ὕλη . . . τὸ ὑποκείμενον γενέσεως καὶ φθορᾶς δεκτικόν.

p. 217. 6. 'ultimate basis of existence': the Arabic is عنصر, a translation of the Greek στοιχεῖον, element (i.e. fire, air, water, earth), but the term στοιχεῖον is also used of matter, e.g. Aristotle, *Met. N* 2. 1088ᵇ27: τὰ στοιχεῖα ὕλη τῆς οὐσίας the elements are the matter of substance.

p. 217. 7. Cf. e.g. Aristotle, *De an.* Γ 4. 430ᵃ7: ἄνευ γὰρ ὕλης δύναμις ὁ νοῦς τῶν τοιούτων (τῶν ἐχόντων ὕλην), for the intellect is the power to become the things possessing matter without their matter.

p. 217. 8. Averroës is here referring to Aristotle's theory (*Met. H* 6. 1045ᵃ30) that in the definition which consists of the genus and the *differentia specifica* the genus represents the matter, the *differentia specifica* the form: ἔστι δὲ τῆς ὕλης ἡ μὲν νοητὴ ἡ δ' αἰσθητή, καὶ ἀεὶ τοῦ λόγου τὸ μὲν ὕλη τὸ δὲ ἐνέργειά ἐστιν, οἷον ὁ κύκλος σχῆμα ἐπίπεδον, i.e. plane figure is the generic element of 'circle'.

p. 218. 1. Cf. Aristotle, *Met. Θ* 8. 1049ᵇ5: φανερὸν ὅτι πρότερον ἐνέργεια δυνάμεώς ἐστιν, i.e. the active element, the form, is prior to the purely passive element, matter.

p. 218. 2. Here Averroës, in opposition to the general trend of his book, drops the pretence that the inner sense (ὑπόνοια) of revealed religion may express the highest truths of reason. Here he follows the unalloyed rationalism of classical philosophy, and professes, as Plato did, that the truth can only be attained by the systematic and strenuous thought of the philosophical few.

p. 218. 3. According to Aristotle, *Met. Λ* 7.

p. 219. 1. i.e. according to the Ash'arites the attributes inhere in an immaterial substratum which has no characteristic of its own, and one might therefore ask: 'Who or what then is the possessor of these attributes?' But I think the question cannot be answered: *individuum est ineffabile*, description and definition express only the universal. And if God, like man, is conscious, the individuality of His consciousness is as difficult to describe and define as the individuality of the human ego. However, al-Ash'ari gives a kind of Neoplatonic solution of this problem, i.e. he affirms that in God the opposites are destroyed, for he asserts according to Shahrastani, op. cit., p. 67, that one may neither say that God's attributes are identical with God, nor different from Him, nor that they are not God, nor not different from Him: لا يقال هى هو ولا غيره ولا لا هو ولا لا غيره.

p. 219. 2. Cf. note 135. 3. Perhaps he is here referring to the Ash'arites Ibn Furak and Baqillani, who, according to Ibn Hazm, op. cit. iv. 214, v. 32, affirmed that God has but one name, although He has many appellations (تسميات)—which implies the magical theory that names exist by nature and express the essential nature of the object named, or to Abu Ishaq al Isfaraini, who held, according to Shahrastani, op. cit., p. 72, 3 that the most proper description of God is that His being compels us to differentiate Him from all other beings, (instead of تميزه) اخص وصفه هو كون يوجب تمييزه عن الاكوان كلها.

p. 219. 3. The hidden highest name, 'the most great name', of God, since it expresses His real essence, would confer unlimited power on the man to whom it was revealed. For 'the most great name of God' cf. Frazer, *The Golden Bough*, vol. iii, p. 390.

p. 220. 1. Cf. Origen, *De princip.* i. 1. 6: 'Deus ... ἑνάς, et mens ac fons ex quo initium totius intellectualis naturae vel mentis est'.

p. 221. 1. Cf. Plotinus, *Enn.* v. 4. 1: It is necessary that above everything there must be something simple, different from everything else, independent in no communion (οὐ μεμιγμένον) with what depends on it.

p. 221. 2. The First is without any conjunction and composition: συμβάσεως ἔξω πάσης καὶ συνθέσεως, Plotinus, *Enn.* v. 4. 1. Plotinus asserts (*Enn.* vi. 2. 17) that even if, in one way, we may call the First the Good (τὸ ἀγαθόν), the Good is not a genus, for it cannot be predicated of anything else, since otherwise this would be equally the Good. According to Aristotle the First has no contrary, οὐ γάρ ἐστιν ἐναντίον τῷ πρώτῳ οὐθέν (*Met.* Λ 10. 1075ᵇ22).

p. 221. 3. Cf. note 195. 1.

p. 221. 4. That neither 'the one' nor 'being' can be a genus is asserted by Aristotle (*Met.* B 3. 998ᵇ22: οὐχ οἷόν τε δὲ τῶν ὄντων ἓν εἶναι γένος οὔτε τὸ ἓν οὔτε τὸ ὄν) since otherwise unity and being would have to be predicated of the differentiae of this genus also.

p. 221. 5. One may call the First, according to Plotinus, *Enn.* vi. 8. 8, principle, ἀρχή; from another point of view, however, so far as this would imply a constituent of its essence, the First is not a principle.

p. 222. 1. Description رسم, ὑπογραφή; ὑπογραφή is a technical term of Stoicism; description does not indicate the essence of a thing as the definition does, but omits its *proprium* (cf. Simplicius, *In Arist. Cat. Comm.*, Kalbfleisch, 29. 21: ὁ μὲν ὑπογραφικὸς λόγος τὴν ἰδιότητα τῆς οὐσίας ἀφορίζει, ὁ δὲ ὁριστικὸς τὸ τί ἦν εἶναι ἑκάστου καὶ τὴν οὐσίαν αὐτήν). The categories cannot be defined, but only described (cf. Simplicius, op. cit. 75. 36).

p. 222. 2. This is part of the Aristotelian definition of substance, i.e. the individual existent, this man, this horse, *Cat.* 5. 2ᵃ11: οὐσία δέ ἐστιν ἡ κυριώτατά τε καὶ πρώτως καὶ μάλιστα λεγομένη, ἣ μήτε καθ' ὑποκειμένου τινὸς λέγεται μήτε ἐν ὑποκειμένῳ τινί ἐστιν. It was objected to this definition—says Simplicius, op. cit. 81. 5—that it is purely negative, that it is like saying that a man is neither a horse nor a dog. But—he answers—first, it is not a definition but a description, and where there is a trichotomy, the denial of two members affirms the third.

p. 222. 3. 'a genus in the accident': i.e. an accident which would constitute a genus.

p. 222. 4. This argument does not seem to me correct. The objection against this definition is not that it does not indicate whether the thing defined exists, for no definition does indicate this; the objection is that it does not indicate what it is that exists ('Sein ist kein reales Prädikat, d. i. ein Begriff von irgend etwas, was zu dem Begriffe eines Dinges hinzukommen könne', says Kant), i.e. of what the individuality of the individual existent consists. There is no answer: *individuum est ineffabile*.

p. 222. 5. And 'being' cannot have a specific difference; see note 221. 4.

p. 222. 6. Cf. the section in Avicenna's *Salvation*, p. 374 ان نوع واجب الوجود لا يقال على كثيرين اذ لا مثل له ولا ضد that the species of the necessary cannot be predicated of a plurality, since it has neither equal nor contrary.

p. 222. 7. That being is predicated analogically is affirmed by Aristotle, *Met.* Γ 2 ad init. Also, according to Plotinus (*Enn.* vi. 2. 17), 'the good' can be predicated analogically; there is in everything possessing the good a gradation *per prius et posterius*, πρώτως καὶ δευτέρως καὶ ὑστέρως, and a subordination, and the whole series depends upon the Good beyond (τοῦ ἐπέκεινα).

p. 222. 8. According to Averroës this is not a real definition, since it does not determine the quiddity of the soul, but only indicates its relation to the body.

p. 223. 1. i.e. if 'being' were an essence, a thing could be defined by it, since it is defined by its essence, but a thing is also qualified by its *proprium*; however, if being were a *proprium*, this *proprium* could not qualify a thing, since 'Sein ist kein Begriff von etwas, was zu dem Begriffe eines Dinges hinzukommen könne'. Quiddity, says Avicenna (*Salvation*, p. 340), is, for example, man, horse, soul, intellect, which is then qualified as being existent and being one. Therefore understanding the quiddity of anything is different from understanding that it is one (the text is corrupt; evidently the word فهمك has been omitted before وفهمك) and therefore unity is neither the essence of anything nor a constitutent of the essence, but a necessary attribute of the essence.

p. 223. 2. Because, in the example in the preceding note, Avicenna mentions man, horse, soul, and intellect; but man and horse, being sensible material substances, are essentially different from soul and intellect, which are intelligible immaterial substances. But, says Plotinus (*Enn.* vi. 1. 2), there cannot be a common genus for the sensible substance, and for the intelligible, since otherwise there would be another substance superior to both, which could be predicated of them.

p. 223. 3. For Farabi's book about demonstration, i.e. his commentary on the *Posterior Analytics*, compare Prantl, *Geschichte der Logik im Abendlande*, ii. 311 sqq., and Steinschneider, *Al-Farabi*, Mém. de l'Acad. Imp. des Sciences de St. Pétersbourg, série VII, t. xiii, n. 4, pp. 43 sqq. It seems to have been a most important work of this philosopher, of whom Maimonides said that, for the understanding of logic, the study of his works alone would be sufficient. In his commentaries on the *Anal. Post.* Averroës often quotes this work and often attacks it. It may be that there existed a Latin translation of it, and that Albertus Magnus knew it, as is perhaps suggested by his words (Prantl, op. cit. 312. 51): 'et haec, quae dicta sunt de scientiis Arabum, sunt excerpta, quorum commentum super hunc posteriorum librum ex sententia Alfarabi Arabis ad nos devenit'. The passage in our book is quoted by Steinschneider, op. cit., p. 53. Farabi's conception would be in agreement with such passages in Aristotle as *Met.* Z 1. 1028ᵃ31–32: τὸ πρώτως ὂν καὶ οὐ τὶ ὂν ἀλλ' ὂν ἁπλῶς ἡ οὐσία ἂν εἴη, πρῶτον πάντων λόγῳ, substance is that which exists primarily, not in a qualified sense, but absolutely, and is primary in definition.

p. 223. 4. It has really nothing to do with the Arabic language. The term موجود means 'existent'; a sentence like 'Socrates is existent' is of the same form as 'Socrates is a votary of the Muses', ἔστι Σωκράτης μουσικός, which, according to Aristotle, *Met.* Δ 7. 1017ᵃ33, means that this is true. In the sentence 'Socrates is existent', 'existent' as a predicate is an accident.

p. 224. 1. He means that the true is not something in the external world, but something existing only in the mind; second predicates refer to something in the mind, primary predicates to something in the external world.

NOTES 131

p. 224. 2. *The Book of the Letters*, كتاب الحروف : about this treatise see Steinschneider, op. cit., p. 118, who quotes this passage (erroneously, however, rendering 'Zufälliges' instead of 'accident'). This book is quoted a few times by Averroës and by others (see Steinschneider, loc. cit., and Prantl, op. cit. ii. 311. 50). The title of this treatise is rather mysterious; perhaps the book treated in part of words and language in the same way as the Stoics, who regarded phonetics and linguistics as a part of dialectics, and a passage in Maimonides (see Steinschneider, loc. cit.) makes this seem plausible. 'The book of letters' is, however, also one of the names by which Aristotle's *Metaphysics* was known among the Arabs, and Farabi himself composed a treatise about the intentions of Aristotle in his *Book of Letters*, i.e. his *Metaphysics*.

p. 224. 3. For Aristotle 'paronymous' words, like 'healthy' from 'health', 'medical' from 'medicine', express a secondary mode of being (see *Met. Γ* 2 ad init.). The word موجود 'existent' is 'derived from', i.e. is the passive participle of, the verb وجد, 'to find', and means originally 'what is found', *ce qui se trouve, was vorgefunden wird*.

p. 224. 4. مثال, σύμβολον. Words, according to Aristotle, are symbols of things (*De interpr.* 2. 16ᵃ28), and primitive words express primary things.

p. 224. 5. There seems to be some confusion in this sentence through Averroës's ignorance of Greek and of the differences between Greek and Arabic. Neither Greek nor Arabic need normally express the connexion between subject and predicate. Σωκράτης μουσικός ascribes to Socrates his being a votary of the Muses, and زيد مريض, literally 'Zaid ill', means that Zaid is ill. However, in both languages the connexion may be expressed by the copula (copula, in Greek συμπλοκή, in Arabic الرابط or الرابطة). The copula is expressed in Greek by εἶναι (and we may say ἔστι Σωκράτης μουσικός), in Arabic by the personal pronoun هو, he, it (and we may say زيد انه مريض or زيد هو مريض, literally, 'Zaid he ill'). Averroës knows that the word used as the copula in Greek is related to the words signifying substance and existence in that language, but he seems to think that in Greek also the copula is expressed by a pronoun. The term هوية (literally 'it-ness') which is translated into Latin as *haeceitas*, is used synonymously with موجود (see, for example, Arist. *Metaph. Δ* 7 on τὸ ὄν in Bouyges's edition); it corresponds to the Aristotelian term τόδε τι (المشار اليه) which originally designates an individual thing existing here and now, and expresses the it-ness or this-ness of a thing, i.e. its individuality. For Averroës existence is the existent, τὸ ὄν, the individual, τόδε τι, it is the substance, ἡ οὐσία, it is the subject, τὸ ὑποκείμενον, of a sentence; for Avicenna existence is to exist, τὸ εἶναι, it is added to the subject as a predicate in such sentences as 'Socrates exists', and as a predicate is an accident.

p. 224. 6. e.g. in 'Socrates exists', 'exists' signifies the true, and one may know about Socrates without knowing whether he exists.

p. 224. 7. i.e. one can know of a compound substance, i.e. a transient individual thing composed of matter and form, without knowing whether it exists; but knowledge of a simple, i.e. an immaterial, eternal substance, implies its existence.

p. 224. 8. Aristotle, *Phys. A* 2 and *A* 3, see especially *A* 3. 186ᵃ24, where Aristotle reproaches Parmenides with treating 'being' as having one meaning, whereas it has many, ἁπλῶς λαμβάνει τὸ ὂν λέγεσθαι, λεγομένου πολλαχῶς.

p. 225. 1. That the existent is one is the thesis of Parmenides, which asserts something of the existent; but since an accident is always attributed to a subject, the subject, if being were exclusively an accident, would have no being: the existent would be non-existent (cf. Arist. *Phys. A* 3. 186ᵃ34: τὸ γὰρ συμβεβηκὸς καθ' ὑποκειμένου τινὸς λέγεται, ὥστε ᾧ συμβέβηκε τὸ ὂν οὐκ ἔσται, ἕτερον γὰρ τοῦ ὄντος).

p. 225. 2. For an eternal being is simple and the genus is like the substratum or matter for the specific differences; e.g. Arist. *Met. Δ* 6. 1016ᵃ26: τὸ γένος . . . τὸ ὑποκείμενον ταῖς διαφοραῖς.

p. 226. 1. Cf. Aristotle, *Met. Δ* 3. 1014ᵇ12: ᾧ μὲν γὰρ ἡ διαφορὰ ὑπάρχει καὶ τὸ γένος ἀκολουθεῖ; where the differentia exists, there the genus also is present.

p. 226. 2. For all the elements in a definition must form a unity, since the definition is a formula which is one and which defines a substance (Arist. *Met. Z* 12. 1037ᵇ24: δεῖ δέ γε ἓν εἶναι ὅσα ἐν τῷ ὁρισμῷ· ὁ γὰρ ὁρισμὸς λόγος τίς ἐστιν εἷς καὶ οὐσίας).

p. 226. 3. According to Aristotle (e.g. *Met. H* 6. 1045ᵃ34: ἀεὶ τοῦ λόγου τὸ μὲν ὕλη τὸ δὲ ἐνέργειά ἐστιν) part of the definition is always matter (i.e. potential), part actuality.

p. 226. 4. The recipient is the matter, the thing it receives the form; one of them, i.e. the matter, e.g. wine or the matter of wine, becomes vinegar by receiving acidity, but actually is wine, having received the form, the sweetness of wine.

p. 227. 1. This sentence is very confused and as a matter of fact it is contradictory, for it affirms that potency can be accidentally its opposite, actuality. The contradiction lies in the theory of Aristotle himself, for whom the relation of matter to form expresses both a relation of sequence, i.e. the relation of priority and posteriority (the wine turning vinegar is the matter of the vinegar) and a static relation, the relation of substance and accidence; and Aristotle identifies matter with potentiality and form with actuality. Now one has the right to say that the wine is potentially the vinegar, but

NOTES

there is no sense in saying that the matter exists potentially in the combination of matter and form which constitutes the actually existing individual, and it is a contradiction to say that the actual existent consists in part of a potential existent, or that the actual existent is a combination of the actual and the potential. According to Averroës the matter, by existing in the actually existing individual, is accidentally actual; the form, by existing in matter, the potential, is accidentally potential.

p. 227. 2. For becoming is found only in substance, and there is no generation and destruction of accidents; cf. Aristotle, *Met. E* 5. 1026^{b}24: τῶν δὲ κατὰ συμβεβηκὸς οὐκ ἔστι γένεσις καὶ φθορά.

p. 227. 3. For plane, line, and point are units, and units are indivisible either in quantity or in form; cf. Aristotle, *Met. Δ* 6. 1016^{b}23: πανταχοῦ δὲ τὸ ἓν ἢ τῷ ποσῷ ἢ τῷ εἴδει ἀδιαίρετον.

p. 227. 4. 'this': i.e. that it cannot have receptivity or matter.

p. 227. 5. Since the potential intellect, which is immaterial, receives the active intellect.

p. 227. 6. For this attribute is its essence or its form, since all transient individuals consist of matter and form.

p. 227. 7. The only potentiality that exists in the heavenly body is its capacity to change its place, but there is no possibility of change in its substance; cf. Aristotle, *Met. Λ* 7. 1072^{b}5. See also p. 142 and notes 142. 4 and 142. 8.

p. 227. 8. Whether this substratum be an eternal heavenly body or a transient material body (man).

p. 228. 1. Cf. Aristotle, *Met. Λ* 10. 1075^{b}17: καὶ τοῖς δύο ἀρχὰς ποιοῦσιν ἄλλην ἀνάγκη ἀρχὴν κυριωτέραν εἶναι, those who assume two principles must assume a higher principle, i.e. an efficient cause.

p. 228. 2. According to Aristotle there is no contrary to the First (see note 221. 2).

p. 229. 1. Cf. the end of Aristotle, *Met. Λ* 10: those who introduce a number of independent principles make the substance of the world episodic (ἐπεισοδιώδη τὴν τοῦ παντὸς οὐσίαν ποιοῦσιν), where he concludes with Homer's words, *Iliad* ii. 204: οὐκ ἀγαθὸν πολυκοιρανίη· εἷς κοίρανος ἔστω, the rule of many is not good; let one man be the ruler.

p. 229. 2. Which would have to be its cause.

p. 229. 3. See page 189.

p. 229. 4. This seems to mean that we can have the concept of colour in our mind without thinking of black and red; which is certainly true, but would seem in contradiction to Ghazali's own nominalism.

p. 229. 5. This seems to mean that any colour in real existence must be a definite colour, red or black or yellow, &c., and so far the definite colours are a condition for the real existence of colour; they are, however, not individually a cause for the real existence of colour. Ghazali repeats here what Avicenna says, *Salvation*, p. 379, that no definite colour is a condition for the concept 'colour'; all definite colours are a condition for colour in real existence, but not individually.

p. 230. 1. This last sentence does not fit in very well here. It is not a part of the proof of the philosophers, but part of Ghazali's arguments against it which Averroës repeats in the following passage.

p. 230. 2. Infinite terms or rather indefinite terms ('infinite' is the rather unhappy translation of Boethius which has become current in scholastic philosophy) are the ὀνόματα ἀόριστα (Arab. الاسماء المعدولة) like *non-homo*, *non-albus* (cf. Arist. *De interpr*. 2. 16ᵃ32). Infinite terms are privative (στερητικός), they are not absolute non-being; cf. the parallel passages in Aristotle, *Phys*. Γ 2. 201ᵇ26 and *Met*. Θ 9. 1066ᵃ15: αἱ στερητικαὶ ἀρχαὶ ἀόριστοι.

p. 231. 1. i.e. if red is the cause of the existence of colour, black cannot be the cause of colour, and therefore there cannot be any specific differentiation between colours; but this is not true (I take 'and this is not true' as the words of Ghazali; Averroës, I believe, restricts himself here to repeating Ghazali's argument).

p. 231. 2. i.e. black and red do not enter into the definition of colour, but any existing colour has to be a definite colour (the speciousness of the whole argument rests on the ambiguity of the term 'condition' which can mean a physical cause or a logical relation, i.e. that genus implies species, that without a species there cannot be a genus, that species is a condition for genus; here 'condition' is taken in a logical sense and is not a 'cause').

p. 231. 3. i.e. since, for the First, essence and existence coincide, any specific difference in the First would have to be a condition, i.e. a cause both for the essence and the existence of the First.

p. 232. 1. This is not true; Ghazali did not say here that for the philosophers existence is added as an accident to the quiddity. Their whole argument, according to him, is built on the principle that in God alone essence, what He is, and existence, that He is, coincide—a theory which Averroës also holds, although he affirms also that, since everything is something, every essence is an existence, and confuses the being of an object of thought—what is meant (and what is non-existent may be meant)—with existence.

p. 232. 2. i.e. existence.

p. 232. 3. For it would mean that black and red exist only in reality, but not as concepts.

p. 232. 4. Averroës wants to express that colours can also be differentiated conceptually, not only when they exist (which nobody will deny). Since for him every essence is an existence, and he must all the same distinguish between colours only thought of and colours in real existence, he speaks of the latter as existing in act; 'in act', however, is simply another expression for 'existing'.

p. 232. 5. The simple and the compound are opposites (see, for example, Arist. *Phys. Γ* 5. 204^{b}11), and once the thesis is accepted that the highest principle is simple (τὸ πρῶτον καὶ κυρίως ἀναγκαῖον τὸ ἁπλοῦν ἐστίν, Arist. *Met. Δ* 5. 1015^{b}12), it follows necessarily that it cannot have any composition.

p. 232. 6. 'Through the term only', i.e. through homonymy. That some things are one formally, others generically, others analogically, i.e. through a relation to some thing, is asserted by Aristotle, *Met. Δ* 6. 1016^{b}31.

p. 233. 1. The first agent, the ultimate form, the ultimate end, the ultimate matter are but different names for God, the One. That God is regarded as the ultimate matter may seem rather strange, but as early as Aristotle, *Met. α* 2, ad init., it is asserted that there is some first principle, ἔστιν ἀρχή τις, and it is proved that none of the four causes can form an infinite series but that they all must end in a first term.

p. 233. 2. 'angels': i.e. the philosophers identify the Aristotelian concept of a separate intellect with the Persian–Jewish concept of an angel. The identification of angels with concepts taken from Greek philosophy takes place when Judaism comes into contact with Greek philosophy, and is found already in Philo Iudaeus, who identifies the angels with the Platonic ἰδέαι and the Stoic λόγοι (cf. Philo, *De somn.* i. 115: ἀθανάτοις λόγοις, οὓς καλεῖν ἔθος ἀγγέλους). In the scholastic philosophy of the thirteenth century this identification of angel and separate intellect by the Arabic philosophers was known, but it was often denied, as by Albertus Magnus, *II Sent. dist.* II. iii; however, Dante, *Conv.* ii. 5, says: 'Li movitori di quello (terzo cielo) sono sustanze separate da materia, cioè intelligenze, le quali la volgare gente chiama angeli ... e chiamale Plato Idee, che tanto è a dire, quanto forme e nature universali. Li Gentili le chiamavano Dei e Dee; avvegnachè non così filosoficamente intendessero quelle, come Plato.'

p. 235. 1. تالٍ 'consequent' is a literal translation of τὸ παρακολουθοῦν, a constant attribute, inseparably connected (cf. Arist. *Cat.* 7. 8^{a}33, *Met. I* 2. 1054^{a}14).

p. 235. 2. i.e. it is not impossible for the First to have a necessary attribute.

p. 235. 3. Its impossibility: i.e. the impossibility that the First should have an essence besides its existence.

p. 236. 1. In this book, which has been edited by Muhyi al-Din Sabri al-Kurdi, A.H. 1331, Ghazali proposes (p. 2) simply to relate the theories of the philosophers, since it is necessary to know their theories before refuting them, as he proposes to do afterwards (i.e. in his *Incoherence of the Philosophers*). The book consists of three parts, Logic, Metaphysics, and Physics, was translated into Latin in the Middle Ages and exercised a considerable influence on medieval Scholasticism. It was published in its entirety in Venice in 1506, and there is a new edition by Muckle of the Metaphysics and Physics (entitled, however, Algazel's *Metaphysics*) published in Toronto, 1933.

p. 236. 2. This refers to the passage, in the book mentioned in the preceding note (Part II, section 3, p. 139), where Ghazali gives the following proof of the thesis that, for the necessary existent, essence and existence are identical (ان يتحد انّيته وماهيته): existence is an accident of the quiddity, and every accident is an effect, for if it were an existent by itself, it would not be an accident of something else. Now the cause of the existence of the necessary existent would have to be either its quiddity or something else: if something else, the existence of the necessary existent would be an accident and an effect, and would not be a necessary existent; however, it cannot be its quiddity itself, for the non-existent cannot be a cause of existence, and the quiddity before its actual existence would have to be a non-existent, since if it were already an existent it would not need a second existence, and if we admit a second existence, we shall have an infinite regress. Therefore there is no cause for its existence, and its essence and existence are identical.

p. 236. 3. That the existence of a thing is prior to its quiddity is Averroës's own theory, based on the Aristotelian thesis that the copula implies being or existence: since everything is something, it has to *be*, prior to its being something; from which it would follow that the non-existent also is or exists, a consequence which Aristotle fully accepts.

p. 236. 4. i.e. it is a concept in the mind.

p. 236. 5. This refers to Aristotle, *Anal. Post.* A 2. 71^{b}9: ἐπίστασθαι δὲ οἰόμεθ' ἕκαστον ἁπλῶς . . . ὅταν τήν τ' αἰτίαν οἰώμεθα γινώσκειν δι' ἣν τὸ πρᾶγμά ἐστιν, ὅτι ἐκείνου αἰτία ἐστί, καὶ μὴ ἐνδέχεσθαι τοῦτ' ἄλλως ἔχειν, we believe that we know something absolutely when we believe we know the cause on which its existence depends, i.e. when we know that this is its cause and that it must be so and not otherwise.

p. 237. 1. I do not think he means asking whether God has a necessary attribute which determines His existence, for this would contradict his previous denial that God has a necessary attribute; I suppose he means asking whether the idea of God (i.e. the concept we have of God, which he calls 'the true') is such that we must judge that He necessarily exists. But of course the whole theory is confused and obscure.

p. 237. 2. i.e. by the Stoic term τί, which signifies anything whatever that

NOTES

can be meant, the false and the non-existent included: Averroës means that 'existent' is here a concept in the mind.

p. 237. 3. Analogy according to Aristotle is the nexus between different genera; even when things are generically different the same genus can be attributed to them by analogy (as an example see e.g. *Met. Θ* 6. 1048^b6).

p. 237. 4. This strange theory is based on Averroës's denial of being or existing as an accident. According to Avicenna, in a sentence like 'Socrates is' 'is' is a predicate and therefore an accident. Averroës sees rightly that 'Sein ist kein reales Prädikat, das zu dem Begriff eines Dinges hinzukommt' (Kant), but he identifies essence and existence, from which it follows that there is no distinction between an essence that exists and one that does not. However, as he has to admit this distinction, he regards 'is' in a sentence like 'Socrates is' (or perhaps the whole sentence) as something in the mind. He sees that this something in the mind must have a counterpart outside the mind, since things exist in reality, and he regards it as existing potentially—a dubious kind of reality which he attributes also to universals as entities outside the mind. This use of 'potential' derives from the ambiguity of the term 'actuality' in Aristotle, for whom 'actuality' may mean really existing and being perceived; a colour, for example, as long as it is not actually perceived is only potentially perceived, and we have therefore the contradiction that although it is actual, i.e. really existing, it is also potential, as long as it is not perceived. Cf., however, note 232. 4.

p. 237. 5. Since there would be no cause for its beginning; according to Aristotle movement must be eternal and can never be interrupted: δεῖ κίνησιν ἀεὶ εἶναι καὶ μὴ διαλείπειν (*Phys. Θ* 6 ad init.).

p. 237. 6. i.e. the movement of heaven, which is eternal as a whole, but temporal in its parts.

p. 237. 7. Aristotle shows (*De caelo B* 3, *De gen. et corr. B* 10, *Meteor. A–Γ*) how earthly changes proceed from the different positions of the heavenly bodies and especially of the sun.

p. 238. 1. Averroës's objection seems to me purely verbal: Avicenna calls the existent necessary through another (i.e. heaven) an existent possible in itself (كل ما هو واجب الوجود بغيره فانه ممكن الوجود بذاته, *Salvation*, p. 367), whereas Averroës calls heaven necessary in its substance, but possible in its local movement, combining in this instance necessity and possibility.

p. 238. 2. The Ash'arite term صفات نفسانية, 'mental qualities', corresponds to the Stoic term ἐννοήματα, i.e. 'universals', but neither for the Ash'arites nor for the Stoics does this term correspond to the Aristotelian term 'forms', εἴδη, since neither the Ash'arites nor the Stoics believed that universal entities existed outside the mind.

p. 238. 3. Koran xxi. 31.

p. 238. 4. Koran xli. 10.

p. 239. 1. The nature of the possible, i.e. matter.

p. 239. 2. This refers to the tradition found in the canonical books of tradition of Muslim (ايمان ‏ا 211) and Ahmad ibn Hanbal (vi. 106) سئل النبى عن الوسوسة فقال تلك محض الايمان: they asked the prophet about the whisperings of Satan and he said 'This is an act of pure faith.'

p. 239. 3. 'an existent the non-existence of which can be supposed': this is rather badly expressed; he ought to have said 'an essence' instead of 'an existent', which would include both Socrates (who does not exist any more) and a non-existent golden mountain.

p. 239. 4. i.e. since the First has no essence, its essence is a non-existent whose existence is asserted.

p. 239. 5. i.e. absolute, unrelated existence is but 'ein leerer Begriff', an empty concept, as Kant would say.

p. 240. 1. i.e. since the causeless implies an entity, viz. an essence which is causeless, this essence cannot be denied, i.e. represented as non-existent.

p. 240. 2. i.e. the philosophers identify quiddity and existence in the First, but do not deny that it has a quiddity, its quiddity being its existence. However, Ghazali is quite right in regarding this as a denial of the quiddity.

p. 241. 1. I do not know whether he means here to imply that necessity is a purely mental attribute. The Stoics define necessity as the true that cannot become false, ἀναγκαῖον δέ ἐστιν ὅπερ ἀληθὲς ὂν οὐκ ἔστιν ἐπιδεκτικὸν τοῦ ψεύδος εἶναι (Diog. Laert. vii. 75). The true, however, is for the Stoics incorporeal, ἀσώματον, and unreal, ἀνυπόστατον (Sext. Emp. Hyp. Pyrrh. ii. 81).

p. 241. 2. This is the Stoic and Ash'arite argument.

p. 242. 1. Averroës seems here to be referring to p. 131, where he says that since the Ash'arites accept eternal attributes in God, there must exist an eternal compound of essence and attribute (and according to Averroës every compound is material), which contradicts their theory that every compound is temporal. Here, however, his argument seems to be that their proof that the whole whose parts are temporal is itself temporal is invalid, because although the individual accidents are temporal there is in them a constant element, namely their being accidents inhering in a substratum and forming a compound with it.

p. 243. 1. An eternal composite: i.e. an eternal simple body having a soul; in other words, heaven.

p. 243. 2. This is a rather curious statement; probably he means that this argument is valid against the method by which philosophers like Avicenna try to arrive at an immaterial and transcendent first principle; cf. also below, p. 257.

p. 243. 3. 'that the essence is the cause of its attributes' is a consequence Averroës himself draws, one which Ghazali denies, and which the Ashʿarites would deny also.

p. 244. 1. The First Principle must be unique and must possess unity.

p. 244. 2. i.e. the quiddity is only denied because it implies plurality; one must, however, admit a quiddity, since its denial is absurd, and therefore a plurality is implied in the First.

p. 244. 3. Cf. Plotinus, *Enn.* v. 5. 10, where infinite power is ascribed to the First, τὸ δ' ἄπειρον ἡ δύναμις ἔχει; for the First as the ultimate source of movement cf. Plotinus, loc. cit.: ἀπ' αὐτοῦ κίνησις ἡ πρώτη.

p. 245. 1. Everything that comes into being possesses matter, ἅπαντα δὲ τὰ γιγνόμενα . . . ἔχει ὕλην (Arist. *Met.* Z 7. 1032ᵃ20); body cannot come into being from the incorporeal (Arist. *De caelo* Γ 6. 305ᵃ16).

p. 245. 2. Generation takes place only within the same species: man begets man (Arist. *Met.* Z 7. 1032ᵃ24); Aristotle and his school admit also a *generatio aequivoca*, but only for certain primitive organisms.

p. 245. 3. There is no absolute becoming, for everything must come into being out of something and this something must itself be ungenerated, ἀγένητον, cf. Aristotle, *Met.* B 4. 999ᵇ5.

p. 245. 4. The doctrine that the principle of the individual is the individual, ἀρχὴ γὰρ τὸ καθ' ἕκαστον τῶν καθ' ἕκαστον (Arist. *Met.* Λ 5. 1071ᵃ20): Peleus is the principle of Achilles.

p. 245. 5. In a univocal way, when the father is regarded as the cause of the son, because both belong to the same species; in an analogical way, when the cause and effect are not really in the same genus. Aristotle says that different things, i.e. things not in the same genus, have identical causes and elements only by analogy (*Met.* Λ 5. 1071ᵃ24: ἄλλα δὲ ἄλλων αἴτια καὶ στοιχεῖα . . ., πλὴν τῷ ἀνάλογον).

p. 245. 6. That fire and water have a special corporeality is not an Aristotelian theory. There is here a reference to a problem not found in Aristotle. Although for Aristotle matter is the absolutely indefinite, he often seems unconsciously to regard it as spatial—which is only natural, for how, if it were not spatially extended, could anything enter into it?—and he never asks the question how matter becomes spatially extended. Plotinus, whose theory of matter is inspired both by Plato's *Timaeus* and by Aristotle, regards magnitude, μέγεθος (*Enn.* ii. 4. 8), as a form which enters into matter, but which itself is incorporeal, ἀσώματον. For Avicenna the first form which enters into matter and is common to all matter is that of corporeality, through which matter receives the three dimensions and continuity and divisibility (cf. my *Ep. d. Met. d. Av.*, p. 64). According to Plato (*Tim.* 53 c sqq.) fire has the shape of a pyramid (tetrahedron), air that of an octahedron, water that of an icosahedron, earth that of a cube; and he explains the transmutability of water, air, and fire by the fact that their surfaces are composed of right-angled scalene triangles; but to an Aristotelian like Averroës such a theory, refuted by his master (see e.g. *De caelo* Γ 8. 306^{b}3 sqq.), could not be acceptable, and it is not easy to see what he means here by 'special corporeality' (cf. also my *Ep. d. Met. d. Av.*, pp. 65–66).

p. 245. 7. Warmth, θερμόν, cold, ψυχρόν, moist, ὑγρόν, dry, ξηρόν are the basic qualities of the elements; cf. Aristotle, *De gen. et corr.* B 2. 329^{b}24. That the production of the elements from each other is caused by the movement of the heavenly bodies is a doctrine found in Aristotle, *Meteor.* A 2. 339^{a}21.

p. 246. 1. For this theory of Avicenna cf., for example, his *Salvation*, p. 461, ll. 1 sqq., and my *Ep. d. Met. d. Av.*, p. 44.

p. 246. 2. He refers here, for example, to Themistius, *Paraphr. in Arist. Met.* Λ, Landauer, 9. 3–10. 5; cf. my *Ep. d. Met. d. Av.*, loc. cit.

p. 246. 3. The principal argument would seem to be that in matter there are realized resemblances, ὁμοιότητες, with the forms of the separate principles. Equivocal generation, therefore, is not in conflict with the thesis that *omne vivum ex vivo* (cf. the passages indicated in the two preceding notes). For the Neoplatonic conception of equivocal generation cf., for example, Plotinus, *Enn.* iv. 3. 8 at the end, and Porphyry, *De Antro Nymph.* 18 where he speaks of the βουγενεῖς ψυχαὶ εἰς γένεσιν ἰοῦσαι. Avicenna depends on this Neoplatonic conception, which has in it Platonic and Stoic elements (in its theory of λόγοι σπερματικοί).

p. 246. 4. This, with what follows, is in agreement with Aristotle, who teaches that proofs are valid only for one and the same genus and may not be transferred from one genus to another (cf. Arist. *Anal. Post.* A 7 ad init.: οὐκ ἄρα ἔστιν ἐξ ἄλλου γένους μεταβάντα δεῖξαι).

p. 247. 1. i.e. if the teleological argument is given for God's existence, and if it is said that the size of the world was chosen for the sake of the order of the world, and that therefore there must be a spiritual principle and the material world cannot be the highest principle.

p. 247. 2. The first effect, i.e. the νοῦς, the first Intellect.

p. 247. 3. Cf. with this argument of Ghazali Carneades' denial that the *convenientia consensusque naturae* implies the acceptance of a divine spiritual principle (Cicero, *De nat. deor.* iii. 11. 18). This passage, which is a refutation of the teleological argument, is contradictory: to say that the special size of the universe exists for the sake of the order of the universe, is to admit the teleological argument, since 'for the sake of' implies an intention. There is an ambiguity in the word 'necessary', which can mean at the same time a necessity in God, a necessary choice for God (who, if He wanted the order of the universe, had to choose this special measure), and the natural necessity of cause and effect without any choice being involved. It is, indeed, one of the difficulties of the teleological argument that it has to assume a necessity of choice in God, since it limits God's choice to what is best and to the means conducive to the best. There is, however, some justification for Ghazali's argument: if, as both Aristotle and Plotinus assert, there is no will in God, but all action of spiritual forces takes place through purely natural necessity (cf. Plotinus, *Enn.* iv. 4. 6), the apparent final causes in this sublunary world will not prove the existence of a conscious spiritual force. Indeed, both Aristotle and Plotinus are guilty of a contradiction, for one cannot admit final causes and at the same time deny conscious intention; unconscious intention is a contradiction in terms. There is here an insuperable difficulty; we cannot rid ourselves of final causes in biology: concepts like that of instinct, for example, imply in their definition the idea of design, since instinctive actions are those which seem to have a design, although they are regarded as being performed by the animal without conscious intention. (According to Cicero, *De nat. deor.* ii. 49. 125, Aristotle gave the various instincts of animals as an argument in his teleological proof for the existence of God.)

p. 247. 4. i.e. why did the Eternal Will create the world at a certain definite moment? (cf. p. 18 and note 18. 3).

p. 248. 1. There seems to be some confusion in this passage: if the distinction between certain sizes is unessential to the order of the Universe, it is not possible to answer the question why the actual size was chosen instead of an equivalent one, and one might say it has not been chosen, but was always there; on the other hand, if the order of the world depends on its actual size, this size seems to have been intentionally chosen; it is true that for the realization of this order no other size was possible, but 'not possible' means here that God had necessarily to choose this definite size. What Ghazali wants to express is this: for an eternal world there cannot be a creator, since creation implies a becoming in time, nor can there have been a design, since design, will, and intention imply temporal priority to the thing designed, willed, and intended.

p. 249. 1. i.e. must be valuable in itself or more valuable than any other thing possible in the same conditions. According to the Ash'arites God is absolutely free, His choice is not determined by anything, and a thing is valuable because God willed it. According to the philosophers, God willed it because it was valuable, the Will of God being determined by the value of the thing.

p. 249. 2. Cf. Plato, *Laws* X 902 e: μὴ τοίνυν τόν γε θεὸν ἀξιώσωμέν ποτε θνητῶν δημιουργῶν φαυλότερον, let us not, then, deem God inferior to human workmen.

p. 249. 3. Since no art or wisdom would be necessary for the artisan.

p. 249. 4. This conception, which implies that nature is the art of God and art the nature of man, presents grave difficulties. On the one hand, how can man, being simply God's creature, himself become a creator, or being simply an effect, himself become a cause? *Natura non nisi parendo vincitur*, says Francis Bacon paradoxically, but he offers no solution. If man is but a *res creata* and a part of nature, how can he conquer nature? For man will not have any more power over nature than the falling stone, as Spinoza believed. On the other hand, if God stands to nature as man to his artefact, God's action will be determined by His own nature and the exigencies of His material. Aristotle himself was unable to distinguish satisfactorily between art and nature (cf. my *Ep. d. Met. d. Av.*, p. 205).

p. 250. 1. i.e. the theologians following the Stoic argument.

p. 250. 2. Mixture, امتزاج, μίξις, cf. Aristotle, *De gen. et corr.* A 16; alteration, استحال, ἀλλοίωσις; ἀλλοίωσις μεταβολὴ κατὰ τὸ πάθος, cf. Aristotle, *Met.* Λ 2. 1069^{b}12.

p. 250. 3. He means that we see the temporal body coming into existence through a cause (however, its matter is eternal). Averroës does not see that he is here accepting Ghazali's assertion that a cause implies a coming into existence.

p. 250. 4. *De Caelo et Mundo*, i.e. *De Caelo*; Averroës is here referring to *De caelo* B 14, where Aristotle explains the spherical shape of the earth by asserting that all its parts tend towards their natural place, which is the centre of the world, and says at B 14. 297^{b}14 sqq.: 'If the earth has been generated . . . it must have come into existence in the shape of a sphere; if the earth, however, is ungenerated and everlasting it must have the same shape as it would have as a result of generation.'

p. 251. 1. There is here some confusion; by 'the beginning of things' he cannot of course mean a beginning in time, but the beginning of a causal series; according to him the materialists admitted as the supreme cause of all change and becoming the eternal movement of the heavens. This would imply the passivity of everything else, and so this cause would not be a supreme cause and the termination of a causal series, but the only cause and a cause simultaneous with its effect. At the same time, however, Ghazali regards the movement of the heavens as a sequence of causes and effects. He seems to have here in mind the theories of such naturalistic Peripatetics as Strato of Lampsacus, of whom Cicero declares (*Acad. pr.* ii. 38. 121): 'negat opera deorum se uti ad fabricandum mundum'.

NOTES

p. 251. 2. 'this causal series', i.e. the series of forms and accidents.

p. 251. 3. Koran vi. 75.

p. 251. 4. i.e. the Ashʿarites regarded God as the sole cause, creating and re-creating the Universe at every instant.

p. 252. 1. i.e. the materialists might say the material world exists by itself without a cause.

p. 252. 2. This may mean that it is necessary to inquire whether the body of the heavens possesses matter, i.e. the principle of possibility.

p. 252. 3. Averroës's objection to this proof seems here to be that it cannot be used as an *a priori* proof—as Avicenna seems to use it, putting it at the beginning of his *Metaphysics* (in the *Recovery*)—but that it is only valid *a posteriori*, after the study of the physical universe. In the next paragraph he is, however, much more sceptical about the value of this argument.

p. 253. 1. i.e. it is not proved that it is a spiritual substance possessing thought.

p. 253. 2. Since the world as a whole is eternal, and according to Aristotle 'eternal' and 'necessary' are convertible (cf., for example, Arist. *De gen. et corr.* B 11. 338ᵃ1: ὥστ' εἰ ἔστιν ἐξ ἀνάγκης, ἀίδιόν ἐστι, καὶ εἰ ἀίδιον, ἐξ ἀνάγκης).

p. 254. 1. i.e. through procreation the animal also participates in eternity.

p. 254. 2. This passage is not found, so far as I know, in any of the Greek texts that have come down to us. It is, however, in harmony with the general trend of Alexander's philosophy (cf., for example, his *Quaest. nat.* ii. 3). In an Arabic work ascribed to Alexander *On the Principles of the Universe* which is not known in Greek or mentioned by Greek authors (cf. note 113. 6, p. 245 in my *Ep. d. Met. d. Av.*), but which on the whole agrees with Alexander's *Quaestiones naturales* i. 1 and ii. 3 and which has been edited by ʿAbd ar-Rahman Badawi (Cairo, 1947) in a collection of treatises entitled *Aristotle among the Arabs* (pp. 253–77), we find (p. 273, l. 18) the following passage: 'just as there is in the one city one leading principle (مدبر i.e. the Stoic ἡγεμονικόν), so we can say that there is one spiritual force which pervades the whole world and unites its parts; and just as there is in a city only one leading principle which is either its prince or its law, so the world is a unique eternal body unified by an unchanging (read p. 274, l. 2 غير متغير) principle which holds it together and keeps it in its order through a spiritual force which pervades all its parts.'

p. 254. 3. The Arabs had collected the *Hist. an.*, the *De part. an.*, and the *De gen. an.* into one work. This refers to Aristotle, *De part. an.*, where it is said (B 10. 656ᵃ8) that the genus man, among the animals known to us, either alone participates in the Divine or participates in it in the highest degree (ἢ γὰρ μόνον μετέχει τοῦ θείου τῶν ἡμῖν γνωρίμων ζῴων ἢ μάλιστα πάντων) and where it is said (Δ 10. 686ª28), that the function of what is most divine is intelligence and thought (ἔργον τοῦ θειοτάτου τὸ νοεῖν καὶ φρονεῖν).

p. 254. 4. On this book cf. Nallino, 'Filosofia "orientale" od illuminativa', in Riv. degli Studi Orientali, x. 433–367, and Nallino, Raccolta di scritti editi e inediti, vol. ii, p. 467. The Oriental Philosophy, which seems to have been unknown to Averroës, is preserved in manuscript in Constantinople. The Theorems and Notices seems to bear the same relation to it as the Salvation to the Recovery of the Soul, i.e. to be a compendium of it. Compare also Madkour's Introduction p. 22 to the first volume of Avicenna's Logic, Cairo 1952.

p. 254. 5. On the principles, i.e. On the principles of the Universe. The argument (op. cit., p. 257, l. 1) is as follows: that which is the cause in everything of the perfection which characterizes its nature must be of a greater excellence, and necessarily the cause of the movement of the divine body must be its longing for the highest pitch of excellence. Cf. Alexander Aphrodisiensis, Quaestiones naturales, ed. Bruns, p. 4, ll. 18 sqq.: μάλιστα γὰρ ὀρεκτὸν τῇ αὑτοῦ φύσει τὸ τῇ αὑτοῦ φύσει καλὸν μάλιστα . . . (that which is most desirable in its own nature is that which has in its own nature the greatest excellence).

p. 255. 1. This would imply that it does not need a cause for its bodily substance, and so invalidate the idea of an eternal creation which Averroës holds also. Of course, strictly speaking, since movement is eternal it will be according to Aristotle necessary and therefore in no need of a cause.

p. 255. 2. The meaning is that the world as a whole is eternal, although individual sublunary things are liable to change. According to Aristotle the world, form, and matter are eternal. But how can matter, the possible, be eternal, since everything eternal is necessary?

p. 255. 3. The actuality of thought is life, says Aristotle, ἡ γὰρ νοῦ ἐνέργεια ζωή (Met. Λ 7. 1072ᵇ28).

p. 255. 4. According to the Stoic principle that every living being is self-conscious, παντὶ ζῴῳ συνείδησις τῆς αὑτοῦ συστάσεως (Diog. Laert. vii. 85).

p. 256. 1. 'God an eternal man'; there is here an allusion to Aristotle, Met. B 2. 997ᵇ8, where Aristotle raises against the Platonists the objection that by assuming eternal ideas, an eternal ideal man, an eternal ideal horse, an eternal ideal health, they are acting like the anthropomorphizers who make of their gods eternal men, ἀιδίους ἀνθρώπους. Compare also Sext. Emp. Adv. phys. i. 46: And again, when the ancients had imagined a long-lived man, they prolonged his lifetime to infinity, and reaching the concept of eternity by the combination of the present, the past, and the future, they declared that God was eternal.

p. 256. 2. i.e. if God is an eternal man, man is differentiated by eternity and temporality.

NOTES

p. 256. 3. According to Aristotle, *De an.* B 1. 412^{b}16 (see also ^{a}27), all life consists in the power of self-motion.

p. 256. 4. Averroës here identifies will with non-rational desire, ἄλογος ὄρεξις, which is found also in animals.

p. 257. 1. An increase in the desire would only cause the act when the desire was an ἄλογος ὄρεξις. According to Aristotle, *De an.* Γ 9 ad fin., moderate men, although they have desire and appetite, do not follow their desire, but obey reason.

p. 257. 2. i.e. this practice is only an internal act of the soul; it is not combined with external actions, e.g. movements, as is the case with the practical arts. For thought as action cf. Aristotle, *De an.* B 5. 417^{b}18 sqq.

p. 258. 1. Analogy قياس (or تمثيل ; مثل is example) is regarded by the Muhammadan jurists as one of the 'roots' of Muhammadan law. When the Koran and the sayings and actions traditionally attributed to Muhammad fail to give an indication which legal practice is to be followed, new legal prescriptions may be obtained through applying to them reasoning by analogy. The Zahirites do not admit the legitimacy of analogical inference. The theory of inference by analogy was first formulated by Aristotle in his theory of reasoning by example (παράδειγμα), *Anal. Pr.* B 24: if it was wrong that the Thebans should fight their neighbours the Phocians, it is equally wrong that the Athenians should fight their neighbours the Thebans, because from the antecedent the general principle may be inferred that it is wrong to fight one's neighbour. The term συλλογισμὸς κατὰ τὸ ἀνάλογον is found in Galen's *Introductio*, and the schoolmen speak of a *ratiocinatio per analogiam*; the term قياس 'analogy', 'reasoning by analogy', comes, in Arabic, to mean syllogism in general. According to the Stoics (cf. Sext. Emp. *Adv. ethic.* 250–1) all knowledge transcending the evidence of the senses proceeds by way of analogical inference, μετάβασις ἀναλογιστική. The practice of judging by analogy in law is not confined to the Muhammadan jurists, but is generally acknowledged. It consists in inferring from the individual case, i.e. the precedent (in Roman law, *exemplum*), the underlying *ratio legis*; if it can be assumed that a complex *ABC* has the judicial consequence *F* because of *A* as its *ratio iuris*, the consequence of *ADE* will equally be *F*.

p. 259. 1. For the rhetorician tries to convince by stirring the emotions (πάθη) of his audience (cf. Arist. *Rhet.* A 2. 1356^{a}10).

p. 259. 2. Cf. e.g. Avicenna's *Salvation*, pp. 267 sqq.; this is the Platonic (cf. Plato, *Phaedo* 61 b) and Neoplatonic (cf. Plotinus *Enn.* i. 2. 3) theory of κάθαρσις: freed from the bodily passions, the soul contemplates the intelligibles and assimilates itself to the Divine.

p. 260. 1. It is interesting to note that Ghazali, the theologian, arranges all his syllogisms in a hypothetical form. In this he follows the Stoic logicians, whose examples are always given in hypothetical syllogisms. Ghazali himself, in his *Touchstone of Knowledge* (Cairo, 1911), p. 88, declares that the hypothetical syllogism is most useful in all juridical matters.

p. 260. 2. Assuming the minor premiss in a mixed hypothetical syllogism (συλλογισμὸς ὑποθετικὸς κατὰ μετάληψιν, قياس شرطي استثنائي) is called by the Arabian logicians استثناء, i.e. literally 'excepting', 'excluding' (the conjunction 'but' introducing the minor—e.g. '*but* it is not in matter'—is called by them حرف الاستثناء, the particle of exception). The Peripatetics call this μετάληψις (the Stoics πρόσληψις) and the minor premiss itself τὸ μεταλαμβανόμενον (المستثنى). The term استثناء seems to be a translation of διάζευξις and διαίρεσις, 'disjunction', and indeed a major of the form 'If it is not day, it is night' is equivalent to the disjunction 'Either it is day or it is night'; but when both major and minor are positive it seems somewhat illogical to regard the minor, as the Arabic logicians seem to, as part of a disjunction. (In Greek also the minor in a disjunctive syllogism is called τὸ μεταλαμβανόμενον.) The other terms used in describing the hypothetical syllogism are all borrowed from the Peripatetics: τὸ ἡγούμενον, the antecedent, is called in Arabic المقدم; τὸ ἑπόμενον, the consequent, التالى; τὸ συμπέρασμα, the conclusion, النتيجة.

p. 260. 3. This refers to p. 88 in the edition quoted in the last note but one. Ghazali there gives the same examples as here, and shows that neither the assumption of the opposite of the antecedent nor the assumption of the positive consequent leads to a conclusion.

p. 260. 4. Cf. e.g. Aristotle, *Met.* Θ 8. 1050ᵇ2: τὸ εἶδος ἐνέργειά ἐστιν. The form is ἐνέργεια (ἐνέργεια in its double sense of 'actuality', 'reality' and 'activity').

p. 260. 5. Cf. e.g. Aristotle, *Met.* Δ 2. 1013ᵃ27: τὸ εἶδος ἐστὶν ὁ λόγος τοῦ τί ἦν εἶναι.

p. 260. 6. For according to Aristotle purpose and form do not differ essentially (cf. *Met.* H 4. 1044ᵇ1: ἴσως τὸ εἶδος καὶ τὸ τέλος ἄμφω τὸ αὐτό).

p. 260. 7. Why the active potencies are only particular and not common, whereas the passive potencies can be either particular or common, I do not know; nor is it clear which potencies are active and which passive—all we know is that they are opposites; there is some confusion in this passage, since the opposition of active and passive potencies is reduced to that of actuality (or activity) and potentiality, or form and matter.

p. 261. 1. Cf. Aristotle, *Met.* H 6. 1045ᵇ17: ἡ ἐσχάτη ὕλη καὶ ἡ μορφὴ ταὐτὸ καὶ ἕν, τὸ μὲν δυνάμει, τὸ δὲ ἐνεργείᾳ: the proximate matter and the form are one and the same, the one potentially and the other actually.

p. 261. 2. According to Aristotle it is only the active intellect which is separate from matter (χωριστὸς καὶ ἀπαθὴς καὶ ἀμιγής, *De an.* Γ 5. 430ᵃ18).

p. 261. 3. Cf. Aristotle, *De an.* B 12, ad init.: ἡ μὲν αἴσθησίς ἐστι τὸ δεκτικὸν τῶν αἰσθητῶν εἰδῶν ἄνευ τῆς ὕλης.

p. 262. 1. This refers to the passage in *De an.* Γ 7. 431ᵃ4–7, where it is said that perception is not a passivity and cannot be compared to the other movements in which there is something imperfect, since activity in the absolute sense is the activity of that which has reached perfection (τοῦ τετελεσμένου). Aristotle, does not, however, offer any further explanation. The theory of perception expounded in this passage is difficult to understand. Perception, according to Aristotle, is an activity of the soul, but when we ask what this activity is, the only answer is that the percept (αἰσθητόν) makes (ποιεῖ) an actual percipient (αἰσθητικόν) of a potential. This would imply that perception is a passivity rather than an activity; but this Aristotle denies. The crux of the problem lies in the term αἰσθητόν, 'the percept or perceived' (not here to be translated by 'the perceptible'), for the percept (whether we take it to mean the perceived object or the perceived matterless form—in the latter case the perception of any material object would be impossible) is here regarded as the cause of perception; but it has also to be its effect, i.e. the perception itself. We find in Aristotle the two tendencies which run through the history of philosophy: (1) to regard the thing perceived in perception both as a cause and as an effect of perception; (2) to reduce the act of perception to a state (a state of the organ, according to Aristotle; the existence of sensations in a consciousness, according to the moderns).

p. 262. 2. Cf. Aristotle, *Met.* Λ 7. 1072ᵇ14–1073ᵃ13: God as pure intellect and pure actuality.

p. 262. 3. Inference, Arabic لزوم, Greek ἐπιφορά (the concept and the term are Stoic). Theophrastus (cf. Alexander of Aphrodisias in *Anal. Pr.* Wallies, 388. 17) had asserted that the minor in the mixed syllogism must itself be accepted through induction, or through another hypothesis, or from self-evidence (ἐνάργεια), or through a syllogism. Compare with Averroës's passage Sext. Emp. *Adv. log.* ii. 329, where the latter discusses Epicurus' proof for the existence of the void: If motion exists, the void exists; but motion does exist, therefore the void exists. The premisses of this syllogism—says Sextus—are not generally accepted; the Peripatetics deny the major, and Diodorus Cronus the minor and the conclusion.

p. 263. 1. The conjunction is that of matter and of absence of thought; the disjunction, διάζευξις, is that reality is either material (or attached to matter) or thought—the proposition 'If it does not think, it is in matter' is equivalent to this disjunction (cf. note 260. 2).

p. 263. 2. i.e. the argument in the form of the mixed hypothetical syllogism should not be as Ghazali gives it, but should run: 'If the First does not think, it is in matter; but the First is not in matter, therefore it thinks'.

p. 264. 1. Cf. e.g. Plotinus, *Enn.* iii. 2. 2: γέγονε δὲ οὐ λογισμῷ τοῦ δεῖν γενέσθαι, ἀλλὰ φύσεως δευτέρας ἀνάγκῃ: i.e. the world has not come into being because of God's reasoning that He had to create it, but because of the necessity that there should be a secondary nature.

p. 264. 2. This argument is nothing but a *petitio principii*. It is true that will implies the possibility of choice between opposites, i.e. that I know that I can do a thing or refrain from doing it (or, as Aristotle has it, e.g. *De an.* Γ 10. 433ᵃ29: πρακτὸν δ' ἐστὶ τὸ ἐνδεχόμενον καὶ ἄλλως ἔχειν), but in a world in which there was no will there would be no choice of opposites.

p. 265. 1. Compare the Epicurean argument (e.g. Lucretius, *De rerum natura*, ii. 1095) that the gods are unable to rule all the events in the infinite world (*regere immensi summam*). Ghazali here means by 'knowledge' knowledge of the purpose and of the means to its attainment; and indeed will seems to imply such a preliminary knowledge (although there is here a difficulty; e.g. I can only will to lift my arm, when I know that I can lift it; but how can I know that through my will I can lift my arm, when I have never willed it?). There may, however, be foreknowledge, even for human beings, of some of the consequences following the attainment of the purpose, although these consequences are indifferent to the willer.

p. 266. 1. i.e. when one denies the divine will and temporal creation, one has to regard God as a natural cause acting by necessity and through mediation, and such a cause cannot know the mediate effects which constitute the world.

p. 266. 2. Cf. Carneades' argument in Sext. Emp. *Adv. phys.* i. 139–42, and Cicero, *De nat. deor.* iii. 13. 32, that the senses imply transiency and death: *omne igitur animal confitendum est esse mortale*.

p. 267. 1. 'representation', i.e. φαντασία; cf. Aristotle, *De an.* Γ 10. 433ᵇ28 sq.: ὀρεκτικὸν δὲ οὐκ ἄνευ φαντασίας· φαντασία δὲ πᾶσα ἢ λογιστικὴ ἢ αἰσθητική. As man is concerned, Averroës here means the φαντασία λογιστική.

p. 267. 2. i.e. God's knowledge, for Ghazali, means God's purpose, God's intention; and intention implies will.

p. 268. 1. 'to every intelligent being', i.e. both in the temporal world and in the eternal.

p. 268. 2. As a matter of fact, Ghazali's assertion that God can only know the purpose of His own action, and that He cannot know the consequences of these actions through mediate causes, would ascribe to Him ignorance of all human actions; and the only way to avoid this consequence would be the Ashʿarite doctrine of regarding God as the real cause of all human actions also. It is noteworthy that Geulinx in his *Metaphysica vera et ad mentem peripateticam* propounds a theory which has a certain resemblance to Ghazali's: according to Geulinx nothing acts which does not know what it is doing; since man does not know how he moves his hand, he cannot do it himself, but God, when a man wills to move his hand, takes this opportunity (*occasio*) to set his hand in motion. All human actions, both for the Ash'arites and for the occasionalists, are performed by God, the difference between the two schools being apparently that whereas for the occasionalists the will of man, e.g. to move his hand, is dependent on himself, for the Ash'arites even this volition is caused by God.

p. 268. 3. i.e. the more knowledge an intellect possesses, the nobler it is.

p. 270. 1. See note 255. 2.

p. 270. 2. See note 255. 3.

p. 270. 3. This is the well-known argument of Zeno (Sext. Emp. *Adv. phys.* i. 104): τὸ ἔμψυχον τοῦ μὴ ἐμψύχου κρεῖττόν ἐστιν.

p. 271. 1. Ghazali follows the same line of reasoning as Alexinus, the Megarian (Sext. Emp. *Adv. phys.* i. 108) in his opposition to Zeno's argument. Alexinus observed: 'One might in this way argue that the Universe was not only animate, but also poetical, grammatical, and possessed of the other arts, since the possession of all these is better than their absence.'

p. 271. 2. This trichotomy is a difficult point in the Aristotelian philosophy. One of the distinctions between natural and voluntary acts is that in inanimate natural things there is a necessity (ἀνάγκη) of becoming which does not exist for activities based on will (προαίρεσις), where there is a choice between two contraries (cf. Arist. *Met.* Θ 5. 1048ᵃ1). On the other hand, there is also in nature the accidental, for—says Aristotle, *De interpr.* 9. 19ᵃ9— in what is non-eternal and transient there is always the possibility of being and non-being (ὅτι ὅλως ἔστιν ἐν τοῖς μὴ ἀεὶ ἐνεργοῦσι τὸ δυνατὸν εἶναι καὶ μή. For the failure of the Aristotelian philosophy to distinguish between nature and art see my *Ep. d. Met. d. Av.*, pp. 204-5.

p. 272. 1. This is rather a strange theory for a philosopher who regards God as the Prime Mover. What Averroës seems to mean here is that God, being incorporeal, cannot set things in motion through the movement of his body as man does. The Sceptics and Stoics held that the incorporeal was incapable of any action (cf. Sext. Emp. *Adv. phys.* i. 151: οὐδὲν δυνάμενον ἐνεργεῖν τὸ ἀσώματον).

p. 272. 2. Cf. note 264. 2. We may add here that this conception is opposed to Aristotle's explicit statement (*Phys.* B 8. 199ᵇ26) that in nature, although it acts according to an end, there is no deliberation (βούλευσις), i.e. no conscious choice (προαίρεσις). It is the characteristic of nature (see note 271. 2) that in it there is no choice between two contraries.

p. 272. 3. Cf. Aristotle, *Met.* Δ 4. 1015ᵃ14: ἡ πρώτη φύσις καὶ κυρίως λεγομένη ἐστὶν ἡ οὐσία ἡ τῶν ἐχόντων ἀρχὴν κινήσεως ἐν αὐτοῖς ᾗ αὐτά: the primary and foremost meaning of nature is the essence of those things that have in themselves, as such, a principle of motion.

p. 272. 4. There is more purpose and more beauty in the works of nature than in those of art, says Aristotle, *De part. an.* A 1. 639^{b}19: μᾶλλον δ' ἐστὶ τὸ οὗ ἕνεκα καὶ τὸ καλὸν ἐν τοῖς τῆς φύσεως ἔργοις ἢ ἐν τοῖς τῆς τέχνης.

p. 272. 5. e.g. naturalistic Peripatetics like Strato.

p. 272. 6. Cf. Aristotle about 'wonderful automata', τῶν θαυμάτων ταὐτόματα, e.g. *Met.* A 2. 983^{a}14; *De gen. an.* B 1. 734^{b}10.

p. 272. 7. Cf. Aristotle, *Met.* A 3. 984^{b}15: νοῦν ... ἐνεῖναι, καθάπερ ἐν τοῖς ζῴοις καὶ ἐν τῇ φύσει τὸν αἴτιον τοῦ κόσμου καὶ τῆς τάξεως πάσης: 'that there is intellect in nature, just as in animals, and that it is the cause of all order and arrangement'.

p. 273. 1. Cf. p. 266.

p. 273. 2. But Averroës does not accept the universal maxim: no universal maxim applies to God's uniqueness. This of course implies that nothing can be attributed to God, since every attribute is a universal.

p. 273. 3. i.e. being dead, like being blind, is a privation, a στέρησις, of that which would naturally be in the possession of the subject: cf. Aristotle, *Met. Δ* 22. 1022^{b}24.

p. 273. 4. i.e. the Aristotelian principle that every individual is generated from what is synonymous with it (ἑκάστη ἐκ συνωνύμου γίγνεται οὐσία), e.g. that man begets man, would thereby be violated.

p. 274. 1. This is the same answer as the Stoics gave to refute Alexinus' argument against Zeno (see note 271. 1): Zeno had chosen—they said—the absolutely superior, τὸ καθάπαξ κρεῖττον, namely reason (Sext. Emp. *Adv. phys.* i. 109).

p. 275. 1. Avicenna says in his *Salvation* (p. 404, l. 4; cf. the parallel passage in his *Recovery, Met.* viii. 6): 'To ascribe to God a plurality of thoughts is just as much attributing to Him a deficiency as to ascribe to Him a plurality of acts: God knows everything, only in a universal way; still no single thing, not even the weight of an atom, is hidden from Him (according to the Koran xxxiv. 3; x. 62). This is something very wonderful, the understanding of which needs great intellectual subtlety.'

p. 275. 2. The example of the eclipse is taken from Avicenna (*Recovery, Met.* viii. 6, and *Salvation*, p. 405).

p. 276. 1. A node is one of two points at which the orbit of a planet intersects the ecliptic; the ascending node is that encountered by the heavenly body in its northward passage, the descending that encountered in its southward passage.

p. 276. 2. 'in its desire to assimilate itself to God'; for Aristotle the heavens move through love for God, and here the Platonic τέλος, 'assimilation', ὁμοίωσις τῷ θεῷ κατὰ τὸ δυνατόν, is added to this conception. For the question whether this assimilation can be realized through movement, whereas God is the eternally stable, see below.

p. 276. 3. The whole of this interesting passage is based on Avicenna, *Recovery, Met.* viii. 6 and the parallel passage *Salvation*, pp. 404 sqq. Avicenna's position about God's knowledge or ignorance of the individual is far from clear, and indeed his thesis that God can know every individual thing in a universal way, being contradictory, cannot be understood. (On the fundamental problem of the relation between the individual and the universal, as an empiricist Aristotle asserts the priority of the individual to the universal, as a Platonist the priority of the universal to the individual, and this contradiction is still more evident in the Neoplatonic commentators; cf. my *Ep. d. Met. d. Av.*, notes 81. 5 and 126. 2). But the conclusion Ghazali, following Avicenna, mentions here does not really concern God's knowledge or ignorance of the individual—His knowledge, indeed, is here assumed— but is the logical outcome of any theory which ascribes to God a timeless eternity, for no actual relation can exist between the timeless and the transitory. If we admit in God omniscience, and foreknowledge of all future events, He will know the sequence of things in an eternal 'now', for He will know time as a sequence of events which are earlier and later (just as we know in the present an eternal and stable sequence of past events). But there is another aspect of time, the passing of the future through the present into the past, i.e. the living indefinable experience of the ever-fleeting, the ever-new 'now'. God, not being in a fleeting present, can never have experience of it. He may know that such-and-such actions are subsequent to my birth, but He cannot know *now* that I am acting or have acted in such-and-such a way, for in God's stable timeless 'now', in God's stillness, there can be no experience of the indefinable fleeting 'now' in which we live and act and die. This was clearly seen by Avicenna. He says (cf. e.g. *Salvation*, p. 406. 14 sqq.): 'If you know eclipses in as far as you exist' (I take this to mean: in as far as you exist without any reference to time) 'or in as far as you exist eternally, and if you have knowledge not of the eclipse in general, but of any eclipse whatever, then the existence or non-existence of any definite eclipse will not produce a change in you or your knowledge, for what you know is that one definite eclipse is later than another; and this knowledge of yours will be true during, before, and after any eclipse. But when you introduce the concept of time, and know at one definite moment that the eclipse is not actual and at another that it is, then your knowledge is not unalterable. The First, however, who is not in time or subject to its rule, can never refer to anything in this or that definite time, since this would imply that He Himself was in it and would imply in Him a new judgement and a new knowledge' (Aristotle had already distinguished, *Met. Θ* 10, between two types of truth, eternal and transitory, cf. my *Ep. d. Met. d. Av.*, pp. 220–1).

p. 276. 4. Possibly this is Avicenna's conception, but his theory (which I shall not try to analyse here) in the chapter mentioned in the preceding note is both confused and contradictory. In any case Avicenna ascribes to God only conceptual knowledge, since for Him there is neither a *hic* nor a *nunc*, and denies sense-perception to Him; he repeats (e.g. *Salvation*, 405. 9) Aristotle's assertion that an individual of any species can only be known by being a 'this', a τόδε τι, المشار اليه, by being pointed at, i.e. through direct perceptual experience, المشاهدة الحسية (cf. e.g. *Cat.* 5. 3^{b}10, where Aristotle says that every individual substance seems to signify a 'this'). However, this view cannot be upheld. It is true that in perception everything perceived stands in relation to a 'here' (a most mysterious relation, since 'here' is the place where my body is, and 'my body' assumes a relation between something non-spatial, i.e. my spiritual self, and a spatial entity). But in thought an individual can be completely determined in space and time without direct reference to any 'here' or 'now', although it may be conceded that without any perception of spatial relations we should not have any conception of space. It may be remarked that *hic* and *nunc* are not in every sense analogous. The 'now', the present moment, is involved in the concept of time, whereas the 'here' does not enter into the definition of space, but needs space for its own definition (the place in which my body is), and is individually subjective, whereas any interaction between individuals assumes the simultaneity of a 'now'. Another point is that if God is deprived of perception of the individual He cannot have knowledge of the universal either. It is one of the fundamental cruces of philosophy that perception and conception seem to imply each other; there is no individual percept that has no qualities (Aristotle knew that there is no 'that' which is not a 'what'), and there is no universal which does not stand either directly or indirectly in some relation to something perceived.

p. 277. 1. Conditions, احوال, πῶς ἔχοντα: see note 3. 6.

p. 278. 1. I have not found this tripartite division in Avicenna who, however, in his *Recovery*, *Met.* iii. 10, has a long discussion about relations (the difficult concept of relation was much discussed in later Greek philosophy, see e.g. the long discussion in Simplicius, *Comm. in Cat.*, Kalbfleisch, 155. 30 sqq.; the Peripatetic Boethus dedicated a whole book to the discussion of this problem, according to Simplicius, op. cit. 163. 6). Avicenna there refutes, for example, the view held by the Greek sceptics, the Muslim theologians and some moderns (Bradley, for example—*Appearance and Reality*[2], pp. 31 sq.—some of whose negative theories may be found in Sextus Empiricus) that relation, since it implies an infinite regress, can have no reality, and I do not know to which Arabic author Ghazali is here referring. The tripartite division which he mentions here is illogical and confused, for there is only room here for two classes of relations, essential (or internal) and non-essential (or external), and the example of Ghazali's second kind of condition implies an essential relation: when a man stops moving, although his capacity to move has not changed, there is an actual change in him from action to rest. This tripartite division seems to refer to the equally confused distinction between πρός τι πὼς ἔχον, πὼς ἔχον, and πρός τι in Stoicism (cf. Simplicius, op. cit. p. 165, 32 and v. Arnim, *Stoic. Vet. Fr.* ii. 132. 21). The first condition would be the πρός τι πὼς ἔχον, i.e. an accidental relation (see loc. cit., l. 26, where 'to the right', δεξιόν, is given as an example); the second would be the πὼς ἔχον, which is a non-essential characteristic of a thing (as an example of such a non-essential characteristic Plotinus, *Enn.* vi. 1. 30, gives acting—τὸ ποιεῖν πὼς ἔχον); the third would be, when a thing in its distinct existence of its own—i.e. when it is a ποιόν—implies a relation to something else, and is therefore essentially relative, like any state, knowledge, and perception (v. Arnim, op. cit. ii. 132. 45 ὅταν μὲν κατὰ διαφοράν τι διακείμενον πρὸς ἕτερον νεύσῃ, πρός τι μόνον τοῦτο ἔσται, ὡς ἡ ἕξις καὶ ἡ ἐπιστήμη καὶ ἡ αἴσθησις).

p. 278. 2. 'like a mere relation', i.e. like a mere external relation.

p. 278. 3. This of course is false; Ghazali has evidently not seen the point. If God had created in us an everlasting knowledge that Zaid will come tomorrow, this knowledge, if true today, would be false tomorrow and ever afterwards. On the other hand, if God had created in us an everlasting knowledge that Zaid has come, or will come, the former would be false up to the moment he has actually come, but true ever afterwards, whereas the latter would be true till he has actually come and false ever afterwards.

p. 279. 1. This sentence is rather confused, but I am well aware of the difficulty of the problem of relations in general and of the problem of knowledge in particular. The words 'whenever the relation becomes different' mean 'whenever the knowledge becomes different' (because of the change in the object of knowledge in reality); again, by 'the thing which has this essential relation' knowledge is understood; according to this view knowledge both *is* a relation and *has* an essential relation to the thing known.

I think knowledge (knowing) can only be conceived as a unique and indefinable relation implying two terms, the knower and the objective thing known; if it is represented—as it so often is—as a separate entity having some independent existence in a mind, two new relations will be needed, one to a mind and the other to the objective thing. I think it is correct to say that when an object known or perceived changes, the percipient who notices this change changes too through the change in his knowing and perceiving. The last part of Ghazali's sentence—i.e. that whenever this differentiation and this sequence arise there is a change—is a tautology.

p. 279. 2. One might answer: 'There might be in God one single cognitive relation to the whole world, just as in one human act of perception or thought a whole consisting of a plurality may be apprehended; my perception of a complex, e.g. the face of a friend, does not consist in my perception of all its parts individually—every complex forms a new unity in which the individual constituents are merged.' Indeed, if the act of perception were identical with the object perceived, not only would the perception of a magnitude be itself a magnitude, but it would consist like the magnitude itself of an infinite number of points (cf. Arist. *De an.* A 3. 407ᵃ6 sqq., where he rejects the view that thought, νόησις, is a magnitude, μέγεθος).

p. 279. 3. That universals are infinite is not accepted by the Aristotelians, and would not fit easily into their conception of a spatially limited universe. They argue, however, against the Stoic theory of a divine providence for all individuals, saying that, since time is infinite, this would imply in God knowledge of the infinite (cf. my *Ep. d. Met. Av.*, p. 145). Cf. note 205. 2.

p. 279. 4. Ghazali misses the point: time is a condition of change; a timeless knowledge is allowed in God, not a temporal changing knowledge.

p. 280. 1. Since human knowledge enters into the essence of the knower.

p. 280. 2. Cf. Aristotle, e.g. *De an.* B 5. 417ᵇ22: τῶν καθ' ἕκαστον ἡ κατ' ἐνέργειαν αἴσθησις, ἡ δ' ἐπιστήμη τῶν καθόλου.

p. 280. 3. He seems to mean: if the human mind possessed a highest genus, e.g. 'being', or 'something' (which are the highest genera according to the Stoics) by which it could comprehend (the word is used equivocally and can mean both 'grasp' and 'include') all the genera and species, it would also comprehend all the individuals; but one should not compare the divine understanding with the human mind, since for the divine intellect the opposition between universal and individual is obliterated.

p. 280. 4. 'a passive intellect and an effect': i.e. our human intellect; it is regarded here as passive and an effect, because in its knowledge it is dependent on reality, our knowledge being posterior to reality; whereas God's knowledge, being the cause of reality, either precedes it (as a cause, but not in time) or, being identical with the things, coexists with them without any priority or posteriority (cf. *Enn.* v. 9. 5: οὐ γάρ ἐστιν οὔτε πρὸ αὐτοῦ οὔτε μετ' αὐτόν, viz. τὰ ὄντα).

p. 280. 5. This theory of God's active or creative knowledge goes back to Plotinus (cf. especially *Enn.* v. 9. 5), who quotes Parmenides' important statement that thought and being are identical, τὸ γὰρ αὐτὸ νοεῖν ἐστίν τε καὶ εἶναι (*Parmenides*, Fr. 3 Diels). According to Plotinus the νοῦς is pure act and is eternal; by its absolute being it thinks and creates (ὑφίστησιν) things, which cannot exist as something outside itself, ἑτέρωθι. Thinking its own self, in its own self it thinks the things, which therefore are identical with it: ἔστιν ἄρα τὰ ὄντα. This theory, the so-called theory of intellectual intuition, is found also in Christian philosophy and theology. Cf. e.g. St. Augustine (*Confess.* xiii. 38. 53): 'nos itaque ista quae fecisti videmus, quia sunt; tu autem quia vides ea, sunt'. Kant expresses this in his *De mund. sens. atque intell. form. et princip.* ii. 10: 'intuitus nempe mentis nostrae semper est passivus ... divinus autem intuitus, qui obiectorum est principium, non principiatum, cum sit independens, est Archetypus et propterea perfecte intellectualis'.

p. 281. 1. Of course one might ask how, if intellect can be only attached to the existent, the non-existent can form an object of thought, or how the intellect can plan the non-existing future, remember the non-existing past, be subject to illusion and doubt. We have, however, seen that for Averroës even the objectively non-existing has some existence, existing subjectively, i.e. in the mind, as a representation. We have here an example of the fatal reification of thought, regarding the act of thought as the existence in the mind of some mental atoms, which has so deeply warped philosophical speculation.

p. 281. 2. *veritas adaequatio intellectus et rei.*

p. 281. 3. Compare the scholastic principle *Esse est Deus*, which is Eckehart's fundamental principle. Both Sufism, i.e. Muslim mysticism, and Western medieval mysticism are based on Neoplatonic conceptions (in Sufism there are also Hermetic and Gnostic elements). The resemblance between those two schools, which are geographically so far apart, is often so great that many affirmations of German medieval mystics like Eckehart, Tauler, or Suso might be taken for translations from some Arabian or Persian mystic.

p. 281. 4. Namely, in plants, animals, men, and heaven.

p. 281. 5. The Muʿtazilites seem to have been aware of the difficulty that to attribute to God a knowledge of the changing affairs of the world implies a change in Him. According to Shahrastani (*Religious and Philosophical Sects*, p. 60), Jahm said, 'God cannot know a thing before creating it, for either (1) God's knowledge is unchangeable, and if He knew that it would be before He created it, He would be in error (the text has 'ignorance', جهل), when it was or had been and He still thought that it would be; or (2) His knowledge would be changeable, but only the created can change.' (Ibn Hazm, op. cit. ii. 130, says that the Muʿtazilites asked: 'When does God know that Zaid has died? For if God knows it eternally, this implies Zaid's eternal death.' Ibn Hazm's answer on this problem runs on the same lines as Ghazali's.) At the same time, according to Shahrastani, Jahm affirmed that God had new knowledge, not, however, in a substratum (لا فى محل) i.e.

not in God Himself). It is to this latter assertion that Ghazali is evidently referring, but it seems to contradict the other assertion that God's knowledge cannot change. Probably Jahm regarded God's knowledge as a separate entity emanating from Him (there is here probably some vague relation to the Philonic Logos-theory), and used 'knowledge of God' in an ambiguous way, meaning at one time an attribute of God, at another an effect of God.

p. 281. 6. See note 2. 6.

p. 281. 7. Cf. 74. 2; and since nothing that changes can be eternal, that which is eternal (i.e. God) cannot be subject to change.

p. 282. 1. i.e. it is impossible that time should have a beginning, although the series of causes is limited. We have already shown the fallacy of this view.

p. 282. 2. i.e. every movement of the spheres is temporal, since all movement implies time and there is a continual beginning and ending of these movements, just as time changes eternally and a new 'now' continually occurs.

p. 282. 3. i.e. according to their system time arises from the timeless; time is the effect of a timeless cause.

p. 282. 4. i.e., if the temporal can proceed from the timeless, should not temporal knowledge, i.e. knowledge of the temporal, proceed from the timeless knower? However, the idea of an emanation of knowledge from the knower seems to make very little sense.

p. 282. 5. 'coloured', for according to Aristotle it is only colour or that which possesses colour that is seen (*De an.* Γ 2. 425^{b}18: ὁρᾶται δὲ χρῶμα ἢ τὸ ἔχον).

p. 282. 6. For this conception of vision cf. e.g. *De sensu* 2. 438^{a}12 sqq.

p. 283. 1. For knowledge as the supreme end of man see, for example, Aristotle, *Met.* A 2; *Eth. Nic.* K 7.

p. 283. 2. Since the terms used are equivocal.

p. 283. 3. i.e. since illumination or light is, according to Aristotle (*De an.* B 7. 419^{a}9), the actuality of the transparent, the substance of the transparent is not changed through the illumination.

p. 285. 1. See note 256. 1.

p. 285. 2. 'man a mortal god', *homo quasi deus mortalis*: this refers to the beautiful words ascribed to Aristotle in Cicero, *De finibus* ii. 13. 40 (fr. 61 Rose): man whose destiny is thought and action is like a mortal god: 'sic hominem ad duas res—ut ait Aristoteles—, ad intellegendum et agendum, esse natum quasi mortalem deum'.

p. 285. 3. St. Thomas Aquinas, who regards it as probable that the stars are moved by angels, asserts, *Sum. c. gent.* ii. 70, that from the religious point of view it is indifferent whether it be declared that heaven is animated or not: 'hoc autem quod dictum est de animatione coeli non diximus quasi asserendo secundum fidei doctrinam, ad quam nihil pertinet sive sic sive aliter dicitur'. However, among the 219 opinions ascribed to the Latin Averroist Siger of Brabant and condemned by the Church in 1277, we find this proposition (prop. 92 in Denifle, *Chart. Univ. P.* i, p. 548): 'quod corpora celestia moventur a principio intrinseco, quod est anima; et quod moventur per animam et per virtutem appetitivam, sicut animal. Sicut enim animal appetens movetur, ita et coelum.' (St. Thomas Aquinas believed that the movement of the stars depended on an external animated principle.)

p. 285. 4. 'by perception': φαίνεται, as Aristotle says, *De caelo B* 8. 289^{b}1; for another example of an argument based on the evidence of the senses, διὰ τῶν φαινομένων, cf. *De caelo B* 14. 297^{b}1. Although in the following Ghazali seems to be referring to Avicenna's *Salvation*, pp. 422 sqq. (and the parallel passages in the ninth book of the metaphysical part of his *Recovery*), his argument differs considerably from the discussion by Avicenna; but in any case its principle is derived from Aristotle's *De philosophia*. Aristotle, in the passage of this lost dialogue quoted by Cicero, *De nat. deor.* ii. 16. 44 (fr. 24 Rose), bases his argument on the disjunction that all movement either takes place by nature or is constrained or is voluntary (*aut natura aut vi aut voluntate*). He rules out the possibility that the stars might be moved by nature, since all movement by nature is either downward or upward, and the stars have a circular movement; their movement cannot take place by constraint, for what could possess a greater force than the stars? It is therefore voluntary.

p. 286. 1. The meaning is: if the fact of being a body implied its movement, every body would be in motion; there must therefore be a cause of motion, i.e. everything moved is necessarily moved by something (Arist. *Phys. H* 1, ad init., 241^{a}34: ἅπαν τὸ κινούμενον ὑπό τινος ἀνάγκη κινεῖσθαι).

p. 286. 2. It is interesting to note that this sentence is a free translation (with, however, a slight, but important difference) of one in Aristotle, *Phys.* Θ 5. 256^{a}14: εἰ δὴ ἀνάγκη πᾶν τὸ κινούμενον ὑπό τινός τε κινεῖσθαι, καὶ ἢ ὑπὸ κινουμένου ὑπ' ἄλλου ἢ μή, καὶ εἰ μὲν ὑπ' ἄλλου [κινουμένου], ἀνάγκη τι εἶναι κινοῦν ὃ οὐχ ὑπ' ἄλλου πρῶτον, εἰ δὲ τοιοῦτο τὸ πρῶτον, οὐκ ἀνάγκη θάτερον: if therefore everything moved necessarily must be moved by something either moved by another or not by another; and if it is by a thing moved, it is necessary that this should be a first mover not moved by something else, and if such a mover is found there is no need for another mover. We see that the Arabic has substituted for a first mover a voluntary mover moving its body by itself, and the argument which Aristotle uses to establish the existence of an unmoved first mover, i.e. God, is used here to prove the existence of an eternal soul which moves the body of heaven by a first movement, i.e. a movement on which all the other movements of the world depend. As a matter of fact there is no reason why Aristotle should have made his first mover transcendent, and why the mover of heaven should not be immanent in the world and be the soul of heaven. Of course, if this argument is offered to prove the soul of heaven, it can no longer be offered to prove the existence of God; and if the existence of God is still accepted, He can no longer be the source of all movement and action, for the soul, even the human soul, does not set in motion through a mover (although for a motive), but by itself, i.e. its will and desire. That the soul cannot be moved is acknowledged by Aristotle himself, *De an.* A 4. 408^{b}30.

p. 286. 3. i.e. the universal relation of the world to God cannot explain motion: if the fact of being created and a body itself implied movement, every body would be in motion.

p. 286. 4. This example is found in Avicenna, *Recovery, Met.* ix. 4.

p. 287. 1. According to Aristotle (*De caelo* A 2), however, the movement of the stars is a natural one, i.e. natural to things which possess an element more sublime than the four sublunary ones. Avicenna also, in his *Salvation*, p. 424, regards the heavenly movement as caused by an inclination (ميل, ὁρμή or ῥοπή) which may be called natural; however, he adds 'This natural inclination is inspired by a soul and renewed by its representation.' (For the problem caused by the contradiction in the Aristotelian texts, cf. my *Ep. d. Met. d. Av.*, note 108. 2; Alexander of Aphrodisias and Averroës deny that the celestial bodies can have φαντασία, i.e. any representations.)

p. 287. 2. This refers to Ghazali's words: 'every mover receives its impulse from the moved itself'; but this is only a verbal quibble, for Ghazali means the same as Averroës.

p. 287. 3. In fact this is a tautology; what he wants to say is that it is self-evident that things have intrinsic natures by which they are moved.

p. 287. 4. i.e. if things had not an intrinsic nature, and everything depended solely on the will of God, as the Ash'arites hold, earth might move upward just as easily as fire.

p. 287. 5. Things which are sometimes at rest, sometimes in motion, can receive by constraint a movement opposed to their natural one, and can therefore execute two opposite movements, cf. Aristotle, *De caelo* A 2. 269^{a}7: a simple body can receive the motion of another body by constraint (βίᾳ), granted that a single body has only one natural movement.

p. 287. 6. Aristotle argued (*De caelo* A 4) that there can be no movement contrary to the circular motion of the stars; heaven cannot be constrained to move by another movement than its own; cf. op. cit. A 3. 270^{a}9. Since, according to Averroës—see below in the text—the motion of the stars is not natural, a proof of the cause of their movement must be given.

NOTES

p. 288. 1. That the soul of the heavenly bodies is only equivocally (ὁμωνύμως) called a soul is stated by Alexander of Aphrodisias, *On the Principles of the Universe*, ed. cit., p. 255.

p. 288. 2. 'Nature' is a most ambiguous word, both in common language and in Aristotle. For the meaning intended here of 'a rational principle' see e.g. Aristotle, *De gen. an.* A 23. 731ᵃ24: εὐλόγως ἡ φύσις δημιουργεῖ 'nature works rationally'.

p. 288. 3. In fact heaven is excluded from physics only so far as its spiritual elements, the separate intelligibles, are in question, since, according to Aristotle (*Met.* E 1. 1025ᵇ26), physics theorizes about substances which are capable of motion and have forms, but about these forms only so far as they are inseparable from matter (cf. also the beginning of *De caelo*).

p. 288. 4. That there cannot be a body outside heaven is argued by Aristotle, *De caelo* A 9. 278ᵇ25 sqq.

p. 289. 1. 'without any act he deliberately chose', since according to Ghazali's theory God's will is not selective (i.e. it does not choose between distinct cases), but creative (i.e. it creates the distinctions themselves).

p. 290. 1. Although we moderns can explain the fact that fire moves upward and stones downward by attributing it to a general characteristic of matter, Averroës is right in asserting that the differentiation of individuals having their special characteristics cannot be deduced from a general principle: there is no answer to the question why this stone is not that stone or that flower. Still, both Averroës and Ghazali, when asked why things are as they are, would answer that everything depends upon the will of God; both would assert that God's eternal will was not comparable with our human will and that God's action was wholly creative. (It is curious to see that, in the matter of God's knowledge, Averroës reproaches Ghazali for not observing that it is wholly creative, whereas in the matter of God's volition he reproaches him for regarding it as wholly creative.) Both would assert also that this was the best of all possible worlds, not only implying by this a deliberation and choice in God, but fixing a limit for His illimitable power.

p. 290. 2. The Ashʿarite view will be discussed below at length.

p. 290. 3. This is Aristotle's own thesis, *De caelo* A 2. 269ᵇ5–14, where he proves that circular motion is natural to the body which has this motion, and 269ᵇ14–17, where he proves that there is a fifth element (i.e. the ether), superior to the sublunary elements, to which the circular movement is natural. If by 'natural movement of the ether' is meant that it moves by itself (Aristotle derives the word αἰθήρ from ἀεὶ θεῖν, 'to run always'), there is no need to accept movers for the spheres.

p. 290. 4. This is based by Aristotle on the principle that a thing can have only one contrary, ἓν ἑνὶ ἐναντίον (cf. *De caelo* A 2. 269ᵃ10), and he holds the strange theory (strange, for circular motion implies a movement in opposite directions) that circular motion has no opposite and that the ether is free from all opposition. Still, according to Aristotle himself the heaven of the fixed stars turns from right to left, that of the planets from left to right.

p. 290. 5. According to the principle that God moves as does the beloved, it would seem that movement *qua* movement was the supreme aim; but Plutarch, *De defect. orac.* xxx, emphasizes the variety and changes (μεταβολαί) implied in movement, and says that, to judge from the motion of the heavens, the Divine really enjoys variety and is glad to survey movement.

p. 290. 6. The heavy, according to Aristotle, is that whose nature it is to move towards the centre, the light that whose nature it is to move away from the centre; according to *De caelo A* 3. 269^{b}30, the body whose movement is circular can have neither weight nor lightness, for neither naturally nor unnaturally can it move either towards or away from the centre.

p. 290. 7. i.e. whether the heavenly bodies have consciousness and which kind of consciousness.

p. 291. 1. According to Aristotle an external force moving heaven would involve an effort, whereas the movement of heaven is ἄπονος, effortless; he says that we should not believe the traditional myth about Atlas (cf. *De caelo B* 1. 284^{a}11–22).

p. 291. 2. Aristotle in his criticism of Thales' view that the earth rests on water (*De caelo B* 13. 294^{a}28) says that then one would have to ask the same question over again: for what supports the water?

p. 291. 3. Cf. Aristotle, *De caelo A* 9. 279^{a}8: ὕλη γὰρ ἦν αὐτῷ τὸ φυσικὸν σῶμα καὶ αἰσθητόν: the matter (of the whole universe) is natural perceptible body.

p. 291. 4. That the elements are transitory, γενητά, is argued by Aristotle, *De caelo Γ* 6.

p. 291. 5. All generation and decay on earth are caused through the motion of the sun along the ecliptic; cf. Aristotle, *Meteor. A* 9.

p. 291. 6. For Aristotle (cf. e.g. *Phys. Γ* 2. 202^{a}8) all motion is based on touch; even in thought the thing thought of is touched by the thinker (cf. *Met. Θ* 10. 1051^{b}24 and *Λ* 7. 1072^{b}20).

p. 291. 7. It is interesting to note that Averroës sees that there is a resemblance between the Stoic theory and the Ash'arite. We have tried to show above that there is, in fact, a relation between these two views.

p. 292. 1. i.e. the Ash'arites, not the Stoics.

p. 292. 2. 'accidental', since it was there only by constraint.

p. 292. 3. i.e. movement *qua* movement, without any reference to a special place or time, is a universal; and if the heavenly bodies desire this movement, they are moved by a concept, something in the soul. Averroës's argument, however, is not only a *petitio principii*, i.e. not only is it used to prove that the heavenly bodies are animated, but it is also contradictory, for it first denies the objective existence of movement absolutely, and then admits that a movement exists in the individual moving thing, although not permanently (this is in opposition to Arist. *Phys. Δ* 4. 228ª20, where it is asserted that the movement which is absolutely one [and particular] is that which is continuous, without any restriction as to time; cf. also Avicenna, *Salvation*, 180. 11). Averroës's assertion is a reminiscence of the animistic view that all movement is based on love or desire, which we discussed above in our note on love. It may be added that this view survives in modern philosophy in one form or another. Schopenhauer, for example, regards movement as the objectivation of will, and at vol. i, p. 119 of his *Die Welt als Wille und Vorstellung* he quotes with approval the passage of St. Augustine, *De civ. Dei* xi. 28: 'si essemus lapides ... non tamen nobis deesset quasi quidam nostrorum locorum atque ordinis appetitus, nam velut amores corporum momenta sunt ponderum, sive deorsum gravitate, sive sursum levitate nitantur: ita enim corpus pondere, sicut animus amore.'

p. 292. 4. This would seem to imply that the souls of the heavenly bodies possess imagination (φαντασία), and indeed Avicenna asserts this. Averroës, however, denies it—see my *Ep. d. Met. d. Av.*, note 109. 6—and we must regard the representation he mentions here as a kind of intellectual act. Alexander of Aphrodisias also denied φαντασία to the intellectual movers: see below, 301. 3.

p. 293. 1. Aristotle did not see this difficulty in ascribing natural motion to heaven (see note 290. 4).

p. 293. 2. In the following passage Ghazali refers to the chapter in Avicenna's *Salvation* (pp. 429 sqq.) about the aim of the movement of heaven; cf. also ib., p. 490.

p. 293. 3. The basic idea of this deeply religious assertion, that God should be loved for His own sake, not out of hope for reward or fear of punishment, is found already in Aristotle, *Eth. Eud. H* 3 ad init., where he lays down as a condition of love a certain equality, ἰσότης, between the lover and the beloved, and where he says that it would be ridiculous to expect God in His majesty to repay the love with which He is loved (cf. Spinoza, *Eth.* v, prop. xix: 'qui deum amat, conari non potest, ut deus ipsum contra amet'). Plotinus, *Enn.* ii. 2. 2, says that the stars, wherever they are, rejoice in surrounding God, and this not by reason, but by a natural necessity (ἕκαστον γὰρ οὗ ἐστι περιειληφὸς τὸν θεὸν ἀγάλλεται οὐ λογισμῷ ἀλλὰ φυσικαῖς ἀνάγκαις).

p. 293. 4. 'The angels in His proximity', i.e. the Hebrew Cherubim, are mentioned in the Koran iv. 170. We have here an example of the identification mentioned above, note 233. 2, of Judaeo–Christian–Muslim concepts with the entities of Aristotelian–Neoplatonic philosophy. Avicenna, *Salvation*, p. 490, does not use the term 'Cherubim' (he uses the term, however, in other writings, for instance, in his *Refutation of the Astrologists*), but says that the spiritual abstract angels, الملائكة الروحانية المجردة, of the highest degree are called intellects, whereas the angels of the second degree, the active angels, i.e. the movers of the stars, are called souls. In Qazwini's *Cosmography* (ed. Wüstenfeld, pp. 55 sqq.) there is given a long list of angels who are inhabitants of heaven, سكان السموات, and at p. 59 the Cherubim are mentioned, who, according to Kazwini, are continuously, day and night, wholly absorbed in adoration of God. He mentions also the movers of the stars, of whom (he says) there are seven, but according to him the exact number of angels is known only to God. Muslim angelology was influenced by Neoplatonism (cf. Plotinus *Enn.* iii. 5. 6), which regarded the stars as gods of a secondary order, subsidiary and related to the intelligible gods and dependent on them, θεοὺς δευτέρους μετ' ἐκείνους καὶ κατ' ἐκείνους τοὺς νοητούς, ἐξηρτημένους ἐκείνων. St. Thomas Aquinas, too, distinguishes between angels who move stars and those who do not; the former he calls *intelligentiae*, e.g. *Contra gent.* iii. 23. Like the Muslim philosophers he regards the differentiation of individual angels as a differentiation of species.

p. 294. 1. 'there is no potency in them'; since they are eternally absorbed in the contemplation and adoration of God, there is no change, no possibility of change in them, 'their assimilation to God is made perfect in stability', تم تشبهه به بالثبات (Avicenna, op. cit., p. 431. 15).

p. 294. 2. When the body of the heavens is actually in one position in the heavenly sphere, it is potentially in another, says Avicenna—op. cit., p. 432. 10—in agreement with Aristotle who says, *Met.* Λ 7. 1072^{b}5, that so far as heaven is moved there is a possibility for it of being otherwise, if not in substance, at least in place.

p. 294. 3. 'specifically', specifically and successively, بالنوع والتعاقب, says Avicenna, op. cit., p. 432. 13; the term 'specifically' according to Averroës—see below in the text—is unintelligible.

p. 294. 4. It is unfortunately not true that the unattainable cannot be desired.

p. 294. 5. This might be thought to be more closely in agreement with the words of Aristotle, *Met.* Λ 8. 1073^{a}23: ἡ μὲν γὰρ ἀρχὴ καὶ τὸ πρῶτον τῶν ὄντων ἀκίνητον καὶ καθ' αὑτὸ καὶ κατὰ συμβεβηκός, κινοῦν δὲ τὴν πρώτην ἀΐδιον καὶ μίαν κίνησιν: the principle and the first of all beings is immovable both essentially and accidentally, setting in motion the eternal and single movement. And indeed Plotinus, *Enn.* iv. 4. 8, says that it is not the proper function of the stars to contemplate the places they pass, for this is not essential to them, since they possess a uniform life, ζωὴν τὴν αὐτὴν ἔχοντα, and their movement is vital rather than local, ὡς μὴ τοπικὸν ἀλλὰ ζωτικὸν τὸ κίνημα εἶναι.

p. 294. 6. Cf. Aristotle, *Met.* Θ 8. 1050^{b}24, where he says that the heavenly bodies suffer no fatigue, since there is not for them, as there is for transitory things, that possibility of the opposite which makes continuity of movement laborious, the substance of the latter being matter and potentiality, not actuality; cf. also *De caelo* B 1. 284^{a}4.

p. 295. 1. Cf. Plotinus, *Enn.* vi. 9. 6: ἀρχὴ δὲ οὐκ ἐνδεὲς τῶν μετ' αὐτό, ἡ δ' ἁπάντων ἀρχὴ ἀνενδεὲς ἁπάντων: a principle is in no need of what is under it, and the principle of everything is in no need of anything. Cf. also Plotinus, *Enn.* iv. 4. 6: ἀλλ' οὐδὲ περὶ τῶν ἀνθρωπίνων αὐτοῖς ἐπίνοιαι καὶ μηχαναὶ ἐξ ὧν διοικήσουσι τὰ ἡμέτερα: the heavenly bodies do not think about human affairs, nor have they the means to administer them.

p. 295. 2. The conception of this circular movement of the stars as based on a desire to assimilate themselves to God, the unmovable, the object of this love, is an extremely strange one, and Theophrastus, whose *Metaphysics*, was known to the Arabs, felt its difficulty. It is difficult to see, he says (*Met.* 5^{a}25), how, having a physical desire, the stars do not pursue rest instead of movement, especially when this view is combined with the Platonic theory of imitation (μίμησις).

p. 296. 1. The comparison is of course wrong: guarding a city against the enemy may be called an approach to God, because the intention of the act is praiseworthy; but then the approach to God is a consequence of the good intention of the act; approach to God, i.e. assimilation to God, is not its primary intention.

p. 296. 2. Koran xvii. 39.

p. 296. 3. e.g. *Phys.* E 4. 228^{a}20; see note 292. 3.

p. 296. 4. Specifically one, i.e. so far as they are movements. This, however, is by no means what Aristotle understands by 'a movement specifically one'. He says (*Phys.* E 4. 228^{a}3) that when Socrates undergoes an alteration (ἀλλοίωσις) specifically (τῷ εἴδει) identical, repeated at different times, these alterations (i.e. movements) will be specifically one, but numerically different, although similar.

p. 297. 1. Compare Plotinus, who asks (*Enn.* iii. 3. 3) 'Has one to attribute the character of every being to its creator, if there is one, or to the creature itself, or should one not ask for a reason at all?' He answers that to ask for a reason why plants are created without perception, or why animals do not behave like men, would be like asking why men are not gods.

p. 298. 1. All this is in agreement with Aristotle's view that the side from where movement in animals starts is the right; cf. e.g. *De inc. an.* 6. 706ᵇ25–707ᵃ13.

p. 298. 2. This rather strange conception is based on Aristotle's view that right and left are only to be found in moving living beings, for only living beings have in themselves a principle of motion (cf. *De caelo* B 2. 285ᵃ27), and that motion starts from the right and tends towards the right. This implies that both the sphere of the fixed stars and the spheres of the planets move towards the right, although they move in opposite directions, and according to Aristotle the northern hemisphere is the lower in relation to the diurnal movement but the upper in relation to the motion of the planets (cf. *De caelo* B 2. 285ᵇ15). Aristotle and Averroës have it both ways; they regard right and left as relative to an observer and as absolutely attributable to the universe (cf. Arist. *Phys.* Γ 5. 205ᵇ33). According to the latter view Averroës holds that only the heaven of the fixed stars tends to the right, and this because the right side is the nobler; according to the former view he holds that all the heavens tend to the right.

p. 298. 3. Since it can only revolve on its axis.

p. 298. 4. Literally: like an ambidextrous foot. According to Aristotle (*Hist. an.* B 1. 497ᵇ31) only man among the animals is ambidextrous.

p. 298. 5. Contrary, namely in their direction—in their approach to the earth and recession from it.

p. 298. 6. Cf. e.g. Aristotle, *De caelo* B 3. 286ᵇ1 sqq.; generation implies more than one revolution of heaven; if there were only one revolution the relations between the four elements would remain stable, but the four elements imply generation by their nature, since none of them is eternal.

p. 299. 1. 'Why does the heaven revolve?', Plotinus asks at the beginning of *Enn.* ii. 2. 1, and the answer is that it is because it imitates the Intellect, ὅτι νοῦν μιμεῖται.

p. 299. 2. This kind of argument, which is very frequent, is used, for example, by Favorinus against the astrologers in Aulus Gellius' *Noct. Att.* xiv. 1: The shortness of human life prevents the perception and interpretation of such relations between events as are assumed by the astrologers.

p. 299. 3. Literally *On the particular influences of the spheres*. But that τὰ ἀστρολογικὰ θεωρήματα is meant can be seen from the fact that in his commentary (comm. 68) on *De caelo* B 10. 291ᵃ29, where Aristotle himself seems to refer to this work (other references are found in *Meteor.* A 3. 339ᵇ7 and A 8. 345ᵇ1), Averroës says: 'Aristoteles autem fecit librum de hoc qui dicitur de regiminibus coelestibus' (*regimina* corresponds exactly to the Arabic تدبيرات, which I have translated by 'influences'). About the astrological meaning of the word θεώρημα Cicero informs us at *De fato* i. 6. 11

where he translates the word θεωρήματα by *percepta*, and where he gives as an example of such a *perceptum* the fact that if so and so is born at the rise of the dog-star, he will not be drowned at sea. The correct English translation for θεώρημα in its astrological meaning would seem to be 'judgement'. 'As it is said' seems to imply that Averroës himself had not seen the book.

p. 299. 4. 'Chaldaeans' in Greco-Roman literature is often almost synonymous with 'astrologers'; cf. e.g. Cicero, *De divin*. i. 1. 2.

p. 300. 1. Cf. Aristotle, *De part. an.* A 1. 641^{b}12.

p. 300. 2. For a great number of signs of providence (the *ratio naturae intellegentis*) indicative of terrestrial things, compare, for example, Cicero, *De nat. deor.* ii. 47. 120 sqq.

p. 300. 3. 'thousand years'; this number makes it plausible that Averroës borrowed the assertion from some Greek author, and indeed Theophrastus, as quoted by Ps.-Philo, *De aeternitate mundi* (145), says that science was invented barely a thousand years ago, μόλις πρὸ χιλίων ἐνιαυτῶν. Compare Lactantius, *De ira* c. 13. 10 (*Stoic Vet. Fr.* ii. 337. 2) : '(Stoici) aiunt enim multa esse in gignentibus et in numero animalium quorum adhuc lateat utilitas, sed eam processu temporum inveniri, sicut iam plura prioribus saeculis incognita necessitas et usus invenerit.'

p. 300. 4. Cf. Aristotle, *Met.* Λ 8. 1074^{a}38; compare also Cicero, *De Divin.* ad init. 'Mysterious indication', رمز , corresponds to Greek μυστήριον, 'divine, inspired truth': cf. e.g. *Corp. herm.* i. 16.

p. 300. 5. This is, of course, a sophism: if rest is taken as the opposite of movement, God is not at rest, since He is not spatially determined; but if rest is taken as the opposite of change it will apply also to God (representing the universe in spatial images, man in general, and Aristotle in particular, have a tendency to regard all change as motion: a moving in and out).

p. 300. 6. 'the indelible tablet' اللوح المحفوظ . The indelible tablet is mentioned in the Koran, lxxxv. 21: 'it is a glorious Koran written on the indelible tablet'. It is regarded by the Muhammadans as the depository of all the events decreed by God. The allegorical interpretation of the philosophers takes the indelible tablet as the symbol of the Universal Soul. Jurjani in his *Definitions*, ed. Fluegel, p. 204, distinguishes four tablets: (1) the first Intellect; (2) the Universal Soul which is identical with the indelible tablet; (3) the particular souls of the heavens in which everything which has shape or form or magnitude in this world is inscribed; (4) matter.

p. 300. 7. There is a passage in Plutarch, *De defect. orat.* 40 (p. 432 c), in which he gives the Posidonian view of prophecy and compares the prophetic faculty, τὸ μαντικόν, with a tablet, not written on, irrational and indeterminate in itself, γραμματεῖον ἄγραφον καὶ ἄλογον καὶ ἀόριστον ἐξ αὐτοῦ, but capable through the reception of representations and forebodings of grasping the future without reasoning, ἀσυλλογίστως. And he says (op. cit. 39) that the prophetic faculty should not surprise us, for the soul possesses also its counterpart, memory, which preserves what has been the present, but no longer is: in a mysterious way the soul lays hold both on the not yet existing and on the no longer existing. Compare also Cicero, *De divin.* i. 56. 128: it is not astonishing that soothsayers can predict things that are nowhere, for everything 'is', although not (really) in time (*sunt enim omnia, sed tempore absunt*).

p. 300. 8. Cf. Farabi, *The Gems of Wisdom* (Dieterici), p. 77. Farabi asserts that neither the tablet nor the pen—see next note—is a concrete thing.

p. 301. 1. 'The Pen' is the name of Sura lxviii of the Koran. In Muhammadan tradition it is affirmed that the first thing God created was the pen with which He wrote down all future events.

p. 301. 2. The images in this sentence are rather mixed; the pen, or rather the burin, is regarded as the instrument of the divine engraver, but is also personified as His knowledge. In any case for the allegorical interpretation the pen is regarded as the active element, i.e. the First Intellect, the tablet as the receptacle or the effect of its action, the Universal Soul.

p. 301. 3. Cf. Alexander of Aphrodisias, *The Principles of the Universe*, ed. cit., p. 255, where it is stated that the heavenly bodies do not need those faculties which serve only for preservation. For Avicenna's theory that the heavenly bodies have representations or imagination cf. my *Ep. d. Met. d. Av.*, pp. 117–18.

p. 301. 4. According to Aristotle (*De an.* Γ 3. 428ᵃ10) all animals have sensations, but not all animals have imagination; for instance, the ant, the bee, and the grub do not possess it.

p. 301. 5. i.e. they possess only the intellectual part of the soul.

p. 301. 6. The will follows the end and not the end the will, says Avicenna, *Salvation*, 446. 2; cf. Aristotle, *Rhet.* Γ 16. 1417ᵃ18: ἡ προαίρεσις ποιὰ τῷ τέλει. The opposite was held by Spinoza, for whom the good, or rather the good for me, is what is desired by me (*Eth.* iii, prop. 39, schol.).

p. 302. 1. This is proved by Avicenna, e.g. *Salvation*, pp. 426 sqq. (cf. the parallel passage, *Recovery*, ix. 4): the Universal Will, الإرادة الكلية, cannot cause a movement from one definite point to another.

p. 302. 2. Avicenna (*Salvation*, p. 463) says that the celestial bodies influence the terrestrial through the qualities which are proper to them and which flow out from them into this world; and they also influence the souls of this world; through this we know that the nature which leads (ἡγεμονεῖ) these terrestrial bodies, like their perfection and their form (read الصورة),

receives its existence from the soul which is dispersed over heaven, or through its collaboration.

p. 302. 3. The accidental finding of a treasure, when one is digging for another reason, is a standard example among the Peripatetics of an event occurring by accident, ἀπὸ τύχης and unpredictable; cf. Aristotle, *Eth. Nic.* Γ 5. 1112ᵃ27 and Alexander of Aphrodisias, *De fato*, 172. 25. 'What can be the connexion between the universe and the finding of a treasure?' asks Cicero, *De divin.* ii. 14. 33.

p. 302. 4. All this is Stoic determinism; compare, for example, Cicero, *De divin.* i. 56. 127: if there were a man who saw the connexion of all causes, he would never fail in any prediction, for he who knows the causes of future events will necessarily know all future events; but since this is only possible for a god, man cannot predict the future except by certain signs.

p. 303. 1. Avicenna affirms in his *Recovery*, *Met.* x. 1, that the souls of the heavenly bodies know the particular individual in a way which is not purely intellectual.

p. 303. 2. Muslim dream-interpretation depends largely on Greek principles, especially on those of the Stoics (Chrysippus, Diogenes of Babylon, Antipater, and Posidonius all wrote books on divination and dreams, cf. Cicero, *De divin.* i. 3. 6). The basic idea of prophetic inspiration is found in the famous passage of Aristotle's *De philosophia* (fr. 10 Rose) quoted by Sext. Emp., *Adv. phys.* i. 20: The conception of gods arose among men from two principles, from what befalls the soul and from the aspect of the heavens; it arose from what befalls the soul because of inspirations in sleep and prophecies. For (he says) when the soul retires in sleep to itself it takes on its proper nature, and prophesies and predicts the future. It is also in this state when, at the point of death, it is severed from its body. Posidonius—cf. Cicero, *De divin.* i. 30. 63—took over this view from Aristotle. One of the three reasons given by Posidonius for the divine inspiration of dreams is the kinship of the human soul with the divine (Cic. op. cit. 64), or, as Cratippus (ap. Cic. i. 32. 70) says: 'Outside the human soul there is a divine soul from which the human takes its origin.' Compare also the passage quoted by Cicero (op. cit. 61) from Plato's *Republic* ix. 571 sq., where the latter says that when, in sleep, the irrational parts of the soul are pacified and the rational part shines forth, a man's dreams will be peaceful and reliable (tum ei visa quietis occurrent tranquilla atque veracia). Avicenna's relation to astrology is much the same as Plotinus', or rather it depends on it. Both Plotinus and Avicenna accept the Stoic idea of a natural sympathy through which all parts of the Universe stand in relation to each other, and changes in one part can give indications of changes in others. But they both reject the extravagant claims of the astrologers (cf. Plotinus, *Enn.* iii. 1. 5 sqq.; Avicenna, e.g., in a short treatise on the question) with arguments derived ultimately from Carneades; and both inconsistently try to safeguard free-will, notwithstanding the dependence of everything on one supreme principle and the emanation of everything from it.

p. 303. 3. Aristotle, in *De divin. per somn.* 2, denies that dreams are divinely inspired (θεόπεμπτα), since animals also dream, and otherwise only the wisest would be able to foresee the future, whereas common men and even the demented and melancholic are capable of doing so. He holds that dreams depend on an unconscious and irrational perception of signs which the imagination symbolizes. Therefore, says he (op. cit. 2. 464^{b}5), the best interpreter (τεχνικώτατος) of dreams is one who can perceive the similarities.

p. 303. 4. Cf. Plutarch, *De gen. Socr.* 24, who says that the chosen few are sometimes, but rarely, in direct contact with the Divine, whereas the common man receives only the signs which form the subject-matter of soothsaying (τὸ θεῖον ὀλίγοις ἐντυγχάνει δι' αὑτοῦ καὶ σπανίως, τοῖς δὲ πολλοῖς σημεῖα δίδωσιν).

p. 304. 1. Cf. note 301. 4.

p. 304. 2. Cf. Aristotle, *Met.* Z 8. The carpenter gives the form of the cupboard, which is always a universal, to the matter, i.e. all art proceeds from universal rules; but such a theory can never explain the individual differences in works of art, and the fact that in his work of art the artist expresses his individuality.

p. 304. 3. 'by nature', i.e. by instinct.

p. 304. 4. According to Aristotle, however, animals have no notion of the universal, but only representation of the particular (τῶν καθ' ἕκαστα φαντασίαν) and memory, cf. *Eth. Nic.* H 5. 1147^{b}5.

p. 304. 5. 'the definition of a thing', i.e. the concept of it.

p. 304. 6. This distinction between a universal representation and the concept (form) is not found in Aristotle.

p. 304. 7. The problem of the instinct of animals seems to have interested the Stoics especially. 'How is it,' asks Seneca (*Epist.* 121. 19), 'that the hen does not flee from the peacock or the goose, but from the hawk, which is much smaller and which it does not even know?' ('quid est, quare pavonem, quare anserem gallina non fugiat, at tanto minorem et ne notum quidem sibi accipitrem?'), and he asks from where the bees get their ingenuity in building their cells, and the unity of their collaboration (22): 'non vides, quanta subtilitas apibus ad fingenda domicilia, quanta dividui laboris obeundi undique concordia.' And the answer is that their art is innate, not acquired: 'nascitur ars ista, non discitur' (cf. n. 334. 3). Origen, *De princip.* iii. 108 (*Stoic. Vet. Fr.* ii. 288. 2), says that some animals have by instinct an imagination which leads them to some specified action, the bees, for example, to the building of cells.

NOTES

p. 304. 8. i.e. the artisan who does not genuinely possess his art, but proceeds empirically.

p. 305. 1. He means that the king who arranges his armies for a battle is not occupied with the individual men, but only with the armies as a whole. Averroës seems here to confound 'whole' and 'universal'.

p. 305. 2. Aristotle says (*Eth. Nic.* Γ 5. 1112ª21) that there can be no deliberation about that which is eternal (since it is eternally fixed, and therefore no will can alter it).

p. 306. 1. Irenaeus (*Contra haer.* i. 9. 4) had protested against the Gnostics that they transferred expressions and terms from their natural sense to an unnatural (λέξεις καὶ ὀνόματα μεταφέρουσιν ἐκ τοῦ κατὰ φύσιν εἰς τὸ παρὰ φύσιν).

p. 306. 2. Both the terms 'universal aim' and 'universal will' which he identifies here have very little sense. If he means, however, that when a man has decided to go immediately to Mecca, no movement occurs, this is not correct: all his subsequent movements depend on this decision and are simply the means to attain his end.

p. 307. 1. i.e. the straight line is perfectly determined, and to follow it one needs no other determination.

p. 307. 2. This is in fact Anselm's (and Augustine's) doctrine of *fides quaerens intellectum*. It would be negligent, in a person capable of understanding, not to proceed from the means to the end, from belief to understanding.

p. 308. 1. The former would be the Stoic view, the latter the Peripatetic.

p. 308. 2. Averroës seems rather undecided about this question, but perhaps he means the same as Cicero, *De nat. deor.* ii. 65. 164: 'licet contrahere universitatem generis humani eamque gradatim ad pauciores postremo deducere ad singulos', i.e. if the gods care universally for man, one may deduce from this that providence extends to every individual man.

p. 309. 1. 'in a created soul', since, for God, knowledge of the infinite is not impossible. For Augustine also (*De civ. dei.* xii. 19) God can comprehend the infinite, and His knowledge transcends number as infinity transcends number: 'infinitas itaque numeri, quamvis infinitorum numerorum nullus sit numerus, non est tamen incomprehensibilis ei, cuius intelligentiae non est numerus'.

On the other hand, Alexander of Aphrodisias (*De fato* xxx. 201. 9) asserts that, since the infinite cannot be measured, the infinite future events cannot be known to the gods. For the gods what is impossible remains impossible, and they do not seek to overcome it, since this would make any assertion meaningless. For this reason it is impossible for the gods to know definitely of a thing contingent by nature that it will be or will not (op. cit. 200. 23)

(Alexander's thesis against Stoic determinism is that there are things contingent by nature and that chance exists). It is rather astonishing that Ghazali, for whom as an Ash'arite there is no objective necessity at all, and for whom there is no certainty in any foreknowledge, since any future event depends solely on God's pleasure, does not attack (as Alexander does) the basic Stoic thesis of the necessary concatenation of all events.

p. 309. 2. i.e. in a body.

p. 309. 3. i.e. through a body.

p. 309. 4. There is here, perhaps, some reference to the difficult problem in Platonic ethics and Greek ethics generally of the dual nature of man, divine through his spiritual, intellectual being, profane through his earth-bound life. If man's aim lies solely in the perfection of his intellect, in a purification from all earthly desire, in a flight of the alone to the Alone (φυγὴ μόνου πρὸς μόνον), his relation to his fellow men would seem irrelevant. But it would be presumptuous in earth-bound man, says Protarchus (cf. Plato, *Philebus* 62 b), to seek only the eternal and divine; to find his way home man should consider also the less pure and less perfect particular knowledge. It is, according to Greek ethics, in and through society that man, being by nature a gregarious animal, will develop his moral character. And since kings ought to be philosophers, some philosophers ought to be leaders of men. Compare Cicero, *De fin*. iii. 20. 68: the wise man should desire to engage in politics and government, since we see that man is designed by nature to safeguard and perfect his fellows; cf. Spinoza, *Eth*. iv. 73 (Spinoza certainly knew the *De finibus*; compare, e.g., *De fin*. iv. 1. 14 with *Eth*. v. 20 demonstr., and *De fin*. iv. 7. 16 with *Eth*. iv. 20 demonstr.).

p. 310. 1. i.e. the soul is all the individuals potentially, because on the one hand in perception it can become all the individuals actually, and on the other it receives from the intellect a knowledge of the permanent (stable, στατικός) intelligibles which comprehend potentially all the individuals.

p. 310. 2. According to Plotinus the soul stands in an intermediary position between the Intellect and the sublunary world; it is a unity-plurality, πλῆθος ἕν, and otherwise could not produce a plurality so far distant from unity (cf. *Enn*. vi. 2. 5).

p. 310. 3. I think Averroës is here referring to the passage p. 309, l. 10, where Ghazali admits the possibility that the soul of heaven may know all particular events, but where he limits this knowledge to the present and therefore partially accepts, partially rejects the philosophical theory, and where by this arbitrary limitation he refutes the philosophical theory of prophecy. Of course Ghazali admits foreknowledge in God of the infinity of all particular events. St. Augustine (*De civ. Dei* v. 9) says that this foreknowledge, according to Cicero, *De divin*., implies fate (*concessa scientia futurorum ita esse consequens fatum ut negari omnino non possit*), and that therefore Cicero rejects it. So did the Peripatetics, as we have seen, and for the same reason. The implication seems to me evident, but St. Augustine is not of this opinion.

p. 310. 4. The irascible soul, θυμός, the concupiscent soul, ἐπιθυμία, i.e. the two irrational parts of the soul according to Plato (cf. *Rep.* iv. 436 a); to contemplate the soul in her primordial purity, she should be viewed in her immortal yearning for the divine which is akin to her, and as cleansed from the incrustation due to her earth-bound state (cf. op. cit. x. 611–12).

p. 311. 1. For an historical view of the division of the sciences from the Alexandrian commentators on Aristotle, especially Ammonius Hermiae, who is the originator of this type of philosophical literature, to the end of the scholastic period, see L. Baur, 'Gundissalinus, de divisione philosophiae', *Beitr. z. Gesch. d. Philos. d. Mittelalt.* iv. 2–3, pp. 325 sqq. Both Farabi and Avicenna wrote treatises on the division of the sciences, Farabi's treatise being called *On the Enumeration of the Sciences* and Avicenna's *On the Divisions of the Intellectual Sciences*. Avicenna's division is based on Ammonius' scheme of διαίρεσις (division) into practical and theoretical sciences; ἐπιδιαίρεσις (secondary division), e.g. the tripartite division of the theoretical sciences into physics, mathematics, and theology; and ὑποδιαίρεσις, subdivision, e.g. the subdivision of the physical sciences. The division of physics into eight parts, each based on a special treatise of Aristotle, is a common feature of the Muslim commentators. The sequence of these parts and the enumeration of the books of Aristotle is taken from Philoponus, in *Phys. comm.* (Vitelli i. 1. 20); Philoponus, however, subdivides the part that treats of animals into a class that treats of them as wholes and a class that treats of their parts.

p. 311. 2. Classes, اصول, i.e. literally 'roots', radices; subdivisions, فروع, i.e. ramifications, rami.

p. 311. 3. Not only is time, according to Aristotle, a consequence of movement (ἀκολουθεῖ τῇ κινήσει ὁ χρόνος, *Phys. Δ* 11. 219ᵇ16), since time is the number of movement, but he seems to regard space as posterior to movement, and not the reverse, for he says (*Phys. Δ* 1. 208ᵇ8): 'The movements of the elements show not only that there is a space, but that it has a certain function (καὶ ἔχει τινὰ δύναμιν).'

p. 311. 4. The same definition is found in Avicenna's *On the Divisions of the Intellectual Sciences*, which Ghazali in his enumeration of the seven subdivisions follows very closely. The Aristotelian definition of medicine is: ἡ ἰατρικὴ τέχνη ὁ λόγος τῆς ὑγιείας ἐστίν or τῆς ἰατρικῆς τέχνης τέλος ὑγίεια (e.g. *Met. Λ* 3. 1070ᵃ30; *Eth. Nic. A* 1. 1094ᵃ8). By regarding medicine as a species of physics, the primary division of the sciences into practical and theoretical is vitiated, as Averroës observes below. Aristotle (*Eth. Nic.*, loc. cit.) gives medicine as an example of a practical science.

p. 311. 5. The possibility of physiognomy is admitted by Aristotle, *Anal. Pr. B* 27. 70^{b}7, when it has first been conceded that body and soul can change at the same time: anger and desire, for example, find their expression in physical movements. Pythagoras (cf. Hippolytus, *Refut.* i. 2. 5) was regarded as the inventor of physiognomy (φυσιογνωμικὴν ἐξεῦρε), and Alexander of Aphrodisias (*De fato* 171. 11) tells a story of Zopyrus, the physiognomist, who from an examination of Socrates' exterior attributed many vices to him—a story also mentioned by Cicero, *Tusc.* iv. 37. 80 and *De fato* 5. 10. The treatise on physiognomy ascribed to Aristotle is not genuine.

p. 311. 6. The telesmatic art is the art of charms, amulets, talismans, &c. (the word 'talisman' is derived, through the Italian *talismano*, from the Arabic طلسم, itself a derivative of τέλεσμα, one of the many Greek words for 'charm' or 'amulet'). The telesmatic art differs from magic in that the magician needs no external instrument. Compare the long chapter dedicated to this art in Ibn Khaldun, *Prolegomena*, ed. Quatremère, *Notices des Manuscrits de la Bibl. Imp.*, vol. xviii, p. 124. Among the Arabs the best known authors on magic are Jabir ibn Hayyan and Maslama ibn Ahmad al-Majriti.

p. 311. 7. In this art there is only a combination of earthly virtues. Averroës—see below—regards it as a kind of conjuring.

p. 312. 1. For alchemy compare also Ibn Khaldun, op. cit., pp. 191 and 229. Jabir ibn Hayyan, mentioned in the last note but one, was regarded among the Arabs as the greatest authority on alchemy, which is sometimes called the science of Jabir.

p. 312. 2. This is not true according to Aristotle, who regards it as purely rational and based on a syllogism of the first figure, when the major and middle terms are convertible (*Anal. Pr. B* 27. 70^{b}32).

p. 312. 3. Ibn Khaldun develops this idea for his refutation of alchemy, op. cit., p. 236: Alchemy is the reproduction of nature by art. We should have to follow in detail all the processes which nature uses in the formation of metals, and know all the particular circumstances of their development and all their effects. These, however, are infinite and beyond man's grasp; it would be as if man were to create a man or an animal or a plant.

p. 313. 1. 'existing by themselves'; this is of course in opposition to the Aristotelian theory that the soul is the form of the body, a theory rejected by Plotinus in the fragment quoted by Eusebius, *Praep. ev.* xv. 10, since according to such a theory the soul could not be separated from the body. Avicenna holds both theories, the Aristotelian theory of the soul as the form of the body and the Platonic and Plotinian of the soul as a substance and an entity separable from the body; he does not seem to be aware of the contradiction.

NOTES   173

p. 313. 2. According to Plotinus (*Enn.* iv. 7. 9), who follows Plato (*Phaedo* 105 c–106 d), the principle of movement and life cannot itself be mortal. Compare also, for example, Avicenna, *Salvation*, p. 302, where it is argued 'that the soul does not die through the death of the body', since body and soul are both substances.

p. 313. 3. In opposition to the Koran, which teaches the resurrection of the flesh; compare, for example, Sura lxxxi. 7, where in speaking of the resurrection the phrase is used 'when souls shall be paired with their bodies'.

p. 313. 4. Hume (*Enquiry concerning Human Understanding*, § 10), who does not believe in laws of nature any more than the Ashʿarites do, and who does not believe in miracles either, defines a miracle as a violation of the laws of nature. He says, however, that it is a miracle that a dead man should come to life, because that has never been observed in any age or country; this, of course, is not a valid reason—many (in a sense, all) things happen quite 'naturally' that have never been observed before. According to this definition, a miracle does not abolish the idea of a law of nature but on the contrary assumes it. Nor is it true that a miracle abolishes the concept of cause and effect. A miracle is attributed to God as a cause, as an immediate interference of God with the causes and the course of nature. Strictly speaking there are no miracles for the Ashʿarites, nor has the word 'nature' any meaning for them; or perhaps one might say that for them all miracles are natural, and all nature miraculous.

p. 313. 5. For the changing of Moses' rod into a serpent see Koran ii. 21.

p. 313. 6. Cf. Koran, Sura liv, which begins: 'the hour draws nigh and the moon is split asunder'. This is sometimes interpreted later as a miracle performed by Muhammad, but it can be explained as one of the signs of the resurrection.

p. 313. 7. Some of the older Muʿtazilites were already regarded as thorough-going rationalists, e.g. Hisham ibn Amr al-Futi and Nazzam (see e.g. Shahrastani, *Relig. and Philos. Sects*, i. 51; 40). For a rationalistic exegesis compare also Cl. Huart, 'Le Rationalisme musulman', in *Revue de l'histoire des religions*, vol. l, p. 201. One must distinguish the rationalistic interpreters from those numerous mystics who give to the religious text a symbolic meaning in accordance with their spiritualistic doctrines.

p. 313. 8. Compare, for example, Avicenna, *Theorems and Notices*, p. 213, and Farabi, *The Gems of Knowledge* (Dieterici), p. 76.

p. 313. 9. Intellectual acuteness (حدس, ἀγχίνοια): the term is defined by Aristotle, *Anal. Post.* A 34. 89^{b}10 as the capacity of a man to arrive at the middle term quickly; such a man, for example, will quickly understand that the moon receives its light from the sun. According to Avicenna, *Salvation*, p. 273, whom Ghazali here follows very closely, intellectual acuteness differs among men qualitatively and quantitatively: on the one hand there are men who are absolutely devoid of it, on the other there are those, the prophets, in whom it reaches such excellence that the forms of the active intellect are immediately imprinted on it.

p. 314. 1. This is a quotation from the mystical verse of the Koran, xxix. 35: 'God is the light of the heavens and the earth; His light is as a niche in which is a lamp, and the lamp is in a glass, the glass is as though it were a glittering star, it is lit from a blessed tree, an olive neither of the west nor of the east, the oil of which would well-nigh give light though no fire were in contact with it, light upon light . . .'.

p. 314. 2. This example is found in Plutarch, *Quaest. conv.* v. 7. 3 (ἐπίνοιαι γὰρ ἀφροδισίων ἐγείρουσιν αἰδοῖα and again τὰ σπέρματα τῶν ἀνθρώπων μᾶλλον ἅπτεσθαι, ὅταν ἐρῶντες πλησιάζωσιν; Thomas Fienus says, *De viribus imaginationis*, p. 59: 'qui imaginatur Venerem, ei coles excitatur et spiritus moventur versus genitalia, et non ad aliam partem'), where 'fascination' (καταβασκαίνειν) and the 'evil eye'—which is admitted and explained, in *Theorems and Notices*, p. 221, and in the psychological part of his *Recovery*, iv. 4, by Avicenna in the same way as by Plutarch, by an explanation which is, I presume, of Stoic origin—are attributed to the influence of the emotions of the soul on the body.

p. 314. 3. The example of the plank is taken from Avicenna, *Theorems and Notices*, p. 219 and *The Recovery*, loc. cit. Ibn Khaldun, who reproduces as he says the theories of the philosophers, also mentions it, op. cit., p. 132. It is interesting to note that the same example is quoted in a well-known passage of the *Pensées* of Pascal (in the section 'Imagination'): 'Le plus grand philosophe du monde, sur une planche plus large qu'il ne faut, s'il y a au dessous un précipice, quoique sa raison le convainque de sa sûreté, son imagination prévaudra.' Pascal took this example from Montaigne, *Essais*, ii. 12: 'Qu'on jette une poutre entre deux tours (de Notre Dame de Paris) d'une grosseur telle qu'il nous la faut à nous promener dessus, il n'y a sagesse philosophique de si grande fermeté qui puisse nous donner courage d'y marcher comme si elle était à terre.' Emile Coué, *De la suggestion et ses applications*, Nancy, 1915, p. 5, also has this example. The example is found in R. Burton, *The Anatomy of Melancholy*, part I, sect. 2, mem. 3, subs. 2, who ascribes it to Peter Byarus. He means evidently Petrus Bairus (Pietro Bairo), a famous Genoese physician and an elder contemporary of Montaigne, who in his book *De pestilentia* (chapter *de cibo et potu*) had a long quotation from Avicenna's *Psychology* with our example. Doubtless Montaigne with his great interest for medicine found it there. Thomas Aquinas has this example, *Contra gentiles* iii. 103. He rejects, however, the consequence Avicenna draws and declares that a spiritual substance cannot make an impression on a body, except by means of local movement. The examples given in our text all concern the involuntary influence of imagination on our body or behaviour; but the magician, as a performer of miracles, acts voluntarily. The fundamental problem of the relation of body and mind, the fact that my immaterial ego is in contact with the physical universe (and, another mystery, that through physical means it can communicate with other immaterial egos), and that through its will it can influence my material body and by its intermediation change the face of the world—this problem, which has struck moderns since Descartes with wonder, was never properly seen by the ancients, although St. Augustine (*De civ. Dei* xxi. 10) said: 'modus quo corporibus adhaerent spiritus omnino mirus est, nec comprehendi ab homine potest; et hoc ipse homo est'. Plotinus, on whom Avicenna's mystical theories largely depend, explains all magical influence by the Stoic concept of a 'sympathy' which all things have for each other (cf. *Enn.* iv. 4. 40–42).

p. 314. 4. This is the theory of Avicenna, found in *The Recovery* and in *Theorems and Notices*, p. 220: certain souls may exercise an influence on other bodies than their own. It is repeated by Ibn Khaldun, op. cit., pp. 132–3. Burton says, loc. cit: 'Nay more, they (i.e. witches and old women) can cause and cure not only diseases, maladies, and several infirmities by this means, as Avicenna, *De anima* libr. iv. sect. 4, supposeth in parties remote, but move bodies from their places, cause thunder, lightning, tempests, which opinion Alkindus, Paracelsus, and some others approve of'. Burton gives in this section a bibliography on the subject of 'The Force of Imagination'. Fienus, whom Burton calls 'the pick of the bunch' ('*instar omnium*'), says, op. cit., p. 25, cf. pp. 40 sqq., that Avicenna's theory was held, for instance, by Albertus Magnus, Marsilius Ficinus, Pomponatius, and Paracelsus. Compare also H. C. Agrippa, *De occulta philosophia*, i. 65.

p. 314. 5. The swallowing up of the earth with its inhabitants as a punishment is mentioned in the Koran (xxxiv. 19); 'God made the wind subservient to Solomon', ibid. xxxiv. 11; 'God struck the inhabitants of Ad and Thamud with a thunderbolt', ibid., e.g. xli. 12, and ' "rained a rain" on the people of Lot', ibid. vii. 82.

p. 314. 6. Warmth, for example, is commonly produced by the soul in its body (says Ibn Khaldun, op. cit., p. 132) in a state of pleasure and joy. Compare also Thomas Aquinas, loc. cit.

p. 315. 1. That philosophy implies virtue is a Stoic idea: 'philosophia studium virtutis est, sed per ipsam virtutem ... cohaerent inter se philosophia virtusque' (Seneca, *Epist.* 89. 8).

p. 315. 2. i.e. without physical contact.

p. 315. 3. i.e. which is not logically impossible, ἀδύνατον ἁπλῶς.

p. 315. 4. 'that they are of this kind', i.e. not logically impossible. The whole sentence is ambiguous, everything depends on what he understands by 'logically impossible'. From what follows it would seem that he does not admit that prophets can interrupt the course of nature, but is unwilling to express it too clearly.

p. 315. 5. See note 152. 1.

p. 315. 6. He is doubtless here referring to the chapter in Ghazali's book *The Preserver from Error* entitled 'On the reality of prophecy and its necessity for all men', where the prophet is regarded as a man who by his special qualities is in contact with the occult, and where it is expressly stated that one should not base one's belief in prophecy on such facts as the changing of a rod into a serpent or the cleavage of the moon.

p. 316. 1. i.e. they are not relative, but cause (say the sceptics) is something relative, for it is a cause of something and occurs to something, e.g. the lancet is the cause of something, i.e. cutting, to something, i.e. flesh; relatives, however, do not exist, but are only subjective (Sext. Emp. *Adv. phys.* i. 207–8).

p. 316. 2. This, the denial of any logical nexus, is the fundamental thesis of Greek empirical medicine: for we find the consequent through experience, but not as implied by the antecedent; and therefore none of the empiricists say that one thing implies another, although they will certainly assert that certain facts follow or precede other facts or are simultaneous with them (εὑρίσκεται μὲν κἀκ τῆς πείρας τὸ ἀκόλουθον, ἀλλ' οὐχ ὡς ἐμφαινόμενον τῷ ἡγουμένῳ. καὶ διὰ τοῦτο τῶν ἐμπειρικῶν οὐδεὶς ἐμφαίνεσθαί φησι τῷδε τινὶ τόδε τι. καίτοιγε ἀκολουθεῖν λέγουσι τόδε τῷδε καὶ προηγεῖσθαι τόδε τοῦδε καὶ συνυπάρχειν τόδε τῷδε): Galen, *De meth. med.* ii. 7 (K. x. 126 F; Deichgräber, op. cit. 123. 24).

p. 316. 3. The example of burning is given by Sext. Emp. *Adv. phys.* i. 241 sqq. The argument given there is that if fire were the cause of burning, it would either burn by itself or need the co-operation of the burning matter; in the former case, it would burn always and in all circumstances, in the latter it would not burn exclusively through its own nature.

p. 317. 1. 'simultaneity': Hume would have regarded this rather as a sequence.

p. 317. 2. According to Stoicism also God is the only active principle and matter is passive or, as Ghazali would say, dead. The Stoic God is immanent in the world; He does not act voluntarily, but Himself is Law, Fate, and Necessity. In a way Aristotelianism also, as we have seen, implies God as the Unique Agent; for He is the one principle of movement, the constant mover of Heaven, on whom all earthly change depends, and in the next sentence in the text Ghazali quite rightly draws this conclusion.

p. 317. 3. Aristotle's own theory of procreation is confused and obscure; life and soul are not body, but cannot exist without body, which either is warmth, not fire (θερμὸν οὐ πῦρ), or *pneuma*, and something more divine than the so-called elements (σῶμα θειότερον τῶν καλουμένων στοιχείων) and related to the matter of stars (ἀνάλογον τῷ τῶν ἄστρων στοιχείῳ); cf. *De gen. an.* B 3. 736^{b}29 sqq. For the theories of Avicenna and Averroës compare my *Ep. d. Met. d. Av.*, pp. 40 and 44 and notes.

p. 317. 4. This is rather a strange argument in a refutation of the causal nexus between phenomena, since it admits and implies such a nexus. The arguments seems somehow related to the equally bad argument of Chrysippus quoted in Cicero's *De fato* 18. 41–19. 45, by which Chrysippus wanted to safeguard free-will without abandoning the idea of a universal causal concatenation, and where he distinguishes between *causae perfectae et principales* and *causae adiuvantes et proximae*. We cannot, he says, give our consent (*assensio*, συγκατάθεσις) to a thing seen without the form of the visible object making an impression on our soul, but this impression is only a *causa adiuvans* of the consent, which depends on our own nature. Compare also Cicero, *Top.* 15. 58, for the Stoic distinction of two types of causes, the efficient, 'unum quod vi sua id quod sub ea subjectum est certo efficit' (αἴτιον δι' ὅ), 'alterum quod naturam efficiendi non habet sed sine quo non potest effici' (αἴτιον οὗ οὐκ ἄνευ or αἴτιον προκαταρκτικόν). In Ghazali's example the light of the sun is a cause of the former type, the opening of the eyelids of the latter. For a further classification of causes by the Stoics see, for example, Clement of Alexandria, *Strom.* viii. 9. 25 (*Stoic Vet. Fr.* ii, pp. 119–21).

p. 317. 5. i.e. the celestial bodies.

p. 317. 6. Whom does he mean? In a well-known passage in Book XII of his great commentary on Aristotle's *Metaphysics* (Bouyges, p. 1498, quoted already by Renan, *Averroes et l'Averroisme*[3], p. 109) Averroës distinguishes the different opinions held by philosophers on the relation between God and the world; according to him, besides the Muslim theologians only the Christian philosophers like John Philoponus professed that all the potentialities of the created reside in God. However, according to Neoplatonism and the Neoplatonic commentators all forms derive ultimately from God, and so all the Muhammadan Aristotelians may be meant here. But it is strange that Ghazali should give them the designation of 'true philosophers'.

p. 318. 1. This is perfectly true; if the only function of the human mind were the registration of isolated sense-impressions, as the empiricists or sensationalists or positivists have it, or if *esse* were *percipi*, there could be no investigation, no search for explanation or causes, since nothing could be known but the experienced and the given. All search, all research, all questioning, all wonder implies belief in causation. All knowledge, as both Plato and Aristotle knew, arises from questioning and wonder: διὰ γὰρ τὸ θαυμάζειν οἱ ἄνθρωποι καὶ νῦν καὶ τὸ πρῶτον ἤρξαντο φιλοσοφεῖν (Arist. *Met.* A 2. 982^{b}12; cf. Plato, *Theaet.* 155 d), and transcends the actually perceived.

p. 318. 2. 'evident', I think, would be better than 'self-evident'; the evident is that whose cause is known, the unknown that of which the cause is not yet perceived. We believe that we know a thing—says Aristotle, *Anal. post.* A 2. 71^{b}9—when we believe that we know its cause. (See above, note 236. 5.)

p. 318. 3. This is Aristotle's argument against the Heraclitean flux (*Phys.* A 2. 185^{b}19): all things would be one, right and wrong, man and horse, would be identical; indeed one would not even speak any more about the identity of all things but about their nothingness: οὐ περὶ τοῦ ἓν εἶναι τὰ ὄντα ... ἀλλὰ περὶ τοῦ μηδέν.

p. 318. 4. This also seems to me to be true. All conceptual thought implies the idea of identity, and all identity in the real implies a conformity to law, a sameness of action under the same conditions, i.e. that in such-and-such conditions a certain entity will necessarily act in such-and-such a way; the concept of fire, for example, implies a fore-knowledge of hypothetical necessities: if fire acted in different ways under the same conditions, the concept of fire would not convey any meaning.

p. 318. 5. Since 'one' and 'being' are convertible (cf. e.g. Arist. *Met.* I 2. 1053^{b}25).

p. 319. 1. In this sentence his belief in absolute causal necessity would seem to be shaken, and indeed Averroës holds with Aristotle that there are accidental events: i.e. when something does not happen always or in the majority of cases, ἐπὶ τὸ πολύ (cf. e.g. *Met.* E 2. 1026^{b}32). From the following, however, it appears the he means here only that under different conditions things may act differently.

p. 319. 2. i.e. the body of someone capable of sensation.

p. 319. 3. Condition (or presupposition, ὑπόθεσις: the word ὑπόθεσις with this sense is found in Theophrast. *Hist. Plant.* 4. 13. 4, where it is said that the root is the presupposition of the tree) is a logical concept; a substratum (ὑποκείμενον) is a real entity, but, as we have seen, ancient philosophy does not distinguish clearly between the logical and the real. As we have seen, too, the theologians do not accept the Platonic–Aristotelian–Stoic concept of matter; they do, however, accept the idea of the inherence of accidents in a substratum (and they accept the Platonic and Aristotelian idea of a *scala naturae*—see below); and in their logic, which is based on Stoic logic and which uses hypothetical propositions for preference, relations of inherence can be included, as in the example given in the text: life is the condition or presupposition of knowledge, i.e. if there is no life there is no knowledge, and there can be knowledge only in the living (from Kant's treatment of the hypothetical judgement, *Kr. d. r. V.*, tr. An. 9. 3, it has often been erroneously assumed that the hypothetical judgement expresses a causal relation, the categorical a relation of inherence).

NOTES

p. 319. 4. Forms, being universals, are not admitted by the theologians; for them there are no universal entities *in rerum natura*, and universals are psychological entities, things of the mind (ἔννοιαι).

p. 319. 5. i.e. they acknowledge that not only is God, who is invisible, a cause, but there are also visible causes.

p. 319. 6. 'sign' (دليل, σημεῖον) is one of the more important concepts of Stoic logic (cf. Sext. Emp. *Hyp. Pyrrh.* ii. 96 sqq.; *Adv. log.* ii. 140 sqq., 149 sqq.). Stoic logic, in opposition to the Platonic and Aristotelian, does not try to establish relations between concepts, but contents itself with finding an external connexion between certain observed facts, e.g. the fact that a woman has milk is a sign or indication that she has conceived. The empirical physicians do not try to explain the connexion, i.e. to find a more universal law from which it may be deduced, nor do they regard this connexion as necessary, but only as probable; and the question how often such a connexion has to be observed to give a reasonable probability was much discussed (the fact that the probability is greater the greater the number of observations can, however, only be explained by the fact that a real causal connexion becomes more probable). The fact that science tries to explain such connexions and does not regard them as a mere expression of empirically stated coincidence, but holds them to be invariable and necessary, shows that we assume them to be based on a causal relation.

p. 319. 7. This is a Stoic proof (cf. Sext. Emp. *Adv. phys.* i. 78 sqq.); instead of 'harmony' one might translate 'sympathy', i.e. the Stoic συμπάθεια which holds all things together and through which, when a finger is cut, the whole body shares in its condition.

p. 319. 8. This is a well-known dictum; cf. note 16. 5. Sextus Empiricus says (*Adv. phys.* i. 204 and *Hyp. Pyrrh.* ii. 19; 23) that the man who denies cause does so either without a cause or with a cause—but in the former case his assertion is worthless.

p. 320. 1. This is a telling question, and I do not know how, for example, Hume would answer it. If causation is really a habit in man, what makes it possible that such a habit can be formed, or what is the objective counterpart of these habits? Is it simply our good luck that nature repeats the same connexions over and over again? The most important question, however, that which the Greek dogmatists asked the empiricists, viz. how many times such a connexion must be observed, before it can be relied upon (cf. e.g. Galen, *On Medical Experience*, Walzer, viii. 8), or before such a habit can be formed, is one he does not ask. Besides, how can we act at all, before such a habit is formed? For we shall not be able to act, not knowing the consequences of our actions, or rather not knowing that we can act at all. Have we to pass through a period of inertia where we observe and wait till in one way or another the habit arises? (see also note 324. 4). Proverbial wisdom, however, has it that once bitten is twice shy, that a burnt childe dreadeth the fire, that he that stumbleth twice at one stone is worthy to break his shin.

p. 320. 2. Koran xxxv. 41–42.

p. 320. 3. Habit ($ἔθος$), says Aristotle (*Rhet. A* 10. 1369^{b}6) is what one does through having done it often.

p. 320. 4. For nature, according to Aristotle (*Rhet. A* 11. 1370^{a}7) is concerned with the invariable, as habit with the frequent, $ἡ\ μὲν\ φύσις\ τοῦ\ ἀεί$, $τὸ\ δὲ\ ἔθος\ τοῦ\ πολλάκις$. However, Aristotle often says that things that happen by nature happen invariably or in a majority of cases (e.g. *Phys. B* 8. 198^{b}35); and Averroës repeats this below in the text.

p. 321. 1. Cf. note 317. 3.

p. 321. 2. He is here referring of course to the Stoics, not the Epicureans. According to Aristotle colours come into existence from the fundamental colours, black and white, through mixture ($μίξις$); cf. *De sensu* 3. 439^{b}18–440^{b}25. About the Stoic theory of colours nothing is known except a few words ascribed to Zeno (*Stoic Vet. Fr.* i. 26. 1–3), according to which colours are the first configurations ($σχηματισμοί$) of matter, or colour is the surface-stain ($ἐπίχρωσις$) of matter.

p. 321. 3. The sun hardens mud and melts wax, says Sext. Emp. *Adv. log.* ii. 194; *Adv. phys.* i. 247; for this whole passage compare Sext. Emp. *Adv. phys.* i. 246–9.

p. 321. 4. This example is also found in Sextus Empiricus, loc. cit.: $ὁ\ ἥλιος\ \ldots\ λευκαίνει\ μὲν\ τὰ\ ἐσθήματα,\ μελαίνει\ δὲ\ τὴν\ ἡμετέραν\ ἐπιφάνειαν$: the sun whitens clothes, but blackens our complexion.

p. 322. 1. The elemental fire, i.e. the fire which has its natural place directly under the heavenly spheres and which surrounds the air (cf. Aristotle, *De caelo B* 4. 287^{a}33; *Meteor. A* 4. 341^{b}14). For Averroës's theory compare my *Ep. d. Met. d. Av.*, p. 182.

p. 322. 2. Compare, however, what Averroës says himself, p. 288.

p. 323. 1. Koran iii. 5. It is hardly necessary, I think, to draw attention to the ambiguity of Averroës's religious views.

p. 324. 1. With the whole of this section compare Sext. Emp. *Adv. phys.* i. 202–4, where it is said that if there were no causes anything might come from anything at any time and place; a horse might come from a man, a plant from a horse, snow might congeal in Egypt, there might be a drought in Pontus, things happening in summer might occur in winter and vice versa; and again, *Hyp. Pyrrh.* iii. 18, where we have again as an example the horse which might come from mice, or, as another example, elephants that might come from ants.

p. 324. 2. It is to be remembered, however, that for the Ash'arites the possible is the realized.

p. 324. 3. The conjecturing power, i.e. حدس, ἀγχίνοια, which we met in Avicenna, see note 313. 9.

p. 324. 4. This is of course an absurd theory, and condemns man to absolute passivity. Such an absolute passivity, however, is the consequence of any sensationalistic theory which reduces causation to a mere sequence of events, since for such a theory the words 'I do', 'I act', 'I think' are completely devoid of sense. Ghazali admits activity in God, but does not define the word; he would hardly be able to hold (as Averroes sees) that God's action is nothing but a habit in Him, i.e. an habitual sequence of events.

p. 325. 1. The formula in itself leaves the question open; if knowledge is simply the recording of external data, there is no objection to Ghazali's theory; it belongs, however, to man to foresee, to intend, and to act, which implies law and a knowledge of law; and this is what Averroës wishes to express, as can be seen from what follows.

p. 325. 2. i.e. if the agent, God, could do anything, and anything could be done to the creature, i.e. the substratum. (However, the omnipotence of the creator already implies the possibility of omniformity in the creature.)

p. 325. 3. i.e. if anything may happen in the future.

p. 325. 4. I do not think that Averroës's position is very acceptable from a theological point of view, for it does not leave any liberty to God whatever, since God must conform to the law. One might perhaps say that God has chosen the law Himself; however, once this law is chosen He can no longer infringe it.

p. 325. 5. 'created', i.e. revealed or inspired.

p. 325. 6. This seems to mean that even revealed or inspired knowledge must be in agreement with what is possible according to the laws of nature.

p. 325. 7. I think this means that if we know that an event is possible—and we may know this either through revelation or through reason or through both—there must be in reality potentialities which make this event possible.

p. 325. 8. This contradicts what he said on p. 320 (see note 320. 4).

p. 325. 9. i.e. knowledge, even divine creative knowledge, implies always a thing known with which it is in agreement.

p. 325. 10. 'the nature of the actually existent', i.e. the fact that Zaid is coming.

p. 325. 11. This seems to mean that knowledge can only refer to facts, an assertion which is surely false.

p. 326. 1. i.e. through God's knowledge, Zaid's coming (for example) is attached to Zaid. This would seem to imply that God's knowledge is the only cause of everything that happens. See, however, the next sentence in the text and the next note. The whole passage is of course very confused; the term 'nature' is used in a very vague and indefinite sense and the concept of creative knowledge involves in fact a *contradictio in adiecto*. The general sense of the passage, however, seems to be that God cannot infringe natural law.

p. 326. 2. i.e. through our ignorance of the causal laws which determine (for example) Zaid's coming.

p. 326. 3. It would seem from the next sentence in the text that opposites are always in equilibrium in themselves, since the cause of their actualization, i.e. the preponderance given to the one over the other, seems to lie in 'the knowledge of the existence of this nature', i.e. God's knowledge that this opposite will be realized.

p. 326. 4. Koran xxvii. 66.

p. 326. 5. Cf. note 320. 4.

p. 326. 6. The consequences mentioned, pp. 323–4.

p. 326. 7. In this section Ghazali abandons the Ash'arite theory of the denial of causation, and reverts to the rationalistic supernaturalism of the Muslim philosophers (i.e. their attempt to justify supernatural facts by rational arguments, by theories, for example, of influences emanating from the soul or of a universal natural sympathy) which ultimately derives from Stoicism. The philosophers limit supernatural possibilities arbitrarily to certain categories; but the Ash'arites, who do not show any logical consistency, assert that, once philosophical principles are admitted, there is no limit to God's omnipotence but the logically impossible and absurd. The whole problem was much discussed in Scholastic philosophy. Leibniz's position on this question is almost identical with the Ash'arite view.

p. 327. 1. Compare Leibniz, *Theod.* 1, 'Discours de la conformité de la foi avec la raison', 3: 'Il se peut qu'il y ait des miracles que Dieu fait par le ministère des anges, où les lois de la nature ne sont point violées, non plus que lorsque les hommes aident la nature par l'art, l'artifice des anges ne différant du nôtre que par le degré de perfection.' It is interesting to see that Newton's discovery of the law of gravitation was used for the explanation of such possibilities; cf. Leibniz, op. cit., 19: '. . . le célèbre M. Locke a déclaré, en répondant à M. l'évêque Stillingfleet, qu'après avoir vu le livre de M. Newton, il rétracte ce qu'il avait dit lui-même, suivant l'opinion des modernes, dans son Essai sur l'entendement, savoir qu'un corps ne peut opérer immédiatement sur un autre qu'en le touchant par sa superficie et en le poussant par son mouvement: et il reconnaît que Dieu peut mettre des propriétés dans la matière qui la fassent opérer dans l'éloignement.'

p. 327. 2. For plants as composed of earth, cf. Aristotle, *De an.* Γ 13. 435^{b}1.

p. 327. 3. Blood is the final form of food, ἐσχάτη τροφὴ τὸ αἷμα, cf. e.g. Aristotle, *De gen. an.* A 19. 726^{b}3.

p. 327. 4. For the theory of sperm as coming from blood see Aristotle, *De gen. an.* A 17–20.

p. 327. 5. In the sperm there is the form of the animal; cf. Aristotle, *De gen. an.* B 1. 733^{b}32 sqq.

p. 327. 6. The theologians and Ghazali admit a *scala naturae*, a necessary order and succession, τὸ ἐφεξῆς, in all things; cf. Aristotle, *Hist. an.* H 1. 588^{b}4 sqq. and also *De an.* B 414^{b}28: sensation, for example, is a condition of intellect, nutrition of sensation, &c. Compare Thomas Aquinas, *Contr. gent.* iii, c. 99, where he declares that God can produce an effect without its proximate causes.

p. 327. 7. Cf. Leibniz, op. cit. 2: 'il est donc vrai que ce n'est pas sans raison que Dieu les (i.e. les lois générales) a données, car il ne choisit rien par caprice, et comme au sort, ou par une indifférence toute pure; mais les raisons générales de bien et de l'ordre, qui l'y ont porté, peuvent être vaincues, dans quelques cas, par des raisons plus grandes d'un ordre supérieur.'

p. 328. 1. According to Aristotle's principle of synonymity, everything comes into existence from the synonymous, e.g. warmth from warmth; cf. *Met.* Z 9.

p. 328. 2. For the spontaneous generation of worms, the so-called 'earth-guts', γῆς ἔντερα, see Aristotle, *De gen. an.* Γ 11. 762^{b}27, and *Hist. an.* Z 16. 570^{a}15; see also *Hist. an.* E 19. 550^{a}1 for the spontaneous generation of grubs, σκώληκες; for the spontaneous generation of mice compare the curious passage in Aristotle, *Hist. an.* Z 37. 580^{b}30, and Pliny, x. 85, who says that according to Aristotle the generation of mice takes place *lambendo, non coitu*. Scorpions according to Aristotle (fr. 367 Rose) are generated from rotten bergamot-mint, ἐκ τῶν σισυμβρίων σαπέντων; as to serpents, they are oviparous (see Arist. *Hist. an.* Z 1. 558^{b}1), and Aristotle nowhere says that they might be generated spontaneously.

p. 328. 3. 'non pas par caprice, et comme au sort, ou par une indifférence toute pure'.

p. 328. 4. Although Aristotle himself does not seem to admit the possibility of the generation of men from earth (see Arist. *De gen. an.* Γ 11. 762^{b}28), there was an old Greek tradition that such a generation had taken place (cf., for example, Plato, *Plt.* 269 b and Herodotus viii. 55).

p. 329. 1. In these two examples, although they are logically impossible, something more than the simultaneous affirmation and negation of one isolated entity is involved: in the definition of will, for example, a relation to knowledge is implied. All definition states a necessary relation between two concepts, and to deny the logical implication is logically impossible since it destroys the definition.

p. 329. 2. There is some confusion here. There is no logical impossibility in the supposition that God creates purposeful actions in a dead man (or in a living animal that acts by instinct). But the Ash'arites hold that God is the sole agent, and that the actions of living men are created by Him, and then the question arises what difference there can be between voluntary and involuntary action in man (for the distinction between voluntary and involuntary action see Galen, *De motu musc.* ii. 5). The same objection was made against the Stoics: if no atom can move without God's will, if everything depends on fate, there is no longer any sense in man's deliberation and will (cf. Plut. *De comm. not.* 34; Alexander Aphrod. *De fato* i. 33; Nemesius, *De nat. hom.* 39). Another unavoidable consequence is that vice occurs not only of necessity or according to fate, but also in accordance with the Reason of God and with what is best (cf. Plut. *De Stoic. rep.* 34).

p. 329. 3. Aristotle expresses the principle of contradiction in the same way: opposites cannot inhere in the same substratum simultaneously (*Met.* Γ 3. 1005^{b}26).

p. 329. 4. Leibniz (op. cit. 19) does not seem to regard this as impossible; he thinks the dogma of the real and substantial participation may be explained perhaps by the fact that one body can have an immediate influence on others; divine omnipotence might perhaps cause one body to be present in others, there being no great difference between immediate influence and presence.

p. 329. 5. I do not know to whom Ghazali is referring; perhaps it is to Ibn Hazm, according to whom God can do also what is logically impossible (cf. op. cit. ii. 181); but as a matter of fact it is the theory which the Ash'arites and Ghazali himself hold, since according to them God at every moment re-creates afresh the whole world, in which there is no stable element nor any connexion. For Aristotle, however, whose theory Ghazali (cf. *Phys. A* 6–10) is going to reproduce, change implies a substratum, a matter which changes and is the underlying stable element to which the changes occur.

p. 330. 1. He should, of course, say 'the illusion of power', for if God acts in us we do not act ourselves, although we may in 'voluntary action' labour under the illusion that we do. 'Power' seems here to be a translation of τὸ ἐφ' ἡμῖν and Ghazali, following al-Ash'ari, who also distinguishes between voluntary action and a reflex action like shivering (see Shahrastani, *Relig. and Philos. Sects*, i. 68), here gives the answer of the Stoics to their critics (see, for example, Aulus Gellius, *Noct. Att.* vii. 2): although everything is determined by fate, everything acts according to its nature; if, for example, you throw down a stone the impulse is given by you, but the stone rolls according to its own nature, and man acts according to his nature when he acts deliberately and by will. The ultimate dilemma, and that not only for the Stoics and the Ash'arites, is this: I am only responsible for those acts which I have freely chosen, and my choice depends on my character (or nature). But there are only two factors which determine my character: the internal initial characteristics transmitted to me by my parents, and the external conditions in which I find myself; and I have freely chosen neither of these factors. The whole problem belongs to that of objective possibility, which I have discussed before: My will implies the possibility of doing or not doing, but only when all the conditions are fulfilled can the possible happen; then, however, it is necessary.

p. 330. 2. I think he means that we attain the knowledge that these movements are performed by a living being like ourself, possessing will. I do not think he means God here.

p. 331. 1. This is badly expressed; what he means is that certain acts which are expected need not necessarily occur.

p. 331. 2. Since the theologians admit definitions, and in the definition, according to Aristotle, the genus takes the place of matter, the specific difference the place of form (cf. e.g. Arist. *Met. Δ* 6. 1016ᵃ28).

p. 331. 3. i.e. in sublunary living beings.

p. 331. 4. The theologians admit, as we have seen (p. 319), that life is a condition of rationality; i.e. they accept the definition of man as a rational animal, but do not regard warmth and moisture, which are the active qualities of the elements (cf. *De gen. et corr. B* 2. 329ᵇ24), as a condition of life, because these qualities do not enter into the definition of life. For the Aristotelians, however, there is a steady progress, an uninterrupted *scala naturae*, from the simple elements through the homogeneous parts (ὁμοιομερῆ) and the organic towards man, in whom earthly nature finds its highest perfection and its supreme end: the lower is a condition of the higher, which is its end (cf. Arist. *De part. an. B* 1. 646ᵃ12). It is warmth (or *pneuma*) which generates life according to Aristotle (*De gen. an. B* 3. 736ᵇ29 sqq.).

p. 331. 5. Every organ is adapted to its function, whose means it is; shape and function are intimately related (cf. Arist. *De an. A* 3. 407ᵇ13).

p. 331. 6. For the hand as an organ of the intellect see Aristotle, *De part. an. Δ* 10. 687ᵃ7 sqq.

p. 332. 1. i.e. every species has its peculiar qualities, ἴδια, which do not define the species although they characterize it (cf. Arist. *Top. A* 4. 101ᵇ19).

p. 332. 2. Koran xxiii. 12–14.

p. 332. 3. We have seen that some Greek authors also believed this.

p. 332. 4. Such a theory is in fact akin to those theories (see e.g. J. S. Mill, *Syst. of Logic*, ii. 7. 5) which derive the laws of thought from experience. Averroës here refers to Ibn Hazm, who (op. cit. ii. 181) distinguishes four classes of the impossible, declares that the third class, that of the logically impossible, e.g. that a man should at the same time sit and stand, is possible for God in another world, although we know necessarily by the actual organization of our mind (بنية العقل) that it is not possible in this. The Ash'arites do not assert that the logically impossible is possible for God (see Ibn Hazm's polemics against them, op. cit. v. 214).

p. 333. 1. It is rather strange that Shahrastani in his *Religious and Philosophical Sects*, pp. 70–71, reproaches Abu Ma'ali (i.e. Juwaini, surnamed the Imam of the two Holy Towns, an Ash'arite and the teacher of Ghazali) for acknowledging a causal nexus in nature and coming near to the philosophical point of view.

p. 333. 2. Koran xxxiii. 62; xxxv. 41; xlviii. 23.

p. 333. 3. Cf. note 332. 4, and see also Ibn Hazm (op. cit. ii. 182), where he says that what is logically impossible for our understanding is so only because God has made it impossible; if God had wished, it would no longer be impossible, and a thing both could be and could not be at the same time, or a body could be at the same time in two places or two bodies in the same place.

p. 333. 4. i.e. since the soul has no spatial magnitude it cannot be localized anywhere.

p. 333. 5. In the following, Ghazali summarizes Avicenna's doctrine found, for example, in his *Salvation*, pp. 259 sqq., from which, however, he deviates in certain points of terminology, as I shall indicate.

p. 333. 6. It seems contradictory to say that although the soul is not impressed on a body its faculties are so impressed; the same difficulty exists for Aristotle also, but the question will be discussed at length below. It may be added that both in Greek and in Arabic the term for sensation, αἴσθησις, حاسّة, can also mean 'sense-organ'.

p. 333. 7. The term 'internal sense' is not found in Aristotle. But Aëtius tells us (*Plac.* iv. 8. 7; *Stoic. Vet. Fr.* ii. 39) that the Stoics called Aristotle's 'common sense' ἐντὸς ἁφή, internal touch (touch, in accordance with their general materialistic view), a term translated by Cicero as *tactus interior* (*Acad. post.* 7. 20); and Alexander of Aphrodisias opposes the objects of φαντασία (for the relation of φαντασία to common sense see note 334. 1) as internal percepts, αἰσθητὰ ἐντός, to the objects of the senses, αἰσθητὰ ἐκτός (*De anima*, Bruns, 68. 31). The expression, 'internal perception', ἡ αἰσθητικὴ ἡ ἔνδον δύναμις, is used in Neoplatonism (cf. e.g. Plotin. *Enn.* iv. 8. 8), and Augustine under Neoplatonic influence speaks of an internal sense which is conscious of its own perception and in which everything the external senses provide is collected (e.g. *De lib. arb.* ii. 4 and ii. 23).

p. 333. 8. The location of sensation in the brain is based on the discovery of the nerves and the anatomical study of the brain by the Greek physicians Erasistratus and Herophilus.

p. 334. 1. Aristotle in his theory of the common sense, ἡ κοινὴ αἴσθησις, made a first and interesting attempt to explain the unity of the perceiver and the thing perceived, i.e. to explain (1) the fact that the same man (the same ego) can perceive sensations of different senses or compare the different sensations of one and the same sense (he did not observe the fact that he is conscious of his own identity, although he attributes to the common sense the faculty of perceiving that we perceive); (2) the fact that, for example, when we perceive yellow honey, we are aware that it is sweet, although we only see it (cf. *De an.* Γ 1. 425ᵃ 22). On the second point Aristotle confuses the unity of the qualities in the external thing (although he does not doubt the objectivity of these qualities) with our conviction that the identical thing which is seen may be touched and eventually tasted (one must distinguish of course between the unity of the external object and our knowledge, or our imagining, that it is a unity of such-and-such qualities) and with some faculty in our soul of unifying the subjective sensations; if, as a matter of fact, the external world were simply a construction out of sensations, there ought to be such a unifying faculty (the primitive and irreducible fact that the self-same thing which is seen can be touched belies the possibility of such a construction, for a visual sensation, even if visually extended, can never be touched, since by definition it is not in the objective space in which we move: heterogeneous sensations cannot be combined). As to φαντασία (representation, imagination), it is primarily, according to Aristotle, a function which transcends the actual sensation (cf. *De an.* Γ 3. 428ᵃ9). Since, however, there is also in the *sensus communis* an awareness of a non-actual sensation (as in the example of honey given above), he cannot delimit φαντασία from common sense; and indeed he ascribes to φαντασία some of the functions he attributes to the *sensus communis*, e.g. awareness that the white object actually perceived has such-and-such non-perceived qualities (cf. *De an.* Γ 3. 428ᵃ28) and also (428ᵇ22) awareness of the common sensibles (which, for instance at *De an.* Γ 1. 425ᵃ17, he attributes to the common sense). The commentators saw the difficulty, and, for example, Ps.-John Philoponus tries—*Comm. in de an. libr.*, Hayduck, 507. 16—to establish a distinction between common sense and φαντασία: common sense is the receptacle of the sensible forms through the medium of the particular sense, αἴσθησις μερική, whereas φαντασία receives them both through the common sense. The confusion in the Aristotelian theory is increased still further in Muslim philosophy through certain Stoic developments, as I shall show, and also through terminological difficulties, the terms used here for the first three internal senses being different translations (whose sense is not absolutely fixed) of the Greek word φαντασία; the word, for example, which I translate by 'representative faculty' (القوة الخيالية) is used by Avicenna (who calls it also (القوة المصوّرة) for what Ghazali calls the 'conservative faculty', whereas Avicenna designates the *sensus communis* by the Greek word (in Arabic transcription, فنطاسيا). For the expression 'judging element' compare note 334. 6.

p. 334. 2. The estimative faculty (القوة الوهمية): the term is one of the different translations of the term φαντασία, but has acquired a special sense—in the Latin translations it is called *vis aestimativa*.

p. 334. 3. The intentions, المعاني (in the Latin translation *intentiones*). The word المعاني, as we have seen—note 3. 6—is a translation of the Greek τὰ λεκτά, and instead of 'intentions' I might have translated it 'meanings' or 'significations'. The term shows that here we have Stoic influence, and indeed the Stoics define λεκτόν through φαντασία: λεκτὸν δὲ ὑπάρχειν φασὶ τὸ κατὰ λογικὴν φαντασίαν ὑφιστάμενον, an intention is what subsists in conformity with a rational presentation (Sext. Emp. *Adv. log.* ii. 70). Now the Stoics distinguish six classes of φαντασίαι (Diog. Laert. vii. 51; *Stoic. Vet. Fr.* ii. 24. 15): the sensational (αἰσθητικαί), the non-sensational (οὐκ αἰσθητικαί), the rational (λογικαί), the non-rational (ἄλογοι), the artful (τεχνικαί), and the artless (ἄτεχνοι), i.e. natural, unmethodical; the non-sensational apprehend through insight (διάνοια) the incorporeals and the other conceptual notions; the rational exist only in man and are thoughts (νοήσεις), whereas the non-rational, which animals possess, have no name (οὐ τετυχήκασιν ὀνόματος). It seems to me from this that the later Stoics may have recognized a non-rational, but at the same time non-sensational, φαντασία on which the instinct of animals depends, and that the Arabs may have applied to this φαντασία, to which the Greeks had not given a distinctive name, the term 'estimative faculty'. In any case, that there is Stoic influence here may be seen from Seneca's epistle 121, where he asserts that animals also have a *constitutionis suae sensus* (*constitutionis suae sensus* is the translation of συνείδησις, the Stoic counterpart of Aristotle's *sensus communis* in so far as *sensus communis* means the consciousness of one's own activity), and to this *sensus* he ascribes all the instinctive actions of animals and, for example, the fact that the hen flees from the hawk, but not from the peacock or the goose (I have not met in classical literature the example of wolf, sheep, and lamb which seems to be a common example among the Arabs and which, e.g., is found in Farabi's *Gems of Wisdom* and in Ghazali's *Vivification of Theology*, vol. iii, p. 7). Cf. note 304. 7.

p. 334. 4. The forms, i.e. the individual sensible forms which exist in the *sensus communis*.

p. 334. 5. According to Avicenna this faculty is located at the end of the middle ventricle of the brain (*Salvation*, p. 266).

p. 334. 6. Aristotle distinguishes between φαντασία αἰσθητική (or βουλευτική) and φαντασία λογιστική (*De an.* Γ 10. 433ᵇ29), sensational and intellectual or deliberative φαντασία (a term which in a way is a *contradictio in adiecto*, since φαντασία is by definition αἰσθητική, an image); but he does not indicate how the animals can perform their actions by mere φαντασία (and desire), without any rational element (on the other hand, he regards sensation already as having a kind of rational element akin to judgement, *De an.* Γ 7. 431ᵃ8, and in *De memoria* 1. 450ᵃ15 he regards *all* φαντασία as having a conceptual element), and John Philoponus simply says (op. cit. 515. 9): 'You must know that what in us is the intellect is in an animal the φαντασία'; from which it would appear that the imaginative faculty can perform what the estimative faculty is supposed to do, and the estimative faculty is therefore superfluous, as Averroës asserts later (p. 336).

p. 334. 7. Here, too, there is some Stoic influence. The Stoics (but not Aristotle) have the term φαντασία συνθετική, 'combining φαντασία' (cf. Sext. Emp. *Adv. log.* ii. 276), and Ps.-John Philoponus (op. cit. 509. 16) distinguishes two kinds of φαντασία, one that accepts the forms and one that combines at will representations of phantastic beings.

p. 334. 8. Avicenna says, loc. cit., that this faculty is located in the middle ventricle of the brain near the vermiform process (فى التجويف الاوسط من الدماغ عند الدودة).

p. 334. 9. See note 335. 2.

p. 334. 10. Galen, *De plac. Hippocr. et Plat.* vii. 3 (K. v. 605), says that anatomical research on the brain has shown that a lesion in the last ventricle affects the sensibility and motive power of the animal more than a lesion of the middle ventricle, and a lesion in the middle ventricle more than one in the first. Aristotle himself regarded the heart as the central organ of sensation (see e.g. *De iuvent.* 2. 469ᵃ11).

p. 334. 11. This is a very questionable logic, especially in view of the fact that representation itself implies memory; but the comparison with water is found also in Avicenna, loc. cit. It is inspired by a passage in Aristotle's *De memoria* 1. 450 ᵇ1–3, where he says that people in violent emotion do not remember well; it is as if a seal were stamped on running water. And Plotinus says, *Enn.* iv. 7. 6, that if one should imagine sense-impressions to be impressed on a liquid like water, they would run away and there would be no memory.

p. 334. 12. Avicenna calls the memorative faculty the retentive-memorative: القوة الحافظة الذاكرة. In this distinction of two memories, one for sensible affections, one for thoughts, there seems to be some Neoplatonic influence, for Plotinus in his subtle and profound discussion of memory (*Enn.* iv. 3. 25–33) distinguishes between them and attributes the former to the lower soul, the latter to the higher (*Enn.* iv. 3. 15–22). He has, however, a much more idealistic view of memory, which, according to him, belongs exclusively to the soul, and at *Enn.* iv. 3. 26 he refutes the Stoic view which compares memory with the imprint of a signet-ring on wax (a view which, however, Chrysippus did not share, cf. Sext. Emp. *Adv. log.* i. 229).

p. 335. 1. What Ghazali relates here of the motive faculties is almost (see note 335. 4) a textual quotation from a passage in Avicenna, *Salvation*, p. 259. It is, although simplified, materially in agreement with Aristotle, cf. e.g. *De an.* Γ 10. 433^{b}13 sqq. Aristotle has simply the term $\phi a \nu \tau a \sigma i a$: the appetitive animal cannot be without $\phi a \nu \tau a \sigma i a$ (433^{b}28).

p. 335. 2. There is here some terminological confusion. Ghazali here copies Avicenna, who understands by 'representative faculty' the fourth internal sense, whereas Ghazali meant by it the first. According to what Ghazali says (p. 334) about the relation between the third internal sense and the motive faculty, one would have expected him to have mentioned this third faculty here. But I admit that the meaning of all these terms is very evasive.

p. 335. 3. This is the only sentence Ghazali adds to this passage.

p. 335. 4. Cf. Aristotle, *De an.* Γ 10. 433^{b}25: all animals move by pushing and pulling, $\mathring{\omega}\sigma\iota\varsigma$ καὶ ἕλξις; there must therefore be in them a fixed point from which the movement starts (cf. also Arist. *Phys.* H 2. 243^{b}15).

p. 335. 5. 'discursive' from 'discourse' (i.e. speech). By this I translate ناطقة, derived from نطق like λογιστικός from λόγος, both the Greek and the Arabic word meaning both 'speech' and 'reason'.

p. 335. 6. This is also stated by Avicenna, loc. cit.

p. 335. 7. 'Conditions' and 'modes' are here synonymous; by these terms the theologians expressed the unreality of universals, which existed only for the mind (cf. note 3. 6).

p. 335. 8. This is a very simplified summary of Avicenna's chapter 'On the faculty of the speculative soul and its degrees', op. cit., p. 269. The idea that the soul receives its vices by inclining to the body and being subjected by it, and its virtue by contemplation of intellectual realities, is derived from Neoplatonism; cf. e.g. Plotinus, *Enn.* i. 6. 5–6.

p. 336. 1. The soul is not really subsistent by itself for Aristotle (it is so for Plotinus), since it is the form of the body; but although it is incorporeal it performs its functions (except the highest, the intellectual) through organs in which it is located, and only the active part of the intellect is separable from the body (how this is possible, when the soul is regarded as a unity, is another question). The arguments that will be given try to prove the intellect's independence of any bodily organ (the terms 'intellect', νοῦς, and 'soul', ψυχή, are often confused).

p. 336. 2. I think Averroës here means by 'imaginative faculty' imagination in the more general sense of φαντασία, common to men and animals.

p. 336. 3. This sentence is rather confusing. Avicenna evidently does not think that the estimative faculty in the animal replaces the cogitative in man, nor could Avicenna mean (if indeed he said that the ancients called the estimative faculty the imaginative) that the estimative faculty and the imaginative are identical, as Averroës seems to imply, but only that the ancients did not distinguish clearly between them.

p. 336. 4. i.e. to the *sensus communis*; shape (σχῆμα), being a kind of magnitude, is one of the common sensibles and is apprehended through motion by the *sensus communis* (Arist. *De an.* Γ i. 425ᵃ16) which, according to the Muslim philosophers, is located in the front part of the brain.

p. 336. 5. i.e. the imaginative faculty is not mere imagination, but perceives what happens in the external world.

p. 336. 6. i.e. they are not derived from sensible experience; this seems to contradict the Aristotelian principle 'nihil in intellectu quod non prius in sensu'.

p. 336. 7. Nothing is found in the *De sensu* about this question, but Averroës is probably referring to *De memoria* 1. 450ᵃ15, where Aristotle says that animals possess φαντασία, because it is primarily a perception and not one of the conceptual faculties, although it is accidentally such a faculty (it seems to be, like memory, something intermediate between perception and thought; cf. ibid. 449ᵇ26).

p. 337. 1. This is the thesis of Avicenna (*Salvation*, p. 285) in the chapter on the immateriality of the substratum of the intelligibles. See below in the text.

p. 337. 2. Some theologians held that thought was located in an atom in the heart. The Stoics also had placed the ἡγεμονικόν in the heart (or in the brain; according to Plutarch, *De comm. not.* 45, the Stoics regarded it as a πόρος στιγμαῖος, a passage not bigger than a point, in the heart).

p. 337. 3. The question of the indivisibility or divisibility of time, space, and matter was discussed copiously by the Muslim theologians. How well the Greek arguments for either point of view were known can be seen from the long discussion of this question by Ibn Hazm, and his refutation of Ash'arite atomism, op. cit., vol. v. 92–108 (the arguments for indivisibility are mainly based on Aristotle). Curiously enough the older theologians were also interested in this question.

p. 337. 4. i.e. of a plurality in the atom, since this atom would have two sides and would therefore be divisible. This is the argument found in

Aristotle, *Phys. Z* 1 (ad init.): indivisibles could not touch, because they would not have parts and therefore their wholes would coincide. It is also given by Avicenna, p. 286, in the chapter mentioned in note 337. 1.

p. 338. 1. Throughout this problem perception and φαντασία are regarded as images on an extended substratum, and, of course, Ghazali is right in regarding it as impossible, as the philosophers hold in the case of other universals, that an abstract entity like hostility should be impressed on a surface.

p. 338. 2. But this is not an argument against the intelligibles, for the philosophers do not hold that intelligibles can be impressed on matter, although inconsistently they hold this to be possible for hostility. On the contrary it is an argument against the materialism which Ghazali has set out to defend.

p. 338. 3. This argument against the philosophers is correct, if by 'knowledge' is meant sensible knowledge, i.e. perception and φαντασία.

p. 338. 4. This is a curious remark, since Ghazali has just argued that there can be no relation between hostility and a body. It can only mean here: 'like the relation of hostility to the body according to the philosophers, a conception I have shown to be false'.

p. 339. 1. i.e. the colour white, for example, is evenly extended over the whole body, and when you take a part of the body you take also a part of the white, and the white of the part is the same white as the white of the body.

p. 339. 2. Here there is another conception of sensation; i.e. it is conceived not as an impression, but as a faculty, a capacity for action (and reception), and therefore shapeless ('without a specific shape', says Averroës, but this seems to me a *contradictio in adiecto*); but how can the shapeless be extended over the extended? There is here a reference to the theory found in Aristotle, *De an. A* 5. 411^{a}26. Cf. note 343. 2.

p. 339. 3. i.e. sight, which is an attribute of the eye, is, like whiteness, found in every part of its substratum, i.e. the eye, but some eyes or some parts of the eye have a greater receptivity for sight than others, and in old age this receptivity of some parts of the eye becomes less and therefore the old see less well than the young (Aristotle says, *De an. A* 4. 408^{b}21, if an old man could acquire the eye of a young man, he would see as well as a young man).

p. 339. 4. i.e. sight and (the same shade of) white have in all individuals the same definition, but they are quantitatively divided, i.e. spatially and through being in different individuals.

p. 339. 5. He probably means by 'that they cannot be divided into any particular part whatever' that, for example, some eyes lose in part their receptivity for sight.

NOTES 193

p. 339. 6. i.e. the part which has vanished acts (or acted) with a greater intensity.

p. 339. 7. Even colours cannot be divided absolutely, for they terminate in a point at which they cannot be seen any more (namely at a certain distance). This refers to Aristotle, *De sensu* 7. 449^{a}22 sqq.

p. 339. 8. This refers to *De sensu* 6. 445^{b}28, where Aristotle says that only the continuous *per se* (καθ' αὐτό) falls into a finite number of equal parts.

p. 340. 1. He means that Ghazali treated estimation as if it were an impression, whereas it is a faculty; Averroës, however, has not shown in any way how Ghazali's argument could be refuted by regarding estimation as a faculty.

p. 340. 2. In the chapter quoted in note 337. 1.

p. 340. 3. This completion is given by Avicenna in the chapter indicated in note 346. 6.

p. 341. 1. Curiously enough this is nowhere explicitly stated by Aristotle. The argument is found in Avicenna (see below). It may be inferred from the passage at the beginning of *De an.* Γ 4, where Aristotle agrees with Anaxagoras that the mind must be unmixed, ἀμιγής, and asserts that it cannot be mixed with the body or have an organ, and cannot have a form of its own, since the appearance of such a form would obstruct everything else. This connects with the passage (*De an.* B 5. 417^{a}2) where he asks why the sense-organs cannot have a perception of themselves.

p. 341. 2. This is the argument given by Avicenna (*Salvation*, p. 290). It is based on the argument found in Aristotle, *De an.* A 3. 407^{a}2 sqq., where Aristotle attacks Plato's conception, found in the *Timaeus*, of the soul as implying magnitude. Aristotle says in substance that, the meaning Plato gives to 'soul' being undoubtedly 'intellect', the unity of the intellect is not the unity of a magnitude. If it were a magnitude, with which of its parts would it think? And if it thought with some only of its parts, the others would be superfluous; besides, if the term 'parts' means points, there would be an infinity of them and infinity cannot be traversed, and if all the parts collectively were in contact with the thing thought, what could be meant by this contact?

p. 342. 1. Cf. Aristotle, *Eth. Nic.* Z 1. 1139^{b}4: ἢ ὀρεκτικὸς νοῦς ἡ προαίρεσις ἢ ὄρεξις διανοητική, καὶ ἡ τοιαύτη ἀρχὴ ἄνθρωπος: will is either desiring reason or reasoning desire, and such a principle is man (in his totality).

p. 343. 1. This in a way contradicts what he said on p. 339, where he regarded this second class as that of things by definition divisible through the divisibility of the substratum, although with different degrees of intensity.

p. 343. 2. The problem of the faculties is discussed in *De an.* A 5. 411^a 26 sqq., where Aristotle asks what it is that holds the soul together if it can be divided by nature through the different operations of its organs. Should we not rather say that each of the operations of the soul belongs to the soul in its entirety? Is not the soul a unity? However, although in this passage he seems to regard the soul as a unity, he regards only the intellect as self-subsistent and imperishable, for, says he, if there were anything that could destroy it, it would be decrepitude (*De an. A* 4. 408^{b}18–20).

p. 343. 3. After the passage where Aristotle asserts that only decrepitude could destroy the intellect, he says that the same thing seems to apply to the sense-organs; and then the sentence quoted by Averroës follows: εἰ γὰρ λάβοι ὁ πρεσβύτης ὄμμα τοιονδί, βλέποι ἂν ὥσπερ καὶ ὁ νέος (loc. cit., ^{b}21).

p. 343. 4. Aristotle says, loc. cit., ^{b}22: 'Decrepitude is not due to some affection of the soul, but to that in which it resides, just as in drunkenness and illnesses.' However, for Aristotle sleep and fainting, λιποψυχία, are not due to any affection of any sense-organ, but to the inactivity of the central sense, the *sensus communis* (cf. *De somn.* 2. 455^{a}26 sqq.).

p. 343. 5. It is found that plants and certain insects live when they are cut in two, and it seems that the same soul resides specifically, although not numerically, in the two parts (Arist. *De an. A* 4. 409^{a}9; cf. *B* 2. 413^{b}16).

p. 343. 6. Koran xvii. 87.

p. 343. 7. The parts, i.e. the organ and the soul: the organ becomes inactive, and the soul remains both in sleep and in death (but can it be active after death?). But this is not the conception of Aristotle, for whom both waking and its opposite, sleep, are common to body and soul (cf. *De somn.* 1. 1) and due, as we have seen, to the inactivity of the central sense; the term 'common sense', however, is ambiguous and may mean either the central organ (in animals that have blood this is the heart) or its counterpart in the soul; both meanings are intended here. For Aristotle (cf. *De gen. an. E* 1. 778^{b}30) sleep is a borderland (μεθόριον; افق is the Arabic term, well known in Muslim mysticism) between life and death, between existence and non-existence. Sleep is the first state of the animal, because through it it passes from non-existence to existence (the Homeric metaphor of Sleep as the brother of Death was well known in Islam, see, for example, Ghazali, *Vivification of Theology*, iv. 291).

p. 343. 8. Koran xxxix. 43.

p. 344. 1. Compare note 342. 1; for Aristotle, however, man in his totality consists of his body and soul, for Ghazali's materialism, in his body exclusively.

p. 344. 2. If the soul is a unity, as Averroës has just asserted, there is certainly such an analogy, as Aristotle also holds (see next note).

p. 344. 3. Both Aristotle and Averroës hold at the same time three different theories about sensation: (1) that sensation is an impression on a sense-organ; (2) that it is a faculty of a soul in which all faculties are united; (3) that it is a faculty of that (for Aristotle, at least, inseparable) synthesis of body and soul which constitutes man. Here Averroës seems to hold that one ought really to say that the eye sees, and that 'a man sees' is only an idiomatic expression. Aristotle, however (*De an. A* 4. 408 ^{b}13), says: βέλτιον γὰρ ἴσως μὴ λέγειν τὴν ψυχὴν ἐλεεῖν ἢ μανθάνειν ἢ διανοεῖσθαι, ἀλλὰ τὸν ἄνθρωπον τῇ ψυχῇ: 'It would perhaps be better not to say that the soul has pity or learns or thinks, but that the man does so through his soul.'

p. 345. 1. 'Judgement of his sight.' For Aristotle there is in sensation already a cognitive element (*De an. B* 10. 424^{a}5; cf. 432^{a}16).

p. 345. 2. Such absurdities are a consequence of all materialization of mental phenomena; compare with this section Plutarch, *De comm. not.* 45. This theory is directed against the materialism, Stoic in origin, of those theologians for whom all reality consists only in body, and for whom the soul is nothing but the material vital spirit (πνεῦμα, spiritus, روح) which is dispersed through the whole body (cf. e.g. Alex. Aphr. *De an. libr. mant.* 115. 6, Bruns; *Stoic. Vet. Fr.* ii. 218. 25) although its principle is in the heart (or the brain). The origin of the argument is unknown to me, and seems to have been so to Averroës, too, but it is based on problems discussed by the Stoics; Chrysippus objected to the impression-theory on the ground that, if the mind thought at the same time of a triangle and a quadrangle, the same body would be at the same time triangular and quadrangular (cf. Sext. Emp. *Adv. log.* i. 229). It may have been offered either by someone who believed the seat of the soul to be an indivisible body, an atom, or by one who believed the soul to be an indivisible immaterial substratum (if the latter, one should not be shocked by the idea that it is said to be in a place; Aristotle himself calls the intellect a τόπος εἰδῶν, *De an. Γ* 4. 429^{a}27, a place for universals, and our modern philosophers say that things are *in* a consciousness). It asserts that, since we cannot assert two opposite ideas at the same time and cannot, for example, possess at the same time ignorance (regarded as something positive) and knowledge, there must be room in the soul for only one of two opposite notions, and therefore it must be indivisible. The last sentence of the passage means that the theologians might retort that in *one* indivisible place ignorance and knowledge could be opposed, since in *one* place they might form a unity—i.e. the notion that ignorance is not knowledge; but their adversary can then object *ad hominem* that the Stoic conception, that the principle of the soul is in the heart or in the brain and that at the same time it is a unique vital force extended over the whole body, is contradictory. This objection seems legitimate, but if such a vital force is acknowledged it destroys the assailant's thesis also. (It is curious to see that Plotinus argues the other way round. He says, *Enn.* iv. 7. 8, that if the soul were the entelechy of the body and therefore dispersed through the whole body, a human being could have only one sentiment and never be in discord with itself. In a little treatise, 'On happiness and on the ten arguments for the substantiality of the soul'—published in Seven Treatises by Avicenna, Haiderabad, H. 1353, and where Avicenna follows largely Plotinus—Avicenna says, p. 8, that if the intelligible form were in a body, it would be impossible to perceive at the same time two opposites.

p. 345. 3. Compare Chrysippus' definition: ἡ ψυχὴ πνεῦμά ἐστι σύμφυτον ἡμῖν συνεχὲς παντὶ τῷ σώματι διῆκον (Stoic. Vet. Fr. ii. 238. 33). Plants and animals are joined through one single ἕξις, junction (Sext. Emp. Adv. log. i. 102; Adv. phys. i. 81: three cohesive forces are distinguished, ἕξις for the inorganic, φύσις for the plants, ψυχή for the animals).

p. 346. 1. Aristotle, e.g. Anal. Pr. A i. 24ᵃ21: τῶν ἐναντίων εἶναι τὴν αὐτὴν ἐπιστήμην.

p. 346. 2. Bodily or in the body; as we have seen, Aristotle also confuses a theory of the common sense as a faculty of the soul subsisting in the body with a theory of the common sense as corporeal. The intellect distinguishes or joins intellectual opposites, the common sense sensible opposites.

p. 346. 3. i.e. this fifth argument.

p. 346. 4. ἀλλὰ κατὰ μίαν δύναμιν καὶ ἄτομον χρόνον μίαν ἀνάγκη εἶναι τὴν ἐνέργειαν, i.e. a single faculty can have only one activity at the same moment (Arist. De sensu 7. 447ᵇ17).

p. 346. 5. This takes place through the common sense.

p. 346. 6. This is proved by Avicenna, op. cit., p. 292, cf. note 341. 1.

p. 347. 1. Cf. note 260. 2; we have the following mixed hypothetical syllogism: if the intellect perceives the intelligibles through a bodily organ, it does not know itself; but it knows itself, therefore it does not perceive the intelligibles through a bodily organ.

p. 347. 2. It would perhaps be better to translate: 'It does not see the eyelid' (since colour is the condition of sight (ὁρᾶται δὲ χρῶμα ἢ τὸ ἔχον) Arist. De an. Γ 2. 425ᵇ18).

p. 347. 3. What is placed on the sense-organs is not perceived, but what is placed on the flesh is (Arist. De an. B 11. 422ᵇ34).

p. 347. 4. This would be difficult for Averroës to explain according to Aristotelian theory, since for Aristotle the sense-organ receives the form of the percept without its matter; nor is there any duality in the act of seeing, for 'to act' here means for Aristotle 'actuality' (the verb becomes a substantive), and either the percipient becomes the percept or the percept the percipient.

p. 348. 1. Through this theory of identity not only is thought about other things abolished, but also self-consciousness itself. It was just because of the duality in all thought that Plotinus denied it to the First. As was said above, the idea that thinking by adding something to reality falsifies it led Aristotle to a theory which annuls thought itself.

p. 348. 2. The sixth proof is identical with the fifth: if the intellect perceived through a bodily organ, it could know neither itself nor its organ, which would be itself or part of itself; it is in this way that the thesis is set out by Avicenna, loc. cit.

p. 348. 3. That of all animals only the crocodile moves the upper jaw was a fact already known to Herodotus (ii. 68). Aristotle mentions the fact in different passages, e.g. *Hist. an. A* ii. 492^{b}23: κινεῖ δὲ πάντα τὰ ζῷα τὴν κάτωθεν γένυν, πλὴν τοῦ ποταμίου κροκοδείλου· οὗτος δὲ τὴν ἄνω μόνον. This is given as an example against induction by Sextus Empiricus, *Hyp. Pyrrh.* ii. 195: since most animals move the lower jaw, only the crocodile the upper, the premiss that every animal moves the lower jaw is false. The general argument against induction (ἐπαγωγή, استقراء) is given op. cit. ii. 204: ἐπεὶ γὰρ ἀπὸ τῶν κατὰ μέρος πιστοῦσθαι βούλονται δι' αὐτῆς (i.e. ἐπαγωγῆς) τὸ καθόλου, ἤτοι πάντα ἐπιόντες τὰ κατὰ μέρος τοῦτο ποιήσουσιν ἢ τινά. ἀλλ' εἰ μὲν τινά, ἀβέβαιος ἔσται ἡ ἐπαγωγή, ἐνδεχομένου τοῦ ἐναντιοῦσθαι τῷ καθόλου τινὰ τῶν παραλειπομένων κατὰ μέρος ἐν τῇ ἐπαγωγῇ· εἰ δὲ πάντα, ἀδύνατα μοχθήσουσιν, ἀπείρων ὄντων τῶν κατὰ μέρος καὶ ἀπεριορίστων: when one tries to reach the universal through induction, one can do this by examining either all the instances or some; if the latter, the induction will be unreliable, since some of the neglected cases may be in opposition to the universal, if the former, one is attempting the impossible, since the particulars are infinite and inexhaustible. Curiously enough, Nemesius, *De natura hominis*, ii (Migne, xl, col. 548), uses exactly the same argument to refute Cleanthes' opposite thesis that nothing incorporeal can partake of the corporeal, μηδὲν ἀσώματον σώματι συμπάσχειν. The *De natura hominis* was known to the Arabs.

p. 348. 4. What follows is a free interpretation of Avicenna's proof (op. cit. p. 292) that, if the intellectual faculty thinks through an organ, it must always be conscious of that organ (يجب ان تعقل آلتها دائماً). Avicenna, however, speaks only of the organ, not of the body (compare Averroës's answer below in the text).

p. 349. 1. Compare William James, *The Principles of Psychology*, vol. i, p. 291: 'In its widest possible sense, however, a man's Self is the sum total of all that he can call his, not only his body and his psychic powers, but his clothes and his house . . ..'

p. 349. 2. The organ of smell (consisting of the two olfactory nerves) is, according to Galen (*De usu part.* viii. 6, Helmreich, i. 469), the only one in the skull placed in the foremost ventricle of the brain.

p. 349. 3. Cf. Aristotle, *Top.* A 1: induction based on common opinions or the opinions of the majority or the wise (ἔνδοξα δὲ τὰ δοκοῦντα πᾶσιν ἢ τοῖς πλείστοις ἢ τοῖς σοφοῖς) has only dialectical value, and its conclusions provide only probability.

p. 350. 1. Aristotle, *De an.* Γ 1 ad init., proves that there cannot be more than five senses.

p. 350. 2. e.g. the *sensus communis* and φαντασία are neglected.

p. 351. 1. This argument, which is given by Avicenna, *Salvation*, p. 294, whom Ghazali follows almost verbally, is found in Aristotle, *De an.* Γ 4. 429^{a}29 (cf. Γ 2. 426^{a}30), with the exception that the tiredness of the intellect is not discussed and thereıore is not ascribed to the imaginative faculty; in fact this addition invalidates the whole argument, for thought is constantly accompanied by imagination (οὐδέποτε νοεῖ ἄνευ φαντάσματος ἡ ψυχή, *De an.* Γ 7. 431^{a}16).

p. 352. 1. For the Greeks forty years is the ἀκμή of a man, both physically and mentally; the Arabs, however, ascribe greater wisdom to the old.

p. 352. 2. i.e. from 'if a is, then either b is or not-b' no inference can be drawn. But Ghazali does not seem to see that through this exception the whole argument is invalidated. Of course, it may be that for different reasons the sense-organs and the intellect decline in old age, and that it is this which the argument sets out to prove; but this is a new thesis or hypothesis. The argument is taken from Avicenna (op. cit. p. 295), who first gives as a proof of the immateriality of the intellect that it does not decline with age whereas the senses do, and who then makes the objection that the intellect also declines through illness and dotage, an objection which he rebuts in the way indicated by Ghazali below in the text. (That the objection was made can be seen from Galen, *Quod animi mores corporis temperamenta sequuntur*, where he asks, 3 (Mueller 9. 11): 'Why, if the soul is immortal as Plato has it, does it leave the body when the brain is too cold or too hot, too dry or too moist, and why does a great loss of blood, or the taking of hemlock or a high fever, make it leave it? And', he adds ironically, 'if Plato were still alive, I should be delighted to learn it from him.') The argument is based erroneously on the passage of Aristotle (*De an.* A 4. 408 ^{b}18) discussed above, over the interpretation of which the commentators differ; there it is said that the senses decline through the decay of the organ, not through the decay of the faculty, and Aristotle admits (408^{b}24) that the intellect declines in old age.

p. 352. 3. The conception of fear as a disease is Stoic. Any permanent disposition to a violent emotion is called by the Stoics νόσημα, disease (cf. *Stoic. Vet. Fr.* iii. 105. 6).

p. 353. 1. According to the Stoics man acquires reasoning power during the first seven years of his life (Aët. *Plac.* iv. 11. 4); in the second seven years, or thereabouts, he acquires the notions of right and wrong (Aët. *Plac.* v. 23. 1). According to Varro—see Censorinus, *De die natali*, 14—life is divided into five equal epochs, each of fifteen years, except the last. The first epoch which lasts to the fifteenth year embraces childhood.

p. 353. 2. Natural heat, i.e. πνεῦμα.

p. 353. 3. This passage is closely related to a passage in Plutarch, *De Ei apud Delphos*, 18 (p. 392 c). I give it here in the translation of Montaigne, who quotes it in his *Apologie de Raymond Sebond* (ad fin.): 'De façon que ce qui commence à naistre ne parvient jamais jusques à perfection d'estre, pour autant que ce naistre n'acheve jamais, et jamais n'arreste, comme estant à bout, ains, depuis la semence, va tousjours se changeant et muant d'un à autre; comme de semence humaine se fait premierement dans le ventre de la mere un fruict sans forme, puis un enfant formé, puis, estant hors du ventre, un enfant de mammelle; aprés il devient garson, puis consequemment un jouvenceau, aprés un homme faict, puis un homme d'aage; à la fin decrepité vieillard: de maniere que l'aage et generation subsequente va tousjours desfaisant et gastant la precedente.' The idea of the Heraclitean flux, the constancy of inconstancy, is a favourite subject in later Greco-Roman philosophy. Compare also, for example, Seneca, *Epist.* 58. 22: 'nemo nostrum idem est in senectute qui fuit iuvenis, nemo nostrum est idem mane qui fuit pridie. corpora nostra rapiuntur fluminum more. quicquid vides, currit cum tempore. nihil ex iis quae videmus manet et ego ipse, dum loquor mutari ista, mutatus sum': none of us is in old age the same as he was in youth, none of us is in the morning the same as he was the previous day. Our bodies are carried away like streams. Everything you see hastens away with time. Nothing of what we see remains. And while I am saying that all this is changing, I myself am changed.

p. 353. 4. This proof is Platonic and Neoplatonic. At the end of the *Cratylus* (440 a) Socrates says: 'Can we truly say that there is knowledge, Cratylus, if all things are continually changing and nothing remains? For knowledge cannot continue to be knowledge unless it remains and keeps its identity. But if knowledge changes its very essence, it will at once lose its identity and there will be no knowledge. And if it is for ever changing, knowledge will for ever not be and there will be no one to know and nothing to be known. But if the knower exists and the known exists and the Beautiful and the Good and everything real exist, then I do not think that we can truly say what we just asserted, that they are, as it were, in flux and transition.' 'Every body is in flux and in perpetual movement'—says Plotinus, *Enn.* iv. 7. 3—'and the world would immediately perish, if everything were body'.

As for Plotinus, we have also the beautiful and important passage in *Enn.* iv. 7. 10: δεῖ δὲ τὴν φύσιν ἑκάστου σκοπεῖσθαι εἰς τὸ καθαρὸν αὐτοῦ ἀφορῶντα ἐπείπερ τὸ προστεθὲν ἐμπόδιον ἀεὶ πρὸς γνῶσιν τοῦ ᾧ προσετέθη γίγνεται. σκόπει δὴ ἀφελών, μᾶλλον δὲ ὁ ἀφελὼν ἑαυτὸν ἰδέτω, καὶ πιστεύσει ἀθάνατος εἶναι, ὅταν ἑαυτὸν θεάσηται ἐν τῷ νοητῷ καὶ ἐν τῷ καθαρῷ γεγενημένον. ὄψεται γὰρ νοῦν ὁρῶντα οὐκ αἰσθητόν τι οὐδὲ τῶν θνητῶν τούτων, ἀλλ' ἀϊδίῳ τὸ ἀΐδιον κατανοοῦντα: 'one should contemplate the nature of everything in its purity, since what is added is ever an obstacle to its knowledge; contemplate therefore the soul in its abstraction, or rather let him who makes this abstraction contemplate himself in this state, and he will know that he is immortal, when he sees himself in the purity of the intellect; for he will see his intellect contemplating nothing sensible, nothing mortal, but apprehending the eternal through the eternal.' These words suggested to Avicenna (in the psychological part of his *Recovery*, v. 7) the example of a man veiled, hanging in mid-air without the possibility of any sensation even of his own body, who would still be conscious of his ego, his immaterial intellect. (This conception sins against the Aristotelian principles that all thought is accompanied by φαντασία and that *nihil in intellectu quod non prius in sensu*; however, so does Aristotle's own conception of the self-consciousness of God.) I do not know whether Avicenna had any direct knowledge of the passage in Plotinus; the beginning of chapter iv in the so-called *Theology of Aristotle* also refers to it. 'He', it says, 'who is able to divest himself of his body and to quiet his senses and their suggestions and movements, will be able to revert with his thought to his own essence and to ascend with his intellect into the intelligible world.' But the Plotinian and Cartesian principle, that one should contemplate things in their purity abstracted from all extraneous matter, though mentioned by Avicenna, is not in the *Theology of Aristotle*.

p. 353. 5. This is an answer any Stoic would have given, since the Stoics, as we have seen, acknowledged three material unifying forces, ἕξις, φύσις, ψυχή. Not only is the identity and unity of our Self a mystery, but the unity and identity of any reality, be it organic or inorganic, is a problem, the whole being more than the parts.

p. 354. 1. i.e. it is not a τόδε τι.

p. 354. 2. Cf. Aristotle, *Anal. Post.* A 4. 73^{b}26: καθόλου δὲ λέγω ὃ ἂν κατὰ παντός τε ὑπάρχῃ καὶ καθ' αὑτὸ καὶ ᾗ αὐτό. φανερὸν ἄρα ὅτι ὅσα καθόλου ἐξ ἀνάγκης ὑπάρχει τοῖς πράγμασιν: I call universal that which is valid of everything, *per se*, and so far as it is this thing; it is therefore clear that everything that is universal pertains to things necessarily. The intellect is receptive of the form and potentially like the form (Aristotle, *De an.* Γ 4. 429^{a}15).

p. 354. 3. The theory of the theologians which will be expounded here is essentially the same as the sensationalism of the Stoics (cf. e.g. Sext. Emp. *Adv. log.* ii. 58–60; *Adv. phys.* i. 393–5). The essence of all nominalistic and sensationalistic theories (ancient or modern—*plus ça change, plus c'est la même chose*) is that thought is reified and regarded as a joining or severing of mental impressions, that in fact thought and representation are identified; and since there are no representations of universal things—you can represent a particular hand, but not a universal hand—the existence of universals is denied (the theories are mostly so confused—one cannot be a consistent nominalist—that they both do and do not deny the universal). Berkeley's theory in his introduction to the *Principles of Human Knowledge*, Intr. §§ 10–12, is practically identical with Ghazali's conception. 'I can consider', he says, 'the hand ... separated from the rest of the body, but whatever hand ... I imagine must have some particular shape. ... I believe we shall acknowledge, that an idea which, considered in itself, is particular, becomes general, by being made to represent or stand for all other particular ideas of the same sort.' But how can a particular idea represent—whatever the word means— all particular ideas of the same sort and become general in this singular fashion, and what do 'the same sort' and 'general' mean on a theory which only acknowledges particular ideas? Ghazali, too, both affirms and denies universals at the same time; he asserts that one shape of hand can represent, or, as he expresses it, can be related to, both a big white hand and a small black hand; he too may be asked how this can come about.

p. 355. 1. i.e. the individual impression which is retained in the soul.

p. 355. 2. 'the thing thought of', this is how I here translate معقول (which can also mean 'intelligible'), since I take it that Ghazali here means something outside the mind.

p. 355. 3. The Aristotelian term 'form' probably means here both sensible form and external shape (it is susceptible of both meanings in Aristotle himself).

p. 355. 4. i.e. the only immaterial being is God.

p. 356. 1. Cf. e.g. Aristotle, *Met.* Z 8. 1033^{b}5: οὐδὲ τὸ εἶδος γίγνεται οὐδ' ἔστιν αὐτοῦ γένεσις. Concepts are timeless, every real thing may be inconstant, but the concept 'inconstancy' is constant.

p. 356. 2. i.e. the absolutely individual cannot be shared, cannot be communicated: *individuum est ineffabile*, this is the basic argument against all nominalism.

p. 356. 3. As I have said before, this theory of identity rests on the confusion of the identity of the thing thought with the identity of the thinker. Zaid and Amr may have an identical thought just as they may perceive an identical thing, for we all live in one common universe; but this does not imply that Zaid and Amr, the thinkers, are identical.

p. 356. 4. This would seem to mean that in the soul also there is a *principium individuationis* through which the soul of Amr, even if it is separated from his body, is distinguished from the soul of Zaid. However, such a view could not be ascribed to the most famous philosopher of them all, Aristotle. (Cf., however, note 14. 4.)

p. 356. 5. i.e. for Ghazali the animality in Zaid is numerically identical with the animality in Khalid. It is as if one said that Zaid carried the numerically identical book that Khalid carried at the same time, but two cannot be one and the same book cannot be in two places at the same time. Ghazali, as Averroës rightly observes, confuses the identity of the individual with that of the universal.

p. 356. 6. Averroës omits to mention the second proof, which is (Ghazali, *Incoherence*, Bouyges, 339. 10) that no immaterial substance can perish (كل جوهر ليس في محل فيستحيل عليه العدم), but of course this second proof is a part of the first. Avicenna, op. cit. 302, has two propositions: (1) that the soul does not die with the death of the body; (2) that the soul is absolutely incorruptible.

p. 357. 1. This is the principal Platonic argument (*Phaedo* 102 a–107 b): a concept can never change into its opposite, and since life belongs to the concept of the soul, it can never be changed into its opposite, death (Plotinus, who wrote a special treatise on Immortality, *Enn.* iv. 7, gives this argument at iv. 7. 11). The argument rests on a confusion between the universal and the individual (it belongs to the paradoxes of the history of philosophy that Plato, for whom all individual things are transitory, regards the human personality, individuality *par excellence*, as eternal), and it certainly cannot prove the immortality of the individual soul; but if it is true that the living can only proceed from the living, life itself would seem to have no origin—and indeed the origin of life and of consciousness remain insuperable cruces for any theory of evolution.

p. 357. 2. This has been shown in Chapter II.

p. 357. 3. Avicenna accepts, as does Plato, the immortality of the soul, but denies with Aristotle its pre-existence (which invalidates, of course, all his Platonic arguments for the eternity of the soul). There can be no pre-existence of the soul, says Avicenna, *Salvation*, pp. 300 sqq.; for either all souls would form a unity before their union with the body, which brings about many impossibilities, as Averroës says, or they would be individually differentiated; but they can only be individually differentiated by matter, i.e. their bodies. But how, then, can they be individually differentiated after death? This is a question to which Avicenna has no satisfactory answer.

p. 357. 4. Here and throughout this passage Averroës leaves his Aristotle and accepts the notions of the Stoics and the Neoplatonists. The passage is rather confused, and Averroës does not seem to distinguish clearly between the souls of the δαίμονες (intermediaries, like the λόγοι σπερματικοί, between God and man) and the disembodied souls of men. According to Plotinus the souls of the δαίμονες have bodies of air or of fire, σώματα ἀέρινα ἢ πύρινα (cf. *Enn.* iii. 5. 6). According to Sext. Emp. *Adv. phys.* i. 71–73, the Stoics held that souls consist of fine particles not less like fire than like πνεῦμα. Compare also for the δαίμονες, e.g. Sext. Emp. *Adv. phys.* i. 87, and especially Plutarch, *De orac. defectu* (cf. G. Soury, *La Démonologie de Plutarque*, Paris, 1942).

p. 358. 1. See note 127. 6.

p. 358. 2. 'the soul creates and forms the body', i.e. it makes its matter a living organism. This sentence is not Platonic, but Plotinian. Plato and Plotinus seem to have been often confused by the Arabs. The sentence refers to *Enn.* iv. 7. 11: ἢ πάθος ἐπακτὸν τῇ ὕλῃ λέγοντες τὴν ζωήν, παρ' ὅτου τοῦτο τὸ πάθος ἐλήλυθεν εἰς τὴν ὕλην, αὐτὸ ἐκεῖνο ἀναγκασθήσονται ὁμολογεῖν ἀθάνατον εἶναι: if it is said that life is a condition imposed on matter, one is forced to admit that the principle which has given this condition to matter must be immortal.

p. 358. 3. The functions attributed by late Greek philosophers to the δαίμονες are ascribed by Muslim authors to the Jinn.

p. 358. 4. The bestower of forms is identified by Avicenna with Aristotle's active intellect.

p. 358. 5. Averroës seems to assume here that the idea of a bestower of forms implies a temporal creation, a change both in the giver and in the receiver; but the only change permitted in the celestial world according to Aristotle is a change of place. However, for the theory of emanation the giving is timeless and changeless. What is in the giver is simultaneous in the receiver, and emanation is a timeless immutable transaction. This is a self-contradictory theory, but Averroës also accepted it.

p. 358. 6. It is not clear from this isolated sentence what is meant here by 'material intellect'; if the counterpart of the active intellect is meant (which is its usual meaning), Averroës here identifies the active intellect with God, as does Alexander of Aphrodisias. But he may understand here by 'material intellect' simply an intellect in contact with this world, whereas the absolutely immaterial intellect, God, is free from all earthly contact. However, Allah knows best!

p. 358. 7. Cf. Aristotle, *Met.* A 3. 984[b]15. Averroës here identifies Anaxagoras' νοῦς with the Aristotelian prime mover.

p. 359. 1. In the last chapter of his *Incoherence* Ghazali attacks the arguments of the philosophers, who in their eschatological theories, taken from late Greek philosophy, deny the resurrection of the flesh and interpret the materialistic conceptions expressed in the Koran symbolically in accordance with their system. According to Ghazali a literal interpretation is possible (cf. *Incoherence*, 355. 4), and the philosophers through their denial of the express words of the Koran place themselves outside the community of Islam. Averroës in his last chapter touches on this problem only slightly, but he aims at defending the philosophers against the accusation of heresy.

His approach to religion is pragmatic and utilitarian. He asserts that religion has no other aim than philosophy in its search for the *summum bonum* and the development of those moral qualities upon which the order of society depends and which the masses never could attain without the guidance of divinely inspired men. His attitude stands midway between the materialistic and utilitarian view of religion which sees in it an astute human invention, aiming at enforcing moral conduct on the masses through the fear of an invisible and omnipresent supervisor (ἐπίσκοπος, see Sext. Emp. *Adv. phys.* i. 54), and the supernatural conception of religion as the revelation of the supreme divine truth. With the latter it considers religion as inspired and expressing the one fundamental truth of the existence of a supreme spiritual deity; with the former it takes the purely pragmatic view of regarding religious dogmas, which are amenable to a rational interpretation and in which an element of pious fraud seems to be involved, as a means of establishing the order and the preservation of society, which forms the condition of all human activity. It had not been difficult for an acute dogmatist like Ibn Hazm to confute this line of thought (cf. op. cit. i. 94), which is based—as I have shown—on Stoic ideas, was already followed by Farabi, and was later adopted by Spinoza in his *Tractatus theologico-politicus*.

p. 359. 2. Indications of a belief in bodily resurrection are few and late in the Old Testament; they are found in Daniel and especially 2 Maccabees, and there is a suggestion of resurrection in Psalm lxxxviii. 11. How well the Arabs were informed about Judaism and Christianity may be seen from the lengthy exposition and criticism of both religions in Ibn Hazm, op. cit. i. 116–ii. 75.

p. 359. 3. Cf. Ibn Hazm, op. cit. i. 35. 5: وكان الذى ينتحل الصائبون, اقدم الاديان على وجه الدهر والغالب على الدنيا, the religion of the Sabaeans was the oldest and the most widely accepted. About the Sabaeans there was some confusion in Islam. They are mentioned in the Koran (ii. 59, v. 73, xxii. 17), but there a sect in Mesopotamia seems to be meant, also called Mandaeans. The sect whose dogmas are described under this name by the Muhammadan authors (e.g. Shahrastani in his *Rel. and Philos. Sects* and Ibn Hazm) was a Gnostic sect in the city of Harran, an ancient city of Hellenistic culture; a strong Neoplatonic influence can be discerned in its tenets and it may have contributed to the spread of Neoplatonic ideas in Islam.

p. 359. 4. i.e. his εὐδαιμονία.

p. 359. 5. For the distinction between ethical and dianoetic virtues compare Aristotle, *Eth. Nic.* A 13. 1103^{a}3.

p. 359. 6. 'The practical virtues', i.e. the moral virtues.

p. 359. 7. Cf. e.g. Francis Bacon, *Advancement of Learning*, i. 5. 1: 'The knowledge of man is as the waters, some descending from above, and some springing from beneath; the one informed by the light of nature, the other inspired by divine inspiration.'

p. 360. 1. Cf. Spinoza, *Tract. theol.-polit.* xiv. 14: 'fidem non per se, sed tantum ratione oboedientiae salutiferam esse'.

p. 360. 2. This is a Stoic doctrine; cf. Seneca, *Epist.* 5. 4: 'hoc primum philosophia promittit: sensum communem, humanitatem et congregationem.' Cf. also Sext. Emp. *Adv. phys.* i. 131: ἡ δικαιοσύνη κατά τινα κοινωνίαν ἀνθρώπων πρὸς ἀλλήλους καὶ ἀνθρώπων πρὸς θεούς νενόηται: justice is a certain brotherhood between men and men, and between men and the gods.

p. 361. 1. Spinoza, op. cit. ii. 1, is opposed to this view: the prophets were not men of special intellectual gifts, but had a strong moral sense and a strong 'imaginatio' (φαντασία); prophecy has never made prophets learned men (op. cit. ii. 3).

p. 361. 2. This well-known saying may possibly come from a Jewish source.

p. 361. 3. Koran xiii. 35.

p. 361. 4. There are, however, many traditions giving a realistic description of Muhammad's vision of heaven during his ascension (معراج). Cf. Asín y Palacios, *La escatología musulmana en la Divina Comedia*, 2nd ed., Apéndice I, p. 425.

p. 361. 5. i.e. the words we apply to the other world are meant in a sense absolutely different from the ordinary; cf. e.g. Spinoza, *Eth.* i, prop. xvii schol.: 'intellectus et voluntas, qui Dei essentiam constituerent, a nostro intellectu et voluntate toto coelo differre deberent, nec in ulla re, praeterquam in nomine, convenire possent; non aliter scilicet, quam inter se conveniunt canis, signum coeleste, et canis, animal latrans.' Even Spinoza does not seem to have seen that this absolutely deprives these words, as applied to the Divine, of any sense. Many traditions were attributed to Ibn Abbas, a paternal cousin of Muhammad; this one seems to have been inspired by an anti-literalist. To the same Ibn Abbas is attributed a tradition of a realistic character about Muhammad's ascension. Cf. Asin, op. cit., p. 432.

p. 362. 1. Simulacrum: εἴδωλον—see for this word and the theory Porphyry, *Sentent.* 32. For the theory of the pneumatic or astral body compare also Plotinus (*Enn.* iii. 5. 6). Proclus (*Inst.* 205) and Iamblichus (*Myst.* 5. 12) call this body ὄχημα.

p. 362. 2. He refers here to Ghazali's *Balance of Action*, Cairo, H. 1328, where, p. 5, Ghazali distinguishes four classes of people as to their opinions about the life hereafter. The third class to which the Sufis belong declare that in death the soul is for ever severed from the body.

p. 362. 3. Universal consent, اجماع, in Islam confers the sanction of legitimacy on a dogma. The idea seems inspired by the Stoic notion of universal consent, 'omnium consensus naturae vox est' (Cic. *Tusc.* i. 15. 35); 'apud nos veritatis argumentum est aliquid omnibus videri' (Seneca, *Epist.* 117. 6).

p. 362. 4. In his 'Ignominies of the Allegorists' (p. 11 of the text in Goldziher's *Gazali's Streitschrift gegen die Batinijja*) Ghazali repeats his attacks on the denial of a bodily resurrection.

p. 363. 1. I have not found the exact sentence in Galen. Galen says, however, *De facult. natur. subst.* iii. 10: those who want to know anything better than do the masses must far surpass all others by nature and by early training; such people, however, can be only very few in number, εἶεν δ' ἂν ὀλίγοι παντάπασιν οὗτοι. It was in the Stoic tradition that the wise man was rare, as rare as the phoenix which is born once in five hundred years (cf. Seneca, *Epist.* 42. 1).

INDEX OF PROPER NAMES
MENTIONED IN THE INTRODUCTION AND NOTES

ibn 'Abbās, 205.
'Abd al-Raḥmān al-Ṣūfī, 96.
Aenesidemus, 63, 79.
Aëtius, 186, 198.
Agathon, 62.
Agrippa, H. C., xxix, 175.
Aḥmad ibn Ḥanbal, 138.
Albertus Magnus, 130, 175.
Albinus, 25.
Alexander of Aphrodisias, 3, 38, 39, 45, 74, 82, 90, 111, 115, 121, 122, 143, 144, 147, 158, 161, 167, 169, 172, 184, 186, 195.
— (from Arabic translations), 85, 89, 122, 143, 159, 166.
Aleximus, 149, 150.
Ammonius Saccas, xxxii.
Ammonius, son of Hermias, 70, 75, 76, 100, 171.
Anaxagoras, 24, 72, 193.
Anselm, 169.
Antipater, 167.
Antiphanes, 31.
Antisthenes, 126, 127.
Apocrypha: Wisdom of Solomon, 124.
Aquinas, St. Thomas, ix, xviii, xx, xxiii, xxvii, xxix, 3, 19, 23, 54. 65, 85, 90, 91, 110, 156, 157, 162, 174, 175, 183.
Aristotle, *Anal. Pr.*, 41, 145, 172, 196.
— *Anal. Post.*, 2, 6, 29, 57, 82, 89, 99, 111, 121, 130, 136, 140, 173, 178, 200.
— *De anima*, 2, 3, 5, 6, 12, 15, 46, 50, 52, 63, 66, 68, 76, 81, 82, 83, 84, 85, 89, 93, 99, 100, 102, 104, 105, 110, 111, 113, 115, 120, 122, 127, 145, 146, 147, 148, 154, 156, 158, 166, 182, 183, 185, 187, 189, 190, 191, 192, 193, 194, 195, 196, 197, 200.
— *Categories*, 29, 30, 32, 33, 48, 58, 61, 109, 111, 112, 129, 152.
— *De. an. incessu*, 24, 164.
— *De. an. motu*, 114.
— *De an. gen.*, 48, 49, 101, 102, 105, 115, 121, 127, 159, 177, 182, 183, 185.
— *De caelo*, i, 2, 3, 6, 8, 17, 18, 19, 21, 22, 23, 24, 26, 32, 34, 37, 40, 42, 43, 44, 57, 59, 60, 76, 84, 92, 94, 137, 139, 140, 142, 157, 158, 159, 160, 163, 164, 180.
— *De div. per somn.*, 168.
— *De gen. et corr.*, 10, 20, 22, 24, 26, 27, 72, 78, 80, 84, 94, 100, 101, 103, 106, 137, 140, 142, 143, 185.
— *De interpr.*, 37, 45, 82, 131, 134, 149.
— *De iuv.*, 189.
— *De memoria*, 49, 89, 189, 191.
— *De part. an.*, 24, 40, 50, 143 f., 150, 165, 185.
— *De philosophia*, xvii, 1, 34, 65 (new fragment), 98, 157, 167.
— *De sensu*, 63, 84, 95, 156, 180, 193, 196.
— *De somno*, 194.
— *Eth. Eud.*, 161.
— *Eth. Nic.*, 4, 62, 103, 156, 167, 168, 169, 171, 193, 204.
— *Hist. An.*, 28, 61, 63, 164, 183, 197.
— *Metaphysics*: 1, 2, 3, 5, 6, 9, 10, 11, 12, 15, 16, 17, 19, 20, 22, 23, 26, 27, 29, 32, 36, 37 f., 39, 40, 41, 42, 43, 44 46, 47, 51, 57, 58, 60, 63, 65, 66, 67, 70, 71, 72, 73, 74, 75, 76, 78, 79, 80, 82, 84, 87, 88, 89, 90, 92, 93, 94, 96, 98, 99, 101, 102, 103, 104, 106, 108, 109, 110, 111, 114, 115, 116, 117, 118, 119, 120, 121, 122, 123, 127, 128, 129, 130, 131, 132, 133, 134, 135, 137, 139, 142, 144, 146, 147, 149, 150, 152, 156, 159, 160, 162, 163, 165, 168, 171, 177, 178, 183, 184, 185, 201, 203.
— *Meteor.*, 21, 25, 49, 57, 69, 78, 83, 115, 137, 140, 160, 164, 180.
— *Physics*, 2, 5, 8, 9, 10, 11, 14, 17, 20, 22, 25, 26, 27, 28, 29, 30, 31, 32, 33, 34, 35, 36, 38, 43, 44, 47, 48, 52, 53, 55, 61, 62, 66, 87, 90, 91, 92, 95, 101, 102, 103, 104, 117, 118, 119, 132, 134, 135, 137, 149, 157, 160, 161, 163, 164, 171, 178, 180, 184, 190, 192.
— *Politics*, 24.
— *Rhet.*, 63, 145, 166, 180.
— *Soph. El.*, 19, 32, 66.
— *Topics*, 2, 7, 20, 22, 33, 56, 78, 88, 116, 185, 197.
— *Fragm.* 367 R., 183.
— *De mundo*, 18, 65, 67, 76, 78.
— *On the particular influences of the spheres*, 164.
— *Problemata*, 98.
— *Theology*, 76, 200.
al-Ash'arī, x, 5, 125, 184.
Ash'arites, xii, xxii, xxiii, xxix, 3, 17, 37, 40, 41, 42, 44, 53, 55, 56, 59, 60, 62, 64, 70, 85, 86, 87, 88, 97, 115, 116, 118, 128, 137, 138, 143, 148, 159, 173, 180, 182, 184, 186, 191.
Athanasius, St., 88.

INDEX OF PROPER NAMES

Atomists, 44.
Augustine, St., xii, xvii, xx, 3, 5, 11, 16, 68, 84, 90, 91, 98, 100, 103, 105, 116, 125, 155, 161, 169, 170, 175, 186.
Averroës, 18, 53, 56, 57, 164, 177, and *passim.*
Avicenna, xii, xiv, xxvii, 13, 25, 26, 48 f., 49, 66, 69, 83, 86, 92, 95, 97, 118, 121, 137, 138 f., 172.
— *Division of the intellectual sciences,* 171.
— *On Happiness,* 196, 197.
— *On Love,* 91.
— *Oriental Philosophy,* 83, 144.
— *Recovery (Shifā'),* 13, 67, 71, 75, 102, 103, 106, 112, 114, 143, 144, 150, 151, 152, 157, 158, 167, 175, 200.
— *Refutation of the Astrologists,* 162, 167.
— *Salvation (Najāt),* 1, 2, 13, 17, 29, 36, 67, 75, 81, 106, 107, 108, 112, 113, 114, 129, 130, 134, 137, 140, 144, 145, 150, 151, 152, 157, 158, 161, 162 ff., 166, 173, 186, 188, 189, 190, 191, 192, 193, 198, 202.
— *Theorems and Notices,* 49, 100, 114, 144, 173, 174, 175.

Bacon, Francis, 204.
al-Baghdādī, 3, 15, 16, 54, 59, 77, 88.
Bairo, Pietro, 174.
al-Bāqillānī, 60 f., 124, 128.
al-Battānī, 96.
Bayle, *Dictionnaire,* 19.
Berkeley, xxxiii, 201.
Bernard of Clairvaux, St., 91.
Boethius, 134.
Boethus, 152.
Bradley, 152.
Brentano, x, xxvii.
Brunetière, F., xiii.
Burton, R., xxix, 92, 174, 175.

Campanella, 91.
Cardano, xxix, 90.
Carneades, x, 77, 86, 140, 148, 168.
Celsus, 97, 124.
Censorinus, xvi, 198.
Cervantes, xiv.
Chalcidius, 38.
Chrysippus, 11, 18, 45, 77, 167, 177, 190, 195, 196.
Cicero, xvii, xxi, 1, 3, 13, 16, 39, 65, 76, 83, 101, 127, 142, 172, 177, 186, 205.
— *De div.,* 39, 98, 165, 166, 167, 170.
— *De fato,* 39, 164 f., 172, 177.
— *De fin.,* 12, 16, 90, 156, 170.
— *De nat. deor.,* 8, 34, 65, 77, 78, 79, 83, 140, 141, 148, 157, 165.
Cleanthes, 65, 197.

Clement of Alexandria, 1, 16, 65, 113, 118, 177.
Corpus Hermeticum, 165.
Coué, Emile, xxix, 174.
Cratippus, 167.
Critolaus, 31.

Damascius, 88.
Dante, 19, 20, 40, 92, 135.
Democritus, 63, 90, 101.
Descartes, xxxiii, 40, 102, 175, 200.
Dio Chrysostomus, 126.
Diodorus Cronus, 36, 39, 147.
Diogenes of Babylon, 167.
Diogenes Laertius, 1, 18, 56, 67, 83, 89, 117 f., 122, 127, 138, 144, 188.
[Dionysius Areopagita], 88, 89, 91.

Eckehart, 155.
Eleatics, xxi, 45, 60, 63.
Empedocles, 44, 72, 91.
Epictetus, 72, 77, 127.
Epicurus, 1, 78, 83, 101.
Erasistratus, 187.
Eryximachus, 91.
Eusebius, 16, 31, 100, 172.

Fakhr ad-Dīn ar-Rāzī, 88.
al-Fārābī, x, 7, 12, 71, 75, 76, 131, 136, 171; 26, 166, 173, 188.
Favorinus, 164.
Ficino, M., 92, 175.
Fienus, Th., 174, 175.
Fludd, R., 90.
Franck, 70.
Frazer, 128.
Fredegisus of Tours, 47.
ibn Fūrak, 128.

Galen, xxix, 16, 50, 56, 57, 61, 66, 83, 145, 176, 179, 184, 189, 197, 198, 206.
— *De demonstr.,* 56.
Gellius, Aulus, 66, 164, 184.
Geulincx, 148.
al-Ghazālī, xxviii, xxix, xxxii, xxv, and *passim.*
— *Aims of the Philosophers,* 146.
— *Alchemy of Happiness,* xxxv.
— *Balance of Action,* 205.
— *Distinction between Faith and Heresy,* 63.
— *Foundation of Dogmatics,* x, 53.
— *Golden means in Dogmatics,* x, 53.
— *Ignominies of the Allegorists,* 206.
— *Just Balance,* 125.
— *Niche for Lights,* 53, 95.
— *Preserver from Error,* 176.
— *Touchstone of Knowledge,* 146.
— *Touchstone of Science in Logic,* 125.
— *Touchstone of Speculation in Logic,* 125.
— *Vivification of Theology,* x, 53, 91, 188, 194.

INDEX OF PROPER NAMES

Gibbon, 98.
Gnosticism, 12, 155.
Goethe, 90.
Gregory of Nyssa, St., 123, 124.
Grotius, 97.

al-Ḥallāj, 7.
abū Hāshim, 59, 88.
ibn Ḥazm, 7, 8, 13, 37, 38, 40, 54, 55 f., 60 f., 82, 85, 100, 124, 128, 155, 184, 185, 186, 191, 204.
Heracliteans, 60.
Heraclitus, 44.
Herodotus, 183, 197.
Herophilus, 187.
Hesiod, 126.
Higden, 90.
Hipparchus, 96.
Hippocrates, 61.
Hippolytus, 172.
Hishām b. 'Amr al-Fuwaṭī, 13, 173.
Hobbes, 90.
Holstenius, 100.
Homer, 96, 126, 133, 194.
abu'l Hudhail al-'Allāf, 54.
Hume, xxx, 64, 120, 173, 176, 179.
Ḥunain ibn Isḥāq, 61.

abū Isḥāq al-Isfara'īnī, 128.
Irenaeus, 169.

Jābir ibn Ḥayyān, 172.
Jahm, 155 f.
James, W., 197.
Jesus, 30, 97.
John Damascene, St., 109 f.
John Philoponus, xvii, 1, 3, 7, 8, 26, 29, 30, 31, 56, 171, 177, 187, 189.
John Scotus Eriugena, 84.
al-Jubbāī, 59.
al-Jurjānī, 165.
al-Juwainī, 18, 186.

Kant, xvi, xix, xx, 8, 10, 11, 17, 80, 96, 125, 129, 137, 138, 155, 178.
Karrāmites, 3, 59.
ibn Khaldūn, 172, 174, 175.
al-Kindī, 90.

Lactantius, 18, 98, 165.
Leibniz, 13, 18, 28, 40, 49, 119, 182, 183, 184.
Leo Hebraeus, 92.
Lucretius, 16, 148.

Mach, E, xxv, 64.
al-Maidānī, 49, 95.

Maimonides, 1, 37, 126.
Marcianus, 77.
Mandaeans, 204.
Marcus Aurelius, 14, 72, 127.
Maslama ibn Aḥmad al-Majrīṭī, 172.
Maximus Confessor, 123 f.
Megarians, xxi, xxii, xxix, 17, 37, 38, 39, 42, 45, 60, 61, 62, 68.
Meinong, x.
Middle Platonism, 48, 88.
Mill, J. S., 185.
Montaigne, xxix, xxxii, 19, 174, 199.
Mu'ammar, 60, 94.
Mucius Scaevola, 98.
Muḥammad al-Murtaḍā, 55.
Muslim, 138.
al-Muṭahhar al-Maqdisī, cf. abū Zaid al-Balkhī.
Mu'tazilites (σχισματικοί), ix, x, xxii, xxiii, 7, 47, 48, 54, 59, 62, 77, 86, 88, 94, 116, 155, 173.
Mysticism, German, 12.

ibn an-Nadīm, 70.
an-Naẓẓām, 30, 38, 48, 54, 173.
Nemesius of Emesa, xxxii, 61, 184, 197.
Neoplatonism, xi, 1, 12, 51, 54. Cf. Plotinus, Proclus, &c.
Neopythagoreanism, 88.
New Testament, 124, 126.
Nicholas of Autrecourt, xxx.
Nietzsche, F., xxiv.
Numenius, xxxii.

Old Testament, 201.
Origen, 8, 12, 14, 97, 98, 116, 124, 128, 168.

Panaetius, 98.
Paracelsus, xxix, 90, 175.
Parmenides, xx. 17, 132, 154.
Pascal, xxix, 174.
Pasicles, 115.
Pelagius, 18.
Philo (of Alexandria), 18, 22, 72, 76, 88, 126, 135, 156.
— *De aetern. m.*, 29, 37, 56, 57, 65, 165.
Philoponus, cf. John Ph.
Plato, 5, 6, 13, 14, 15, 19, 30, 50, 52, 58, 68, 72, 82, 91, 105, 106, 119, 142, 145, 167, 170, 171, 177, 183, 199.
— *Tim.*, 1, 11, 14, 23, 28, 30, 31, 34, 52, 56, 64, 72, 114, 139, 140, 193.
Plautus, xxxiii.
Pliny, 183.
Plotinus, xi, xvi, xviii, xxv, xxvi, xxix, xxxi, xxxii, 5 f., 12, 13, 14, 15, 21, 25, 29,

INDEX OF PROPER NAMES

34, 49, 52, 63, 64, 65, 72, 73, 74, 78, 79, 84, 85, 87, 88, 91, 93, 94, 95, 106, 108, 109, 110, 112, 113, 114, 115, 119, 120, 121, 122, 128, 129, 139, 140, 141, 145, 148, 153, 154, 161, 162, 163, 164, 167, 170, 172, 173, 175, 186, 189, 190, 195, 196, 197, 199, 202, 203, 205.
Plutarch, xxviii, xxxii, 18, 31, 38, 40, 72, 98, 127, 160, 165, 168, 174, 184, 199, 202.
[Plutarch], 39.
Pomponatius, 175.
Porphyry, xxxiv, 63, 76, 100, 121, 140, 205.
Posidonius, 165, 167.
Proclus, xvii, xxvi, 1 f., 2 9, 31, 74, 75, 87, 91, 106, 205.
Ptolemy, 20, 74, 85, 96.
Polybus, 61.
Pythagoras, 172.
Pythagoreans, 20. Cf. Neopythagoreans.

al-Qazwīnī, 162.
Qur'ān, 18, 23, 24, 53, 54, 55, 66, 72, 76, 78, 79, 82, 83, 86, 90, 92, 97, 98, 118, 121, 125, 126, 138, 143, 150, 162, 163, 165, 166, 173, 174, 175, 180, 182, 185, 186, 194, 204, 205.

Renan, E., xii.
Russell, B., xxii.

Sabaeans, 204.
Sceptics, ix f., xxix, 60, 63, 81, 149.
Schopenhauer, 19, 161.
Seneca, 13, 16, 72, 77, 127, 168, 175, 188, 199, 205, 206.
Sextus Empiricus, 4, 16, 29, 30, 32, 38, 45, 49, 53, 63, 65, 67, 68, 71, 72, 77, 79, 86, 87, 89, 99, 102, 118, 122, 138, 144, 147, 148, 149, 150, 152 f., 167, 176, 179, 180, 188, 189, 190, 195, 196, 197, 200, 202, 205.
ash-Shahrastānī, 2, 4, 7, 38, 88, 94, 125, 128, 155, 173, 184, 186, 204.

Siger of Brabant, 157.
Simplicius, xviii, 7, 20, 23, 30, 31, 37, 65, 70, 74, 84, 121, 129, 152, 163.
Spinoza, xi, xiv, xx, 19, 20, 37, 90, 92, 102, 106, 126, 161, 166, 170, 204, 205.
Stobaeus, 31.
Stoic terms, ix f., xvii, xxiii, xxiv, 1, 4, 17 f., 45, 48, 52, 56 f., 57 f., 81, 85, 87, 89, 92, 117, 122, 126, 137, 138, 149, 150, 154, 160, 176, 180, 182, 188, 189, 191, 200, 202.
Stoicorum Veterum Fragmenta, 4, 11, 18, 22, 30, 31, 32, 37, 38, 39, 40, 45, 57, 65, 76, 89, 90, 153, 165, 168, 177, 180, 186, 188, 195, 196, 198.
Strato, 83, 101, 142.
Ṣūfism, 12, 60, 155.
Suidas (Suda), 76.
Suso, 155.

Tauler, 12, 155.
Taurus, 66.
Telesio, 91.
Tertullian, 97.
Thales, 160.
Themistius, 32, 76, 94, 102, 126, 140.
Theophilus, St., 123.
Theophrastus, xvii, xxviii, 21, 147, 163, 165, 178.
ibn Ṭufail, 12, 73.

ibn Uthmān al-Khayyāṭ, 7.

Varro, 98.

abū Ya'qūb, 73.

Zacharias of Mitylene, 100.
Ẓāhirites, 145.
'abū Zaid al-Balkhī', 8, 54, 57, 62. Cf. Muṭahhar al Maqdisī.
Zeno of Citium, 102, 180.
Zeno the Eleatic, i, 63, 149.
Zopyrus, 172.

INDEX OF SUBJECTS MENTIONED IN THE NOTES

accident as a universal, 33.
accidental, 22.
actions, classification of, 117.
actual, 2.
actuality, 67, 137.
actualizer, 1.
agent, eternal, 1.
alchemy, 172.
analogy, 145.
angels, 23, 135, 162.
annihilation of the world, 54, 59.
aporetic, 53.
apprehension, immediate intuitive, 11; cf. intuition.
art, 149, 168, 192.
artisan, 120, 169.
ascension of Muhammad, 205.
ass, Buridan's, 19.
assimilation to God, 151, 163.
astrology, 164 f., 167.
astronomy, 82.
atomism, 38, 184, 191; cf. matter; time.
attributes, 115 f., 135 f., 138 f.
autodidactus, 49.

badness, 114.
becoming, 10, 48, 58, 62 f.
being, 80, 89, 110 f., 122, 129, 137; non-being, 5, 47; cf. existence.
blood, 182.
body, 102; celestial b., 77, 161, 166 (cf. stars); pneumatic or astral b., 205; rectilinear, 22; terrestrial, 166.
brain, 187, 188 f.

causation, 60, 64, 67; denial of c., 79, 178, 179, 181, 182.
cause, 74, 79, 106, 177 (stoic); efficient c., 70; final c., 21; material c., 104, 105; receptive c., 116; timeless c., 156; *see also* first cause.
change, 3, 10, 27, 58, 62, 71, 184.
circularity, 27.
colour, 107, 134, 135, 137, 156, 180, 193.
command, divine, 77.

common man, 168.
— notions, 2, 6.
— sense, 187 f., 194; cf. internal sense.
compenetration, 110.
conjecturing power, 173 f., 181.
consent, universal (*ijmā'*), 205 f.
convention, 6.
copula, 131.
corruptibility of the world, 56 f.
creation, eternal, 9, 55, 75, 76, 100; *ex nihilo*, 65; temporal, 148.
creationism and traducianism, 49, 52.

dator formarum, 25, 83, 203.
deliberation, 169.
demiurge, 1.
demonstration, 1, 116, 130.
description, 84, 129.
desire, 5, 145.
determinism, 167.
differentiating principle, 17.
dimension, 32.
disposition, 4.
divination, 167.
divisible, 15.
dreams, 167, 168.
dualism, 24.

eclipse, 150.
ecliptic, 21.
effect, 5, 68, 115.
ego, 12 f., 117, 120, 175, 200; cf. self-consciousness.
elements, 22, 83.
emanation, 63, 73, 75, 85, 92, 94, 100, 115, 203.
Empirical physicians, 176, 179.
Empiricism, 16.
essence and existence, 136 ff.; cf. existence.
estimation (*aestimatio*), 188, 193.
Eternity, 1; of the world, 56, 67; timeless, 1, 54.
ethics, 170.
event, 4.
evidence, 16.

INDEX

existence, 112; potential e., 58; possible and actual e., 10; non-e., 10, 46, 47, 48, 52; cf. being, essence.
existent, necessary, 106.
extension, 31.

faith, 124.
fallacy, 3.
falsehood, 42.
φαντασία (cf. imagination, representation), 122, 161, 188 f.
fate, 38.
fear, 198.
fire, 180.
first agent, 135.
— cause, 9, 95.
— effect, 95.
— principle, 93, 139.
flux, 60, 199.
Form; acceptance of, 189.
— as active element, 127.
— as thoughts, 68.
— bestower of (active intellect), 200, 203; cf. *dator formarum*.
— change in, 48.
— different definitions of, 81, 90.
— distinctions in, 14.
— entry into matter, 23.
— eternity, immortality of, 44, 61, 91, 144.
— God providing, 25, 69.
— God the, 91.
— humanity, 99.
— imperishable, 32.
— individuality, individual, 51, 86, 133, 188.
— in blood, 182.
— in colouredness, 89.
— in sperm, 183.
— intellect receptive of, 200.
— intelligible, 196.
— mind and, 193.
— non-becoming of, 44.
— non-self-subsistence of, 52.
— One through, 12, 14.
— of object, 62.
— of percept, 196.
— perception of, 84.
— perfection of, 166.
— proximate, 146.
— pure, 81, 125.
— relation of matter and, 24, 48, 52, 65, 71, 81, 93, 94, 96, 119, 121, 132, 139.
— soul as, 49, 120, 172.
— specific difference in place, 185.
— substances having, 159.
— sweetness in wine, 132.
— transient, 133.
— unity based on, 15.
— universal, as universals, 25, 51, 121, 179.
formative faculty, 83.

generation (cf. procreation), 139; spontaneous g., 140, 183.
generosity, 114.
God, acts of, 5.
— attributes of, 4, 108, 109.
— cause of human actions, 198.
— efficient cause, 70.
— essence and existence coincide, 134.
— eternal agent, 1.
— eternal man, 144.
— generosity, bounty, 64, 114.
— joy, happy condition, 114.
— knowledge, 119, 121, 151, 152, 153, 155, 159, 170, 181; active or creative knowledge, 154; self-knowledge, 7; his knowledge of the infinite, 169; his knowledge of individuals, 81, 85, 89.
— life of, 114.
— mercy of, 98.
— new decisions in the mind of G., 1, 3.
— new volitions in G., 3.
— no composition in G., 88.
— omnipotence of, 181.
— omniscience of, 86, 151.
— only active principle (Stoicism), 176.
— providence of, 82.
— power and majesty of, 77.
— power to do one of the contraries, 5.
— prime mover, 20, 91.
— self sufficient, 118.
— simplicity of, 87.
— supreme end, 20, 91.
— synectic cause, 65.
— uniqueness of, 87, 108, 150.
— unity of, 4, 108, 109 f., 112, 113.
— will of, 113, 141, 148, 159; eternal will of, 3, 6.
— words of, 4.

habit, 179, 180.

INDEX

hand, 115, 185.
heart, 191.
heaven, 23.
heresy, 203.
hypothetical propositions, 178; cf. syllogism.

ideas, Plato's theory of, 88, 99.
identity, 12, 14, 60, 178, 199 f., 201.
immortality, 12, 202.
impossible, 36, 40.
indestructible, 1.
imagination, 35, 83, 89, 161, 166, 174 f. (influence on body), 187, 191.
impressed, 49.
inclination, 158.
individuality, 49.
induction, 197.
inference, 147.
infinite, actual, potential, 8; number, 7; time 8, 10; God's knowledge of, 109
infinite series, 26 (cf. regress), 13, 14.
instant, 30.
instinct of animals, 168.
intellect, 13, 72, 84, 120; active, 3, 15, 74, 81, 83, 115, 146, 203; first, 74, 166; immaterial, 3, 74, 81, 203; material, 3, 74, 81, 203; passive, 3, 13, 74, 154; potential, 3, 15, 74; practical, 113; separate, 135; theoretical, 113.
intention, first, 111; second, 111, 113, 120 f.; intentions, 188.
internal sense, internal perception, 186.
interpretation, allegorical, 165, 166.
intuition, intellectual, 155; cf. apprehension.

Jinn, 203.
judgement, 83.
jump, 30, 38.

Kings philosophers, 170.
knowledge, 153; creative, 84; relational, 50; traditional, 16; self-k., 122 f.; unity of, 123; God's knowledge, *see* God.
Kumūn, 48.

law, 41.
liberum arbitrium, 18.
life and death, 68 f.
light, 15, 49.

Logic: Aristotelean, 1, 2; Stoic, 178, 179.
logical and ontological, 103, 104.
love, 20, 91 f., 151, 161.
lumen naturale, ix, 7.

macrocosm, 90.
magic, 172, 175.
man a mortal God, 156.
materialists, 105, 142.
matter, 3, 95, 106, 116 f., 119, 139, 178, 191; proximate, 25, 146.
meaning, 4.
measure, 35.
mediation, 71, 97.
medicine, 82, 171.
memory, 89, 166, 189 f.
microcosm, 90.
miracles, 97, 124, 173, 175.
motion, 160; circular, 158 f.; essential and accidental, 26; self-m., 145.
motive faculties, 190.
movement, 157, 161; principle of, 2; two definitions of, 42.
Mover, eternal, 79, 93; prime, 26, 149; unmoved, 2, 75.
mystical, intuitive apprehension, 11.

nature, 83, 142, 149 f., 159, 180, 182; atomic structure of n., 38.
necessity, 138; objective, 45; logical and factual, 40, 103.
negative theology, 88.
nominalism, 15, 51.
nothingness, 58, 59.
notiones transcendentales, 80.

optimism, Aristotelean, 20.
organ, 185.

paradox of continuity, 33.
paronomasia, 109, 131.
particular, 168.
Pen, 166.
perception, 83, 84, 89, 147, 154.
physiognomy, 172.
plants, 182.
plurality, 23, 71, 106.
pluralization, 63.
pneuma, 90.
possibility, 16, 95; objective, 37, 38, 39, 45, 185; subjective, 10; coextensive with reality, 38, 44.

INDEX

possible, 2, 10, 36, 40, 180.
potency, active, 146; passive, 146; as a dormancy, 39.
potentiality, 1, 2, 10 f.
principium continui, 28.
principium identitatis indiscernibilium, 13.
principium individuationis, 117, 201.
principium melioris, 16.
principle of contradiction, 7, 184; of movement, 2; of synonymity, 183; determining p., 2, 17; first principles, 6.
priority and posteriority, 29.
privation, 32, 48, 63, 150.
process and result, 68.
procreation, 83, 105, 143; cf. generation.
progress, 165.
prophets, 124, 165, 167, 174, 176, 205.
providence, 22, 82, 123, 154, 165; cf. God.
purpose, 5.

quality, 69.
quiddity, 109, 130.

ratio recta (ὀρθὸς λόγος), 7, 49.
reality, 110; dichotomy of r., 103; trichotomy of r., 66, 104.
recipient, 46.
regress, infinite, 60, 87.
relation, 60, 81, 115, 122, 124, 152 f.
religion, 98, 180, 203 f.
representation, 148, 166, 168; cf. φαντασία.
resurrection of the body, 173, 203, 204, 206.
rhetorician, 145.
right and left, 23.

scala naturae, 183, 185.
sciences, 97, 171; division of, 171.
self-consciousness, 12 f., 73, 113, 120, 122, 144, 200; cf. ego.
sensation, 122, 187, 194 f.
sensationalism, 181.
shape, 191.
sign, 179.
simultaneity of cause and effect, 29.
sleep, 194.
something, 4, 46.
sophistry, 15.
soul, 12 ff., 50, 102, 159, 171, 172, 186, 190; universal, world, s. of heaven, 83, 84, 165, 166, 170; pre-existence of, 12, 202.
space, 35, 171, 190.
sperm, 183.
sphere, 20, 21, 92.
spirit, 195.
stars, 22, 78, 96, 157, 158 ff.; cf. body, celestial.
state, world as, 72, 76.
Stoic philosophy, and Ghazāli, 129.
—— and ijmā', 205 f.
—— classification of actions, 117.
—— divine command, 77.
—— middle terms between belief and unbelief, 117.
—— pneuma, 90.
—— self-preservation, 89.
—— synectic cause, 65.
—— τί (entity, thing), 116.
—— universal divine Law, 76.
—— universe a unified body, 89.
—— world as a state, 76.
cf. cause.
substance, 112.
substratum, 25.
sun, 20, 57.
supernaturalism, 182.
syllogism, dialectical, 116; disjunctive, 57, 146; hypothetical, 57, 145 ff.
sympathy, 167, 175.

tablet, indelible, 165.
teleological argument, 140 f.
telesmatic art, 172.
theology, negative, 88, 89; *per analogiam, per eminentiam*, 89.
time, 8, 11, 28, 31 (subjective), 34 (definition), 35 (and movement), 62 (time atom), 151, 154, 156, 171, 191.
treasure, 167.
truth, 15, 45, 103, 110.
ungenerated, 1.
universal, 4, 50, 52, 109, 121, 154, 168, 179, 190, 200, 202.

virtue, 175, 204.
vision, 156.
whole and part, 27.
will, 5, 6, 18, 20, 63, 145, 148, 166, 169; God's will, *see* God.
World, ungenerated, 1.

SOME CONTRADICTIONS IN ARISTOTLE'S SYSTEM

System *teleological* and denial of God's will, 6.

Common notions as probable and as a criterion of truth, 6.

The *potential infinite* can never be actualized, whereas the potential is what can be or has to be actualized, 8.

The *potential* as what can be actualized and as what has to be actualized, 36, 37–40.

Theory of a *first cause* and the acceptance of an infinite series of causes, 9.

Time as what has no beginning nor end, whereas there are finite times, 10.

The dubious nature of *time*, 8, 11.

Soul as possessing and not possessing *individuality*, 12.

God as the supreme *Agent* and the supreme *End*, 20.

Matter as the principle of plurality, and the plurality of the immaterial heavens, 23.

Forms and matter as ungenerated, whereas only the individual exists, 25.

The transitory individual as composed of two non-existing eternal elements, form and matter, 25.

Matter as the possible and eternal, whereas everything eternal is necessary, 26.

God's existence as timeless and as simultaneous with the world, 29.

The denial of an intermediary between being and non-being, and the theory of the potential, 38.

The potential as identical with the actual, 6, 40.

Monistic and pluralistic views, 75, 93.

Matter regarded as something corporeal, 93, 117, 139.

Identification of action (ἐνέργεια) and end (ἐντελέχεια), 43.

Privation as a negation and a positive existent, 47.

The contradiction in Aristotle's theory of becoming, 48.

All reality is individual, all knowledge universal, 65.

Relation of individual and universal, 99.

Confusion of logical and ontological necessity, 103.

Dubious nature of the universal, 111, 121.

The difficulty in the assertion that the non-existent is, 112.

Identification of knowledge and things known, 122.

God as an individual universal or a universal individual, 125.

The ambiguous relation of matter to form, 132.

The difficulty of the distinction between art and nature, 142.

Difficulties in Aristotle's theory of perception, 147.

Difficulty in the trichotomy of things becoming, 149.

Different conceptions of the cause of movement of the stars, 158.

Right and left as relative to the observer and as absolutely attributable to the universe, 164.

Confusion in the theory of the common sense, 187.

Contradiction in the conception of φαντασία, 187.

Difficulties in regarding the soul as a unity, 193.

Ambiguity of the term 'common sense', 194, 196.

Three different conceptions of sensation, 194.

That all thought is accompanied with φαντασία is in contradiction to the concept of pure self-consciousness, 200.

ARABIC/GREEK INDEX TO THE NOTES

abadī ἄφθαρτον, 1.
a'ḍā μόρια, 48.
'adam στέρησις, 32.
aḥdatha causative of γίγνεσθαι, 54.
aḥkām νοήματα, 4.
al-ajrām al-basīṭa τὰ ἁπλᾶ σώματα, 83.
'alā-l-aktharī ἐπὶ τὸ πολύ, 2.
'āmm κοινόν, 2.
al-ān τὸ νῦν, 10.
'alā-l-aqallī ἐπὶ τὸ ἔλαττον, 2.
'aql hayūlānī νοῦς ὑλικός, 3.
asfal κάτω, 22.
al-aṣlaḥ τὸ βέλτιστον, 18, 22
asmā maʿdūla ὀνόματα ἀόριστα, 134.
azalī ἀγένητον, 1.

bu'd διάστημα, 31.
burhān ἀπόδειξις, 60.

ḍafīra πλόκαμος, 96.
dahr αἰών, 54, 105.
dalīl σημεῖον, 179.
dhāt οὐσία, 109.
— τὶ, 110.
dhauq γεῦσις, 11.

fā'il qarīb ἐγγύτατον αἴτιον, 83.
farḍ κατόρθωμα, 117.
fauq ἄνω, 22.
fi'l ἐνέργεια, 43.
fiṭra lumen naturale, 7.
fiṭra fā'iqa ὀρθὸς λόγος, 7.
bi-l-fiṭra φύσει, 7.

ghā'ib ἀναίσθητον, 35.
ghair ma'lūm ἀκατάληπτος, 54.
ghair ma'rūf ἀκατάληπτος, 54.
ghanī αὐτάρκης, 118.
ghāya τέλος, 24.

ḥads ἀγχίνοια, 173, 181.
ḥāl πῶς ἔχον, 4.
— διάθεσις, 4.
ḥāla πῶς ἔχον, 79.
ḥarām ἁμάρτημα, 117.
ḥāssa αἴσθησις, 186.
ḥifẓ σωτηρία, 28, 78.

imtizāj μίξις, 142.
istiḥāla ἀλλοίωσις, 142.
istikmāl ἐντελέχεια, 43.
istiqrā' ἐπαγωγή, 197.
istithnā' διάζευξις, διαίρεσις, 146.

ittiṣāl σύνδεσμος, 28.

jā'iz ἀδιάφορον, 117.
juz' μέρος, 27.
juz'ī μερικός, 28.

kullī ὁλικός, 28.

lāḥiq συμβεβηκός, 117.
laḥiqa συμβαίνειν, 117.
lāzim συμβεβηκὸς καθ' αὑτό, 117.
luzūm ἐπιφορά, 147.

ma'ānī λεκτά, 4, 60.
mafhūm κατάληπτος, 45.
māhiyya τὸ τὶ ἐστιν, τὸ τί ἦν εἶναι, 109.
mail ὁρμή, ῥοπή, 158.
makrūh ἀποπροηγμένον, 117.
malaka ἕξις, 4.
ma'lūm κατάληπτος, 112.
mandūb, προηγμένον, 117.
maqdūr εἱμαρμένον, 38.
mashhūr ἔνδοξον, 2.
mithāl σύμβολον, 131.
mizāj κρᾶσις, 50.
mubāḥ ἀδιάφορον, 117.
mudabbir ἡγεμονικόν, 143.
muḥāl ἄτοπον, 43.
al-muktasab τὸ ἐφ' ἡμῖν, 38.
munshār πρίων, 24.
muntabi' τυπούμενον, 49.
— ἐνσφραγιζόμενον, 49.
muqaddam ἡγούμενον, 146.
murajjiḥ ἐπικλῖνον, 2.
muṣādara' alā-l-maṭlūb ἅπτεσθαι τῆς ζητήσεως ἐξ ἀρχῆς (petitio principii), 55.
al-mushār ilaihi τὸ τόδε τι, 131.
mustaḥibb προηγμένον, 117.
mustathnī μεταλαμβανόμενον, 146.
mutakallimūn διαλεκτικοί, 4.
mutalāḥiqan ἅμα κατὰ χρόνον, 54.
mutasāwiqan ἐφεξῆς, 54.
muwāti'a συμφωνία, 16.

nāmūs νόμος, 41.
naql μεταφορά, 19.
natīja συμπέρασμα, 146.
natīja mā yurāmu τὸ ἐξ ἀρχῆς αἰτεῖσθαι, 105.

al-qābil τὸ πάσχον, 25.
qidam ἀϊδιότης, 1.
qiyās sharṭī munfaṣil διεζευγμένον ἀξίωμα, 57.
qiyās sharṭī muttaṣil συνημμένον ἀξίωμα, 57.

ARABIC/GREEK INDEX TO THE NOTES

al-quwwa al-mudabbira τὸ ἡγεμονικόν, 12.
al-quwwa al-muṣawwira ἡ δύναμις ἡ διαπλαστική, 83.

rābiṭ, rābita συμπλοκή, 131.
rasm ὑπογραφή, 84, 129.
rūḥ πνεῦμα, 195.
ar-ruṭūba al-jalīdiyya min al-'ain τὸ ὑαλοειδὲς ὑγρὸν τοῦ ὀφθαλμοῦ, 63.

sailān τὸ ῥεῖν, 60.
shay' τὶ, 4, 110, 123.
ṣifāt nafsāniyya ἐννοήματα, 137.
aṣ-ṣuwar al-ḥissiyya τὰ αἰσθητὰ εἴδη, 93.

ṭab' φύσις, 6, 7, 77.
tābi' παρακολουθοῦν, 135.
tabi'a διώκειν, 50.
ṭafra ἅλμα, 30.

taḥqīq συγκατάθεσις, 1.
taklīf προστακτικόν, νόμος, 77.
at-tālī τὸ ἑπόμενον, 146.
tanzīh ἀφαίρεσις, 88.
'alā-t-tasāwī ἐπὶ τὸ ἴσον, 2.
taṣdīq συγκατάθεσις, 1.
ṭilasm τέλεσμα, 172.
min tilqā ἀπὸ ταὐτομάτου, 5.

ufq μεθόριον, 194.
'unṣur στοιχεῖον, 127.

waḍ' θέσις, 6, 77.
wāhib aṣ-ṣuwar χορηγὸς τῶν λόγων (dator formarum), 25.
al-wajh al-awwal πρώτη θέσις, 111.
al-wajh ath-thānī δευτέρα θέσις, 112.
wājib κατόρθωμα, 117.
bi-lā wasṭ ἄμεσον, 13.

GREEK/ARABIC INDEX TO THE NOTES

ἀγένητον *azalī*, 1.
ἀγχίνοια *ḥads*, 173, 181.
ἀδιάφορον *mubāḥ*, 117.
ἠδιάφορος *jāʾiz*, 117.
ἀϊδιότης *qidam*, 1.
αἴσθησις *ḥāssa*, 186.
αἰσθητὰ εἴδη, τὰ— *aṣ-ṣuwar al-ḥissiyya*, 93.
αἰτεῖσθαι, τὸ ἐξ ἀρχῆς *natīja mā yurāmu*, 105.
αἴτιον, τὸ ἐγγύτατον— *al-faʾil al-qarīb*, 83.
αἰών *dahr*, 54, 105.
ἀκατάληπτος *ghair maʿlūm*, 54.
— *ghair maʿrūf*, 54.
ἀλλοίωσις *istiḥāl*, 142.
ἄλμα *ṭafra*, 30.
ἅμα κατὰ χρόνον *mutalāḥiqan*, 54.
ἁμάρτημα *ḥarām*, 117.
ἄμεσον *bilā waṣṭ*, 13.
ἀναίσθητον *ghāʾib*, 35.
ἄνω *fauq*, 22.
ἀξίωμα, διεζευγμένον— *qiyās sharṭī munfaṣil*, 57.
ἀ., συνημμένον— *qiyās sharṭī muttaṣil*, 57.
ἁπλᾶ σώματα, τὰ— *al-ajrām al-basīṭa*, 83.
ἀπόδειξις *burhān*, 60.
ἀποπροηγμένον *makrūh*, 117.
ἅπτεσθαι τῆς ζητήσεως ἐξ ἀρχῆς *muṣādara ʿalā-l-maṭlūb*, 55.
ἄτοπον *muḥāl*, 43.
αὐτομάτου, ἀπὸ τοῦ— *min tilkā . . .*, 5.
ἀφαίρεσις *tanzīh*, 88.
ἄφθαρτον *abadī*, 1.
αὐτάρκης *ghanī*, 118.

βέλτιστον, τό— *al-aṣlaḥ*, 18, 22.

γεῦσις *dhauq*, 11.
γίγνεσθαι (causative of . . .) *aḥdatha*, 54.

διάζευξις *istithnāʾ*, 146.
διάθεσις *ḥāl*, 4.
διαίρεσις *istithnāʾ*, 146.
διαλεκτικοί *mutakallimūn*, 4.
διάστημα *buʿd*, 31.
διώκειν *ṭabiʿa*, 50.
δύναμις διαπλαστική *al-quwwa al-musawwira*, 83.

εἱμαρμένον *maqdūr*, 38.
ἔλαττον, ἐπ᾿— *ʿalāʾ l-aqallī*, 2.
ἔνδοξον *mashhūr*, 2.
ἐνέργεια *fiʿl*, 43.
ἐννοήματα *ṣifāt nafsāniyya*, 137.
ἐνσφραγιζόμενον *munṭabiʿ*, 50.

ἐντελέχεια *istikmāl*, 43.
ἕξις *malaka*, 4.
ἐπαγωγή *istiqrāʾ*, 197.
ἐπικλῖνον, τὸ— *al-murajjiḥ*, 2.
ἐπιφορά *luzūm*, 147.
ἑπόμενον, τὸ— *at-tālī*, 146.
ἐφ᾿ ἡμῖν, τὸ— *al-muktasab*, 38.
ἐφεξῆς *mutasāwiyan*, 54.
ἔχον, τὸ πὼς— *ḥāl*, 4.
— — *ḥāla*, 79.

ἡγεμονικόν *mudabbir*, 143.
ἡγεμονικόν, τὸ— *al-quwwa al-mudabbira*, 12.
ἡγούμενον, τὸ— *al-muqaddam*, 146.

θέσις *waḍʿ*, 6, 77.
θέσις, πρώτη— *al-wajh al-awwal*, 111.
θ., δευτέρα— *al-wajh ath-thānī*, 111.

ἴσον, ἐπ᾿— *ʿalā-t-tasāwī*, 2.

κατάληπτος *maʿlūm*, 112.
— *mafhūm*, 45.
κατόρθωμα *farḍ*, 117.
— *wājib*, 117.
κάτω *asfal*, 22.
κοινόν *ʿāmm*, 2.
κρᾶσις *mizāj*, 50.

λεκτά *maʿānī*, 4, 60.
λόγος, ὀρθὸς— *fiṭra fāʾiqa*, 7.
lumen naturale *fiṭra*, 7.

μεθόριον *ufq*, 194.
μερικός *juzʾī*, 28.
μέρος *juzʾ*, 27.
μεταλαμβανόμενον, τὸ— *al-mustathnī*, 146.
μεταφορά *naql*, 19.
μίξις *imtizāj*, 142.
μόρια *aʿḍāʾ*, 48.

νοήματα *aḥkām*, 4.
νόμος *nāmūs*, 41.
— *taklīf*, 77.
νοῦς ὑλικός *ʿaql hayūlānī*, 3.
νῦν, τὸ— *al-ān*, 10.

ὁλικός *kullī*, 28.
ὀνόματα ἀόριστα *asmāʾ maʿdūlā*, 134.
ὁρμή *mail*, 158.
οὐσία *dhāt*, 109.

παρακολουθοῦν *tābiʿ*, 135.

πάσχον, τό— al-qābil, 25.
petitio principii muṣādara ʿalā-l-maṭlūb, 55.
πλόκαμος ḏafīra, 96.
πνεῦμα rūḥ, 195.
πολύ, ἐπὶ τό— ʿalā-l-aktharī, 2.
πρίων munshār, 24.
προηγμένον mandūb, 117.
— mustaḥibb, 117.
προστακτικόν taklīf, 77.

ῥεῖν, τό— sailān, 60.
ῥοπή mail, 158.

σημεῖον dalīl, 179.
στέρησις ʿadam, 32.
στοιχεῖον ʿunṣur, 127.
συγκατάθεσις taḥqīq, 1.
— taṣdīq, 1.
συμβαίνειν laḥiqa, 117.
συμβεβηκός lāḥiq, 117.
συμβεβηκὸς καθ᾽ αὑτό lāzim, 117.
σύμβολον mithāl, 131.
συμπέρασμα natīja, 146.

συμπλοκή rābiṭ, rābiṭa, 131.
σύνδεσμος ittiṣāl, 28.
συμφωνία muwāṭīʾa, 16.
σωτηρία ḥifẓ, 28, 78.

τέλεσμα ṭilasm, 172.
τέλος ghāya, 24.
τὶ dhāt, 110.
— shay, 4, 110, 123.
τί ἦν εἶναι, τό— māhiyya, 109.
τί ἐστιν, τό— māhiyya, 109.
τόδε τι, τό— al-mushār ilaihi, 131.
τυπούμενον munṭabiʿ, 49.

ὑαλοειδὲς ὑγρὸν τοῦ ὀφθαλμοῦ, τό— ar-ruṭūba al-jalīdiyya min al-ʿain, 63.
ὑπογραφή rasm, 84, 129.

φύσει bi-l-fiṭra, 1.
φύσις ṭabʿ, 6, 7, 77.

χορηγὸς τῶν λόγων (dator formarum) wāhib aṣ-ṣuwar, 25.